Police Ethics

KV-621-727

The International Library of Essays in Public and Professional Ethics
Series Editor: Seumas Miller and Tom Campbell

Police Ethics

Edited by

Seumas Miller

Charles Sturt University, Australia

ASHGATE

© Seumas Miller 2006. For copyright of individual articles please refer to the Acknowledgements.

All rights reserved. No part of this publication may be reproduced, stored in a retrieval system or transmitted in any form or by any means, electronic, mechanical, photocopying, recording or otherwise without the prior permission of the publisher.

Published by
Ashgate Publishing Limited
Gower House
Croft Road
Aldershot
Hampshire GU11 3HR
England

Ashgate Publishing Company
Suite 420
101 Cherry Street
Burlington, VT 05401-4405
USA

Ashgate website: http://www.ashgate.com

British Library Cataloguing in Publication Data
Police ethics. - (The international library of essays in
    public and professional ethics)
    1.Police ethics
    I.Miller, Seumas
    174.9'3632

Library of Congress Cataloging-in-Publication Data
Police ethics / edited by Seumas Miller.
        p. cm. – (The international library of essays in public and professional ethics)
    ISBN 0-7546-2572-9 (alk paper)
    1. Police ethics. 2. Police discretion. 3. Police corruption. I. Miller, Seumas. II. Series.

    HV7924.P63 2005
    174'.93632–dc22

                                                                                    2005045342

    ISBN 10: 0 7546 2572 9
    ISBN 13: 978-0-7546-2572-8

Printed in Great Britain by TJ International Ltd, Padstow, Cornwall

Contents

PART VI RIGHTS OF SUSPECTS

Acknowledgements

The editor and publishers wish to thank the following for permission to use copyright material.

AEI Press for the essay: Edwin J. Delattre (2004), 'Tragedy and "Noble Cause" Corruption', in Edwin J. Delattre, *Character and Cops: Ethics in Policing*, Washington, DC: AEI Press, pp. 181–204; 204a. Reprinted with the permission of the American Enterprise Institute for Public Policy Research, Washington, DC.

Blackwell Publishing for the essay: John Kleinig (1998), 'Selective Enforcement and the Rule of Law', *Journal of Social Philosophy*, **29**, pp. 117–31.

Cambridge University Press for the essay: John Kleinig (1996), 'Moral Foundations of Policing', in John Kleinig, *The Ethics of Policing*, Cambridge: Cambridge University Press, pp. 11–29; 29a–d.

Greenwood Publishing Group for the essay: Howard S. Cohen and Michael Feldberg (1991), 'A Social Contract Perspective on the Police Role', in Howard S. Cohen and Michael Feldberg, *Power and Restraint:The Moral Dimension of Police Work*, New York: Praeger Press, pp. 23–38.

The Institute for Criminal Justice Ethics for the essays: R.E. Ewin (1990), 'Loyalty: The Police', *Criminal Justice Ethics*, **9**, pp. 3–15; Howard Cohen (1986), 'Exploiting Police Authority', *Criminal Justice Ethics*, **5**, pp. 23–31; Jerome H. Skolnick (1982), 'Deception by Police', *Criminal Justice Ethics*, **2**, pp. 40–54; Jerome H. Skolnick and Richard A. Leo (1992), 'The Ethics of Deceptive Interrogation', *Criminal Justice Ethics*, **11**, pp. 3–12. Reprinted by permission of The Institute for Criminal Justice Ethics, 555 West 57th Street, Suite 607, New York, NY, 10019-1029.

John Jay Press for the essays: William C. Heffernan (1985), 'The Police and their Rules of Office: An Ethical Analysis', in William C. Heffernan and Timothy Stroup (eds), *Police Ethics: Hard Choices in Law Enforcement*, New York: John Jay Press, pp. 3–24; James F. Doyle (1985), 'Police Discretion, Legality, and Morality', in William C. Heffernan and Timothy Stroup (eds), *Police Ethics: Hard Choices in Law Enforcement*, New York: John Jay Press, pp. 47–68.

Oxford University Press for the essay: P.A.J. Waddington (1991), 'Deadly Force', in P.A.J. Waddington, *The Strong Arm of the Law*, Oxford: Clarendon Press, pp. 75–120; 120a. By permission of Oxford University Press.

Pearson Education for the essay: Jerome H. Skolnick (1975), 'A Sketch of the Policeman's "Working Personality"', in Jerome H. Skolnick (ed.), *Justice Without Trial*, (2nd edn) New

York: John Wiley and Sons, pp. 42–70. Copyright © 1986. Reprinted with permission of Pearson Education, Inc., Upper Saddle River, NJ.

Rowman and Littlefield for the essay: Jeffrey Reiman (1996), 'Is Police Discretion Justified in a Free Society?', in J. Kleinig, *Handled with Discretion: Ethical Issues in Police Decision Making*, Lanham, MD: Rowman and Littlefield, pp. 71–83.

Sage Publications for the essays: Carl B. Klockars (1980), 'The Dirty Harry Problem', *The Annals of the American Academy of Political and Social Science*, **452**, pp. 33–47; Gary T. Marx (1982), 'Who Really Gets Stung? Some Issues Raised by the New Police Undercover Work', *Crime and Delinquency*, **8**, pp. 165–93.

Springer for the essays: Seumas Miller (2004), 'Moral Rights and the Institution of the Police', in T. Campbell and S. Miller (eds), *Human Rights and the Moral Responsibilities of Corporate and Public Sector Organisations*, Dordrecht: Kluwer, pp. 167–88; Gerald Dworkin (1985), 'The Serpent Beguiled Me and I did Eat: Entrapment and the Creation of Crime', *Law and Philosophy*, **4**, pp. 17–39.

The Stationery Office for the essay: Lord Scarman (1981), 'Two Principles of Policing', in Lord Scarman, *The Scarman Report*, Harmondsworth: Penguin, pp. 102–5.

Sweet & Maxwell for the essay: Laurence Lustgarten (1986), 'Police Discretion', in L. Lustgarten, *The Governance of Police*, London: Sweet and Maxwell, pp. 10–24.

Waterside Press for the essays: John Kleinig (2004), 'The Problematic Virtue of Loyalty', in Peter Villiers and Rob Adlam (eds), *Policing a Safe, Just and Tolerant Society*, Winchester: Waterside Press, pp. 78–87; William C. Heffernan (2003), 'Three Types of Police Leadership', in Robert Adlam and Peter Villiers (eds), *Police Leadership in the Twenty-first Century*, Winchester: Waterside Press, pp. 134–45.

Every effort has been made to trace all the copyright holders, but if any have been inadvertently overlooked the publishers will be pleased to make the necessary arrangement at the first opportunity.

Series Preface

'Ethics' is now a considerable part of all debates about the conduct of public life, in government, economics, law, business, the professions and indeed every area of social and political affairs. The ethical aspects of public life include questions of moral right and wrong in the performance of public and professional roles, the moral justification and critique of public institutions and the choices that confront citizens and professionals as they come to their own moral views about social, economic and political issues.

While there are no moral experts to whom we can delegate the determination of ethical questions, the traditional skills of moral philosophers have been increasingly applied to practical contexts that call for moral assessment. Moreover this is being done with a degree of specialist knowledge of the areas under scrutiny that previously has been lacking from much of the work undertaken by philosophers.

This series brings together essays that exhibit high quality work in philosophy and the social sciences, that is well informed on the relevant subject matter and provides novel insights into the problems that arise in resolving ethical questions in practical contexts.

The volumes are designed to assist those engaged in scholarly research by providing the core essays that all who are involved in research in that area will want to have to hand. Essays are reproduced in full with the original pagination for ease of reference and citation.

The editors are selected for their eminence in the particular area of public and professional ethics. Each volume represents the editor's selection of the most seminal essays of enduring interest in the field.

SEUMAS MILLER AND TOM CAMPBELL
Centre for Applied Philosophy and Public Ethics (CAPPE)
Australian National University
Charles Sturt University
University of Melbourne

Introduction

This book collection is a contribution to the literature on police ethics, and specifically the philosophical literature on ethical issues that arise in policing.

Many occupations exist to secure some fundamental *end* or goal, and this end is a human *good*. For doctors the end or goal is health, for lawyers justice, for journalists truth. Arguably, the central and most important end of policing is the protection of moral rights. The achievement of this fundamental end requires specialized skills, knowledge and individual judgement. However, there is a crucial further defining feature of policing, namely the routine and inescapable use of harmful methods, including coercive force, deception and the infringement of privacy. This combination of good ends and morally problematic means is a distinctive feature of policing.

Ideally, members of occupations *internalize* the fundamental ends which define their particular profession. This process of internalization may only be implicit. These ends may guide the actions of (say) doctors, even though they may not be very often explicitly aware that this is so.

Most important, members of such occupations, if they are to be successful practitioners, must identify with these defining ends. That is, their *self-worth* comes to depend in part on their capacity to realize these ends. The good teacher is one who not only has a capacity to impart knowledge, she also suffers a loss in self-esteem when she fails to successfully exercise this capacity. Similarly, the good police officer is one who not only has a capacity to detect crime and apprehend criminals, he also suffers a loss in self-esteem when he fails to successfully exercise this capacity.

Occupations are not only in part defined in terms of the end to which they ought to be directed, they are also in part defined in terms of the characteristic activities that members of the occupation engage in. In the case of the police, these characteristic activities are quite diverse, and include law enforcement activities, such as investigating and apprehending criminals, and peace-keeping activities, such as intervening in bar-room brawls or domestic disputes. When members of an occupation not only habitually engage in these activities, but do so skilfully and in a manner that secures the ends of the occupation, they are successful practitioners who can be said to possess the characteristic virtues of that occupation.

Individual police officers belong not only to an occupational group whose members have specialized knowledge and skills, they belong to a group which displays a high degree of solidarity. This is in part due to the trust that individual police officers need to be able to place in one another, given the dangers that they face in their work.

Significant interest in police ethics as an area of academic inquiry began in the early 1980s and became in large part centred in the Institute of Criminal Justice Ethics at John Jay College of Criminal Justice in New York. The main academic journal in this area, *Criminal Justice Ethics*, was published by the Institute, though recently it has become a joint publication of the Institute and the Centre for Applied Philosophy and Public Ethics at Charles Sturt University in Australia. Important early collections, such as William Heffernan and Timothy Stroup's volume, *Police Ethics: Hard Choices for Law Enforcement*, were published or sponsored by John Jay College. Probably the most influential authored book on police ethics in this early period was Edwin Delattre's *Character and Cops: Ethics in Policing*. The collection, *Moral Issues in Policework*, by Frederick A. Elliston and Michael Feldberg was also widely used.

During the 1990s various other authored books and collections emerged, including Howard Cohen and Michael Feldberg's *Power and Restraint*; John Alderson's *Principled Policing*; Seumas Miller, John Blackler and Andrew Alexandra's, *Police Ethics*; and the most comprehensive treatment of the subject to date, namely, John Kleinig's *Ethics of Policing*. Since then there has been a steady stream of books including, from the United Kingdom, Peter Neyroud and Alan Beckley's *Policing, Ethics and Human Rights*; Peter Villiers and Robert Adlam's *Policing a Safe, Just and Tolerant Society*; and from Australia, Seumas Miller (with John Blackler), *Ethical Issues in Policing*.

Part I of this collection is entitled *Theories of Policing*, and in it a variety of philosophical theories of policing are on display, including a social contract theory, and a rights-based theory. It also includes an essay by Egon Bittner (Chapter 1) in which he outlines his famous definition of policing in terms of the use of coercive force.

In Part II, *Police Authority and Discretion*, the focus is on various ethical problems that arise in relation to both the individual authority of police officers and the independence or sphere of authority of police organizations vis-à-vis government in particular. Issues include the problematic concept of operational autonomy and its importance in relation to, for example, the need for investigatory independence of police from government, and the concept of the original authority attaching to the office of constable in the United Kingdom and Australia. The related and much discussed concept of police discretion is the subject of a number of the essays. I note two influential books on this topic, K.C. Davis's *Police Discretion* and John Kleinig's volume *Handled with Discretion*.

Police Culture is the title of Part III, and this is another theme much discussed in policing literature. Here I note, in particular, Jerome Skolnick's classic essay 'A Sketch of the Policeman's "Working Personality"' (Chapter 12), taken from his volume *Justice Without Trial*.

The morally problematic features of police culture have often been noted, for example, feelings of loyalty on the part of fellow officers to protect the criminal actions of police. However, loyalty and other elements of police culture also serve to further legitimate police purposes, for example, by ensuring that fellow officers are assisted in dangerous situations.

Part IV deals with *Police Corruption*. Police corruption in general is the topic of the Sherman and Cohen essays in Chapters 17 and 18 respectively. Accounts of noble cause corruption in policing follow in Chapters 19 and 20 from Klockars and Delattre.

Corruption takes many forms in policing, including theft, bribe-taking, 'testilying', and fabricating or withholding evidence. Notoriously, the use of coercive and deadly force by police is on occasion not only morally unjustified – indeed a violation of the rights of suspects – it is also an act of corruption; it corrupts morally and legally legitimate processes and purposes. Consider in this connection use of the so-called 'third degree' to extract a confession from suspects.

In Part V, our attention is turned to one of the key harmful methods deployed by police, namely 'coercive force' and especially *Deadly Force*. Among the issues addressed are the various moral justifications for police use of deadly force, including self-defence, defence of the rights of others, and the use of deadly force to enforce the law. Arguably, the latter justification is not simply a special case of one of the other two justifications. Consider an offender who has committed a property crime, but is using the threat of force to prevent his arrest. In using coercive force to arrest the offender the police officer is not necessarily acting in self-defence or in defence of others.

Part VI deals with the *Rights of Suspects* that are infringed by some of the harmful methods deployed by police, such as deception, undercover work, surveillance, and entrapment. Here I note in particular the work of Gary T. Marx, including his book, *Undercover: Police Surveillance in America*.

Some of these above-mentioned police methods are less harmful than others, and some are morally justified in some circumstances but not in others. Thus an intrusive bodily search can not only be an invasion of privacy, it can also have a psychologically damaging effect. And this can be so, even if the search was morally justified. Again, police deception in the investigative stage might be morally justifiable, but not in the testimonial stage in the courtroom.

While police ethics as an area of academic inquiry is still in a developmental phase, a body of literature is now available, and it is increasing in response to, for example, the increasing educational needs of police practitioners. I hope that this volume is found to be a useful selection from that literature.

References

Alderson, John (1993), *Principled Policing*, Winchester: Waterside Press.

Cohen, Howard, and Feldberg, Michael (1991), *Power and Restraint: The Moral Dilemma of Police Work*, New York: Praeger Press.

Davis, K.C. and Wilson, John P. (1975), *Police Discretion*, St Paul, MI: West Publishing Company.

Delattre, Edwin (1989), *Character and Cops: Ethics in Policing*, Washington DC: AEI Press.

Elliston, Frederick A. and Feldberg, Michael (1985) (eds), *Moral Issues in Policework*, Totowa, NJ: Rowman and Allanheld.

Heffernan, William and Stroup, Timothy (1985) (eds), *Police Ethics: Hard Choices for Law Enforcement*, New York: John Jay Press.

Kleinig, John (1996a), *The Ethics of Policing*, Cambridge: Cambridge University Press.

Kleinig, John (1996b) (ed.), *Handled with Discretion*, Lanham, MD: Rowman and Littefield.

Marx, Gary T. (1988), *Undercover: Police Surveillance in America*, Berkeley, CA: University of California Press.

Miller, Seumas with Blackler, John (2005), *Ethical Issues in Policing*, Aldershot: Ashgate.

Miller, Seumas, Blackler, John and Alexandra, Andrew (1997, 2nd edn 2005), *Police Ethics*, St Leonards, NSW: Allen and Unwin.

Neyroud, Peter and Beckley, Alan (2001), *Policing, Ethics and Human Rights*, Devon, UK: Willan Publishing.

Skolnick, Jerome (1977, 3rd edn. 1993) (ed.), *Justice Without Trial*, New York: Macmillan.

Villiers, Peter and Adlam, Robert (2004) (eds), *Policing a Safe, Just and Tolerant Society*, Winchester: Waterside Press.

Part I
Theories of Policing

[1]

The Capacity To Use Force As
The Core Of The Police Role

Egon Bittner

We have argued earlier that the quest for peace by peaceful means is one of the culture traits of modern civilization. This aspiration is historically unique. For example, the Roman Empire was also committed to the objectives of reducing or eliminating warfare during one period of its existence, but the method chosen to achieve the *Pax Romana* was, in the language of the poet, *debellare superbos,* i.e., to subdue the haughty by force. Contrary to this, our commitment to abolish the traffic of violence requires us to pursue the ideal by pacific means. In support of this contention we pointed to the development of an elaborate system of international diplomacy whose main objective it is to avoid war, and to those changes in internal government that resulted in the virtual elimination of all forms of violence, especially in the administration of justice. That is, the overall tendency is not merely to withdraw the basis of legitimacy for all forms of provocative violence, but even from the exercise of provoked force required to meet illegitimate attacks. Naturally this is not possible to a full extent. At least, it has not been possible thus far. Since it is impossible to deprive responsive force entirely of legitimacy, its vestiges require special forms of authorization. Our society recognizes as legitimate three very different forms of responsive force.

First, we are authorized to use force for the purpose of self-defense. Though the laws governing self-defense are far from clear, it appears that an attacked person can counterattack only after he has exhausted all other means of avoiding harm, including retreat, and that the counterattack may not exceed what is necessary to disable the assailant from carrying out his intent. These restrictions are actually enforceable because harm done in the course of self-defense does furnish grounds for criminal and tort proceedings. It becomes necessary, therefore, to show compliance with these restrictions to rebut the charges of excessive and unjustified force even in self-defense.[63]

The second form of authorization entrusts the power to proceed coercively to some specifically deputized persons against some

[63] "Justification for the Use of Force in the Criminal Law," *Stanford Law Review,* 13 (1961) 566-609.

specifically named persons. Among the agents who have such
highly specific powers are mental hospital attendants and prison
guards. Characteristically, such persons use force in carrying out
court orders; but they may use force only against named persons
who are remanded to their custody and only to the extent required
to implement a judicial order of confinement. Of course, like everybody else, they may also act within the provisions governing self-
defense. By insisting on the high degree of limited specificity of
the powers of custodial staffs, we do not mean to deny that these
restrictions are often violated with impunity. The likelihood of
such transgressions is enhanced by the secluded character of
prisons and mental institutions, but their existence does not impair the validity of our definition.

The third way to legitimize the use of responsive force is to institute a police force. Contrary to the cases of self-defense and the
limited authorization of custodial functionaries, the police authorization is essentially unrestricted. Because the expression "essentially" is often used to hedge a point, we will make fully
explicit what we mean by it. There exist three formal limitations
of the freedom of policemen to use force, which we must admit
even though they have virtually no practical consequences. First,
the police use of deadly force is limited in most jurisdictions.
Though the powers of a policeman in this respect exceed those of
citizens, they are limited nevertheless. For example, in some
jurisdictions policemen are empowered to shoot to kill fleeing
felony suspects, but not fleeing misdemeanor suspects. It is scarcely necessary to argue that, given the uncertainties involved in defining a delict under conditions of hot pursuit, this could hardly
be expected to be an effective limitation.[64] Second, policemen may
use force only in the performance of their duties and not to
advance their own personal interest or the private interests of
other persons. Though this is rather obvious, we mention it for
the sake of completeness. Third, and this point too is brought up
to meet possible objections, policemen may not use force maliciously or frivolously. These three restrictions, and nothing else,
were meant by the use of the qualifier "essentially". Aside from

---

[64] "At common law, the rule appears to have been that an officer was entitled to make a
reasonable mistake as to whether the victim had committed a felony, but a private person
was not so entitled. Thus strict liability was created for the private arrester, and he could not
justifiably kill, if the victim had not actually committed a felony. Several modern cases have
imposed this standard of strict liability even upon the officer by conditioning justification of
deadly force on the victim's actually having committed a felony, and a number of states have
enacted statutes which appear to adopt this strict liability. However, many jurisdictions,
such as California, have homicide statutes which permit the police officer to use deadly force
for the arrest of a person 'charged' with felony. It has been suggested that this requirement
only indicates the necessity for reasonable belief by the officer that the victim has committed a
felony." *Ibid.*, pp. 599-600.

these restrictions there exist no guidelines, no specifiable range of objectives, no limitations of any kind that instruct the policeman what he may or must do. Nor do there exist any criteria that would allow the judgment whether some forceful intervention was necessary, desirable, or proper. And finally, it is exceedingly rare that police actions involving the use of force are actually reviewed and judged by anyone at all.

In sum, the frequently heard talk about the lawful use of force by the police is practically meaningless and, because no one knows what is meant by it, so is the talk about the use of minimum force. Whatever vestigial significance attaches to the term "lawful" use of force is confined to the obvious and unnecessary rule that police officers may not commit crimes of violence. Otherwise, however, the expectation that they may and will use force is left entirely undefined. In fact, the only instructions any policeman ever receives in this respect consist of sermonizing that he should be humane and circumspect, and that he must not desist from what he has undertaken merely because its accomplishment may call for coercive means. We might add, at this point, that the entire debate about the troublesome problem of police brutality will not move beyond its present impasse, and the desire to eliminate it will remain an impotent conceit, until this point is fully grasped and unequivocally admitted. In fact, our expectation that policemen will use force, coupled by our refusals to state clearly what we mean by it (aside from sanctimonious homilies), smacks of more than a bit of perversity.

Of course, neither the police nor the public is entirely in the dark about the justifiable use of force by the officers. We had occasion to allude to the assumption that policemen may use force in making arrests. But the benefit deriving from this apparent core of relative clarity is outweighed by its potentially misleading implications. For the authorization of the police to use force is in no important sense related to their duty to apprehend criminals. Were this the case then it could be adequately considered as merely a special case of the same authorization that is entrusted to custodial personnel. It might perhaps be considered a bit more complicated, but essentially of the same nature. But the police authority to use force is radically different from that of a prison guard. Whereas the powers of the latter are incidental to his obligation to implement a legal command, the police role is far better understood by saying that their ability to arrest offenders is incidental to their authority to use force.

Many puzzling aspects of police work fall into place when one ceases to look at it as principally concerned with law enforcement

38

and crime control, and only incidentally and often incongruously concerned with an infinite variety of other matters. It makes much more sense to say that the police are nothing else than a mechanism for the distribution of situationally justified force in society. The latter conception is preferable to the former on three grounds. First, it accords better with the actual expectations and demands made of the police (even though it probably conflicts with what most people would say, or expect to hear, in answer to the question about the proper police function) ; second, it gives a better accounting of the actual allocation of police manpower and other resources; and, third, it lends unity to all kinds of police activity. These three justifications will be discussed in some detail in the following.

The American city dweller's repertoire of methods for handling problems includes one known as "calling the cops." The practice to which the idiom refers is enormously widespread. Though it is more frequent in some segments of society than in others, there are very few people who do not or would not resort to it under suitable circumstances. A few illustrations will furnish the background for an explanation of what "calling the cops" means.[65]

Two patrolmen were directed to report to an address located in a fashionable district of a large city. On the scene they were greeted by the lady of the house who complained that the maid had been stealing and receiving male visitors in her quarters. She wanted the maid's belongings searched and the man removed. The patrolmen refused the first request, promising to forward the complaint to the bureau of detectives, but agreed to see what they could do about the man. After gaining entrance to the maid's room they compelled a male visitor to leave, drove him several blocks away from the house, and released him with the warning never to return.

In a tenement, patrolmen were met by a public health nurse who took them through an abysmally deteriorated apartment inhabited by four young children in the care of an elderly woman. The babysitter resisted the nurse's earlier attempts to remove the children. The patrolmen packed the children in the squad car and took them to Juvenile Hall, over the continuing protests of the elderly woman.

While cruising through the streets a team of detectives recognized a man named in a teletype received from the sheriff of an adjoining county. The suspect maintained that he was in the

---

[65] The illustrations are taken from field notes I have collected over the course of fourteen months of intensive field observations of police activity in two large cities. One is located in a Rocky Mountain State, the other on the West Coast. All other case vignettes used in the subsequent text of this report also come from this source.

hospital at the time the offense alleged in the communication took place, and asked the officers to verify his story over their car radio. When he continued to plead innocence he was handcuffed and taken to headquarters. Here the detectives learned that the teletype had been cancelled. Prior to his release the man was told that he could have saved himself grief had he gone along voluntarily.

In a downtown residential hotel, patrolmen found two ambulance attendants trying to persuade a man, who according to all accounts was desperately ill, to go to the hospital. After some talk, they helped the attendants in carrying the protesting patient to the ambulance and sent them off.

In a middle-class neighborhood, patrolmen found a partly disassembled car, tools, a loudly blaring radio, and five beer-drinking youths at the curb in front of a single-family home. The home-owner complained that this had been going on for several days and the men had refused to take their activities elsewhere. The patrolmen ordered the youths to pack up and leave. When one sassed them they threw him into the squad car, drove him to the precinct station, from where he was released after receiving a severe tongue lashing from the desk sergeant.

In the apartment of a quarreling couple, patrolmen were told by the wife, whose nose was bleeding, that the husband stole her purse containing money she earned. The patrolmen told the man they would "take him in," whereupon he returned the purse and they left.

What all these vignettes are meant to illustrate is that whatever the substance of the task at hand, whether it involves protection against an undesired imposition, caring for those who cannot care for themselves, attempting to solve a crime, helping to save a life, abating a nuisance, or settling an explosive dispute, police intervention means above all making use of the capacity and authority to overpower resistance to an attempted solution in the native habitat of the problem. There can be no doubt that this feature of police work is uppermost in the minds of people who solicit police aid or direct the attention of the police to problems, that persons against whom the police proceed have this feature in mind and conduct themselves accordingly, and that every conceivable police intervention projects the message that force may be, and may have to be, used to achieve a desired objective. It does not matter whether the persons who seek police help are private citizens or other government officials, nor does it matter whether the problem at hand involves some aspect of law enforcement or is totally unconnected with it.

40

It must be emphasized, however, that the conception of the centrality of the capacity to use force in the police role does not entail the conclusion that the ordinary occupational routines consist of the actual exercise of this capacity. It is very likely, though we lack information on this point, that the actual use of physical coercion and restraint is rare for all policemen and that many policemen are virtually never in the position of having to resort to it. What matters is that police procedure is defined by the feature that it may not be opposed in its course, and that force can be used if it is opposed. This is what the existence of the police makes available to society. Accordingly, the question, "What are policemen supposed to do?" is almost completely identical with the question, "What kinds of situations require remedies that are non-negotiably coercible?" [66]

Our second justification for preferring the definition of the police role we proposed to the traditional law enforcement focus of the role requires us to review the actual police practices to see to what extent they can be subsumed under the conception we offered. To begin we can take note that law enforcement and crime control are obviously regarded as calling for remedies that are non-negotiably coercible. According to available estimates, approximately one-third of available manpower resources of the police are at any time committed to dealing with crimes and criminals. Though this may seem to be a relatively small share of the total resources of an agency ostensibly devoted to crime control, it is exceedingly unlikely that any other specific routine police activity, such as traffic regulation, crowd control, supervision of licensed establishments, settling of citizens' disputes, emergency health aids, ceremonial functions, or any other, absorb

---

[66] By "non-negotiably coercible" we mean that when a deputized police officer decides that force is necessary, then, within the boundaries of this situation, he is not accountable to anyone, nor is he required to brook the arguments or opposition of anyone who might object to it. We set this forth not as a legal but as a practical rule. The legal question whether citizens may oppose policemen is complicated. Apparently resisting police coercion in situations of emergency is not legitimate; see Hans Kelsen, *General Theory of Law and State*, New York: Russel & Russel, 1961, pp. 278-279, and H. A. L. Hart, *The Concept of Law*, Oxford: Clarendon Press, 1961, pp. 20-21. Common law doctrine allows that citizens may oppose "unlawful arrest," 6 *Corpus Juris Secundum*, Arrest #13, p. 613; against this, the Uniform Arrest Act, drafted by a committee of the Interstate Commission on Crime in 1939, provides in Section 5, "If a person has reasonable grounds to believe that he is being arrested by a peace officer, it is his duty to refrain from using force or any weapons in resisting arrest regardless of whether or not there is a legal basis for the arrest." S. B. Warner, "Uniform Arrest Act," *Vanderbilt Law Review*, 28 (1942) 315-347. At present, at least twelve states are governed by case law recognizing the validity of the Common Law doctrine, at least five have adopted the rule contained in the Uniform Arrest Act, and at least six have case law or statutes that give effect to the Uniform Arrest Act rule. That the trend is away from the Common Law doctrine and in the direction of the Uniform Arrest Act rule is argued in Max Hochanadel and H. W. Stege, "The Right to Resist an Unlawful Arrest: An Outdated Concept?" *Tulsa Law Journal*, 3 (1966) 40-46. I am grateful for the help I received from 35 of the 50 State Attorney General Offices from whom I sought information concerning this matter.

anywhere near as large a share of the remaining two-thirds. But this is precisely what one would expect on the basis of our definition. Given the likelihood that offenders will seek to oppose apprehension and evade punishment, it is only natural that the initial dealings with them be assigned to an agency that is capable of overcoming these obstacles. That is, the proposed definition of the role of the police as a mechanism for the distribution of non-negotiably coercive remedies entails the priority of crime control by direct inference. Beyond that, however, the definition also encompasses other types of activities, albeit at lower level of priority.

Because the idea that the police are basically a crimefighting agency has never been challenged in the past, no one has troubled to sort out the remaining priorities. Instead, the police have always been forced to justify activities that did not involve law enforcement in the direct sense by either linking them constructively to law enforcement or by defining them as nuisance demands for service. The dominance of this view, especially in the minds of policemen, has two pernicious consequences. First, it leads to a tendency to view all sorts of problems as if they involved culpable offenses and to an excessive reliance on quasi-legal methods for handling them. The widespread use of arrests without intent to prosecute exemplifies this state of affairs. These cases do not involve errors in judgment about the applicability of a penal norm but deliberate pretense resorted to because more appropriate methods of handling problems have not been developed. Second, the view that crime control is the only serious, important, and necessary part of police work has deleterious effects on the morale of those police officers in the uniformed patrol who spend most of their time with other matters. No one, especially he who takes a positive interest in his work, likes being obliged to do things day-in and day-out that are disparaged by his colleagues. Moreover, the low evaluation of these duties leads to neglecting the development of skill and knowledge that are required to discharge them properly and efficiently.

It remains to be shown that the capacity to use coercive force lends thematic unity to all police activity in the same sense in which, let us say, the capacity to cure illness lends unity to everything that is ordinarily done in the field of medical practice. While everybody agrees that the police actually engage in an enormous variety of activities, only a part of which involves law enforcement, many argue that this state of affairs does not require explanation but change. Smith, for example, argued that the imposition of duties and demands that are not related to crime control dilutes the effectiveness of the police and that the growing

42

trend in this direction should be curtailed and even reversed.[67] On the face of it this argument is not without merit, especially if one considers that very many of those activities that are unrelated to law enforcement involve dealing with problems that lie in the field of psychiatry, social welfare, human relations, education, and so on. Each of these fields has its own trained specialists who are respectively more competent than the police. It would seem preferable, therefore, to take all those matters that belong properly to other specialists out of the hands of the police and turn them over to those to whom they belong. Not only would this relieve some of the pressures that presently impinge on the police, but it would also result in better services.[68]

Unfortunately, this view overlooks a centrally important factor. While it is true that policemen often aid sick and troubled people because physicians and social workers are unable or unwilling to take their services where they are needed, this is not the only or even the main reason for police involvement. In fact, physicians and social workers themselves quite often "call the cops." For not unlike the case of the administration of justice, on the periphery of the rationally ordered procedures of medical and social work practice lurk exigencies that call for the exercise of coercion. Since neither physicians nor social workers are authorized or equipped to use force to attain desirable objectives, the total disengagement of the police would mean allowing many a problem to move unhampered in the direction of disaster. But the non-law-enforcement activities of the police are by no means confined to matters that are wholly or even mainly within the purview of some other institutionalized remedial specialty. Many, perhaps most, consist of addressing situations in which people simply do not seem to be able to manage their own lives adequately. Nor is it to be taken for granted that these situations invariably call for the use, or the threat of the use, of force. It is enough if there is need for immediate and unquestioned intervention that must not be allowed to be defeated by possible resistance. And where there is a possibility of great harm, the intervention would appear to be justified even if the risk is, in statistical terms, quite remote. Take, for instance the presence of mentally ill persons in the community. Though it is well known that most live quiet and unobtrusive lives, they are perceived as occasionally constituting a serious hazard to themselves and others. Thus, it is not surprising that the police are always prepared to deal with these persons

---

[67] Smith, *op. cit. supra*, Note 1.

[68] The authors of the *Task Force Report: Police* note that little has been done to make these alternative resources available as substitutes for police intervention; *op. cit. supra*, Note 56 at p. 14.

at the slightest indication of a possible emergency. Similarly, though very few family quarrels lead to serious consequences, the fact that most homicides occur among quarreling kin leads to the preparedness to intervene at the incipient stages of problems.

In sum, the role of the police is to address all sorts of human problems when and insofar as their solutions do or may possibly require the use of force at the point of their occurrence. This lends homogeneity to such diverse procedures as catching a criminal, driving the mayor to the airport, evicting a drunken person from a bar, directing traffic, crowd control, taking care of lost children, administering medical first aid, and separating fighting relatives.

There is no exaggeration in saying that there is topical unity in this very incomplete list of lines of police work. Perhaps it is true that the common practice of assigning policemen to chauffeur mayors is based on the desire to give the appearance of thrift in the urban fisc. But note, if one wanted to make as far as possible certain that nothing would ever impede His Honor's freedom of movement, he would certainly put someone into the driver's seat of the auto who has the authority and the capacity to overcome all unforeseeable human obstacles. Similarly, it is perhaps not too farfetched to assume that desk sergeants feed ice cream to lost children because they like children. But if the treat does not achieve the purpose of keeping the youngster in the station house until his parents arrive to redeem him, the sergeant would have to resort to other means of keeping him there.

We must now attempt to pull together the several parts of the foregoing discussion in order to show how they bring into relief the main problems of adjusting police function to life in modern society, and in order to elaborate constructively certain consequences that result from the assumption of the role definitions we have proposed.

At the beginning we observed that the police appear to be burdened by an opprobrium that did not seem to lessen proportionately to the acknowledged improvements in their practices. To explain this puzzling fact we drew attention to three perceived features of the police that appear to be substantially independent of particular work methods. First, a stigma attaches to police work because of its connection with evil, crime, perversity, and disorder. Though it may not be reasonable, it is common that those who fight the dreadful end up being dreaded themselves. Second, because the police must act quickly and often on mere intuition, their interventions are lacking in those aspects of moral sophistication which only a more extended and more scrupulous consideration can afford. Hence their methods are comparatively crude. Third, because it is commonly assumed that the risks of the kinds of breakdowns that require police action are much more heavily concentrated in the lower classes than in other segments of society, police surveillance is inherently discriminatory. That is, all things being equal, some persons feel the sting of police scrutiny merely because of their station in life. Insofar as this is felt, police work has divisive effects in society.

Next, we argued that one cannot understand how the police "found themselves" in this unenviable position without taking into consideration that one of the cultural trends of roughly the past century-and-a-half was the sustained aspiration to install peace as a stable condition of everyday life. Though no one can fail being impressed by the many ways the attainment of this ideal has been frustrated, it is possible to find some evidence of partially effective efforts. Many aspects of mundane existence in our cities have become more pacific than they have been in past epochs of history. More importantly for our purposes, in the domain of internal statecraft, the distance between those who govern and those who are governed has grown and the gap has been filled with bureaucratically symbolized communication. Where earlier compliance was secured by physical presence and armed might, it now rests mainly on peaceful persuasion and rational compliance. We found the trend toward the pacification in governing most strongly demonstrated in the administration of justice. The banishment of all forms of violence from the criminal process, as administered by the courts, has as a corollary the legalization of judicial proceedings. The latter reflects a movement away from peremptory and oracular judgment to a method in which all decisions are based on exhaustively rational grounds involving the use of explicit legal norms. Most important among those norms are the ones that limit the powers of authority and specify the rights of defendants. The legalization and pacification of the criminal process was achieved by, among other things, expelling from its purview those processes that set it into motion. Since in the initial steps, where suspicions are formed and arrests are made, force and intuition cannot be eliminated entirely, purity can be maintained by not taking notice of them. This situation is, however, paradoxical if we are to take seriously the idea that the police is a law enforcement agency in the strict sense of legality. The recognition of this paradox became unavoidable as early as in 1914, in the landmark decision of *Weeks* v. *U.S.* In the following decades the United States Supreme Court issued a series of rulings affecting police procedure which foster the impression that the judiciary exercises control over the police. But this impression is misleading, for the rulings do not set forth binding norms for police work but merely provide that *if* the police propose to set the criminal process into motion, *then* they must proceed in certain legally restricted ways. These restrictions are, therefore, conditional, specifying as it were the terms of delivery and acceptance of a service and nothing more. Outside of this arrangement the judges have no direct concerns with police work and will take notice of its illegality, if it is illegal, only when offended citizens seek civil redress.

Because only a small part of the activity of the police is dedicated to law enforcement and because they deal with the majority of their problems without invoking the law, a broader definition of their role was proposed. After reviewing briefly what the public appears to expect of the police, the range of activities police actually engage in, and the theme that unifies all these activities, it was suggested that *the role of the police is best understood as a mechanism for the distribution of non-negotiably coercive force employed in accordance with the dictates of an intuitive grasp of situational exigencies.*

It is, of course, not surprising that a society committed to the establishment of peace by pacific means and to the abolishment of all forms of violence from the fabric of its social relations, at least as a matter of official morality and policy, would establish a corps of specially deputized officials endowed with the exclusive monopoly of using force contingently where limitations of foresight fail to provide alternatives. That is, given the melancholy appreciation of the fact that the total abolition of force is not attainable, the closest approximation to the ideal is to limit it as a special and exclusive trust. If it is the case, however, that the mandate of the police is organized around their capacity and authority to use force, i.e., if this is what the institution's existence makes available to society, then the evaluation of that institution's performance must focus on it. While it is quite true that policemen will have to be judged on other dimensions of competence, too— for example, the exercise of force against criminal suspects requires some knowledge about crime and criminal law—their methods as society's agents of coercion will have to be considered central to the overall judgment.

The proposed definition of the police role entails a difficult moral problem. How can we arrive at a favorable or even accepting judgment about an activity which is, in its very conception, opposed to the ethos of the polity that authorizes it? Is it not well nigh inevitable that this mandate be concealed in circumlocution? While solving puzzles of moral philosophy is beyond the scope of this analysis, we will have to address this question

46

in a somewhat more mundane formulation: namely, on what terms can a society dedicated to peace institutionalize the exercise of force?

It appears that in our society two answers to this question are acceptable. One defines the targets of legitimate force as enemies and the coercive advance against them as warfare. Those who wage this war are expected to be possessed by the military virtues of valor, obedience and *esprit de corps*. The enterprise as a whole is justified as a sacrificial and glorious mission in which the warrior's duty is "not to reason why." The other answer involves an altogether different imagery. The targets of force are conceived as practical objectives and their attainment a matter of practical expediency. The process involves prudence, economy, and considered judgment, from case to case. The enterprise as a whole is conceived as a public trust, the exercise of which is vested in individual practitioners who are personally responsible for their decisions and actions.

Reflection suggests that the two patterns are profoundly incompatible. Remarkably, however, our police departments have not been deterred from attempting the reconciliation of the irreconciliable. Thus, our policemen are exposed to the demand of a conflicting nature in that their actions are supposed to reflect military prowess and professional acumen.

In the following, we will review certain well-known aspects of police organization and practice in an attempt to show that the adherence to the quasi-military model by our police forces is largely a self-defeating pretense. Its sole effect is to create obstacles in the development of a professional police system. On the basis of this review we will attempt to formulate an outline of a model of the police role in modern society that is recognizably in accord with existing practices but which contains safeguards against the existence and proliferation of those aspects of police work that are generally regarded as deplorable. In other words, the proposed suggestions will be innovative only in the sense that they will accent already existing strength and excise impeding ballasts.

[2]

A Social Contract Perspective on the Police Role

Howard S. Cohen
Michael Feldberg

Police ethics, like all professional ethics, must be grounded in a broader moral perspective. A moral perspective is a point of view that highlights the moral and ethical dimensions of actions and events. The perspective helps us examine human actions in a moral light, so that we can make value judgments about what is good or bad, or what is right or wrong. From a moral perspective, the field of police ethics particularly has some clear rights and wrongs. For example, refusing a bribe is not only following department rules or the dictates of law but is doing the right and honorable thing. Except for the special case in which a police officer was acting as part of an anti-corruption investigation, there is no moral perspective that could justify taking a bribe.

Most of the time, our judgments do not require a very refined moral perspective. Each of us has a notion of common decency that is widely accepted in our society. We have learned it from our parents and our teachers. It is incorporated into religious teachings and espoused by national leaders. We pick it up from observation, experience and instruction. This is not to say that what we have learned is a carefully articulated moral theory, but "common decency" does provide a shared sense of right and wrong. Most of us believe that it is wrong to steal, to cheat at cards or to do violence to innocent children. It is right to keep your promises, to help people in need and be fair in your dealings with others.

Common decency can take most of us a long way as we deal with life's difficulties or deal with other people. However, when we think

24   Standards of Police Ethics

of making moral judgments about police, we quickly realize that we cannot easily comprehend their actions or their moral situation in terms of common decency alone. Police have more power than the average citizen and are authorized to use force where others are forbidden. They are expected to keep social order, even when the rest of us have the impulse to carouse, to protest or even to riot. Finally, they are expected to operate in dangerous circumstances, risking their safety so we can have ours. Their duties and their working environment often place the police in situations where common decency has broken down. Holding them to its standards can be irrelevant or worse in extreme circumstances, such as negotiating with hostage-takers. It is often inappropriate to judge police work by the standards we would use for common social interaction or even business dealings.

Our assumption is that we need a different, more appropriate moral perspective for evaluating police work. It is important to remember that police work is a public function; that is, a political and governmental function. Police work is a form of public service, much as fire-fighting, emergency medical care or primary education are public services. In modern society, providing police service is a fundamental duty of government. Seen in this light, the moral basis of police work can be found in the moral basis of government activity itself.

A BRIEF HISTORY OF SOCIAL CONTRACT THEORY

Social contract theory provides an appropriate moral foundation for understanding and evaluating police practices. The theory lies at the very foundation of our society's social arrangements and its form of government. The nation's most important political documents, the Declaration of Independence and the Constitution, deeply reflect the influence of seventeenth- and eighteenth-century social contract philosophy. Thomas Jefferson, chief drafter of the Declaration, was a careful student of the English political theorists Thomas Hobbes and John Locke, leading articulators of social contract theory. It seems appropriate, therefore, that our theory of police ethics should be grounded in a broader political theory that has shaped the structure and practice of American government. After all, the police are among the most visible agents of government and, for most of us, agents of government that are highly identifiable on the street.

A Social Contract Perspective   25

This contractual perspective on the police is especially helpful because it is the perspective that underlies our own form of government—a perspective articulated in the Declaration of Independence and the Constitution. As noted previously, the idea of the social contract, as it has come into our own political history, was articulated most clearly by two seventeenth-century English political writers, Thomas Hobbes and John Locke. Caught up in two separate seventeenth-century revolutions in which English monarchies were being challenged and even overthrown, these two men asked the question, "What is the basis of political authority?" With some variation, Hobbes and Locke each developed the image of government as the outcome of an agreement among citizens. More precisely, the theory of the social contract treats *both government itself and the authority it exercises* as the products of a bargain or compact struck between rulers and citizens. That bargain identifies the rights and obligations of each party to the relationship.

Although the social contract perspective is deeply ingrained in American political culture, we have not, of course, taken it over from seventeenth-century England without change. It is important to remember that both Hobbes and Locke thought of society as a society of property holders. They did not include in their thinking about political rights and political participation women, the poor or those in bondage. Social contract theory does not speak to issues of democracy or universal suffrage. It addresses, rather, issues about the sources and limits of governmental authority.

Thomas Hobbes argued that political authority derived from the presumed consent of the governed rather than from a divine right bestowed by God on a hereditary monarch. Hobbes made this argument in his best-known work, *Leviathan* (1649),[1] as England was headed for civil war over a struggle between Charles I, who claimed to rule by divine right, and Parliament, which tried to subject Charles to its laws. Eventually, Parliament won out and ordered Charles beheaded. Oliver Cromwell, at the invitation of Parliament, assumed political authority as the head of state. Cromwell's authority could not be grounded in the divine right of a king—he had no blood connection to a hereditary monarch— but Hobbes defended Cromwell's authority by arguing that it rested in the *office* of the ruler rather than his *personhood*.[2]

Political authority, as Hobbes conceived it, was given over by each person in society, unanimously and collectively, to an individual or individuals who could protect them from each other and protect them from a life that would otherwise inevitably be "solitary, poor, nasty, brutish and short."[3] In exchange for taking on the obligation to protect the lives of citizens and to create the secure conditions that would permit a reasonable life for each of them, citizens grant the ruler authority to make laws and the power needed to enforce them. During the revolutionary years of the 1640s, the terms in which Hobbes described the origins of government authority (improved chances for citizens' lives and security in exchange for their grant of authority and power to the ruler) must have seemed a reasonable bargain—at least to property holders. Nevertheless, one criticism that has since been applied to Hobbes's ideas is that they imposed few limits on the behavior or power of the ruler. So long as he provided security for the lives and property of citizens, he could choose virtually any of the means by which he governed.

John Locke was also writing about these issues in another revolutionary era, although the "Glorious Revolution" of 1688 was hardly as perilous as the civil war forty years earlier. In 1660, after the Cromwell years, Parliament restored the Stuarts to the English throne: Charles II, son of the beheaded former king, ruled until his own death in 1685; his brother, James II, succeeded him. The restoration of the Stuart monarchy in effect reopened the question of whether kings ruled by divine right or by consent of the governed. All of the issues between king and Parliament that had been contested in the 1640s were contested again. Supporters of the king published vigorous defenses of divine right theory. A friend of the parliamentary party, Locke penned his *First Treatise on Civil Government* (1688),[4] which systematically attacked the writings of divine right apologist Robert Filmer. Locke's better-known *Second Treatise*[5], published in 1691, was dedicated to the reign of William and Mary of Orange, who Parliament invited to England from the Netherlands in 1685 to replace the exiled James II. Once again, Parliament's forcible removal of a monarch needed justification and, like Hobbes, Locke did this through a theory of political legitimacy based on the notion of consent of the governed.

In the *Second Treatise*, Locke identified the purpose of government as providing safety and security to the governed, and he attempted to demonstrate why any reasonable person would accept these services from government rather than trying to provide them for himself or herself. Locke's version of the social contract establishes a more limited form of government than that envisioned by Hobbes. No doubt conditions in England in Locke's time were less severe, and a rational person would be less inclined to give so much power to an authority when the alternative was not so dire. The American Founding Fathers were deeply influenced by Locke's concept of a limited government, based on a social contract, and grounded in the consent of the governed. They found in the *Second Treatise* both the justification for separation from England in 1776 and the blueprint for a federal form of national government in 1787.

The Declaration of Independence asserts, in effect, that the government of England was no longer keeping its bargain with the citizens of the American colonies. The Declaration begins with Locke's assertion that "all men are created equal" and that they have rightful claims to life, liberty and property (Jefferson substituted "happiness" for "property" in the Declaration).[6] In Locke's view, the rights are inalienable, that is, cannot be either taken or even given away, because they are not granted by government (people would have them even in a "State of Nature," that is, a condition in which government did not exist). Nor, even after government is formed, are the individual's rights simply surrendered completely to that government. The purpose of government as the American Founding Fathers described it is simply to "secure" those rights that citizens already possess but have difficulty maintaining on their own. This is why people consent to give over or transfer their own authority to government—why they choose to become part of society rather than spend all their energies in the struggles of self-defense and defense of their material goods. Government, in a sense, is the agent of the citizens, providing collective security more effectively than sovereign individuals could do for themselves.

The Founding Fathers took from Locke the idea that, when a government no longer protects the individual's rights to life, liberty and property, it breaks its contract with the citizenry. In turn, citizens have a right, even a duty, to replace that government with another that will do a more effective job of providing for "safety and happiness." In a few short paragraphs, the authors of the Declaration presented the outlines of Locke's account of governmental authority before going on to list in detail the ways in which they felt the English government had abused or undermined it.

Locke's influence extended to the creation of the Constitution as well. The Constitution bears Locke's stamp in the sense that it structures the federal government along the lines of the three main governmental functions outlined in the *Second Treatise*: legislative, executive and judicial.[7] The Constitution goes beyond Locke's thinking in that it separates these functions into different branches of government, and places them in a system of checks and balances. Locke was not troubled by the possibility of joining all three functions into a single office or constitutional monarch, but the American experience under the reign of King George III would have made such an arrangement unthinkable by 1787, when the Constitution was drafted.

The Lockean underpinnings of the Constitution are also apparent in the general line of defense of the Constitution that appeared in the *Federalist Papers*, a series of newspaper editorials written by Alexander Hamilton, James Madison and John Jay meant to encourage electors in the various states to adopt the proposed Constitution of 1787, rather than continue American government under the Articles of Confederation.[8] The Federalist argument in favor of the Constitution begins from the problem of security in a hostile world, in effect, the problem of life in the state of nature (that is, life without government). In *Federalist Paper* No. 15, Hamilton stressed the importance of "safety and happiness" for society, and argued that both were threatened by the "anarchy" that he saw emerging under the weak form of national government authorized under the Articles of Confederation.[9] By creating a stronger central government, the Constitution promised to become the new social compact that would free the United States from that anarchy. The Federalists urged its adoption on the grounds that it provided the judicious balance of "stability and energy of government" on the one side, with liberty and representation on the other (*Federalist* No. 37).[10]

THE POLICE AND SOCIAL CONTRACT THEORY

Although both Locke and the Founding Fathers speak of government in general rather than police in particular, the social contract perspective permits a more detailed account of the powers and obligations of specific government agents. It is possible, from the perspective of the social contract, to explain the difference between the proper exercise of police authority (such as arresting a person who is the subject of a warrant) and the abuse of police authority (demanding cash from local tavern owners not to check the I.D.s of their young-looking patrons), between equal protection of citizens (not picking out black teenagers for harassment) and special privileges for some citizens (letting a personal friend or relative walk away from a drunk-driving offense), and between protecting citizens' liberty and security (proactive patrolling of high-crime areas) and jeopardizing the safety and security of the citizenry (conducting a high-speed auto chase on a busy city street).

It is worth looking a little more closely at John Locke's understanding of the social contract in order to see exactly how the responsibilities and obligations of public officials, particularly the police, can be derived from this perspective. Most of the interest by political theorists in the social contract has focused on questions of the source of sovereign authority in the people, the responsibilities of the citizenry to obey authority and the limits of authority in circumstances of revolutionary change. Less discussed, but of primary importance here, is the question of the obligations of those in authority to the citizenry. Locke, as we noted earlier, developed his conception of political authority in contrast to the idea of authority enunciated by the kings and queens of Europe, who claimed they inherited their thrones from God's biblical grant of the earth to Adam and his descendants. Similarly, Locke rejected the idea that political authority was that of ''a father over his children, a master over his servant, a husband over his wife [or] a lord over his slave.''[11] Rather, political authority is its own kind of power relationship. As Locke wrote:

Political power I take to be a right of making laws with penalties of death, and consequently all less[er] penalties, for the regulating and preserving [of] property, and of employing the force of the community, in execution of such laws, and in defense of the commonwealth from foreign injury; and all this only for the public good.[12]

To explain the extent and limits of this right of the "political power" to make and enforce laws, Locke introduced the concept of the State of Nature.[13] As we have noted, the State of Nature is Locke's name for the idea of human society without civil government—without a political authority. Locke asks us to consider what life would be like in a situation in which every person has freedom (everyone makes their own decisions) and equality (no one has authority over anyone else).[14] In such a condition, he suggests, people would live their lives without common authority: no law, no rules and no regulations. In our time, this would mean no taxes and no municipal services, such as public schools, libraries, fire departments and police. Each person would be free from the authority of others; there would be no public officials to compel us to drive on the right side of the road (if there were roads). Conversely, there would be no city hospital to go to if we were hurt, no police to call if our property were stolen, or no army to summon if our land were invaded. Each would be responsible for his or her survival and protection. In a State of Nature, in other words, we would each be on our own.

In such a State of Nature, individuals would have *liberty*.[15] For Locke, liberty means both freedom from restraints imposed by others (nobody has the right to stop you from doing what you want as long as you are not interfering with anyone else's rights), and freedom to decide what you want to do or be and pursue it.[16] In Locke's State of Nature, each person has the liberty to create a life and acquire property as he or she sees fit. No government official can confiscate that property through taxation or by eminent domain simply by claiming that it is needed for the common good. In other words, private property is strictly private, and no one else can have a claim on it.

Although it is true that each individual is free from the authority of others in the State of Nature, there are still some limits on how we ought to behave. Locke expressed this by saying that, even in a State of Nature, we are each subject to the "Law of Nature."[17] The Law of Nature, which we can know through our capacity to reason, tells us that "no one ought to harm another in his life, health, liberty or possessions."[18] Everyone is bound to "preserve himself" and, "as much as he can, preserve the rest of mankind." This law is not a creation of legislatures but something inherent in Nature, and so applies to people even where there are no governments or, even where governments do exist, no common jurisdiction.

Because Nature has its own law, people who are "harmed" by others have recourse. Everyone has the right to enforce the Law of Nature. That is, in a State of Nature, each individual also has the right of self-protection and the right to enforce his or her own rights.[19] If someone takes my property, I have the right to take it back and to impose a penalty on the person who took it. I do not have to obtain a warrant from a court to search for my missing goods, and I need not wait for a police officer to conduct the investigation. Nor do I need a court to tell me what penalty to impose on the individual who stole my goods, should I find that person (or decide that I probably found him or her).

A Social Contract Perspective

After all, in a State of Nature, where there is no common authority (government), institutions such as courts and the police do not exist.

The State of Nature is not particularly likely to be a tranquil, co-operative society. Although it is possible that people without a common authority might live peacefully, it is also possible, indeed likely, that some people will attempt to take advantage of the physical weakness of others. The strong would try to steal property from and even enslave the weak. In those circumstances, the State of Nature simply becomes a state of war[20] (Hobbes called it the "war of all against all"). The threat of war highlights the greatest deficiency of the State of Nature: individuals in it lack security.[21]

In the State of Nature, there is no one in authority to help me enforce my rights, protect my property and maintain my liberty. If others more powerful than I decide to interfere with my liberty or take my property, how can I stop them? There is no authority I can call on for help—no sheriff to ride into town at high noon and shoot the "bad guys" for me. I have the right to retaliate against them, of course, but since my tormentors are more powerful than I, how can I exercise this right? I could get a gun, an "equalizer," but so could my tormentors. Self-defense is not effective here. In a State of Nature, I would always be looking over my shoulder, watching out to see that no one was threatening my property or encroaching on my liberty. I would be preoccupied with self-protection. Each time I accumulated anything of value, I would feel like an exposed target. As soon as my life became a little more comfortable, it would also become a little more insecure.

Since a life like this would be intolerable, reasonable people would look for a better way to live together. In Locke's words:

Men being . . . by nature all free, equal and independent, no one can be put out of his estate and subjected to the political power of another without his own consent, which is done by agreeing with other men, to join and unite in a community for their comfortable, safe and peaceable living, one amongst another, in secure enjoyment of their properties, and a greater security than any that are not of it.[22]

Free, rational people see the advantages of a more secure life and therefore would voluntarily choose to leave the State of Nature for life in an organized community, that is, political (civil) society. Locke calls the process by which individuals make the choice to live in political society a "compact,"[23] or social contract. In every bargain or contract, individuals exchange something they have and are willing to part with for something they want but lack. In a State of Nature, people have liberty and lack security. Reasonable people would trade some of their liberty for increased security.

As we noted earlier, the liberty that individuals have in a State of Nature includes the liberty to enforce their own rights. That is, they have the freedom to protect themselves and their property from threats by others. Of course, for the relatively weak, these rights are difficult to enforce; even for the strong, it is almost impossible to protect oneself all the time, or to fight off coalitions of others who outweigh or outnumber even the strongest individual.

Since in a bargain one gives up something he already has in order to get something he does not, under the social contract each individual transfers to an authority the liberty to enforce his own rights (not much of a sacrifice) in exchange for greater security (an indisputable benefit). The contract is the means by which individuals designate an agent (the state or government) to act on their behalf. This agent exercises the individuals' rights to safety and security by making rules for common living (for example, that no one may take the property of another without due process of law; no person may kill another except in self-defense; no one may enter the home of another uninvited). The end result is a trade-off: although individuals in civil society may have less liberty to pursue their private ends, they have greater security to enjoy the fruits of their labor. Their agent, government, has assumed the burden of protecting their lives, their property and their remaining liberty to develop their lives as they see fit.

Because Locke thinks of the social contract as a bargain, he insists that each individual who is a party to it should be thought of as having consented to it.[24] It is consent that binds individuals to the decisions made and actions taken by political authorities.[25] This consent may be explicit or tacit.[26] Tacit consent is given by those who "enjoy" or benefit from the laws of a political society. Locke regards mere benefit as a reasonable sign of consent, because he thinks it would be a contradiction to accept society's protection but deny the grounds on which it rests.[27] In other words, everyone is a party to the social contract, without exception, even if some refuse to recognize this condition. Given Locke's focus on property holders, we can understand the force of the tacit consent argument. Surely the benefits of protection of property are considerable in most societies. The argument is less compelling for the dispossessed. It is not so clear that a rational person with nothing—and nothing to lose—would agree to civil society over the State of Nature. Having noted this point, though, it is also worth remembering that the obligations of those in authority to "citizens" and "aliens" alike are not diminished by their inclusion in or exclusion from the social contract. All fall under the jurisdiction of the common authority.

Locke's conception of consent of the governed helps to clarify another point: the social contract is not a historical document.[28] To be sure, Locke thinks there may have been times in history when free people did come together and agree to create a government.[29] However, his point is that each rational person voluntarily consents to the necessary existence of political authority. The social contract—the deal struck among all those who comprise society—is only a hypothetical bargain. We do not actually sign a contract when we are born or when we become old enough to vote. Rather, we live together *as if* we had. When we contemplate the advantages and disadvantages of the State of Nature compared to civil society, we as rational individuals would of course consent to enter civil society. It is a significantly better way to live. In practice, however, no one asks us whether we wish to join society. We are assumed to have done so.

The social contract is a bargain with a specific purpose: preservation of life, liberty and property. Consequently, we owe allegiance only to those governments that achieve that purpose. Such governments have very specific obligations to their citizens. First, they must establish and make known the laws of common living—the legislative function.[30] Second, they must provide "an indifferent judge, with authority to determine all differences according to established law"—the judicial function.[31] Third, they must "back and support the sentence when right"—the executive function.[32] Locke thus proposed the division of roles among the legislature, judiciary and executive—the "separation of powers"—that characterizes the American constitutional system.

For Locke, individuals consent to a common authority in order that these three functions are carried out. Government has a very specific charge from its citizens, rather than *carte blanche* to organize society in ways that serve the interests of those who govern. In other words, the social contract is a limited bargain. Individuals do not give up all their rights to the common authority. They only give up the rights to make law, adjudicate their own disputes and enforce their own rights, that is, act as legislator, detective, arresting officer, prosecutor, judge, jury and executioner in their own case. They also give up these rights only on the condition that they receive improved security in exchange. If life under a government were less secure than life in a State of Nature (as it is for some in authoritarian states), then free, rational people would not agree to the contract.

Even if government were not cruel but merely incompetent, that is, if it were unable to provide security because it was run by weak, unintelligent or corrupt individuals, it would also fail to fulfill its obligations under the social contract. For government to provide security, it must be energetic enough to make rules and enforce them. Its representatives must be strong enough to assure that the rules are obeyed. Unless government is strong enough to protect individual rights, no one is secure.

Social contract theory is compatible with several forms of government. As long as government carries out its three central functions, it may be a democracy, an oligarchy, a monarchy (hereditary or elective) or any combination of these.[33] In Locke's version of the contract, we consent to the functions and responsibilities of government, rather than its form. Of course, in the contemporary United States, few of us would consent to anything other than a democracy.

In a democratic society, political debates sometimes revolve around whether the government has become too strong, whether too much individual liberty has been exchanged for security and whether each citizen has equal access to the benefits of government security. At other times, individuals concerned about social disorder or crime worry that government has provided for too much liberty or that criminals have too many rights. Given that liberty and security are seen as trade-offs (that is, that they are elements exchanged in a bargain), it is not surprising that each generation wishes to re-examine the terms under which the social contract is made, or that certain groups in society would question whether all members of society benefit equally from the bargain. We know, of course, that they do not, and the press for civil rights by various social groups can be understood in these terms. Indeed, Locke would encourage each individual to go through this rational exercise in allegiance.[34]

THE POLICE OFFICER AS SPORTS REFEREE: A USEFUL ANALOGY

One way to think about the role of government under Locke's conception of social contract is to think about government as if it were a referee at a sporting event, say a professional hockey or basketball game, or the umpire in major league baseball. The executive branch in particular (of which the police are a part) and sports referees share the quality of having authority and power. As referee, the executive interprets rules (the laws), enforces them and arbitrates disputes among "players" (citizens). As with referees, the public seems to enjoy booing the performance of government, but most seem to abide by its decisions.

We are introducing the referee analogy here because it is implicit in the Lockean conception of governmental function (he speaks of the government as an "Umpire") and because it helps to clarify the specific obligations of authorities to the citizenry. However, it is important to remember that this analogy only works at a very broad conceptual level. It is not an analogy that differentiates police functions from those of judges, prosecutors, prison guards, parole officers and others with authority in law enforcement organizations. The police are sometimes, literally, referees, but in many other of their functions they are not. Nevertheless, if one thinks of the laws as, in a general sense, the "rules of the game," then law enforcement has some structural similarities to refereeing.[35] The analogy is a heuristic; it permits us to think about the obligations of police in a different, but more familiar light—the obligations of sports referees. We have found this analogy especially helpful in introducing these concepts in police-training classes. The value of the comparison is that we can use our understanding of "good refereeing" to understand the elements of "good" law enforcement and to see how they are derived from the social contract perspective.

A referee's purpose is to make certain that the game is played fairly and within the rules. To achieve this end, a referee must have certain attributes and attitudes. For one, the referee must be neutral: above the game and disinterested in its outcome. He must not favor some players at the expense of others. He must not care who wins. Imagine what would happen if a basketball referee were rooting for one of the competing teams, or if the umpire calling balls and strikes had bet on the home team. Imagine a hockey referee with a prejudice against Canadian players who refused to call penalties on American players. Favoritism, prejudice and self-interest can each distort a referee's capacity to judge a game fairly.

When players feel that a referee is unfair, the contest can deteriorate so that players play and enforce their own rules, which increases their chances of getting hurt. A player who thinks that the referee is not protecting his or her interests, or is favoring the other side, will often try to even the odds by cheating, breaking the rules or retaliating against opponents he feels are getting away with unseen or uncalled violations. Sometimes we see in hockey or basketball the retaliatory punch thrown by a distraught player who feels that he was fouled but the referee was unwilling to blow the whistle on the violator. When a player believes that the referee is not neutral or fair, such retaliation is an almost inevitable result.

Put another way, the referee must maintain control over the game both to keep it flowing smoothly and to keep the players from retaliating for real or imagined fouls. That is, the referee enforces the official rules so that players refrain from imposing their private version of justice. As parties to a social contract (membership in the league implies agreement to follow the rules set by the league), players agree to give the referee a monopoly on deciding which actions are violations and which are not. If the referee cannot maintain the respect of the players, the players will challenge his or her monopoly on authority, and the crowd will "get on the referee's back," reinforcing the disrespect shown by the players. So too with governments; if they cannot maintain law and order in society, vigilante groups arise to enforce their own rights, or racketeers offer protections to those who can, or who are forced to, pay for it.

The police are the most visible government agents playing the role of social referee. Police departments and individual officers both derive their authority and power from the social contract. The contract illuminates the police role, and it also illuminates the moral obligations the police assume because of their role. As social referees, the police have power and authority like that of a sports referee: they must maintain their authority and control of the game (keeping public order); they must stay neutral and above the game (not play favorites, do special favors or receive rewards); they must enforce the rules (enforce the law); they must protect the players' interest (protect property and ensure public safety); and they must keep the players from taking the rules

A Social Contract Perspective   37

into their own hands (settle disputes fairly, terminate fights and prevent violence).

Just as professional sports leagues evaluate their referees each season to determine whether they are performing their duties adequately, as parties to the social contract, we are entitled to evaluate the performance of our agents (government officials in general and police in particular) in regard to their success at "refereeing" society. The perspective of the social contract allows us to derive five ethical standards from which to make moral assessments of police work. The next chapter delineates those standards, explains why they are useful for evaluating police work and explores some of the ways in which police work may or may not live up to the standards.

NOTES

1. Thomas Hobbes, *Leviathan* (New York: E.P. Dutton, 1950).

2. For an excellent account of this period, see Christopher Hill, *The Century of Revolution: 1603–1714* (New York: Norton, 1961).

3. Hobbes, p. 104.

4. John Locke, *Two Treatises of Government, A Critical Edition with an Introduction and Apparatus Criticus*, ed. Peter Laslett (Cambridge, England: Cambridge University Press, 1970).

5. Ibid.

6. Declaration of Independence.

7. Constitution of the United States.

8. *The Federalist Papers*, ed. Clinton Rossiter (New York: New American Library, 1961).

9. *Federalist Papers*, No. 15, pp. 105–13.

10. *Federalist Papers*, No. 37, pp. 224–31.

11. Locke, *Second Treatise*, Sec. 2, p. 268.

12. Ibid., Sec. 3, p. 268.

13. Ibid., Sec. 4, p. 268.

14. Ibid., Sec. 4.

15. Ibid., Sec. 6, pp. 270–71.

16. Isaiah Berlin, "Two Concepts of Liberty," *Four Essays on Liberty* (Oxford, England: Oxford University Press, 1969).

17. Locke, *Second Treatise*, Sec. 6, pp. 270–71.

18. Ibid.

19. Ibid., Sec. 8, p. 272.

20. Ibid., Sec. 16, pp. 278–79.

21. Ibid., Sec. 19, pp. 280–81.

22. Ibid., Sec. 95, pp. 330–31.
23. Ibid., Sec. 97, p. 332.
24. Ibid., Sec. 96, pp. 331–32.
25. Ibid., Sec. 97, p. 332.
26. Ibid., Sec. 119, pp. 347–48.
27. Ibid., Sec. 120, pp. 348–49.
28. Ibid., Sec. 101, p. 334.
29. Ibid., Sec. 103, pp. 335–36.
30. Ibid., Sec. 124, pp. 350–351.
31. Ibid., Sec. 125, p. 351.
32. Ibid., Sec. 126, p. 351.
33. Ibid., Sec. 132, p. 354.
34. Ibid., Sec. 94, pp. 329–30.
35. Technically speaking, referees are also like judges: they assign punishments. They function as police when they *detect* rules violations, and as judges when they assess the penalty for violations (i.e., free throws, points deducted, plays recalled, etc.). The analogy between police and referees has also been acknowledged from the other perspective. Earl Strom, a well-known professional basketball referee, is quoted as saying: "I would crouch down and look for things to happen. I was like a cop and, for some reason, people liked that." Jeff Coplon, "Profiles (Earl Strom)" *The New Yorker*, October 1, 1990.

[3]

Moral foundations of policing

John Kleinig

Police are occupied with peacekeeping – but preoccupied with crime fighting.

Jesse Rubin[1]

As long as human societies have existed, the police function has been needed. Social coordination and harmony have never flourished without some form of executive authority. Sometimes the executive task has been shared among many; at other times, and increasingly with the division of social labor, it has devolved upon selected individuals, organized and coordinated to provide that service effectively and efficiently. What we now most generally refer to as policing usually dates itself from the formation, in 1829, of the London Metropolitan Police, a legislatively mandated organization designed to provide round-the-clock service to a community confronted by diverse needs and fears. The "principal object" of the Metropolitan Police was "the Prevention of Crime,"[2] and although, along with the detection and conviction of offenders, this has ever since been the central and distinctive concern of police organizations, it is clear even from the first instruction manual that police were expected to have a much wider social role as "problem busters" or "crisis managers."

On what *moral* basis can we justify the existence of an organization with the powers customarily vested in police? By what morally preferable alternative means might we contemplate the provision of police services? How widely should police authority and responsibility be permitted to extend? It is to these general questions of political morality that the present chapter is directed.

Like many others who have considered these questions, I begin with social contract theory, because some version of that theory permeates most liberal democratic thinking, and appears to offer good prospects for a theory of accountable policing. Yet, as will become clear, I am not altogether comfortable with naked contractualism, because it belies much of our communal and historical experience as inheritors and perpetuators of cultural traditions, albeit traditions that can and indeed ought to be open to the scrutiny of those who are their bearers. And so I offer an account of the police role as "social peacekeeping," understood not so much as a function of social homogeneity as of social cooperation in the pursuit of the varied ends to which, as individuals and groups, we may choose to devote ourselves. To understand those ends, however, we need an appreciation of cultural histories and traditions, and must focus not only on the present and future, but also on the past that has yielded, and gives much significance to, the present.

2.1   CONSENT AND TRADITION

The justificatory framework for what we now understand by policing antedates its organizational manifestations by well over a century. In his *Second Treatise Of Civil Government*,[3] John Locke maintained that life outside of civil government – life in what he calls "a state of nature" – would be beset by certain "inconveniencies," deficiencies that would prompt rational individuals, desirous of preserving their fundamental rights, to forsake this natural state for a civil one. Although, according to Locke, humans are endowed by their Creator and by virtue of their rational nature with certain basic rights – to life, liberty, and property – their ability to exercise and secure those rights is severely hampered by several features of the human condition. These deficits of the human condition include ignorance, carelessness, partiality, and lack of power, almost surely guaranteeing that life in a state of nature will be characterized by fear, insecurity, and arbitrary interferences. In such circumstances, Locke believes that it would make sense to exchange certain of one's freedoms for the greater security of rights promised by some form of civil government.

Locke is not content to present only a general argument for government, one designed to do no more than reconcile a theory of fundamental rights with the exercise of governmental power. He is quite specific about the particular deficiencies attending a state of nature and about the kinds of governmental institutions that would rectify them. In Chapter 9 of the *Second Treatise*, he identifies three kinds of deficiencies, and nominates their institutional remedies. First of all, the Law of Nature, that fundamental standard of right and wrong, is inadequate to the task of guiding and coordinating the everyday affairs of humankind. Although this moral law is discernible to the eye of reason, our partiality, ignorance and negligence distort or obscure its dictates, and it needs to be supplemented by "an *establish'd*, settled, known *Law*, received and allowed by common consent to be the Standard of Right and Wrong, and the common measure to decide all Controversies between [people]." A legislature is called for.

But a shared law, whether natural or positive, is not sufficient to rectify the defects of a state of nature. Laws need to be applied to particular cases, and in a state of nature this will be done idiosyncratically and arbitrarily. It

Moral foundations of policing 13

is, Locke believes, a manifest fact of human experience that those who need recourse to law are likely to be biassed in their interpretation of its provisions; and where their own interests are not immediately involved, their commitment to its application is likely to be half-hearted. So, Locke writes, there needs to be instituted *"a known and indifferent Judge,* with Authority to determine all differences according to the established Law." A judiciary is called for.

Without power, however, the authority to make and apply law will come to nothing. In a state of nature, Locke observes, offenders are unlikely to offer themselves for punishment or penalization, and those who have been wronged or who stand to gain from the law may not have the power to make good their claims or position. Civil government will provide *"Power* to back and support the Sentence when right, and to *give* it due *Execution."* Institutions for law enforcement are called for.

Locke thus provides a neat and persuasive justification for the emergence of those various agencies of law enforcement – police, corrections, probation, and parole – that represent for many citizens the most immediate and visible expression of governmental authority and power. And, not surprisingly, it is social contractarianism that figures most prominently in contemporary justifications of the institution of policing.[4]

The contractarian strategy for governmental and police authority can be seen as *moral,* and not merely pragmatic if viewed in the light of the moral problem that generates it. Put in Lockean terms, it is the problem that government, any form of government, just because it places constraints and limits on beings who have certain inherent moral rights, is morally suspect. The core of that tradition, and indeed of most liberal thinking, is that mature individuals have a status that casts a moral shadow over any constraint that is placed on them. There is a moral onus on those who limit the freedom of others to provide a justification for that limitation.

Yet the social contract theory, though deeply entrenched in our cultural rhetoric of individual rights and government by consent, cannot be simply presumed to provide the whole, or even an unambiguous, justificatory story. There are hard questions that need to be faced, both generally and specifically. At the most general level there are problems concerning the existence, interpretation, range and basis of the rights that government is supposedly instituted to guarantee; the underlying conception of the bearers of those rights; and the quality and validity of the consent that liberal democracies are able to secure. More specifically, there are problems concerning the particular forms to be taken by the various institutions of government, and the most appropriate way of separating and delegating social responsibility. The role of police cannot be presumed to be timelessly settled by, say, Locke's simple tripartite division.

We cannot expect to address all these issues here; yet neither ought we to ignore them, if we wish to provide an account of policing that is attuned to both the realities of everyday life and the demands of moral theory. And so I

14   *Professional ethics*

shall indicate only briefly why an account such as Locke's needs to be amplified, amended, and supplemented if it is to retain its place within an account of police authority.

2.1.1 *The purposes of government*

According to Locke, the chief end of government is the protection of individual life, liberty, and property. No longer is that simple statement sufficient. At the time it was enunciated, it represented an assertion of individual moral claims against the oppressiveness of feudal, monarchical, and other authoritarian regimes. Since then, particularly with the formation of more democratic political structures and the rise of potentially oppressive forces outside of government (industrial and corporate powers), there has been a general shift toward the positive contribution that government may be able to make to human welfare. The right to government protection against invasions of life, liberty, and property has been reinterpreted to include the government securement or provision of what will enable those rights to be enjoyed, supplemented by other social, political, and welfare rights.

There has been, of course, no unanimity about the wisdom or justifiability of the foregoing shift, and in our current social environment the political divisions that exist between "left" and "right" manifest the tension that exists between those with more and less expansive views of the role that government should take in providing for human well-being. This tension can create confusion and difficulty for police officers, who, as agents of government, may at some times be unclear about what is expected of them and at other times be expected to offer services that they may not think it their business to provide.

2.1.2 *The bearers of rights*

The picture of human nature and human social life presented by early social contract theorists carries with it the strong suggestion that our capacities for speech, imagination and reflection preexist their civil (and social[5]) embodiment, and that civil society is simply a mechanism for preserving what is already in – albeit precarious – existence. But human life is much more deeply embedded in relatively complex social structures than this account suggests. Humans as we conceive of them do not emerge from the womb fully formed, nor do their distinctive capacities develop, like pubic hair, out of a genetic blueprint, as the (mostly) natural outcome of physiological maturation. What is most characteristically and distinctively human is the result of a long process of learning. And this process of learning is essentially social. It requires the ongoing engagement of human beings, and if it is to be at all successful, this social environment must be characterizable in certain relatively determinate ways. Determining the exact nature of these social conditions must be a matter for empirical research as well as normative reflection. But it will almost certainly include an environment characterized by care, stability, moral sensitivity, diversity of experience, interaction with others, attention to individuality, and so on.

What this means is that human social life cannot be completely resolved into relations governed by consent. Our social existence is governed as much by inherited traditions[6] – linguistic, cultural, moral, and political – as it is by structures and institutions for which our consent may and should be sought. In an important sense, we become the bearers of traditions before we become consenting agents, and the consenting agents we become will be determined in part by the traditions within which we have been nurtured. Of course, traditions are neither fixed nor inaccessible to critical scrutiny, and they may, over time, be abandoned or transformed. Indeed they *ought* to be responsive to changing situations and the progress of thought. But there is a dynamic tension here, a dialectic, that excludes a simple either/or attitude to consent and tradition.

Police work itself, and the authority vested in it, is not (and has not historically been) simply the outcome of some social contract, but it is also the expression and to some extent the perpetuator of an ongoing form of social life. What was "initiated" in 1829 was as much the outcome of a long tradition as it was a deliberate choice to create something "new."

To some extent police are expected to act as conservators of a tradition. What is more, for police themselves the work is not simply an acceptance of contractual responsibilities, but also a participation in ongoing traditions. The loyalty that police have for each other, like the loyalty of citizens to their country, is no mere fidelity to the terms of a contract, but the outcome of commitment to a way of life that has become partially constitutive of their identity. The education of police is not just the impartation of skills, but induction into a form of life. It is characterized as much by ritual and tradition as by expertise. Consent is not excluded, but it is conditioned.

Our participation in a variety of communities – families, ethnic and religious communities, political associations, and professions – informed by their distinctive traditions, brings with it the possibility of conflict, and draws attention to the importance of a personal formation that fosters individuality, and of structures that will provide opportunities for consent (and dissent). A personality constructed out of traditions that offer minimal freedom of choice risks fragmentation when those traditions come into conflict. And though refuge from such conflict can possibly be found within the walls of some single, all-encompassing tradition, such as a religious tradition, this option, though available to individuals, cannot easily be generalized. Social life of any diversity will carry within itself the seeds of struggle and accommodation.

2.1.3 *The manipulation of consent*

Were atomistic or individualistic social contractarianism considered the sole justification for our acceptance of governmental authority, our existing insti-

tutions and structures would be in dire moral straits. For the opportunities
for consent and the quality of consent generally available to us would cast
serious doubt on the validity of those institutions and structures.

Within most liberal democratic communities, consent is thought to be
executed by means of the franchise. At periodic elections, and in the processes leading up to them, citizens have the opportunity to register their will,
and to have their individual preferences count equally with those of others
in determining representation, and, less directly, social policy. The franchise
is not, perhaps, the only vehicle through which the popular will may be
expressed. Referenda, petitions, demonstrations, and media publicity all
provide channels through which advocacy, consent and dissent may be
expressed. Yet they are generally considered secondary to that provided by
the franchise.

All, however, are limited as vehicles of consent. Voters are not given
much choice about the particular form of government they will have, the
limits of its mandate, or the institutions through which it will exercise its
authority. They are, rather, socialized into an existing range of structures,
expectations and institutions, and their choices are to a significant extent
limited by these. And when we come to actual practices of government –
the influence of party machines, the prepackaging of policies, the gerry-
mandering of electorates, and manipulation by the media – we see much
that compromises the integrity of the freedom that is supposedly honored
by atomistic contractarian consent. In other words, government by consent operates within a framework provided by already existing ways of
social being and doing. Although these traditions are in some measure responsive to change, and, in fact, do change over time, they are not as
open to criticism and revision as simple atomistic contract theory would
lead us to expect.

Locke himself was aware of the awkward fit between his notion of an
original contract and its application to an ongoing civil society. He knew
there was a problem "how far any one shall be looked on to have consented,
and thereby submitted to any government where he has made no expressions of it at all." He found refuge in a notion of "tacit consent," supposedly
given when a person has benefitted from the provisions of an existing governmental authority.[7] But though consent may sometimes be tacitly given,
what Locke extends it to accommodate, and what full-fledged contractarian
justifications of the existing order must also require, almost certainly
stretches the concept beyond the bounds of its legitimate use.[8] Perhaps the
idea of tacit consent has some residual point in hypothetical contractarian
theories, which focus on some account of what (suitably defined) rational
beings *would* consent to. Here, though, it has to be recognized that one vital
connection with classical contract theory – *actual* consent – is missing.

We may, however, give a more generous (albeit problematic) interpretation to the Lockean notion of "tacit consent." If we see such tacit consent not
as a substitute for the "original consent" that brings people into civil society,
but as a "sign" that an ongoing civil order is fulfilling the contractarian

mandate (what rational beings would consent to) and therefore may lay claim to our obedience, we give some weight to the ongoing customs, traditions, values, and expectations of a community over and above what has been explicitly agreed to by its members. True, there will be an ongoing dialectical interplay between the expectations of tradition and the moral requirement of consent, but it will generally have the form of a fraternal debate rather than of negotiations between rival powers.

Even though traditional and contractual expectations may well achieve some sort of mutual accommodation, it is important to recognize their theoretically different character. Traditional expectations are more immediately rooted in affective bonds and communal ties than they are in voluntaristic, deliberative accords. Contractual expectations, on the other hand, are explicitly deliberative and calculative. In practice the distinctions begin to blur. Like love and marriage, loyalty and fidelity, friendship and partnership – indeed, like morality and law – traditional and contractual relations, and the rights and obligations that go with them, exist in something of a dynamic tension, each having its place in human social life, and neither easily sustainable without the other.

Police work must take account of this fuller background to governmental authority. Were policing to involve no more than a mechanical enforcement of laws defined by a legislature, as Locke sometimes seems to envisage, there would be some reason to ground it in an explicit contract. But police work has evolved into far more than this. Strict law enforcement comprises only a part of that work, and perhaps only a small part, and even in that part the need to exercise discretion in how law is enforced requires that police appeal to something beyond the explicit terms of any contract. If police are not to lapse into private decisions about how they are to act, they must be attuned to the cultural traditions and *mores* that inform the world they serve.

2.2 POLICE AUTHORITY

The "inconveniencies" of the state of nature are generally said to provide a sufficient reason for rational individuals to cede some part of their freedom to governmental control. But if what I have thus far argued is on the right track, this justification is too simple. We are initiated into a world of social rights and obligations before we acquire the capacity to appreciate the nature and accept the responsibilities of contract, and to a large extent these traditional rights and obligations provide a framework within which our contractual rights and obligations are voluntarily acquired. True, the traditions themselves may be revised, but, like Theseus's ship, they are reconstructed gradually, while we are still aboard, and using materials that have been fashioned en route. Some contemporary contract theories of government, by focusing on hypothetical rational consent rather than actual consent, have tended to marry these dual sources of social rights and responsibilities, for in such theories the canons of rationality have become the bearers of tradition.[9]

But whether we focus on traditional rights and obligations or on those rights and obligations for which some more contractualized justification can be sought, governmental action is to be understood, in the first instance, as an exercise of *authority* rather than of naked *coercive power*.[10] I say, "in the first instance," because the ability to enforce its will is of course integral to the idea of government. Social contract theory was developed in response to that recognition as a way of reconciling the coercive power of government with a particular conception of the rights of human personality. But governmental coercion, to the extent that it has not degenerated into dictatorial coercion, is a normatively constrained form of coercion. Although authoritatively sanctioned, the coercive dimension of government obtrudes itself only when the normative force of its requirements fails, when the "majesty" of law is denied or not heeded. Government does not merely command us, it obligates us, albeit with the threat of sanctions should we transgress its requirements.

These are, of course, normative rather than merely descriptive observations. Although, for reasons to be indicated below, the persistence of governmental *authority* will almost surely depend on the government's conformity to this understanding, unless it is perceived to have right as well as might it will lose its character as the source of law and social order, and it will become indistinguishable from the gunman, bully or tyrant for whom threat is the modus operandi. What is more, even when the might of governmental authority is exercised, it is not simply might per se, but a normatively constrained force, deemed appropriate to the normative requirement that has been disobeyed.[11] Individual actions of government or its agents may be more readily characterizable as those of the authoritarian or "tough," but so long as these do not become too pervasive, the institution will retain its authoritative character.[12]

The notion of authority has a certain complex unity, though many writers have been more inclined to focus on the complexity than on the unity. It is quite common, for example, to differentiate three kinds or forms of authority: (1) positional, or de jure, authority (someone's being *in* authority); (2) actual, or de facto, authority (someone's *having* authority); and (3) expert authority (someone's being *an* authority).[13] And, by those who have made such a differentiation, it is usually claimed that these different kinds of authority are conceptually independent. Someone who is *in* authority may not *have* authority or be *an* authority. Someone who *has* authority may not be *in* authority or be *an* authority. Someone who is *an* authority may not *have* authority or be *in* authority. And it is indeed sometimes useful to make these distinctions. But they should not be allowed, as they frequently are, to obscure the centripetal forces that make them all instances of *authority*.

Authority is not a property that people possess, like body weight or skin color or recessive genes, though it is just possible that these could, rightly or wrongly, enter into attributions of authority.[14] Authority is centrally and essentially a *normative social relation*, an accorded status. Someone who is in authority or is an authority or who has authority is someone who is acknowledged by others as being in a position to do or require or know whatever happens to be the object of that authority. Someone with authority possesses a normative resource such as a right, entitlement or power. There is a consensual but not exclusively contractual element to the possession of this resource. Tradition no less than contractual agreement may sustain authority. In liberal societies, individual political authority, both de jure and de facto, may depend to a significant degree on something approaching contractual consent. But parental authority may be acknowledged for moral or customary reasons that cannot easily be construed contractually. Of course, like all traditional roles and statuses, that of parental authority may be reviewed and be reconceptualized. But the authoritative standing of parents does not initially depend on a negotiated understanding.

What links positional, actual and expert authority is not simply their being socially sustained; there is a certain content to that social support. Underlying every recognition of authority is the presumption that the person (or officeholder or group member) is "in the know." The bearer of authority is presumed to be informationally equipped to engage in or require certain conduct or to pronounce on particular matters. It is not usually necessary that authorities be "experts" in the usual sense; experts, to be sure, are "in the know," but to be "in the know" you do not have to be an expert. It is often argued that the most important quality a police officer can possess is a reasonably informed "common sense," and a recognition that officers manifest this in their work may be sufficient to sustain the presumption that a police officer is relevantly "in the know."

What we are talking about here is a *presumption* of knowledge that sustains authority, not the *possession* of knowledge that would justify it. One of the arts (or wiles) of politicians – and probably of many others in or with authority – is to maintain the appearance of being "in the know" even if there is no substance to back it up. Or, no less problematic, it is to seek to discredit those who *are* "in the know," so that they will lose or fail to achieve the authority warranted by the knowledge they in fact possess.

Police authority, as a form of governmental authority, will to some extent depend on the recognition accorded to "the powers that be." If the government of the day loses credibility, this may well be reflected in the authority the police are seen to possess.[15] But the authority of police officers will also depend on the way in which they conduct themselves, on whether *they* are perceived to be "in the know" with respect to the matters over which they have jurisdiction.[16]

Several factors make the public recognition of police authority highly volatile. As enforcers of law and maintainers of public order, they may be the executors of unpopular policies, and their activities may be perceived as being more oppressive than authoritative. And because there may be uncertainty or conflicting views about their social role, and hence about the matters on which they are expected to be "in the know," there may be a hiatus between police service and public expectations. Further, because a good deal of police work involves discretionary judgment, there is considerable room for judgments that are, or may appear to be, arbitrary, inconsistent, or unfair.

This volatility is exacerbated by two additional factors: the fact that police are given primary responsibility for the social use of coercive power, and the unifying significance of the police uniform.[17] Along with the coercive power that is given to police there also goes a heavy responsibility. We do not lightly waive our right to self-defense. And in cases in which a police officer abuses his or her authority, the uniform makes for a ripple effect. Because a police officer loses or at least obscures his or her particular identity under the uniform, what that officer does is frequently taken to characterize the police as a whole. And so, when police administrators attempt to take refuge in the idea that police corruption is to be construed on the model of "a few bad apples in the barrel," their failure to convince can sometimes be attributed not merely to the fact that the corruption is more systemic than officially acknowledged, but also to the unifying symbol of the uniform.

2.3   PRIVATE VERSUS PUBLIC POLICING

To this point I have assumed that policing is appropriately regarded as a governmental activity – whether national, state, or municipal. Even if it is insisted that the allegiance of police is to law rather than to the partisan concerns of an incumbent power, nevertheless law, whether federal, state, or local, is an expression of ongoing governmental authority, and police services are generally paid for from public revenues.

It is one thing to argue that a viable social community needs police services, but it is quite another to assume that these should be publicly provided. If, as it appears, it is not self-evident that the provision of educational and medical services is a governmental responsibility, why should we assume that police services ought to be provided from the public purse? The question is not posed *in vacuo*. There has been a growing demand for private policing, a demand that has already been realized in a variety of private investigational and security services.[18] And volunteer groups of various kinds have assumed or supplemented various police functions.

Policing may be "private" in more than one way.[19] It may be privately organized and privately paid for, privately organized and publicly paid for, publicly organized and privately paid for, and privately organized as a nonpaid or not-for-profit service. Some of the discussion to follow is more appropriately associated with one rather than another form of "private policing."

The argument for privately organized and paid-for police services can be mounted in several ways. Most radically, it can take the form of an anarchist eschewal of governmental power, a considered belief that any concentration of power will ultimately jeopardize the rights that it is intended to secure. A detailed exploration of this position belongs elsewhere.[20] Less radically, it can be argued that the policing function can be most efficiently handled by private contractors. This practical argument may have its source in two different considerations. The more general one is that government bureau-cracies tend to be less efficient than private service providers, since competi-tion ensures an optimal use of available resources. The more specific reason is that the existing publicly provided resources are inadequate and need to be supplemented from private sources. This, presumably, is the view of businesses that make use of private security services: they judge that their needs are in excess of what is publicly available. Communities, too, might supplement their existing personnel resources by employing private con-tractors. More significantly, it may be the view of certain groups in the community, in places in which it is considered that "the social contract" leaves them with less than they might have expected, that "private" or "community-owned" police services should replace those that have been publicly provided.[21]

The more general claim, that the private provision of police (and other) services is likely to be more efficient, and therefore better, looks more plausi-ble in theory than in practice. If it is seen as an argument for the exclusively private provision of police services, serious questions of justice will have to be confronted. Those who cannot afford police services, and who may well be most in need of them, will be left unprovided for.[22] Historically, we have seen no reason to believe that such people will be adequately shielded by the "Invisible Hand."[23] As a community we have not been able to tolerate the provision of educational and medical services on this basis. The trickle-down theory is just what it says, and those who do not have their own access to resources suffer significantly in comparison with those who do. Even less, I believe, could we tolerate what would become the maldistributive outcome of private police services.

What may seem to be more plausible is the public funding of private police services, the contracting out of police work to private agencies that must tender for their services.[24] But recurrent scandals surrounding govern-mental recourse to private defense and building contractors suggests that this, too, may not be anything more than a theoretically attractive solution: The real marketplace is no paragon of efficiency or justice. The problems may not be insuperable, for the government holds the purse strings and it may also set standards and determine levels of accountability. In the correc-tional area, at least, there is some evidence to suggest that private agencies may do *no worse* than those over which the government has direct control. For the internal politics that so often characterizes governmental activity may be just as, if not more, destructive of the delivery of just and efficient services as the bridled workings of the profit motive. Still, this is hardly an encouraging prospect.

An intermediate position, according to which private policing is taken as the norm, and is supplemented by the public coverage of those unable to afford it, might also be contemplated, though it, too, may leave much to be desired. As public medical patients have often observed, the quality of treat-ment they receive, whether from public practitioners or from medical per-sonnel who also care for private patients, is often markedly lower. We have no reason to believe that it would be otherwise in respect of the publicly covered clients of private police service providers.

In considering the demerits of private policing, we should not pass over or ignore the serious deficiencies of public policing. Were that not the case, the arguments for the private provision of police services would hardly be worth mounting. And it may well be the case that the argument for one rather than another of the foregoing alternatives will look stronger or weaker depending on the prevailing social environment. Just as our beliefs concerning the appropriate form and role of government have undergone change as social circumstances have changed, so too may our beliefs about the best way of satisfying our police needs.

A more attractive option may be to view private police services as supplementary to those that have been publicly provided. It can be argued that some social activities make greater demands on police services than the public purse is able to finance, and that these might reasonably be provided on a private basis. This is what in effect happens when individuals and companies hire or employ security personnel or private detectives, and it is in some ways analogous to private payment for educational and medical services over and above those that can be secured through other means. Although this practice may sometimes lead to jurisdictional conflicts or even to conflicts of interest, some version of it may represent a judicious response to the scarcity of social resources. Of course, there is a serious problem for the community whose *basic* police needs cannot be fully met from the public purse.

Even if it is possible to develop an argument for the provision of some private police services, important problems will have to be confronted. But they may have their source in jurisdictional and industrial factors as much as any private/public distinction. We already find such problems in the relations between firefighters, ambulance personnel, and police officers, and between local, state, and federal police officers. Their activities converge in various situations, and some determination of authority and responsibility must be made. That determination is probably made more easily in the case of private and public agencies, because it is generally accepted that the institutions of government take precedence. But in any case it will be necessary to develop structures of accountability that will minimize the "inconveniencies" that generally make the state of nature such an unattractive alternative to civil society.

2.4   THE POLICE ROLE

To this point I have assumed that Locke's executors of the legislative will are police officers as we generally understand them to be. But in a complex society this executive function is in fact much more dispersed. Internal Revenue agents, housing and FDA inspectors, "meter maids," court officers, public safety officers and bailiffs, among many others, have executive functions in the Lockean sense. Their roles are often more circumscribed and clearly defined than those of police officers, and for the most part they do not have the same individual resources of coercive force as police officers.

So what, then, is the *police* role? It should first be noted that in speaking of a "role" we are referring to more or less determinate social relations that are governed by certain norms. Roles are not constituted simply by habits or patterns of conduct. They are structured by obligations and responsibilities, rights and privileges. We may occupy various roles – familial, occupational, and associational – and our roles may change over time. To be the occupant of a role we must be aware of the relations associated with it and the norms governing it. We do not play roles blindly. In the case of many roles, we expect, partly because of the norms involved, and partly because of the importance accorded to those roles, that those who occupy them will not only be aware of, but also be committed to what the roles demand of them.[25]

Can we provide any general account of the "police" role that will give coherence to our understanding of policing and an indication of its appropriate scope and limits? On one reading of Locke, the role of police is centrally concerned with effecting the rule of law. From this executive goal there flow the various duties and privileges of police officers. But although there is significant support for this understanding within the police community and in popular police mythology, the reality of police work suggests otherwise. Studies have revealed that only a small proportion of police work is devoted to crimefighting.[26] Most police time is spent in various social service activities – intervention in family crises, searching for lost children, rescuing animals, directing traffic, supervising crowds, visiting schools, assisting the elderly, and so on – or in various administrative tasks. No doubt some police specialist groups spend much more of their time in strict law enforcement activities; but for the majority of police officers that is not so.

It does not of course follow from this that the police function ought not to be conceived of as crimefighting. It is at least arguable – and many police officers do argue – that policing has been deflected from its raison d'être, and needs to be reorganized round what they see as its central functions: the prevention of crime and the prosecution of criminals. Yet there is nothing sacrosanct about the crimefighting model, or the Lockean tradition. In the same way as we now have an expanded conception of the role that government may legitimately play in our lives, we may also have an expanded conception of the role that police should have in our communities. Just as government is seen as having a welfare as well as a protective function, so we may see police as having a social service as well as a law enforcement purpose.

The issues here are as much empirical as ideological. For they concern not only the appropriate bounds of governmental authority but also the optimal way in which that authority may be expressed. Some might want to argue that the optimal use of those with police powers is to be found in their exclusive attention to law enforcement, other social services being provided by specialists with different training and skills. But this division of labor is almost certainly at odds with the structure and demands of social life. There is much to be said for a strict division of labor in a factory setting, where the processes are limited and controlled, but in the complex environment of urban and suburban society a firm division of this kind is unrealistic. So-called domestic disputes, for example, are not either exclusively law enforcement or exclusively social work matters. They may be both (and other things), and it may be difficult to tell in advance which need is most pressing, or how it is best addressed.[27] Crowd and traffic control, too, may involve a convergence of functions. So too may the search for a missing person. There is something to be said for a response that is able to accommodate a variety of social needs.[28]

In order to deal with this complexity, but also to provide some sort of normative shape for the police function, writers on police matters have developed a variety of models of police work.[29] These models are designed to provide ways of structuring our understanding of the police role so that its legitimate limits can be determined. The strengths and weaknesses of these models highlight some of the major issues in contemporary police work.[30]

2.4.1 *The crimefighter*[31]

The major attractions of this self-explanatory model are its pedigree and simplicity. Classical social contract theory perceives such a role for police. Just as an army is needed to protect us from the barbarian without, a police force is required to protect us from the barbarian within. Thus the role has a clear rationale and a simple definition.

But there are serious practical and moral problems with the model. Violations of law vary in their seriousness, and violators differ in their depravity. Even if all violators of criminal law act in a manner that is properly considered antisocial, they do so in different ways. There is a morally relevant distinction to be drawn between the person who cheats on his taxes and the mugger, between the shoplifter and the rapist, between the person who parks illegally and the carjacker. The crimefighter model tends to obscure this. Criminals are "the enemy," "the bad guys," and police and the law-abiding community are "the good guys." This strong dichotomy between "them" and "us," normal in wartime and so easily cultivated in police circles, frequently fosters a form of police conduct that is inimical even to the purposes of crimefighting. For police come to see their role punitively, and not simply custodially; they are inclined to treat suspects as though they are guilty criminals; and, not surprisingly, skepticism and cynicism often characterize police attitudes toward the public at large.

As in military engagements, police work runs a risk of excess. Indeed, the problem may be exacerbated in police work because, unlike defending armies, which often (and no doubt prefer to) operate on or beyond territorial borders, police conduct their crimefighting activity in the midst of our ongoing social life. The dangers of innocents being caught in the "crossfire" are considerable. Privacy may be invaded, entrapment may be induced, life and limb may be jeopardized.

One way of ameliorating this problem is to set crimefighting activity into a wider framework of social service so that police will be less inclined to dichotomize their social world and so to jeopardize some of the values, such as liberty and justice, that they are employed and empowered to preserve. One of the difficulties here is that many police *like* to see themselves as crimefighters, and even though their actual work is much more diversified, the attitudes associated with the crimefighting model frequently pervade these other activities.

Even if crimefighting ought not to be seen as the raison d'être of police work, we need to remember that, aside from the armed forces, the police constitute our major social repository of coercive power. And for this reason any model of policing that fails to take into account their authority to employ force will be inadequate. This is so even with regard to those police who, in some societies, are generally unarmed.

However, as the following models indicate, the coercive possibilities of the police role can be accommodated within a wider understanding than that provided by the crimefighter.

2.4.2 *The emergency operator*[32]

Howard Cohen states that, besides law enforcement, peacekeeping and the provision of social services constitute "the authoritative social interventions characteristic of police work."[33] He notes, however, that since there are other social agents, public and private, who provide these latter services as professionals (social workers, psychologists, clergy, and so on), it is not clear what appropriate place remains for police involvement in their provision. It is Cohen's contention that as long as police are limited to offering emergency assistance of these kinds, they may be accorded authority to do so. They have what he calls a "stand-in authority": "they make decisions and take action where designated authorities cannot or will not."[34]

I do not believe that Cohen wishes to limit this sort of authority to police[35] or to suggest that this is the only authority they have. Rather, stand-in authority places an appropriate limit on police involvement in the provision of social services. Whereas others may also act as emergency stand-ins, the ubiquity and experience of the police in dealing with people will make them the most appropriate stand-ins where professionals are not available.

Once we accept that only a small proportion of police work is involved with crimefighting, Cohen's position might be taken to imply a serious downgrading of much police activity. Police social service authority will be seen as temporary and provisional, the product of an untimely conjunction of events rather than of any particular social skills or expertise that police possess. Perhaps this is as it should be. Nevertheless, as Joseph Betz points out, there is a dimension to the provision of these services that Cohen's account overlooks. The fact that police will often be succeeded by professionals (doctors, social workers, marriage counselors, and so on)

> does not mean that the police had no role in the situation if the doctor or
> marriage counselor got there first. The police do not stand in for them; the
> police handle the situation when it is not yet a problem which the doctor or
> marriage counselor can handle. . . . They have their own full authority for their
> own kind of situation, not half of somebody else's authority for someone else's
> problem.[36]

Cohen's apparent downgrading of police peacekeeping and social service authority may well serve only to reinforce the view that real police work and police authority is constituted by crimefighting, for only in that role will police be perceived as having more than stand-in authority. And that would go contrary to Cohen's intentions. As Betz puts it: "Police are not crimefighters out of their element doing social work; they are emergency resource personnel who usually do social work but are competent in crime control as well because of their monopoly on coercive force."[37]

But even with this emended understanding of police authority, the characterization of police as emergency operators seems both too broad and too narrow. It is too broad because many other emergency resource personnel can be so designated – ambulance operators, firefighters, and so on. It is too narrow, because much police work does not seem to be easily characterizable as a response to some social emergency – community-oriented policing, for example, in which the avoidance of emergency situations might seem to be more to the point.[38] The second element in Betz's account might therefore seem to provide the appropriate distinguishing feature, their monopoly on coercive force. So argues Egon Bittner.

2.4.3   *The social enforcer*

Bittner believes that the unifying feature of police work, and the source of police authority, can be found in the likely need for coercive intervention: "The role of police is to address all sorts of human problems when and insofar as the problems' solutions may require the use of force at the point of their occurrence."[39]

Bittner's model has several attractions. It seems to do justice to many of the situations in which police are involved. Not only in their crimefighting role, but also in many emergency situations, police are appropriately involved in part because they are repositories of coercive power. Domestic and other confrontations may require forcible intervention, and access to coercive force may be needed at demonstrations and accidents to ensure crowd and traffic control. The model preserves the strong identification that police feel with their possession of coercive power while at the same time extending their role beyond that of crimefighting. And at a theoretical level, the model coheres well with the traditional liberal understanding of police agencies as communal reservoirs of coercive power.

But there are also serious drawbacks to the model. As it stands, Bittner's account is too broad. Police are not the only members of society whose authority to use coercion is recognized. Parents are usually accorded the authority to use some coercion in relation to their children; school teachers, too, may be granted limited coercive authority. "Bouncers" in nightclubs may use force to remove the unruly; and in similar vein there are various private security agencies with recognized coercive powers. Even citizens are granted powers of arrest and detention in certain circumstances. But Bittner's account is also too narrow. Many police activities – for example, informing a woman of her spouse's death in an accident, giving safety lectures to school groups, searching for missing amnesiacs, opening locked car doors, and running youth programs – do not call attention to their access to coercive force.

An even greater problem for Bittner's model is that it focuses too directly on the coercive dimension of police authority. Although it is true that police are authorized to use force where necessary to carry out their responsibilities, we should not confuse their role with means that are available to them in their performance of that role. That confusion perpetuates one of the features of police work that many people find most problematic, the tendency of police to resolve issues by means of force and threat. Citizens frequently complain that their encounters with police are intimidating, that threat is used when negotiation would have been more appropriate, and that force is resorted to when mediation was called for. Certain features of police culture have reinforced this: the emphasis on physique and "street smarts" and a disdain for formal education, the macho values that are fostered and savored, the encouragement often given to "come on strong,"[40] and the resistance to and masculinizing of female officers. We need a model of police work that acknowledges the nonnegotiable force at police disposal without transforming it into the police raison d'être.

2.4.4 *The social peacekeeper*

It is this characterization that seems to me to offer the best potential for accommodating in a practical and normatively satisfactory way the varied tasks that police are called upon to perform.[41] One of its virtues lies in its deep historical roots, allowing us to see its contemporary manifestations in evolutionary rather than revolutionary terms, as the historical bearer of a tradition rather than as some johnny-come-lately bandaid for our social problems. Continuity blends with change, history with contemporary need.

The origins of the model can be found in the Anglo-Saxon notion of the king's peace, a zone of tranquillity that was originally local, personal, and seasonal, but which was gradually extended to encompass the whole realm, not merely during the life of the king, but in perpetuity.[42] Breaches of the king's peace were crimes, subject to fines. In republican society, the king's peace became the public peace, a social environment characterized by ordered liberty. Modern-day police have become its guardians.

On this understanding, the peacekeeper model does not stand over against the crimefighter model or social service model (as is the case in many discussions[43]), but it embraces them. It is grounded in the recognition that there are many things that may and do disturb the peace or tranquillity of a community, not just crime, but disaster, noncriminal social conflict, the movement of people, and even large gatherings. The role of the police is to ensure or restore peaceful order.

Communal peace as I understand it here is not simply a matter of some externally imposed structure (law enforcement), but of a perceived security, of ordered liberty. It has a significant psychological as well as a behavioral dimension. Police, to use Wayne Hanewicz's terminology, are there to distribute psychologically satisfying closure on social conflict.[44] Perhaps that puts it too reactively: the role of police is not simply to resolve social conflict, but, so far as possible, within a reflective and ongoing framework of values and traditions, to minimize its likelihood. Police have preventive, deterrent, and crowd/traffic control functions as well as mediatorial and law enforcement ones.[45]

Perhaps the foregoing is still expressed too negatively. The functions of police are not limited to keeping a lid on the sources of social disorder. Within the bounds of the resources that are available to them, they may engage in forms of social assistance that actually enhance the quality of social life, not only deterring crime and disorder and dissipating fear, but actually fostering social trust and cooperation. That, indeed, is often seen as a key element in community policing.

Such peacekeeping is not to be confused with pacification. Although police generally function as agents of government, it is to democratic governmental authority that the peacekeeper model is intended to apply. In so-called police states, in which police function to impose the will of government against the people, their function is one of pacification rather than of social peacekeeping.

Hanewicz suggestively links the peacekeeping function of police with a deeper human need for ordered experience. Ordered experience, he claims, is not simply a desirable end, but essential to human life as we wish it to be. At the most fundamental level, it is provided by conceptualization – that by which we render the perceptual field intelligible; at the social level, the "need is met in its most elementary form by predictability in behavior, by commitments, roles, social institutions."[46] But these commitments, roles, and social institutions are not fully self-sustaining for the same reason that Locke considered the state of nature to be deficient. There is need for an independent "other" to ensure or restore the order that we need, to help maintain and create conditions under which trust can grow. Police constitute part of that "other," and, given adequate training in discretionary responsiveness as it relates to public law and policy, they are able to contribute to the need we have for a peaceably ordered social environment.

So understood, the peacekeeper model is broad enough to encompass most of the work that police do, whether it is crimefighting, traffic control, or intervention in crisis situations. But what is more important is the irenic cast that it gives to police work. Although the model has room for the use of nonnegotiable force, its instrumental or subservient character is emphasized. The use of coercion to enforce the law or settle disputes is not appropriate just because police are socially recognized repositories of coercive power or because they have coercive power at their disposal, but because in their peacekeeping role such means have become necessary. If police are seen as possessors of authority and not simply as wielders of coercive power, and if that authority is vested in their perceived ability to preserve and restore a peaceable social order, then their use of coercion becomes a last (albeit sometimes necessary) resort rather than their dominant modus operandi.

Again, my purpose in emphasizing "peacekeeping" is not to downplay the importance of "crimefighting." Law enforcement is indeed the "hard edge" of police work. Crime can generally be considered to constitute the most serious and worrisome disturbance to a peaceable social environment. But just as the peacekeeping perspective refocuses our attention from coercive force to authority, it does the same for law enforcement, when that is viewed as an element of peacekeeping.

There is one final reason not to downplay the importance of crimefighting, a reason rooted in the historical origins of the peacekeeper model in the notion of the king's peace. The king, as protector of the realm, was concerned primarily with a public rather than a private order and peace. What we speak of as "civil" or "private" disputes are not generally the concern of police. Their commitment is to a broader peaceableness, to fostering and maintaining an order that is not exclusive to the concerns of particular individuals, but focuses on concerns that have wider social ramifications. Crimes, though often committed against individuals, are seen as violative of that wider social order. "The People" take action. Civil claims or breaches focus on action in its private aspect, and police involvement will normally be limited to what might be called the public ramifications of such actions.

The problem, of course, is that the private–public distinction, problematic enough in theory, is sometimes even more difficult to make in practice. Domestic disputes are now seen as falling within the domain of police concern, but school demonstrations generally do not. What happens in such cases is that police must judge whether a particular form of disorder has reached a point at which wider social order is implicated. In many cases, unfortunately, police–community relations have been strained by poor or controversial judgments in this area.

It is primarily in terms of social peacekeeping that I shall understand the police role in this book. Having regard to the values we associate with peace, a climate of trust in which our human selves may flourish in community with others, I suggest that, if taken seriously, this conception could provide the basis for a profoundly renovating and conciliatory style of policing through which both police and community might be brought together in a joint and mutually supportive enterprise.

MORAL FOUNDATIONS OF POLICING

1.   Jesse Rubin, "Police Identity and the Police Role," in Robert F. Steadman (ed.), *The Police and the Community* (Baltimore: Johns Hopkins University Press, 1972), p. 25.

2.   Metropolitan Police, *General Instructions* (1829), part 1, excerpted in John Kleinig, with Yurong Zhang (comps. and eds.), *Professional Law Enforcement Codes: A Documentary Collection* (Westport, CT: Greenwood, 1993), p. 27. Usage of the term "police" was settled by Patrick Colquhoun's *A Treaty on the Police of the Metropolis* (London: C. Dilly, 1796), and the role of police as formulated in the *General Instructions,* had already been enunciated in Saunders Welch, *Observations on the Office of Constable: With Cautions for the More Safe Execution of That Duty: Drawn from Experience* (London: printed for A. Miller, 1754). For a history of the Metropolitan Police, see David Ascoli, *The Queen's Peace: The Origins and Development of the Metropolitan Police 1829–1979* (London: W. Hamilton, 1979). Policing in the United States is usefully chronicled in Robert Fogelson, *Big-City Police* (Cambridge, MA: Harvard University Press, 1977).

3.   John Locke, *Second Treatise of Civil Government* (1690). The material that follows is drawn particularly from chs. 2 and 9.

4.   See, for example, Jeffrey H. Reiman, "The Social Contract and the Police Use of Deadly Force," in Frederick A. Elliston and Michael Feldberg (eds.), *Moral Issues in Police Work* (Totowa, NJ: Rowman & Allanheld, 1985), pp. 237–49; Howard Cohen and Michael Feldberg, *Power and Restraint: The Moral Dimension of Police Work* (New York: Praeger, 1991).

5.   Locke, unlike Hobbes, does at least acknowledge that social life of a limited kind may preexist the conveniences of civil government. But it is not clear that he appreciates to what extent the individuals who subsequently come together in civil society are "socially constructed."

6.   Albeit traditions that may have survived the scrutiny and obtained the consent of a past generation.

7.   Locke, *Second Treatise*, ch. 8, sect. 119.

8.   See, for example, the discussion in A. John Simmons, *Moral Principles and Political Obligations* (Princeton, NJ: Princeton University Press, 1979), ch. 4.

9.   For failing to recognize this in his *A Theory of Justice* (Cambridge, MA: Harvard University Press [Belknap Press], 1971), John Rawls was strongly criticized. In subsequent work he has acknowledged that his argument needs to be understood against a background of liberal commitments. See, for example, his *Political Liberalism* (New York: Columbia University Press, 1993).

10   There is an impressive statement and defense of this general position in H. L. A. Hart's critique of John Austin. See his *The Concept of Law* (Oxford: Oxford University Press [Clarendon Press], 1961), ch. 1.

11   Embedded in the notion of *authoritative* coercion is the idea of proportionality.

12   Anyone can bully or tyrannize. Authoritarianism is a coercive abuse of authority. See my *Philosophical Issues in Education* (New York: St. Martin's, 1982), pp. 217–18.

13   See, for example, R. S. Peters, "Authority," *Proceedings of the Aristotelian Society* 32 (1958), pp. 207–24. Somewhat earlier, Max Weber made a slightly different distinction between "traditional," "legal-rational," and "charismatic" authority. See *The Theory of Social and Economic Organisation*, trans. A.M. Henderson and Talcott Parsons, rev. ed.- (London: W. Hodge, 1947), pp. 324ff.

14   It used to be thought that police officers should meet certain height requirements, the idea being, in part, that an imposing figure would more likely command respect and obedience.

15   The causal connection probably works in the opposite direction as well. If police abuse their authority, this can lower the authoritative standing of the governing power.

16   In the film version of his story *(Serpico*, starring Al Pacino), Frank Serpico reports that what impressed him about police officers as a child, and influenced his decision to go into police work, was that, in a situation where others were confused, "they knew!"

17   See D. F. Gundersen, "Credibility and the Police Uniform," *Journal of Police Science and Administration* 15, 3 (September 1987), pp. 192–5.

18   See, for example, Clifford D. Shearing and Philip C. Stenning, "Modern Private Security: Its Growth and Implications," in Norval Morris and Michael Tonry (eds.), *Crime and Justice: An Annual Review of Research,* vol. 3 (Chicago: University of Chicago Press, 1981); Clifford D. Shearing and Philip Stenning (eds.), *Private Policing* (Beverly Hills, CA: Sage, 1987); Marcia Chaiken and Jan Chaiken, *Public Policing – Privately Provided* (Washington, DC: NIJ / OCRU, 1987).

19.   We should, perhaps, not forget that the primary agent of arrest was originally "the private person." The balance in "power to arrest" shifts to constables, sheriffs, and so forth, only during the nineteenth century See Jerome Hall, "Police and Law in a Democratic Society," *Indiana Law Journal* 28, 2 (Winter 1953), esp. pp. 135–7. Although it is not with this sense of "private policing" that I am here concerned, there are connections, since pre-nineteenth-century policing was "characterized" by a lack or limitedness of public control.

20.   An acute discussion of its inadequacies, by someone who was ideologically inclined to it, can be found in Robert Nozick, *Anarchy, State and Utopia* (Oxford: Blackwell Publisher, 1974), pt. 1. Also, see John Hospers, *Libertarianism: A Political Philosophy for Tomorrow* (Los Angeles: Nash Publishing, 1971), ch. 11.

21.   See Bill Lawson, "Crime, Minorities, and the Social Contract," *Criminal Justice Ethics* 9, 2 (Summer /Fall 1990), pp. 16–24.

22.   For an argument to the effect that a policy of allowing the police acceptance of gratuities would be tantamount to encouragement of private and unequally distributed police services, see Michael Feldberg, "Gratuities, Corruption, and the Democratic Ethos of Policing: The Case of the Free Cup of Coffee," in Elliston and Feldberg, *Moral Issues in Police Work,* esp. pp. 270–6.

23.   Adam Smith thought that the universal pursuit of self-interest would "frequently" do more to promote the good of society than a deliberate promotion of the public interest. By intending their own gain, individuals are "led by an invisible hand to promote an end which was no part of [their] intention" (*The Wealth of Nations* [Edinburgh: Adam & Charles Black, 1863], p. 199). For a critique, see Christopher McMahon, "Morality and the Invisible Hand," *Philosophy & Public Affairs* 10 (1981), pp. 247–77.

24.   This was recently attempted, though the officers appointed were given considerably fewer powers than regular peace officers. See "Sussex Approves Use of Guards to Replace Police," *New York Times,* 21 April 1993, p. B7; Robert Hanley, "Sussex Force Only Looks Like Police," *New York Times,* 14 June 1993, pp. B1, B4.

25.   The normative dimension of roles is often absent from sociological discussions. For a seminal treatment that emphasizes the normative character of roles, see Dorothy Emmet, *Rules, Roles and Relations* (London: Macmillan Press, 1967).

26.   See James Q. Wilson, *The Varieties of Police Behavior* (Cambridge, MA: Harvard University Press, 1968), p. 19; Thomas Bercal, "Calls for Police Assistance," *American Behavioral Scientist,* 13 (1970), p. 682; Albert J. Reiss, Jr., *The Police and the Public* (New Haven, CT: Yale University Press, 1971), p. 75; Elaine Cumming, Ian M. Cumming, and Laura Edell, "The Policeman as Philosopher, Guide and Friend," *Social Problems,* 12 (Winter 1965), pp. 276–86. A British study yielded similar results: Maurice Punch and Trevor Naylor, "The Police: A Social Service," *New Society* 24 (17 May 973), pp. 358–61. Although these studies are now somewhat dated, it is unlikely that the situation has changed significantly. See David H. Bayley, *Police for the Future* (New York : Oxford University Press, 1994), ch. 2.

27.   For the most significant recent research on this particular issue, see Lawrence W. Sherman, with Janell D. Schmidt and Dennis P. Rogan, *Policing Domestic Violence: Experiments and Dilemmas,* New York: Free Press, 1992.

29c

28. The fact that situations requiring a police presence do not divide neatly into community-service and law-enforcement categories constitutes the weakness of Bernard L. Garmire's suggestion that "contradictory roles that the police are expected to perform" be handled by a firm division of labor — "two agencies under one department," with staff selected on the basis of their suitability for one or the other function. See "The Police Role in an Urban Society," in Steadman, *The Police and the Community*, pp. 1–11.

29. Models may be descriptive or normative; that is, some attempt to give a general characterization of the way in which police work *is* done, whereas others attempt to provide a characterization that will circumscribe the legitimate authority of the police role. Here I am *concerned* with normative models.

30. There is no decisive reason why police work should conform to any *one* model, though a single model may provide unity of understanding and help to obviate some of the role conflict that police often experience.

31. Sometimes this is referred to as the Law Enforcement or Military Model. Its dominance is suggested by (a) the fact that when officers refer to "real police work," they generally mean crimefighting, (b) the strongly hierarchical organization and trappings of many police departments -- uniforms and badges of rank, salutes, inspections and parades, the carrying of weapons, and so forth, and (c) popular representations of police work on television and in movies. Although some recent TV series have attempted to take a broader view of the police role, most are still heavily slanted toward crimefighting.

32 Sometimes referred to as the Firefighter Model.

33. Howard Cohen, "Authority: The Limits of Discretion," in Elliston and Feldberg (eds), *Moral Issues in Police Work*, pp. 27–41. Though the purposes of peacekeeping and providing social services are stated rather than argued for, they are almost certainly broad enough to encompass the range of activities in which police currently find themselves engaged.

34. Cohen, "Authority: The Limits of Discretion," p. 38.

35. It is at least arguable that the kind of "stand-in authority" that Cohen accords to police is partially grounded in a more fundamental obligation that we all have when bystanders in crisis situations. Police will function somewhat as "professional citizens."

36. Joseph Betz, "Police Violence," in Elliston and Feldberg (eds.), *Moral Issues in Police Work*, p. 192. A similar point is made by Egon Bittner, "The Capacity to Use Force as the Core of the Police Role," in Elliston and Feldberg (eds.), *Moral Issues in Police Work*, p. 20.

37. Betz, "Police Violence," p. 187.

38. However, if we see community-oriented policing as problem-oriented policing – as a number of current writers do – then a rather more plausible rendition can be given of the social service role of police. They are there not just for "crises" and "emergencies" but for problem solving. See John E. Eck and William Spelman, "Who Ya Gonna Call? The Police as Problem-Busters," *Crime & Delinquency* 33, 1 (January 1987), pp. 31–52; Herman Goldstein, *Problem-Oriented Policing* (New York: McGraw-Hill, 1990); Malcolm K. Sparrow, Mark H. Moore, and David M. Kennedy, *Beyond 911: A New Era for Policing* *(New* York: Basic, 1990).

39. Bittner, "The Capacity to Use Force as the Core of the Police Role," p. 21. For a lengthier treatment, see his *The Functions of the Police in Modern Society* (Washington, DC: U.S. Government Printing Office, 1967). Cf. the very similar account of Peter Manning: "Police agencies may be defined as those agencies that stand ready to employ force upon the citizenry on the basis of situationally determined exigencies" *(Police Work: The Social Organization of Policing* [Cambridge, MA: MIT Press, 1977], p. 40).

40. Arthur Niederhoffer reports: The new man is needled when he shows signs of diffidence in arresting or asserting his authority. Over and over again, well- meaning old timers reiterate, "Ya gotta be tough, kid, or you'll never last" *(Behind the Shield: The Police in Urban Society* [New York: Doubleday, 1969], p. 56).

41.   In order to sustain this peacekeeping function, various supporting personnel will no doubt have to be employed - forensic specialists, police surgeons, detectives, and various managerial and administrative staff. Some of them will properly have "peace officer" status, others will simply be civil service employees.

42.   See Hubert Hall, "The King's Peace," *The Antiquary* 18 (November 1888), pp. 185–90; Sir Frederick Pollock, "The King's Peace," in *Oxford Lectures and Other Discourses* (London: Macmillan Press, 1890), pp. 65–82; Julius Goebel, Jr., *Felony and Misdemeanor: A Study in the History of Criminal Law* (1937; reprint, Philadelphia: University of Pennsylvania Press, 1976), pp. 7–12; Jack K. Weber, "The King's Peace: A Comparative Study," *The Journal of Legal History* 12 (September 1989), pp. 135–60.

43.   Michael Banton distinguishes between police as "law officers" and "peace officers" *(The Policeman in the Community* [New York: Basic, 1964], pp. 6–7, 127ff), and is followed by Egon Bittner, who divides the police role into "law enforcement" and "keeping the peace" ("The Police on Skid-Row: A Study in Peace Keeping," *American Sociological Review* 32, 5 [October 1967], p. 700). Bernard L. Garmire distinguishes their "law-enforcement" and "community-service" functions ("The Police Role in an Urban Society," p. 4), Jesse Rubin their "peacekeeping," "crimefighting," and "community service" functions ("Police Identity and the Police Role," p. 23), and Maurice Punch and Trevor Naylor their "crime prevention and detection" and "social service" functions ("The Police: A Social Service," *New Society* [17 May 1973], p. 358).

44.   Wayne B. Hanewicz, "Discretion and Order," in Elliston and Feldberg (eds.), *Moral Issues in Police Work*, pp. 43–54.

45.   One of the original intentions of putting police into uniform was to deter public disorder. Police were not employed simply to catch criminals.

46.   Hanewicz, "Discretion and Order," p. 47. The two levels are not separate. Conceptualization does not occur in vacuo, but only as we are incorporated into a social milieu characterized by language, culture, traditions, predictability, and so on.

[4]

Moral Rights and the Institution of the Police

SEUMAS MILLER

In this chapter I discuss the relationship between moral rights and the institution of the police.[1] I argue that the protection of moral rights is the central and most important moral purpose of police work, albeit a purpose whose pursuit ought to be constrained by the law. So while police institutions have other important purposes that might not directly involve the violation of moral rights, such as to enforce traffic laws or to enforce the adjudications of courts in relation to disputes between citizens, or indeed themselves to settle disputes between citizens on the streets, or to ensure good order more generally, these turn out to be purposes derived from the more fundamental purpose of protecting moral rights, or they turn out to be (non-derivative) secondary purposes. Thus laws against speeding derive in part from the moral right to life, and the restoring of order at a football match ultimately in large part derives from moral rights to the protection of persons and of property. On the other hand, handing out summonses to assist the courts is presumably a secondary purpose of policing.

It is important to state a number of things at the outset. First, this is a *normative* account of policing, not a *descriptive* account; it is an account of what policing *ought* to be about, not what it has been or is about. Moreover, it is a normative theory of the *institution* of the police, that is, of the proper ends and distinctive means of the institution of the police. So it is not a theory about specific police methods or strategies; it is not a theory of, so to speak, best practice in policing. Accordingly, I will not here have anything much to say about disputes between crime-fighter and peace-keeper models of the role of police officers, or in relation to arguments concerning community-based policing or zero-tolerance policing. That said, a normative theory of the institution of the police will have important implications for questions of police methods and strategies, though often these will not be straightforward or obvious. At any rate, such questions are not my concern here.

---

[1] See the *United Nations Code of Conduct for Law Enforcement Officials*. Most of the articles in this code specify the human rights constraints on police officers. However, Article 1 stresses the duty to protect persons, and the commentary (under c) notes the duty of police to provide aid in times of emergency.

T. Campbell and S. Miller (eds), Human Rights and the Moral Responsibilities of Corporate and Public Sector Organisations, pp. 167–188.

Naturally, whether or not a descriptive theory of an institution is warranted depends on empirical facts. Moreover, the falsity of the *descriptive* theory would put pressure on the acceptability of any *normative* theory of institutions. If it turned out that no institution of that kind at any time or place *in fact* involved to any extent the pursuit of the moral good proposed in some normative theory of that institution, then this would make it implausible to claim that the institution, nevertheless, in general *ought* to aim at that good.

Second, I am assuming a particular notion of moral rights. Moral rights are of two kinds. First, there are human rights; moral rights that individuals possess solely by virtue of being humans, for example, the right to life and the right to freedom of thought. Second, there are institutional (moral) rights; moral rights that individuals possess in part by virtue of rights generating properties that they have as human beings, and in part by virtue of their membership of a community or morally legitimate institution, or their occupancy of a morally legitimate institutional role. Thus the right to vote is an institutional right, since it exists in part by virtue of possession of the rights generating property of autonomy, and in part by virtue of membership of a political community. Again, the right to arrest and detain someone for assault is a moral right possessed by police officers. This right is in part dependent on membership of a morally legitimate police institution, but it is also in part dependent on the human right of the victim not to be assaulted.

Moreover, I am assuming the following properties of moral rights. First, moral rights generate concomitant duties on others, for example, A's right to life generates a duty on the part of B not to kill A. Second, human rights, but not necessarily institutional moral rights, are justifiably enforceable, for example, A has a right not to assaulted by B, and if B assaults, or attempts to assault, A, then B can legitimately be prevented from assaulting A by means of coercion. Third, bearers of human rights in particular do not necessarily have to assert a given human right in order for the right to be violated, for example, an infant may have a right to life even thought it does not have the ability to assert it (or for that matter to waive it).

Third, the conception of policing that I am offering is a teleological conception; it is a conception in terms of the ends or goals of policing. Moreover, it is a teleological conception according to which the most important end or purpose of policing is the protection of moral rights.

Fourth, on the view that I am advocating, while police ought to have as a fundamental purpose the protection of moral rights, their efforts in this regard ought to be constrained by the law. So I am insisting that police work ought to be guided by moral considerations – namely, moral rights – and not simply by legal considerations. This enables me to avoid the problems besetting theories of policing cast purely in terms of law enforcement or protection of the state.[2] Such theories are faced with the obvious problem posed by authoritarian states, or sometimes even democratic states, that enact laws that violate human rights, in particular. Consider

---

[2] John Alderson, *Principled Policing* (Winchester: Waterside Press, 1998) at times seems to advocate a view close to the one that I am proposing. However, at other times he seems to be elaborating the view that human rights are merely side constraints on policing, rather than a *raison d'etre* for police work. See especially Chapter One.

the police in Nazi Germany, Soviet Russia, or Iraq under Saddam Hussein. These police forces upheld laws that violated the human rights of (respectively) Jews, Soviet citizens, and Iraqi citizens (including Shi'ite Muslims' religious rights). By my lights the officers in these police forces simultaneously violated human rights, and abrogated their primary professional responsibility as police officers to protect human rights.

Further, on the view that I am advocating police engaged in the protection of moral rights ought to be constrained by the law, or at least ought to be constrained by laws that embody the will of the community in the sense that: (a) the procedures for generating these laws are more or less universally accepted by the community, for example, a democratically elected legislature, and; (b) the content of the laws are at least in large part accepted by the community, for example, they embody general policies with majority electoral support or reflect the community's moral beliefs.[3] So I am in part helping myself to a broadly contractarian moral constraint on policing, namely the 'consent' of citizens; although by my lights consent is not the *raison d'etre* for policing, rather it provides an additional (albeit necessary) condition for the moral legitimacy of policework. Moreover, I am refraining from providing police with a licence to pursue their possibly only individually subjective view of what counts as an enforceable moral right. What counts as an enforceable moral right is an objective matter. Nevertheless, someone or other has to decide what are to be taken to be enforceable moral rights and what are not to be so taken, and in my view ultimately this is a decision for the community to make by way of its laws and its democratically elected government. Here I take it that in a properly constituted democracy the law embodies the will of the community in the sense adumbrated above.

And there is a further point here. The law concretises moral rights and the principles governing their enforcement, including human rights as well as institutional moral rights. To this extent the law is very helpful in terms of guiding police officers and citizens in relation to the way that abstract moral rights and principles apply to specific circumstances.

In short, in my view police ought to act principally to protect certain moral rights, those moral rights ought to be enshrined in the law, and the law ought to reflect the will of the community. Should any of these conditions fail to obtain, then there will be problems. If the law and objective (justifiably enforceable) moral rights

---

[3] Here I am assuming that large fragments of a legal system can consist of immoral laws, and yet the system remains recognisably a legal system. See Ronald Dworkin, *Law's Empire* (Oxford: Hart Publishing, 1998) p. 101. I am also assuming that for a legal system to express the admittedly problematic notion of the will of the community, it is at least necessary that the overwhelming majority of the community (not just a simple majority) support the content of the system of laws taken as a whole – even if there are a small number of individual laws they do not support – and support the procedures for generating laws, for example, they have a democratically elected legislature. See Seumas Miller, *Social Action: A Teleological Account* (New York: Cambridge University Press, 2001) pp. 141-151. Finally, I am assuming that the fact that a party or candidate or policy or law secured (directly or directly) a majority vote is an important (but not necessarily decisive) consideration in its favour, and a consideration above and beyond the moral weight to be given to the existence of a consensus in relation to the value to be attached to voting as a procedure.

come apart, or if the law and the will of the community come apart, or if objective moral rights and the will of the community come apart, then the police may well be faced with moral dilemmas. I do not believe that there are neat and easy solutions to all of such problems. Clearly, if the law and/or the citizenry requires the police to *violate* moral rights then the law and/or the citizenry will be at odds with the fundamental purpose of policing. Accordingly, depending on the circumstances, the police may well be obliged to disobey the law and/or the will of the community. On the other hand, what is the appropriate police response to a citizen violating someone else's objective moral right in a community in which the right is not as a matter of fact enshrined in the law, and the right is not supported by the community? Consider in this connection women's rights to (say) education under an extremist fundamentalist religious regime such as the former Taliban regime in Afghanistan.[4] Under such circumstances an issue arises as to whether police are morally obliged qua police officers to *enforce* respect for the moral right in question. Again, I suggest that they may well be obliged to intervene to enforce respect for such a moral right.

Normatively speaking, then, the protection of fundamental moral rights – specifically *justifiably enforceable* moral rights – is the central and most important purpose of police work. As it happens, there is increasing recourse to human rights legislation, in particular, in the decisions of domestic as well as international courts. This is an interesting development. However, it must also be pointed out that the criminal law in many, if not most, jurisdictions already in effect constitutes human rights legislation. Laws proscribing murder, rape, assault, and so on, are essentially laws that protect human rights. So it is clear that whatever the historical importance of a statist conception of human rights – human rights as protections of the individual against the state – a statist conception is inadequate as a *general* account of human rights. Human rights in particular, and moral rights more generally, also exist to protect individual citizens from their fellow citizens, and individual citizens from organisations other than the organisations of the state.

In this connection please note that I do not say that the protection of (legally enshrined, justifiably enforceable) moral rights is the *only* goal of policing; merely that it is the *central and most important* goal. Nor do I hold that police are, or ought to be, preoccupied with seeing to it that *all* moral rights are secured. Roughly speaking, police are, or ought to be, engaged in moral rights work to the extent to which the moral rights in question are ones that justify and require the use of coercive force for their protection.[5] Some moral rights are not justifiably enforceable, for example, a wife's moral right to the sex her husband promised her when they got married. Other moral rights do not necessarily, or in general, require the use of coercive force for their protection. For example, a physically disabled person might have a moral right to appropriate access to public buildings such as libraries and government offices, and such access might necessitate the provision of

---

[4] Regarding the role of the religious police of the Taliban in the Department of the Promotion of Virtue and Prevention of Vice see Ahmed Rashid's *Taliban, The Story of the Afghan Warlords* (London: Pan Books, 2001) Chapter Eight.

[5] Though no doubt all human rights need protection from time to time.

sloping paths as opposed to stairs. But the securing of this right for the disabled might call only for action on the part of the local council; there might be no need for the police to be involved.

Here the distinction made by Henry Shue is relevant. Shue distinguishes between three sorts of duties that correlate with what he calls basic rights.[6] These are the duties to: (i) avoid depriving; (ii) protect from deprivation; (iii) aid the deprived.

In relation to police work, (ii) above, the duty to protect from deprivation is especially salient. Police are typically engaged in protecting someone from being deprived of their right to life, liberty or property. Note that in providing such protection police are different from other occupations in that they are entitled to employ the use of, or more often, the threat of the use of, coercive force. This is, of course, not to suggest that police always or even typically use coercive force, or threaten to use it; rather the claim is that this recourse to coercion is a distinctive and routine feature of policing, and is in some sense 'the bottom-line' when it comes to realising the proper ends of policing.

At any rate, the account of the institution of the police that I am offering promises to display the distinctive defining features of the institution of the police; namely, its use of coercive force in the service of legally enshrined moral rights. On this account the institution of the police is quite different from other institutions that are either not principally concerned with moral rights, or that do not necessarily rely on coercion in the service of moral rights. Consider business. Many business organisations do not have the securing of moral rights as a primary purpose; nor should they. On the other hand, moral rights are an important side constraint on business activity. Now consider welfare institutions. There is a human right to a subsistence living, and aiding the deprived (to use Shue's terminology) is a fundamental purpose of welfare institutions. However, aiding the deprived does not necessarily or routinely involve the use of, or threat of the use of, coercive force. Thus welfare institutions are different in kind from policing institutions.

It might be argued that contemporary military institutions meet our definition of the institution of the police. Consider so-called humanitarian armed intervention in places such as Somalia, Bosnia, Rwanda, Kosovo and East Timor. Whether or not each of these armed interventions was principally undertaken to protect human rights is a matter of controversy. At any rate, I make three points in response.

First, the nature and evolution of military and policing institutions is such that the lines have often been blurred between the two. Thus, in the British colonies the police historically had a paramilitary role in relation to what was regarded as a hostile population. The Royal Irish Constabulary is an example of this. Indeed, according to Richard Hill:

> Coercion by army and by police have always been distinguished by differences of
> degree, rather than kind, and through most of the history of policing there was no clear
> demarcation between the two inter-woven strands of control situated towards the
> coercive extremity of the control continuum ... Historically, constables were generally
> considered to be a reserve military body for mobilisation by the state in potential or

---

[6] Henry Shue, *Basic Rights* (Princeton: Princeton University Press, 1996) p. 52.

actual emergency; conversely soldiers were frequently called upon to conduct duties generally considered to be of a 'policing' nature.[7]

But from this is does not follow that there are not good reasons for a *normative* theory of *contemporary* policing in liberal democracies to make distinctions between the fundamental role of the police and that of the military. Such reasons would include the well-documented and high problematic character of para-military police forces, including in relation to the violation by such forces of individual moral rights, and the tendency for such forces to become simply the instrument of governments rather than the protectors of the rights of the community and the servants of its laws.

Second, while contemporary military forces may undertake humanitarian armed interventions from time to time, this is not, or has not been, their fundamental purpose; rather national self defence has avowedly been their purpose.

Third, to the extent that military institutions do in fact take on the role of human rights protection by means of the use of coercive force, then they are being assimilated to police institutions. It is no accident that recent humanitarian armed interventions are referred to as episodes of international *policing*.

There are some other objections to my account of the institution of the police. I try to deal with the most important of these later on in this chapter.

In the first section of the chapter I offer a brief account of moral rights and the cognate notion of social norms. In the second section I present my theory of policing as the protection of legally enshrined moral rights by means of coercive force. In the third and final section I deal with some residual issues arising from the use of harmful methods in policing, including methods that under normal circumstances would themselves constitute human rights violations.

1. MORAL RIGHTS AND SOCIAL NORMS

Moral rights are a basic moral category; but they are far from being the only moral consideration. Here we note that moral rights comprise a relatively narrow set of moral considerations. There are many moral obligations that are not, and do not derive from, moral rights, for example, an obligation to assist a friend who is depressed, or not to cheat on one's boyfriend.

The point of human rights is to protect some basic human value or values. On James Griffin's account, human rights arise from the need to protect what he calls personhood.[8] At the core of his notion of personhood is individual autonomy. Certainly, autonomy is a basic human value protected by a structure of human rights. However, I have some reservations about Griffin's account; specifically, it might turn out to be too narrowly reliant on autonomy. Perhaps the right not to be

---

[7] Richard S. Hill, *Policing the Colonial Frontier: The Theory and Practice of Coercive Social and Racial Control in New Zealand, 1767-1867* (Wellington, NZ: Government Printer, 1986) Part One p. 3.

[8] James Griffin, 'Human Rights' this volume pp. 31-43.

tortured does not simply derive from a right to autonomy; perhaps it derives, at least in part, from the right not to suffer extreme pain intentionally inflicted by another.[9]

At any rate, whatever the correct theoretical account of human rights might be, I assume that Griffin is right to set out a relatively limited set of moral considerations as being human rights. These will include the right to life, to physical security, to freedom of thought, expression and movement, and to freedom to form human relationships, including freedom to choose one's sexual partner. They will also include the right to a basic subsistence; so they will include rights to food, water, and shelter.

However, moral rights will include a range of other moral rights that go beyond human rights and that might be termed 'institutional moral rights'. As mentioned above, these are moral rights that depend in part on rights generating properties possessed by human beings qua human beings, but also in part on membership of a community or of a morally legitimate institution, or occupancy of a morally legitimate institutional role. Such institutional moral rights include the right to vote and to stand for political office, the right of legislators to enact legislation, of judges to make binding judgments, of police to arrest offenders, and of patients to sue doctors for negligence.

Here we need to distinguish between: (a) institutional rights that embody human rights in institutional settings, and therefore depend in part on rights generating properties that human beings possess as human beings (these are institutional *moral* rights), and; (b) institutional rights that do not embody human rights in institutional settings (these are not necessarily institutional *moral* rights, but rather *mere* institutional rights). The right to vote and the right to stand for office embody the human right to autonomy in the institutional setting of the state; hence to make a law to exclude certain people from having a vote or standing for office, as happened under apartheid in South Africa, is to violate a moral right. But the right to make the next move in a game of chess, or to move a pawn one space forward, but not (say) three spaces sideways, is entirely dependent on the rules of chess; if the rules had been different, for example, if the rules prescribed that each player must make two consecutive moves or pawns can move sideways, then the rights that players have would be entirely different. In other words these rights that chess players have are *mere* institutional rights; they depend entirely on the rules of the 'institution' of the game of chess. Likewise, (legally enshrined) parking rights, including reserved spaces, one hour parking spaces, and so on, in universities are *mere* institutional rights, as opposed to institutional *moral* rights.

A large question that arises at this point is the status of property rights. Are such rights institutional *moral* rights or *mere* institutional rights. It would seem that at least *some* property rights are institutional *moral* rights by virtue of being in part dependent on rights generating properties that human beings have qua human beings. Specifically, some property rights depend on the rights generating properties of: (1) the need to have exclusive use of certain physical material eg this food and water, and physical space eg this shelter, and; (2) individual or collective *labour*,

---

[9] This is a point made by Tom Campbell in discussion.

including labour that *creates* new things eg tools or ornaments that an individual or particular group has made. Some of these property rights might be individual rights eg to personal effects, some might be collective rights eg to occupy a certain stretch of territory and exclude others from it. At any rate, I will assume that some property rights are institutional *moral* rights.

Some (but not all) moral rights, including many (perhaps all) human rights are, or ought to be, embodied in the laws governing a community. This is most obvious in the case of many of the so-called negative rights, such as the right to life, the right to physical security, and the right to property. Murder, assault, rape, theft, fraud, and so on, are criminal offences. Moreover, the police have a clear and central role to investigate and apprehend the perpetrators of these crimes – the rights violators – and bring them before the courts for trial and sentencing.

Naturally, there are large fragments of the legal system concerned with matters other than criminality. For example, there are all manner of disputes of a non-criminal nature that are settled in the civil courts. These often involve important questions of *justice* that are not human rights issues. On the other hand, many of these disputes involve institutional moral rights, for example, who gets what part of the estate of some deceased relative or of the property formerly jointly owned by a husband and wife now involved in divorce proceedings. Moreover, in so far as a dispute is, or gives rise to, an issue of justice, then moral rights are involved at least in the sense that the disputants have a moral right to a just outcome.

To the extent that law enforcement by police is enforcement of moral rights, whether enforcement of criminal law or not, the police are undertaking their fundamental role (on my account). On the other hand, the police do have a legitimate role in relation to law enforcement, where the laws in question do not embody moral rights. This is a matter to which we return later in this chapter. Suffice it to say here that the law enforcement role of the police in relation to matters other than the enforcement of moral rights is, in our view, either a derived role or it is a secondary role.

It is also the case in Anglo-Saxon countries, in particular, that there are some human rights that are not embodied in the law. In Australia it is not unlawful to refrain from assisting someone who is drowning or starving. Yet the right to life is a human right, and therefore there is a concomitant moral obligation to assist someone who is drowning or starving, or at least to do so in situations in which in assisting such a person would not put oneself at risk of harm.

The moral and legal issues in this area are complex. However, in my view it ought to be unlawful to refrain from assisting persons whose lives are at immediate risk, and whom one can assist with minimal cost to oneself. Indeed, there ought to be a variety of so-called Good Samaritan laws, and the reason for this is that human rights ought to be protected, and some Good Samaritan laws protect human rights.

So I hold that in general violations of human rights ought to be criminalised. If this were the case – and it already is to a considerable extent – then the police would have a central role in relation to the enforcement of human rights by virtue of having a role in relation to the enforcement of the criminal law.

One of the interesting implications of this is that there would be a shift in the line of demarcation between the so-called police service role and the law enforcement role (especially criminal law enforcement role) of police. Typically, the police service role is contrasted with the law enforcement role; the rescue operations of Water Police or of police dealing with dangerous mentally deranged persons are supposedly service roles, not law enforcement roles. In one sense the contrast here is already overdrawn; the law with respect to water craft needs to be enforced, as does the law in relation to dangerous mentally deranged persons. Moreover, questions of policing *methods* should not be confused with questions of what actions ought to be criminalised and what ought not. In relation to some criminal offence, for example, juvenile gangs engaged in assaults, it might be more productive for police to engage in preventative strategies, such as restorative justice techniques, rather than simply arresting/charging and locking up offenders. More important, in so far as Good Samaritan laws with respect to so called positive moral rights were enacted, then many police activities previously regarded as service roles would become in part law enforcement roles (indeed roles of enforcing criminal laws). But it is important to stress here that the criminalisation of violations of certain positive moral rights is entirely consistent with an overall reduction in acts regarded as criminal, for example, decriminalisation of laws in relation to cannabis and prostitution. After all, smoking cannabis and selling sex are not activities which in themselves necessarily violate anyone's moral rights.

Thus far I have sought to make a connection between moral rights and the law on the one hand, and law enforcement and the institution of the police on the other. This has enabled me to present, albeit thus far in very general terms, the view that the fundamental point of policing is to enforce certain moral rights viz. justifiably enforceable moral rights. However, there are other competing views. One such influential contrasting view holds that the law embodies social morality in general.[10] On this view, in so far as the role of the police was to enforce the law, then their role would be to enforce social morality. Should this view be preferred to mine?

The notion of social morality is to be understood as the notion of the framework of moral values and principles that a society accepts and conforms to, that is, the framework of *social norms*.

Elsewhere I have offered and defended a detailed account of the notion of a social norm.[11] Roughly speaking, according to that account, a social norm is a regularity in behaviour among a group of individual persons such that: (a) each (or at least most) believes that each (including him/herself) morally ought to conform, and; (b) the belief of almost any individual that each (including him/herself) morally ought to conform is in part dependent on almost everyone else's belief that each morally ought to conform. So conformity to social norms is based on an interdependence of attitude – specifically, interdependence of moral beliefs.

Given the above account of social norms, it is easy to see why citizens feel that they ought to obey many of the laws of the land, and in particular criminal laws. For

---

[10] I take it that Lord Devlin's account is a version of this view. See Patrick Devlin, *The Enforcement of Morals* (Oxford University Press, 1965).

[11] Miller, *Social Action op.cit.*, Chapter Four.

the criminal law is typically in large part an explicit formulation (backed by penal sanction) of a society's social norms. Citizens believe that they ought not to flout the laws against murder, theft, rape, assault and so on, because these citizens have internalised a system of social norms which proscribes such behaviour. Putting matters simply, for the most part any given citizen does not commit murder in part because s/he believes it is wrong for s/he to murder, and in part because others believe it is wrong for s/he to murder.

Unfortunately, there are some citizens who have not internalised the system of social norms, or who have not sufficiently internalised that system. Accordingly, there is a need to buttress the system of social norms by the construction of a criminal justice system. The latter system involves the detection of serious moral wrongdoing, and the investigation, trial and punishment of offenders.

Accordingly, it is tempting to view the role of the police as the enforcement of social morality understood as the structure of social norms in force in the community. This picture is an appealing one. However, it is inadequate in two respects.

Firstly, the notion of a social norm, and of social morality, are relatively wide notions; considerably wider than the notion of a basic moral requirement that ought to be enshrined in the criminal law (or the legal system more generally). Note also that the notion of an action or omission required by a social norm is considerably wider than the notion of a duty correlative to a moral right. For the notion of a social norm – and therefore of social morality – embraces regularities in behaviour (including omissions) that are the subject of some moral attitude. So they include behaviour that is outside the purview of the criminal law, or indeed the law more generally. For example, social norms prescribe and proscribe sexual behaviour that is not necessarily, or even generally, the subject of any legal requirement. Moreover, there is a great danger in widening the law to embrace all of social morality. Consider in this connection the threats to individual autonomy posed by puritanical polities such as Calvin's Geneva or agencies such as the Department for the Promotion of Virtue and the Prevention of Vice under the Taliban regime in Afghanistan.[12]

Secondly, the notion of a social norm – and of social morality – is an essentially subjective notion; it refers to the values and principles that are *believed in*, and in conformed to *as a matter of contingent fact*, by the members of some presumably morally sentient community. So social morality stands in contrast with objective notions, such as the notion of human rights. Or at least there is a contrast here for those of us who believe that the notion of a human right is an objective notion. It might be thought, nevertheless, that the subjective character of social morality is no obstacle to its being deployed – via the notion of the criminal law in particular – to define the proper role of the institution of the police. After all, the criminal law is itself subjective in the above sense. The criminal law is a de facto set of laws; it is not necessarily the set of laws that *ought to* exist by the lights of some objective

---

[12] Rashid, *op.cit.*, Chapter Eight.

moral standard.[13] And it might be thought that the proper role of the police is to enforce the law in general, and the criminal law in particular, as it is; not as it morally ought to be.

Once again, this is an issue to be addressed in more detail later in this chapter. Here I simply record my view that a normative account of the role of the police must be cast in terms of objective notions, not subjective ones. The de facto role of the police in apartheid South Africa was the enforcement of the laws of apartheid, and of the Serbian police, for example, the so-called Red Berets of the Serbian Interior Ministry of Belgrade, the ethnic cleansing of Muslims in Bosnia, but these are not the morally legitimate roles of police forces.[14]

The upshot of the discussion thus far is that the view of police simply as enforcers of social morality is untenable. We cannot make a connection between the notion of social morality and the criminal law (especially) on the one hand, and the criminal law and the enforcement of the criminal law by the police on the other, and thereby erect a normative theory of the role of policing as the enforcement of social morality. Rather we ought to prefer the related, but competing view, that the fundamental role of the police is to protect legally enshrined (justifiably enforceable) moral rights, and for two reasons. First, the notion of justifiably enforceable moral rights is a suitably narrow one to qualify as the fundamental purpose of policing, unlike the notion of social morality. Second, the notion of justifiably enforceable moral rights is an objective notion, again unlike the notion of social morality. Putting matters simply, justifiably enforceable moral rights are an *objective* set of *fundamental* (actual or potential) social norms that are capable of being enshrined in enforceable law. As such, justifiably enforceable moral rights are an appropriate notion to provide the moral basis for policing, or at least the central and most important moral basis for policing.

So much for the discussion of human rights and social norms, and their relationship to the institution of the police. In the next section I consider in detail the relation between moral rights and the institution of the police.

2. MORAL RIGHTS AND THE INSTITUION OF THE POLICE

I have elsewhere provided a teleological normative account of social institutions.[15] According to that account, the ultimate justification for the existence of fundamental human institutions such as government, the education system, the economic system, and the criminal justice system, is their provision of some moral or ethical good or goods to the community. The existence of universities is justified by the fact that the academics that they employ discover, teach and disseminate the fundamental human good, knowledge. The existence of an economic system, including the free market system, is justified by the fact that it contributes to the fundamental human good, material well-being. The existence of governments is justified by the fact that they

---

[13] The criminal law is not simply a set of laws. For some theoretical accounts of the criminal law see A. Duff (ed.), *Philosophy and the Criminal Law* (Cambridge University Press, 1998) and Dworkin, *op.cit.*

[14] See Laura Silber and Allan Little, *Yugoslavia: Death of a Nation* (London: Penguin, 1997) p. 224.

[15] *Social Action op. cit.*, Chapter Six.

provide the fundamental social good, leadership of the community, and thereby contribute to prosperity, security, equitable distribution of economic goods, and so on. In short, the point of having any one of these institutions is an ethical or moral one; each provide some fundamental human or social good(s).

Moreover, these moral goods, or at least believed moral goods, are, normatively speaking, the *collective* ends of institutions, and as such they conceptually condition the social norms that govern, or ought to govern, the constitutive roles and activities of members of institutions, and therefore the deontic properties (institutional rights and duties) that attach to these roles. Thus a police officer has certain deontic powers of search, seizure and arrest, but these powers are justified in terms of the moral good, legally enshrined human rights (say) that it is, or ought to be, the role of the police officer to maintain.

It is also worth noting here that there is no easy rights versus goods distinction. Human rights certainly function as a side constraint on the behaviour of institutional actors. But equally the securing of human rights can be a good that is aimed at by institutional actors.

Further, a defining property of an institution is its substantive functionality (or telos), and so a putative institutional entity with deontic properties, but stripped of its substantive functionality, typically ceases to be an institutional entity, at least of the relevant kind; would-be surgeons who cannot perform surgery are not surgeons. Equally, would-be police officers who are incapable of conducting an investigation, or who cannot make arrests or exercise any form of authority over citizens, are not really police officers. Here, by substantive functionality, I have in mind the specific defining ends of the institution or profession. In the case of institutions, including professions, the defining ends will be collective ends; they will not in general be ends that an individual could realise by his or her own action alone. In short, the theory of institutions, and of any given institution, is a *teleological* theory.

Further, institutions in general, and any given institution in particular, require both a teleological *descriptive* theory, and a teleological *normative* theory. Naturally, whether or not our commitment to teleological descriptive theories of institutions is warranted depends on empirical facts. If it turned out, for example, that most or all institutions did not have collective ends that were regarded either as intrinsic moral goods, or the means to intrinsic moral goods (derived moral goods) – that is, the participating agents did not in fact seek to realise the relevant putative defining collective ends – then my teleological descriptive theory would be false; I would have to abandon it. Moreover, the falsity of the teleological *descriptive* theory would put pressure on the acceptability of any teleological *normative* theory of institutions. If it turned out that no institution at any time or place *in fact* involved to any extent the pursuit of the relevant kind of collective end that was an *objective* (intrinsic or derived) moral good, then this would make it implausible to claim that institutions nevertheless in general *ought* to aim at collective ends that are objective (intrinsic or derived) moral goods.

Thus far I have spoken in terms of the theory of institutional action where institutions have been taken to be different and separate 'entities'. However, there is also a need for a theoretical account of the *interrelationships* between different institutions. It is clear that on our teleological account of institutions any given institution is to be understood in terms of the collective end or ends to which its activities are and/or ought to be directed. However, there still remains the question of the relationships between institutions. One issue concerns the extent or degree of any required relationship. Another concerns the nature of the required relationship. As far as the extent of the relationships is concerned, in the post-Enlightenment West this interaction between institutional organisations belonging to the same society has typically taken place in the context of a commitment to a basic separation between them. Governments must stand apart from corporations lest public and private interests are confused, and corporations must stand apart from one another in the interests of competition. In communist regimes, by contrast, the doctrine of organisational (or at least institutional) separation, including separation of powers, has not been adhered to. Japan constitutes an interesting third model. While Japan is obviously in some sense a liberal democratic state, there has been an extent of government, corporation and bureaucracy linkage that is at odds with the notion of institutional separation. Moreover, there is some evidence that in recent years in the western liberal democracies the doctrine of institutional separation is under threat in the face of policies coming under the banner of so-called economic rationalism. Such policies include the privatisation of law enforcement agencies and prisons, and the out-sourcing of administrative functions.

As far as the *nature* of the relationship between institutions is concerned, this is presumably to be determined primarily on the basis of the extent to which the differential defining collective ends of institutions are complementary rather than competitive, and/or the extent to which they mesh in the service of higher order ends. In this connection consider the complementary ends of the institutional components of the criminal justice system *viz.* the police (whose end or purpose is to gather evidence and arrest suspects), the courts (whose end or purpose is to try and sentence offenders) and the prisons (whose end or purpose is to punish, deter and rehabilitate offenders). Consider also that certain institutions, for example, the government and the police, might be meta-institutions in the sense that they have a role in relation to pre-existing institutions, for example, the family, and the economic system. That role might be to assist or to protect these pre-existing institutions, or at least their members.

Having discussed social institutions in general I now need to turn to the institution of the police in particular.

In times of institutional crisis, or at least institutional difficulty, problem solving strategies and policies for reform need to be framed in relation to the fundamental ends or goals of the institution; which is to say they need to be contrived and implemented on the basis of whether or not they will contribute to transforming the institution in ways that will enable it to provide, or better provide, the moral good(s) which justify its existence. However, in relation to policing, as with other relatively modern institutions – the media is another example – there is an unclarity as to what precisely its fundamental ends or goals are. Indeed it is sometimes argued that there can be no overarching philosophical theory or explanatory framework that spells out the fundamental nature and point of policing, and that this is because the activities that police engage in are so diverse.

Certainly, the police are involved in a wide variety of activities, including control of politically motivated riots, traffic control, dealing with cases of assault, investigating murders, intervening in domestic and neighbourhood quarrels, apprehending thieves, saving people's lives, making drug busts, shooting armed robbers, dealing with cases of fraud, and so on. Moreover they have a number of different roles. They have a deterrence role as highly visible authority figures with the right to deploy coercive force. They also have a law enforcement role in relation to crimes already committed. This latter role involves not only the investigation of crimes in the service of truth, but also the duty to arrest offenders and bring them before the courts so that they can be tried and – if found guilty – punished. And police also have an important preventative role. How, it is asked, could we possibly identify any defining features, given this diverse array of activities and roles?

One way to respond to this challenge is to first distinguish between the activities or roles in themselves and the goal or end that they serve, and then try to identify the human or social good served by these activities. So riot control is different from traffic control, and both are different from drug busts, but all these activities have a common end or goal, or at least set of goals, which goal(s) is a moral good(s). The human or social goods to be aimed at by police, will include upholding the law, maintaining social order, and preserving human life.[16]

Indeed, policing seems to involves an apparent multiplicity of ends or goals. However, some ends, such as the enforcement of law, and the maintenance of order, might be regarded as more central to policing than others, such as financial or administrative goals realised by (say) collecting fees on behalf of government departments, issuing speeding tickets and serving summonses.

But even if we consider only so-called fundamental ends, there is still an apparent multiplicity. For example, there is the end of upholding the law, but there is also the end of bringing about order or conditions of social calm, and there is the end of saving lives. Indeed Lord Scarman relegates law enforcement to a secondary status by contrast with the peace-keeping role.[17] Moreover, the end of enforcing the law can be inconsistent with bringing about order or conditions of social calm. As Skolnick says: 'Law is not merely an instrument of order, but may frequently be its adversary'.[18]

Can these diverse and possibly conflicting ends or goals be reconciled? I suggest that perhaps they can, and by recourse to the notion of justifiably enforceable moral rights. The first point here is that the criminal law in particular is, or ought to be, - fundamentally about ensuring the protection of certain moral rights, including the rights to life, to liberty, to physical security, to property and so on. The moral rights enshrined in the criminal law are those ones regarded as fundamental by the wider society; they constitute the basic moral norms (social norms) of the society.

---

[16]Different theorists have seen one of these goals as definitive. See, for example, J. Skolnick and J. Fife, *Above the Law: Police and the Excessive Use of Force* (New York: Free Press, 1993).
[17]Lord Scarman, *The Scarman Report* (Penguin, 1981).
[18] Jerome Skolnick, *Justice Without Trial* (New York: Macmillan, 1966).

Naturally, some of these are contentious, and as society undergoes change these moral norms change – for example, in relation to homosexuality – but there are a core which there is reason to believe will never change or ought not to change, for example, the rights to life, freedom of thought and speech and physical security.

Notice here that I am offering a normative teleological account of the institution of policing, but one that is reliant on a descriptive teleological theory. The descriptive theory tells us that the criminal law in particular in modern democratic states is principally concerned to protect basic social norms which turn out in large part to be objective moral rights. The teleological theory alerts us to the possible discrepancy between the criminal laws as they are, and as they ought to be. Specifically, some criminal laws might seek to embody social norms that are not moral rights, or even objective moral standards of any kind. Or criminal laws, or the law more generally, might fail to embody justifiably enforceable moral rights, including some human rights. This is so in relation to some so-called positive human rights. As we pointed out earlier, such human rights call for Good Samaritan laws to be enacted.

The second point is that social order, conditions of social calm and so on, which are at times contrasted with law enforcement, are in fact, I suggest, typically necessary conditions for moral rights to be respected. A riot or bar room brawl or violent domestic quarrel is a matter for police concern precisely because it involves, at least potentially, violation of moral rights, including the rights to protection of person and property. Consider in this connection interregnum periods of disorder between the ending of military hostilities and the establishment of civil order, such as the looting, revenge killings and so on that took place on a large scale at the close of the recent war in Iraq.

The third point to be made here pertains to the enforcement of those laws that do not appear to embody justifiably enforceable moral rights. Many of these laws prescribe actions (or omissions) the performance (or non-performance) of which provides a social benefit. Consider the laws of taxation. The benefits provided by taxation include the provision of roads and other services to which arguably citizens do not have a moral right, and certainly not a justifiably enforceable moral right. On the other hand, taxes also enable the provision of benefits to which citizens do have a justifiably enforceable moral rights, for example, medicine for life-threatening diseases, basic welfare.

The fourth point to be made here pertains to the justification for enforcement of the law by police. I have argued that certain legally enshrined moral rights are justifiably enforced by police, as are laws that indirectly contribute to the securing of these rights. The moral rights in question are justifiably enforceable moral rights. Now clearly there are laws that are not of this sort. Many of these laws are fair and reasonable, and the conformity to them enables collective goods to be provided. But what is the justification for their enforcement by police? I suggest that the fact that they provide collective benefits and/or that they are fair and reasonable do not of themselves provide an adequate justification for their enforcement. Perhaps consent to the enforcement of just and reasonable laws that enable the provision of collective benefits provides an adequate moral justification for such enforcement. Here there is an issue with respect to the degree and type of enforcement that might be in this way justified; deadly force may not be justified, even if it is consented to in relation to fair and reasonable laws that enable collective benefits to be provided. Moreover, as is well known, there is problem in relation to consent. Evidently, there is not in fact explicit consent to most laws, and the recourse to tacit consent seems not to offer a sufficiently strong and determinate notion of consent.

At any rate, I want to make two points here in relation to what is nothing more than a version of the traditional problem of the justification for the use of coercive force by the state to enforce its laws.[19] First, self-evidently there is no obvious problem in relation to the enforcement of laws that embody *justifiably enforceable* moral rights, including human rights. Moreover, there may well be other laws that can justifiably be enforced (up to a point) on the grounds that not only are they fair, reasonable and productive of social benefits, but in addition citizens have consented to their enforcement (up to that point). Second, I want to suggest that notwithstanding our first point, there are fair, reasonable and socially beneficial laws with respect to which enforcement is not morally justified. Further, there may not be an adequate justification for enforcement of some of these laws, even if enforcement were to be consented to. The reason for this is that the nature and degree of enforcement required to ensure compliance with these laws – say, use of deadly force – is not morally justified.[20] Certainly recourse to deadly force – as opposed to non-deadly coercive force – is not justified in the case of many unlawful actions; specifically, unlawful actions not regarded as serious crimes. Indeed, this point is recognised in those jurisdictions that have made it unlawful for police to shoot at many categories of 'fleeing felons'.[21] It is more often than not now unlawful, because immoral, to shoot at (say) a fleeing pickpocket.

At any rate, I cannot pursue these issues further here.. Rather I will simply assume that the general human and social good that justifies the institution of the police is the protection of justifiably enforceable moral rights. Accordingly, such moral rights ought to be respected by social norms, and ought to be enshrined in the law, especially the criminal law.

But policing has a further important distinguishing feature. The end or moral good to be secured by the institution of the police is the protection of justifiably enforceable moral rights. But that is not all that needs to be said; I need also to speak of the *means* by which this end is to be achieved.

Egon Bittner has propounded a very different theory of policing to the one I have suggested. However his account is insightful. Bittner focuses attention on the means deployed by police to secure those ends. Bittner has in effect defined policing in terms of the use or threat of coercive force.[22] Bittner defines police-work as: 'a

---

[19] See Dworkin, *op. cit.*, p. 190.

[20] This is consistent with their being a moral obligation to obey these laws; we are speaking here of the justification for the *enforcement* of such laws. For an account of the moral justification for obeying the law see *Social Action op.cit.*, pp. 141-51. See also David Luban, *Lawyers and Justice: An Ethical Study* (Princeton University Press, 1988), Chapter Three.

[21] See Seumas Miller, 'Shootings by Police in Victoria: The Ethical Issues' in T. Coady, S. James, S. Miller and M. O'Keefe, (eds), *Violence and Police Culture* (Melbourne University Press, 2000).

[22] Egon Bittner, *The Functions of Police in Modern Society* (Cambridge, Mass: Gunn and Hain, 1980).

mechanism for the distribution of non-negotiable coercive force employed in accordance with the dictates of an intuitive grasp of situational exigencies'.[23]

Bittner's account of policing is inadequate because it fails to say anything about the goals or ends of policing. Moreover, coercion is not the only means deployed by the police. Other typical means include negotiation, rational argument, and especially appeal to human and social values and sentiment. Indeed, whole taxonomies of police roles have been constructed on the basis of different mixes of methods and styles of policing. There are Peace-keepers and Crime-fighters, and there are Social Enforcers and Emergency Operators.[24] Here I need to stress that I am not advocating one or other of the possible configurations of these mixes. Hitherto, I have spoken of the ends of policing, and especially the fundamental purpose of ensuring the protection of justifiably enforceable moral rights. Now I am speaking of the means – and associated roles – by which to achieve that purpose. Clearly, there are different ways to achieve a given end; there are different means, including different role mixes, by which to realise the fundamental end of policing as we have described it. Whether to emphasise the Crime fighter or the Peace-keeper role, for example, ought to be settled in large part on the basis of which is the most efficient and effective means to ensuring the protection of (justifiably enforceable) moral rights. To this extent my theory of policing is neutral on questions of police methodology, and in relation to disputes between advocates of law enforcement roles and service roles for police.

To return to Bittner: Bittner in drawing attention to coercion has certainly identified a distinctive feature of policing and one that separates police officers from, say, criminal justice lawyers and politicians.

Further, Bittner in stressing the importance of coercion draws our attention to a fundamental feature of policing, namely, its inescapable use of what in normal circumstances would be regarded as morally unacceptable activity. The use of coercive force, including in the last analysis deadly force, is morally problematic; indeed it is ordinarily an infringement of human rights, specifically the right to physical security and the right to life. Accordingly, in normal circumstances the use of coercive force, and especially deadly force, is morally unacceptable. So it would be morally wrong, for example, for some private citizen to forcibly take a woman to his house for questioning or because he felt like female company.

Use of coercive force, especially deadly force, requires special moral justification precisely because it is in itself at the very least harmful, and possibly an infringement of human rights; it is therefore in itself morally wrong, or at least, so to speak, a *prima facie* moral wrong. Similarly locking someone up deprives them of their liberty, and is therefore a *prima facie* moral wrong. It therefore requires special moral justification. Similarly with deception. Deception, including telling lies, is under normal circumstances morally wrong. Once again use of deception requires special moral justification because it is a *prima facie* moral wrong. Intrusive surveillance is another *prima facie* moral wrong – it is an infringement of privacy.

---

[23] Bittner, *op.cit.*

[24] See, for example, John Kleinig, *The Ethics of Policing* (Cambridge, UK: Cambridge University Press, 1996) pp. 22f.

Therefore intrusive surveillance requires special moral justification. And the same can be said of various other methods used in policing.

The point here needs to be made very clear lest it be misunderstood. Police use of coercion, depriving persons of their liberty, deception and so on, are morally problematic methods; they are activities which considered in themselves and under normal circumstances, are morally wrong. Therefore they stand in need of special justification. In relation to policing there is a special justification. These harmful and normally immoral methods are on occasion necessary in order to realise the fundamental end of policing, namely the protection of (justifiably enforceable) moral rights. An armed bank robber might have to be threatened with the use of force if he is to give himself up, a drug dealer might have to be deceived if a drug ring is to be smashed, a blind eye might have to be turned to the minor illegal activity of an informant if the flow of important information he provides in relation to serious crimes is to continue, a paedophile might have to be surveilled if evidence for his conviction is to be secured. Such harmful and normally immoral activities are thus morally justified in policing, and morally justified in terms of the ends that they serve.

The upshot of our discussion thus far is that policing consists of a diverse range of activities and roles the fundamental aim or goal of which is the securing of (justifiably enforceable) moral rights; but it is nevertheless an institution the members of which inescapably deploys methods which are harmful; methods which are normally considered to be morally wrong. Other institutions which serve moral ends, and necessarily involve harmful methods, or *prima facie* wrongdoing, are the military - soldiers must kill in the cause of national self-defence – and political institutions. Australia's political leaders may need to deceive, for example, the political leaders of nations hostile to Australia, or their domestic political enemies.

I have suggested that policing is one of those institutions the members of which need at times to deploy harmful methods; methods which in normal circumstances are morally wrong. In response to this we need first to ask ourselves why it is that morally problematic methods, such as coercion and deception are inescapable in policing. Why could not such methods be wholly abandoned in favour of the morally unproblematic methods already heavily relied upon, such as rational discourse, appeal to moral sentiment, reliance on upright citizens for information, and so on?

Doubtless, in many instances morally problematic methods could be replaced. And certainly overuse of these methods is a sign of bad police-work, and perhaps of the partial breakdown of police-community trust so necessary to police work. However, the point is that the morally problematic methods could not be replaced in *all* or even *most* instances. For one thing the violations of those moral rights which the police exist to protect are sometimes violations perpetrated by persons who are unmoved by rationality, appeal to moral sentiment, and so on. Indeed, such persons, far from being moved by well-intentioned police overtures, may seek to coerce or corrupt police officers for the purpose of preventing them from doing their moral and lawful duty. Hence the truth of the claim that the use of coercive force in particular remains the bottom line in policing, no matter how infrequently coercion is in fact used. For another thing, the relevant members of the community may for one reason or another be unwilling or unable to provide the necessary information or evidence, and police may need to rely on persons of bad character or methods such as intrusive surveillance.

So the use of harmful methods cannot be completely avoided; indeed the routine use of such methods in policing is unavoidable. It remains important to realise that these methods are in fact morally problematic; to realise that coercion, depriving someone of their liberty, deception, invasion of privacy and so on are in fact in themselves harmful. Indeed, these methods constitute *prima facie* wrongdoing, and some of them constitute – under normal circumstances – human rights violations. In the final section of this chapter I consider some of the elements of this means/end problematic in policing.

3. MORAL RIGHTS IN POLICING: MEANS AND ENDS

In drawing attention to the use of harmful methods by police I am far from denying the moral acceptability of these methods. The key point is that the use of any particular harmful method be morally justified in the circumstances. When police officers act in accordance with the legally enshrined, and morally justified, principles governing the use of harmful methods they achieve three things at one and the same time. They do what is morally right; their actions are lawful; and – given these laws are the result of properly conducted democratic processes – they act in accordance with the will of the community.

Nevertheless, the use of harmful methods in the service of moral ends – specifically the protection of (justifiably enforceable) moral rights – gives rise to a number of problems in policing. Here I will mention only four.

Firstly, the working out of these moral principles and the framing of accompanying legislation is highly problematic in virtue of the need to strike a balance between the moral rights of victims and the moral rights of suspects.

Obviously suspects – people who are only suspected of having committed a crime, but who have not been tried and found guilty – have moral rights. Suspects have a right to life, a right not to be physically assaulted, and a right not to be subjected to psychological harassment or intimidation. More generally, suspects have a right to procedural justice, including the right to a presumption of innocence and a fair trial.[25]

On the other hand, the police and the criminal justice system do not principally exist to protect the rights of suspects. They exist to protect the rights of victims and to ensure that punishment is administered to offenders.[26] Accordingly, if the police believe on the basis of evidence that a particular person is guilty of a serious crime then the police are obliged to do their utmost to arrest and charge the suspect, and provide sufficient evidence to enable his or her successful prosecution.

---

[25] Here I am assuming that rights to procedural justice are institutional *moral* rights.

[26] This is putting things simply, even simplistically, but it makes no difference to the main point I am seeking to make here. Consider in this connection the restorative justice movement; it sees itself as an alternative to punishment oriented conceptions of the criminal justice system.

However, there is inevitably a certain tension between these two moral requirements of the police – the requirement to respect the moral rights of suspects (including the duty to make available evidence that may assist a suspect) and the requirement to apprehend, and provide evidence to ensure the conviction of, offenders. And the procurement of such evidence may inevitably involve the kinds of justified, but harmful, actions we have been speaking of.

This tension has to be somehow resolved by framing laws that strike a moral balance between on the one hand ensuring that the rights of suspects are protected, and on the other providing the police with sufficient powers to enable them to successfully gather evidence and apprehend offenders (especially rights violators).

This tension, and any resolution of it, is further complicated by the social, institutional and technological contexts in which they operate. A set of laws might be thought to have struck an appropriate ethical balance between the moral rights of suspects and the provision of necessary powers to police, until one considers the criminal justice institutional context. For example, if putting young offenders into the system merely has the effect of breeding criminals, then this needs to be a factor taken into consideration in framing laws, including laws governing the nature and extent of police powers. Similarly, technological developments, such as surveillance technology and high-level encryption products, can justify either restrictions on police powers or extensions to police powers.

A second problem in this area arises when the three desiderata mentioned above come apart. That is, a problem arises when what the law prescribes is not morally sustainable, or at least is not morally acceptable to the community or significant sections of the community. Dramatic examples of the gap between law and the morality of significant sections of the community include the discriminatory race laws in South Africa under apartheid, the laws against homosexuality in Britain earlier this century, and the current laws in relation to prostitution and cannabis in parts of Australia. Other kinds of examples include obvious loopholes and deficiencies in the law. For example, legislation in relation to telephone interception in this country might be thought to reflect appropriate moral principles, yet other forms of surveillance using new technology are not yet subject to laws reflecting these principles.

In all these kinds of situations police are placed in an invidious position, and one calling for discretionary ethical judgment. It is a lose/lose situation. In the first kind of example, while they are under a moral obligation to enforce the law, they may be unsure that the laws they are enforcing are in fact morally justifiable. Certainly, they are aware that the laws in question are regarded as immoral by significant sections of the community. Recourse to justifiably enforceable moral rights, including human rights, is helpful in this context. For in so far as such rights provide an objective moral standard, and in so far as this objective moral standard comes to be widely accepted, then the uncertainty arising from subjective moral standards will cease to be a problem.

In the second kind of example, the law may allow police to engage in activities they believe to be immoral and which the community believes to be immoral, and yet engaging in these activities may enable them to secure convictions they would otherwise be unable to secure. Clearly the resolution of this problem lies in bringing the law into line with objective moral principles.

A third problem in this area remains even after the provision of laws that strike the appropriate moral balance mentioned above, and even when laws are not in need of revision. This problem seems to arise out of inherent features of police work.

There is a necessity for police to be given a measure of professional autonomy to enable them to exercise discretion. Thus individual police officers have a significant measure of legal authority.[27] They are legally empowered to 'intervene – including stopping, searching, detaining and 'apprehending without a warrant any person whom [they], with reasonable cause suspect of having committed any such offence or crime'[28] – at all levels of society.

Moreover, the law has to be interpreted and applied in concrete circumstances. There is a need for the exercise of discretion by police in interpretation and application of the law. Further, upholding and enforcing the law is only one of the ends of policing, others include maintaining of social calm and the preservation of life. When these various ends come into conflict, there is a need for the exercise of police discretion, and in particular the need for the exercise of discretionary *moral* judgment.

The unavoidability of the exercise of discretionary moral judgment in policing means that it will never be sufficient for police simply to learn, and act in accordance with, the legally enshrined moral principles governing the use of harmful methods. On the other hand, our normative teleological account of policing in terms of the goal of protecting (justifiably enforceable) moral rights provides the theoretical means to satisfactorily resolve some of these dilemmas requiring discretionary moral judgment.

A fourth, and final, problem concerns the proper scope of the institution of the police. It is evident that transnational crime is on the increase. Accordingly, national law enforcement agencies are increasingly involved in transnational (and therefore trans-jurisdictional) law enforcement collaboration. Further, there has been a growth in private policing, including in the area of criminal investigations of fraud and white-collar crime. It might be thought that these developments threaten an institutional conception of policing. Given these developments, does it still make sense to talk of the institution of the police? I suggest that it does still make sense. Very briefly, while the notion of an institution is tied to the realisation of certain ends, it is not necessarily the notion of a compartmentalised entity unrelated to other like institutions. We can still think of a specific organisation as an institution, notwithstanding the fact that it has strong and important collaborative connections with like institutions, and notwithstanding the fact that other somewhat dissimilar organisations perform similar roles. Of course, this says nothing about the desirability of these developments. On the teleological account of institutions that I am offering, whether or not transnational collaboration and/or private sector

---

[27]On general issues of autonomy and accountability in policing in Australia see David Moore and Roger Wettenhall, (eds), *Keeping the Peace: Police Accountability and Oversight* (University of Canberra, 1994).
[28]*NSW Crimes Act* No. 40 Section 352, Sub-section 2(a) (1990).

188   SEUMAS MILLER

policing, is to be welcomed or spurned depends on its contribution to the moral good that justifies the institution of the police, namely, the protection of legally enshrined, justifiably enforceable, moral rights.

Centre for Applied Philosophy and Public Ethics
Charles Sturt University and The Australian National University

Part II
Police Authority
and Police Discretion

[5]

Two principles of policing

Lord Scarman

4·55   Before I deal with these criticisms, it will, I think, be helpful
to refer to two well-known principles of policing a free society which
are relevant to my Inquiry:

   (1) 'Consent and balance', words which I take, with respect and
       gratitude, from the written evidence of the Chief Constable of
       Avon and Somerset;
and
   (2) 'Independence and accountability'.

(1) Consent and balance

4·56   The function of our police has been authoritatively defined as:

The prevention of crime . . . the protection of life and property, the
preservation of public tranquillity.[1]

   This three-fold function requires 'consent and balance', words
which I take to mean that, if the police are to secure the assent of the

---

1. Extract from Sir Richard Mayne's instructions to the 'New Police of the Metropolis'
in 1829.

Two principles of policing

community which they need to support their operations, they must strike an acceptable balance between the three elements of their function.

4·57   What is the balance which they would seek to achieve? An authoritative answer has again been given: the primary duty of the police is to maintain 'the Queen's peace', which has been described as the 'normal state of society',[1] for in a civilized society, normality is a state of public tranquillity. Crime and public disorder are aberrations from 'normality' which it is the duty of the police to endeavour first to prevent and then, if need be, to correct. It follows that the police officer's first duty is to cooperate with others in maintaining 'the normal state of society'. Since it is inevitable that there will be aberrations from normality, his second duty arises, which is, without endangering normality, to enforce the law. His priorities are clear: the maintenance of public tranquillity comes first. If law enforcement puts at risk public tranquillity, he will have to make a difficult decision. Inevitably there will be situations in which the public interest requires him to test the wisdom of law enforcement by its likely effect upon public order. Law enforcement, involving as it must the possibility that force may have to be used, can cause acute friction and division in a community – particularly if the community is tense and the cause of the law-breaker not without support. 'Fiat justitia, ruat caelum'[2] may be apt for a Judge: but it can lead a policeman into tactics disruptive of the very fabric of society.

4·58   The conflict which can arise between the duty of the police to maintain order and their duty to enforce the law, and the priority which must be given to the former, have long been recognized by the police themselves, though they are factors to which commentators on policing have in the past often paid too little attention. The successful solution of the conflict lies first in the priority to be given in the last resort to the maintenance of public order, and secondly in the constant and common-sense exercise of police discretion. Indeed the exercise of discretion lies at the heart of the policing function. It is undeniable that there is only one law for all: and it is

1. *The Home Office*, Sir Frank Newsam, Allen and Unwin, 1955 (2nd edition).
2. 'Let justice be done, though the heavens collapse.'

The Police

right that this should be so. But it is equally well recognized that successful policing depends on the exercise of discretion in how the law is enforced. The good reputation of the police as a force depends upon the skill and judgement which policemen display in the particular circumstances of the cases and incidents which they are required to handle. Discretion is the art of suiting action to particular circumstances. It is the policeman's daily task.

(2) Independence and accountability

4·59   The independence of the police is the other principle of policing a free society to which I wish to refer. Neither politicians nor pressure-groups nor anyone else may tell the police what decisions to take or what methods to employ, whether to enforce the law or not in a particular case, or how to investigate a particular offence. The exercise of police judgement has to be as independent as the exercise of professional judgement by a doctor or a lawyer. If it is not, the way is open to manipulation and abuse of the law, whether for political or for private ends.

4·60   There are, nevertheless, limitations on the power of the police. First and foremost, the law. The police officer must act within the law: abuse of power by a police officer, if it be allowed to occur with impunity, is a staging-post to the police state. But there is also the constitutional control of accountability (see Part V, paragraphs 5·55–71, infra). The police must exercise independent judgement: but they are also the servants of the community. They enforce the law on behalf of the community: indeed they cannot effectively enforce it without the support of the community. The community pays them and provides them with their resources. So there has to be some way in which to secure that the independent judgement of the police can not only operate within the law but with the support of the community. At present, outside London, that mechanism is provided by the local police authority. A Chief Constable is independent, but accountable to his local police authority. The Metropolitan Police are differently placed. The Commissioner is accountable not to a local police authority but to the Home Secretary and, through him, to Parliament. Both these arrangements have been subject to criticism in the course of the Inquiry. I

104

Two principles of policing

examine those criticisms later (Part V, paragraphs 5·55–71, infra).
Suffice it to say for the present that the second basic principle of
policing a free society which is of essential relevance to my Report is
the independence of the police, coupled with the need to ensure that
the police operate not only within the law but with the support of the
community as a whole. Accountability and effective consultative
machinery are needed to ensure this support.

E · Findings on the main criticisms of the police

4·61   Approaching the police problem with the two principles to
which I have referred very much in mind, I now state my findings on
the main criticisms of the police which have been developed by
represented parties in the course of the Inquiry.

(1) 'Racial prejudice'

4·62   The direction and policies of the Metropolitan Police are not
racist. I totally and unequivocally reject the attack made upon the
integrity and impartiality of the senior direction of the force. The
criticisms lie elsewhere – in errors of judgement, in a lack of
imagination and flexibility, but not in deliberate bias or prejudice.
The allegation that the police are the oppressive arm of a racist state
not only displays a complete ignorance of the constitutional arrangements for controlling the police: it is an injustice to the senior
officers of the force.

4·63   Such plausibility as this attack has achieved is due, sadly, to
the ill-considered, immature and racially prejudiced actions of some
officers in their dealings on the streets with young black people.
Racial prejudice does manifest itself occasionally in the behaviour of
a few officers on the streets. It may be only too easy for some officers,
faced with what they must see as the inexorably rising tide of street
crime, to lapse into an unthinking assumption that all young black
people are potential criminals. I am satisfied, however, that such a
bias is not to be found amongst senior police officers. They recognize that those black people in Brixton who are engaged in crime

[6]

THE POLICE AND THEIR RULES OF OFFICE: AN ETHICAL ANALYSIS

WILLIAM C. HEFFERNAN

Before assuming their positions, police officers must take an oath to uphold the Constitution of the United States and the laws and ordinances of their jurisdiction. The oath stands as a personal commitment to honor the rules of the policeman's office. At least two of these rules deserve special consideration. First, full enforcement legislation—New York City's is typical of its kind—requires, among other things, that an officer "preserve the public peace, . . . protect the rights of persons, . . . enforce and prevent the violation of all laws and ordinances in force in the city, and for these purposes . . . arrest all persons guilty of violating any law or ordinance. . . ."[1] Second, the laws of criminal procedure, particularly the Fourth and Fifth Amendments, function as special constitutional rules of the policeman's office. In considering the combined force of his oath and these rules, an officer could conclude that he has made a promise, has committed himself

William C. Heffernan is Associate Professor of Law at John Jay College of Criminal Justice of the City University of New York. Together with Timothy Stroup, he founded John Jay's Institute for Criminal Justice Ethics, and he now serves as editor of the Institute's journal, Criminal Justice Ethics. *Professor Heffernan's articles on jurisprudence and professional ethics have appeared in the* University of Chicago Law Review, Buffalo Law Review, Criminal Justice Review, *and* International Journal of the Sociology of Law.

4 Fidelity to Law

personally, in taking the oath. The content of the commitment—that is, the terms of his promise—requires the enforcement of all laws governing his jurisdiction. Among these are laws, directed at him, requiring full enforcement, with the procedural limits set by the Constitution, of all substantive laws in force in his jurisdiction. By taking the oath, the officer could conclude, he has promised to obey the rules of his office.

In this essay, I shall ask whether it is ever morally permissible for a police officer to violate his oath and thus legitimately operate outside the rules of his office. This question is an important one partly because legal sanctions are practically never brought to bear on police officers who engage in low-level, noncorrupt violations of their rules of office. If, for instance, an officer decides not to enforce a minor criminal statute or if he undertakes an illegal search that results in no physical harm to the person searched, then there is virtually no chance that he will be subject to administrative discipline for his conduct. Furthermore, if his search produces contraband—a gun, perhaps, or drugs—a sanction will be visited on the state via the exclusionary rule, but none on the officer himself. Legally, police officers have little to fear when they report violations like these of their rules of office; and, of course, unless a statement is legally required, such violations almost always go unreported.

The question about a moral obligation to honor the oath is also important because police officers often claim there is none. Those who follow this line of reasoning would grant that a moral wrong is committed if any of the rules of office is violated for self-interested reasons—to obtain graft, for instance, or, in the case of nonenforcement, simply to avoid extra work. However, they would argue that violations of the rules are frequently justified when they are prompted by disinterested motives. If the goal of nonenforcement is to conserve police resources to combat more serious crime or to give an offender a break, then, according to many officers, nonenforcement can be morally acceptable despite the existence of the rules of office and the oath to honor them. A similar argument is also advanced in support of violations of the Fourth Amendment that result in no physical harm to the person searched or arrested. These, too, some police claim, can contribute to the conservation of law enforcement resources and can also make it possible to punish those who are barely touched by the courts. Disinterested violations are thus often acceptable in police eyes, while self-interested ones of course are not.

In the first section of the essay, I take seriously police officers' claims that their deviations are morally justified. I try to develop a systematic

The Police and Their Rules of Office: An Ethical Analysis   5

argument that is implicit in their defenses of their conduct, and I then
outline a typology of the disinterested, low-level violations in which
they engage. In the second section, I return to the significance of the
oath of office. There, I argue that, while promises cannot be accorded
absolutely binding force, they can be overridden only by the most
serious considerations. Those considerations are not present in most
cases of police violations of the rules of office, and the oath, I argue,
should therefore take precedence. In the final section, though, I suggest one situation in which the oath can be at least provisionally
dishonored, and I advance some proposals for resolving the status of
this rule violation and for guaranteeing uniform police practices while
the resolution is being sought.

OFFICERS' JUSTIFICATIONS FOR DISINTERESTED VIOLATIONS OF THEIR RULES OF OFFICE

In conversations about their work,[2] police officers consistently seek
to justify their rule deviations by appealing to what they believe to be
the ultimate aims of the criminal justice system in which they operate.
Their arguments are of course advanced in ad hoc fashion; however,
one can discern the following systematic pattern that is contained in
them. They claim, first, that the goal of criminal justice is to guarantee a
minimally just social order—not *just* in a distributive sense, but *just* in
the sense that citizens are protected, with minimal state interference,
from the threat of the infliction of serious harm by their fellow citizens.
Police officers next argue that current laws, including their rules of
office, help achieve this just social order when they are applied to
serious offenses such as robbery, burglary, or rape. However, when
less serious offenses are at stake, then, by this argument, neither the
law nor its current application by the courts helps to achieve the
ultimate goal of criminal justice. For low-level offenses, police officers
take steps on their own to help achieve the goal. The aims of criminal
justice are in this way promoted, and the rule violations thus justified.

When police officers who offer this argument are reminded that it
involves a violation not merely of their rules of office but also of their
oath to follow those rules, they claim that even the latter violation is
justified by the imperative of achieving the goals of criminal justice.
The officers grant that the rules contemplate only a limited police
contribution to these goals. However, they argue that, when other
agencies fail to deal with low-level offenses that are properly the
concern of criminal justice, the police must then assume a complete

6   Fidelity to Law

responsibility for this by taking the steps they do. The steps are limited in scope. No physical harm is inflicted. No financial gain is realized by a police officer. Justice is done and order maintained in ways that are compatible with the ultimate goals of criminal justice, though not with the legal procedures specified for reaching them.

Some police officers—and even some scholars—classify these rule deviations as special forms of discretionary conduct.[3] This surely is false, for the law states that the police must not do what they in fact do. Alternatively, some police officers argue that their conduct constitutes a type of civil disobedience. This, too, must be rejected. To engage in civil disobedience, one must aim at changing the law, not evading it. True, police officers would like to change the rules of their office in order to legalize their conduct. However, they do not engage in rule violations in order to bring about this result. The fact that these violations are not reported (except insofar as the law requires this for arrests—and, then, police officers can be confident that this will not result in sanctions against *them*) is sufficient to demonstrate that the police conduct cannot be classified as civilly disobedient.

It is best instead to place this pattern of conduct in a category apart from others—to say that its unifying feature is the disinterested violation of one's rules of office. Whenever a police officer engages in this, he invokes the general authority underlying his role to achieve a result that he believes to be compatible with the ultimate purposes of criminal justice but which he, as an agent of a legal system, has not been authorized to bring about. Given this definition, one could say that judges, prosecutors, prison officials, and parole officers have also been known to engage in disinterested rule violations. On occasion, any of these agents can violate the specific legal duties of his role in order to achieve what he believes to be the ultimate goal of the system in which he works.

As far as the police are concerned, there are at least four types of disinterested rule violations that deserve serious consideration. We have already seen that two goals—the preservation of order and the meting out of condign punishment—underlay the police violations. In turn, there were two proscribed enforcement practices—the violation of constitutional rights and selective enforcement of the law—by which these goals were reached. If we combine these categories, we can discover the four types of disinterested rule violations: (1) the meting out of justice via violations of the Constitution, (2) the meting out of justice via selective enforcement of the law, (3) the promotion of social order via violations of the Constitution, and (4) the promotion of social order via selective enforcement of the law. Brief descriptions of

The Police and Their Rules of Office: An Ethical Analysis   7

each are provided below, and, in order to emphasize the extent to
which the police actually do engage in these violations, the descriptions contain references to current studies of the police.

(1) *Meting Out Justice Via Violations of the Constitution.* Illegal searches
or arrests are sometimes undertaken in order to punish persons whom
officers believe to be both systematically engaged in crime and relatively immune to the formal processes of the courts. Professor Davis
tells of an interview in which "one officer proudly told us . . . that he
'knows' that X is a big narcotics dealer, so that whenever X comes out
on the street the officer searches him and often finds some excuse to
arrest him."[4] Illegal searches and arrests are probably motivated partly
by an officer's desire to "clean up" his beat. [See violation (3).] However, Kenneth Culp Davis's[5] and James Q. Wilson's[6] research indicate
that they can also be prompted by a belief that "known" criminals
should receive their due. As police officers are quick to point out, this is
a mild type of punishment since a suspect will at most lose one night's
rest. But, as they also point out, one night is frequently all that is lost
even for a valid arrest, given the reluctance of many judges to impose
prison terms on those who appear before them.

(2) *Meting Out Justice Via Selective Enforcement of the Law.* Deliberate
decisions *not* to enforce the law are perhaps the commonest way in
which officers seek to give citizens their due, though decisions of this
type involve illegal clemency while decisions in (1) involve illegal
punishment. As Jerome Skolnick notes,

> the policeman sees himself as a merciful administrator of jus-
> tice. . . . Vice control men feel, for example, that any "breaks" a
> particular defendant deserves have already been meted out
> according to personal discretionary standards of the police,
> appropriate in their operational environment.[7]

Whenever nonenforcement is motivated by a desire to see that citizens
receive their due, the act of enforcement will itself become punitive.
While the policeman's rules of office treat arrest as a morally neutral
act, this cannot be the case when an officer practices selective enforcement in order to mete out justice. When this is done, then *all* arrests
must involve a moral decision as to whether a suspect deserves punishment or not.

(3) *Promotion of Social Order Via Violations of the Constitution.* Police
officers frequently claim that the courts do not understand the critical
contribution that preventive frisks can make to the maintenance of
public order. Two premises are contained in the police claim. First,
police believe that criminal activity can be more efficiently detected—

8   Fidelity to Law

that is, with a lower ratio of police effort to evidence (not necessarily
admissible evidence) obtained—when preventive frisks are undertaken
than when they are not.[8] Second, the police also believe that the courts
have erred in construing terms such as *probable cause* and *articulable
suspicion* without reference to the ability of experienced police officers
to spot those who engage in criminal conduct. In particular, they point
out that they often are able to detect likely possessors of illegal firearms
even though they lack the legal requisites to make a forcible stop. As
Wilson has noted, many policemen believe that they would be "derelict in their duty" if they did not detain such people for questioning.[9]
According to the police, current law defeats the goals of criminal justice
under these circumstances, so the police employ their own authority to
override the rules of their office.

   (4) Promotion of Social Order Via Selective Enforcement of the Law. Police
officers also base enforcement decisions on their appreciation of the
prospects of maintaining order. As was true in the previous violation,
two factors are at stake in this decision, though in this case their
importance is reversed. On the one hand, policemen who decline to
enforce the law often do not even think of the full enforcement legislation they have violated. Certainly the violations are so frequent that
few are viewed as worthy of individual justification. On the other
hand, considerations of efficiency are particularly important in this
case. As Wilson has noted, in deciding whether to enforce the law a
police officer often asks himself, among other things, whether or not
an arrest is more likely to promote order than would the investment of
his energy in some other kind of activity.[10] The categories contained in
this formula are open-ended: a policeman could define *order* in terms of
the reduction of serious felonies or the minimization of rowdiness in
public places, and the meaning of *activity* would be limited only by the
policeman's imagination and fidelity to his rules of office. The vagueness of the formula's terms, though, only serves to increase the number of situations in which a police officer could reasonably conclude
that an arrest would do less to promote public order—as the officer
defined that term—than would the investment of his energy elsewhere. If, for instance, a policeman were to arrest someone, without a
citizen's complaint, for smoking marijuana in a completely deserted
public place, he could then expect to spend at least two to three hours
booking his suspect and could possibly spend an equal amount of time
making court appearances. In considering whether to make the arrest,
the officer could therefore reasonably conclude that his investment of
energy in it would be highly inefficient as compared with, say, preventive patrol, since the arrest would be less likely than patrol to produce

The Police and Their Rules of Office: An Ethical Analysis 9

order—again, *order* according to the officer's definition, though in this case he could use the term to refer both to reducing felonies and to minimizing public rowdiness. Obviously, there are other low-level offenses in which the marginal efficiency of an officer's conduct would be difficult to determine. Obviously, too, where serious offenses are concerned, efficiency would be only one consideration among many in determining how to allocate police resources. In cases such as marijuana possession, though, an officer following the efficiency formula could reasonably decline to make an arrest and instead invest his energy elsewhere.

The four different types of disinterested rule violations have thus been outlined. It is now possible to inquire more critically into the moral status of the practices underlying them.

THE SIGNIFICANCE OF THE OATH AND OF AN OFFICIAL'S OBLIGATION OF FIDELITY TO HIS LEGAL DUTIES: AN ARGUMENT AGAINST VIOLATIONS (1), (2), AND (3)

To justify the violations, a police officer would have to show that he is not bound by his oath and that he is not obligated, despite his role as a public official, to obey the laws that define the rules of his office. I shall argue that neither every promise nor every law must be honored, but I shall also argue that strong reasons—particularly strong when an oath and an official's legal duties are at stake—must be given if either is to be overridden. The question, then, is whether the police justifications outlined earlier provide compelling reasons in support of the violations.

The oath is what a prospective policeman offers the state in exchange for the employment he receives. In my conversations with them, police officers have tended to dismiss the significance of their promise to enforce the Constitution and the laws of their jurisdiction. But the practical significance of the oath is amply demonstrated by the fact that any prospective officer who declined to take it or who made public in advance his intention to adhere to it selectively would surely be denied the position he seeks. Furthermore, as with any promise that serves as the basis for an ongoing beneficial exchange, the promise signified by the oath remains morally binding for as long as the benefit is conferred. Sometimes, of course, promises that create exchanges can be onerous as well as beneficial, as when a promisee relies to his detriment on the future performance of a promisor and the latter encounters unexpected difficulties while trying to complete the agreed-upon task. Police officers, though, do not normally experience this kind of situa-

10   Fidelity to Law

tion since, except for unusual circumstances, there is nothing for them
to complete. They can withdraw from their promise on virtually a
moment's notice, and the state can then replace them, without detriment to itself, with someone else. Unlike some other promisors, then,
policemen are not imprisoned by their agreement but can instead
cancel it with ease if they find that they cannot in good conscience
discharge its terms.

A police officer might claim that, whatever the original status of his
promise, there are good reasons to infer he is no longer bound by it, at
least as far as low-level, disinterested rule violations are concerned.
The reasons advanced by the officer would vary according to the
violations. With regard to infringements of constitutional rights, the
officer might point out, these are always reported when an arrest is
made, yet, as the officer would further point out, administrative or
legal action is practically never taken provided no physical harm has
been suffered by the suspect. In the case of selective enforcement,
officers seldom report their omissions; but an officer might nonetheless point out that his supervisors are probably aware of the general
pattern of selective enforcement and that they impose no sanctions on
those who practice it. In both cases, the officer would argue, the failure
of administrators and prosecutors to take action concerning low-level
violations allows for the inference that the terms of the promise have
been amended to include these.

Though generally correct as a factual claim, this point does not
support the conclusion that police officers draw from it. The officers'
argument presupposes that their superiors and district attorneys can
validly amend the terms of their promise. But this is not the case. The
promisee in this instance is the state, and the state exists as an entity
only through the formal acts of its officials, not through the informal
expressions of approval that are sometimes provided by its subordinate employees. The state officers who possess the authority to vary
the terms of the promise are, in this case, legislators and judges.
Furthermore, there are two ways in which they could do so: first, by a
declaration that the rules of the policeman's office have been modified,
and second, by failure to act when the police have provided them with
notice of their violations. The first has not occurred in most jurisdictions, although (lest it be supposed that this is an impossibility) it
should be noted that New Mexico has amended its statutes to allow
selective enforcement.[11] The second is a more problematic criterion
since it is not certain exactly *how* the police could provide notice of their
violations. At the very least, the following would be required. Police
administrators would have to report—without necessarily endors-

The Police and Their Rules of Office: An Ethical Analysis 11

ing—to legislative committees on widespread practices of rule violations in their department.

As far as the courts are concerned, notice of the violations would
have to be provided via prosecutions for dereliction of duty or applications for injunctions to require the police to honor their rules of office.
In no sense can police administrators be said to have been given this
kind of notice to either legislatures or the courts of disinterested, low-
level police violations, so in no sense could the violations be said to
have been condoned. In fact, in the one case where notice *has* been
provided—suppression hearings in criminal actions involving the
Fourth Amendment—the violations have been consistently condemned, though of course the result of a suppression hearing can only
be the imposition of a sanction on the state, not on an individual police
officer. In whatever way that one considers the question, then, there is
no reason to believe that the terms of the promise have been varied to
legitimize the police violations.

The policeman's obligation as a public official to obey the rules of his
office is logically independent of his obligation as a promisor. The
former is created by the position he holds and the expectations it
engenders, the latter by a special commitment that has ethical significance apart from any official role. When allowance is made for these
differences, though, one can also point out that both obligations arise
out of a relation of trust and that both therefore require strong reasons
for violating that trust. Arguably, the obligation to obey the law stands
on a lesser footing than does the one to keep promises. However, we
must remember that we are dealing here with an official's relation to
legal duties that create monopoly powers for all who perform his role.
Because of the role's monopoly powers, an official's breach of its duties
carries with it a significantly greater danger of public disruption than
do the great majority of citizen violations of laws that apply to all.
Furthermore, a public official can always opt for the relatively low-cost
alternative of resigning his office rather than disobey its duties, while a
citizen confronted with an undesirable law can chose only between the
more painful alternatives of possible criminal prosecution or emigra-
tion. For these reasons, an official's conscientious violation of the rules
of his office can be justified only in unusual circumstances.

In what circumstances, then, could a violation—of the oath or of an
official's obligation of fidelity to the law—be justified? As far as promising is concerned, there are arguably many situations in which a promise can be set aside in favor of other conduct. Similarly, an official's
legal duties can arguably be ignored in favor of urgently needed action
that is neither required of nor forbidden to him. But that is not the kind

12   Fidelity to Law

of promise-breaking that we considered in violations (1)–(4). In all of those, the promise and rules of office were not simply set aside, they were instead directly contradicted by the actions that police officers took. Furthermore most of the violations went unreported, and the others were reported to administrators who of course had no authority to vary the terms of the promise. Finally, the police officers did not resign their positions following the violations but instead continued to receive benefits that were predicated on the assumption of official adherence to the law.

When a promise is directly contradicted, the promisee left unaware of the violation, and the benefits accruing from the promise retained, then the circumstances in which the relation of trust created by the promise can be justifiably broken are narrow indeed. First, if a promisee—a tyrant, for instance—is clearly an evil person, then a promisor can enter in bad faith into a relation of trust with the intention of using his position to counteract the harm that the promisee seeks to commit. This is the only situation in which a promise can be justifiably initiated in bad faith and the only one in which there is no duty subsequently to report a violation or return benefits. All of these otherwise unacceptable steps are justifiable only because they are necessary to combat a great evil. We may assume that American police cannot avail themselves of this justification, although police in other countries perhaps could.

Second, the terms of a promise can be breached and benefits accruing from it retained if harm, which is both immediately threatened and unforeseen by both parties until the threat arises, can be averted only by using the position created by the promise to reduce the threat. In this case, as in the first, there is an appeal to a good for which the promise was not created. Here, though, the promisor assumes that the promisee would wish him to perform the proscribed act and that only the press of circumstance or some difficulty in gaining the attention of the promisee makes explicit amendment of the terms of the promise impossible. In this case, then, the violation would have to be reported and the position resigned if the promisee did not offer subsequent ratification of it, though the justifiability of breaching one's promise could not be affected by the promisee's refusal. In one sense this justification is unavailable to the police since they already possess the authority under the Fourth Amendment to intervene in situations where there is the probability of harm to themselves or others. In another sense, though, the police might seek to claim this justification—provided, that is, that they reported their conduct to the proper authorities. Sometimes the police confront situations, as in violations (1) and (3), in

The Police and Their Rules of Office: An Ethical Analysis 13

which there is only the possibility—but no probability—of imminent harm. An example of this would be a "gun run" where an officer acts on an anonymous tip that a suspect is armed. The officer pursuing this tip would be aware of possible danger to himself but would also know that he lacks the authority under the Constitution to execute a frisk upon approaching the suspect. Even in a case of *possible* harm like this, though, the police could not invoke the justification just suggested, for while the threat posed by the specific gun run could not have been foreseen until the officer was obligated to act, the threat posed by that *type* of run certainly could have been foreseen before the obligation arose. In cases like these, Fourth Amendment standards may expose the police to a greater threat of harm than they wish to bear; but since this can be anticipated, the "imminent harm" rationale cannot justify violation by police of their oath of office.

Third, while the first two examples involve compelling instances of promise-breaking, there is, I think, a final justification for direct violation of a promise and retention of benefits even when imminent harm is not threatened. In this case, the justification would be available only when two conditions are met—first, when the promisor has reason to believe that doing so would fulfill better an implied purpose of the promise (without interfering with other purposes that can be implied) than would adherence to the terms themselves, and second, when the promisee's consent cannot easily be obtained, thus making it likely that the promise's purposes would be significantly defeated if unilateral action were not taken by the promisor. Here, because the breach is not prompted by the threat of imminent harm to the promisor or to a third party, only the promise itself can serve to justify the breach. And here, because the promise has been reinterpreted so that one of its underlying purposes is made to take precedence over its terms, the breach could at best be considered provisionally justified, with final justification available only through ratification by the promisee. Weak as this is, it is the only justification that a police officer can cite, since the others can be used only in more extreme conditions than those in which the police operate. I shall argue that, even under this standard, a provisional justification is available only for the fourth violation. The first three must be rejected as wholly unacceptable.

The police, it will be recalled, defend their violations on the ground that these fulfill better the underlying goals of criminal justice than does fidelity to their rules of office. This line of reasoning, it should now be clear, is incompatible with the violation of a promise and the retention of benefits while doing so. One cannot point to a good to justify the direct violation of the terms of one's promise. Absent the

14   Fidelity to Law

condition of imminent harm suggested before, only a good that was clearly implied in the promise itself can provide even a provisional justification for the violation; otherwise, withdrawal from the promise would be required. The police defense of their conduct can therefore be set aside on the ground that it is incompatible with the institution of promising. Instead, we must ask whether any of the goods pursued by the police in the course of their violations can be said to be implied by the terms of their promise and so offer a possible justification for their conduct.

The violations were motivated by two different goods—the meting out of justice [violations (1) and (2)] and the promotion of social order [violations (3) and (4)]. Each should be examined in terms of the goals that the police oath of fidelity to the law is meant to fulfill.

(a) The Police as Dispensers of Justice: Violations (1) and (2). Whatever the status of the police as promoters of public order, there is certainly no reason to infer from their oaths or their rules of office that the state intends them to use their positions to dispense justice. Their rules of office contain a catalogue of highly specific duties plus one that is a catch-all requiring them to enforce all laws and ordinances and make arrests of all violators.[12] The duties mentioned point unmistakably toward a contemplated role of police as gatherers of evidence and determiners of probable violations of the law. They do not, however, allow for the inference that the police may dispense justice to private citizens. That function has clearly been delegated to other agents of the criminal justice system. In the absence of any formal indication that the police were intended to fulfill it, they may not do so and remain faithful to their oath.

As we have seen, the police claim that the courts fail to perform adequately their function as dispensers of justice. This is certainly an argument that deserves to be taken more seriously than it often is. It cannot, however, serve as a ground for violation of the oath or the official's obligation of fidelity to the law. If a police officer believes that the current rules of his office are subverting the aims of criminal justice, then he should either resign his position or else protest those rules while still honoring them in his work.

These comments, it should be noted, are as relevant to the granting of clemency [violation (2)] as they are to the infliction of punishment via transgressions of the Constitution [violation (1)]. Other agents of the criminal justice system—prosecutors, jurors, and judges—are explicitly vested with authority to excuse defendants from legal liability in the face of evidence of guilt. But a police officer may not do this even for petty offenses such as traffic infractions. No matter how appealing a police officer may find the act of granting clemency, nonenforcement

The Police and Their Rules of Office: An Ethical Analysis   15

of the law *for the sake of granting mercy* is incompatible with the police-man's promise to honor his rules of office.

(b) *The Police as Promoters of Order: Violations (3) and (4)*. By contrast, the police rules of office do allow for the inference that one of the implicit purposes of the promise is to promote public order. This point, if it is not already clear, can be made so by reference to that portion of the full enforcement catalogue of duties which requires the police to "preserve the public peace, . . . suppress riots, mobs and insurrec-tions [and] dispose of unlawful and dangerous assemblages. . . ." For the violations under consideration, then, we can begin by noting a potential tension between the general good of maintaining order, which the police promise implicitly seeks to promote, and the specific means—protection of rights [violation (3)] and full enforcement [viola-tion (4)]—which the promise prescribes for reaching it. The fact of the tension could not by itself justify preference for the end rather than the means. Because of the promise, the opposite priority should prevail. However, if the means assigned the police are not only inadequate but actually counterproductive, and if another approach could be adopted that fulfills better the goal of maintaining order without interfering with other goals implied by the promise, then even the direct violation of the promise might be considered provisionally justified. This is the defense that can be offered for violation (4). It is not, however, avail-able for violation (3).

As we have seen, the police defend violations (3) and (4) on the ground that adherence to their rules of office would reduce the pros-pects of achieving public order, while the violations actually enhance these. If there were a larger force, the police claim, then fidelity to the rules could perhaps lead to achievement of the goal. Given current staff levels, though, the police contend that they must consider ques-tions of efficiency in deciding how to allocate their time. In violation (4), for instance, an officer would forgo formal action in the face of clear-cut evidence of guilt in order to preserve his energy for possible infractions by citizens that pose a greater threat to public order. Similar considerations of efficiency would underlie violation (3). There, a police officer would decide to make an illegal search or arrest of a "well-known" criminal in the hope of deterring either the suspect or others like him from engaging in a genuine crime. In both cases, the decision, which is prompted by the level of police staffing, would be based on a desire to achieve the police goal of maintaining order in the most efficient possible way.

In violation (3), though, a police officer must actively and illegally harm a citizen so as to promote order, while in violation (4), the officer would fail to perform a legal duty for the same reason. If we assume

16   Fidelity to Law

that the officer has made a reasonable calculation of efficiency (that is, that his actions tend to promote a conception of order that is consistent with the one implicit in his rules of office), then breaking promises through omission should be considered provisionally acceptable as long as it reaches its goal better than adherence to the prescribed means and also does not interfere with other implied promises of the police. The same cannot be said for violation (3). There, an officer must subvert a basic purpose of policing—the protection of individuals from illegal harm—in order to achieve another goal. Police officers might argue that the minor harm suffered by victims of illegal searches and arrests is outweighed by the potentially serious harm these can avert. Balancing considerations of this kind are not, however, compatible with the violation of a promise and the retention of benefits for it. Only harm which is both imminently threatened and unforeseen by the parties until the threat of it arises can justify this kind of promise-breaking—and we have already seen that this rationale cannot be applied to the third violation. Once this justification is taken away, the third violation can be seen to rest on a balancing consideration to which the police may not, because of their promise, legitimately appeal.

We may conclude, then, that the police cannot justify violations of their promises in situations (1), (2), and (3). This proposition has important implications for administrators and individual officers. For the former, it provides a compelling reason to welcome, rather than resist, administrative bodies that actively investigate violations in cases (1) through (3). The possibility that departmental morale will be jeopardized by such investigation must be deemed a secondary consideration when compared with the importance of the oath of office and the administrators' obligation to make sure that it is honored. For individual officers, whether or not they are threatened with sanctions for noncompliance, the implications are equally serious. Because of the promise, violations (1) through (3) are impermissible—the first two because the police promise does not even imply that they may dispense justice, the third because the promise, while it does envision a police role as maintainers of order, seeks to have them do so without inflicting harm on others. Individual officers therefore must either honor their oath or else they must resign their position rather than accept benefits for direct violation of a promise.

RESOLVING THE STATUS OF THE FOURTH VIOLATION

In classifying violation (4) as "provisionally justified," I was suggesting that police officers can legitimately omit enforcement of certain

The Police and Their Rules of Office: An Ethical Analysis 17

statutes for the sake of promoting order *without* seeking the prior approval of the state. The violation seems sufficiently compatible with the implied purpose of the promise and seems also sufficiently clearly to involve no threat to its other purposes that would warrant unilateral action by the police. Unilateral action, though, can be acceptable for only a limited period of time. If the police were to continue ad infinitum in their violations without even alerting the state, much less seeking guidance from it, then their conduct would at some point become unjustified. Clearly, it is the police who have a responsibility—as promise-breakers—to seek that guidance. In this section, I shall suggest how they can fulfill that responsibility and what administrators and individual officers should do in the interim while clarification of the status of their conduct is being sought.

(a) *Seeking Guidance from the State.* Given the seriousness of the oath of office, one would expect police administrators to be anxious to seek guidance from the state concerning their subordinates' practices. The reverse, though, is closer to the truth. As calls to legal divisions of police departments reveal, administrators are anxious to advance theories that would justify the legality of nonenforcement, but they are equally wary of subjecting any of these theories to actual legal tests. I have been told by lawyers for the New York City Police Department, for instance, that since legislators systematically underappropriate funds for the police, the legislators therefore must expect and approve of selective enforcement by the police.[14] As we have seen, though, legislative *inaction* can be construed as ratification of a breach of a promise only if unmistakable evidence of the breach has first been presented to the state. This, of course, is something that New York's police administrators have failed to do. I have also been told that since the courts have held that municipalities are not liable (on grounds other than sovereign immunity) in tort for the consequences of decisions by police and fire departments *not* to provide requested services, the courts have therefore recognized the legality of nonenforcement.[15] But while an explicit court declaration on the legal duties of the police could resolve this issue, a determination that municipalities are not civilly liable for police failure to provide a service that is clearly not required by their rules of office does not suffice.

There are two ways in which state guidance should be sought. First, administrators could apply to the legislature for changes in the statutes that define the duties of their office. In particular, they could describe in detail, without necessarily endorsing, the pattern of nonenforcement practices that currently prevails in their departments. This would provide legislators with notice of the phenomenon, and failure to take

18   Fidelity to Law

legislative action concerning it might then be construed as condoning
it. Next, the administrators could ask the legislature to promulgate
general guidelines for nonenforcement and then to delegate to departmental boards the authority to refine these guidelines and to publicize the circumstances in which low-level statutes would or would
not be enforced. This would be the most satisfactory way of making
final the provisional justification of nonenforcement for the sake of
promoting order.

Second, administrators could actively seek a court test of nonenforcement practices. This is a step they have assiduously avoided so
far. Recently, for instance, an application for an injunction against the
New York City police chief was sought by women identifying themselves as victims of spousal assaults to require the chief of police to
issue an order to subordinates that spouses be arrested when there is
probable cause to believe an assault has been committed.[16] Here, at
least, was an opportunity for judicial determination of the validity of
one type of nonenforcement. However, once the trial court ruled
against the department's motion to dismiss, the department's lawyers
entered into a stipulation that made moot any further litigation on the
question.[17] Police administrators' responsibilities require, I think, that
they do the opposite. Because of the significance of the oath, administrators should welcome such suits, avoid out-of-court settlements, and
seek a decision in the highest court of their jurisdiction. Even this
might not resolve the issue since the courts frequently decline to
compel administrators to perform their statutorily defined duties while
also declining to hold that these have ceased to be legal duties.[18] It is for
this reason that an application to the legislature would serve as a more
satisfactory means of resolving the status of the fourth violation.

(b) *Interim Planning by Administrators.* What, though, should administrators do while the efforts at clarification are pending? I would
suggest, as others have,[19] that a departmental board should be created
to determine and publicize nonenforcement policies. The alternative to
this kind of centralized planning—ad hoc decisions by individual
police officers as to which laws are to be enforced—would produce a
patch-work pattern of enforcement, thus resulting in differential treatment of citizens who commit the same offense.

The board should be guided by the general formula which, it was
suggested, is implicit in all type (4) violations—that the police can, on
occasion, promote public order more efficiently by not enforcing the
law (and investing their energy elsewhere) than by enforcing it. The
meaning of this formula did not seem particularly problematic when
the only example used involved a policeman's choice between invest-

The Police and Their Rules of Office: An Ethical Analysis   19

ing his energy in a marijuana arrest in a deserted public place or investing it in some other kind of activity that, he believed, would contribute more to maintaining public order. The marijuana arrest was the only example needed to demonstrate the principle that an officer could reasonably believe that order can sometimes be more efficiently maintained by deviating from, rather than adhering to, his rules of office. However, a departmental board would of course have to move beyond elementary cases. In doing so, the board would have to clarify what *kind* of public order it desires, choosing between alternatives such as reducing serious felonies and minimizing public rowdiness. Furthermore, empirical studies would be needed to determine the relative efficiency of nonenforcement practices where, unlike the marijuana example, it is indubitably clear that the police could find more effective ways of using their energy than enforcing the law. In these cases, enforcement would have to be compared with various possible uses of time spent on nonenforcement. Conceivably, enforcement might be deemed more efficient than some and less than others, thus making the decision hinge on the likelihood of capitalizing on the more efficient kinds of nonenforcement.

I would suggest the following guidelines for the board. First, the board should be empowered to determine—and this of course would be subject to judicial review, thus making possible a court test of selective enforcement—whether a statute is not to be enforced at all (in all likelihood, few would be subject to so sweeping a regulation) or whether its enforcement is to be limited according to criteria defined in advance for police officers. Second, because it is the police who are violating their promise, the burden of proving efficiency should be borne by those who argue for nonenforcement rather than those who argue for enforcement. Furthermore, the weight of that burden should vary inversely with the grade assigned an offense by the legislature. A burden of the preponderance of the evidence might be established for violations. A heavier burden should be used for misdemeanors, and all felonies (except perhaps for the lowest grade) should be immune from consideration. Finally, I would also suggest that, except for unusual circumstances, priority should be given to reducing felonies rather than general preservation of the public peace.

We have assumed up to now that the departmental board would use only the efficiency formula in reviewing low-level offenses. This of course was an oversimplification since the board would have to consider other factors, such as community need and consistency of action, in determining enforcement policy. The latter factor is particularly important and may sometimes conflict with the achievement of effi-

20   Fidelity to Law

ciency. Prostitution, for instance, may be easier to contain by arresting prostitutes than by arresting their customers. (There are great difficulties in gaining admissible evidence against the latter.) Or, to take a different, though related, problem, some neighborhoods may favor strict enforcement of disorderly conduct or public intoxication statutes, while others may so resent this that public order would be endangered more by the enforcement than by nonenforcement. In both of these cases, variable, and thus inconsistent, police action could well be more in keeping with the norm of efficiency than would a policy of uniform enforcement. In both, though, it could also be argued that the similarity of offending conduct requires a uniform response despite the possibility of a relative loss of efficiency. I would suggest that a heavy burden should be placed on those who argue for permitting inconsistency and that differential enforcement should be rejected *per se* for all offenses above the lowest-grade misdemeanor.

(c) *Interim Action by Individual Police Officers.* If administrators were to undertake interim planning, then one would have only to suggest to police officers that they adhere to the guidelines given them. However, police administrators, while claiming for their subordinates the right not to enforce the law, have consistently declined to establish guidelines to carry this out. Their reason for doing so is understandable, since they want to preserve maximum leeway for police action. The consequences of their omission have, however, been very disturbing. Citizens have been subject to variable enforcement practices, and the variations have often been particularly pronounced as between whites and blacks, rich and poor, and old and young. Individual police officers in turn have not known when to enforce certain low-level statutes, and they have of course been exposed to extra danger in their work because of citizen resentment of the variable enforcement practices of their peers. How, then, should officers conduct themselves in the absence of guidance from above?

As a preliminary matter, it should be noted that the interim is likely to persist—and to become the defining state of police work—as long as administrators fail to seek guidance from the state in either of the ways suggested before. This does not mean, though, that individual officers should therefore avoid nonenforcement. The duty of a promisor is to notify the promisee of any breach of his promise. This, an officer can—and should—do by informing his superior of his policy of nonenforcement. Assuming that his superiors believe this to be a provisionally justified violation of the policeman's oath, they should then not impose penalties but instead use the information gained to present to the legislature a detailed portrait of department-wide patterns of non-

The Police and Their Rules of Office: An Ethical Analysis 21

enforcement. That administrators have failed—and are likely to continue to fail—to do this cannot be considered the fault of an individual officer. While an officer cannot validly conclude that failure to take administrative sanctions against him indicates that the terms of his promise have been amended, he can at least fulfill his obligation as one who has breached that promise in order to achieve one of its underlying purposes by notifying his superiors of his conduct.

The general criteria underlying an officer's nonenforcement practices should, I think, be identical with those appropriate for a departmental board. In acting on his own, each police officer takes on the functions of such a board, and he therefore should be guided by the standards of efficiency, communal need, and formal consistency that were suggested before. Formal consistency, though, is especially difficult to attain when each officer is free to decide on his own policies. An officer could encounter a situation in which his peers consistently fail to enforce the law while the officer believes that, on balance, there is good reason to enforce it. And the reverse could also be encountered— the officer might believe that nonenforcement is appropriate while his peers generally enforce the law. The critical point in both cases is that the victim of variable enforcement has a legitimate grievance in receiving unfavorable treatment *even when*, on balance, it could be concluded that all people engaging in his conduct deserve such treatment. This is not a conclusive reason for failing to make an arrest. However, it is a factor that must be considered by an individual officer in deciding whether or not to arrest—and it is a factor that could be made irrelevant by a system of administrative planning for selective enforcement. In sum, the officer acting on his own must operate as if he were a planning board, while taking into account the invidious treatment that can be accorded citizens because there is none.

CONCLUSION

In this paper, I have described four types of disinterested violations by police officers of the rules of their office. Officers frequently claim that, despite the oath they have taken to honor these rules, the violations constitute a justifiable breach of their promise since each achieves better one of the aims of criminal justice than would adherence to the rules. I have argued that this cannot constitute a justification for violation of a promise *and* the retention of benefits accruing from it. To gain even a provisional justification under these circumstances, I have suggested, a police officer must show that, by deviating from the terms

22 Fidelity to Law

prescribed by the promise, he can achieve better one of the implicit aims of the promise (*not* one of the aims of the entire system in which he works) and must show that he can do so without detracting from any of the promise's other aims. Under this standard, three of the violations must be rejected as unacceptable breaches of the oath, and police administrators and officers, I have argued, should show due regard for the seriousness of the oath by taking strong action with regard to these violations. The fourth violation—selective enforcement of low-level criminal statutes in order to maximize the efficiency of police efforts in maintaining public order—can be considered provisionally justified. I have therefore proposed ways in which this provisional justification could be made permanent and have also suggested steps that administrators and officers could take pending that final resolution.

NOTES

1. *New York City Charter* § 435, as amended, 1950.

2. My conversations have been with ten New York, New Jersey, and federal law enforcement officers who have enrolled during the last two years in my John Jay seminar on the law of search and seizure. In each semester that I have taught the course, I have devoted two hour-and-a-quarter classes to consideration of the justifiability of police officers' disinterested violations of their rules of office. During the first class, I have confined myself to developing the implications of the officers' arguments. During the second, I have reminded the officers of the significance of the oath and have also noted their special relation to the law. These, however, are only two of many ethical perspectives on disinterested rule violations that I have mentioned. I have not suggested that these were my own.

Of the officers with whom I have spoken, none has rejected as unjustified at all times any of the rule violations discussed in this paper. All have agreed that the second, third and fourth are widespread, and they have agreed that the fourth is the commonest of the violations. There has been some divergence of opinion as to the frequency with which the first occurs. Three officers have cited routine instances of it; the others have granted that it sometimes occurs but have also claimed that it is far less common that the others.

I have never asked anyone directly whether or not he has committed any of the these violations. All officers have volunteered that they engage in the fourth. Five have stated in class that they follow a policy of using violation 3, and three of these have stated that they also engage regularly in violation 1. One of the latter officers would frequently remark—half in jest, I think—"Well, we're the good guys, you know."

3. For scholars who have employed this classification, see Mortimer and Sanford Kadish, *Discretion to Disobey* (Stanford, Calif.: Stanford University Press,

The Police and Their Rules of Office: An Ethical Analysis   23

1973), pp. 73–80; and James Q. Wilson, *Varieties of Police Behavior* (Cambridge, Mass.: Harvard University Press, 1968), pp. 83–139.

4. Kenneth Culp Davis, *Police Discretion* (Minneapolis, Minn.: West, 1975), p. 16.

5. Ibid., pp. 20–22. There Davis discusses the "hatred" the Chicago police seemed to feel for pimps who live off the earnings of their women while remaining virtually immune to the formal processes of law. Purposeful harassment serves as a means by which the officers give these pimps their due.

6. Wilson, *Varieties of Police Behavior*, p. 36. In summarizing police attitudes, Wilson remarks "[t]o be just to these [i.e. street] people means to give each what he deserves and to judge what he deserves by how he acts and talks. This is close to the ancient conception 'distributive' justice, which holds that things and honors should be divided among persons according to merit or so that inequality in person is reflected by a proportional inequality of treatment." Wilson is mistaken, I think, when he suggests that officers are concerned with *distributive* justice, and his citation of *Nicomachean Ethics* V, 3 reveals the way in which he has made a mistake. Aristotle's references to "shares" in that passage indicates that he is concerned with the distribution of a limited good, and this is the sense in which the term has been used by modern writers. Police officers are instead concerned with imposing condign punishment, which involves a different, though nonetheless important, type of justice.

7. Jerome Skolnick, *Justice Without Trial* (New York: Wiley, 1966), pp. 197–98. See also Wilson, *Varieties of Police Behavior*, pp. 50,52.

8. There is some empirical evidence supporting this conclusion. The San Diego Police Study of 1973 concludes that "some level of field interrogation, as opposed to none, provides a deterrent effect on suppressible crimes in localized areas." John E. Bodstun et al., *San Diego Field Interrogation: Final Report* (Washington, D.C.: Police Foundation, 1975), p.5. In the San Diego study, the police were permitted to initiate frisks only after they had first questioned a suspect. Violation 3 includes frisks made on less than articulable suspicion and initiated upon approaching a suspect. Because of this distinction, the police should find it easier to detect criminal activity than they did in San Diego, though of course violations would also do more to exacerbate police-citizen relations.

9. Wilson, *Varieties of Police Behavior*, pp. 40–41.

10. Ibid., p. 84.

11. See New Mexico Statutes § 29-1-1, as amended, 1979, which states that it is "the duty of every sheriff . . . to investigate all violations of the criminal laws of the state of New Mexico . . . and it is also declared the duty of every such officer to diligently file a complaint or information *if the circumstances are such as to indicate to a reasonably prudent person that such action should be taken. . . ."* (emphasis added)

24   Fidelity to Law

12. An example of the catalogue can be found at New York City Charter § 435, as amended, 1950.

13. Ibid.

14. This is also one of the arguments advanced by Professor Davis in support of the legality of selective enforcement. See *Police Discretion*, pp. 80–82.

15. The cases cited to me by New York City Police Department lawyers were Motyka v. City of Amsterdam, 15 N.Y. 2d 134 (1965) and Riss v. City of New York, 22 N.Y. 2d 579 (1968). Not surprisingly, the department's lawyers did not cite Runkel v. Homelsky, 286 A.D. 1101 (1959), aff'd. 3 N.Y. 2d 857 (1960) and Schuster v. City of New York, 5 N.Y. 2d 75 (1961). In both of the latter cases, the courts held that a municipality can be liable for police failure to provide requested protection.

16. See Bruno v. Codd, 90 Misc. 2d 1047 (1977).

17. Bruno v. Codd, 64 A.D. 2d 582 (1978) (reversing the Supreme Court Special Term on other grounds); aff'd. at 47 N.Y. 2d 582 (1979).

18. See, for instance, Jones v. Beame, 45 N.Y. 2d 402 (1978); James v. Board of Education, 42 N.Y. 2d 357 (1977); Matter of Abrams v. New York City Transit Authority, 39 N.Y. 2d 990 (1976); Matter of Community Action Against Lead Poisoning v. Lyons, 36 N.Y. 2d 686 (1975).

19. See, for instance, Davis, *Police Discretion*, pp. 98–120; and Joseph Goldstein, "Police Discretion Not to Invoke the Criminal Process: Low Visibility Decisions in the Administration of Justice," *Yale Law Journal* 69 (1960): 588–89.

[7]

POLICE DISCRETION
Laurence Lustgarten

One of the concepts central to nearly all literature concerning the
police is that of discretion. Joseph Goldstein's classic article[1] introduced two important ideas: that the police are virtually unique
among bureaucratic organisations in that the degree of discretion
is greatest at the lowest level of the hierarchy, and that decisions
by policemen in their dealings with the public are of "low visibility"—inaccessible to their ostensible superiors and effectively
unreviewable by any authority, particularly where they have
decided *not* to arrest someone. Discretion here is used in the sense
familiar to administrative law: in K.C. Davis' words, it exists
"where effective limits on a public officer's power leave him free to
make a choice among possible courses of action or inaction."[2] This
"room for decisional manoeuvre" is a matter of degree, which
varies with the precision of the standards governing an official's
discretion.[3]

Yet the points Goldstein emphasised may themselves in part be
merely a reflection of a more fundamental fact: that in taking the
sort of decision that is the quintessence of their work, the police
are guided by virtually no legal standards at all. More precisely,
whilst the police may not violate general criminal or civil law,—
e.g. by accepting a bribe or assaulting someone without lawful
excuse,—they act within an almost infinite range of lawful possibilities. Consider the choices open to a constable summoned to the
scene of a minor fight between two men who in law have been
guilty at least of common assault. They include:

1. Breaking it up, with an informal warning to the participants
   and no other action.
2. Breaking it up, inquiring into the cause and attempting to
   conciliate or mediate between them.
3. Formally cautioning either or both.
4. Attempting to inquire into the cause of the fight, arresting
   only the one he believes was responsible.
5. Arresting both participants, on any of a wide range of

[1] Goldstein (1960), *passim*.   [2] Davis, (1969), p. 4.   [3] Jowell, (1973), p. 179.

charges relating to public order and/or varying degrees of
assault as seem to him appropriate.

Even in this apparently simple situation, the range of permissible choices is extraordinary, and will depend on how the constable, or those who train and supervise him, perceives his task. If
it is solely and simply law enforcement, the first two possibilities
are excluded: the law has been broken and the offenders must be
penalised. If considerations of maintaining the peace and public
good will predominate, any of the responses is permissible and
may depend upon the character of the people involved, where the
fight took place, reactions of others in the neighbourhood, and
numerous other highly idiosyncratic factors. Still other factors,
notably the dangers of overloading the capacity of the criminal justice system and the cost of processing offenders, will also be relevant, particularly if the legal infraction is seen as minor.

All the suggested options are within the range of the constable's
legal powers. To say therefore that he must uphold the law, or is
responsible to the law, is in practical terms meaningless. His discretion involves either making value judgments about the worthiness of the people involved, or public feeling, or the seriousness of
the incident, or the long-term gains and losses involved in sanctions of varying severity.

Since the constable has acted within the law whichever course he
chooses, the question that must be asked is why the choice should
be his. He is not making a technical or professional decision
beyond the competence of the untrained lay persons, but a sensitive, very specific human judgment. So to describe what is entailed
is to emphasise, not to demean, its importance.

The sheer idiosyncracy, the fact that every decision will require
the weighing of different factors means it may be difficult to subject it to preordained rules drawn up by hierarchical superiors.[4]
The speed with which the choice must be made is largely responsible for this, for where other highly personal judgments are
governed by complex rules—for example, entitlement to supplementary benefit—decisions often take days. However, police discretion at this level differs qualitatively from the exercise of
discretion by other public officials only in the specific character of
the human relations elements of the decision, not because it is
"legal".

Much has been made of the "original authority" and "indepen-

---

[4] For an argument that the police are unique in that everything they do is of such
case-by-case specificity that it is impossible to formulate general norms of conduct, see Bittner (1974), p. 18 *et seq.*

12   *Police Discretion*

dence" of constables (see below, p. 25). This would seem to imply an unrestricted power of the constable to exercise his discretion according to his best judgment. One has only to state this to see its unreality: the very existence of an organised police force precludes it. Constables are part of a highly disciplined organisation with a quasi-military structure. They are subject to voluminous standing orders. More important, their decision to arrest is subject to review by hierarchical superiors, who may reject a charge or, indeed, require an arrest where a caution has been proposed. Despite the rhetoric, the constable's discretion is greatest, paradoxically, when he chooses *not* to invoke the law, for that will seldom come to his superiors' notice. But the restrictions which membership in the police organisation impose on the constable appeared most clearly in the well-known case of P.C. Joy. From this case precisely the wrong conclusion is sometimes drawn.[5] P.C. Joy had arrested an M.P for a traffic offence and wished to prosecute him. His superiors overruled his judgment and contented themselves with a caution. The perseverant constable then undertook a successful private prosecution. Whilst this incident may vindicate the existence of the right to private prosecution in English law, its primary lesson is how tightly the constable's wings are clipped by the structure within which he works. P.C. Joy's superiors were able to substitute their discretion for his; so far as the Kent Constabulary were concerned, the offender was *not* prosecuted.

The courts have come to understand the reality of the hierarchical control of constables. In 1979 the indefatigable Mr Blackburn (below, pp. 62–66), tried yet again to challenge the enforcement of the obscenity laws by the Metropolitan Police. He argued that instructions issued by the commissioner, requiring officers on the ground to refer all potential prosecutions to a centralised squad, were an unlawful restriction on the constable's power of arrest. This claim was rejected: there was in fact no restriction on the power of arrest, and the lawfulness of an administrative requirement that ensured uniformity of practice throughout the force was unassailable.[6] The point was addressed even more directly in *Hawkins* v. *Bepey*.[7] Chief Inspector Hawkins of the Kent Police died after instituting a prosecution of the defendants, who presented

---

[5] A brief account of this incident, which received extensive press coverage at the time, is found in Gillance and Khan (1975).
[6] *R.* v. *Metropolitan Police Commissioner, ex p. Blackburn, The Times,* December 1, 1979. (Q.B.D.)
[7] [1980] 1 All E.R. 797.

the ingenious argument that since the proceedings had been taken by a specific individual, his death required that they be terminated. The High Court, *per* Watkins J., would have none of it. Quoting what was almost certainly the precise instruction that had led to the countermanding of P.C. Joy, he noted that there were standing instructions in the force that all informations should be laid by chief inspectors or inspectors. The chief constable issued such instructions pursuant to his power of direction and control of the force (s.5(1) of the Police Act 1964; see below p. 74) and there is "a sound administrative, if not other, reason for it." "The real prosecutor" was therefore the chief constable or the force itself[8]— not the person who instituted proceedings nor, *a fortiori*, the arresting officer.

These decisions simply recognise the reality of the organisational structure within which the constable functions. They do not, however, make incursion upon the legitimate and necessary, indeed inescapable, discretion the constable must exercise. Statutes confer discretionary powers directly upon constables, and establish factual preconditions for their exercise. Thus section 1 of the Police and Criminal Evidence Act 1984 gives a constable power to search any vehicle if he has reasonable grounds to suspect that he will find a stolen or prohibited article, and section 24 grants him power to arrest without warrant anyone whom he has reasonable grounds to suspect is guilty of an arrestable offence, or is about to commit one. The factual condition precedent is his knowledge of certain events and of the behaviour of the person searched or arrested. For the power to be validly exercised, those facts must be known to be, or at least reasonably suspected to be true, by the constable—and by no one else, including a superior officer.[9] This point was emphasised by Lawton L.J. in the *Central Electricity Generating Board* (C.E.G.B.) Case.[10] The Board had sought mandamus against the Chief Constable of Devon and Cornwall, who had refused to order his men to clear a site of demonstrators whose non-violent resistance was obstructing its exploration of the site as a possible nuclear power station. His Lordship's remarks require extended quotation:

---

[8] *Ibid.* p.800.

[9] These limits appear in sharp relief when contrasted with anti-terrorism legislation, in which the requirement of reasonableness does not appear. As construed by the House of Lords in *McKee* v. *A.G. for Northern Ireland* [1985] 1 All E.R. 1, reversing the Northern Ireland Court of Appeal, an instruction by a superior officer to arrest the plaintiff as a suspected terrorist was sufficient to make the arrest valid under the Prevention of Terrorism Acts.

[10] [1980] 1 All E.R. 797, 826.

14   *Police Discretion*

> "[The Board's] application, in my judgment, showed a mis-
> conception of the powers of chief constables. They command
> their forces but they cannot give an officer under command an
> order to do acts which can only lawfully be done if the officer
> himself with reasonable cause suspects that a breach of the
> peace has occurred or is imminently likely to occur or an
> arrestable offence has been committed. [The Chief Constable
> could] order some of his constables to watch what was going
> on in the field when the Board wanted to exercise their statu-
> tory powers; but what he could not do was to give unqualified
> orders to his officers to remove those who were obstructing
> the Board's work. Any orders he gave would have to have
> qualifying words to the effect that those obstructing should be
> removed if, but only if, [an offence was imminent]."[11]

The technical legal reason behind the restriction on the chief
constable's power is that, not being *in situ*, he cannot make the
requisite factual evaluation which must form the reasonable belief
necessary to make a valid arrest. The corollary—a matter of vital
importance for police governance—is that no superior officer can
take away the discretion granted to the individual constable by
statute,[12] either by requiring him to arrest, or forbidding him to
arrest, a particular individual or anyone who falls into some prede-
fined category. A chief constable cannot tell his subordinates,
"Arrest those demonstrators" or "Do not search the car of my
friend X, notwithstanding that you reasonably suspect him of
being in possession of stolen goods." It is at this point, and this
point only, that the constable's statutory discretion becomes
"independence," in the precise sense of freedom from interference in the exercise of that discretion. If the balance of power
between chief constables and democratic representatives was to be
altered, and police authorities once again[13] exercised executive
control of their forces, that change would leave the discretionary
power of constables totally unaltered. In other words, democratic
control of the force as an organisation—its priorities, allocation of
resources and methods of operation—could not, as a matter of
constitutional law, detract from the discretion Parliament has conferred on constables. The elected body would in this respect
become, so to speak, successor in title to the chief constable; and

[11] *Ibid.* p.835.
[12] In the latest *Blackburn* case, see above, n. 6, the Court also averred that a commanding officer could not take away the constable's power of arrest.
[13] The contention that nineteenth century borough watch committees possessed
and exercised such powers is elaborated in detail in Chap. 3.

Police Discretion   15

all the encumbrances imposed upon him—notably that explained by Lawton L.J. in the C.E.G.B. case—would become theirs.

Political Implications of Discretion

The discretion not to enforce the law—which in terms of the working constable means not to arrest someone who has in a strict sense broken the law—may also arise from the substantive breadth and vagueness of the law itself. J.R. Spencer has noted the characteristic preference of the English judiciary for broadly defined offences, mitigated by "common sense" discretion not to prosecute.[14] This is particularly important in controversial public order matters, where notions of breach of the peace, threatening behaviour, obstruction and the like are so wide that virtually any action can, depending on its context, be plausibly branded criminal so as to justify an arrest.[15] The result is that the police invariably underenforce the law. This is normally regarded as simple common sense, essential to avoid dragging the law into disrepute, yet the result is to turn conventional thinking about policing on its head. The equation of policing with enforcement of the Law—the august embodiment of state sovereignty—becomes untenable. For most less serious offences under-enforcement is the norm; precisely for that reason, enforcement can be a serious abuse of power.[16] The "common sense"[17] which tempers full enforcement may readily become a cloak for conscious or unconscious discrimination on the basis of political opinion, personal appearance, demeanour, social status or race. Under-enforcement becomes selective enforcement.

In only one reported case has this critical issue been even implicitly raised in the courts. In *Arrowsmith* v. *Jenkins*[18] the defendant, a well-known peace campaigner, challenged the validity of her conviction for a violation of the Highways Act. She had addressed a meeting at a site where others had spoken many times without prosecution. The Divisional Court dismissed the issue in half a sentence: so long as personal guilt was established, non-enforcement against others was legally irrelevant. It is unclear from the

[14] Book Review, 51 *U.Chi.L.Rev.* 1265 (1984).

[15] Other examples offered by Thomas (1982) include obscenity, "reckless" driving, and offences concerning "indecent" matter.

[16] Non-enforcement can also be a serious abuse, as the incident involving P.C. Joy showed. But that problem arises only where enforcement is the norm, which for reasons given in the text is not generally the case.

[17] It is in this sense that Lord Scarman (1981, para. 4.51, 4.58) uses the term "discretion" to which he attributes such importance.

[18] [1962] 2 Q.B. 561.

16   *Police Discretion*

brief report how forcefully the point was argued, but its curt dismissal evinces an extraordinary indifference to political freedom.
The result is to leave the police with vast power which can be
abused with no possibility of legal review. The need for the political process to step into the breach is therefore imperative.

Other decisions, whilst not overtly biased, may cumulatively
produce collective distortion. Research indicates, for example,
that working class and black youths are less likely than middle
class and white youths to be cautioned than arrested for the same
offence.[19] It is doubtful even in the latter instance that many individual officers say to themselves, "He's black so I'll go harder on
him". Yet the resulting structural bias is familiar enough to analysts of race relations, who have documented how, in a wide range
of areas like housing and employment, unconscious stereotypes
and unthinking habits produce unintentional, but no less effectively unequal, treatment of black people, a phenomenon known
as institutional racism. "Institutional class-ism" lacks the same
verbal resonance, but is equally illegitimate and socially damaging.
The problem cannot realistically be attacked, however, by abolish-
ing discretion and requiring full enforcement[20]; the question is
rather what mechanisms, internal or external to the police organisation, can be devised to ensure its fair exercise. That discretion
may be exercised in a manner systematically unfair but also lawful
is something the courts do not seem to comprehend; since the bias
has political implications—its victims are almost invariably people
on the Left, those the police define as "troublemakers," and
ethnic minorities—control of this sort of discretion must be
regarded as a political question.

A Case Study

In April 1985, the following report appeared in the press:

> "Police in London's East End are to institute a much tougher
> policy against racial harassment or racial attacks on the Ben-
> gali minority.
> Commander Malcolm Sullivan, of Tower Hamlets police,
> promised yesterday to lower the threshold of what constitutes
> an arrestable offence where an attack was racially motivated.

[19] Landau (1981); Fisher and Mawby (1982).
[20] Some American states have enacted statutes which require full enforcement of
all criminal prohibitions. As K.C. Davis (1975), Chap. 3 notes in his study of
police discretion, these are simply dead letters.

> He said that where, previously a victim . . . might have had
> to pursue the case privately as a common assault, local police
> were now more likely to interpret such minor assaults as
> actual bodily harm"[21]

This episode illustrates better than any other the breadth and
political character of legitimate police discretion. Racist attacks
have been the subject of concern for many years, but it took years
of victimisation and campaigning before the issue was taken
seriously by the Home Office and years more before the police
were seen to take it seriously.[22] Ethnic minorities, particularly
Asians, and above all Bengalis in the East End, have been the victims of offences ranging from broken windows to murder. Perhaps
the most common and frightening experience is being beaten up by
groups of whites. A frequent and bitter allegation is that those
complaining to the police have been told that they would have to
pursue the matter privately.

As a matter of technical law, assault is a common law offence
committed when a person causes another to apprehend immediate
force, which need amount to little more than unlawful touching.
Assault occasioning actual bodily harm (A.B.H.) is a statutory
offence punishable by up to five years imprisonment and is therefore, unlike common assault, an arrestable offence.[23] The degree
of violence necessary to satisfy the requirement of A.B.H. is relatively low: bruising will suffice.[24] Virtually all racist attacks can
therefore be classified as A.B.H., so that the police will undertake
responsibility for tracking down and prosecuting the perpetrators.
The expense and complexity of proceedings, not to mention the
inability of the ordinary person to conduct an investigation,
ensures that classifying an incident as common assault means
ignoring it.

It cannot be said that previous police practice was unlawful. It is
within their discretion to charge or prosecute for less than the
maximum offence that the facts of an incident might justify, and

---

[21] *The Guardian,* April 10, 1985.

[22] Evidence was first systematically compiled by Stepney Trades Council, whose
1978 Report *Blood on the Streets* was wilfully ignored by government and police.
It took several more years of violence before the Home Office officially acknowledged the problem in its paper on *Racial Attacks* (1981).

[23] "Arrestable offence" is defined in s.24 of the P.C.E.A. 1984 to include *inter alia*
any offence which may attract a sentence of five years of imprisonment. (This
definition does not alter previous law). A.B.H. is an offence created by s.47 of
the Offences Against the Person Act 1861.

[24] *Taylor* v. *Granville* [1978] Crim.L.R. 482, Q.B.D.

18   *Police Discretion*

there is no suggestion that racially motivated attacks alone have been treated in this way. The revised practice, which followed on from an announcement of the commissioner some weeks previously that racial attacks would be one of the force's priorities in 1985, expresses a judgment that because of the psychological and other effects on ethnic minority communities, and on their relations with the rest of the society, racially motivated assaults will be regarded as more serious than the same physical injury where such motivation was absent. This is also a lawful position to take, but it be distorting words to call it a legal decision. It is a political act—one based on a more sensitive appreciation of the position of a particular group in society, responsive to their organised representations and those of their sympathisers. It is the sort of judgment that advocates of greater democratic control would hope their proposals would produce more generally; indeed greater and earlier police responsiveness of this type would probably have defused the movement for such a programme.

This episode illustrates three important points. First, "the law" does not produce one right answer. Secondly, its administrators can respond to perceived social needs whilst staying within its mandate, a response which can take account of the different social situations of identifiable groups.[25]

Thirdly, the rigid distinction between law and politics is exposed as hollow. In constitutional terms, this is of the highest importance, for the existence of that distinction is the intellectual underpinning of the doctrine of constabulary independence and hence of the current political structure of police governance. Yet in the above example, the substantive law never changed, only the (legally valid) way in which it has been applied. This application, though pursuant to a general policy, occurs at the level of the individual case: a particular assailant will now be treated as having committed a more serious offence if the facts warrant it. The only specifically legal element is the presence of the requisite fact (the degree of physical injury) necessary to bring the assault within the higher category of offence. This alone cannot be treated as a matter of discretion subject to police judgment. All else is political, in the sense of reflecting judgment of social utility and morality that are contro-

---

[25] Jefferson and Grimshaw (1984a), *passim* had previously argued that such a response was not possible, because of the restrictive nature of the "legal mandate" of the police. This argument had always seemed implausible in any number of contexts, and is now explicitly discredited in relation to the problem they had addressed. Their view that something they call a "socialist conception of justice" must be accepted before a response to needs of disadvantaged minorities can be addressed is thereby also rendered suspect.

versial. Just as police discretion is inevitable, so is its ineradicably political character.

Discretion and Capability

Discretion of a very different sort exists at the highest manager-ial level of policing as well. Indeed this discretion is much the most important, for it concerns the orientation and capability of the par-ticular force as a whole. The concept of capability[26] is crucial here. "You do not have a drug problem until you have a drug squad" runs an adage well known among police officers. The police do not encounter offences "at random." The organisation of the force will structure the occasions on which generalist beat constables or members of specialist squads will receive complaints or infor-mation about crime. The particular types of offences and geo-graphic patterns of their commission thus emerging will skew the crime figures and hence the definition of "the crime problem." This prominence will in turn purportedly justify particular empha-sis on these offences or areas. In this light, many crimes are seen to be *interchangeable.* Particularly in relation to offences which depend primarily upon self-initiated police work (like drugs or cor-ruption), or which public willingness to report is dependent upon the belief that the police are likely to respond sympathetically (as with rape) or effectively (minor burglary or criminal damage), a change in police attitudes or manpower allocation may produce an apparent increase in one whilst another declines.[27]

Among these critical managerial decisions are:

1. The fundamental style or method of policing—reactive; community-based; "hard" or "soft"; degree of involvement with other agencies.
2. Deployment of manpower, both in terms of the number and quality of constables assigned to a particular area and of the establishment of specialist units, *e.g.* drugs, fraud, Special Patrol Group or equivalent.
3. Emphasis given to a particular offence, *e.g.* the anti-porno-graphy drive launched by the Chief Constable of Greater Manchester, or a response to concern expressed by affected

[26] The term is taken from Grant (1980).
[27] "Decline" is relative. If the "objective" frequency of a particular offence is rising rapidly, a decline in police capability in relation to it may only slow the rate of increase in reported offences, not produce a drop in the absolute number reported. "Interchangeability" of course refers to official statistics of crime, not to its true but unknowable incidence.

sections of the public about, *e.g.* racist attacks, rape, or street robbery.
4. Acquisition, and the rules governing the use of, new technology and weaponry.

Some of these decisions require solely the application of professional experience and expertise. Most, however, are *political* decisions. The word is used, not in the sense of partisanship but to describe the essence of public choice: decisions which entail judgments about moral values, favour certain interests over others, and require weighing competing claims for scarce resources. At this level, policing is politics, just as taxation or education are politics. The choices should be informed by knowledge, and the specialists given the task of carrying out the political decisions should be listened to with care if those decisions are not to be based solely on ideology and hope. But to regard these sorts of decisions as exclusively "legal" is to misunderstand them fundamentally and thereby deliver substantial political power by default to the chief constable to whom they are entrusted.

A False Distinction

In recent contemporary debate about police governance, a distinction has emerged between "policy" and "operations." Those relatively rare police authorities which have sought to exercise their influence have generally found chief constables willing to discuss the former but steadfastly refusing to speak about the latter, and it is a mark of the unique influence and the critical political position occupied by the Consultative Committee established in Lambeth in the wake of Lord Scarman's Report that the local commander has been willing to extend his consultation to detailed operational matters.[28]

The precise pedigree of the distinction is unclear. It appeared by implication in the Police Authorities (Powers) Bill introduced by Jack Straw M.P. in 1980, attracting some bipartisan interest. This would have enabled police authorities to determine "policies." Lawyers will recall its appearance in the speech of Lord Wilberforce in *Anns* v. *London Borough of Merton*.[29] It is possible that this rigid division can coherently be maintained in the relatively uncontentious area of negligence law, but a glance at the above

---

[28] See the papers by Commander Marnoch and Canon Walker, Chairman of the Consultative Committee, in Brown (1985).
[29] [1978] A.C. 728, 754–755.

examples of executive discretionary decisions will show that it
breaks down entirely in relation to policing.

More precisely, some of the crucial "policy" decisions are about
"operations." The method of policing, for example, will determine whether the force relies on computerised information collected by various forms of pressure on those at the edges of
criminal involvement, leading to isolated "swoops" on suspects
but otherwise remaining aloof from the public, or an intensive
commitment to street patrols leading to personal knowledge of
most of the people in the area, involvement in community welfare
projects and co-ordination with other "care and control" agencies
in crime prevention.[30] The choice could be described as policy, but
its concrete manifestations are in the day-to-day contacts with the
public—abrasive or supportive—and it is these which may produce
dissatisfaction and demands for change. "Swamp '81" in Brixton is
only the most spectacularly disastrous example; public strip-
searching, excessive force in dealing with youths congregating on
the street, or an attempt to gain access to confidential school
records of a particular pupil are more typical examples of causes of
antagonism.

The distinction becomes even less tenable when one examines
the decision to set up a drug squad. This involves allocation of
manpower and related resources that would otherwise be used in
alternate ways. In other words, it represents a decision that drugs
deserve greater or increased attention compared to traffic control,
burglary or rape. It may also have serious consequences for relations with various groups within the community—innocent persons
who feel harassed by searches; women or householders who feel
that the safety of the streets or their property is not receiving sufficient protection. The decision is highly controversial, and a
classic example of a political choice. Yet it could equally be well
characterised as "operational"—it merely involves reassignment
of a limited number of constables to particular duties.

Finally, it is important to recognise that the distinction was
developed in a radically different constitutional context, in which
the actions of public officials are challenged in the courts on
grounds of alleged negligence. These officials serve a Minister (or
a local authority) who in traditional constitutional theory is
responsible to Parliament and thus ultimately to the electorate for
the policy adopted. The exemption of policy from judicial scrutiny
reinforces the process of political accountability along the gener-

---

[30] See further Baldwin and Kinsey (1982), Chaps. 2, 3, 8 and 9.

22   *Police Discretion*

ally accepted lines. Moreover, the choices often involve complex technical judgments which the courts are not competent to make. This leaves the secondary and less value-laden area of "operations" subject to judicial evaluation under standards of negligence. However, in the policing debate the distinction is stood on its head, for "policy" is what is sought to be brought under democratic control and "operations" defines the no-go area; the issue is not the scope of judicial control but the exclusion of representative institutions from their normal commanding role. In sum, in the context of policing it would be a distinct gain if this proposed line of demarcation vanished from public debate.[31] A more precise delineation of the sphere from which political control should be excluded must be formulated, a task taken up in Chapter 10.

Conclusion

Substantive vagueness of the law and limited resources thus create enormous discretion, at the lowest and highest levels, for the police. Underpinning both, however, is an even more important consideration. The purposes of policing are much less obvious than may first appear. Few have been able to share Peel's single-minded view that the main task of the police is the prevention of crime. For Sir Richard Mayne, who issued the founding instructions to the New Police in 1829, the tasks were more complex and diffuse: "the prevention of crime . . . the protection of life and property, the preservation of public tranquility." Mayne's formulation was quoted with approval by Lord Scarman, who added a critical rider. The aims, he argued, may conflict; and where this occurs, preservation of public tranquility must come first.[32] This view has had great influence on the new regime in charge of the Metropolitan Police, which embraced it in the principles of Policy and Guidance for Professional Behaviour issued to the Force in April 1985. Yet the police officer, at whatever level, taking this injunction to heart may well ask, but what of my duty to the law? Am I to turn a blind eye to infractions in the name of public tranquility? If so, does that give any minority, if sufficiently aroused, the power to nullify Parliament's command? Sir Robert Mark made this point when criticising Scarman, who had faulted the police for not exercising the same sensitivity to public feeling in

---

[31] The Canadian Royal Commission of Inquiry into abuses by the R.C.M.P. also concluded that the policy/operations division was untenable in the security field; see Marshall (1984), pp.125–127.

[32] Scarman (1981), paras. 4.56–4.57.

Conclusion 23

their manner of law enforcement in Brixton as they show elsewhere. This, said Mark, meant one law for blacks and another for whites.[33]

Mark's absolutist position has the virtue of simplicity: the law is the law is the law. Law is somehow "above" politics (a dirty word): the courts are its oracles and the police derive their mandate from it. The difficulty with this stance is that it is a recipe for intolerable conflict or, more likely, for its authoritarian resolution. A political and social order which values freedom cannot take law as its foundation: it must rest on voluntary allegiance. If the majority's law is pushed too far or too hard, that consent evaporates and the ensuing coercion will assuredly curb the liberties of the majority as well. The paramountcy of law is not the highest social good.

One critical point, which Lord Scarman explicitly recognised,[34] is that whilst a judge cannot take this view, the constable must. The judge derives his mandate from the law, the constable from the polity. Law enforcement can no more be an absolute than the environment can remain pure in an industrial economy.

Yet Scarman failed to reflect sufficiently upon the implications of his insight. Once it is accepted that strict law enforcement must give way to more important considerations, the idea that the police can somehow stand apart from politics and from the process of public choice becomes untenable. And the problem is much broader. Once it is admitted that discretion in policing is inevitable, and that the choices involved in police managerial discretion are political, there inevitably follows the question, who determines how the discretion shall be exercised? To answer this one needs both a theory of governance—of constitutional allocation of power—and a conception of policing that enables one to identify the ways, if any, in which it occupies a place in constitutional structure different from other public services. These matters are taken up below.

At this point, however, a fundamental axiom must be stated. It is simply that police discretion is not a seamless web. There are different types of discretion, exercised at different levels within the police service. Some are quintessentially political, and should be exercised by elected representatives in the accepted democratic manner. Some involve application of legal standards to specify factual circumstances, for example the degree of suspicion necessary to justify a search of a particular person. To analogise such dis-

---

[33] *Observer*, November 29, 1981.
[34] *Op. cit.* para. 4.57.

cretion to a judicial function merely confuses thought.[35] It is an executive discretion in relation to the administration of criminal law, a function of particular importance to personal freedom and the legitimacy of the state, which should therefore remain free of political control to remove any possibility of its perversion in the service of person or partisan ends. (It is equally important that such perversion is not practised by the police themselves: hence there remains wide scope for political bodies to review police behaviour on both individual and systematic bases). Many, perhaps most, lie somewhere in-between, like the choices available to the constable attending the assault incident. For consistency they require general guidance as to the primary aims to be pursued and the relative weight to be given to various factors which point in different directions, but as a practical matter the decisions will be taken by individual constables in specific circumstances. The essential task is to identify the *degree* of political control appropriate to particular kinds of decision.

[35] The 1962 Royal Commission fell into this trap, describing this aspect of the constable's work as "quasi-judicial" (Cmnd. 1728, para. 86). The House of Lords in *Holgate-Mohammed* v. *Duke*, [1984] A.C. 437 has finally scotched this error, and treated constables as exercising executive discretion. See below, pp. 69–71.

[8]

THE PERVASIVE FALSE PRETENSE OF FULL ENFORCEMENT

K.C. Davis

The overall picture.

The five gross deficiencies in the methods by which the Chicago police make enforcement policy, just summarized in the concluding section of the preceding chapter, all stem directly from the pervasive system of falsely pretending that all statutes and ordinances are fully enforced. The police assume that full enforcement is required by an Illinois statute and by four Chicago ordinances, and when either insufficient resources or good sense requires nonenforcement they also assume that they must do what they can to conceal the nonenforcement. So the only open enforcement policy is one of full enforcement. The top officers accordingly assume that they never have any enforcement policy to make. So they do not make enforcement policy. The false pretense thus causes the patrolmen to become the primary makers of policy, for when they are confronted with an enforcement problem, they cannot escape a decision to act or not to act.

PRETENDED FULL ENFORCEMENT

Because of the false pretense of full enforcement, no studies are ever made to guide the
formulation of enforcement policy, and no
professional staffs are ever needed for that
purpose. And because the police falsely pretend to have no enforcement policy except
one of full enforcement, no occasion arises
for ascertaining community desires about
enforcement policy, or for coordinating police enforcement policy with the policy of
prosecutors and judges.

The false pretense of full enforcement has
all these devastating consequences. It is a
central and pervasive reality, especially in
the minds of all officers above the patrolman
level. The pretense of full enforcement is a
prominent part of what officers have said to
us in our interviews with 300 of them. For
the typical officer, especially supervisory officers, the pretense relieves him from the
work of directly addressing his mind to
questions of enforcement policy, since such
questions may be so easily assumed to be already resolved in favor of full enforcement
on all occasions.

The false pretense has not been created by
the present personnel of the Chicago police
department. They have inherited it. It
probably started during the second half of

PRETENDED FULL ENFORCEMENT

the nineteenth century and may have been full-blown by 1900. Everyone now in the department grew up on it and has naturally assumed it ever since.

The cause of the false pretense is clearly the combination of full enforcement legislation (statutes and ordinances) with the lack of resources for full enforcement and the common sense of some nonenforcement.

This chapter discusses the full enforcement legislation, and then describes the accomplishment of patrolmen in departing from that legislation. The story is largely one of police wisdom in escaping from the full enforcement legislation, but with extreme damage from the supposed necessity for concealing the truth about enforcement policy. I shall analyze that damage, and then I shall present the reasons for disclosing enforcement practices. In the next chapter, a legal analysis will show the legality of an open system of selective enforcement, which is what I strongly recommend.

The full enforcement legislation.

The Illinois revised statutes of 1845 imposed the duty on every constable, when a crime was committed in his presence, "forthwith to apprehend the person" and bring

[54]

PRETENDED FULL ENFORCEMENT

him before some justice of the peace. In 1874 the statute was expanded to cover "every . . . policeman." The present provision is ch. 125, § 82: "It shall be the duty of every sheriff, coroner, and every marshal, policeman, or other officer of any incorporated city, town or village, having the power of a sheriff, when any criminal offense or breach of the peace is committed or attempted in his presence, forthwith to apprehend the offender and bring him before some judge, to be dealt with according to law . . . ." The statute has been interpreted to apply to misdemeanors as well as felonies, People v. Davies, 354 Ill. 168, 188 N.E. 337 (1934), but no other judicial interpretation relevant to the present context has been found.

The duty imposed by that statute is combined with ch. 38, § 33–3: "A public officer or employee commits misconduct when, in his official capacity, he commits any of the following acts: (a) Intentionally or recklessly fails to perform any mandatory duty as required by law. . . . A public officer or employee convicted of violating any provision of this Section forfeits his office or employment." In addition, he is subject to fine and to imprisonment up to five years in the penitentiary.

[55]

PRETENDED FULL ENFORCEMENT

The Chicago Municipal Code contains four ordinances which call for full enforcement by the police. One is § 11–9, which provides that the police board "shall, through the Superintendent of Police . . . . enforce all laws, ordinances of the city and orders of the City Council and of the Mayor." Whatever applies to the superintendent must apply to all the police, since he acts through them. A second ordinance is § 11–24: "The members of the police force of the city, when on duty, shall devote their time and attention to the discharge of the duties of their stations, according to the laws of the state and ordinances of the city and the rules and regulations of the department, to preserve order, peace, and quiet and enforce the laws and ordinances throughout the city." Even if the provision may be properly read to mean that "The members . . . shall . . . enforce the laws and ordinances . . ." that meaning seems a bit unclear. But the provision clearly says that the members shall devote their time to discharge of their duties according to the laws of the state, and the Illinois statute imposes the "duty" to apprehend an offender for a crime committed or attempted in the presence of an officer. The ordinance also requires discharge of duties

[56]

PRETENDED FULL ENFORCEMENT

according to "rules and regulations of the department" and those rules and regulations require full enforcement, as we shall shortly see.

A third ordinance, § 11–31, provides: "Any member of the police force who shall refuse or neglect to perform any duty required of him, when such refusal or neglect to perform any such duty shall tend to hinder, obstruct, or impair in any way the proper and strict enforcement of any law or provision of this code or the efficiency of the police force, is hereby declared to be no longer qualified to be a member of the police force, and shall be discharged from said police force and the service of the city in the manner provided by law." The key word is "duty," and again the meaning depends on the Illinois statute and on the department's rules and regulations.

And the same is true of the fourth ordinance, § 11–32: "Any member of the police department who shall neglect or refuse to perform any duty required of him by the provisions of this code or the rules and regulations of the department of police . . . may, in addition to any other penalty or punishment imposed by law, be fined not more than one hundred dollars for each offense."

[57]

PRETENDED FULL ENFORCEMENT

One cannot escape the conclusion that the four ordinances, even though they are dependent on the statute and on the regulations, say rather clearly that the police have an obligation to enforce all statutes and ordinances. The statute and the ordinances together will be referred to as "the full enforcement legislation."

Formal administrative action supporting the full enforcement legislation.

The formal (but not the actual) power to make rules and regulations to govern the department is not in the department but is in the Chicago police board, which, in December of 1973, issued a 34-page printed pamphlet entitled "Chicago Police Department—Rules and Regulations." Part II states six "goals of the department," the fourth of which is "Enforcement of all laws and ordinances." Part V, on "rules of conduct," states 55 "prohibited acts," the third of which is "any failure to promote the Department's efforts to implement its policy or accomplish its goals." Part VI states penalties for violating the rules and regulations—oral reprimand, written reprimand, extra duty without compensation, suspension without pay, and institution of charges before the police board. The rules and regulations thus

[58]

PRETENDED FULL ENFORCEMENT

mean that all officers have a duty to "enforce all laws and ordinances." That is
clearly the formal enforcement policy.

Formal instructions from the superintendent to his subordinates are in the form of
"general orders," "special orders," and to
some extent "training bulletins." General
order 70–4, issued in 1970, is on the subject
of "district watch commanders." It provides in part III: "The district watch commander will . . . direct the enforcement of all laws and ordinances and the
rules, regulations, and orders of the Department during his tour of duty." The general
order contains no exception to the words "all
laws and ordinances."

Another example is general order 70–10,
also issued in 1970 (but now repealed), on
the subject of "district vice officers." It
provided in part III, B: "The duties of district vice officers will include the enforcement of all statutes and ordinances relating
to gambling, prostitution, narcotics, and liquor laws . . . ." No exception to the
words "all statutes and ordinances" was
mentioned.

One wonders about possible negative implications of some orders. For instance, patrolmen are unanimous in refusing to arrest

[59]

PRETENDED FULL ENFORCEMENT

for social gambling in absence of complaint or unusual circumstance, and the superiors are well aware of that policy. No general order even mentions social gambling. But general order 73–10, issued in 1973, is on the subject of "lottery gambling enforcement program," and the first sentence is: "This order . . . continues an intensified enforcement program aimed at eliminating lottery gambling." Would a perceptive officer know that an order to bear down on lotteries may mean that bearing down on other forms of gambling is not stressed?

Officers we have interviewed have often told us that the policy of the department has always been to avoid any statement in writing that directs or authorizes any officer to engage in nonenforcement in any circumstances. Even a deputy superintendent has said to me explicitly that superior officers never instruct subordinates not to enforce. Our search of the general orders and special orders almost completely supports that statement. Exceptions are very slight. A training bulletin, III, 38, issued in 1962, has one sentence that seems to authorize nonenforcement: "The keynotes in the enforcement of any curfew ordinance are the application of common sense and good judgment." A training bulletin on traffic violators,

[60]

PRETENDED FULL ENFORCEMENT

VII, 10, 1966, provides: "In consideration of the safety of others, it may be more practical to allow a traffic violator to escape rather than jeopardize others in a high-speed chase." Another traffic enforcement training bulletin, VII, 48, 1966, is unusually daring when it says that "you will be selective in your enforcement. You can then patrol an area at the time accidents are happening, at the locations where they occur and be able to observe the violations that cause them." See also another training bulletin, VIII, 26, 1967.

We spent a good deal of time interviewing in the training division of the department, but we found no attempt to teach selective enforcement policy. The absence of such instruction was finally confirmed by interviews with instructors and with recruits. Some of the instruction affirmatively emphasizes the policy of full enforcement. The recruit has to learn about nonenforcement from his colleagues after he is on the job. Yet a recruit is exposed to nonenforcement if he reads The Challenge of Crime in a Free Society, as he is supposed to do. Some nonenforcement is inevitably mentioned in class discussions, as for example a discussion of how a juvenile gang fight at a high school dance was satisfactorily handled without an

[61]

PRETENDED FULL ENFORCEMENT

arrest. A police woman trainee specifically said that in her training courses she had never heard a discussion of discretion not to arrest.

The police accomplishment.

The police generally realize but are reluctant to acknowledge that the legislative bodies have often overshot very considerably in enacting criminal legislation, and they may also realize that the legislative excesses are compounded by the full enforcement legislation. Nevertheless the rule of full enforcement is in the forefront of their minds: "We have an obligation to enforce everything." Even so, the legislative bodies lack the practical power to repeal the common sense of confident, secure, and experienced officers.

The common sense of the officers very often prevails over the legislative excesses in the criminal legislation, as compounded by the full enforcement legislation. That is the police accomplishment.

The second section of the first chapter of this essay contains "twenty quick samples of nonenforcement of criminal statutes and ordinances." All twenty of those samples are relevant here. No matter what the legislative body has made a crime and no matter what the literal words of the full enforce-

[*62*]

PRETENDED FULL ENFORCEMENT

ment legislation say, patrolmen do not arrest
for all offenses committed in their presence.
Patrolmen are in fact often lenient. They
know that some legislation is almost never
enforced, and they know that common sense
requires that it be almost never enforced.
Even when the crime is committed in their
presence, they do not ordinarily arrest for
such crimes as fornication in a public park,
quiet drinking in the park, smoking in an el-
evator, spitting on the sidewalk, or social
gambling with a friend. Patrolmen ordinarily refrain from making such arrests, in
absence of special reasons to make them, despite the words of the ordinance that an officer who fails to perform such a duty is "no
longer qualified to be a member of the police
force, and shall be discharged from said police force." That is, I think, a police accomplishment.

Let us consider for a moment some examples of police leniency toward normal children, in violation of the literal terms of the
full enforcement legislation. A 9-year-old
lights a firecracker for which he has just
traded some marbles. Should the patrolman, no matter what the circumstances,
take him into custody? He is required to if
he follows the literal meaning of the full enforcement legislation. A 12-year-old gets a

[*63*]

PRETENDED FULL ENFORCEMENT

new bicycle and promptly rides it on the sidewalk, in violation of an ordinance applying to anyone 12 years old or more. Should the patrolman explain the ordinance to him and not take him into custody for the first offense? A 13-year-old, by rare good marksmanship, throws a rock forty yards and breaks the only unbroken window in an abandoned building, and is therefore technically guilty of vandalism. A 14-year-old is guilty of an offense when his older friends first introduce him to beer. A 16-year-old brings his girl friend home a little too late and violates the curfew laws, which make no exceptions for human circumstances.

The police spend more than half their law enforcement time on minor crimes, and some minor crimes are rather puny ones that clearly do not call for full enforcement on all occasions. An ordinance, § 193–7.10, makes it a crime to smoke in "any street car, elevated train, or subway," and imposes a penalty of not more than $5. The superintendent of the Chicago police told me that the evening before we were talking he had asked a fellow passenger in an elevated train to put out his cigaret; the man refused until the superintendent identified himself. What the superintendent said indirectly was that he did not apprehend one who was commit-

[*64*]

PRETENDED FULL ENFORCEMENT

ting a crime in his presence. Should he have apprehended the man, or should he have used his own good judgment, as he did? The fact is that he did not do his "duty" under ch. 125, § 82, for he did not "apprehend the offender and bring him before some judge." The superintendent violated ch. 38, § 33–3, for which the penalty may be imprisonment up to five years. He failed under § 11–9 of the ordinances to "enforce all . . . ordinances . . ." Under § 11–31 he is "no longer qualified to be a member of the police force." And he violated his "duty" under the police board's formal rules and regulations to "enforce all . . . ordinances" and is therefore subject to discharge.

What utter nonsense! Could any rational legislative body have possibly intended any such results? The police accomplishment in escaping the full enforcement legislation is a very considerable one, for which the police deserve much credit.

The system of criminal justice would be insufferable without that police accomplishment.

Even though the police insist on interpreting the full enforcement legislation literally, they also insist on following what they re-

PRETENDED FULL ENFORCEMENT

gard as their own common sense. This means that they violate their own interpretation of the full enforcement legislation. And I regard that as an accomplishment. *The police wisdom has on a wide scale overridden the legislative unwisdom embodied in the literal terms of the full enforcement legislation.* The police are properly lenient to many offenders. They do adapt their enforcement practices to the dominant community attitudes they are able to perceive. They do often refuse to make arrests for offenses committed in their presence. They have even established many patterns of nonenforcement.

Three possible courses of action for the police.

Confronted with their own literal interpretation of the full enforcement legislation, the police could theoretically follow any one of three possible courses of action: (1) Full enforcement in fact, along with truthful statement of it, (2) selective enforcement, along with pretense of full enforcement, and (3) selective enforcement, along with truthful statement of it. (A fourth possibility of full enforcement, along with a pretense of selective enforcement, is not worth considering.)

(1) In an ideal world, the first might be the best, if some leeway were left for discre-

[*66*]

PRETENDED FULL ENFORCEMENT

tionary leniency. But in an ideal world, the criminal legislation would be tailored to what is practically enforceable, and our present legislation falls short by a wide margin. Either we must cut back the legislation or we must allow some nonenforcement of our excessive legislation—or a little of each. I favor cutting back the legislation, but I do not *expect* that. Our legislative bodies probably lack the capacity to legislate the needed refinement. The only practical way for legislative bodies to accomplish the objective of full enforcement is probably by delegating power to a rulemaking agency to cut back the excessive statutes to what can and should be enforced, and that agency might well be the police. Over a period of time the police could formulate rules that would be susceptible of full enforcement—if the rules contained enough vaguenesses and escape clauses to permit needed individualizing. But, as I show in chapter 5, the police already have that kind of rulemaking power, without an explicit delegation of it. If we start with the first of the three theoretical courses of action and make the necessary modifications in it, we wind up with the third one.

We cannot enforce our present legislation fully unless we cut it back either by amend-

[67]

PRETENDED FULL ENFORCEMENT

ing it or by changing it through rulemaking. The very idea of changing legislation through rulemaking sounds repugnant and obviously illegal—until one takes into account the expressions of legislative intent that are inconsistent with the legislation, and those expressions are set forth and analyzed in chapter 4.

The first course of action is the one we have tried over a period of more than a century, and no information has come to light that it works in even a single one of the 40,000 police agencies over the country. We know from experience that the first course does not work. That is why we apparently do not have it anywhere.

(2) What we have in Chicago is the same as what apparently all other American communities have—selective enforcement, along with the pretense of full enforcement. The Chicago police provide selective enforcement because they *cannot* provide full enforcement and because full enforcement often seems to them to be contrary to common sense. They pretend to have full enforcement because they interpret the full enforcement legislation literally. They assume they cannot tell the truth about their own practices. Yet many harms stem from their false pretense.

[*68*]

PRETENDED FULL ENFORCEMENT

(3) The only one of the three courses of action that can produce a satisfactory system is selective enforcement, along with truthful statement of it. We already have selective enforcement. The needed change is from falsity to truth, not merely because truth is in general preferable to falsity (as it surely is for a police agency) but because so many harms flow from the falsity.

The assumption of the Chicago police that falsity is necessary seems to me untenable. I have asked each of the top six officers of the department this question: "Do you really mean that you are unwilling to tell the public the truth about what you are doing?" None said directly: "Yes, I am unwilling," but all said that indirectly in one form or another. All have been brought up on the system of pretending full enforcement. That is the only system any of them has ever known. They assume that that system is necessary. Yet none gave a satisfactory reason in support of it. The best any could do was to say: "If parents of teenagers learn that we don't arrest for smoking marijuana, for instance, we'll be in for a bad time. We're not going to ask for unnecessary trouble." To that, my question was: "Does that mean you are opposed to letting the public influence your enforcement poli-

PRETENDED FULL ENFORCEMENT

cies?" The answer: "We'll just have unnecessary difficulty if we create a lot of issues
we don't now have." I agree that dictator-
ship can be more efficient than a democratic
process, but I favor public participation.
Parents of teenagers should have a voice in
police enforcement policy about marijuana,
even at the cost of some "difficulty" to the
police. The false pretense effectively shuts
off that voice.

Reasons for getting rid of the false pretense.

I cannot discuss sound reasons for *keeping*
the false pretense of full enforcement, for I
know of none, except that it is the product
of accretions of history. The problem seems
to be the rare one where all the reasons are
on one side.

Five reasons against the false pretense are
discussed in the first paragraph of this chapter—the false pretense prevents the top officers from making enforcement policy and
requires patrolmen to be the principal makers of such policy, it prevents studies of enforcement policy, it deters employment of
specialized staffs to make enforcement policy, it discourages open processes that would
invite community participation and criticism, and it cuts off coordination of police

[70]

PRETENDED FULL ENFORCEMENT

enforcement policy with the policy of prosecutors and judges.

Two additional reasons against the system
of false pretense, rather obvious ones, are
that deliberate deception of the public by the
police is morally objectionable, and that direct and purposeful violation by the police of
what they believe to be the law is contrary
to the heart of the fundamental principle we
call "the rule of law."

Beyond those negative reasons against the
system of the false pretense, I shall discuss
three main affirmative reasons for full and
honest disclosure of enforcement policy to
the public: (1) Any public agency, because
it is a public agency, should make its policies
known. (2) Fairness requires that those affected have a chance to know the enforcement policies. (3) The public, in my opinion, will prefer the truth about selective enforcement to continuing the false pretense of
full enforcement.

(1) All public officers at times have a
tendency to assume that the agency they
work for is their establishment and that
what they do is their business and nobody
else's. But the top officers of the Chicago
police department are not the proprietors of
a private business. They work for the pub-

[71]

PRETENDED FULL ENFORCEMENT

lic. In a democratic system, the members of the public—the electorate—are their bosses. And the bosses have a right to know what is going on.

Legislative bodies are increasingly requiring administrative openness. The Freedom of Information Act requires all federal agencies to open their records to public inspection. In state governments, a wave of "government in the sunshine" legislation is tending to cover the country, and the movement has not yet run its course. But openness of government agencies, whether or not required, has long been the policy of the best administrators. We Americans don't want dictators; we want a chance to know and a chance to criticize what our public servants are doing. Otherwise, we believe, government by bureaucrats is likely to be in the interest of the bureaucrats and not in the interest of the public.

(2) Fairness requires that those affected by law should have a chance to know what the law is. When a legislative body enacts a statute or an ordinance making an act a crime, concealment of the statute or ordinance would be outrageous, as all who are committed to our general system of government are likely to agree. Similarly, repeal of criminal legislation should also be knowa-

[72]

PRETENDED FULL ENFORCEMENT

ble; to require one to comply with legislation that has been repealed would be unfair. So one who cannot know of the repeal would be unjustly treated.

Criminal law has two sides—the formality and the reality. The formality is found in statute books and in opinions of appellate courts. The reality is found in the practices of enforcement officers. Drinking in the park is a crime according to the ordinance, but quietly drinking at a family picnic without disturbing others is not a crime according to the reality of the law, because officers uniformly refuse to enforce the ordinance in such circumstances. When the formality and the reality differ, the reality is the one that prevails. When the officer says, "I won't interfere if you drink quietly," the words of the ordinance, the formality, are superseded by the enforcement policy, the reality.

If, then, I am right that concealing criminal statutes and ordinances from those affected would be outrageous, as well as concealing the repeal or partial repeal of statutes or ordinances, concealing the reality of the law, the enforcement policy, would be even more outrageous, because the reality is what counts.

[73]

PRETENDED FULL ENFORCEMENT

Of course, I do not say that enforcement strategies or allocations of police manpower must be disclosed. If extra men are assigned to a high crime area, disclosure might defeat the purpose. But when the policy is that an officer will not arrest for a crime committed in his presence, that reality of the law should be disclosed, for nonenforcement is the practical equivalent of repeal or partial repeal of the criminal legislation.

Some say that unenforced legislation may have a deterrent effect that will be destroyed by disclosure of the lack of enforcement and that therefore disclosure is undesirable. The consensual sex crimes are an example. If the police can't and don't enforce, should they nevertheless pretend to enforce and thereby induce some compliance? The question seems to be subject to difference of opinion, but I think honesty of a government agency is the best policy. I think the man and woman who want to live together without marriage should be entitled to know that, in absence of special circumstances, the police have not enforced the fornication statute for many decades.

(3) In our interviews we have learned that the Chicago police uniformly believe that the public would disapprove any nonen-

PRETENDED FULL ENFORCEMENT

forcement policy they might learn about.
My opinion is that the reasons for nonenforcement are often entirely sound and that
when the reasons are sound a persuasive
statement of them is likely to win public approval. The public can understand the reasons for nonenforcement, including limited
police resources, longterm legislative acquiescence in selective enforcement, the need
for enforcement priorities, and the propriety
of leniency in some circumstances.

Specific experience of the Chicago police
supports my view. When Chicago policemen
during the 1960s arrested a group of prominent men for playing poker at the home of
one of them, Superintendent O. W. Wilson
announced to the press that he was sorry
and that he was giving instructions not to
arrest for social gambling. The public did
not rise up and say that Wilson had no authority to change the Illinois statute making
gambling a crime and making no exception
for social gambling. Instead, the public response was uniformly favorable. The statute remained on the books, but those who
wanted to engage in social gambling were
more secure. Similarly, a Chicago newspaper reported February 16, 1966: "Chicago
Police Supt. Orlando W. Wilson said Tues-
day that city policemen will continue to ig-

PRETENDED FULL ENFORCEMENT

nore jaywalking. On the basis of a two-month study of cities that enforce jaywalking laws, he explained, his men will leave well enough alone. He said that Chicago's pedestrian death rate is substantially lower than in cities that have had enforcement programs for years." Wilson did not ask for repeal of the ordinance, and as of 1975 it remains on the books, unenforced. Repeal of the ordinance would no doubt have been better, but the present point is that no outcry came from the public that the Superintendent was usurping legislative power. The public accepted and still accepts the nonenforcement.

Superintendent O. W. Wilson even had the courage to say in general terms that selective enforcement is essential. In a widely circulated pamphlet entitled "On This We Stand," he said on behalf of the police department at page 2: "The police must necessarily exercise discretion in the enforcement of the laws because of the limited resources available to them . . . Enforcement must be selective to be most effective . . . It must be selective as to time and place . . . It must also be selective as to the relative importance of crimes." What he said was true when he said it and it remains true today. The public did not criti-

[76]

PRETENDED FULL ENFORCEMENT

cize him adversely for speaking the truth. The public today would not criticize his successors adversely if they were to substitute the truth for their false pretense.

Of course, the public may object to nonenforcement of particular statutes or ordinances. I, for one, strongly object to some of the present selective enforcement practices; I feel shocked to learn that one caught in the act of burglary may be immune from arrest because he is giving the police information about narcotics dealers. And I am shocked that the police customarily do not arrest for attempted bribery of police officers even when they have witnesses to the attempted bribery. I also believe that arrests should normally be made for serious crimes whenever witnesses are available to testify to the crime, whether or not the victim of the crime is willing to sign a complaint. Various other enforcement policies I disagree with and I think the public generally may. But that is not a reason against disclosure of those policies; instead, it is a reason *for* such disclosure. Every policy, unless confidentiality is necessary, should have to run the gauntlet of public criticism. If it does not survive, then it should not survive.

[77]

PRETENDED FULL ENFORCEMENT

Altogether, I think the reasons against the false pretense of full enforcement are very powerful, and that nothing stands in the way of an open policy of selective enforcement, except the police belief that such an open policy would violate the full enforcement legislation. That is the subject of the next chapter.

[9]

POLICE DISCRETION, LEGALITY, AND MORALITY

James F. Doyle

Despite cherished myths that we enjoy "a government of laws and not of men," our theories and practical experience increasingly tell us otherwise. At least they tell us that we are the beneficiaries or victims, as the case may be, of government that is permeated by official discretionary power. They also give us reason to believe that official discretion pervades all levels and all agencies of government, whether legislative, executive, administrative, or judicial. That police are no exception to this generalization is now widely acknowledged, though myths about a government of laws and not of men still cling tenaciously to police activity.

One reason for the persistence of these myths, no doubt, is that the discretionary power of police is so awesome, including as it does the power to use coercive and even deadly force, to invoke or not invoke the dreaded mechanisms of the criminal process, to conduct investigations using such methods as secret surveillance, to destroy or confiscate property, and many other similar powers. Allan Silver made tacit reference to these awesome powers when he wrote that "practical men

James F. Doyle is Professor of Philosophy at the University of Missouri (St. Louis). He has edited Educational Judgments *and has published articles in* Philosophy, Archiv fur Rechts-und Sozialphilosphie, Logique et Analyse, *and* Journal of Value Inquiry.

48   Discretion

have never underestimated, though they have often distorted, the importance of the police."[1] Kenneth Culp Davis, who has done more than anyone else to dispel the myths I spoke of, has been even more emphatic about the challenge posed by the discretionary power of police:

> The police are among the most important policy-makers of our entire society. And they make far more discretionary determinations in individual cases than [does] any other class of administrators; I know of no close second.[2]

While exercising awesome power, police also tend to have a more tangible presence in the community than do most other officials. Whether or not they wish to do so, they play a powerful symbolic role as the "visible personification of the law"[3] in the eyes of the ordinary citizen. Somewhat paradoxically, police also play a role as outsiders or adversaries who are socially distanced from the rest of society. These two roles, and the threat of conflict between them, further explain why the mythology of a government of laws still clings to police activity. Moreover, in practice if not in theory, it is much easier to endorse this mythology than to try to legitimate the discretionary power of police.

Both the theoretical and practical challenge posed by the legitimation of police discretion must be faced, however, and sooner rather than later. This challenge is part of an ongoing crisis of authority, confidence, and public trust that affects all agencies of government, and especially the police. In this paper I propose to consider two different but related questions about legitimation of police discretion. First, can the discretion exercised by police be reconciled with the requirements of *legality*, in general as well as in particular cases? Here *legality* means more than merely not violating the law; in fact that kind of legality is taken for granted in this paper. *Legality* in the sense I am using it is a generally accepted standard of the authority and sometimes the validity of legal regulation of conduct. The second question is this: Can the discretion exercised by police be reconciled with requirements of *morality*, in general as well as in particular cases? The moral requirements in question are those of *critical public morality*, which I interpret as a justifiable standard for official conduct that is distinct from both legality and conventional moralities.

These questions should take precedence over others that might be raised because they are about the possibility of principled legitimation of police discretion. That is, they invoke principles of legality or principles of morality that are applicable to any attempt to legitimate police discretion. However, they do not rule out other questions that also have a bearing on this issue, and several of these will be considered in the course of the discussion. For example: To what extent can police discretion be legitimated by such factors as the professionalism, bureaucratic organization, or quasimilitary discipline of police? To what extent is the discretion exercised by police influenced by the discretion, expectations, and demands of nonpolice? To what extent are police subject to institutional and organizational constraints in their exercise of discretion?

Thus far I have referred to police discretion as if there were general agreement about its nature and scope, but in fact this is not the case. We find in scholarly and public debates about this subject, not only conflicting views of discretion,[4] but even conflicting views of police and police activity.[5] In the first section of this paper I want to consider and try to resolve some of these conflicts before taking up the questions about legitimation of police discretion which are the subject of the paper's second and third sections.

THE NATURE OF POLICE DISCRETION

A basic choice we confront in discussing police discretion is between narrower and broader views of police and police activity. A good example of a narrower view is one recently defended by David Bayley: "Police are a group authorized in the name of territorial communities to utilize force within the community to handle whatever needs doing."[6] I call this a narrower view, not because it makes the utilization of force a defining criterion (this is true of most views), but because it limits police to those who are *authorized in the name of territorial communities* to engage in police activity. By this criterion of political and legal authorization, ordinary police agencies along with special police agencies such as the Bureau of Customs and the Immigration Border Patrol would count as police, but private security forces and others who engage in police activity would be excluded.

Contrast this narrower conception of police with a broader one such as Peter Manning's (which is largely a reiteration of Egon Bittner's): "Police agencies may be defined as those agencies that stand ready to employ force upon the citizenry on the basis of situationally determined exigencies."[7] Manning explains the significance of this broader definition as follows: "Included here are the variety of forces found in most complex societies that share with the formally constituted police the right to use violence: security guards, private detectives, reserve constables, and the like (usually loosely controlled by the full-time

50   Discretion

police force), regardless of their relationship to the law as a resource for rationalization of their actions."[8] The contrast drawn here between narrower and broader views of police is approximately between *being publicly authorized* to engage in police activity and *having effective power* to engage in such activity.

Corresponding to these different views of police are narrower and broader views of police activity and its functions. The myths I spoke of at the beginning about a government of laws and not of men have spawned other myths that are specific to police activity. One of these myths is that the sole or at least primary function of the police activity is to carry out a legal mandate to enforce criminal law. This is really a whole series of related myths, one of which is that police activity is entirely the creature of legal authorization and direction. What this myth obscures is the fact that police, besides being agents of the law (and most are in some degree), are also agents of the state or its subdivisions, or of persons or groups protected by the state. The myth that police are politically neutral in their activity bears little relation to reality. Intertwined with this myth is what has been called the myth of full enforcement, according to which police have a legal mandate to enforce fully all criminal laws. This myth is also pernicious in several different ways. It obscures the fact that actual enforcement of criminal law nowhere approaches full enforcement and is also highly selective.[9] It also places police in the untenable position of being exclusively or primarily responsible for controlling crime when in fact they neither have, nor can have, such control. Manning's observation about the limited ability of police to control crime is pertinent here: "They cannot control crime any more than they can alter the economic system, the political system, the educational system, or fundamentally affect the birthrate or patterns of migration."[10] The growing emphasis on police-community relations can be seen as a way of disguising the utter lack of realism of these myths about police activity.

Among broader and more realistic classifications of police functions, the one I find most useful for present purposes has been recommended by Albert J. Reiss.[11] He argues that police agencies are organized around one or more of four major tasks or functions. One of these is enforcement, including preventive enforcement, of criminal laws, traffic laws, and other kinds of law, both public and private. A second function is preserving public peace, maintaining public order, and protecting life, health, and property. Third is the function of providing assistance, service, and information to members of the public and other governmental agencies. The fourth function is inspecting premises or activities and granting licenses or permits of various kinds.

Interpreted generously, these four broad functions probably cover most of what police, broadly construed, actually do in their official capacity. History tells us not to adopt a static view of police functions, however, because they vary from one time and social condition to another.

One argument for adopting a broader rather than narrower view of police and police activity is that our view of police discretion is then likely to be more realistic. That is, we will then be less inclined to underestimate the difficulties of legitimating the discretion actually exercised by police. A second argument for adopting a broader view of police and police activity is that this is more in keeping with one of the ways in which the concept of official discretion is most commonly used. This usage was first given currency by Kenneth Culp Davis: "A public officer has discretion whenever the effective limits on his power leave him free to make a choice among possible courses of action or inaction."[12] On this broad interpretation, to have discretion is to have *effective power* to make certain kinds of choices and to act on them, whether or not one is *formally empowered* to do so. Effective discretionary power may be greater or less than formal discretionary power, but it is important to recognize that they are not necessarily congruent. In considering police discretion we must be concerned, not only with the formal power of police, but also with their effective power.

Another way to make the same point is to say that police discretion is not necessarily limited to the discretionary power they are *authorized* to exercise. However, whether discretion is authorized or not depends on the mode of authorization one has in mind. We can distinguish at least four different modes of authorization that may apply to police discretion. The most obvious mode is authorization through *express* delegation of discretionary power by appropriate legislative, executive, administrative, or judicial authority. A second mode of authorization is *implicit* or *implied* delegation of discretionary power, based logically on what the delegating authority has actually said or done. This is stronger than yet a third mode of authorization whereby discretionary power is delegated by *default*—that is, by an evident failure on the part of the delegating authority to anticipate the necessity for discretion and to provide for it, either expressly or implicitly. Delegation is even more tenuous in a fourth mode that we might call *asserted* authorization. In this mode the asserted authority to exercise discretion is considered to be delegated to the extent that other officials and the public acquiesce in it. The exercise of discretionary power on this basis would clearly be the most vulnerable and controversial mode of authorized discretion, at least insofar as authorization depends on delegation.

52   Discretion

At least two other criteria besides delegation are relevant to the distinction between authorized and unauthorized discretion. One of these is the criterion of *competence*, which makes authorized discretion depend not so much upon delegation but upon having discretionary responsibilities (powers) of an office and being able to perform these responsibilities competently. Even express authorization of discretionary power is open to challenge to the degree that it is not based on the competence of those to whom the power is delegated. A second, related criterion of authorized discretion is that the discretion be exercised *in compliance with relevant standards*. Familiar examples are the standards of reasonable cause, probable cause, due care, due consideration, good faith, public interest, conflict of interest, fair price, natural justice, and the like. It is standards of this sort on which charges of abusing discretion, exceeding discretion, and maladministration are usually based, and these are all forms of unauthorized discretion.

One other useful distinction between kinds or degrees of discretion is between *weak* and *strong* discretion. Ronald Dworkin has made much of this distinction in his theory of judicial discretion,[13] and I here adapt it to the purpose of shedding light on police discretion. One form of weak and thus fairly uncontroversial discretion is the freedom, and sometimes the duty as well, to exercise *judgment* rather than mechanically apply rules to a case. This form of official discretion is closest to the ordinary discretion we generally admire in people: that is, discretion as discernment, discrimination, sound judgment, and the ability to be discrete. This is the kind of discretion we speak of as being the better part of valor. Moreover, this form is traditionally appealed to as the basis of fairness and equity; to quote Roscoe Pound, equity was originally "discretionary interference with the operation of general rules in order to do justice in particular cases."[14]

Another form of weak official discretion that perhaps is not so familiar is the freedom to make choices that are *not generally open to review or reversal* by others. Dworkin considers this a weak form of official discretion because it is a necessary feature of legal and other decision-making systems that offer a high degree of *finality* in the disposition of cases and settlement of disputes. It is also a form of discretion that is cultivated in all the professions as a qualification and privilege of their members.

A good example of weak discretion in both of these senses is the discretionary intervention by police in a violent domestic conflict, followed by their discretionary resolution of the conflict. This is typical of many situations in which police must have both sound judgment and, for all practical purposes, the last word if they are to be effective.

Police Discretion, Legality, and Morality 53

Thus it seems safe to say that police often and probably routinely exercise both of these weak forms of discretion. Whether they exercise what Dworkin calls strong discretion is not so easy to decide, however. This is discretion as the freedom to make choices without being subject to independent standards for making such choices. Some of Dworkin's critics have questioned whether judges could ever have this strong form of discretion, but the question I want to consider is whether police exercise this form of discretion. Many critics of police discretion appear to have this strong form in mind, so the question I am raising is of more than academic interest. One might argue that merely by taking an oath of office police become subject to *some* independent standards for their choices, however vague and incomplete these standards may be. A relevant reply to this argument, however, is a point made earlier, that being *formally* subject to independent standards of choice—say, by taking an oath of office—is not the same as being *effectively* subject to such standards.

In light of this distinction, it is evident that police often have strong discretion in the sense of being free to make official choices without being *effectively* subject to independent standards for making such choices. A notorious example is the discretionary use of undercover informants by police. This and similar examples of discretionary power may have prompted the writers of the well-known *Task Force Report: The Police* to describe the decision-making process of police as "unarticulated improvisation."[15] Even if this is not a fair description of all discretionary decision making by police, it stands in sharp contrast to Dworkin's description of official discretionary decision making as "articulate consistency."[16] What Dworkin meant by this phrase is that officials have a responsibility to make and justify each discretionary decision on the basis of general considerations of principle and policy that also support their other decisions. This view has important implications for the possibility of legitimating police discretion, and I shall consider it in more detail in the next section.

Some of the strong discretionary power of police is *authorized* in one or more of the ways I described earlier, though certainly not all of it is. In any case, what the preceding analysis has shown is that we cannot rely on authorization alone to determine whether police discretion can be legitimated. One reason is that authorization provides only a presumption of legitimation, and it may be a very weak and easily defeated presumption. Another reason is that other factors besides authorization are relevant to legitimation of police discretion. Among these other factors are competence, compliance with appropriate standards, and being effectively subject to independent standards for

54   Discretion

making decisions. These independent standards surely include the requirements of legality, at least to the extent that police perform legal functions and help to determine the operation and effects of law. Legality as a general standard of legal systems should apply as much to police as it does to other agents of law, and this holds true not only of the formally constituted police but of private security forces, detectives, and others who engage in police activity under the color of law. But if the nature and scope of police discretion are as I have described them, can this discretion be reconciled with the requirements of legality? This is the main question I want to consider in the next section.

LEGALITY AND POLICE DISCRETION

We owe to H. L. A. Hart one of the clearest and most succinct statements of the requirements of legality:

> The requirements that the law, except in special circumstances, should be general (should refer to classes of persons, things, and circumstances, not to individuals or to particular actions); should be free from contradictions, ambiguities, and obscurities; should be publicly promulgated and easily accessible; and should not be retrospective in operation are usually referred to as the principles of legality.[17]

Hart's statement may suggest that the requirements of legality apply only to the process and results of *lawmaking*. However, the distinction between lawmaking, on the one hand, and administering, applying, and enforcing law, on the other, is more analytic than practical. The requirements that the law be general, consistent, clear, public, prospective, predictable, stable, and accessible apply to all of these phases of law, and this is the reason why they apply also to police discretion.

Though Hart considers these principles of legality to be important, he has warned us not to overestimate their practical significance. According to Hart, they are only formal principles of procedural justice in the legal regulation of conduct. In other words, they are not principles of substantive justice governing the content, ends, and outcomes of the law. This means, for Hart, that the law can fulfill the requirements of legality and nonetheless be grievously unjust and even iniquitous in its outcomes.[18]

This conclusion has been disputed by Lon Fuller, however, on the basis of a richer and more robust conception of legality than Hart had defended.[19] According to Fuller, law is best thought of as a more or less distinct social activity, the reason for being and "internal morality" of which are expressed by principles of legality. To the extent that making, administering, applying, and enforcing law fail to meet the requirements of legality, they fail to *be* law in the strict sense and become something else such as despotism or anarchy. Fuller specified eight different ways in which law can be deficient in, or opposed to, legality. It can: (1) fail to promulgate and publicize its norms; (2) fail to treat particular cases in accordance with its publicized norms; (3) fail to maintain the stability of its norms; (4) fail to create general norms; (5) fail to make its norms intelligible; (6) fail to make its norms consistent with one another; (7) fail to avoid retrospective punishments; and (8) fail to avoid imposing duties and responsibilities which normal people cannot meet.

This list, which was not intended to be exhaustive, bears a strong resemblance to Hart's summary statement of the principles of legality. Where Fuller and Hart mainly differ is over the question whether these are substantive moral principles of law or only procedural principles that are morally neutral. Between the two of them, I share Fuller's conviction that these requirements of legality would have no normative force as procedural standards of law apart from the social ends or outcomes they are supposed to serve. For example, it is difficult to see why the law should avoid imposing obligations that are retroactive, or that normal people cannot perform, unless such procedures are generally thought to lead to unjust legal outcomes. At the same time, I agree with Hart that legality is not the same as morality, even if Fuller is right that legality is not morally neutral. I want to give further consideration to this claim of Fuller's about the relation between legality and morality in the next section of the paper, after evaluating possible answers to the question whether police discretion can be reconciled with the requirements of legality.

How we answer this question depends in part on the general role we assign to official discretion in the legal regulation of conduct. Arthur Rosett has identified, in judicial opinions and elsewhere, at least five different views of the role of discretion, and each of them has become influential enough to constitute a doctrine or theory.[20] According to the first of these theories, any system of legal regulation is bound to be incomplete, since the application of general rules and policies to particular cases will inevitably reveal gaps or empty spaces that must be filled by discretionary choices. Like nature, it seems, legal regulation abhors a vacuum; but unlike nature, it fills a vacuum with discretion. This theory has supported the view that discretion is the *absence* of law; that is, where discretion begins marks the end of law.

56   Discretion

The usual legalistic response to official discretion—including police discretion—interpreted as the absence of law is, as Rosett points out, "to inject a healthy dose of familiar legal structure: standards, process, review."[21] He argues, however, that "this sort of reform has had the ability to *displace* discretion, but not to *replace* it with formal legality. The formal play is acted out, but the decisions are moved off-stage to be made elsewhere."[22] What is recognized here is that the exercise of official discretion is often a zero-sum problem which legalistic responses at best only appear to solve. Police discretion in particular may simply be driven underground or displaced laterally in the direction of greater citizen discretion, prosecutorial discretion, and official discretion in other agencies. A revealing example of this is the ongoing attempt by courts and other legal agencies to impose an effective exclusionary rule on police activity.

A second theory holds that official discretion is *antithetical* to law unless it is expressly delegated by higher authority. This view of discretion may be reinforced by doctrines of libertarianism, constitutionalism, legislative supremacy, or even popular sovereignty, and its logic is that "that which is not expressly permitted is forbidden." One institutional response to this view of discretion as exercised by police is to transform police organizations into bureaucracies of elaborately delegated authority and formal accountability. As a response to police discretion viewed as antithetical to law, however, this cure is often worse than the disease. And as Rosett shows, this response tends to put a premium on strict procedural compliance at the expense of considerations of substantive justice.

Somewhat more positive is the theory that official discretion is a way of providing *relief* from tendencies of legal regulation to become excessively and even inhumanly mechanical and inflexible. Construed in this way, as Rosett says, "equitable discretion is the power of the official to be fair in the face of the rules."[23] However, this positive view of discretionary flexibility on the part of officials such as police must be tempered by the recognition that it can also undermine legality. This is especially true where the need for relief from rules is generated by unduly harsh, severe, demanding, or indiscriminate rules and policies. An example of this is the policy of making police responsible for reducing crime rates. Such rules and policies may call forth so much discretionary flexibility—in the form of either dispensations to those who can help promote police goals, or deprivations imposed on those who are not helpful—that requirements of legality such as generality, consistency, publicity, and stability are flagrantly violated. It often appears that rules and policies are deliberately made much more severe and unyielding than is reasonable in order to create a need for massive police discretion. Legality is poorly served by such a policy.

Another positive theory views official discretion as a necessary *supplement* to law—not to fill gaps, as in the first theory, but to give *practical effect* to legal regulation in particular cases. As Rosett observes, this involves interpreting and adjusting rules and policies in terms of the contingencies of actual situations. This generally calls for discretionary judgment, as does the activity of fact-finding that accompanies the application of rules and policies to particular cases. Another supplementary role of discretion is in fashioning dispositions and remedies for particular cases. Here, what is needed is not only discretion in the sense of sound judgment but discretion to make choices that are generally not reviewable. This is especially true in the case of police, because they often need to be able to act promptly and decisively without fear of second-guessing by others. Experience shows, however, that police discretion which serves these functions as a necessary supplement to law is particularly difficult to regulate in the interests of legality.

Finally, official discretion has been viewed as a *form* of law because it provides a way of incorporating the special competence (including expertise, ingenuity, insight, sensitivity, etc.) of officials into legal regulation of conduct. Rosett has explained why this role of discretion has usually been overlooked, and the price we pay for doing so:

> In restricting all discretion to avoid the depredations of bad persons the system loses the capacity to fully realize the virtues of good people in power. Harnessing talent, increasing responsiveness, improving the content of decisions are all aims that justify taking risks.[24]

This view of discretion as an alternative form of law is similar to the characterization by Sanford Kadish and Mortimer Kadish of what they call "deviational discretion."[25] This is the discretion on the part of officials such as police to deviate from prevailing legal norms in the interests of more responsive, humane, enlightened, or reasonable regulation of conduct by law. The Kadishes consider such discretion to be a form of law if those who exercise it are able to legitimate it on the basis of overriding considerations of principle such as "lesser-evil" or "justifiable nonenforcement." Whether such discretion should be considered *strong* in the sense I described in the previous section depends on whether those who exercise it are *effectively* subject to independent legitimating principles.

In addition to assigning a general role to discretion in the legal

58   Discretion

regulation of conduct, each of these theories suggests a strategy for reconciling discretion with the requirements of legality. We might consider these different strategies as they apply specifically to police discretion. The first two theories—that discretion fills gaps in law and that it is antithetical to law—reflect a justified concern with what I described in the preceding section as strong discretion, unauthorized discretion, and discretion which, though authorized, should not be. However, the strategies suggested for reconciling these forms of police discretion with the requirements of legality generally hold little promise of success. In keeping with the first theory, Davis has argued that police discretion ought to be legally "confined, structured, and checked" as fully as possible in the interests of legality. The legality that results is likely to be purely formal and even illusory, however, unless these legalistic techniques are part of a broader, more positive strategy that will encourage rather than frustrate responsible exercise of discretion by police. The same holds true of the bureaucratic strategies suggested by the second theory.

More promising is Davis's suggestion that "any agency which has discretionary power necessarily has the power to state publicly the manner in which the agency will exercise the power."[26] In other words, to use Davis's own definition of discretion, if police have effective power to choose among possible courses of action or inaction, they must also have effective power to articulate publicly how they will exercise this power to choose. By exercising this power, police would take a significant step toward reconciling their discretion with the requirements of legality. In fact, "articulate publicity" on the part of police is probably a precondition for meeting the other requirements of legality such as generality, clarity, consistency, prospectivity, and congruence. Moreover, such publicity would help disabuse police, politicians, and the general public of biased and unfounded assumptions about police activity. Manning has explained why publicity is a necessary precondition to the reconciliation of police discretion and legality:

> It can now be seen that many commonsense assumptions previously made about policing, such as the assumption that it can prevent crime, control narcotics, deter offenders through patrol, or produce a public sense of well being, are quite functional for the maintenance of police morale and the officer's sense of personal efficacy but are not representative of *actual* police goals. That is, if they are police goals, the police are failing in a

catastrophic fashion; if they are not police goals, then the public is being seriously misled.[27]

Even if articulate publicity is a precondition for reconciling police discretion with the requirements of legality, it is far from being the whole story. The other three theories of the role of discretion—namely, that it is necessary to provide relief from law, to give practical effect to law, and as a form of law—suggest additional strategies that are necessary in this endeavor. One strategy suggested by the first of these theories is to thwart the tendency of overzealous politicians, legislators, and moralists to enact harsh standards and sanctions and then expect police and other agencies to moderate this harshness to a level that they and the public can tolerate. The need for discretionary relief and flexibility on the part of the police should be a bona fide practical need and not one that is artificially and even hypocritically created.

A related strategy suggested by the other two theories is to make the individual and organizational competence of police more nearly congruent with their discretionary power and responsibility in society. One way to achieve a higher degree of congruence is to adopt a more realistic view of the nature and scope of police discretionary power and responsibility. This means dispelling most of the prevailing myths about police activity and replacing them with enlightened public standards of what police, broadly conceived, can and cannot be expected to do. In order for these discretionary responsibilities of police to be realistic, however, they must be matched by the competence of police to exercise this discretion. Here, *competence* involves both being *empowered* to exercise this discretion and having the proven *ability* to exercise it, and the requisite competence in both senses must be achieved by police organizations as well as by individual police.

As the preceding analysis has suggested, the competence of police to exercise discretionary power encompasses much more than their technical proficiency, quasi-military discipline, and bureaucratic organization. If Dworkin is right, and if police can justifiably be compared to other agents of the law, then they have a responsibility to be conscious of the grounds of their decisions, and to fit these grounds into a coherent view of police activity and its goals. It is not enough to say that police have a responsibility to enforce substantive law while respecting the procedural law that applies to their activity. This statement may be true, but it sheds little light on the question of the competence that police actually need if they are to perform this broad responsibility. For example, they need to appreciate the limits of legal

60 Discretion

rule-making and rule-following, because these limits help explain why the exercise of discretion is necessary in police activity. They also need to understand the various roles that discretion may play, for better or worse, in police decision-making. Finally, they need to be able to make discretionary decisions, and explain and justify them, on the basis of normative considerations that can be "consistently articulated" to others.

What can we conclude about the effectiveness of these general strategies to bring about a reconciliation of police discretion with the requirements of legality? If they were vigorously adopted and orchestrated, they would surely go some way toward achieving this reconciliation, but my own view is that they would not go far enough. My skepticism is based on the fact that police cannot begin to fulfill the requirements of legality unless other officials and even private citizens are also committed to legality. The law may not be a seamless web, but legality is dependent for its realization on the cooperation and shared responsibility of all agents of the legal system. Police alone, either individually or collectively, can do very little to achieve a higher degree of legality than other agents of the law are able and willing to achieve. Even official incentives to achieve a higher degree of legality are lacking where such practices as plea bargaining prevent exposure of unjustifiable discretion and encourage police to conform more to other officials' expectations than to expectations of the general public. In short, the institutional and organizational environment of police activity is on the whole not conducive to a reconciliation of police discretion with the requirements of legality.

Another reason for doubt is that police are agents, not only of the law, but of the state and other social sources of power and responsibility. This means that other standards of official action besides legality are applicable to police activity; and where these other standards conflict with legality, the conflict may be, and often is, resolved at the expense of legality. Fuller tried to obviate this kind of conflict by characterizing legality as a morality, "a special morality of role attaching to the office" of those who exercise official power and responsibility.[28] Although, with Hart, I would insist on distinguishing morality and legality, I endorse Fuller's insight that officials are necessarily subject to standards of morality as well as legality. Anthony D'Amato has explained this necessary connection as follows: "The very definition of who is an official (and whether the official thus located is entitled to continue to be regarded as an official) may be dependent upon a congruence between morality and official actions or decisions."[29] This view suggests the possibility that police discretion can at

Police Discretion, Legality, and Morality 61

least be reconciled with relevant requirements of morality, even if it cannot be reconciled with legality. I want to evaluate this possibility of moral legitimation of police discretion in the next section.

THE MORAL LEGITIMATION OF POLICE DISCRETION

In considering whether police discretion can be morally legitimated, we must first decide what moral standards are appropriate for this purpose. A further, more philosophical question is whether the moral standards deemed most appropriate are themselves justifiable, at least to the extent that we could reasonably expect them to merit general endorsement. The most obvious candidates for moral standards of this sort are those that have come to be widely recognized as standards of the ethics of police activity. Here we must make a further choice, however, among (1) moral standards that police organizations and associations have themselves officially endorsed as ethical codes for police activity, (2) moral standards that govern police activity insofar as it is considered a professional activity engaged in by members of a distinct profession, and (3) moral standards derived from a critical public morality (as distinct from conventional and private moralities) which are applicable to all official conduct, including what police do or fail to do in their official capacity. These different options testify to both the ambiguity of the term *police ethics* and the difficulty of deciding whether police discretion can be morally legitimated.

For purposes of this paper I shall ignore codes of ethics that have been officially endorsed by police organizations and associations, main-ly because they tend to reflect the mythology of police activity which I criticized earlier. More promising are the moral standards that are applicable to police activity insofar as police are plausibly viewed as members of a distinct profession. Without describing these moral standards in detail, it seems safe to say that they would require that police be responsive to the real human needs of other people and not merely to their own personal or group interests. Perhaps no profession today can take much pride in the degree of altruism exhibited by its members, but concern for the well-being of others continues to be one of the distinguishing marks of the professions and one of the moral standards of professional activity. Another related standard is that members of professions base their professional decisions and actions on a theoretical as well as practical understanding of their activity. In the case of police, this would include a theoretical understanding of the historical and cultural development of police activity, its social goals

62   Discretion

and effects, the causes of crime and other social disorders, the operation of the legal system, the rationale of punishment, and many other
related matters.

To the degree that police are able to meet these and other recognized
standards of professional activity, they have a strong claim to the kind
of discretionary authority and power that have traditionally been accorded to the professions and their members. That is, police would
have a strong claim to a high degree of individual and organizational
autonomy in the way they perform their professional responsibilities.
However, Jeffrey Reiman has argued that professionalization of police
does not and cannot make them comparable to other professions in
this respect. He explains the fundamental difference between the
police and other professions as follows:

> The informal organizational pressure for police autonomy, self-
> evaluation and freedom from external scrutiny pose problems
> of an entirely different nature than those posed by similar pres-
> sures among, say, doctors and lawyers. The explanation of this
> difference lies in the fact that the authority of doctors and
> lawyers rests on special expertise which once learned is in a
> tangible sense truly theirs while the authority of the police re-
> sides in their ability to exercise power which is perpetually
> loaned to them by the community and which is never theirs.[30]

According to this argument, the authority of other professionals
bestows autonomy on them because it is based on complex knowledge
and skills that become permanent attributes of theirs. The authority of
police does not bestow autonomy on them, however, because it is
based on *conditional* authorization and competence to perform the
responsibilities of police activity. No matter how professional police
become in the way they perform their responsibilities, they never cease
to be *agents* of the state, the community, or some other social authority,
and thus they cannot be autonomous professionals.

This argument against the autonomy of police is most compelling
when applied to their power to employ force and to curtail people's
freedom. This is the kind of power that makes police somewhat comparable to military professionals, and this analogy in turn makes quasi-
military organization and discipline rather than autonomy seem appropriate for the police. Also counting against the professional autonomy
of police is the fact that they have no control over the final disposition
of legal cases which they initiate by invoking criminal or other legal
processes. Without this control, they also have less incentive to exercise their law enforcement powers in a professional manner. Despite

Police Discretion, Legality, and Morality 63

these institutional and organizational constraints, however, police usually have other powers and responsibilities that make them more comparable to professionals on whom society bestows a relatively high degree of autonomy. This is especially true of their activity as investigators, peacekeepers, protectors, and providers of various services to the public.

The foregoing considerations support the general conclusion that professionalization of the police gives them a claim to autonomy in some kinds of police activity but not in others. Where professional autonomy is justified, moral legitimation of police discretion is possible on the basis of appropriate standards of professional ethics—provided, of course, that police are effectively subject to these standards in their choices and actions. Where autonomy is not justified, however, the professional ethics of police would at best only reinforce any legitimation of their discretionary power that is possible on other kinds of moral grounds.

I turn, then, to the third possibility mentioned earlier, which is the possibility of reconciling police discretion with standards of critical public morality. These are moral standards that are applicable to all exercise of official power by individuals or organizations, and this is why they are deemed public rather than private. Moreover, their justification is based on ethical considerations of what is morally at stake in the exercise of official power, and this is why they are called critical moral standards, to distinguish them from conventional moral standards which lack these ethical credentials.

Thomas Nagel has argued that at least some requirements of critical public morality are different from those of the morality of private individuals and moreover are not derivable from the latter. The main reason for this difference, he claims, is "the degree to which ruthlessness is acceptable in public life—the ways in which public actors may have to get their hands dirty," and this "depends on moral features of the institutions through which public action is carried out."[31] As Nagel points out, public organizations and institutions have no "insides," no private lives, and they serve purposes larger than those of particular individuals and groups. These and other features serve to justify greater emphasis in public morality on results rather than means, on what is achieved rather than how it is, thereby "permitting the public employment of coercive, manipulative, or obstructive methods that would not be allowable for individuals."[32] Counterbalancing this emphasis on results rather than means, however, is the moral requirement that "public policies and actions have to be much more impartial than private ones, since they usually employ a monopoly of certain

64   Discretion

kinds of power and since there is no reason in their case to leave room
for personal attachments and inclinations that shape individual
lives."[33]

If this exposition of critical public morality is accurate as far as it goes,
then no official can evade the moral tensions, ambiguities, and dilemmas that are necessarily involved in exercising public power over
others. Nagel has well described what is perhaps the main difficulty in
meeting the requirements of public morality:

> One of the hardest lines to draw in public policy is the one that
> defines where the end stops justifying the means. If results
> were the only basis for public morality then it would be possible
> to justify anything, including torture and massacre, in the ser-
> vice of sufficiently large interests.[34]

This constant effort to adjust means to ends so that the ends themselves are not subverted, while also adjusting personal and group
loyalties to public standards of impartiality, is what critical public
morality requires of all officials. This requirement imposes special
moral responsibilities on police because of the awesome powers they
may exercise over other members of society.

Can the exercise of discretionary power by police be reconciled with
justifiable requirements of public morality, and especially with the
more stringent responsibilities that this morality imposes on the police? Before trying to answer this question in a general way, we might
consider the various kinds of discretionary decisions that police are
called upon to make. For this purpose, Herman Goldstein has provided a useful classification of the main kinds of these discretionary
decisions.[35] They consist of decisions about (1) goals and objectives of
police activity; (2) methods of police intervention; (3) alternative forms
of disposition of cases by police; (4) methods of police investigation; (5)
police procedures, both in the field and in internal administration; and
(6) police activity related to issuing licenses and permits. Each of these
kinds of discretionary decisions may be made at the individual as well
as organizational level. How much discretion is involved varies considerably from one kind of decision to another, but it need not vary
with the rank of the decision-maker. In fact Goldstein observes that,
"unlike the military, on which they claim to model themselves, police
agencies allow their lowest-ranking officers to make some of their most
important decisions."[36]

Police who make the kinds of discretionary decisions cited above are
clearly subject to standards of critical public morality. The question is
whether their discretion can be morally legitimated on the basis of

these standards. In answering this question, discretionary decisions about the goals and objectives of police activity are the crucial ones to consider, because they determine the individual and organizational priorities which in turn influence all the other kinds of decisions. Police activity can be guided by many different goals and objectives, and until these have been deliberately chosen, reconciled with one another, and translated into coherent police policies, other kinds of discretionary decisions will tend to be ad hoc, arbitrary, or biased. A common result of this tendency is that police decide to employ means which erode and eventually undermine the goals and objectives they are supposed to serve. As Rubén Rumbaut and Egon Bittner recently pointed out, bureaucratic, technological, and legalistic responses to police discretion have tended to obscure the need for police to make, and be guided by, decisions about ends as well as means:

> The problems of policing are not simply problems of finding "efficient" and "effective" means; they are problems of ends, of competing social values, interests, and priorities, the resolution of which raise fundamental moral and political issues to be decided by an informed citizenry, not only scientific or technical issues to be decided by experts and technocrats. Hence, the most hopeful prospect of substantive police reform is the influence an informed public can exert on the direction of change in police agencies.[37]

Following up on this suggestion by Rumbaut and Bittner, I see no reason in principle why individual police and police agencies cannot make decisions about what they will attempt to do that are guided and justified by standards of public morality. At the very least, their discretionary decisions would have to be compatible with broader, publicly derived goals of society at large. In addition, these decisions by police should be able to win the support of a broad spectrum of other officials and private citizens. Only in this way can police share the responsibility for "dirty hands"—that is, for the unavoidable ruthlessness, coerciveness, and repressiveness of police activity—with other members of society for whom and over whom they exercise power. A third requirement is that discretionary decisions about goals should not commit police to the use of means that would call into question the worthiness of the goals pursued. This implies, for example, that the goals endorsed by police should not compel them to engage in highly invasive intelligence gathering, persistent harassment, capricious enforcement, or degradation of members of the public. Finally, these decisions by police, like all their other decisions, should be impartial

66 Discretion

both in the way they are made and in the justification provided for them.

Critical public morality as I have sketched it here provides standards of official conduct which many critics of the police may consider too permissive. Be that as it may, these standards provide the most promising basis that I can see for the moral legitimation of police discretion, both in theory and in practice. This kind of moral legitimation does not rule out, but in fact complements, the more limited means of legitimating police discretion through making the police effectively subject to standards of professional ethics and standards of legality.

NOTES

1. Allan Silver, "The Demand for Order in Civil Society: A Review of Some Themes in the History of Urban Crime, Police, and Riot," in *The Police: Six Sociological Essays*, ed. David J. Bordua (New York: Wiley, 1967), pp. 6–7.

2. Kenneth Culp Davis, *Discretionary Justice* (Urbana: University of Illinois Press, 1969), p. 222. See also his *Police Discretion* (St. Paul, Minn.: West, 1975).

3. Quoted in Drew Humphries and David F. Greenberg, "The Dialectic of Crime Control," in *Crime and Capitalism*, ed. David F. Greenberg (Palo Alto, Calif.: Mayfield, 1981), p. 228.

4. See Arthur Rosett's observation that "our thinking about discretion has been hampered by the very slipperiness of the concept," in "Connotations of Discretion," *Criminology Review Yearbook*, vol. 1, ed. by Sheldon L. Messinger and Egon Bittner (Beverly Hills, Calif.: Sage, 1979), p. 379.

5. One very broad conflict is between descriptive and normative views of police and police activity, discussed by Newton Garver in "The Ambiguity of the Police Role," *Social Praxis* 2 (1974): 309–23.

6. David H. Bayley, "Police Function, Structure, and Control in Western Europe and North America: Comparative and Historical Studies," in *Crime and Justice: An Annual Review of Research*, vol. 1, ed. by Norval Morris and Michael Tonry (Chicago: University of Chicago Press, 1979), p. 113.

7. Peter K. Manning, *Police Work: The Social Organization of Policing* (Cambridge, Mass.: MIT Press, 1977), p. 40.

8. Ibid.

9. See, e.g., Joseph Goldstein, "Police Discretion Not To Invoke the Criminal Process: Low Visibility Decisions in the Administration of Justice," *Yale Law Journal* 69 (1960): 551–94.

Police Discretion, Legality, and Morality 67

10. Manning, *Police Work*, p. 373.

11. Albert J. Reiss, Jr., "Discretionary Justice," in *Handbook of Criminology*, ed. Daniel Glaser (Chicago: Rand McNally, 1974), p. 634.

12. Davis, *Discretionary Justice*, p.4.

13. Ronald Dworkin, *Taking Rights Seriously* (Cambridge, Mass.: Harvard University Press, 1978), pp. 31–39.

14. Roscoe Pound, "The Decadence of Equity," *Columbia Law Review* 5 (1905): 21.

15. The President's Commission on Law Enforcement and Administration of Justice, *Task Force Report: The Police* (Washington, D.C.: Government Printing Office, 1967), p. 18.

16. Dworkin, *Taking Rights Seriously*, p. 88.

17. H. L. A. Hart, "Philosophy of Law, Problems Of," *The Encyclopedia of Philosophy*, ed. Paul Edwards, 8 vols. (New York: Macmillan Co., 1967), 6: 273–74.

18. Ibid., p. 274.

19. Lon Fuller, *The Morality of Law*, rev. ed. (New Haven, Conn.: Yale University Press, 1969), Chapter 2.

20. Rosett, "Connotations of Discretion," passim.

21. Ibid., p. 388.

22. Ibid. (my emphasis).

23. Ibid., p. 390.

24. Ibid., pp. 400–401.

25. Sanford Kadish and Mortimer Kadish, *Discretion to Disobey* (Stanford, Calif.: Stanford University Press, 1973), pp. 42 ff.

26. Davis, *Police Discretion*, pp. 109–10.

27. Manning, *Police Work*, p. 373 (his emphasis).

28. Fuller, *The Morality of Law*, p. 206.

29. Anthony D'Amato, "The Limits of Legal Realism," *Yale Law Journal* 87 (1978): 512.

68   Discretion

30. Jeffrey H. Reiman, "Police Autonomy vs. Police Authority: A Philosophical Perspective," in *The Police Community*, ed. Jack Goldsmith and Sharon S. Goldsmith (Pacific Palisades, Calif.: Palisades Publishers, 1974), p. 229.

31. Thomas Nagel, "Ruthlessness in Public Life," in *Public and Private Morality*, ed. Stuart Hampshire (Cambridge: Cambridge University Press, 1978), p. 82.

32. Ibid., p. 84.

33. Ibid.

34. Ibid., p. 89.

35. Herman Goldstein, *Policing a Free Society* (Cambridge, Mass.: Ballinger, 1977), pp. 94–101.

36. Ibid., p. 101.

37. Rubén G. Rumbaut and Egon Bittner, "Changing Conceptions of the Police Role: A Sociological Review," in *Crime and Justice: An Annual Review of Research*, vol. 1 (see note 6), p. 284.

[10]

Is Police Discretion Justified in a Free Society?

Jeffrey Reiman

By "police discretion" I understand the freedom of police officers to decide whether or not to arrest an individual when the conditions that would legally justify that arrest are present and when the officer can make the arrest without sacrificing other equally or more pressing legal duties. So I do not count as police discretion the choice of which individual to arrest when the arrest of several is similarly legally justified but the arrest of only one is physically possible. And of course I exclude all the other important, and I think inescapable, acts of judgment that police officers must make (for example, deciding whether the conditions legally justifying arrest are present). Our question, then, is this: Is it justifiable in a free society to allow police officers freedom to determine whether or not to arrest someone when they legally and physically can make the arrest? The short answer is no. The long answer will require a look at the nature of free societies and the sort of law enforcement they demand.

Before proceeding to this, I want to qualify my thesis in one important way. Police are commonly charged with the dual task of enforcing law and maintaining order. In pursuit of the latter aim, they disperse unruly crowds, quiet noisy neighbors, break up fights before they begin, clear the streets of drunks or prostitutes, and so on. In the context of such order maintenance, the police power to arrest is not so much a power to limit citizens' freedom as it is a power to get troublesome individuals to desist from offending behavior or to clear the area. As long as arrest is used only in this way, I think it is acceptable for police to refrain from exercising their arrest power – even where the facts justify its exercise – if they judge that milder means will serve the goal of order maintenance. Thus it seems to me that discretion does have a place here.[1] But when arrest is used to set in motion a series of events aimed at seriously limiting citizens' freedom, or when the threat of arrest itself seriously limits citizens' freedom, I contend that police ought not to have discretion. A brief detour through the history of political philosophy will help explain why.

Plato is well known for the (it is to be hoped!) unrealistic claim, argued at great length in the *Republic*, that a good state will be possible only when philosophers become kings or kings philosophers.[2] In this good state, there are to be few laws, since Plato thinks of laws the way he thinks of medication: more than just a minimum betokens and promotes a permanently sickly constitution. More particularly, the philosopher-king does not need laws because he or she knows the good, and thus can determine in each new case exactly what is right to do. (I'm not being politically correct here; Plato actually argued for equal opportunity for women to become philosopher-kings.) It would make no sense to tie the philosopher-king's hands with laws, since laws bring about only generally good outcomes and they might prevent the philosopher-king from doing exactly what is right in each new particular situation.

But the *Republic* is not Plato's last word. His last dialogue, and thus his last word – at least on the topic of the good state – is the *Laws*. And the title should make clear that here, near the close of his life, Plato took a far more positive view of the role of and need for laws than he did as an idealistic young man. Midway (in content and in time) between the *Republic* and the *Laws*, stands Plato's dialogue called the *Statesman*. In it, we see unfold before our eyes the shift from the rule of the philosopher-king to the rule of law. It will be instructive to see what reasons ground this shift in Plato's views.

The dialogue in the *Statesman* takes place between a character called "the Eleatic stranger," and another called "the younger Socrates" (not to be confused with the Socrates who leads the discussion in the *Republic*). The stranger starts by speaking of the true statesman, the one who possesses the "royal art" of ruling wisely and justly, and young Socrates balks when the stranger suggests that such a statesman may rule without laws. The stranger then explains that

> the best thing of all is not that the law should rule, but that a man should rule, supposing him to have wisdom and the royal power. . . . Because the law does not perfectly comprehend what is noblest and most just for all and therefore cannot enforce what is best. The differences of men and actions,

Is Police Discretion Justified in a Free Society? 73

and the endless irregular movements of human things, do not admit of any universal and simple rule.[3]

The stranger likens the royal art to other arts such as those practiced by physicians or physical trainers. If these individuals truly possess their arts, it would be absurd to bind them by preestablished rules. If a physician gave a prescription to a patient, only later to discover a better way of curing his ailment, we would hardly insist that the physician stick to the earlier treatment. We would allow, even want, him to do just what his art taught him was best in this particular case. So too, the practitioner of the art of ruling. Says the stranger, "Then if the law is not the perfection of right, why are we compelled to make laws at all? The reason of this has next to be investigated."[4]

Turning to this, the stranger points out that, like other arts, the royal art can never be mastered by more than a few individuals. Thus, there may be rulers who falsely claim to have that art and who therefore say that it is for the best that they rule without laws. Such false rulers are called tyrants, and their lawless rule is as bad as the genuine ruler's rule is good. Moreover, the fact that few are likely to possess the royal art, combined with the possibility of tyrants pretending to have it, makes people suspicious of anyone who would rule without law, even those who have the art. People "can never be made to believe that any one can be worthy of such authority. . . ; they fancy that he will be a despot who will wrong and harm and slay whom he pleases."[5] This suspicion creates instability, which, itself invites tyranny as worried citizens flock to demagogues for protection. In short, because there is no clear identifying mark of the true philosopher-king, no one can be allowed to rule without laws. Says the stranger, "as the State is not like a beehive, and has no natural head who is at once recognized to be the superior both in body and in mind, mankind are obliged to meet and make laws. . . ."[6]

Plato calls rule by laws "second best."[7] It cannot do justice (full, complete, perfectly tailored justice) to the complexity and variability of human affairs, in the way that a genuine philosopher-king unconstrained by laws could. But given how few true philosopher-kings there are, how difficult it is to recognize one and above all how dangerous it would be if a phony philosopher-king ruled without laws, we must settle for second best – meet and make laws and hold everyone strictly accountable. Ironically, the laws are good for the same reason that makes them only second best, namely, because they limit the power of the ruler. They protect the citizens from the rulers, and the citizens pay for this protection by giving up the possibility of perfectly good solutions to their complex and variable problems.

Plato teaches, then, three lessons about the rule of law: First, the function of the rule of law is not only to render justice to the citizens, but also to protect them from their governors. Second, the justification of the rule of law cannot be that it produces the best results in every case; its justification is that it gives generally good albeit imperfect results while protecting against tyranny. Law represents, to use a term not found in the Platonic corpus, a trade-off: the possibility of perfect outcomes is traded off for security against the worst outcomes. Third, this trade-off, and thus the rule of law itself, would not be necessary if states were like beehives, in which those who are truly fit to rule are naturally marked and easily recognized.

From these Platonic lessons about the rule of law, we can draw some morals about police discretion, since police discretion begins where the rule of law ends: police discretion is precisely the subjection of law to a human decision beyond the law. Like rule by philosopher-kings unfettered by law, police discretion makes possible a tailoring of justice to the complexity and variability of human affairs. Thus, one moral to draw is that if we give up police discretion, we also give up the possibility of some results that are better than what we get by strict application of the law. The second moral is that if we allow police discretion, we give certain citizens a special discretionary power over others which can be used in tyrannical ways. Consequently, if police discretion is to be justified, we must be confident that it is more likely to be used to arrive at benefits superior to those the rule of law provides than to be used tyrannically. And, finally, this confidence will be rash to the degree in which states are unlike beehives. The final moral, then, is that the less we are able to pick out those who are truly fit to exercise authority, the less confident we should be about allowing discretionary law enforcement.

Though these Platonic morals regarding police discretion continue to have relevance today, for us they are only a starting point. They do not give us the whole moral truth about police discretion – at least, not in terms that are adequate to modern political theory, nor in terms adequate to the project promised in my title. Plato's republic was not, and was not meant to be, a free society. To shift our perspective and look at the problem from the standpoint of the conditions and nature of a free society is to move a greater distance than might immediately be apparent. My purpose, then, in starting with Plato is, in addition to distilling some general truths about the rule of law and its opposite, to use Plato as a backdrop against which the features of modern political theorizing, with its emphasis on the value of freedom, can most clearly be seen. For this, we must shift to modern thinkers like Hobbes and Locke, and contemporaries like Rawls. Though all of these are broadly in the "social contract" tradition, their contractarianism as such is of secondary importance for our concerns. Far more important for our purposes is the way in which they view the state and the task of political philosophy.

Interestingly, both Hobbes and Locke start where the last of the Platonic morals left off. They echo, and in fact extend, Plato's observation that the human society is unlike a beehive, in that there are no naturally marked and thus easily identifiable natural rulers. The crucial chapter 13 of Hobbes's *Leviathan*, the chapter in which he introduces his grim account of the state of nature and the reasons for getting out of it by creating a political commonwealth, begins:

> Nature hath made men so equall, in the faculties of body, and mind; as that though there bee found one man sometimes manifestly stronger in body, or of quicker mind then another; yet when all is reckoned together, the difference between man, and man, is not so considerable, as that one man can thereupon claim to himselfe any benefit, to which another may not pretend, as well as he. For as to the strength of body, the weakest has strength enough to kill the strongest. . . .
>
> And as to the faculties of the mind . . . , I find yet a greater equality amongst men, than that of strength.[8]

And chapter 2 of Locke's *Second Treatise of Civil Government*, the chapter in which he introduces his own not-so-grim view of the state of nature, begins by making the same point as Hobbes:

> To understand political power right, and derive it from its original, we must consider, what state all men are naturally in, and that is, a *state of perfect freedom* to order their actions . . . as they think fit . . . , without asking leave, or depending on the will of any other man.
>
> A *state* also *of equality*, wherein all the power and jurisdiction is reciprocal, no one having more than another; there being nothing more evident, than that creatures of the same species and rank, promiscuously born to all the same advantages of nature, should also be equal one amongst another. . . .[9]

To these modern thinkers, human social life is less like a beehive than even Plato thought. For Plato, we are not like a beehive because natural rulers are not naturally marked and easily recognized. This led to suspicion and fear of a false ruler who might tyrannize people, and from there to preference, albeit reluctant, for the rule of law as second best. For Hobbes and Locke, and I daresay for us as well, we are not like a beehive because there *are* no natural rulers. No one has – by virtue of innate ability or some other trait – natural fitness to rule others. There are no natural rulers to recognize, no queen bees, no philosopher-kings. And this has new and profound implications for understanding the danger of tyranny and the attraction of the rule of law.

In the state of nature, each has authority over herself and none has authority over others. Let us call authority over oneself "personal authority," and authority over others, "political authority." In the state of nature, then, there is no political authority, only everyone's full and equal personal authority. If there is no natural political authority, such political authority as exists is artificial – created by us. It should be clear that personal and political authority are mutually exclusive categories. The creation and enlargement of political authority is necessarily at the expense of personal authority (and vice versa). Since any political authority that exists is humanly created, it is either taken by force from, or freely given by, those over whom it is exercised. Note that this is a claim in political theory, not in psychology. Neither the taking nor the giving of authority need be consciously or intentionally done.

Since political authority detracts from personal authority, it results from either a forced taking or a free giving up of some of an individual's personal authority. If political authority is taken by force, then it has no moral claim on those over whom it is exercised. Consequently, for political authority to be morally legitimate, for it to exercise a claim on citizens, it must be freely given. But the political authority essential to a state cannot be freely given in the form of an actual voluntary donation by citizens: the benefits of a state depend on its already being in existence when people are born so that they can be protected and educated to the point at which they could make the donation. Thus, the test of whether political authority is legitimate becomes the theoretical one of whether it would be *reasonable* for citizens to make this donation. And that question is answered positively if what citizens get from political authority amounts to the best possible bargain for what they give up for it.

Here lies the analytic power and normative force of the social contract: it embodies the terms on which it would be reasonable for humans equal and complete in their personal authority to grant to some individuals political authority over them. This is why it has never been important that the contract and the state of nature are historical fictions. The contract spells out conditions under which citizens' surrender of some of their equal personal authority is reasonable, and thus, though it is the purest fiction, it provides a standard for legitimate political authority over free people.

Is Police Discretion Justified in a Free Society?   77

An important implication of this contractarianism is that legitimate political authority is literally concocted out of the parts of free people's personal authority that they surrender to the political commonwealth. The lawmaker's authority to make laws is derived from the authority that free people have to make decisions about how they should live, and the law enforcer's authority to back laws up with force is derived from the authority that free people have to use force in defense of their authority to govern their own lives, and so on. Thus, Locke says of the extent of the political authority in a legitimate state:

> It is *not*, nor can possibly be absolutely *arbitrary* over the lives and fortunes of the people: for it being but the joint power of every member of society . . . ; it can be no more than those persons had in a state of nature before they entered into society, and gave up to the community.[10]

And Rawls can say of liberal democracies that "political power, which is always coercive power, is the power of the public, that is, of free and equal citizens as a collective body."[11]

A corollary of this point is that authority exercised by political officials beyond that which it would be reasonable for people to surrender in forming a state is illegitimate. And "illegitimate" here means morally indistinguishable from the sorts of invasions that characterized the state of nature and which, once a state exists, are called "tyrannical" or "criminal." If political authority is understood as the authority that free people reasonably deposit in a state; authority exercised beyond that amount is stolen, taken by force. The force may be that of habit or tradition or ignorance, but forced taking rather than free giving it remains. Thus, authority exercised beyond what is rationally granted is morally indistinguishable from tyranny or crime – that is, from the sorts of coercive invasions the avoidance of which makes the state reasonable in the first place. Rather than citizens having an obligation to respect such authority, they have the right to resist it. Says Locke:

> Where-ever law ends, tyranny begins . . . ; and whosoever in authority exceeds the power given him by the law, and makes use of the force he has under his command, to compass that upon the subject, which the law allows not, ceases in that to be a magistrate; and, acting without authority, may be opposed, as any other man, who by force invades the right of another.[12]

It should be evident now that the political authority that governs a free society has a very different moral structure from that which governs Plato's republic. This will be clearest if we imagine, contrary to fact, that

Plato's philosopher-king was dedicated, above all, to promoting the free-dom of his or her subjects. Then we could picture the philosopher-king's authority as a kind of unlimited, all-purpose power to do whatever is needed to realize, or even maximize, people's freedom. This is not how political authority in a free society should be understood, however. The most important difference is that political authority that is created by free people is not authority to do whatever is necessary to realize any particu-lar goal, even the maximization of freedom. It is rather a specific, limited grant of authority to do certain things, and only certain things.

Another way to put this difference is as follows. The Platonic ruler is authorized to accomplish a goal, and thus his authority is limited not in its scope but only in the purposes to which it can be directed. By contrast, the modern ruler of a free society is authorized to perform certain specified actions, and thus her authority is limited in its scope. The political officials of a free society are not empowered to do whatever is necessary to bring about some overriding purpose, even the maximization of freedom itself. They have only the authority that they have been given, and they must keep within that even if exceeding it would better achieve popular goals. In this respect, we can understand the efforts of the founders of the American republic, first, to list in the Constitution the specific powers granted to the central government, and then, when it became obvious that the central government could not realistically be limited that way, to list in the first ten amendments to the Constitution specific areas in which the government could not tread even in the service of desirable goals.

From this discussion of political authority there follows a very simple conclusion for police discretion: there are only two ways in which it can be justified in a free society, either by explicit grant from the citizens or by showing that it would be reasonable for the citizens to make such a grant. I take it that there has been no such explicit grant to police. Judges, by contrast, are, or at least once were, explicitly given sentencing ranges within which to choose the most just outcome all things considered. But the police are simply and explicitly authorized to enforce the laws that the people's representatives enact, and no more.

Would it, however, be reasonable for the people to grant the police some range of freedom of decision about whether or not to enforce laws when they legally and physically can do so? Here it seems to me that the answer is no. It would not be reasonable for four very important reasons: First, doing so renders the laws themselves vague and uncertain. Rather than stating forthrightly what will and what will not be permitted, laws subject to discretionary enforcement effectively contain the additional wild-card proviso "if a police officer judges it appropriate, and so on." Second, adding this proviso amounts to amending the laws as passed by the people's representatives. Third, police discretionary power is almost certain to be used frequently in ways that discriminate (in effect, if not in intent) against the poor and powerless and unpopular in our society[13] – undermining the legitimacy of the law where it is most in need of legitimacy. Fourth, granting police freedom to decide whether or not to enforce the law gives police officers the opportunity to use that freedom as leverage over other citizens.

Notice that with this fourth reason the danger of tyranny lies not so much in the police officer's power to arrest, and thus limit citizens' liberty, but in the new power police officers have when it is for them to decide whether to arrest. It might be thought that as long as the police arrest only those who are legitimately subject to arrest, then the discretionary power not to arrest only reduces state interference with the individual below what is legitimate – and thus cannot be tyrannical. But this overlooks the fact that discretion to arrest or not is itself a power over citizens, separate from the power to arrest as such. Over and above their power to enforce the laws, discretion gives the police an additional power beyond what the law authorizes, the power to use their law enforcement authority as a threat. That such threats are the common fare of TV police dramas, and sometimes the only means that real cops have to wring information out of small-time drug dealers or prostitutes and the like, hardly shows that this is right or appropriate to the government of a free society. If we are not ready to endorse a law requiring all citizens to give the police whatever information they want, then such use of discretion as leverage to get information amounts to allowing police to exercise a power over some citizens that we would not allow them to exercise over all. Nor does public acceptance of this phenomenon amount to a public grant of the authority to do it. What it suggests, rather, is that most people don't mind if the police treat drug dealers and prostitutes in a tyrannical fashion.

Bear in mind, I do not doubt that treating drug dealers or prostitutes in a tyrannical fashion may be effective in achieving larger goals, such as catching more serious criminals. But political authority in a free society is not an unlimited grant to do whatever is needed to accomplish good goals (as Miranda warnings and search and seizure protections testify). If most people want the police to exercise discretion in enforcing drug or other vice laws, then the people must say so through their representatives, and this will require in turn that the new authority be justified in open public discussion. And, in fact, my opinion is the same about any area in which it might be thought good to grant the police discretion. Put the grant into the law, or forget about it.

Before concluding, I want to draw support for my argument from another modern political theorist who, while not a social contractarian, played an important role in the thinking of the founders of the American republic. I refer to "the celebrated Montesquieu" to whom Madison, writing in *Federalist* paper 47 attributes that "invaluable precept in the science of politics," the doctrine of the separation of powers.

Montesquieu presents this precept in the context of his discussion of the conditions of political liberty. It is interesting that Montesquieu understands this liberty as "a right of doing whatever the laws permit," and not in the Millian sense, as a freedom from laws. Like Locke, Montesquieu speaks from an older, though still modern, tradition, in which freedom exists as long as all are governed by publicly promulgated laws and only by those laws.[14] He too, then, accepts that the rule of law is the bulwark of liberty. About this bulwark and its maintenance, he writes:

> The political liberty of the subject is a tranquility of mind arising from the opinion each person has of his safety. In order to have this liberty, it is requisite the government be so constituted as one man need not be afraid of another.
>
> When the legislative and executive powers are united in the same person . . . , there can be no liberty. . . .
>
> Again there can be no liberty, if the judiciary power be not separated from the legislative and executive. . . . Were it joined to the executive power, the judge might behave with violence and oppression.[15]

Police discretion is in effect a mixing of legislative and judiciary power with executive power, and thus likewise a threat to political liberty. It mixes legislative power by deciding which laws really are to be enforced, and it mixes judiciary power by deciding who is to come under the laws that are enforced. Now, though neither Montesquieu nor Madison says so explicitly, I think the idea behind the separation of powers is simply that the more people who have to participate in an act of government, the less likely it is that it will be an evil or tyrannical act. Thus, liberty will be best protected if police, judges, and lawmakers each do what they are mandated to do.

I conclude, then, that police discretion has no rightful place in a free society. Where it appears appropriate, I believe this is so because it compensates for flaws elsewhere in the system. For example, police sometimes hesitate to use their powers of arrest because they know that an arrestee may have to spend the night in a detention cell and will get a potentially damaging arrest record even if he is finally not charged or is eventually acquitted.[16] But this could be dealt with by making sure that there is adequate prosecutorial and judicial staff to process arrestees quickly, and by providing for the expunging of arrest records that do not result in a conviction – something long overdue in a society that believes that people are innocent until proven guilty.

Where such institutional flaws are not the problem, then, I contend that seemingly appropriate exercises of police discretion reflect flaws in our laws. For any area in which it would be good to grant police discretion, it will be possible to spell out the rules governing that discretion and build them into the laws (thus eliminating it as discretion in the sense I have been using it here, that is, as freedom to decide whether to apply the law). It follows, then, that for any area in which it is contended that police should have discretion, this will be either to compensate for institutional flaws or inadequate legal draftsmanship. At best discretion solves a problem at the wrong place in the criminal justice system.[17]

Moreover, to the extent that sections of the public are content with police discretion and do not build it into the laws, a dangerous duplicitousness is at play. The people through their representatives say one thing, and through their tacit acceptance say another. They make categorical laws to vent publicly their moral outrage, and then allow the police effectively to redraft the laws once they are out of public sight.

Earlier and in passing, I suggested that there is a difference between Locke's and Montesquieu's view of the relation between law and liberty and Mill's view. Mill's view is that law limits liberty, and thus to enlarge liberty we should shrink the reach of the law. Locke's and Montesquieu's view is that law limits the arbitrary acts of others, and thus to protect liberty we should insist that officials act according to the laws and exercise no authority beyond them. Both views are correct: the simple fact is that a free society should have few and clear criminal laws which the police should be expected to enforce wherever they apply, whenever it is physically possible to do so, as long as doing so is not in conflict with enforcing even more important laws or with explicit legislative guidelines. The police already have enormous powers over citizens that other citizens lack. They should not be given the additional power of being able to use their authority to arrest at their own discretion.

Moreover, the laws should not express society's moral aspirations, but its real will – the terms on which it is truly prepared to act. If the legislators are making more laws than the police can enforce, they should make fewer laws or employ more police officers. The laws should express the actual treatment that the society wants, and police enforcement of those laws should be as automatic as possible. The reduction of discretion should be carried throughout the system. We should have sentencing guidelines for judges, though I would hope for something quite a bit less brutal than the current combination of guidelines plus mandatory minimum sentences. And we should correct the recent lamentable tendency of this combination to shift discretion from judges (who exercise discretion in open court and who are at least somewhat insulated from political pressures) to prosecutors (who exercise discretion out of public view and who are political through and through). Reasonable sentencing guidelines for judges should be matched with reasonable charging guidelines for prosecutors.[18] If these, as well as reasonable arrest guidelines for police, were built into the law, we would have moved a great distance toward realizing the requirements of a free society as understood by liberal political philosophers from Locke to Rawls.

NOTES

I wish to express my appreciation to the participants in the workshop for their many helpful comments, objections, and recommendations. In particular, I thank Professor William Heffernan of John Jay College for his challenging and useful commentary on this essay.

1. I was convinced of the need to make this qualification of my thesis by Professor James Fyfe of Temple University.

2. *Republic* in *The Dialogues of Plato*, trans. B. Jowett (New York: Random House, 1937), vol. I, p. 737.

3. *Statesman* in *The Dialogues of Plato*, trans. B. Jowett (New York: Random House, 1937), vol. II, p. 322.

4. Ibid.

5. Ibid., p. 329.

6. Ibid.

7. Ibid., p. 325.

8. Thomas Hobbes, *Leviathan* (Buffalo: Prometheus, 1988), p. 63.

9. John Locke, *Second Treatise of Civil Government* (Indianapolis: Hackett, 1980), p. 8, emphasis in original.

10. Ibid., p. 70, emphasis in original.

11. John Rawls, *Political Liberalism* (New York: Columbia University Press, 1993), p. 216.

12. Locke, *Second Treatise*, p. 103, emphasis in original.

13. See, for example, Dennis D. Powell, "A Study of Police Discretion in Six Southern Cities," *Journal of Police Science and Administration* 17, no. 1 (1990), pp. 1-7;

Is Police Discretion Justified in a Free Society? 83

as well as the studies reported in Jeffrey Reiman, *The Rich Get Richer and the Poor Get Prison: Ideology, Class and Criminal Justice*, 4th ed. (Needham, MA: Allyn & Bacon, 1995), pp. 105-8. For a general overview of the problem and recent attempts to solve it, see Samuel Walker, *Taming the System: The Control of Discretion in Criminal Justice, 1950-1990* (New York: Oxford University Press, 1993), esp. ch. 2, "Police Discretion."

14. Writes Locke: "for *law*, in its true notion, is not so much the limitation as *the direction of a free and intelligent agent* to his proper interest, and . . . freedom is not, as we are told, *a liberty for every man to do what he lists:* (for who could be free, when every other man's humour might domineer over him?) but a *liberty* to dispose, and order as he lists, his person, actions, possessions, and his whole property, within the allowance of those laws under which he is, and therein not to be subject to the arbitrary will of another, but freely follow his own" (*Second Treatise*, p. 32, emphasis in original).

15. Charles-Louis de Montesquieu, *The Spirit of the Laws* (New York: Hafner, 1949), pp. 151-52. Interestingly, Montesquieu recommends that judges too be deprived of discretion in applying the law: ". . . judges are no more than the mouth that pronounces the words of the law, mere passive beings, incapable of moderating either its force or its rigor" (p. 159).

16. For a sensitive description of cases in which police hesitate to arrest individuals accused by people of doubtful credibility, see H. Richard Uviller, "The Unworthy Victim: Police Discretion in the Credibility Call," *Law & Contemporary Problems* 47, no. 4 (1984), pp. 15-33.

17. I think the same can be said to those who think that the police ought at least to have discretion not to enforce unjust laws. It is easy enough to point to some outrageously unjust law and say it would be better if police were free not to enforce that law. But we are concerned with general policies. And that implies that what must be argued for is a general right of police to decide which laws are unjust enough not to be enforced. For this to be justified, we would need (at the very least) evidence showing that in general the police will be better judges of the justice of the laws than the legislators who make them – whereas the evidence of discrimination by the police argues in the opposite direction. Moreover, it would most likely better serve the cause of justice if police were to enforce unjust laws so that the society would have to face the consequences of its unjust legislation, than if police correct injustice through publicly invisible acts of nonenforcement. It is the legislature that should correct unjust legislation, not the police – another case in which police discretion corrects for a problem that should be corrected elsewhere. Beyond this, it is, I think, inappropriate to apply to the police the model of justifiable civil disobedience. When private citizens engage in civil disobedience, they characteristically submit to the judgment of the law, and thus they pose no threat to the rule of law itself (this is one reason that their disobedience is *civil*). When police or other public officials fail to enforce the law, then the rule of law itself is undermined. At a minimum, if the police refrain from enforcing a law because they believe it to be unjust, they should make their nonenforcement public, in the way that civil disobedients make their disobedience public. Then we might hope that lawmakers would be pressured to respond by improving the law.

18. An interesting proposal to this effect is made in Note, "Developments in the Law: Race and the Criminal Process," *Harvard Law Review* 101(1988), pp. 1550-51.

[11]

Selective Enforcement and the Rule of Law

John Kleinig

"Is it justifiable in a free society to allow police officers freedom to determine whether or not to arrest someone when they legally and physically can make the arrest?" This is the question to which Jeffrey Reiman has recently answered an unambiguous "no."[1] It is not the first time that the question has been answered this way,[2] though Reiman's robust defense must once again give pause to those who, like myself, believe that some discretion in this regard ought to be allowable.

One of the merits of Reiman's discussion lies in his attempt to embed his defense within the larger framework of political philosophy. Using as his base Plato's account of the rule of law in *The Statesman*, Reiman makes three observations. First, the purpose of laws is not simply to ensure justice to citizens, but also to protect us from the vagaries of rulers; second, the rule of law generally works out well, though not perfectly: what it loses in just results in particular cases it gains in the protection that it provides against tyranny; and third, this trade-off is necessitated by the fact that "ideal rulers" are not only few and far between, but cannot be readily identified.[3]

What Plato holds to be true is reinforced by contemporary political theorizing. Here the very idea of an "ideal" or "natural" ruler is called into question. The probability of tyranny is thus increased, and the practical importance of the rule of law is heightened. In a world that lacks natural rulers, each person must be accorded an equality of status and be recognized as having a natural authority over only his or her own actions. Political authority, if it is to be justified at all, can be justified only if it can be seen as a reasonable bargain on the part of those who are subject to it. It constitutes a reasonable bargain only if it is constrained by rules that exclude its arbitrary exercise. And this, Reiman insists, amounts to an acceptance of the rule of law.[4]

Political authority as we now understand it is not primarily goal-oriented, but contractual. It does not authorize those in power to achieve some desirable end by whatever means they consider appropriate, but is a limited *authorization* to secure certain specified ends (as enshrined in law) by means that are limited. That being so, Reiman argues, any discretionary authority that police exercise can be justified in only two ways: either as an explicit grant by citizens or as the conclusion of an argument showing that it would be reasonable to make such a grant. He takes it that there is no basis for believing the former: police are "simply and explicitly authorized to enforce the law that the people's representatives enact, and no more."[5]

Is there any good reason to think that people *should* give police some discretion about whether or not to enforce the law? Reiman offers four reasons for thinking that no good grounds exist for giving them that discretion: (1) it would render the laws "vague and uncertain"; (2) it would effectively give police the power to amend laws that the people's representatives had passed; (3) it would almost certainly be used discriminatorily; and (4) it would be used coercively as a form of leverage. In what follows I shall attempt to meet the challenge posed by Reiman's arguments, and shall argue that it is reasonable to allow to police a limited discretionary authority in regard to their enforcement of law.

Law Enforcement and Order Maintenance

First of all, however, I need to address what I believe to be a very problematic qualification that Reiman makes near the beginning of his discussion. There he notes that police are "commonly charged with the dual task of enforcing law and maintaining order," and that in fulfillment of the latter goal "they disperse unruly crowds, quiet noisy neighbors, break up fights before they begin, clear the streets of prostitutes, and so on."[6] In situations such as these, he believes it appropriate that police exercise discretion—perhaps by choosing not to arrest where the law would allow them to.

This is no small concession. If we are to believe James Q. Wilson, "[t]he patrolman's role is defined more by his responsibility for *maintaining order* than by his responsibility for enforcing the law."[7] Wilson characterizes order maintenance as intervention in situations that disturb or threaten to disturb the public peace, an account that sits well with Reiman's examples.[8] So, despite Reiman's unambiguous "no" to his initial question, a great deal of police work may in fact constitute an exception to it. This surely represents not only an "important" (his term) but a dramatic qualification of his opposition to selective enforcement. For there is nothing in his later arguments that provides a basis for such exceptions. It is, moreover, these added dimensions of the police task (whether characterized as order maintenance, peacekeeping, or social service functions) that have provided one of the traditional rationales for selective enforcement.

But that is not all. Wilson makes it clear that the order maintenance function no longer figures in cases in which "there is no dispute."[9] When an infraction of the law is observed, such as a traffic violation, it is no longer possible to appeal to order-maintenance as a reason for not enforcing the law (in the sense of making an arrest or issuing a ticket). Yet I believe that selective enforcement *may* be justifiable in these cases as well—where there is no victim or there are believed to be extenuating circumstances. And perhaps Reiman would also want to make exceptions in such cases. But if that is so he cannot make them under the rubric of the police order-maintenance function.

Selective Enforcement and the Rule of Law 119

The Rule of Law

As Reiman rightly observes, the idea of "a government of laws, not men" is of ancient pedigree.[10] Not only Plato but also Aristotle was convinced that "the rule of law is preferable to that of any individual."[11] And in liberal democratic regimes, the rule of law has been appealed to as the main bulwark against tyranny. Any theoretical doubts that people have had about its appropriateness have usually been allayed by the spectacle of what happens in societies that have rejected it.

Nevertheless, appeals to the rule of law are neither as transparent nor as compelling as Reiman seems to believe. First of all, there is considerable debate about what is encompassed by the rule of law, and for this reason it can be questioned whether a rule of law excludes the recognition of limited discretionary authority; and second, there is a tension between the rule of law and democratic expectations.

The rule of law is a political ideal. Essentially, it sets forth conditions for government that are intended to preserve the governed from the tyranny of arbitrary power. For some writers this is understood *formalistically*, as requiring no more than the existence of and subscription to fixed and preannounced formal rules, rules that are articulated with sufficient clarity to enable exercises of governmental authority to be predicted with some certainty.[12] But for other writers, the rule of law is interpreted more *substantively* to require that rules promulgated by governmental authority be broadly concordant with a particular conception of human entitlements. Thus "rule of law values" (as catalogued by Michael Moore)—the separation of powers, equality and formal justice, liberty and notice, substantive fairness, procedural fairness, and efficient administration—are intended to secure citizens not only against arbitrariness but also against oppressive rules.[13]

Reiman does not explicitly join this debate, though he is clearly concerned about both oppression and arbitrariness. He accepts that respect for human freedom and human equality need to be preserved in—indeed, constitute the *raison d'être* for—civil society. It could be that freedom and equality can be protected not only by adherence to the rule of law but also by commitment to a conception of human rights or personal sovereignty, the latter pressed as political demands additional to that of the rule of law. But I think that he implicitly accepts the richer, more substantive view of the rule of law, for he quotes with approval Locke's contention that *"where-ever law ends, tyranny begins,"* and that the person who "exceeds the power given him by the law . . . may be opposed, as any other man, who by force invades the right of another."[14] This strongly suggests that Reiman sees the rule of law as securing us not merely against arbitrariness but also against (other?) violations of our rights.[15]

Because of this, Reiman believes that in a free society adherence to the rule of law will preclude the grant of discretionary authority to police. It is only if such authority has been explicitly granted, or if it is reasonable to

120 John Kleinig

expect it to be granted, that we may reconcile police discretion with the rule of law. He takes it that the former has not occurred, and believes the latter to be lacking in merit.

Consider now the second issue: the coherence of the rule of law with democratic or contractual processes. Reiman seems to take it for granted that there is an easy fit between the rule of law and its modern expression in liberal democratic society. Yet a little reflection indicates that this is not the case. The rule of law, at least according to Reiman's conception, seems to require that laws be applied exceptionlessly. Democratic and contractarian theories, on the other hand, emphasize the value of the majority will, and that will need not be limited to or even be compatible with the substantive requirements of law. After all, the rulers envisaged in Plato's *The Statesmen* or Aristotle's *Politics*, though enjoined to rule through law rather than the deliverances of individual judgment, were not conceived of as democratically elected incumbents.

The seriousness of this potential tension between the rule of law and democratic values is not unrelated to the way in which we construe both the rule of law and democracy. If democracy and the rule of law are both thought of formalistically—as no more than a crude majoritarianism, on the part of one, and a law of rules, on the part of the other—then the tension could be quite significant. But if democratic rule is anchored instead in the values of equality and freedom, and the rule of law is likewise anchored in a theory of human rights, the rule of law may be seen as expressing one of the conditions under which (liberal) democratic aspirations may be realized.

Have people actually withheld discretionary authority from the police? Reiman might have referred to the full enforcement statutes that have been passed in many states.[16] If the people have not spoken, then their representatives certainly have, and they have charged police with responsibility to arrest anyone who violates a law.[17] What more appropriate evidence could we want in a democratically ordered society? Strong as this consideration is, however, I am not entirely convinced that we should take it as our only— or even as decisive—evidence of what the people have chosen.

First of all, a great number of violations are dealt with informally by police, and for the most part their choice not to arrest or summons or cite does not meet with public disapproval. We all know that many of those who are stopped for traffic offenses—such as speeding or having defective tail lights—are let off with a warning rather than a summons, and yet, unless the case is an egregious one, we do not complain. Maybe our failure to protest can be put down to naked self-interest—the recognition of our own propensity to speed or our failure to make regular checks of our car's condition, and the desire that we should be treated leniently if caught. But I think there is rather more to it than that. For we also recognize that people exceed the speed limit or fail to ensure that their car is not in violation of laws relating to its condition for many different reasons, and in some of these cases we would feel that an injustice had been done were a ticket to be

Selective Enforcement and the Rule of Law 121

issued or the driver arrested. For the most part, we would be more upset were someone who was speeding for a "legitimate" reason to be ticketed than we would be were someone not to be ticketed for a comparable offense for which there were no "legitimating" reasons.

Reiman alludes to the possibility of a public acceptance of discretion, but says that it does not amount to a public grant of authority. In the circumstances which he has in mind—the nonarrest of drug dealers and prostitutes on condition that they become informants[18]—I am at least sympathetic. But this is probably a special case; at least it is a more controversial one. What we might ask is whether the circumstances in which the discretion is exercised are such that the discretion could (though not necessarily will) be sustained in a public forum. In the case of the circumstances under which the services of drug dealers and prostitutes are obtained, I can imagine that there would be a significant division of opinion. But in the cases to which I earlier alluded, in which traffic laws are violated, I think that the argument for publicly defending an exercise of discretion not to arrest or ticket is much stronger.

Second, there is some reason to view full enforcement statutes only as broad statements of purpose and not as rigid requirements. This is not to say that they would be modified if challenged. They are, however, products of a political process, a process that is sometimes best served if statements are made in categorical and unqualified terms. Lending credence to this view is the finding that despite provisions for doing so, full enforcement statutes are rarely enforced and, further, this fact per se brings with it no public outcry. It is only when the discretion is exercised in what seem to be *inappropriately* lenient ways that complaints are heard.[19] Although we are all aware that the police exercise discretion, when it is not felt to be oppressive it is rarely opposed. Furthermore, it is not uncommon for the police to publicize in broad terms the fact that they selectively enforce the law.[20] What generally sticks in people's craw is not less than full enforcement per se, but the discriminatory way in which that is sometimes practiced and the disregard for victims that it sometimes displays.

Third, although legislation sometimes mirrors a social consensus (or at least social majority), it does not always do so. It may be progressive or lag behind social change. There are many reasons for the hiatuses that occur between legislation and social values – some understandable, some reprehensible – and sometimes police are left with the task of making informal adjustments so that social peace may be preserved. Statutes outlawing sodomy, adultery, and fornication may remain on the books for political reasons, yet police would alienate significant sections of their community and generate considerable social turmoil were they to enforce them.

For these reasons, I do not think it unreasonable to argue that the purpose of full enforcement statutes is not so much to require that every law be enforced on every occasion on which it can be, but to place an onus on police to enforce.[21] The difference is important. Those who violate the law know that police have a defeasible obligation to enforce it. Enforcement is

122 *John Kleinig*

not optional; but neither is it mandatory. It is a defeasible obligation on the part of police to investigate law breaking and to take some action with regard to all violations that are called to their attention.

As I noted earlier, there is a sense in which full enforcement statutes are politically necessary. To pass laws and not require that they be enforced or to indicate explicitly that whether or not they will be enforced will be left to the discretion of the police, would be to undermine their force as law. *Even if* it is left to the discretion of police whether or not to enforce the law by means of arrest or summons, the law needs to be magisterially asserted. Otherwise those who break the law will not see their fate as a consequence of their violating the law but only as a matter of negotiation between themselves and the police. Allowing police discretion to enforce the law selectively is not intended to sanction the latter.

Let us now look in more detail at Reiman's four objections.

Vagueness and Uncertainty

Reiman's first claim is that any acceptance of discretion will render the law "vague and uncertain." Why should we think this to be the case? If the law says that the speed limit is 55 mph, and police do not generally ticket people unless they are traveling 10 mph over the speed limit, the law is not thereby rendered vague and uncertain. Nor does it suggest that the speed limit is really 65 mph and not 55 mph. A person who is traveling at 70 mph will be charged with traveling 15 mph over the speed limit, not 5 mph. And a person who happens to get picked up for traveling at 60 mph cannot complain that he wasn't traveling over 65 mph, and therefore should not have been picked up. Of course, he might wonder why he, of all the people who travel over 55 and under 65 mph, was picked up. But if at 60 mph this person was creating a risk, then there does not seem to be any problem about the police picking him up and not others.

This having been said, it might still be reasonable for us to agree that the police generally wait until people are about 10 mph over the limit before they move in. The reasons here are practical. Our speedometers may be slightly off. The instrumentation used by the police may not be completely accurate. The road may be straight and clear, and visibility good, and no risk may be involved. We may have simply allowed the car to drift above the speed limit, easy to do when one has been driving for a while. It involves a better use of police resources to target those who are more than 10 mph over. And, finally, there may be all sorts of personal reasons why we were traveling above the limit—to get someone to hospital, because we are late picking up the children, we need to get to a bathroom, and so on.[22] Unless there is some special reason to give the law strict liability status, its rigid application in some of these cases would be obnoxious, and would do little to advance the purpose of the law. Laws are not contextless requirements but embedded in social purposes, and although they provide clear guidelines, they are not, or at least should not be, impervious to the social

Selective Enforcement and the Rule of Law 123

purposes that have informed them. "Overreach" of the law, as Klockars calls it, the working of injustice because laws are expressed too specifically or generally, is correctable by means of discretionary judgments. The correction doesn't make the law vague or uncertain, but allows factors relevant to the law's purpose (both in general and in particular cases) to be incorporated into its enforcement.

Another way of putting this is to say that humans are rational beings, capable of understanding not only the terms of laws (their letter), but also the purposes (or spirit) that led to their promulgation. A person who is "given a break" when traveling at 63 mph, because he was responding to an anxious call from his wife, is not going to go on his way less certain about the law, because he understands not only the letter of the law but also the spirit that infuses it.

Confusion of Powers

Would selective enforcement in effect give police the power to amend the law, and thus subvert the purposes that have made the doctrine of a separation of powers so valuable to sustaining liberal democratic structures? Reiman certainly thinks so, and he is not alone in this. The virtue that informs the doctrine of separation of powers is the dispersal of power and thus a diminished likelihood of its being used tyrannically: "liberty will be best protected if police, judges, and law makers each do what they are mandated to do."[23] Whereas it is the task of the legislature to make and amend the law, it is the task of the police to enforce it.[24]

It is worth noting that the matter of separation has been discussed at great length in regard to judicial decision making. There has been a longstanding controversy between defenders of a mechanical jurisprudence, strict constructionists, who believe that the task of judges is to "discover" the law and then to apply it, and those "activists" who believe that judges have a more creative role to play. That debate has been closely linked to another debate, namely, whether "law" should be understood positivistically as rules promulgated by a duly constituted authority, devoid of normative presumptions, or whether law must be thought of normatively, as embodying not merely formal requirements but as also expressive of or at least subject to certain normative "principles," the latter to be understood as either political or legal. Some members of the positivist group would want to limit judicial discretion to those cases not covered by law, and which can be settled *only* by appealing to extralegal (moral or political) principles.[25] Members of the second group, on the other hand, see judicial discretion as both generated and guided by the normative principles that inform law.[26] In other words, the law, though anchored to the words of a text (or texts), is not a contextless set of assertions, but needs to be understood and applied with an eye to the broader social canvas in which it is embedded. This is not to endorse "Humpty Dumpty,"[27] but it is to oppose a contextless literalism.

I believe that the debate over police discretion has significant parallels

124 John Kleinig

to that concerning judicial discretion, and that the reasons which favor the
latter also favor the former. But two factors are sometimes thought to indicate crucial differences. One concerns publicity. The other concerns competence. With regard to the first, whereas the discretionary decisions of
judges are "public," and therefore open to scrutiny, those of individual
police officers are often "private" and therefore veiled from public scrutiny. This clearly poses a problem, for if police are to be given the power
to make discretionary judgments, they need to be accountable for exercises of that power, and that will be very difficult to achieve if their decisions are made out of public view.[28]

But what I think we should conclude from this—and what is to some
extent manifest in practice—is that police discretion needs to be much more
carefully circumscribed than judicial discretion. We should note what this
means and what it doesn't. Since police discretion is private in the sense
that much of what police do is unsupervised, this will remain the case
whether or not they have the formal power to act in a discretionary manner. So removing, circumscribing, or not granting them the power to make
discretionary judgments about whether or not to arrest will have no effect
on the visibility of their conduct. The question we must ask then is: Is it
better that police not have that formal discretionary power (even though
they may privately act as though they do), or that they be granted a formal
discretionary power, although one that is circumscribed (even though we
may not be able to keep a close eye on how they use it)?

How we answer this question goes to the very heart of our aspirations
for policing. If we see the largely paramilitary structure of contemporary
policing as necessary or desirable, then, whether or not it is possible to provide better supervision, the denial of discretionary authority will better reflect the discipline of police work. But if we wish to encourage greater professionalism in policing, then the answer will most likely be the grant of
discretionary authority, along with efforts to educate police in its wise use.[29]

In addition, we should note that although it may be practically difficult
to give the decisions of individual police officers the same kind of scrutiny
as the decisions of judges, there is nothing to stop the general practice of
police decision making from being publicly reviewed, and nothing to stop
certain general kinds of discretionary decisions from being discussed in a
public forum. Indeed, there often is such discussion when the assumed
discretion is exercised in a way that is thought to be harmful to the legitimate interests of those involved—whether they be citizens who believe that
they have been discriminatorily targeted, suspects who feel they have been
harshly treated, or victims who consider that their legitimate expectations
have not been met. I have no problem with greater publicity in this regard,
and indeed would think it highly desirable.

As noted, police discretion generally is more tightly circumscribed than
judicial discretion, both because of significant court cases that have limited
the way in which police may go about their work and because of internal
constraints that have been placed on police procedures. What Kenneth Culp

Selective Enforcement and the Rule of Law 125

Davis popularized as "administrative rule making" colors much of what they may do.

What I have said in relation to publicity also bears on the question of competence. Judges certainly are more experienced "practitioners" of the law than police. Yet the strategies adopted to make police discretion more public or less arbitrary—the openness of discretionary policies to public discussion, and the promulgation of discretionary guidelines—also serve to deal with the lesser sophistication of police.

But Reiman, I suspect, would oppose the grant of discretion *even were* there to be such discussion, *even were* it to be generally agreed that some such discretion would be utilitarianly desirable, and *even were* discretionary guidelines to be publicly promulgated. His reason for this would probably be that powers that should be separate would here be conjoined, that the checks and balances so important to preserving a free society would here be compromised. But this assumes a separation of powers that has never existed; nor could it have. Judges are appointed by politicians; police chiefs are appointed by mayors; funding for the judicial and executive branches of government is usually determined by the legislative branch; and so on. The question is not so much: What separation can we achieve? but: What of importance is secured by whatever arrangement that exists? What we want and need is not a complete separation of powers but sufficient separation—sufficient, that is, for independence and strength—so that we can ensure that the values of a free society are nurtured and preserved. I do not see any virtue in the separation of powers *in abstracto*, but only insofar as it is able to safeguard citizens against tyranny. If it is possible to do well (even better) with less than complete separation, then there should be no decisive objection to that being so.

Of course it would be different if police acted as though they had the discretionary authority to add to our current stock of laws. That indeed would make the exercise of discretion tyrannical. But what we have in mind in talking of selective enforcement is a lessening of the grip of law, an easing of the burdens it imposes, and this, provided that, as a result, victims do not go unrequited, should not be seen as an instance of tyranny. Indeed, I am arguing almost the opposite, viz., that a form of tyranny (or certainly harshness) may reside in always applying the law as written in the circumstances as given.

Reiman is correct to identify the issue of police discretion as an area of concern. But the appropriate response, I believe, is not to condemn that discretion as a transgression of proper boundaries, but to bring it into the public domain for monitoring and discussion, as necessary.

What I think should be more worrying from Reiman's perspective is some form of departmentally sanctioned discretion—where, for example, a police chief promulgates as departmental policy a qualification of the law as written. Suppose, for example, the law forbids the possession of marijuana, but the police chief informs members of the department that no action should be taken against those who have less than 1 oz. of marijuana in

126 *John Kleinig*

their possession. Here, it might be argued, the chief exercises a form of discretion that effectively "amends" the law as written. Is *this* justifiable?

Although it may not be legally provided for, I do not see why it should not be morally justifiable, though there are clearly problems if a decision of this kind is cloaked in secrecy. Although a public *announcement* might well send the wrong message, it is not too difficult to see how a police department could justify this way of husbanding its resources.

Davis gives the example of a police department that, in the face of a law prohibiting gambling, promulgates to its members the following rule:

> In the absence of special circumstances, we do not ordinarily arrest for social gambling in the absence of (a) a complaint, (b) a profit from the gambling other than gambling winnings, or (c) extraordinarily high stakes. When we receive a complaint, we ordinarily investigate, but for first offenders we may break up social gambling without making arrests.[30]

What is going on here? I think it is reasonable to suggest that the legislature did not have as its focus the weekly game of cards played by a group of friends, where only a few dollars change hands over the course of an evening—although there is nothing in the statute to exclude such activities from its purview.[31] With good reason we might also suggest that were the legislature to have attempted to qualify its prohibition so that activities such as these were excluded from its purview, it would have gotten into legislative quicksand. It could not have used the above wording, since it invites inquiries into the meaning of "special circumstances," "extraordinarily," and "ordinarily," and even then is expressed permissively. As Reiman recognizes, human behavior and the circumstances in which it occurs are extraordinarily diverse, and good legislative practice usually involves the drawing of relatively bright lines.[32] My contention is that a police organization that has one ear open to the legislature and one to the community will be able to develop reasonable guidelines for the exercise of discretion.[33]

The foregoing case also touches upon another point that often guides police discretion: the presence or absence of a complaint. Of course, the presence or absence of a complainant is not a decisive feature in deciding whether to go ahead with an arrest, for sometimes victims refuse to lay a complaint for reasons that have nothing to do with the seriousness of a situation.[34] Yet, in the absence of a complaint that would assist in any case for prosecution, arrest may achieve very little. So, although police may have a legally sufficient reason for making an arrest, they may choose not to arrest if the charges are minor and the case will otherwise have a very uncertain future. Scarce resources are expended that might have been more productively used elsewhere.

Discrimination

It is the possibility of using discretion in a discriminatory way that

Selective Enforcement and the Rule of Law 127

troubles me most. It troubles me, not just because of the *possibility* of discretion being exercised discriminatorily, but because *appeals to discretionary power have often been used* to cloak discrimination. Yet we may wonder whether removal of whatever assumed discretionary competence that police have with regard to arrest will resolve this problem, or even go any way toward alleviating it.

As I indicated earlier, the unsupervised nature of much police work will not change just as a result of some change in policy with respect to arrest/nonarrest. If police deviate from discretionary guidelines by claiming that they are only exercising a discretion they have, they will just as readily claim that they have or do not have legally clear grounds for arrest when they act discriminatorily under a full enforcement policy. The poor and ethnically different will still tend to attract disproportionate attention, and not just because they may be in violation of the law more frequently. For the source of discrimination is not to be found in the power to use discretion but in the disposition to act with prejudice, and there is probably no greater difficulty involved in showing that guidelines for exercising discretion were ignored than in showing whether legally sufficient grounds for arrest were present.

Once again, to the extent that it is possible, the best counter to poorly or discriminatorily exercised discretion is not to outlaw it but to reeducate its users and to require that, where decisions or patterns develop that appear discriminatory, they be justified. Given the absence of supervision, this will not guarantee anything, but it may function to deter the development of entrenched practices of discrimination. Ultimately, the issue is not one of having or not having full enforcement laws. It is a matter, rather, of police who want to make fair decisions.

Improper Leverage

Reiman is concerned that discretionary authority will be used in a tyrannical fashion. In particular, he is concerned that the additional power that discretion to arrest gives to police beyond their power to arrest enables them to coerce people into doing things that they would otherwise be unwilling to do. In other words, it allows for the tyrannical exercise of power. He instances the cooption of someone as an informant in exchange for nonarrest.[35]

Why does this constitute a tyrannical use of power? Reiman writes that

> if we are not ready to endorse a law requiring all citizens to give the police whatever information they want, then such use of discretion as leverage to get information amounts to allowing police to exercise a power over some citizens that we would not allow them to exercise over all.[36]

One thing to note about this criticism is that it is leveled at a particu-

128 *John Kleinig*

lar use of discretion, and not at selective enforcement as such. The police
officer who allows a speeding motorist to go unsummonsed after a stern
reprimand about the dangers of speeding is not exploiting that power to
gain something to which he would not otherwise have had access. We
could, therefore, forbid police from using their power as leverage without denying them the power to enforce the law selectively.

So why does Reiman use this argument? It seems to me that the importance of the argument is that it gives *some* plausibility to the idea that
the power not to arrest might contribute to tyranny. It is necessary to
give plausibility to that claim because, at first blush, the power not to
arrest those who have done that which would justify arrest appears to
be the very antithesis of a *tyrannical* use of power. I am sure that the
motorist who gets off with just a warning or reprimand feels relieved
rather than oppressed.[37] Tyranny would be involved were the officer to
take the view that even though the speed limit was 55 mph, he would
ticket people who were traveling only at 50 mph. Or because the color of
their car was displeasing to him. Those would be tyrannical police acts.
So the additional leverage that a police officer may gain as a result of his
discretionary authority is necessary to give some credence to the idea
that it is a tyrannical power.

But as far as I know, defenders of police discretion have not argued
that police should be able to impose *greater* burdens on others than the
law allows. The argument for selective enforcement is always an argument that police should be permitted, in appropriate circumstances, to
impose less than a full enforcement policy would dictate.

Maybe a greater burden could be imposed in cases in which informants are coopted. But I do not think it necessary that this should occur.
Note that there is a considerable difference between there being a law
requiring that we give police whatever information they want, and the
choice offered to offenders to avoid arrest by becoming informants. In
the first case, the threat of arrest attends the refusal to provide information per se. In the second case, the threat of arrest attends the violation of
some other law, but may be removed if a person is willing to provide
information. To the person in the latter situation, becoming an informant
may represent an acceptable bargain and, if there are no significant victims involved, the arrangement may represent good social value. If the
person does not wish to become an informant, then the arrest that follows will be sufficiently justified by the initial offense, and does not need
additional support from the refusal to provide information.

Most of us are aware that police frequently gain informants by means
such as these. Yet for the most part their use evokes from us no angered
or resentful response. Reiman takes our reaction to manifest no more
than the lack of respect we have for drug dealers and prostitutes, and
our acquiescence in their being treated "in a tyrannical fashion."[38] But I
think we need to distinguish two different kinds of case. One is the situation in which the police officer says something like: "If you are pre-

Selective Enforcement and the Rule of Law 129

pared to give me a certain piece of information, I won't take you in." The other is where the officer uses arrest as a *continuing threat* in order to have the person become an ongoing informant. In such cases, where the offender might be looking at a few years in prison, and becoming an informant has significant risks and no clear endpoint, the arrangement may well be seriously exploitative of a vulnerable person.

What Reiman establishes, I think, is that the discretion not to arrest can be easily misused, and needs to be monitored. Officers who make use of informants should be required to submit for approval the uses they make of them and the conditions under which they retain their services.[39]

Conclusion

It is important that a free society be governed by rules, not men. But the adherence to rules need not be mechanical, for the rules, apart from curbing governmental arbitrariness, also serve important social purposes beyond themselves. If those wider purposes are not being served, then either the rules should be amended or, if that poses problems, there should be granted to those who administer them the power to make discretionary judgments concerning their application and enforcement. Provided that those who make such judgments can be held accountable for them, it should be possible to secure a greater just freedom than would be the case were no such discretion permitted.

An earlier version of this paper was read at the International Perspectives on Crime and Justice Conference in Dublin, June 21, 1996. In addition, I have benefited from the comments of William Heffernan, Tziporah Kasachkoff, Steve Bradley Read, and Jeffrey Reiman.

Notes

[1] Jeffrey Reiman, "Is Police Discretion Justified in a Free Society?" in John Kleinig (ed), *Handled With Discretion: Ethical Issues in Police Decision Making*, Lanham, MD: Rowman & Littlefield, 1996, p. 71. I shall assume that what Reiman has in mind includes not only arrest but also other formal procedures (citation, summons) that might be provided for as responses to particular breaches, and that what he proposes to exclude are departmental policies of nonenforcement, or individual decisions not to enforce (by ignoring or merely reprimanding).

[2] A powerful statement can be found in Ronald J Allen's critique of Kenneth Culp Davis's *Police Discretion*: "The Police and Substantive Rulemaking: Reconciling Principle and Expediency," *University of Pennsylvania Law Review*, 125 (1976), pp. 62- 118, and his rejoinder to Davis's reply: "The Police and Substantive Rulemaking: A Brief Rejoinder," *University of Pennsylvania Law Review*, 125 (1977), pp. 1172-81. Davis's critique, however, is primarily legal, and only secondarily philosophical. Cf also Joseph Goldstein, "Police Discretion Not to Invoke the Criminal Process: Low Visibility Decisions in the Administration of Justice," *Yale Law Journal*, 69 (1960), 543-94.

[3] Reiman, "Is Police Discretion Justified in a Free Society?" p 74.

[4] Ibid, pp. 76-77.

[5] Ibid, p. 78.

130 *John Kleinig*

⁶ Ibid, p. 71.

⁷ James Q Wilson, *Varieties of Police Behavior: The Management of Law and Order in Eight Communities*, Cambridge, MA: Harvard University Press, 1968, p. 16.

⁸ Ibid Wilson also allows that "some or all of these examples of disorderly behavior involve infractions of the law" (ibid., p. 17).

⁹ Ibid, p. 17.

¹⁰ Though the phrase was coined by John Adams (*Constitution of Massachusetts: Declaration of Rights*, Art 30 [1780]).

¹¹ Aristotle, *Politics*, Bk 3, Ch. 16.

¹² See, for example, Friedrich von Hayek, *The Road to Serfdom*, Chicago: University of Chicago press, 1944, p 54.

¹³ Michael S Moore, " A Natural Law Theory of Interpretation," *Southern California Law Review*, 58 (1985), pp. 313-18.

¹⁴ Locke, *Second Treatise of Civil Government*, quoted by Reiman on p 77.

¹⁵ Henry Jordan's famous remark regarding Vince Lombardi—"he treated us all the same, like dogs"—captures the problem of formalism

¹⁶ See Allen, "The Police and Substantive Rulemaking: Reconciling Principle and Expediency," pp 71-72.

¹⁷ We should not lose sight of the distinctively North American character of this argument For the British police, a limited selective enforcement is well entrenched in the legal tradition. It is explicitly acknowledged in the judgment of Lord Devlin in *Shaaban bin Hussein v. Chong Fook Kam* (1969) 3 AER 1626, and in the *obiter* of Lord Denning in *R. v. Metropolitan Police Commissioner ex parte Blackburn* 1968 2 WLR 893, at 902, and again in *R. v. Metropolitan Police Commissioner ex parte Blackburn* 1973 QB 241, at 254. Cf. also *Arrowsmith v. Jenkins* 1963 QB. It is also explicitly provided for by the Police and Criminal Evidence Act in cases where a "reasonable suspicion" exists that a person has committed an offense.

¹⁸ Reiman, "Is Police Discretion Justified in a Free Society?" p 79.

¹⁹ There has, for example, been some public concern expressed about the police issuing only warnings in domestic dispute and sexual abuse cases, presumably out of a desire not to disrupt families See, for example, James J. Fyfe, "Structuring Police Discretion," in Kleinig (ed.), *Handled with Discretion*, pp. 183-205; anon., "Police forces allow rapists to go free with a caution," *The Times* (London), Feb. 18, 1996, pp. 1, 2.

²⁰ For example, the IACP "Police Code of Conduct" includes among the fundamental duties of a police officer: "serving the community; safeguarding lives and property; protecting the innocent; keeping the peace; and ensuring the rights of all to liberty, equality and justice" Then, under the heading "Discretion," it notes *inter alia* that "it is important to remember that a timely word of advice rather than arrest . . . can be a more effective means of achieving a desired end."

²¹ It might also be argued that if "the people" were really serious about full enforcement they would also provide the resources for full enforcement But since they do not provide the resources for full enforcement, they could not be serious about it. However, I do not think that this argument will work. Law enforcement has to be weighed against other social priorities, and the people's representatives might reasonably allocate a lesser amount of resources than will be sufficient for full enforcement *while yet believing that, within the limitations of those resources, full enforcement should be practiced.*

²² Carl Klockars offers a whole brace of such reasons in *The Idea of Police*, Beverly Hills, CA: Sage, 1985, p 97.

²³ Reiman, "Is Police Discretion Justified in a Free Society?" p 80.

²⁴ Some legal regimes are quite explicit about this However, I take it that the basis for the doctrine is to be found in political or moral theory and not in the existence of legislation that affirms it.

²⁵ HL.A. Hart represents a notable example. See *The Concept of Law*, Oxford: Clarendon, 1961.

²⁶ Ronald Dworkin sees the principles as essentially political See his *Taking Rights Seriously*, London: Methuen, 1967; Steven J. Burton believes that the background prin-

Selective Enforcement and the Rule of Law 131

ciples are essentially legal. See his *Judging in Good Faith*, Cambridge: Cambridge University Press, 1992.

27   "' . . There's glory for you!'
     'I don't know what you mean by "glory,"' Alice said.
     Humpty Dumpty smiled contemptuously. 'Of course you don't – till I tell you. I meant "there's a nice knock-down argument for you!"'
     'But "glory" doesn't mean "a nice knock-down argument,"' Alice objected.
     'When *I* use a word,' Humpty Dumpty said, in rather a scornful tone, it means just what I choose it to mean – neither more nor less.'
     'The question is,' said Alice, 'whether you *can* make words mean so many different things'
     'The question is,' said Humpty Dumpty, 'which is to be master—that's all.'"
                                  Lewis Carroll, *Through the Looking-Glass*, Ch. 6.

28 The problem is said to be exacerbated by the fact that whereas judges are highly educated and experienced practitioners, those who will exercise most discretion in policing will be those with least training and experience

29 It is at least arguable that efforts being made to loosen the paramilitary structure of policing, the development of more "educative" training systems, and attempts to attract recruits with higher educational levels, signal a publicly accepted commitment to policing that acknowledges the need for wise discretion

30 Kenneth Culp Davis, *Police Discretion*, St Paul, MN: West, 1975, pp 141-42. Reiman would probably see nonarrest in such cases as a legitimate expression of the police order-maintenance function. However, I do not see any significant difference between this case and one in which a police department chooses not to enforce an anti-drug law in cases where small quantities of marijuana are involved, or a can of beer is being consumed in public.

31 Allen considers it out of place to appeal to an alleged "purpose" of a statute as a basis for limiting its scope The legislature may have had a number of purposes in mind, and a limiting "interpretation" that takes one purpose into account may "amend" the statute with respect to other "conceivable" purposes ("The Police and Substantive Rulemaking: Reconciling Principle and Expediency," p. 80). But it is not enough that the purposes be merely "conceivable." We need some reason to think that the other purposes would have been legitimately satisfied by a rule of the kind in question.

32 We need to remember that the drafting of legislation is through and through *political*, and that legislators expect that those charged with enforcement of the law will use good judgment in acting on it

33 In his response to Davis Allen complains that such cases are plausible (to the extent that they are) only because, as it happens, the police department makes a commonsensical decision There is nothing, however, to prevent a chief from deciding not to prosecute rapists when the victim has been dressed "provocatively" ("The Police and Substantive Rulemaking: A Brief Rejoinder," p. 1176). But of course there is everything to prevent *that* assumption of discretionary power—there are victims who will be unrequited and as public that is almost certain to protest. Poor discretionary guidelines may be instituted, but if they are open to scrutiny they are likely to be modified or removed.

34 Domestic disputes are a good example

35 Reiman, "Is Police Discretion Justified in a Free Society?" p 79.

36 Ibid

37 One of Allen's complaints against police "rulemaking" is that the discretionary rules are not likely to come up for public or judicial scrutiny And the reason for that is that "no individual will be affected adversely by such rules" ("The Police and Substantive Rulemaking: Reconciling Principle and Expediency," p. 85). The charge that they are tyrannical needs to be made out.

38 Ibid In many such cases I would think it would more likely be exploitative than tyrannical.

39 Many police departments do in fact have informant policies in place

Part III
Police Culture

[12]

A Sketch of the Policeman's "Working Personality"

Jerome H. Skolnick

A RECURRENT theme of the sociology of occupations is the effect of a man's work on his outlook on the world.[1] Doctors, janitors, lawyers, and industrial workers develop distinctive ways of perceiving and responding to their environment. Here we shall concentrate on analyzing certain outstanding elements in the police milieu, danger, authority, and efficiency, as they combine to generate distinctive cognitive and behavioral responses in police: a "working personality." Such an analysis does not suggest that all police are alike in "working personality," but that there are distinctive cognitive tendencies in police as an occupational grouping. Some of these may be found in other occupations sharing similar problems. So far as exposure to danger is concerned, the policeman may be likened to the soldier. His problems as an authority bear a certain similarity to those of the schoolteacher, and the pressures he feels to prove himself efficient are not unlike those felt by the industrial worker. The combination of these elements, however, is unique to the policeman. Thus, the police, as a result of combined features of their social situation, tend to develop ways of looking at the world distinctive to themselves, cognitive lenses through which to see situations and events. The strength of the lenses may be weaker or stronger depending on certain conditions, but they are ground on a similar axis.

[1] For previous contributions in this area, see the following: Ely Chinoy, *Automobile Workers and the American Dream* (Garden City: Doubleday and Company, Inc., 1955); Charles R. Walker and Robert H. Guest, *The Man on the Assembly Line* (Cambridge: Harvard University Press, 1952); Everett C. Hughes, "Work and the Self," in his *Men and Their Work* (Glencoe, Illinois: The Free Press, 1958), pp. 42–55; Harold L. Wilensky, *Intellectuals in Labor Unions: Organizational Pressures on Professional Roles* (Glencoe, Illinois: The Free Press, 1956); Wilensky, "Varieties of Work Experience," in Henry Borow (ed.), *Man in a World at Work* (Boston: Houghton Mifflin Company, 1964), pp. 125–154; Louis Kriesberg, "The Retail Furrier: Concepts of Security and Success," *American Journal of Sociology*, 57 (March, 1952), 478–485; Waldo Burchard, "Role Conflicts of Military Chaplains," *American Sociological Review*, 19 (October, 1954), 528–535; Howard S. Becker and Blanche Geer, "The Fate of Idealism in Medical School," *American Sociological Review*, 23 (1958), 50–56; and Howard S. Becker and Anselm L. Strauss, "Careers, Personality, and Adult Socialization," *American Journal of Sociology*, 62 (November, 1956), 253–363.

Analysis of the policeman's cognitive propensities is necessary to understand the practical dilemma faced by police required to maintain order under a democratic rule of law. We have discussed earlier how essential a conception of order is to the resolution of this dilemma. It was suggested that the paramilitary character of police organization naturally leads to a high evaluation of similarity, routine, and predictability. Our intention is to emphasize features of the policeman's environment interacting with the paramilitary police organization to generate a "working personality." Such an intervening concept should aid in explaining how the social environment of police affects their capacity to respond to the rule of law.

We also stated earlier that emphasis would be placed on the division of labor in the police department, that "operational law enforcement" could not be understood outside these special work assignments. It is therefore important to explain how the hypothesis emphasizing the generalizability of the policeman's "working personality" is compatible with the idea that police division of labor is an important analytic dimension for understanding "operational law enforcement." Compatibility is evident when one considers the different levels of analysis at which the hypotheses are being developed. Janowitz states, for example, that the military profession is more than an occupation; it is a "style of life" because the occupational claims over one's daily existence extend well beyond official duties. He is quick to point out that any profession performing a crucial "life and death" task, such as medicine, the ministry, or the police, develops such claims.[2] A conception like "working personality" of police should be understood to suggest an analytic breadth similar to that of "style of life." That is, just as the professional behavior of military officers with similar "styles of life" may differ notably depending upon whether they command an infantry battalion or participate in the work of an intelligence unit, so too does the professional behavior of police officers with similar "working personalities" vary with their assignments.

The policeman's "working personality" is most highly developed in his constabulary role of the man on the beat. For analytical purposes that role is sometimes regarded as an enforcement speciality, but in this general discussion of policemen as they comport themselves while working, the uniformed "cop" is seen as the foundation for the policeman's working personality. There is a sound organizational basis for making this assumption. The police, unlike the military, draw no caste distinc-

[2] Morris Janowitz, *The Professional Soldier: A Social and Political Portrait* (New York: The Free Press of Glencoe, 1964), p. 175.

tion in socialization, even though their order of ranked titles approximates the military's. Thus, one cannot join a local police department as, for instance, a lieutenant, as a West Point graduate joins the army. Every officer of rank must serve an apprenticeship as a patrolman. This feature of police organization means that the constabulary role is the primary one for all police officers, and that whatever the special requirements of roles in enforcement specialties, they are carried out with a common background of constabulary experience.

The process by which this "personality" is developed may be summarized: the policeman's role contains two principal variables, danger and authority, which should be interpreted in the light of a "constant" pressure to appear efficient.[3] The element of danger seems to make the policeman especially attentive to signs indicating a potential for violence and lawbreaking. As a result, the policeman is generally a "suspicious" person. Furthermore, the character of the policeman's work makes him less desirable as a friend, since norms of friendship implicate others in his work. Accordingly, the element of danger isolates the policeman socially from that segment of the citizenry which he regards as symbolically dangerous and also from the conventional citizenry with whom he identifies.

The element of authority reinforces the element of danger in isolating the policeman. Typically, the policeman is required to enforce laws representing puritanical morality, such as those prohibiting drunkenness, and also laws regulating the flow of public activity, such as traffic laws. In these situations the policeman directs the citizenry, whose typical response denies recognition of his authority, and stresses his obligation to respond to danger. The kind of man who responds well to danger, however, does not normally subscribe to codes of puritanical morality. As a result, the policeman is unusually liable to the charge of hypocrisy. That the whole civilian world is an audience for the policeman further promotes police isolation and, in consequence, solidarity. Finally, danger undermines the judicious use of authority. Where danger, as in Britain, is relatively less, the judicious application of authority is facilitated. Hence, British police may appear to be somewhat more attached to the rule of law, when, in fact, they may appear so because they face less danger, and they are as a rule better skilled than American police in creating the appearance of conformity to procedural regulations.

[3] By no means does such an analysis suggest there are no individual or group differences among police. On the contrary, most of this study emphasizes differences, endeavoring to relate these to occupational specialities in police departments. This chapter, however, explores similarities rather than differences, attempting to account for the policeman's general disposition to perceive and to behave in certain ways.

THE SYMBOLIC ASSAILANT AND POLICE CULTURE

In attempting to understand the policeman's view of the world, it is useful to raise a more general question: What are the conditions under which police, as authorities, may be threatened? [4] To answer this, we must look to the situation of the policeman in the community. One attribute of many characterizing the policeman's role stands out: the policeman is required to respond to assaults against persons and property. When a radio call reports an armed robbery and gives a description of the man involved, every policeman, regardless of assignment, is responsible for the criminal's apprehension. The *raison d'être* of the policeman and the criminal law, the underlying collectively held moral sentiments which justify penal sanctions, arises ultimately and most clearly from the threat of violence and the possibility of danger to the community. Police who "lobby" for severe narcotics laws, for instance, justify their position on grounds that the addict is a harbinger of danger since, it is maintained, he requires one hundred dollars a day to support his habit, and he must steal to get it. Even though the addict is not typically a violent criminal, criminal penalties for addiction are supported on grounds that he may become one.

The policeman, because his work requires him to be occupied continually with potential violence, develops a perceptual shorthand to identify certain kinds of people as symbolic assailants, that is, as persons who use gesture, language, and attire that the policeman has come to recognize as a prelude to violence. This does not mean that violence by the symbolic assailant is necessarily predictable. On the contrary, the policeman responds to the vague indication of danger suggested by appearance.[5] Like the animals of the experimental psychologist, the po-

---

[4] William Westley was the first to raise such questions about the police, when he inquired into the conditions under which police are violent. Whatever merit this analysis has, it owes much to his prior insights, as all subsequent sociological studies of the police must. See his "Violence and the Police," *American Journal of Sociology*, **59** (July, 1953), 34–41; also his unpublished Ph.D. dissertation *The Police: A Sociological Study of Law, Custom, and Morality*, University of Chicago, Department of Sociology, 1951.

[5] Something of the flavor of the policeman's attitude toward the symbolic assailant comes across in a recent article by a police expert. In discussing the problem of selecting subjects for field interrogation, the author writes:

A. Be suspicious. This is a healthy police attitude, but it should be controlled and not too obvious.
B. Look for the unusual.
  1. Persons who do not "belong" where they are observed.

46   *Justice without Trial*

liceman finds the threat of random damage more compelling than a predetermined and inevitable punishment.

Nor, to qualify for the status of symbolic assailant, need an individual ever have used violence. A man backing out of a jewelry store with a gun in one hand and jewelry in the other would qualify even if the gun were a toy and he had never in his life fired a real pistol. To the policeman in the situation, the man's personal history is momentarily immaterial. There is only one relevant sign: a gun signifying danger. Similarly, a young man may suggest the threat of violence to the policeman by his manner of walking or "strutting," the insolence in the demeanor being registered by the policeman as a possible preamble to later attack.[6] Signs vary from area to area, but a youth dressed in a black leather jacket and

   2. Automobiles which do not "look right."
   3. Businesses opened at odd hours, or not according to routine or custom.
C. Subjects who should be subjected to field interrogations.
   1. Suspicious persons known to the officer from previous arrests, field interrogations, and observations.
   2. Emaciated appearing alcoholics and narcotics users who invariably turn to crime to pay for cost of habit.
   3. Person who fits description of wanted suspect as described by radio, teletype, daily bulletins.
   4. Any person observed in the immediate vicinity of a crime very recently committed or reported as "in progress."
   5. Known trouble-makers near large gatherings.
   6. Persons who attempt to avoid or evade the officer.
   7. Exaggerated unconcern over contact with the officer.
   8. Visibly "rattled" when near the policeman.
   9. Unescorted women or young girls in public places, particularly at night in such places as cafes, bars, bus and train depots, or street corners.
  10. "Lovers" in an industrial area (make good lookouts).
  11. Persons who loiter about places where children play.
  12. Solicitors or peddlers in a residential neighborhood.
  13. Loiterers around public rest rooms.
  14. Lone male sitting in car adjacent to schoolground with newspaper or book in his lap.
  15. Lone male sitting in car near shopping center who pays unusual amount of attention to women, sometimes continuously manipulating rearview mirror to avoid direct eye contact.
  16. Hitchhikers.
  17. Person wearing coat on hot days.
  18. Car with mismatched hub caps, or dirty car with clean license plate (or vice versa).
  19. Uniformed "deliverymen" with no merchandise or truck.
  20. Many others. How about your own personal experiences?

From Thomas F. Adams, "Field Interrogation," *Police*, March–April, 1963, 28.
  [6] See Irving Piliavin and Scott Briar, "Police Encounters with Juveniles," *American Journal of Sociology*, 70 (September, 1964), 206–214.

motorcycle boots is sure to draw at least a suspicious glance from a policeman.

Policemen themselves do not necessarily emphasize the peril associated with their work when questioned directly, and may even have well-
developed strategies of denial. The element of danger is so integral to
the policeman's work that explicit recognition might induce emotional
barriers to work performance. Thus, one patrol officer observed that
more police have been killed and injured in automobile accidents in the
past ten years than from gunfire. Although his assertion is true, he neglected to mention that the police are the only peacetime occupational
group with a systematic record of death and injury from gunfire and
other weaponry. Along these lines, it is interesting that of the two hundred and twenty-four working Westville policemen (not including the
sixteen juvenile policemen) responding to a question about which assignment they would like most to have in the police department,[7] 50
per cent selected the job of detective, an assignment combining elements of apparent danger and initiative. The next category was adult
street work, that is, patrol and traffic (37 per cent). Eight per cent selected the juvenile squad,[8] and only 4 per cent selected administrative
work. Not a single policeman chose the job of jail guard. Although these
findings do not control for such factors as prestige, they suggest that
confining and routine jobs are rated low on the hierarchy of police
preferences, even though such jobs are least dangerous. Thus, the policeman may well, as a personality, enjoy the possibility of danger, especially its associated excitement, even though he may at the same time be
fearful of it. Such "inconsistency" is easily understood. Freud has by
now made it an axiom of personality theory that logical and emotional
consistency are by no means the same phenomenon.

However complex the motives aroused by the element of danger, its
consequences for sustaining police culture are unambiguous. This element requires him, like the combat soldier, the European Jew, the
South African (white or black), to live in a world straining toward
duality, and suggesting danger when "they" are perceived. Consequently, it is in the nature of the policeman's situation that his concep-

[7] A questionnaire was given to all policemen in operating divisions of the police
force: patrol, traffic, vice control, and all detectives. The questionnaire was administered at police line-ups over a period of three days, mainly by the author but also
by some of the police personnel themselves. Before the questionnaire was administered, it was circulated to and approved by the policemen's welfare association.

[8] Indeed, the journalist Paul Jacobs, who has ridden with the Westville juvenile
police as part of his own work on poverty, observed in a personal communication
that juvenile police appear curiously drawn to seek out dangerous situations, as if
juvenile work without danger is degrading.

tion of order emphasize regularity and predictability. It is, therefore, a conception shaped by persistent *suspicion*. The English "copper," often portrayed as a courteous, easy-going, rather jolly sort of chap, on the one hand, or as a devil-may-care adventurer, on the other, is differently described by Colin MacInnes:

> The true copper's dominant characteristic, if the truth be known, is neither those daring nor vicious qualities that are sometimes attributed to him by friend or enemy, but an ingrained conservatism, and almost desperate love of the conventional. It is untidiness, disorder, the unusual, that a copper disapproves of most of all: far more, even than of crime which is merely a professional matter. Hence his profound dislike of people loitering in streets, dressing extravagantly, speaking with exotic accents, being strange, weak, eccentric, or simply any rare minority—of their doing, in fact, anything that cannot be safely predicted.[9]

Policemen are indeed specifically *trained* to be suspicious, to perceive events or changes in the physical surroundings that indicate the occurrence or probability of disorder. A former student who worked as a patrolman in a suburban New York police department describes this aspect of the policeman's assessment of the unusual:

> The time spent cruising one's sector or walking one's beat is not wasted time, though it can become quite routine. During this time, the most important thing for the officer to do is notice the *normal*. He must come to know the people in his area, their habits, their automobiles and their friends. He must learn what time the various shops close, how much money is kept on hand on different nights, what lights are usually left on, which houses are vacant . . . only then can he decide what persons or cars under what circumstances warrant the appellation "suspicious." [10]

The individual policeman's "suspiciousness" does not hang on whether he has personally undergone an experience that could objectively be described as hazardous. Personal experience of this sort is not the key to the psychological importance of exceptionality. Each, as he routinely carries out his work, will experience situations that threaten to become dangerous. Like the American Jew who contributes to "defense" organizations such as the Anti-Defamation League in response to Nazi brutalities he has never experienced personally, the policeman identifies with his fellow cop who has been beaten, perhaps fatally, by a gang of young thugs.

[9] Colin McInnes, *Mr. Love and Justice* (London: New English Library, 1962), p. 74.

[10] Peter J. Connell, "Handling of Complaints by Police," unpublished paper for course in Criminal Procedure, Yale Law School, Fall, 1961.

A Sketch of the Policeman's "Working Personality"   49

SOCIAL ISOLATION

The patrolman in Westville, and probably in most communities, has come to identify the black man with danger. James Baldwin vividly expresses the isolation of the ghetto policeman:

. . . The only way to police a ghetto is to be oppressive. None of the Police Commissioner's men, even with the best will in the world, have any way of understanding the lives led by the people they swagger about in twos and threes controlling. Their very presence is an insult, and it would be, even if they spent their entire day feeding gumdrops to children. They represent the force of the white world, and that world's criminal profit and ease, to keep the black man corraled up here, in his place. The badge, the gun in the holster, and the swinging club make vivid what will happen should his rebellion become overt . . .
It is hard, on the other hand, to blame the policeman, blank, good-natured, thoughtless, and insuperably innocent, for being such a perfect representative of the people he serves. He, too, believes in good intentions and is astounded and offended when they are not taken for the deed. He has never, himself, done anything for which to be hated—which of us has? and yet he is facing, daily and nightly, people who would gladly see him dead, and he knows it. There is no way for him not to know it: there are few things under heaven more unnerving than the silent, accumulating contempt and hatred of a people. He moves through Harlem, therefore, like an occupying soldier in a bitterly hostile country; which is precisely what, and where he is, and is the reason he walks in twos and threes.[11]

While Baldwin's observations on police-Negro relations cannot be disputed seriously, there is greater social distance between police and "civilians" in general regardless of their color than Baldwin considers. Thus, Colin MacInnes has his English hero, Mr. Justice, explaining:

. . . The story is all coppers are just civilians like anyone else, living among them not in barracks like on the Continent, but you and I know that's just a legend for mugs. We *are* cut off: we're *not* like everyone else. Some civilians fear us and play up to us, some dislike us and keep out of our way but no one —well, very few indeed—accepts us as just ordinary like them. In one sense, dear, we're just like hostile troops occupying an enemy country. And say what you like, at times that makes us lonely.[12]

MacInnes' observation suggests that by not introducing a white control group, Baldwin has failed to see that the policeman may not get on

[11] James Baldwin, *Nobody Knows My Name* (New York: Dell Publishing Company, 1962), pp. 65–67.
[12] McInnes, *op. cit.*, p. 20.

well with anybody regardless (to use the hackneyed phrase) of race, creed, or national origin. Policemen whom one knows well often express their sense of isolation from the public as a whole, not just from those who fail to share their color. Westville police were asked, for example, to rank the most serious problems police have. The category most frequently selected was not racial problems, but some form of public relations: lack of respect for the police, lack of cooperation in enforcement of law, lack of understanding of the requirements of police work.[13] One respondent answered:

As a policeman my most serious problem is impressing on the general public just how difficult and necessary police service is to all. There seems to be an attitude of "law is important, but it applies to my neighbor—not to me."

Of the two hundred and eighty-two Westville policemen who rated the prestige police work receives from others, 70 per cent ranked it as only fair or poor, while less than 2 per cent ranked it as "excellent" and another 29 per cent as "good." Similarly, in Britain, two-thirds of a sample of policemen interviewed by a Royal Commission stated difficulties in making friends outside the force; of those interviewed 58 per cent thought members of the public to be reserved, suspicious, and con-

[13] Respondents were asked "Anybody who knows anything about police work knows that police face a number of problems. Would you please state—in order—what you consider to be the two most serious problems police have." On the basis of a number of answers, the writer and J. Richard Woodworth devised a set of categories. Then Woodworth classified each response into one of the categories (see table below). When a response did not seem clear, he consulted with the writer. No attempt was made to independently check Woodworth's classification because the results are used impressionistically, and do not test a hypothesis. It may be, for instance, that "relations with public" is sometimes used to indicate racial problems, and vice versa. "Racial problems" include only those answers having specific reference to race. The categories and results were as follows:

Westville Police Ranking of Number One Problem Faced by Police

	Number	*Per Cent*
Relations with public	74	26
Racial problems and demonstrations	66	23
Juvenile delinquents and delinquency	23	8
Unpleasant police tasks	23	8
Lack of cooperation from authorities (D.A., legislature, courts)	20	7
Internal departmental problems	17	6
Irregular life of policeman	5	2
No answer or other answer	56	20
	284	100

strained in conversation; and 12 per cent attributed such difficulties to the requirement that policemen be selective in associations and behave circumspectly.[14]

A Westville policeman related the following incident:

Several months after I joined the force, my wife and I used to be socially active with a crowd of young people, mostly married, who gave a lot of parties where there was drinking and dancing, and we enjoyed it. I've never forgotten, though, an incident that happened on one Fourth of July party. Everybody had been drinking, there was a lot of talking, people were feeling boisterous, and some kid there—he must have been twenty or twenty-two—threw a firecracker that hit my wife in the leg and burned her. I didn't know exactly what to do—punch the guy in the nose, bawl him out, just forget it. Anyway, I couldn't let it pass, so I walked over to him and told him he ought to be careful. He began to rise up at me, and when he did, somebody yelled, "Better watch out, he's a cop." I saw everybody standing there, and I could feel they were all against me and for the kid, even though he had thrown the firecracker at my wife. I went over to the host and said it was probably better if my wife and I left because a fight would put a damper on the party. Actually, I'd hoped he would ask the kid to leave, since the kid had thrown the firecracker. But he didn't so we left. After that incident, my wife and I stopped going around with that crowd, and decided that if we were going to go to parties where there was to be drinking and boisterousness, we weren't going to be the only police people there.

Another reported that he seeks to overcome his feelings of isolation by concealing his police identity:

I try not to bring my work home with me, and that includes my social life. I like the men I work with, but I think it's better that my family doesn't become a police family. I try to put my police work into the background, and try not to let people know I'm a policeman. Once you do, you can't have normal relations with them.[15]

Although the policeman serves a people who are, as Baldwin says, the established society, the white society, these people do not make him feel accepted. As a result, he develops resources within his own world to combat social rejection.

[14] Royal Commission on the Police, 1962, Appendix IV to *Minutes of Evidence*, cited in Michael Banton, *The Policeman in the Community* (London: Tavistock Publications, 1964), p. 198.

[15] Similarly, Banton found Scottish police officers attempting to conceal their occupation when on holiday. He quotes one as saying: "If someone asks my wife "What does your husband do?", I've told her to say, "He's a clerk," and that's the way it went because she found that being a policeman's wife—well, it wasn't quite a stigma, she didn't feel cut off, but that a sort of invisible wall was up for conversation purposes when a policeman was there" (p. 198).

POLICE SOLIDARITY

All occupational groups share a measure of inclusiveness and identification. People are brought together simply by doing the same work and having similar career and salary problems. As several writers have noted, however, police show an unusually high degree of occupational solidarity.[16] It is true that the police have a common employer and wear a uniform at work, but so do doctors, milkmen, and bus drivers. Yet it is doubtful that these workers have so close knit an occupation or so similar an outlook on the world as do police. Set apart from the conventional world, the policeman experiences an exceptionally strong tendency to find his social identity within his occupational milieu.

Compare the police with another skilled craft. In a study of the International Typographical Union, the authors asked printers the first names and jobs of their three closest friends. Of the 1,236 friends named by the 412 men in their sample, 35 per cent were printers.[17] Similarly, among the Westville police, of 700 friends listed by 250 respondents, 35 per cent were policemen. The policemen, however, were far more active than printers in occupational social activities. Of the printers, more than half (54 per cent) had never participated in any union clubs, benefit societies, teams, or organizations composed mostly of printers, or attended any printers' social affairs in the past 5 years. Of the Westville police, only 16 per cent had failed to attend a single police banquet or dinner in the past *year* (as contrasted with the printers' *5 years*); and of the 234 men answering this question, 54 per cent had attended 3 or more such affairs *during the past year.*

---

[16] In addition to Banton, William Westley and James Q. Wilson have noted this characteristic of police. See Westley, *op. cit.*, p. 294; Wilson, "The Police and Their Problems: A Theory," *Public Policy*, 12 (1963), 189–216.

[17] S. M. Lipset, Martin H. Trow, and James S. Coleman, *Union Democracy* (New York: Anchor Books, 1962), p. 123. A complete comparison is as follows:

Closest Friends of Printers and Police, by Occupation

	Printers N = 1236 (%)	Police N = 700 (%)
Same occupation	35	35
Professionals, business executives, and independent business owners	21	30
White-collar or sales employees	20	12
Manual workers	25	22

These findings are striking in light of the interpretation made of the data on printers. Lipset, Trow, and Coleman do not, as a result of their findings, see printers as an unintegrated occupational group. On the contrary, they ascribe the democratic character of the union in good part to the active social and political participation of the membership. The point is not to question their interpretation, since it is doubtlessly correct when printers are held up against other manual workers. However, when seen in comparison to police, printers appear a minimally participating group; put positively, police emerge as an exceptionally socially active occupational group.

POLICE SOLIDARITY AND DANGER

There is still a question, however, as to the process through which danger and authority influence police solidarity. The effect of danger on police solidarity is revealed when we examine a chief complaint of police: lack of public support and public apathy. The complaint may have several referents including police pay, police prestige, and support from the legislature. But the repeatedly voiced broader meaning of the complaint is resentment at being taken for granted. The policeman does not believe that his status as civil servant should relieve the public of responsibility for law enforcement. He feels, however, that payment out of public coffers somehow obscures his humanity and, therefore, his need for help.[18] As one put it:

Jerry, a cop, can get into a fight with three or four tough kids, and there will be citizens passing by, and maybe they'll look, but they'll never lend a hand. It's their country too, but you'd never know it the way some of them act. They forget that we're made of flesh and blood too. They don't care what happens to the cop so long as they don't get a little dirty.

Although the policeman sees himself as a specialist in dealing with violence, he does not want to fight alone. He does not believe that his specialization relieves the general public of citizenship duties. Indeed, if possible, he would prefer to be the foreman rather than the workingman in the battle against criminals.

The general public, of course, does withdraw from the workaday world of the policeman. The policeman's responsibility for controlling dangerous and sometimes violent persons alienates the average citizen perhaps as much as does his authority over the average citizen. If the

---

[18] On this issue there was no variation. The statement "the policeman feels" means that there was no instance of a negative opinion expressed by the police studied.

policeman's job is to insure that public order is maintained, the citizen's inclination is to shrink from the dangers of maintaining it. The citizen prefers to see the policeman as an automaton, because once the policeman's humanity is recognized, the citizen necessarily becomes implicated in the policeman's work, which is, after all, sometimes dirty and dangerous. What the policeman typically fails to realize is the extent he becomes tainted by the character of the work he performs. The dangers of their work not only draws policemen together as a group but separates them from the rest of the population. Banton, for instance, comments:

. . . patrolmen may support their fellows over what they regard as minor infractions in order to demonstrate to them that they will be loyal in situations that make the greatest demands upon their fidelity. . . .

In the American departments I visited it seemed as if the supervisors shared many of the patrolmen's sentiments about solidarity. They too wanted their colleagues to back them up in an emergency, and they shared similar frustrations with the public.[19]

Thus, the element of danger contains seeds of isolation which may grow in two directions. In one, a stereotyping perceptual shorthand is formed through which the police come to see certain signs as symbols of potential violence. The police probably differ in this respect from the general middle-class white population only in degree. This difference, however, may take on enormous significance in practice. Thus, the policeman works at identifying and possibly apprehending the symbolic assailant; the ordinary citizen does not. As a result, the ordinary citizen does not assume the responsibility to implicate himself in the policeman's required response to danger. The element of danger in the policeman's role alienates him not only from populations with a potential for crime but also from the conventionally respectable (white) citizenry, in short, from that segment of the population from which friends would ordinarily be drawn. As Janowitz has noted in a paragraph suggesting similarities between the police and the military, ". . . any profession which is continually preoccupied with the threat of danger requires a strong sense of solidarity if it is to operate effectively. Detailed regulation of the military style of life is expected to enhance group cohesion, professional loyalty, and maintain the martial spirit." [20]

SOCIAL ISOLATION AND AUTHORITY

The element of authority also helps to account for the policeman's social isolation. Policemen themselves are aware of their isolation from

[19] Banton, *op. cit.*, p. 114.
[20] Janowitz, *op. cit.*

the community, and are apt to weight authority heavily as a causal factor. When considering how authority influences rejection, the policeman typically singles out his responsibility for enforcement of traffic violations.[21] Resentment, even hostility, is generated in those receiving citations, in part because such contact is often the only one citizens have with police, and in part because municipal administrations and courts have been known to utilize police authority primarily to meet budgetary requirements, rather than those of public order. Thus, when a municipality engages in "speed trapping" by changing limits so quickly that drivers cannot realistically slow down to the prescribed speed or, while keeping the limits reasonable, charging high fines primarily to generate revenue, the policeman carries the brunt of public resentment.

That the policeman dislikes writing traffic tickets is suggested by the quota system police departments typically employ. In Westville, each traffic policeman has what is euphemistically described as a working "norm." A motorcyclist is supposed to write two tickets an hour for moving violations. It is doubtful that "norms" are needed because policemen are lazy. Rather, employment of quotas most likely springs from the reluctance of policemen to expose themselves to what they know to be public hostility. As a result, as one traffic policeman said:

> You learn to sniff out the places where you can catch violators when you're running behind. Of course, the department gets to know that you hang around one place, and they sometimes try to repair the situation there. But a lot of the time it would be too expensive to fix up the engineering fault, so we keep making our norm.

When meeting "production" pressures, the policeman inadvertently gives a false impression of patrolling ability to the average citizen. The traffic cyclist waits in hiding for moving violators near a tricky intersection, and is reasonably sure that such violations will occur with regularity. The violator believes he has observed a policeman displaying exceptional detection capacities and may have two thoughts, each apt to generate hostility toward the policeman: "I have been trapped," or "They can catch me; why can't they catch crooks as easily?" The answer, of course, lies in the different behavior patterns of motorists and "crooks."

---

[21] O. W. Wilson, for example, mentions this factor as a primary source of antagonism toward police. See his "Police Authority in a Free Society," *Journal of Criminal Law, Criminology and Police Science*, 54 (June, 1964), 175–177. In the current study, in addition to the police themselves, other people interviewed, such as attorneys in the system, also attribute the isolation of police to their authority. Similarly, Arthur L. Stinchcombe, in an as yet unpublished manuscript, "The Control of Citizen Resentment in Police Work," provides a stimulating analysis, to which I am indebted, of the ways police authority generates resentment.

The latter do not act with either the frequency or predictability of motorists at poorly engineered intersections.

While traffic patrol plays a major role in separating the policemen from the respectable community, other of his tasks also have this consequence. Traffic patrol is only the most obvious illustration of the policeman's general responsibility for maintaining public order, which also includes keeping order at public accidents, sporting events, and political rallies. These activities share one feature: the policeman is called upon to *direct* ordinary citizens, and therefore to restrain their freedom of action. Resenting the restraint, the average citizen in such a situation typically thinks something along the lines of "He is supposed to catch crooks; why is he bothering me?" Thus, the citizen stresses the "dangerous" portion of the policeman's role while belittling his authority.

Closely related to the policeman's authority-based problems as *director* of the citizenry are difficulties associated with his injunction to *regulate public morality*. For instance, the policeman is obliged to investigate "lovers' lanes," and to enforce laws pertaining to gambling, prostitution, and drunkenness. His responsibility in these matters allows him much administrative discretion since he may not actually enforce the law by making an arrest, but instead merely interfere with continuation of the objectionable activity.[22] Thus, he may put the drunk in a taxi, tell the lovers to remove themselves from the back seat, and advise a man soliciting a prostitute to leave the area.

Such admonitions are in the interest of maintaining the proprieties of public order. At the same time, the policeman invites the hostility of the citizen so directed in two respects: he is likely to encourage the sort of response mentioned earlier (that is, an antagonistic reformulation of the policeman's role) and the policeman is apt to cause resentment because of the suspicion that policemen do not themselves strictly conform to the moral norms they are enforcing. Thus, the policeman, faced with enforcing a law against fornication, drunkenness, or gambling, is easily liable to a charge of hypocrisy. Even when the policeman is called on to enforce the laws relating to overt homosexuality, a form of sexual activity for which police are not especially noted, he may encounter the charge of hypocrisy on grounds that he does not adhere strictly to prescribed heterosexual codes. The policeman's difficulty in this respect is shared by all authorities responsible for maintenance of disciplined activity, including industrial foremen, political leaders, elementary schoolteachers, and college professors. All are expected to conform rigidly to

[22] See Wayne R. La Fave, "The Police and Nonenforcement of the Law," *Wisconsin Law Review* (1962), 104–137, 179–239.

the entire range of norms they espouse.[23] The policeman, however, as a result of the unique combination of the elements of danger and authority, experiences a special predicament. It is difficult to develop qualities enabling him to stand up to danger, and to conform to standards of puritanical morality. The element of danger demands that the policeman be able to carry out efforts that are in their nature overtly masculine. Police work, like soldiering, requires an exceptional caliber of physical fitness, agility, toughness, and the like. The man who ranks high on these masculine characteristics is, again like the soldier, not usually disposed to be puritanical about sex, drinking, and gambling.

On the basis of observations, policemen do not subscribe to moralistic standards for conduct. For example, the morals squad of the police department, when questioned, was unanimously against the statutory rape age limit, on grounds that as late teen-agers they themselves might not have refused an attractive offer from a seventeen-year-old girl.[24] Neither, from observations, are policemen by any means total abstainers from the use of alcoholic beverages. The policeman who is arresting a drunk has probably been drunk himself; he knows it and the drunk knows it.

More than that, a portion of the social isolation of the policeman can be attributed to the discrepancy between moral regulation and the norms and behavior of policemen in these areas. We have presented data indicating that police engage in a comparatively active occupational social life. One interpretation might attribute this attendance to a basic interest in such affairs; another might explain the policeman's occupational social activity as a measure of restraint in publicly violating norms he enforces. The interest in attending police affairs may grow as much out of security in "letting oneself go" in the presence of police, and a corresponding feeling of insecurity with civilians, as an authentic preference for police social affairs. Much alcohol is usually consumed at police banquets with all the melancholy and boisterousness accompanying such occasions. As Horace Cayton reports on his experience as a policeman:

> Deputy sheriffs and policemen don't know much about organized recreation; all they usually do when celebrating is get drunk and pound each other on the back, exchanging loud insults which under ordinary circumstances would result in a fight.[25]

[23] For a theoretical discussion of the problems of leadership, see George Homans, *The Human Group* (New York: Harcourt, Brace and Company, 1950), especially the chapter on "The Job of the Leader," pp. 415–440.

[24] The work of the Westville morals squad in analyzed in detail in an unpublished master's thesis by J. Richard Woodworth. *The Administration of Statutory Rape Complaints: A Sociological Study* (Berkeley: University of California, 1964).

[25] Horace R. Cayton, *Long Old Road* (New York: Trident Press, 1965), p. 154.

58   *Justice without Trial*

To some degree the reason for the behavior exhibited on these occasions is the company, since the policeman would feel uncomfortable exhibiting insobriety before civilians. The policeman may be likened to other authorities who prefer to violate moralistic norms away from onlookers for whom they are routinely supposed to appear as normative models. College professors, for instance, also get drunk on occasion, but prefer to do so where students are not present. Unfortunately for the policeman, such settings are harder for him to come by than they are for the college professor. The whole civilian world watches the policeman. As a result, he tends to be limited to the company of other policemen for whom his police identity is not a stimulus to carping normative criticism.

CORRELATES OF SOCIAL ISOLATION

The element of authority, like the element of danger, is thus seen to contribute to the solidarity of policemen. To the extent that policemen share the experience of receiving hostility from the public, they are also drawn together and become dependent upon one another. Trends in the degree to which police may exercise authority are also important considerations in understanding the dynamics of the relation between authority and solidarity. It is not simply a question of how much absolute authority police are given, but how much authority they have relative to what they had, or think they had, before. If, as Westley concludes, police violence is frequently a response to a challenge to the policeman's authority, so too may a perceived reduction in authority result in greater solidarity. Whitaker comments on the British police as follows:

As they feel their authority decline, internal solidarity has become increasingly important to the police. Despite the individual responsibility of each police officer to pursue justice, there is sometimes a tendency to close ranks and to form a square when they themselves are concerned.[26]

These inclinations may have positive consequences for the effectiveness of police work, since notions of professional courtesy or colleagueship seem unusually high among police.[27] When the nature of the policing enterprise requires much joint activity, as in robbery and narcotics enforcement, the impression is received that cooperation is

[26] Ben Whitaker, *The Police* (Middlesex, England: Penguin Books, 1964), p. 137.
[27] It would be difficult to compare this factor across occupations, since the indicators could hardly be controlled. Nevertheless, I felt that the sense of responsibility to policemen in other departments was on the whole quite strong.

high and genuine. Policemen do not appear to cooperate with one another merely because such is the policy of the chief, but because they sincerely attach a high value to teamwork. For instance, there is a norm among detectives that two who work together will protect each other when a dangerous situation arises. During one investigation, a detective stepped out of a car to question a suspect who became belligerent. The second detective, who had remained overly long in the back seat of the police car, apologized indirectly to his partner by explaining how wrong it had been of him to permit his partner to encounter a suspect alone on the street. He later repeated this explanation privately, in genuine consternation at having committed the breach (and possibly at having been culpable in the presence of an observer). Strong feelings of empathy and cooperation, indeed almost of "clannishness," a term several policemen themselves used to describe the attitude of police toward one another, may be seen in the daily activities of police. Analytically, these feelings can be traced to the elements of danger and shared experiences of hostility in the policeman's role.

Finally, to round out the sketch, policemen are notably conservative, emotionally and politically. If the element of danger in the policeman's role tends to make the policeman suspicious, and therefore emotionally attached to the status quo, a similar consequence may be attributed to the element of authority. The fact that a man is engaged in enforcing a set of rules implies that he also becomes implicated in *affirming* them. Labor disputes provide the commonest example of conditions inclining the policeman to support the status quo. In these situations, the police are necessarily pushed on the side of the defense of property. Their responsibilities thus lead them to see the striking and sometimes angry workers as their enemy and, therefore, to be cool, if not antagonistic, toward the whole conception of labor militancy.[28] If a policeman did not believe in the system of laws he was responsible for enforcing, he would have to go on living in a state of conflicting cognitions, a condition which a number of social psychologists agree is painful.[29]

[28] In light of this, the most carefully drawn lesson plan in the "professionalized" Westville police department, according to the officer in charge of training, is the one dealing with the policeman's demeanor in labor disputes. A comparable concern is now being evidenced in teaching policemen appropriate demeanor in civil rights demonstrations. See, e.g., Juby E. Towler, *The Police Role In Racial Conflicts* (Springfield: Charles C Thomas, 1964).

[29] Indeed, one school of social psychology asserts that there is a basic "drive," a fundamental tendency of human nature, to reduce the degree of discrepancy between conflicting cognitions. For the policeman, this tenet implies that he would have to do something to reduce the discrepancy between his beliefs and his behavior. He would have to modify his behavior, his beliefs, or introduce some outside factor to justify

60   *Justice without Trial*

This hypothetical issue of not believing in the laws they are enforcing simply does not arise for most policemen. In the course of the research, however, there was one example. A Black civil rights advocate (member of CORE) became a policeman with the conviction that by so doing he would be aiding the cause of impartial administration of law for Blacks. For him, however, this outside rationale was not enough to sustain him in administering a system of laws that depends for its impartiality upon a reasonable measure of social and economic equality among the citizenry. This recruit identified with the Black community. He challenged directives of the department; the departments claimed his efficiency was impaired. He resigned under pressure in his rookie year.[29a]

Police are understandably reluctant to appear to be anything but impartial politically. The police are forbidden from publicly campaigning for political candidates. The London police are similarly prohibited, and before 1887 were not allowed to vote in parliamentary elections, or in local ones until 1893.[30] It was not surprising that the Westville Chief of Police forbade questions on the questionnaire that would have measured political attitudes.[31] One policeman, however, explained the chief's refusal on grounds that, "A couple of jerks here would probably cut up, and come out looking like Commies."

During the course of administering the questionnaire over a three-day period, I talked with approximately fifteen officers and sergeants in the Westville department, discussing political attitudes of police. In addition, during the course of the research itself, approximately fifty were interviewed for varying periods of time. Of these, at least twenty were interviewed more than once, some over time periods of several weeks. Furthermore, twenty police were interviewed in Eastville, several for periods ranging from several hours to several days. Most of the

the discrepancy. If he modified his behavior, so as not to enforce the law in which he disbelieves, he would not hold his position for long. Practically, then, he may either introduce an outside factor or modify his beliefs. The outside factor would have to be compelling to reduce the pain resulting from the dissonance between his cognitions. For example, he would have to convince himself that the only way he could make a living was by being a policeman, or modify his beliefs. See Leon Festinger, *A Theory of Cognitive Dissonance* (Evanston, Ill.: Row-Peterson, 1957). For a brief explanation of Festinger's theory see Edward E. Sampson (ed.), *Approaches, Contexts, and Problems of Social Psychology* (Englewood Cliffs, N.J.: Prentice-Hall, 1964), pp. 9–15.[29a] I thank Gwynne Pierson for pointing out the inaccuracy of the first edition's report of this incident.

[30] Whitaker, *op cit.*, p. 26.
[31] The questions submitted to the chief of police were directly analogous to those asked of printers in the study of the I.T.U. See Lipset et al., *op. cit.*, "Appendix II–Interview Schedule," 493–503.

time was *not* spent on investigating political attitudes, but I made a point of raising the question, if possible making it part of a discussion centered around the contents of a right-wing newsletter to which one of the detectives subscribed. One discussion included a group of eight detectives. From these observations, interviews, and discussions, it was clear that a Goldwater type of conservatism was the dominant political and emotional persuasion of police. I encountered only three policemen who claimed to be politically "liberal," at the same time asserting that they were decidedly exceptional.

Whether or not the policeman is an "authoritarian personality" is a related issue, beyond the scope of this discussion partly because of the many questions raised about this concept. Thus, in the course of discussing the concept of "normality" in mental health, two psychologists make the point that many conventional people were high scorers on the California F scale and similar tests. The great mass of the people, according to these authors, is not much further along the scale of ego development than the typical adolescent who, as they describe him, is "rigid, prone to think in stereotypes, intolerant of deviations, punitive and anti-psychological—in short, what has been called an authoritarian personality." [32] Therefore it is preferable to call the policeman's a conventional personality.

Writing about the New York police force, Thomas R. Brooks suggests a similar interpretation. He writes:

> Cops are conventional people. . . . All a cop can swing in a milieu of marijuana smokers, interracial dates, and homosexuals is the night stick. A policeman who passed a Lower East Side art gallery filled with paintings of what appeared to be female genitalia could think of doing only one thing—step in and make an arrest.[33]

Despite his fundamental identification with conservative conventionality, however, the policeman may be familiar, unlike most conventional people, with the argot of the deviant and the criminal. (The policeman tends to resent the quietly respectable liberal who comes to the defense of such people on principle but who has rarely met them in practice.) Indeed, the policeman will use his knowledge of the argot to advantage in talking to a suspect. In this manner, the policeman *puts on*

[32] Jane Loevinger and Abel Ossorio, "Evaluation of Therapy by Self Report: A Paradox," *Journal of Abnormal and Social Psychology*, 58 (May, 1959), 392; see also Edward A. Shils, "Authoritarianism: 'Right' and 'Left'," in R. Christie and M. Jahoda (ed.), *Studies in Scope and Method of "The Authoritarian Personality,"* (Glencoe, Ill.: The Free Press, 1954), pp. 24–49.

[33] Thomas R. Brooks, "New York's Finest," *Commentary*, 40 (August, 1965), 29–30.

62   *Justice without Trial*

the suspect by pretending to share his moral conception of the world through the use of "hip" expressions. The suspect may put on a parallel show for the policeman by using only conventional language to indicate his respectability. (In my opinion, neither fools the other.)

A COMPARATIVE GLANCE AT POLICE ROLE AND CULTURE

Must this theory of the policeman's working personality be limited to the police under observation, or can it be generalized to a wider police population? Unfortunately, there are few systematic studies of police for comparison. American studies, as well as reports of police chiefs, indicate that the policeman typically perceives the citizenry to be hostile to him.[34] Thus, for example, a recent survey made by James Q. Wilson of an urban American police force concludes:

> Criticisms of the way a big-city police department was run were largely confined to the younger, most recently promoted sergeants, but "alienation" —an acute sense of citizen hostility or contempt toward officers—was found in almost all age groups. Over 70 per cent of the over 800 officers scored high on an index of perceived citizen hostility—more, indeed, than thought the force was poorly run (though these were over half the total).[35]

This finding of Wilson's, so close to those reported here, is not surprising, and therefore not forceful in persuading the reader that the findings are generalizable. The common pattern of activities of American urban police, for instance, their enforcement of traffic laws, suggests that findings in one city would be similar to those in another. Furthermore, since the Westville police are high caliber, greater citizen hostility would be anticipated in other American cities where the enforcing authorities are less respected and therefore more likely to generate citizen hostility. Assuming that hostility is correlated with social isolation, this feature of police life also is likely to be more pronounced in other American urban areas.

Suppose, however, we were to consider the "working personality" of police who constitute part of a relatively homogeneous society, and who also enjoy an international reputation for honesty, efficiency, and legality. A study of such a police force has been completed by Michael Banton, who observed five police departments in Scotland and in the

[34] Cf. *Parker on Police*, ed. O. W. Wilson (Springfield: Charles C Thomas, 1957), pp. 135–146; O. W. Wilson, "Police Authority in a Free Society," *Journal of Criminal Law, Criminology and Police Science*, **54** (June, 1963), 175–177; Michael J. Murphy, "Stereocracy v. Democracy," *The Police Chief* (February, 1962), 36, 38.

[35] James Q. Wilson, "Police Attitudes and Citizen Hostility" (unpublished draft, Harvard University, September, 1964), p. 24.

United States.[36] The main object of his inquiry is the urban Scottish constable, roughly the equivalent of the American patrolman or "cop on the beat." Comparing the social isolation of American and British police, Banton writes:

> Before my visit to the United States I thought that for a variety of reasons American police officers might well experience more social isolation than their British counterparts. I assumed that the heavier incidence of violent crime, the high proportion of 'cop-haters,' the 'shoot first, ask afterwards' tactics American police have to use on occasion, and the lower prestige of police work, would cause policemen to feel more like outcasts or like troops in occupation of enemy territory. Such an expectation was in accordance with an impression to be gained from a study of Westley's dissertation, where it is said: 'The exigencies of the occupation form the police into a social group which tends to be in conflict with and isolated from the community; and in which the norms are independent of the community' (Westley, 1951, p. 294). The locality in which Westley's research was conducted turns out, however, to be far from representative of the present-day situation, and a reconsideration of his evidence from a comparative rather than a purely American perspective reveals a whole series of influences which operate in a contrary fashion. *American police may seem isolated from the community to an American observer because he compares them with other occupational groups in the same society; they may at the same time seem to an outsider much less isolated than policemen in other societies.*[37]

Banton accounts for the relatively greater isolation of British police by emphasizing the consequences of the exemplary character of the British policeman's role. British police, as portrayed by Banton, are reserved, dignified, impersonal, detached. For them, the role is the man, and the example to be set is taken seriously. He writes:

> Most officers with twenty years' service in a county force can remember the days when a policeman who proposed to marry was required first to submit the name of his fiancee to his superiors so that they could ascertain whether she was a fit and proper person for the role of policeman's wife.[38]

Although the element of danger is not so ultimate for the British policeman, it nevertheless exists. "In Edinburgh," writes Banton, "violence means to a policeman, I suspect, either fists or stones, or at the worst, assault with sticks or iron bars. It does not mean guns or knives." [39] Furthermore, the theme of the police being a "race apart" is a recurring one in Scotland, which Banton attributes to the requirement that

---

[36] Banton, *op. cit.*
[37] *Ibid.*, p. 215 (italics added).
[38] *Ibid.*, p. 195.
[39] Banton, personal communication, 24 August, 1964.

64   *Justice without Trial*

policeman must examine critically every statement made to them.[40] In our interpretation, these reports suggest that the policeman, wherever located, is in a position of vulnerability. Exposure to physical danger represents the height of vulnerability, a situation the British policeman encounters less often than the American. He does, however, experience the possibility of lesser physical danger and of attacks upon his professional competence. The policeman's role is therefore exceptional insofar as he must be so often on the defensive. Banton finds one of his subjects defining "the police mind" as follows: ". . . you suspect your grandmother and that's about the strength of it."

Although the elements of authority and danger have similar consequences for the British and American policeman, the processes bringing about social isolation seem different. British police are inclined to take the initiative in separating themselves from society. They tend to internalize authority, to perform an exemplary role, and thereby are instruments of their own isolation. Even in Great Britain, however, there seem to be differences between the Scottish police studied by Banton and the British police in general. Although the 1962 Royal Commission concluded that a social survey conducted by the Home Office constituted an overwhelming vote of confidence in the police, that interpretation has been widely criticized. For example, the survey disclosed that 42.4 per cent of the public thought policemen took bribes, 34.7 per cent that the police used unfair methods to get information, 32 per cent that they might distort evidence in court and 17.8 per cent that on occasions they used too much force.[41] The Royal Commission, however, felt that since almost half of those interviewed did not believe that the police took bribes, used unnecessary violence, employed unfair means of getting evidence, or gave false evidence in court, it was reasonable to "assert, confidently, on the basis of this survey, that relations between the police and the public are on the whole very good." [42] This interpretation is obviously overoptimistic. Police relations, especially with certain segments of the public, are clearly strained.

In America there has not been a comparable national survey. There have, however, been enough complaints to such groups as the U. S. Civil Rights Commission to suggest that American police are no more beloved or trusted than their English counterparts.[43] The chief difference may be that in America hostile public attitudes isolate policemen

[40] Banton, *op. cit.*, pp. 207–208.
[41] Whitaker, *op. cit.*, p. 15.
[42] *Ibid.*, p. 103.
[43] Commission on Civil Rights Report, Book 5, *Justice* (Washington, D.C.: U.S. Government Printing Office, 1961), pp. 5–44. In New York, a number of civil rights groups have formed an unofficial citizens' board to review charges of police brutality. (*New York Times*, May 23, 1964.)

who would prefer to be more friendly. Although the Westville policeman has been presented as a man who is conservative, suspicious, relatively isolated from the community at large, clannish, and resentful of
public apathy, this is only part of the portrait of a complex being. The
Westville policeman sees himself as a relatively congenial person, able to
make friends. Policemen were asked to rank eight qualities in the order
they felt these qualities best described them.[44] Here we find the quality
of "congeniality and the ability to make friends" ranking high. In Great
Britain also, the social survey finds police rueing their lack of friends,
especially the rural police. Of these, 74 per cent thought they would
have more friends if they had a different job. On the whole, 66.8 per
cent of policemen said that the job adversely affected their outside
friendships.[45]

Unfortunately, the nature of his work often inhibits the policeman
from indulging his gregariousness in a personally meaningful way. He
would like to be friendlier but, of the public over whom he is an authority, he must be suspicious of strangeness, oddity, indeed any sort of
change. The elements of danger and authority in the policeman's work
evidently impede gregarious tendencies and, in general, account for similar cognitive inclinations in American and British police. To be sure,
differences exist in the salience and character of these elements and in
the processes by which danger and authority affect the policeman's way
of looking at the world. Nevertheless, both elements seem to be present, specific outcomes such as social isolation are similar and, most
importantly, the British and American police seem to see the world
similarly.

COGNITIVE SIMILARITY AND THE RULE OF LAW

If the proposition is largely correct that elements of the policeman's
role result in broadly similar "working personalities" in British and
American police, is the validity of this conclusion affected by observations that British police conform to rules of legal procedure more closely
than American? [46] Should not the similarity of cognitive inclination
manifest itself in the behavior of the policeman? Although a number of
factors, such as relations of the police organization to the community

[44] These categories were taken from an unpublished paper, "Articulated Values of
Law Students." The categories were suggested by the eight-value system elaborated
by Harold Lasswell. See, e.g., H. D. Lasswell and A. Kaplan, *Power and Society* (New
Haven: Yale University Press, 1950).

[45] Whitaker, *op. cit.*, p. 127.

[46] See Bruce Smith, *Police Systems in the United States* (New York: Harper and
Brothers, 1960, second rev. ed.), pp. 3, 11, *et. passim*; and Sir Patrick Devlin, *The
Criminal Prosecution in England* (New Haven: Yale University Press, 1958), *passim*.

66   *Justice without Trial*

and a less moralistic substantive criminal law, may help to account for such behavioral differences, this final discussion is confined to the effect of the general social environment. The discussion that follows is limited to the question of how differences in general social environment can influence the relation between the elements of danger and authority in the direction of apparently greater compliance with the rule of law.

It is important to note that the *actual* degree of difference often stated is open to serious question. A reader of memoirs of British police is impressed by the extent to which they describe violations of the judges' rules.[47] One officer writes: "You can see that if we worked according to the strict letter of the Rules we would get nowhere. . . . We have to break the law to enforce it. . . ."[48] Evidently, the British policeman does not conform to rules so much as he knows how to present the appearance of conformity. By contrast, when the American policeman varies from canons of procedural regularity, his misbehaviors tend to be more visible. Reared in a society with finer social distinctions, the British policeman is schooled in etiquette to a degree unknown to most Americans. Victor Meek, a former inspector of the Metropolitan Police, describes how an English policeman investigating a burglary manages to "stop" relatively large numbers of people, at the same time avoiding the appearance of procedural irregularity. He writes:

You see, when a policeman has stopped a hundred people, which number has included perhaps ten proved guilty persons, he has learned the behaviour under these conditions of ninety innocent people and of ten thieves. In the next hundred stopped he will have twenty thieves, in the next perhaps thirty. Not altogether because thieves are thicker but because his "Police here," or "Excuse me a moment, Sir," are enough to satisfy him, by the reaction of the person stopped, whether he is dealing with a sheep or a goat, whether chummy is in the clear or loaded. So to the sheep his next remark is "I am very sorry to bother you but my watch has stopped. Can you please tell me the time?" The answer will naturally be "If you want to know the time I thought you had to ask another policeman," and the mutual appreciation of this witticism sends chummy away chuckling and quite unaware that Section 66 [49] has been tried on him.[50]

[47] See, e.g., Victor Meek, *Cops and Robbers* (London: Gerald Duckworth and Co., Ltd., 1962); William Gosling, *Ghost Squad* (Garden City: Doubleday, 1959); and a "Letter from English policeman on use of judges' rules," in William Thomas Fryer (ed.), *Selected Writings on the Law of Evidence and Trial* (St. Paul: West Publishing Co., 1957), pp. 845–846.

[48] Fryer, *ibid.*

[49] "Any constable may stop, search and detain any vessel, boat, cart or carriage in or upon which there shall be reason to suspect that anything stolen or unlawfully obtained may be found, and also any person who may be reasonably suspected of having or conveying in any manner anything stolen or unlawfully obtained."

[50] Meek, *op. cit.*, p. 86.

The British policeman's ability to make fine social discriminations, plus his training in etiquette, enable him to distinguish not only among those who are more likely to commit crimes but also among those who are more likely to report procedural irregularities. As Meek says, ". . . the names and address of a Section 66 complainer is doubly worth passing on to a good copper of the manor on which chummy lives or works." [51]

Thus, when we envision the "discretion" of the British policeman, we should certainly keep in mind more than the issue of whether he decides to invoke the law. A key distinction between the English and American policeman is that the former tends to be more *discreet* in an interactional sense as well as *discrete* in an administrative one, thereby avoiding the censure that is often the lot of the American policeman. Indeed, as the rest of this study of a "professionalized" American police force is read, the reader may find it interesting to speculate as to what constitutes central elements of professional training. We believe the materials to follow will suggest that the training of etiquette, including the ability to make fine social distinctions, is such an element; more, indeed, than the development of an actual regard for the rule of law.

CONCLUSION

The combination of *danger* and *authority* found in the task of the policeman unavoidably combine to frustrate procedural regularity. If it were possible to structure social roles with specific qualities, it would be wise to propose that these two should never, for the sake of the rule of law, be permitted to coexist. Danger typically yields self-defensive conduct, conduct that must strain to be impulsive because danger arouses fear and anxiety so easily. Authority under such conditions becomes a resource to reduce perceived threats rather than a series of reflective judgments arrived at calmly. The ability to be discreet, in the sense discussed above, is also affected. As a result, procedural requirements take on a "frilly" character, or at least tend to be reduced to a secondary position in the face of circumstances seen as threatening.

If this analysis is correct, it suggests a related explanation drawn from the realm of social environment to account for the apparent paradox that the elements of danger and authority are universally to be found in the policeman's role, yet at the same time fail to yield the same behavior regarding the rule of law. If the element of danger faced by the British policeman is less than that faced by his American counterpart, its ability to undermine the element of authority is proportionately weakened.

[51] *Ibid.*, p. 85.

68   *Justice without Trial*

Bluntly put, the American policeman may have a more difficult job because he is exposed to greater danger. Therefore, we would expect him to be less judicious, indeed less discreet, in the exercise of his authority. Similarly, such an explanation would predict that if the element of actual danger or even the perception of such in the British policeman's job were to increase, complaints regarding the illegal use of his authority would also rise.

There have been spectacular cases supporting this proposition. One of these, resulting in a government inquiry which suspended two top police officers, took place at Sheffield on March 14, 1963. Several detectives brutally assaulted four men in five successive and separate relays with a truncheon, fists, and a rhinoceros whip. The report of the Inquiry concludes that the police were undoubtedly guilty of "maliciously inflicting grievous bodily harm of a serious nature on two prisoners." [52] The assaults were described as "deliberate, unprovoked, brutal and sustained . . . for the purpose of inducing confessions of crime." The detectives had been formed into a "Crime Squad" which felt it had the authority to use "tough methods to deal with tough criminals and take risks to achieve speedy results." The leading offender told the Inquiry "that criminals are treated far too softly by the Courts, that because criminals break rules, police may and most do so to be a jump ahead, that force is justified as a last resort as a method of detection when normal methods fail, and that a beating is the only answer to turn a hardened criminal from a life of crime." [53]

Perhaps the most interesting feature of the report are the mitigating factors the Inquiry took into account. They found that the detectives were overworked (in a city where crime was on the rise); that the detectives were, and felt, under pressure to obtain results; that the use of violence had been encouraged by hints beforehand by senior officers; that senior officers instituted, witnessed, and joined in the violence and were wholly inadequately dealt with by the chief constable; and that the detectives were told to give a false account in court by a senior officer, who concocted it. The entire report suggests that the detectives who engaged in the beatings were not unusual men. There was no evidence of mental instability on their part, neither of psychosis, psychopathy, nor neurosis. Not one man on the force reported the incident, although several had learned of it. The report gives the feeling that while the event itself was exceptional, the conditions leading to it, such as overwork, pressure to produce, and encouragement by superiors,

---

[52] Sheffield Police Appeal Inquiry, Cmnd. 2176, November, 1963.
[53] *Ibid.*, p. 5.

were ordinary. Although the report does not use the language of social science, it strongly suggests that the structural and cultural conditions in the police force supported this sort of response.

Also interesting is the evident racial bias of the Sheffield police. One of them testified he carried his rhinoceros whip to deal with "coloured informants." The racial issue is significant for the British police as a whole. The *New York Times* reported on May 3, 1965 that although the London police force is six thousand men short of full strength, not one colored applicant has been accepted, even though fifteen West Indians, six Pakistanis and six Indians tried to join the force in the preceding three years. The official reason given is that the applicants did not meet the qualifications. Apart from three part-time constables in the Midlands, however, there was, at the time of the report, not one colored policeman in Britain, even though Pakistanis, Indians, and West Indians, all officially classified as colored by the British, account for nearly 2 per cent of the population.

Suggestions have been made to enlist colored policemen for colored neighborhoods, or to bring in trained colored policemen from the Commonwealth. Others have asked for the introduction of colored policemen in white neighborhoods, especially in London. The *New York Times* story closes with a suggestion by one critic, Anthony Lester, that British police chiefs take a trip to New York to see how Negro policemen fit in. "Policemen have a different status here than in the States," he is reported to have said. "They are more a father figure, a symbol of authority with their tall helmets and slow walk. It's difficult to get people to accept colored men in this job. They have had no Negro officers in the Army, no way of getting used to taking orders from colored men."

To complete the analogy of similarity of police action with similarity of social conditions, problems of police behavior also appear to be correlated with the restriction of marihuana use, a recent police phenomenon in England. Colin MacInnes argues, in a letter published in the fall of 1963, that when the London police began vigorously enforcing the marihuana law:

. . . it looks as if the hallowed myth that English coppers never use violence, perjury, framing of suspects—let alone participate in crimes—is at last being shattered in the public mind. Now, what has been foolish about this legend is not that coppers *do* do these things—as all police forces do and must—but that national vanity led many to suppose that our coppers were far nicer men than any others.[54]

[54] "The Silly Season," *Partisan Review*, **30** (Fall, 1963), 430, 432.

70   *Justice without Trial*

Although MacInnes' statement may be overly strong, it does suggest that those who too clearly contrast American and British police in favor of British are probably generally wrong. Of course, there are always individual as well as group differences in police behavior. However, even if conduct varies more than MacInnes indicates, and conduct will vary with relations of the police organization to the community, the character of the substantive criminal law being enforced, and the social conditions of the community, it is nevertheless likely that the variables of danger and authority in the policeman's role, combined with a constant pressure to produce, result in tendencies general enough and similar enough to identify a distinctive "working personality" among police. The question becomes one of understanding what the police do with it. Given this conception of the policeman's "working personality" as background, the chapters that follow analyze the sources of police attitudes and conduct as observed in the setting of specific assignments.

[13]

Car Panels [detail]

Police Culture

**Steve James and
Ian Warren**

The organisational cultures of the agencies of social control have become a fertile field
for scholarly attention. Long gone are conceptions of social control as a purely reactive
enterprise which is structured solely by the phenomena it attempts to control. The
capacities of social control agencies to construct their roles and practices, and to give
particular kinds of social, political and moral meaning to those roles and practices, are
axiomatic features of contemporary control discourse. But few social control agencies
have been subject to quite the degree of cultural analysis as has policing. The
application of concepts of 'culture' to an understanding of police behaviour and
misbehaviour has been a distinctive component of police scholarship over the last two
decades or so. At the same time, 'cultural' explanations of police behaviour have
appeared increasingly in the popular imagery of policing. The development of analyses
of policing which seek to move beyond idiographic conceptions of police behaviour
has been welcome; the sterility of older conceptions of police misbehaviour as
functions of individual venality and pathology has been all too apparent, and such
conceptions have little general currency.

Culture has been invoked as an (or more often the) explanatory variable in the
generation of police corruption, brutality and abuse of power,[1] gender and minority
discrimination within policing,[2] the failure of internal police complaints investigation,[3]
the development of authoritarianism among police personnel,[4] the failure of attempts to
reform police organisational structures, and the meddling of police in the political
process and the corruption of that process.[5] However, the concept of a distinctive
culture within policing which determines all manner of misbehaviours by police is in
grave danger of becoming a cliché. It will be argued that the appropriation of a highly
qualified analytical device drawn originally from anthropology by both popular and
scholarly commentators on policing has resulted too often in an undifferentiated entity
known as 'police culture' which is treated synonymously as the cause and effect of
police misbehaviour.[6]

The purpose of the present chapter is three–fold: to outline briefly the development
of the concept of police culture; to describe the emergence of the concept in Australian
policing commentary; and to raise a number of critical questions about the application
of the concept to our understanding of police behaviour and misbehaviour.

Steve James and Ian Warren

The Development of the Concept of Police Culture

The origins of cultural explanations for police behaviour can be traced to attempts by sociologists in the 1960s to explain an enduring anomaly in policing: the breaking of rules by the people whose primary occupational and social purpose is to enforce rules. Systematic scholarly attention directed at policing is a relatively recent endeavour. The evolution of modern policing, traditionally associated with the introduction by Robert Peel of the London Metropolitan Police in 1829,[7] was for many years assumed to be a rational and successful response to the burgeoning need for more effective means of crime control following the Industrial Revolution.[8] This assumption fitted nicely the premises of a classical conception of effective criminal justice, in which a visible police presence deterred general law breaking and the investigative and apprehension capacities of police offered specific deterrence. In fact, the historical record suggests persuasively that Peelite policing was neither necessarily successful nor accepted by the communities most subject to its activities – the working class.[9] But regardless of its popular reception, a number of factors combined to render policing practically invisible as an object of academic interest for many years. In particular, it was assumed that police did not make many or any crucial decisions in a control context. This assumption was to some extent a function of the low regard in which police were held as lower–class workers recruited more on the basis of their brawn (and in the United States, their local political affiliations[10]) than their brains, characteristics which rendered them less interesting as criminal justice decision–makers compared with the activities of the legislature and the courts. Equally importantly, academics essentially accepted the arguments propagated for many years by police themselves that they were merely servants of the law, acting within the law at all times. Goldstein wrote in 1977:

> In the past the prevalent assumption of both the police and the public was that the police had no discretion – that their job was to function in strict accordance with the law. In fostering this image of themselves as ministerial officers, doing precisely what they were mandated by law to do, the police were responding to their understanding of what was expected of them by legislatures, by the courts, and by a substantial segment of the general public.[11]

But this was and has always been a facade, erected for political and defensive purposes by police departments who did not want their real and extensive decision–making discretion publically recognised and hence held accountable. Policing has necessarily required the exercise of discretion, given its diverse mandate and the many options it has available to it for the execution of that mandate. And much of that decision–making has been problematic. While criminal justice scholars may have been blinkered until the 1960s, other observers of policing (in particular municipal policing in the United States and in Britain) were well aware of the abuse of power by police.[12] According to Jerome Skolnick, writing in 1966, the accumulated evidence of police misbehaviour in the United States raised the issue: 'For many municipal police forces in the United States, the observer's question is... not whether police operate under the constraints of due process of law, but whether they operate within bounds of civilized conduct.'[13]

The belated scholarly recognition that systematic discretionary decision–making by police occurred[14] was accompanied in the United States during the 1960s by a plethora of government inquiries and academic critiques of widespread police misbehaviour.[15] The search began for a comprehensive understanding of why and how police behaved outside the confines of the rules and regulations that formally governed their mandate. Two largely unrelated scholarly developments took place. Psychologists began to hypothesise about the existence of modal personality patterns amongst police officers which would explain their behaviour. At the same time, sociologists explored the impact of organisational and occupational factors upon police behaviour.

4

Psychology's contribution produced a flowering of interest in the 'authoritarianism' of police personalities, an interest which began with the publication of Arthur Niederhoffer's work on anomie and cynicism among police.[16] Authoritarianism, with its alleged elements of (inter alia) conservatism, authoritarian aggression, power and 'toughness', destructiveness, cynicism and stereotypy, appeared to capture well the popular images of police behaviour.[17] It also helped explain why police discriminated against certain groups within the community, behaved aggressively and at times brutally, and fostered a conservative and 'macho' image. However, despite initial research findings in support of police manifesting high levels of authoritarianism,[18] and the resurrection of the hypothesis from time to time,[19] Lefkowitz has produced a persuasive review arguing that across all relevant empirical studies police were found to be no more authoritarian on the standard personality measurements than members of other occupational groups.[20] At the same time, Lefkowitz agreed with most commentators that police do in fact exhibit modal behavioural patterns, although the constellation of characteristics was by no means exclusively negative.[21] But psychological discourse on police behaviour became locked into something of a futile debate about the causes of patterns of police behaviour between those who argued for the dominance of introduced personality patterns (traits) into police and those who argued that behavioural patterns were generated by socialisation into structured policing environments. The debate foundered somewhat, with many personality theorists unable to draw upon a tradition of the examination of structural determinants of behaviour.[22] For such a tradition, we need to turn to sociological endeavours.

One of the earliest attempts to offer a structural understanding of police, and still a remarkably persuasive one, was that by Jerome Skolnick. For Skolnick, the inevitability of the exercise of discretion by police, and the abuse of that discretion, are functions of a structural conflict between the demands of efficient and effective law enforcement on the one hand, and the rule of law on the other:

> The police in democratic society are required to maintain order and do so under the rule of law. As functionaries charged with maintaining order, they are part of the bureaucracy. The ideology of democratic bureaucracy emphasizes initiative rather than disciplined adherence to rules and regulations. By contrast, the rule of law emphasizes the rights of individual citizens and constraints upon the initiative of legal officials.[23]

As a consequence, police violate the principles and guidelines of due process and the rule of law in order to achieve what they believe are the fundamental purposes of policing. But Skolnick recognised that discretionary decision–making (and one of its consequences – the violation of due process) needs to take place within an organisational and occupational context which structures, supports and rationalises rule–breaking. While he did not explicitly describe this context as a 'culture' of policing, he identified many of the conditions and factors which have been viewed subsequently as the defining characteristics of a police culture. Drawing on the literature on the sociology of occupations, Skolnick argued that workers develop particular ways of perceiving, understanding and responding to their occupational environment, 'distinctive cognitive tendencies' which result from factors unique to each occupation.[24] He isolated danger and authority as the most salient factors, and argued that 'the police, as a result of combined features of their social situation, tend to develop ways of looking at the world distinctive to themselves, cognitive lenses through which to see situations and events.'[25] He called the result the 'working personality' of police.

For Skolnick, the exposure of police to danger in their working environment forges a strong sense of suspiciousness, a tendency to be constantly alert to signs of violence and offending. This suspiciousness isolates police from the community, both the law–abiding members who cannot share the same conceptions of danger, and the law–

Steve James and Ian Warren

breaking objects of police attention. It simultaneously leads to a heightened sense of solidarity amongst police workers. At the same time, police are vested with considerable authority to execute their duties, including the enforcement of what in the United States context Skolnick describes as 'puritanical morality'. The community resents and resists the exercise of such authority, which in turn reinforces the police sense of suspiciousness, isolation and solidarity. Crucially, exposure to real or anticipated danger 'undermines the judicious use of authority':[26]

> The combination of danger and authority found in the task of the policeman unavoidably combine to frustrate procedural regularity... Danger typically yields self–defensive conduct, conduct that must strain to be impulsive because danger arouses fear and anxiety so easily. Authority under such conditions becomes a resource to reduce perceived threats rather than a series of reflective judgements arrived at calmly...As a result, procedural requirements take on a 'frilly' character, or at least tend to be reduced to a secondary position in the face of circumstances seen as threatening.[27]

Skolnick argued that while his working personality thesis offers a generalisable description of structuring forces in policing across different societies, it also allowed for significant variation. He proposed, for instance, that the exposure of British police to less danger in their working environment compared with their American counterparts meant that the tendency of danger to weaken procedural regularity was less evident, and that British police in general operated more within the rule of law than American police. He also predicted that were police anywhere to be more exposed to danger (or to perceive that they were in more danger) in their working environment, then we could expect an increase in complaints about illegal police behaviour.

Skolnick's recognition of the differential operation of structural and interactive factors on police work has, as we will argue, not always been manifest in the contemporary discourse on police culture and violence. The challenge for all sophisticated commentators on police behaviour has been the need to recognise and explain both the continuities and the divergences in the behavioural patterns in policing. Many of the seminal contributors to what has become the 'cultural' explanation of police behaviour and misbehaviour were at pains to point out the inevitable degree of differentiation in police work and the behaviours which anchor that work. The work of James Q. Wilson is instructive in this regard.[28] In his celebrated taxonomy of police behaviour, Wilson argued that while certain legal and organisational elements which influence police behaviour are generally common across all police services, substantial variation exists according to particular social, political and organisational factors. For Wilson, his archetypal police organisations – the 'watchman', 'legalistic' and 'service' styles – are products of complex interactions between organisational structure and leadership, local political context, and the nature and behaviour of the local constituency. Wilson's work is known well enough not to require elaboration here, but of particular relevance is that each of Wilson's styles of policing dictate different levels of discretionary decision–making, different focal concerns of the police, and variations in the potential for abuse of police power and denial of due process.

The last contribution to seminal but 'pre–cultural' explanations of police behaviour and misbehaviour to be raised here is that by Reiss in his work on police violence.[29] While he recognised the organisational determinants of police brutality as crucial, Reiss devoted a considerable part of his formulations to the situational and interactional factors which appear to produce brutality beyond the routine use of force. Simply put, he argued that victim characteristics (that is, victims of police brutality) interact with various conceptions of normality and legitimacy that police bring with them to confrontational encounters. From his observational studies, Reiss argued that those most vulnerable to police brutality manifest some degree of defiance of police authority, or represent deviation from 'normal' standards of behaviour held by police

6

(such as intoxicated people, drug addicts and homosexuals).[30] Importantly, variations of treatment for people who were seen by police to defy their authority appeared dependent upon the extent to which police officers believed they could clearly establish that they were in control; thus, when the question of authority remained unresolved, police responses were more likely to be violent.

The formulations outlined above established the broad parameters for an examination of the occupational and organisational determinants of police behaviour and misbehaviour. Much of the contemporary discourse on police behaviour remains anchored in such formulations and their variations.[31] The focal concerns of police scholars began to shift towards explaining how these determinants are transformed into working guidelines for police which sit alongside (and often contradict) formal prescriptive regulations governing police behaviour and practice, and how they are reproduced for subsequent generations of police officers. Two related themes were explored: the need to comprehend organisational life by reference to its informal rules and structures as well as its formal characteristics,[32] and the socialisation of workers into organisational life.[33] By the end of the 1970s, the concept of a distinctive police 'culture' had emerged from the clutter of sociological formulations to serve as the dominant articulation of the importance and impact of organisational structure and meaning upon police workers and police work. The concept by its very nomenclature is evocative and offers a number of simultaneous utilities. It provides a neat description of the complexities of police organisational and occupational life. It strongly implies the coercive power that all cultures are presumed to exert over the behaviour of their members.[34] It suggests a ready–made mechanism by which workers learn (or are forced) to conform to the imperatives of that life; 'culture' implies a process of 'culturation', a process of induction or indoctrination into the real world of working rules and guidelines.[35]

Let us summarise this section by reporting how Jerome Skolnick (with James Fyffe) currently views police culture nearly thirty years after his original work.[36] Skolnick begins by reasserting his contention that policing develops, like all other occupational groups, 'recognizable and distinctive rules, customs, perceptions, and interpretations of what they see, along with consequent moral judgements', which govern police action.[37] The crucial determinants of these rules and customs derive from the capacity of police to exercise authority and force within the context of perceived danger in their work life and in the face of citizen resentment of and resistance to the use of coercive force. Other occupations can be objectively identified as more dangerous or injurious, but it is to police that society gives the right (albeit grudgingly) to exercise force on its behalf, and it is the police who are expected to engage with danger and threat. Police suspiciousness of the conditions (or pre–conditions) for dangerous or threatening situations fosters a preference for predictable, conventional and stable events and people, and a dislike and intolerance of unpredictable, erratic and deviant events and people. Police are as a consequence generally politically and socially conservative in their ideologies. Other related consequences follow. The solidarity engendered by shared perceptions of danger and social isolation leads police to adopt something of a 'siege mentality', reflected in beliefs by police that they are misunderstood and unappreciated by the community at large (and in many cases by their own department).[38] In turn, a code of silence operates to protect even malpracticing police from external (and internal) scrutiny and criticism. The triggers for police abuse of power and force revolve around interactions which represent perceived challenges to police conceptions of normality and convention, and to their status as legitimate holders and wielders of authority. Besides the tendency to exercise more coercive authority and force against people who match stereotypes of deviance and dangerousness, police react aggressively to people who defy or deny their authority.

Steve James and Ian Warren

Culture in Australian Policing

Explanations for police behaviour and misbehaviour which invoke the concept of a distinctive police organisational culture have become a prominent part of the Australian discourse on policing in recent years. While the application of the concept to Australian policing by academics and others has perhaps predictably lagged behind scholarship in the United States, it began to creep into learned commentary in the 1980s.[39] However, it was arguably the Fitzgerald Commission of Inquiry in Queensland in the late 1980s which introduced the concept into popular parlance, and opened up its widespread adoption.[40] Fitzgerald made considerable use of the concept in his attempts to explain the misbehaviour of members of the Queensland Police, and it is the rare piece of contemporary Australian commentary upon police misbehaviour which does not invoke Fitzgerald's formulations.[41] Indeed, Finnane has argued that: 'The analysis of police culture and its effects (by Fitzgerald) is the most sustained official attack on police organization and practices in the history of Australian policing'.[42]

Fitzgerald sets the scene for the gravity and impact of organisational culture upon police impropriety:

> The Queensland Police Force is debilitated by misconduct, inefficiency, incompetence, and deficient leadership. The situation is compounded by poor organization and administration, inadequate resources, and insufficiently developed techniques and skills for the task of law enforcement in a modern complex society. Lack of discipline, cynicism, disinterest, frustration, anger and low esteem are the result. **The culture which shares responsibility for and is supported by this grossly unsatisfactory situation** includes contempt for the criminal justice system, disdain for the law and rejection of its application to police, disregard for the truth, and abuse of authority.[43] (emphasis added)

Fitzgerald concentrates upon three themes within police culture: the opportunities it offers for misconduct; the protection it offers for malpracticing police; and its reproduction in organisational life. For Fitzgerald, misconduct opportunities appear to be both attitudinal and structural. They are attitudinal in the sense that police perceive that they are combatants in an unequal fight with criminals, whose rights are zealously protected by the criminal justice system. Thus, police develop the conception that those rights can and indeed may need to be subverted for the sake of achieving the kinds of 'effective' justice believed to be expected by the community. Structurally, police have many opportunities to subvert rights, particularly through the mechanisms of false and forced confessions, perjury, and the manufacture of other kinds of evidence to secure convictions in court, without much fear of discovery and sanction. Besides abandoning due process in their pursuit of effectiveness, Fitzgerald notes that police have other opportunities available to behave corruptly for personal gain, through bribery, theft of forfeited goods, protection of illegal activities and so forth.[44]

Protection is offered to malpracticing police in both of these arenas of misconduct through the 'police code', a set of unwritten rules underpinned by an exaggerated need for internal solidarity and loyalty which demands, inter alia, that police do not criticise one another, and do not scrutinise each other's behaviours too critically.[45] As a consequence, police witnesses to police misconduct keep silent, 'whistleblowers' are ostracised or worse, investigations of police misconduct are obstructed, and external supervision of police behaviour is rejected.

The reproduction of the police culture takes place through the indoctrination of recruits who are 'young, often immature and with little experience of work or the broader society'.[46] They then:

> * receive inadequate instruction in public ethics and proper relationships ... with training substantially carried out by older police at least some of whom are officers imbued with the police culture;

8

* are provided with virtually no exposure to role models except other members of the Police Force;
* observe the influence of the police elite, their commitment to that culture and their exploitation of it, and the rejection and condemnation of those who do not conform; and
* initially lack the confidence or authority to act inconsistently with that culture, and later become immersed in that culture and compromised either by their behaviour or by acquiescence or inaction.[47]

While these themes offer echoes of propositions and hypotheses in the wider literature on police culture, they are presented more pithily, more trenchantly, and, we will argue, more simplistically, in the Fitzgerald formulations than is usual elsewhere. In particular, it is important to note here that the *Fitzgerald Report* was a response to a specific socio-political era in Queensland's history, and the extent to which its precise formulations are generaliseable across other Australian policing systems must be questioned. Nevertheless, the *Report* has clearly served to entrench the notion that culture in policing is an explanatory variable well worth applying to police behaviour in a variety of arenas. We turn now to brief examples of such applications in the Australian context.

Sutton has recently written on the structural and attitudinal difficulties facing women's entry into and success within policing.[48] Prominent amongst these is the failure by women to accommodate to and be accommodated by the police culture, a critical constituent of which is according to Sutton a powerful masculinist orientation that privileges strength and glamourises violence. Bird has raised the question of whether 'racism is an element of Australian police culture'.[49] Like many other commentators on the Australian policing of Kooris and ethnic minorities, she draws her conclusions (coyly in favour of the 'yes' proposition) from the well-documented overrepresentation of Kooris in police arrest and subsequent court statistics, as well as from a host of ethnographic accounts of the discriminatory verbalisations and actions of police.[50] White has indicted police culture as a determinant in the mistreatment of young people by police.[51] Young people are, according to White, particularly vulnerable to the application by police of culturally-determined practices such as the prediction of dangerousness and the invocation of delinquent stereotypes.

Finally in this section, we offer as illustrations a range of popular representations and a coronial finding on the nature and role of culture as a structuring and explanatory tool in relation to a number of recent critical policing issues in Victoria. In 1993, a number of Victorian police officers were convicted and sentenced for corrupt activities following Operation Cobra, an internal investigation by police which lasted for some eight years and was estimated to cost some $30 million before it was over.[52] In an interview with the *Sunday Age*[53], one of the officers, Paul Strang, gave a vivid account of aspects of culture within the Victoria Police. It is worth reproducing snippets from that account here:

He soon learned the golden rule of policing: don't rat on your mates.
Even as a young policeman, he knew that in the police community, loyalty to fellow coppers was more important than anything.
'When you went to a new police station, people would ring up to find out about you (from your previous station). Your name was on the network. Your future in the job was decided on your reputation. You got the white ball or the black ball. There was no way around it, it was part of the culture.'
He said excessive force and falsifying criminal confessions were standard tools in policing in the 1970s.
After a stint at the South Melbourne CIB, Mr Strang was appointed to one of the toughest squads in the force, the Consorting squad – once known as the 'Fletcher Jones Boys' because they could 'fit anybody'. They were the elite group who had to keep tab on Australia's hardest gangsters. They had instructions to fight fire with fire and they were notorious for bending the rules to get the job done.

9

Steve James and Ian Warren

> '...I went to see him (a senior officer) and he said: Paul, you are going to enter a special
> environment, you are going to work with some very capable men. They may do things
> you may not like, but they will get the desired results. If you feel uncomfortable with
> them in any situation, I will ask you to come and see me before you do anything else and
> I will handle the matter.'[54]

At the time of writing (July 1994), Victorian Police have shot dead seven people in
1994, and a total of 23 people since 1986, a rate which exceeds the total of police
shootings in all other states.[55] There has been, predictably, something of a media frenzy
of speculation about the causes of the fatalities, and culture has been a prominent
invocation. For the co-ordinator of a state–wide legal service for people with
disabilities (a number of whom have been included in the fatalities), 'the fault lay with
the police attitude to the mentally ill.': 'We're looking at a change in police culture,
where we've got baton charges at demonstrations, pressure points being applied and
police requesting sprays.56 John Lannigan, the assistant secretary of the Victorian
Council for Civil Liberties, argues that 'a 'redneck' counter–culture has been allowed to
flourish (among police in Victoria)'.[57] The *Adelaide Advertiser* reports that 'researchers
point to an allegedly 'gung–ho' ethos of aggression and violence in Victorian police
which embodies itself in a tendency towards open, 'frontal' confrontations likely to
provoke violent reactions.'[58] Even senior police invoked culture: The assistant
commissioner for operations, Mr Brian Church, said police culture had several positive
aspects. However he conceded there were several negatives, including the danger that
police became insular and developed a seige mentality.[59] In a return to more
conventional cultural characteristics, the notion of a 'culture of fear' among police in
Victoria was raised following high–profile killings of police and others in incidents such
as the Hoddle, Queen, Russell and Walsh Street murders; this fear has allegedly resulted
in a greater preparedness to use firearms.[60]

In June 1994, the Victorian State Coroner, Hal Hallenstein, handed down the first of
his findings related to seven police shootings in Victoria[61] In a brief reflective section at
the end of the findings, the coroner muses about the difference between the Victoria
Police and the New York Police in their philosophies and practices relating to the use
of firearms, and adds yet another twist to the concept of police culture:

> At one level the differences between two police forces in an area in which their polices are
> basically the same could be described as police culture. Police culture in the New York
> City Police Department rates very highly a police member's personal safety which
> generally carries with it the avoidance of confrontation risks to the public, the police
> member and the suspect. Police culture in Victoria involves a sense of public duty in
> which a police member's duty requires and worth is proved by acceptance of personal risk
> and display of personal courage in order to end by confrontation a situation which
> threatened the public, police members and the suspect.[62]

Police Culture: Some Questions and Issues

The emergence of the concept of a distinctive police organisational or occupational
culture has been, we agree, a valuable evolution in the scholarship on policing. It makes
considerable sense to recognise that occupational behaviour is governed in part by
factors beyond the formal prescriptive rules and guidelines imposed by due process and
the overt organisational structure of policing. It has been necessary to break free of the
limitations imposed upon the understanding of police behaviour by an exclusive
concern for the individual characteristics of police officers. In a common sense way,
anyone who has had systematic dealings with policing and police officers 'knows' that
there are codes and guidelines for police behaviour which do not appear in training
curricula, police regulations and police annual reports. Nevertheless, the very

popularity of the concept and its widespread application to police misbehaviour presents some difficulties. The danger exists, we believe, that its utility as an explanatory and structuring device for understanding police behaviour has become distorted by its invocation as *the* cause of behaviour (or more tyically, misbehaviour); such an application may serve to obscure other relevant factors and variations in police behaviour. In addition, we argue, there are some logical problems in several representations of the concept. These dangers and limitations do not require that the concept be abandoned. They do suggest however that we exercise a good deal of caution in our handling of it.

Our first caveat concerns the extent to which variation in police culture is ignored. This may sound like a paradox of sorts, given that virtually all commentators in the literature begin their arguments by acknowledging that substantial variations exist both within and between police organisations in terms of cultural characteristics. But after this initial acknowledgement, it is all too common for variation to be ignored in the search for continuities and generalisations. Variations exist as a function of the different histories, formal structures and contemporary socio–political contexts across police departments, and as a function of occupational specialisations within policing.[63] The appropriate application of cultural understanding to police behaviour must pay, we argue, at least as much analytical and empirical attention to discontinuities in police behaviour as it does to continuities.[64] In a related vein, much of the contemporary discourse (and virtually all of the popular discussion) on police culture is related to its role in the production and reproduction of police misbehaviour. While this is to some extent understandable, it serves to identify culture as a set of negative imperatives upon police practice. We discuss below some of the conceptual problems which arise from this imputation of 'production' and 'imperative', but here we want to assert that cultural analysis ought to be harnessed equally to the explanation of police propriety (however defined) as it is to police misconduct.[65]

The second and more significant problem we see with many representations of the culture concept is the tendency to embody it both as a prescriptive structure for action and as a rationalising framework through which the meanings of action are located. Fitzgerald's formulations illustrate the tendency. For Fitzgerald, it was the corrupt culture of the Queensland Police (and of the surrounding body politic) which 'caused' the varieties of misconduct uncovered. The informal code which defines culture offered simultaneously the opportunities and imperatives for misconduct and the protection and reproduction of malpracticing police officers. This seems to us to represent a conceptual confusion. On the one hand, the code is seen as a rationalising device, a schema of values in which it is considered permissible to (commonly) deny due process for organisational ends, and (less commonly) engage in corruption for personal gain. On the other hand, the code is seen as a set of prescriptive and sanctionable rules, through which police are driven to action (active misconduct) or inaction (protection of fellow workers through silence and obstruction of scrutiny). There are distinctly different implications for police propriety which flow from these two interpretations. In the first case, the structural opportunities for misconduct do not need to be an inherent component of culture; the role of culture is to legitimate the taking of the opportunities which can exist quite independently of culture. In the second interpretation, the opportunities become imperatives which govern action, and are logically an integral part of the culture. This interpretation is clearly the more subversive of police propriety, as it virtually demands that police engage in police misconduct as a function of the cultural framework within which they work.[66] We have reservations about accepting such a deterministic conception on several different grounds.

Shearing and Ericson have recently mounted a persuasive case against what they call 'cultural determinism' in conceptions of police culture.[67] They argue that in the

Steve James and Ian Warren

conventional rule-based paradigm of explaining behaviour, scholars have failed to find 'empirically locatable rules that generate action',[68] so they have sought implicit rules which best describe observed actions:

> To produce these implicit rules theorists formulate rules that 'fit' the activity. These observer-generated rules are then conceived of as implanted in people, via some process of internalization, so that they become 'need dispositions' that generate the activity from which the rules were derived in the first place.[69]

Shearing and Ericson describe this as 'tautological reasoning' and deficient, particularly given the empirical reality that police behaviour is variable and by no means always congruent with the alleged rules.[70] They posit a complex alternative conception in which people are not conceived of as 'cultural dopes, blindly following internalised rules but rather (one which) acknowledges them as active participants in the construction of action'.[71] They argue that the contours of police culture are shaped not by rigid rules and prescriptions but by the stories and metaphors told and retold within policing, which foster the development of subjective meanings within which police can locate their choices of action or inaction. This conception:

> ...permits us to understand how it is that action can be both guided and improvisational because it recognizes that any process for enabling human action must have an open-ended character that fosters the sensitiveness and openness required for creative choices. It accepts that while people's activity is directed, in the sense that a theatrical performance is directed, they none the less muddle through, improvise, and make things up as they go along. It recognises that police stories provide officers with the tools they can use to get them through the business of police work without minimizing the fact that this still requires individual initiative and daring.[72]

From a distinctly different theoretical basis, the philosopher Muscari has also attacked the deterministic nature of the orthodox conception of police culture.[73] Muscari acknowledges that structural factors, both formal and informal, do contribute to human action, and he accepts the likelihood that specific police cultural factors have an influence upon police misconduct. But he argues that the emphasis upon cultural/structural factors is disproportionate:

> ...(I)t takes the structural factor too much to heart and offers a logic of explanation which makes the element-to-element-to-whole so overridingly important that the individual can only be distinguished at the cost of triviality or misrepresentation... Without a sharper distinction between the agent who engages the structure and the structure itself, such a perspective cannot reconstruct a situation as it might have been grasped by the individual... (t)he current pattern of explanation has woven within its fabric an inherent tendency to turn social structures into causal patterns which siphon power from particular persons and transfer it to the code or medium that link them together.[74]

Muscari's intention is to reinstate the individual as a rational, accountable, moral decision-maker who is influenced but not 'annexed'[75] by structural and cultural factors.[76]

We draw no definitive conclusions from the arguments of Shearing, Ericson and Muscari outlined above, other than to agree with their general assertions that a conception of police culture which ignores the complexity of the relationship between cultural values and actions, which overstates the deterministic capacity of police culture and which ignores the role of the individual member as an active and creative participant in that culture, is ultimately deficient. We look forward to further developments in the discourse on police culture in Australia which take into account these qualifications.

12

NOTES

1. J. Skolnick, J. Fyffe, *Above the Law: Police and the Excessive Use of Force*, New York, 1993.
2. J. Sutton, 'Women in the Job', in P. Moir, H. Eijkman (eds), *Policing Australia: Old Issues, New Perspectives*, South Melbourne, 1992, pp 67–101; Skolnick, Fyffe, op. cit.
3. I. Freckelton, H. Selby, 'Piercing the Blue Veil: An Assessment of External Review', in D. Chappell, P. Wilson (eds) *Australian Policing: Contemporary Issues*, Sydney, 1989.
4. L. Brown, A. Willis, 'Authoritarianism in British Police Recruits: Importation, Socialization or Myth? *Journal of Occupational Psychology*, vol. 58, 1985, pp. 97–108.
5. ibid.
6. C. Geertz, *The Interpretation of Cultures: Selected Essays*, New York, 1973.
7. See T. A. Critchley, *A History of Police in England and Wales*, London, 1978.
8. C. Reith, *The Blind Eye of History: A Study of the Origins of the Present Police Era*, London, 1952.
9. See: M. Bogden, T. Jefferson, S. Walklate, *Introducing Policework*, London, 1988; P. Cohen, 'Policing the Working-class City', in B. Fine, R. Kinsey, J. Lea, S. Picciotto, J. Young (eds) *Capitalism and the Rule of Law*, London, 1979, pp 118–136; M. Sturma, 'Policing the Criminal Frontier in Mid–nineteenth Century Australia, Britain and America', in M. Finnane (ed) *Policing in Australia: Historical Perspectives*, Kensington, New South Wales, 1987, pp. 15–34.
10. See G. Kelling, M. Moore, 'The Evolving Strategy of Policing', *Perspectives in Policing No. 4*, United States Department of Justice, 1988, pp. 1–15.
11. H. Goldstein, *Policing a Free Society*, Cambridge, Massachusetts, 1977, p. 93.
12. Cohen, op. cit.; Kelling, Moore, op. cit.
13. J. Skolnick, *Justice Without Trial: Law Enforcement in Democratic Society*, 2nd edition, New York, 1975, p. 4.
14. See: K. Davis, *Discretionary Justice: a Preliminary Inquiry*, Baton Rouge, Louisiana, 1969; W. Lafave, *Arrest: The Decision to Take a Suspect into Custody*, Boston, 1965.
15. Goldstein, op. cit., p. 5.
16. A. Niederhoffer, *Behind the Shield: The Police in Urban Society*, New York, 1967.
17. R. Balch, 'The Police Personality: Fact or Fiction?', *The Journal of Criminal Law, Criminology and Police Science*, vol. 63, 1972, pp. 106–119.
18. W. Hanewicz, 'Police Personality: A Jungian Perspective', *Crime and Delinquency*, vol. 24, 1978, pp. 152–172.
19. Brown, Willis, op. cit.
20. J. Lefkowitz, 'Industrial–Organisational Psychology and the Police', *American Psychologist*, vol. 31, 1977, pp. 3–26.
21. See, for instance: Balch, op. cit.; C. Haney, 'Employment Tests and Employment Discrimination: A Dissenting Psychological Opinion', *Industrial Relations Law Journal*, vol. 5, 1982, pp. 1–86; D. Katz, R. Kahn, *The Social Psychology of Organizations*, New York, 1978; Lefkowitz, op. cit.; L. Sherman, 'Causes of Police Behaviour: The Current State of Quantitative Research', *Journal of Research In Crime and Delinquency*, 1980, pp. 69–100.
22. Skolnick, op. cit., p. 6.
23. ibid., p. 42.
24. ibid., p. 42.
25. ibid., p. 44.
26. ibid., p. 44.
27. ibid., p. 67.
28. J. Q. Wilson, *Varieties of Police Behavior: The Management of Law and Order in Eight Communities*, Cambridge, Massachusetts, 1968.
29. A. Reiss, 'Police Brutality: Answers to Key Questions' in A. Niederhoffer, A. Blumberg (eds) *The Ambivalent Force: Perspectives on the Police*, San Francisco, 1970, pp. 321–330.
30. ibid., pp. 329–330.
31. For a useful summary, see M. Brogden, T. Jefferson, S. Walklate, *Introducing Policework*, London, 1988, pp. 34–42.
32. See, for instance, A. Reiss, D. Bordua, 'Environment and Organization: A Perspective on Police' in D. Bordua (ed) *The Police: Six Sociological Essays*, New York, 1967.
33. See, for instance: R. Bennett, 'Becoming Blue: A Longitudinal Study of Police Recruit Occupational Socialization', *Journal of Police Science and Administration*, vol. 12, 1984, pp. 47–58; M. Hopper, 'Becoming a Policeman: Socialization of Cadets in a Police Academy', *Urban Life*, vol. 6, 1977, pp. 149–170; J. Van Maanen, 'Police Socialization: A Longitudinal Study of Job Attitudes in an Urban Police Department', *Administrative Science Quarterly*, vol. 20, 1975, pp. 207–228.
34. See P. Manning, 'The Police Occupational Culture in Anglo–American Societies', in L. Hoover, J. Dowling (eds) *Encyclopedia of Police Science*, New York, 1989.
35. See T. Dunham, G. Alpert (eds) *Critical Issues in Policing: Contemporary Readings*, Prospect Heights, Illinois, 1989. Section II: Slection, Training and Socialization.

Steve James and Ian Warren

36   Skolnick, Fyffe, op. cit.
37   ibid., p. 90.
38   ibid., p. 106.
39   See, for instance, R. Hogg, M. Findlay, 'Police and the Community: Some Issues Raised by Recent
      Overseas Research', in I. Freckelton, H. Selby (eds) *Police in Our Society*, Sydney, 1988, pp. 48–49.
40   Fitzgerald , op.cit.
41   See, for instance: K. Bryett, A. Harrison, *Policing in the Community*, North Ryde, Sydney, 1993, p.
      41; M. Palmer, 'Controlling Corruption', in Moir, Eijkman, op. cit., p. 110; Sutton, op. cit., pp.
      67–101; R. White, 'Young People and the Policing of Community Space', *Australian and New
      Zealand Journal of Criminology*, vol. 26, 1993, pp. 207–218.
42   M. Finnane, 'Police Corruption and Police Reform: The Fitzgerald Inquiry in Queensland,
      Australia', *Policing and Society*, vol. 1, 1990, pp. 159–171; p. 167 (parenthesis added).
43   ibid., p. 200 (our emphasis).
44   Fitzgerald argues that 'effectiveness' has been long seen by Queensland Police as synonymous with
      conviction rates; for an argument in support of this proposition, see R. Settle, *Police Power: Use and
      Abuse*, Northcote, 1990, pp. 14–36.
45   Fitzgerald, op. cit., p. 202.
46   ibid., p. 201.
47   ibid., p. 211.
48   Sutton, op. cit., pp. 67–101.
49   G. Bird, 'Policing Multicultural Australia', in Moir, Eijkman, op. cit., p. 363.
50   See also: Human and Equal Opportunity Commission, *Report of the National Inquiry into Racist Violence
      in Australia*, Canberra, 1991, pp. 79–135; C. Cunneen, 'Aboriginal Young People and Police
      Violence', *Aboriginal Law Bulletin*, vol. 2, 1991, pp. 6–9; B. Etter, 'The Police Culture: Overcoming
      Barriers', a paper delivered at the The Police, Aboriginal & Torres Strait Islander Peoples' National
      Conference, Perth, June 22–24, 1993; Office of the NSW Ombudsman, *Race Relations & Our Police: A
      Discussion Paper*, Sydney, 1994; C. Ronalds, M. Chapman, K. Kitchener, 'Policing Aborigines', in M.
      Findlay, S. Egger, J. Sutton (eds) *Issues in Criminal Justice Administration*, Sydney, 1988, pp. 168–183.
51   White, op. cit., pp. 207–218.
52   *Sunday Age*, 17 October 1993.
53   ibid.
54   ibid.
55   *Age*, 17 May, 20 May, 1994.
56   ibid.
57   ibid. (parenthesis added)
58   *Adelaide Advertiser*, 26 May 1994.
59   *Age*, 21 May 1994.
60   *Age*, 21 May 1994; *Sunday Age*, 22 May 1994.
61   State Coroner Victoria, *Coroner's Findings: Investigation into the Death of Gerhard Alfred Paul Sader*,
      Melbourne, 1994.
62   ibid., p. 321.
63   Most if not all of the seminal contributors to the discourse on police culture cited above attest to
      these variations.
64   See, for instance, J. Greene, G. Alpert, P. Styles, 'Values and Culture in Two American Police
      Departments: Lessons from King Arthur', *Journal of Contemporary Criminal Justice*, vol. 8, 1992,
      183–207.
65   For an innovative examination of the potential of using police cultural characteristics as a tool for
      police reform, see A. Goldsmith, 'Taking Police Culture Seriously: Police Discretion and the Limits
      of the Law', *Policing and Society*, vol. 1, 1990, pp. 91–114.
66   We would also argue here that a sharp distinction needs to be drawn between opportunities for
      misconduct pursued for organisational purposes and those pursued for personal gain. Conflating the
      two forms poses problems both for understanding through cultural analysis and for remedial strategies
      (see Settle, op. cit.).
67   C. Shearing, R. Ericson, 'Culture as Figurative Action', *British Journal of Sociology*, vol. 42, 1991, pp.
      481–506.
68   ibid., p. 482 (footnotes omitted).
69   ibid., p. 482.
70   ibid., p. 500 (parenthesis added; quotation marks omitted).
71   ibid., p. 500 (quotation marks omitted).
72   P. Muscari, 'Police Corruption and Organizational Structures: An Ethicist's View', *Journal of Criminal
      Justice*, vol. 12, 1984, pp. 235–245.
73   ibid., p. 241.

14

74   ibid., p. 242.
75   See also W. K. Muir, *Police: Street Corner Politicians*, Chicago, 1977.

[14]

Loyalty: The Police

R. E. EWIN

Moral philosophers, not only professional moral philosophers but also others who think about what morality is, have shown a tendency to ignore virtues, vices, and the general issue of motivation. They have been inclined to work in terms of duties and what might be called moral mathematics. When it comes to practice, most of us recognize that *what* is done, while it might matter a great deal, is not always the only thing that matters; *how* it is done can matter a great deal, too. A helping hand with a kind smile and an indication that the helper cares about the person being helped is usually a lot more efficient in improving somebody's position and disposition than is a helping hand given with an air of superiority or an attitude that suggests that one is no more than a social worker simply earning a living. So important can the motivation be that the same bodily movements, with different motivations, can amount, for all important purposes, to different actions: a kind attempt to help, even if unsuccessful, is still a kind action and can do a great deal to raise the morale of the person who needed help. Motivation *matters* in ethical life;[1] the sort of motivation on which somebody tends to act distinguishes not only between the kind person and the cruel one but also between the kind person and the conscientious one. One's motivation has a great deal to do with what one's character is, with whether one is a decent person or not. Motivation is what makes morality a human matter rather than a merely mechanical one.

What concerns me in this paper is a connection between motivation and various duties, especially duties that arise in the context of an institution such as a police force. I shall want to spread my net wider than that and discuss such issues as the role of loyalty in human life, but the focus will come back to the professional loyalties of police officers and, particularly, the discussion of the police culture in the Fitzgerald Report.[2]

Loyalty as Motivation to Duty

What is it that motivates people to perform their duties? Perhaps what matters, in the end, is *that* the duty is done more than *why* it is done, but motivation will have a lot to do with whether duty is done at all and with how well it is done. Motivation affects efficiency as well as morality and must, therefore, be given considerable thought by anybody concerned with an organization in which people are to perform their duties.

R.E. Ewin, author of Liberty, Community, and Justice, *is Associate Professor of Philosophy at the University of Western Australia.*

There are many different motivations that might lead people to do their duty. Not all are equally good or efficient in motivating dutiful action, and, given the mixed bag that people are, we need to think in terms of motivating those who are less than paragons of virtue if we are concerned with the problem in a practical way. One plausible suggestion is that the best motivation in such cases will be loyalty.[3] Loyalty is important to all of us. It affects what we will take as our interests: inside the family I might find my interests conflicting with my son's, but, outside the family, loyalty is likely to make me see his interests as ours or even as mine. In this way it makes clashes within *our* group (whichever group that might be for the purposes of the moment) less likely or easier to resolve and hence helps to make it possible for us to live as social beings even if it also sometimes helps to provoke clashes between rival groups of social beings. One might even say that loyalty is part of the integrity of a social being; it affects who and what we see ourselves as being. A loyal police officer, seeing what he or she is partly in terms of being a police officer, will not perceive the tasks of office simply as an externally imposed job but as integral to his or her personal responsibility.

Loyalty affects our display of those virtues that we have. Threats to the interests of a member of a group to which I am loyal might call forth from me a reaction that

Loyalty is part of the integrity of a social being.

is courageous; the same reaction to threats to the interests of a member of a rival group might be merely silly since those risks would not be worthwhile for a member of my group. No doubt there are some risks that one should take for anybody in suitable circumstances, but that is not true of all risks in all circumstances. One needs to be very careful in identifying the groups since each of us is a member of many different groups for many different purposes: I might, for example, display courage by bailing out a member of my sailing club or university department with a risky loan but might properly, without displaying lack of courage, decline to do the same for a member of a rival group; I would show no moral fault in not helping in such a case even though I might show great generosity or other virtue if I helped. But if the threat to the interests of the other person is a mugging, then I need to identify with the group of the law-abiding and take muggers as the rival group. Improper action can result from improper identification of the relevant group. That is to say, loyalty can go wrong.

Courage is not, of course, the only virtue affected in this way by loyalty. Looking after my son's interests, if I am thinking in terms of my family, is prudent rather than generous, but, still thinking in the same terms, I cannot be prudent in looking after the interests of my neighbor's children although I might be generous. Again, in different circumstances, the loyalties expressed might not be to family, but to neighborhood, and, in such cases, my neighbor and his children would be part of my

group. Their interests, to that extent, would be taken as my own. I can be grateful for help given to other people only if I identify with them in some way. I can admire and praise those who help others, but I can be *grateful* only for what is done to help me or somebody with whom I can identify.[4] Because loyalty and identification with a group affect who is seen as having a *prima facie* claim on a share in the distribution of goods, loyalty can affect the display of a sense of justice. And so on for the other virtues. Loyalty, therefore, plays a very important part in our moral lives, and it will play an important part in a police force in enabling significant virtues to flourish.

Loyalty is the instinct to sociability that keeps us from the radical form of the Hobbesian natural condition, the war of each against all.[5] It is a matter of emotional ties and commitments far more basic than cold contractual relationships. Those commitments come out, in part, in that aspect of loyalty that consists in a willingness on the part of the loyal person to subordinate his or her interests to those of the object of loyalty. That reduces disputes caused by conflicts of interests. That willingness to fit in and accept some limitations makes possible the acceptance of moral prohibitions and requirements that are generally regarded as necessary for social life. Loyalty is a reliable *motivation* for people to accept those aspects of living in a group. It enables us to live in groups, and, even if relations between the groups are not always cordial, loyalty makes it possible for us to live as people rather than simply as beasts of the forest or plain.[6] If morality is the working out of peaceful rela-

Loyalty is a matter of emotional ties and commitments far more basic than cold contractual relationships.

tions between people, then loyalty is at the start of it; loyalty is basic, and is therefore important to all of us.

And loyalty will matter to a group such as the police more than it matters to most. If one is to go out in the company of a partner to face considerable dangers, for example, one needs to know that that partner will treat one's interest as his or her own, that his or her courage will come into play when one is threatened.

Loyalty Is Not Simply a Virtue

But for all of that, one cannot say simply that loyalty is a virtue or that it guarantees good behavior or a happy outcome. One cannot even say simply that loyalty is a good thing or, without qualifications, that loyalty should be encouraged. The evidence that loyalty can go wrong, that it can lead to immoral behavior apparently just as readily as it can lead to laudable behavior, is all around us: we see it most obviously and most frequently in various forms of chauvinism or racism . There might be some inclination to explain this another way: the display of a lot of virtues depends on their association with other virtues if excess is to be avoided, and if the virtue, rather than a distortion of it (missing the Aristotelian mean), is to be exhibited at all. So it might be suggested that loyalty, too, needs to be associated with other virtues if it is not to go wrong and take excessive forms. But a difference nevertheless remains between loyalty and virtues.

If I am *completely* lacking in prudence, then my physical and mental well-being and my financial state will be such that I am unable to help others and be kind, or to pay my debts and be just. If I am *completely* lacking in courage, if I give up at the first sign of opposition or difficulty, then I can display no virtue at all. If I am *completely* lacking in justice, then I shall not distinguish the mugger from the victim when deciding whom to help and will thus fail in kindness, I shall misapply the criteria for which risks are worthwhile and thus fail in courage, and I shall misapply the criteria for *proper* concern for my own interests and be selfish rather than prudent. And so on. This is not to deny that some virtues might be better developed than others in any given person, but it does at least seem plausible to claim that nobody could have any of the standard virtues without having all of them to some extent. And yet, quite clearly, we can have loyalty without having those virtues. Emotional commitment to other people, particularly evil people, does not depend on possession of virtues. Loyalty is still possible in gangs devoted to vice. A large part of my point is that loyalty does need the virtues if it is not to go wrong, but it can quite clearly exist without them. It does not fit the pattern of that group of qualities of character, even if it underlies them and can be expressed through exhibitions of them. It underlies some vice as well, and can be expressed through that.

Loyalty always excludes some as well as including

others; one is loyal to X as opposed to Y, and one cannot be loyal to the human race as a whole unless in response to an invasion by Martians or an attempt by killer bees to take over the world. Because of that exclusive element, loyalty can lead to injustice and to callousness. Loyalty is an *emotional* tie that can lead people to be unreasonable and to overlook or override proper claims on them. My example for this is the police culture in Queensland as described by Fitzgerald.[7] What Fitzgerald refers to as "the police code" is a crucial element in this culture and has nothing to do with any Code of Ethics such as one might expect police to subscribe to in taking on their profession.

The unwritten police code is an integral element of police culture and has been a critical factor in the deterioration of the Police Force. It has allowed two main types of misconduct to flourish. A practical effect of the code is to reduce, if not almost to eliminate, concern at possible apprehension and punishment as a deterrent to police misconduct. The code exaggerates the need for, and the benefits derived from, mutual loyalty and support. The natural attraction of those characteristics for other members of the group has been exploited by the elite to its own advantage.

   Under the code it is impermissible to criticize other police. Such criticism is viewed as particularly reprehensible if it is made to outsiders. Any criticism which does occur is kept under the control of those who have authority and influence within the Force. Any dissidents are able to be dealt with for a breach of the code, with the approval of other police.[8]

Fitzgerald goes on to give an example of the police code at work:

A senior officer recommended that a Police Sergeant's notice of resignation should not be left to become effective automatically after a month in accordance with then current legislation but that the period should be shortened by 10 days. There was no discernible legitimate reason for such a step. The Government had publicly announced that it intended to legislate during that 10 day period in order to impede police who had been involved in misconduct from resigning and receiving benefits. In any event, the application to resign, which had been completed by the Sergeant, did not state any reasons for his resignation. In fact he had been committed for trial in connection with serious criminal offences of dishonesty associated with his police duties, and was subsequently convicted and imprisoned. A section of the form recording his application to resign called for his senior officer to state the general basis for the resignation and to add his assessment of the intending resignee's work performance and conduct. The section of the form signed by the applicant's superior officer on this occasion was in turn effectively endorsed by his senior officer's recommendation which read:

"1. The Sergeant has been committed for trial on criminal charges.

2. Through his general appearance, punctuality and attention to his duties the Sergeant set an example for junior staff as well as other N.C.O.'s.

His attitude and enthusiasm both as an officer performing general duties, and as a beat sergeant directing, advising and supervising subordinates, was without fault."

Few will have trouble discerning a contradiction between 1 and 2.[9]

And Fitzgerald goes on to give a number of other examples. General acceptance amongst police officers that they can act with impunity in such matters makes possible forays into organized crime that, otherwise, would have been stamped out as soon as they appeared. The loyalty that makes police officers willing to cover up for each other is what makes possible this criminality and the consequent undermining of the police force. As such procedures become institutionalized, only those police officers willing to go along with them will remain in the force, and, as public perception of these activities in the police force becomes common, only those who seek such activities will join the force and others will regard members of the force with suspicion and contempt.

Disloyalty is always reviled, but not all failures to act from loyalty are disloyal.

Fitzgerald makes clear that senior officers are not excluded from his accusations, and, indeed, suggests that they are responsible for the institutionalization of the police code. He also suggests that this is not merely a matter of accident:

Particular responsibility and enthusiasm for the police culture is to be found amongst some members of an elite within the Force, including senior officers, union officials and those with special appointments and functions, particularly detectives and other non-uniformed police. Members of the elite have been the major beneficiaries of the culture which they promote and exploit. . . .

Skilled police are acutely conscious of how laws can be circumvented or broken without penalty. The better they are

at their job, the more they learn. It is no accident that the police officers most admired for their skill by colleagues include some who become corrupt.[10]

It is to be expected, then, given that the most skillful are likely to rise in their profession, that there will be corruption in the higher levels of a police force such as Queensland's Police Force is in Fitzgerald's account. And that makes it hard for anybody who wants to blow the whistle:

There was throughout the evidence at this Inquiry a refrain that honest police did nothing because they did not know where to turn. Statements were even made that information and co-operation were withheld from previous inquiries because of a lack of confidence and trust either in those responsible for providing assistance to the tribunals or in the capacity of the tribunals to discover and expose the truth and have their reports implemented.[11]

And he also writes:

An instinct for survival and advancement in an institution and administration in which it was impossible to tell who could be trusted and who could be told made it imprudent, to say the least, to speak out. It was safer and easier and more consistent with responsibilities to family and self to say and do nothing despite a pledge to uphold the law.[12]

With nowhere safe to turn, with the possibility of being framed by experts if they blew the whistle, honest police were in a position in which there was very little that they could do.

Even a well-intentioned approach can lead to trouble. Apart from straightforward examples of corruption such as theft and bribery, Fitzgerald suggests another sort of wrongdoing that can arise from a desire on the part of police officers to do their job and serve the community well:

The criminal justice system is zealous in its concern for the rights of accused, but the rights and protection which are accorded to accused are obstacles which impede the conviction and punishment of those who are considered guilty, make the work of police more difficult and reduce their chances of a successful prosecution. Police see successful prosecutions as one of the few positive aspects of their work. Some accused persons and their associates (and sometimes their lawyers) engage in improper conduct, which exacerbates the difficulties and frustration of the police. Perhaps because the problems are too difficult or the implications too horrendous, the community has simply turned away from what, on reflection, is readily obvious. . . Steps to redress what is perceived to be an unequal contest are readily open to police officers. Evidence of guilt which is manufactured or falsified or improperly obtained diminishes the effect of the presumption of innocence and such requirements as proof beyond reasonable doubt and unanimous verdicts, and greatly decreases the prospects of acquittal for those whom [sic] the police decide are guilty.[13]

Here it is not self-seeking behavior that causes the problem, but a desire, laudable if given a different expression, to get the job done efficiently. The outcome, nevertheless, is the corruption of the criminal justice system of which the police force is a part and an improper assumption of power by the police force in a way that strikes at important parts of democratic life.

Disloyalty is always reviled, but not all failures to act from loyalty are disloyal. Given the basic place that loyalty has in our lives, it can take good or bad forms. Disloyalty rules out the possibility of taking good forms. Sometimes one has no loyalty and properly has no loyalty. How could I be loyal to somebody I have never heard of? We cannot properly expect loyalty of everybody all the time. We cannot expect one person to subordinate his or her interests to those of another without consideration of who the other person is and what the circumstances are. Sometimes one is reasonably expected to subordinate one's interests to those of an object of loyalty and at other times not. As a consequence, not all failures to act out of loyalty or to subordinate one's interests to those of a proper object of loy-alty are expressive of faults in one's loyalty. So we judge that there has been a *fault* in loyalty, that there has been disloyalty, only when a properly based trust has been breached. We judge that somebody is disloyal if he or she selfishly puts his or her own interests first rather than subordinating them to those of the object of loyalty. The person who did that might have acted out of simple selfishness or out of cowardice or out of spite or from some other motivation. But in any case of disloyalty, the person is expressing at the same time some other vice in putting his or her own interests first when it was not proper to do so.[14] Disloyalty is always expressed with another vice.

Given Fitzgerald's account of the Queensland Police Force, a police officer who blew the whistle could not be claimed to have acted out of loyalty to his or her colleagues (though he or she might have acted out of loyalty to the profession or to the community), but he or she has not been *disloyal* to them, either, because the trust was not properly based. The colleagues might regard the trust as properly based[15] if they took what they had been doing as an accepted part of the system,[16] and especially if the whistle-blower had taken advantages from that part of the system, but that is a matter of their having a different judgment of what is a proper basis for trust and does not go against my point. Disloyalty is a vice, but one cannot say simply that loyalty is a virtue.

How Can Loyalty Develop These Bad Forms?

All of these problems arising from loyalty, Fitzgerald says, were built into the police culture of Queensland. How could that be? The answer is not simply that police officers in Queensland were evil people; as Fitzgerald notes, "The basis of the unacceptable aspect of the police code upon which the misconduct which is woven into the culture depends can be traced to the distortion of acceptable traits."[17]

Some of the causes have to do specifically with police life, or perhaps with police life in Queensland.

Most police are recruited as school leavers. Recruits are therefore young, often immature and with little experience of work or the broader society.

When they join the Force, they enter an insular environment where they work and socialize almost exclusively with their colleagues. Their experience of the broader society is therefore not widened greatly. Contact with members of the public tends to be in situations of distress, conflict and hostility.[18]

And this problem is exacerbated by other developments:

Police work almost exclusively, and socialize extensively, with other police and, with increasing numbers of females in the Police Force, more regularly marry police. As in other occupations, children of police officers follow their parents into the "job."

Faced with public indifference, mistrust, hostility and resentment, police come to depend on their fellows for physical security, friendship, sympathy, emotional support and a feeling of self-worth. In difficult times, police officers naturally turn to the people who have become their closest friends, and the mechanisms are there to make sure they have support.

In the result, the Police Force has increasingly turned in on itself and away from the community apart from superficial campaigns to allay community concerns and win recognition despite its adherence to its culture.[19]

And eventually we reach the stage at which the *point* of a police force is forgotten:

[A typical senior police officer's] loyalty to the Police Force and the people in it will have come to outweigh what was only ever a vague and abstract loyalty to the community. In important respects, he will have rejected the values of the outside community, and be prepared to go to extraordinary and sometimes illegal lengths to protect what he believes to be the interests of the Police Force and of his police brothers. Loyalty to the Force has become the purpose, rather than the means, of fulfilling his duty.[20]

One can see how loyalties would grow strong in the police force, and especially how the fact that police usually mix with members of the public in unhappy circumstances, might provoke an unfavorable attitude to the police that would encourage them to take a "them and us" attitude, identifying themselves very strongly as police and as a group sharply separate from the general public.

One can see, indeed, just how easy it is for antagonistic attitudes to develop between police officers and members of the general public. Controlling traffic on points duty is one of the things that police do, but their work is not usually thought of in those terms. In the more spectacular areas of their work, police and the criminal justice system that they administer are, in a very important way, the last resort. Education, town planning, antipoverty projects, provision of leisure activities and medical services, and so on are all designed to help people to live peaceful and law-abiding lives together. When all of those steps fail and people still commit serious crimes, then the last resort has to be used: the police force and the criminal justice system come into play. The people that police officers meet in that aspect of their work are not likely to be impressive in their probity. Insofar as the people that police officers meet are either other police or hardened criminals, experience is likely to suggest that people outside the police force are not of a very high quality.

Most of us do not meet police in those circumstances. We meet them when it is an issue of whether our automobile is roadworthy, or when we have been driving it at a speed in excess of the speed limit or while having had too much to drink. The police then appear to

us as bureaucratic enforcers of unnecessary regulations, as killjoys, as jumped-up jacks-in-office, or in various ways as people of whom we have a low opinion.[21] This can bring forth aggressive behavior that is not likely to improve the view police have of the rest of us, and fawning behavior as an alternative will not produce a more favorable view. The offer of a bribe might produce a reaction of contempt from an upright police officer, and that contempt, after a while, can turn into the view that the people outside the police force deserve no better than that the bribes be accepted.

But there are more general problems here to do with the nature of loyalty itself. Loyalty can take different sorts of objects.[22] One can be loyal to people, as one might be loyal to a friend with whom one had been through a lot or who had been a great help when one had had troubles. One can similarly be loyal to groups of people with whom one has grown up or groups one has deliberately joined or groups with whom one has been through danger[23] or hard times, and so on. One can be loyal to principles where principles are quite separate from people or groups of people; one is loyal to the

Loyalty to principles and loyalty to people can come into conflict.

principles if one sticks to them even when it is difficult to do so. Loyalty to principles and loyalty to people can come into conflict, as they sometimes do when the primary noticeable loyalty is to a group, but to a group structured by certain principles: somebody who thinks that the members of the group are departing from its principles might be led by loyalty to the principles to oppose the members of the group. (The different sorts of objects of loyalty can, of course, be mixed, as they are likely to be in loyalty to such a group.)

We can have clashes of loyalties that are clashes of loyalties to objects of the same kind, or clashes that are between loyalties to objects of different kinds. I might be a member of two groups and feel loyalty to each even though the loyalties come into conflict. Each might need financial support, for example, and I might be in such a position that I can offer the support to only one of them. The problem, by and large, does not seem to be a great one: I sort it out by considering such issues as which of the groups has the greater need of my support, which I feel I owe more, or which is more important in the grand scheme of things. At least in the normal run of things, the two groups will be commensurable in these respects, and I shall be able to make a decision even if the thinking involved in making it might be difficult. I shall, no doubt, be disappointed at not being able to support a group to which I feel loyalty but I have, clearly, not been disloyal to it even if more devoted members of that group feel let down that I chose the other; the problem was not a lack in my loyalty, but the practicalities of the situation. There might be so little lack in my loyalty in

> "My leader (group, country) right or wrong" is an attitude that causes a lot of trouble.

such a case as to cause me severe emotional stress when I have to make the choice.

Or I might, at times, find that two principles to which I have been loyal come into conflict. That will give me cause for thought and require that I go through a certain amount of re-thinking and re-ordering of my principles. Again, the problem is, at least in theory, resolvable, and there is no basis for an accusation of disloyalty simply in the fact that I cannot follow both principles or continue to subscribe to both in the forms in which I had previously subscribed to them.

Or the clash might be between loyalty to principles and loyalty to a group. An example bearing directly on the issue at hand would be the problem of a police officer wondering whether to blow the whistle on inefficiency or corruption in the force. That sort of problem would be at its most difficult when the person on whom the whistle might be blown was a partner, somebody with whom one had been through hard times and danger, because the loyalty to such a partner is a personal loyalty rather than a loyalty to the principles governing police work. Such partners help each other in times of danger, and that can be stretched very readily to covering up improper activities. The issue will not be an easy one.

The way I have described these cases makes it sound as though sorting out a clash of loyalties is a purely cold, rational procedure that might be carried out using a

computer. And, faced with such a case, we concentrate our attention on the case itself, thinking about its features rather than about what in ourselves makes us treat those features as important. But loyalty is not simply a matter of calculation; it is a matter of emotional commitment, and a clash of loyalties can be a clash of strong emotional commitments that play a fundamental part in somebody's life. Psychiatric upset can follow, and we often greatly admire those who have the strength to handle such cases and make a decision.[24]

On the one hand, one might be inclined to say that one should always stick to principles and be loyal to those, having adopted them after due thought. Blind, chauvinistic loyalty is what leads to a lot of the problems caused by loyalty; blind loyalty, it might be said, is always loyalty to a person or to a group of people whose lead one will follow. "My leader (group, country) right or wrong" is an attitude that causes a lot of trouble, so we might be led to think that *bad* loyalty, the loyalty that causes problems, is loyalty to people or groups and that the good loyalty, the virtue (if such it be), is loyalty to principles. After all, it makes no sense to say "My principles, right or wrong"; if I recognize that they are wrong, then they cease to be my principles. And loyalty to principles, it might be said, cannot be blind, because principles are adopted after rational consideration. But it takes no more than a moment's reflection to recognize the falsity of that claim. Principles can be held because I was brought up to believe in them and never gave them very much thought, and simply applying those principles mechanically, without ever reflecting on them, will be just as much a blind loyalty as any other loyalty.

And it is not clear that the principles always should win out in any such conflict of loyalties. A minor breach of principles by somebody who gave in to temptation and whose career would be ruined by disclosure might not, perhaps, be the occasion for blowing the whistle if one owes loyalty to that person. If the grounds for loyalty are slight and the offense is great, then, no doubt, one should turn in whoever it is. There will be many cases where it is not clear which way the decision should go. But there will also be cases, especially where draconian penalties might be involved, in which one should give precedence to the person.

And surely loyalty to a person should lead one to give that person the benefit of any doubt. Police officers have to mix with criminals to do some of their work, have to seek information that sometimes requires undercover work of an apparently illegal sort in order to gain information from minor criminals that might lead to the arrest of major criminals, and so on. Loyalty to a police officer accused of criminal activity that might be explicable in such a way might well, and properly, lead other police officers to accept the explanation.

Fitzgerald says:

To the obvious benefit of those with something to hide, the police code also ensures that critical activities of police officers are largely immune from scrutiny. The police code effectively requires that it be assumed that whatsoever is done by a police officer legitimately occurs in the course of his duty. It is patent how absurd that is, and what the consequences are certain to be, given the nature of police work and the nature and extent of each police officer's authority and discretion. Police, especially detectives, have to mix with criminals, including informants whom they cultivate as part of their duties. Such contacts are a primary source of police misconduct. Skilled experienced police are usually the ones exposed to the hardened criminals with most to lose and most to offer, and are therefore exposed to maximum temptation.

Police claim that total secrecy concerning informants is necessary. It is said that a police officer should not be called upon to name his informants in any circumstances: to do so would impair the relationship, make it more difficult to obtain information, and even imperil the informant. It is asserted that there must be no supervision of contacts and arrangements between police and informants (or criminals who conceivably might be informants), including payments which are exchanged and other benefits which are granted (including discretions which are exercised in relation to proceedings against informants): police work, so it is said, would be inhibited if such contacts and arrangements were monitored.[25]

Perhaps these claims do go too far. At least supervision within the police force ought to be possible, provided that the senior officers can be trusted.[26] But the point that I am after now is the one made by Fitzgerald and quoted earlier: "The basis of the unacceptable aspect of the police code upon which the misconduct which is woven into the culture depends can be traced to the distortion of acceptable traits."[27] There will be room for a loyal fellow officer to look for the acceptable trait and interpret the behavior in its light. One does not expect loyalty to blind such a person to the obvious, but one might reasonably expect that it would lead him or her to give the colleague the benefit of any doubt. After enough of this giving of the benefit of the doubt, the officer who had given it might find that he or she could not make the behavior of the other public without himself or herself being accused of having connived at the misconduct or at least gone along with it.

There are several different possible objects of loyalty

for police officers in the context of their work. A police officer might be loyal to his or her partner personally or to the police force (which might be taken in a number of ways) or to a police code of ethics or to the government or to the community the police force exists to serve. Conflicts of loyalty can arise from these different possible objects of loyalty, and it is not always clear how they should be resolved. This is the area in which police officers, especially those thinking of blowing the whistle, will have to sort out the appropriate group or object for their loyalties in the circumstances.

A conflict between loyalty to one's partner and loyalty to the police force or to the police code of ethics looks as though it is straightforward but will not always be so.[28] If I owe my life to my partner, then I *should* feel strong ties; I would be less than a decent human being if I simply kept on asking what he or she had done for me today or pointing out that, much as my life means to me, I am not inclined to pay much for it now that I have it and am safe again. A decent human being really *should* feel close ties in such a case and should at least feel torn about whistleblowing, even when the partner's offense is a serious one. This is not to suggest that the Police Code of Ethics should have a clause saying that one must not turn one's partner in when one knows that he or she is guilty of a serious offense, but one does not want to discourage this completely appropriate feeling of personal loyalty in police or in people generally. Without ties of loyalty and trust between partners, police work would be much harder to do. It is at least a mitigating factor in judging the offense of covering up the initial wrongdoing. On top of that, there will be other cases of

Without ties of trust and loyalty between partners, police work would be much harder to do.

lesser offenses when a young and inexperienced officer has given in to temptation or been trapped in a situation in which he or she thought wrongdoing was the only way to escape false accusations, and one might reasonably judge that the good of the police force would best be served by not losing that officer, who was unlikely to offend again in that way after the experience.

Given that a police force exists to serve the community and not purely for the purposes of its members, it might seem straightforward that loyalty to the community should take precedence over loyalty to the police force or its code of ethics. But mishaps are easy in this area, too, and the point is not a straightforward one. A police officer who had formed a low opinion of the community at large might, out of loyalty to the force, make sure that he did a good job anyway. Loyalty to the community, on the other hand, might lead to improper behavior. With expensive lawyers and legal niceties ranged against them, police who wanted to serve the community might bypass the law.[29]

The Role of Judgment in Loyalty and in Virtues

Loyalty, at least on the face of it, then, cannot simply be regarded as a virtue. Loyalty can go dramatically wrong, as it does when it takes some of the forms of jingoism. *Any* virtue can go wrong, of course: genuine courage, undeniably a virtue, can lead one into dangerous situations, and if one's efforts are unsuccessful, it can lead to problems for others. The possibility of mistake in a particular case can never be excluded. Prudence can lead one to miss opportunities that might, as things turn out, be opportunities one would like to have had. Courage and prudence are, nevertheless, clearly virtues. But the position with respect to loyalty is not the same as that with respect to courage or prudence because of the different roles that judgment plays in those qualities of character.[30]

Possession of a virtue is a complex matter; it is a matter of capacities of various sorts being brought together in a person. Kindness is not one simple attribute of a person, let alone a simple attribute that is either present in complete form or completely absent; it is a mixture of emotional elements, an inclination to choose certain sorts of ends in one's actions (notably ends that involve helping other people), and various other elements. One element in all virtues is good judgment.[31] The sort of good judgment at issue is a general capacity opposed to something like stupidity or lack of foresight; it is not the same as infallibility and does not exclude the possibility of occasional mistakes. The point is about qualities of character, not merely about particular actions. In the case of kindness, one needs to be able to judge what help it is one's business to give, failure in which judgment makes one a busybody rather than a kind person; one needs to be able to judge what will really help, and whether one's capacities allow one to do that sort of thing, failure in which judgment makes one a well-meaning burden rather than a kind person; and, to give just one more example, one needs to be able to make judgments of propriety. Kindness is not a matter of requirement in the way that justice is, but judgments of justice can enter: a kind person helps the victim, not the mugger, even if the victim is giving as good as he or she gets and appears to be winning the fight.

This is not a matter of cold-blooded calculation. It need not be a matter of calculation of any sort but may simply be a recognition of what we have come to regard as important features of such a situation, in much the same way as an experienced chess player will recognize various positions on the board without any need to calculate. But, before we can simply recognize the situation in this sort of way, we do have to learn and understand why it is the victim and not the mugger who should be helped. Not caring about these features of the situation (which is different from simply being mistaken about them in any given case) means that one lacks the virtue of kindness even if one means well. Meaning well is, no doubt, better than meaning ill, but constantly getting in people's way with ill-judged attempts to help when one does not know what is going on and should mind one's own business falls a long way short of the proper virtue of kindness. Judgment of when giving help is worthwhile or proper is part of the possession of the virtue of kindness. It is also part of the possession of the virtue of courage: I must, for example, be able to judge which risks are worth taking and which are not if I am actually to be courageous rather than foolhardy. Swimming through shark-infested waters involves taking risks, but it is not courage that leads me to act if I swim through shark-infested waters simply to get my name in *The Guinness Book of Records*. In that case, I am simply foolhardy.

Judgment does not seem to have that sort of role to play in loyalty. The judgments involved in the examples above are *internal* to kindness and courage. Certainly we can make judgments about what is worthy of loyalty and what is not, but that is a judgment *external* to the loyalty and referring to it, so cannot itself be *part* of the loyalty. The central judgment in the case of courage is the judgment that the risks are worth taking given the end. We speak of earning loyalty and of owing loyalty, so that idea might give us a judgment that could be part of loyalty as good judgment is part of courage or kindness. In fact, it will not do so. The judgment that something is owed *as a matter of loyalty* would make the idea of loyalty circular if treated as itself a part of that idea. The judgment that something was owed *as a matter of justice* is relevant to the justice of doing it but not especially relevant to whether performing the action is a display of loyalty. We speak of earning and owing gratitude as we do of earning and owing loyalty, and gratitude, like loyalty, is the sort of thing one discovers one has begun to feel rather than the kind of thing one cold-bloodedly decides to have, but the judgment that something is owed as a debt of gratitude is not necessary to loyalty (gratitude is by no means the only possible ground of loyalty) and, anyway, gratitude can give rise to exactly the same sorts of problems as does loyalty: a proper gratitude is fine, but a gratitude that leads one to ignore the perfectly legitimate interests of some people and improperly further the interests of the person to whom one feels gratitude produces exactly the same sorts of problems as does a bad loyalty. One might note that loyalty is usually expected to lead to the favoring of the interests of the object of loyalty over other interests.

The problem about the role of judgment in loyalty goes deeper than that. Loyalty is an emotional bond, not a calculating form of commitment, and the person who

The person who acts only after calculating that the act is owed is, to that extent, not a typically loyal person.

acts only after calculating that the act is owed as a matter of loyalty is, to that extent, not a typically loyal person. Judgment of what is owed is not part of loyalty as it is part of justice. Emotional ties will bear only so much weight, and loyalty will, no doubt, eventually disappear if too much is loaded on it, but the loyal person, unlike the calculating person, sticks through the hard times when good judgment of fairly ordinary sorts would suggest that one should leave.[32] One has nothing to gain from staying. Loyalty makes one stay, nevertheless; it

motivates one to do what duty requires or to do things for the good of another that are not required by duty.

If I am loyal to you, then I shall be expected to give some precedence to your interests, both over my own interests (at times and to some extent) and over the interests of other people. To that extent, loyalty involves setting aside what good judgment would otherwise require. Perhaps somebody else would do a better job of painting my house, but loyalty to my son makes me employ him. And it is not only my judgment of my own interests that is set aside, but, perhaps, also my judgment of what is morally proper. Loyalty involves giving

Because loyalty is not limited by good judgment, it can take good or bad forms.

some precedence to the interests of the object of loyalty, so, if I act out of loyalty to you, it may involve doing some injustice to those over whose interests I give precedence to yours. In that way, it can set aside good judgment about justice or good judgment that might have led one to be kind to somebody other than the object of loyalty. If my son does something sufficiently reprehensible, then, no doubt, I shall eventually turn him over to the police, but my loyalty to him would make me feel torn about any such decision, and we should expect at least that parents, and others with loyalties, would feel similarly torn if they had to treat the object of their loyalty in such a way. Somebody who acted completely in terms of reason and did not even feel torn in such a situation would be a remarkably cold fish, and the usual judgment of them would be that they showed a significant emotional lack. It is part of loyalty, in a very important way, that it overrides to some extent reason in the form of some important sorts of good judgment and that the person who is loyal does not calculate too much what is owed as a matter of loyalty. The way in which loyalty requires that one set aside good judgment to some extent means that good judgment cannot play the part in loyalty that it does in virtues such as courage. Because loyalty is not limited by good judgment, it can take good or bad forms; good judgment marks courage off from foolhardiness.

One cannot simply say that loyalty is a bad thing. It seems to lend itself very readily to excesses, such as chauvinistic loyalties leading to unjust discrimination against people who are not in the group and to insensitivity to the feelings and legitimate interests of those people. We can see such excesses when loyalties to a football team lead its supporters to such misjudgments as that the result of a football match is sufficiently important to justify beating up and even killing supporters of the opposition team, and, generally, in the problems of jingoistic attachment to a group. Such things are the bad face of loyalty. Nevertheless, even though we can be improperly attached to groups and even though attachment to groups can lead us to improper action, it does matter that we be prepared to attach ourselves to groups and to have the appropriate loyalties. We are social beings, and loyalty is the raw emotional material of that sociality. Without any inclination to loyalty, to identify our interests with those of others and to see ourselves as members of groups, we should be left to live in the Hobbesian natural condition. We need loyalties if we are to be human; they are part of a complete human emotional life. On the other hand, loyalties can lead to serious problems when they go wrong. And if judgment is not part of loyalty as it is part of virtues such as kindness and courage, then we cannot mark off the good loyalty as something separate from the bad loyalty; the judgment that the object of the loyalty is a proper object and that the form of the loyalty is proper will remain something external to the loyalty itself. Loyalty we must have, but it needs to be controlled, and we need to make sure that it has proper objects.

What Is to Be Done?

How can loyalty be controlled in the required way? For that needs to be done, especially in a police force, given the relationship between loyalty and the flourishing of virtues such as courage.

Loyalty can be generated by a variety of things, and it seems clear that the loyalty responds to what generated it. As I pointed out earlier, loyalty always involves some exclusion: one is loyal to X rather than to Y, with Y thus being excluded. At times, the reverse can also be true: that a group of people is excluded (whether or not they are properly excluded) can make them feel a common cause in response to what they see as oppression and can result in the growth of loyalty amongst them. That loyalty, provoked by a dislike and perhaps distrust of the other group, is likely to be marked by behavior that ignores legitimate interests and concerns of the other group.

When loyalty within a police force is generated in that way, problems can be expected. The loyalty will be very much to other members of the police force, not to the police force as an institution that exists to serve the community. As a result, the loyalty is likely to show itself in protection of those members of the force against any threats from outside in just the sort of way Fitzgerald suggests after describing the way in which members of the Queensland Police Force were isolated from the rest of the community and felt themselves to be looked down upon by the rest of the community.

A feeling of rejection, especially if it is soundly based in the fact that one is rejected, cannot be removed simply by fiat. One thing that would help to remove the threat of a bad loyalty amongst police officers would be to have a police force that was not looked down on by the rest of the community, but it is easier to say that than to change the community's views. Change takes time and is likely to be helped by the removal of the isolation of police officers from others. Visits of police officers to schools, having police officers run road safety classes for school children, and other such ventures will all help.

Increasing crime rates help to make people in general think more favorably of the police and their work. One thing that seems to have affected relations between police officers and members of the public in some parts of Australia in recent years is the setting up of Community Watch schemes in which members of a neighborhood agree to keep an eye on each other's houses and goods and to call the police if there is any suspicious activity, with police officers cooperating in the setting up of such schemes and giving lectures to the groups on methods of making a house secure and other such matters. Cooperation of this sort helps to break down the division that Fitzgerald found between police officers and others and to make it less likely that the loyalty that comes simply from a feeling of rejection will arise.

Loyalty can arise from a desire for self-preservation and a feeling that one is in so deep that one must stay with this group and their ways. This might arise with young recruits to a police force who are unsure of how things are done, who feel that they are in no position to blow a whistle because they do not really understand the practicalities of police work and will merely make themselves look silly. As an academic might simply take a

pencil from the office and use it for non-academic purposes without giving the matter any thought, a young
police officer might accept the occasional offer of a free
hamburger as one of the perks of office and develop
slowly from there.[33]

Several things might be done about that. Attempts
might be made to make sure that more of the recruits are
not young people with no experience of work or life
outside the police force, which could be done by strenu-
ously seeking older recruits and by making it easier to
enter the police force some way up the scale. More
encouragement might be given to police officers to
pursue further studies, and not only in matters of direct
relevance to police work: a higher standard of education
will usually help to make people less gullible and less
easily led into thoughtless wrongdoing, even if it might
sometimes make them more efficient at thoughtful
wrongdoing.

And more could be done with the young recruits.
Counseling, the absence of which is noted by Fitzgerald,
might become a regular part of the recruitment and
training procedure, not just a once-and-for-all lecture
during training but a recurrent matter over the first few
years of service. An explicit code of ethics[34] would help
to provide a focus for such counseling. And an experienced, independent person to whom young officers

could go to speak privately about their worries would
give them the benefit of experience without the worries
of looking silly in front of their colleagues or suffering
reprisals for questioning what other officers were doing.

One will never be able to guarantee that only good
people enter the police force or that nobody will suc-
cumb to the temptation that is likely to come a police
officer's way. My concern has not been with grand
schemes of that sort but with the roles that loyalty can
play in a police force. Loyalty, I have argued, is necessary to all of us, and it is probably necessary to any police
force that is to be effective. Certainly one should expect
it to grow amongst people who face danger together and
depend on each other, or even simply amongst people
who work together over a long period of time and face
similar problems. Loyalty is a necessary thing, and in
that way is a good thing for a police officer to have, but
it can go wrong as, according to Fitzgerald, it went
wrong in Queensland. Because judgment does not play
the role in loyalty that it plays in virtues such as courage
and kindness, there is no *internal* limitation on loyalty
that restricts it to the good; limitations that do that must
be external to the loyalty. In this final section I have been
concerned to suggest some methods for applying external limitations that will help to avoid having loyalty
develop in the wrong directions.

NOTES

1 *Cf.* Wren, *Whistle-Blowing and Loyalty to One's Friends*, in
Police Ethics: Hard Choices in Law Enforcement 28 (W. C. Heffernan & T. Stroup, eds. 1985) on the shallowness of the
external viewpoint and the moral judgments it produces.

2 I shall use this popular name to refer to the Report of a
Commission of Inquiry Pursuant to Orders in Council, the report
of the Commission of Inquiry into Possible Illegal Activities
and Associated Police Misconduct, presented to the Premier of
Queensland on 3rd July, 1989, and published by the Government of Queensland in the same year. A. Fitzgerald was Chairman of the Commission. The report alleged substantial and institutionalized involvement of the Queensland Police Force in
organized crime. It resulted in the departure from the scene of
several senior police officers and several senior politicians,
some of whom have since been charged with criminal activities. It is also widely believed that the report was the main
factor in explaining the change of government in Queensland
(after more than two decades of National Party rule) in the
election at the end of 1989.

3 The connection between loyalty and duty is so strong that
they are sometimes run together, to the detriment of the idea
of loyalty. M. D. Bayles, for example, in Professional Ethics 77-
83 (1981), has a section the ostensible subject of which is loyalty

but the real subject of which is no more than the content of professional duties. This reduction of loyalty to duty is an extreme
form of the externalist view rejected by Wren (*supra* note 1) and
has the consequence that loyalty and duty could not come into
conflict, as, quite clearly, they can. I shall go on to argue that,
as well as an idea of duty, we need and expect loyalty as a
motivation amongst a group of people such as a police
force.

4 The point is not always obvious. Suppose I am grateful to
you for helping Jones because this relieves me of the burden of
having to do it myself. We might say here that I am grateful
precisely because I have no loyalty to Jones. Nevertheless, I am
grateful to *you* because you have done something for *me, viz.,*
relieved me of a burden.

5 T. Hobbes, Leviathan 185 (C. B. Macpherson ed. 1968).

6 *Id.* at 186.

7 The Fitzgerald Report, *supra* note 2, ch. VII. Use of the terms
"police culture" and "police code" in the way Fitzgerald uses
them is not peculiar to him. *See, e.g.,* Savitz, *The Dimensions of
Police Loyalty*, 13 Am. Behav. Scientist 694-95 (1970), for such
uses and for reference to other literature.

8 Fitzgerald Report, *supra* note 2, at 202. This emphasis on secrecy in a police force has been noticed by many others. Savitz, *supra* note 7, at 695, cites numerous sources covering a long period of time.

9 Fitzgerald Report, at 202.

10 *Id. at* 200-01.

11 *Id.* at 205.

12 *Id.*

13 *Id.* at 206.

14 Disagreements in the judgments about propriety will help to explain some disagreements about whether somebody was disloyal in much the same way as differing judgments about whether the risks were worth taking can explain differing judgments about whether somebody was cowardly.

15 An example of the way in which differing judgments about propriety can lead to differing judgments about whether somebody has been disloyal.

16 Or they might think that the officer in question should be loyal to them *personally*, not to the police force and to them as members of the police force.

17 Fitzgerald, *supra* note 2, at 32.

18 *Id.* at 201. Similar points can apply in the case of a military culture.

19 *Id.*, p. 210. Others note the isolation of the police: Wren, *supra* note 1, at 26, notes that their role as guardians and regulators of other people's conduct sets them apart, and that their work schedule tends also to seal them off. He notes there the crucial point that police officers *perceive themselves* to be alienated from the rest of the community, which can give rise to problems even if the perception is ill-based. Savitz, *supra* note 7, at 694-95, also notes the significance of occupational isolation.

20 Fitzgerald Report, *supra* note 2, at 210.

21 Savitz, *supra* note 7, at 694, refers to "the policeman's job (enforcing minor statutes which generates resentment and hostility . . .)", citing support from J. Skolnick: Justice Without Trial (1966). He also suggests how this might start off a chain of worsening relations—"Failing to secure the deference which they feel they are owed by the public has resulted in numerous instances of hostile or brusque officer responses in observed police-citizen transactions"—and he cites support from Black and Reiss, *Patterns of Behavior and Citizen Transactions*, in U. S. Government Printing Office, 2 Studies in Crime and Law Enforcement in Major Metropolitan Areas (1967).

22 Despite John Ladd's contention that loyalty must always be to a particular person in a particular role. See his entry on loyalty in 5 The Encyclopedia of Philosophy 97-98 (P. Edwards ed. 1967).

23 Both Wren, *supra* note 1, and Savitz, *supra* note 7, amongst many other writers, note the significance of facing danger in generating police loyalty

24 An example might be R.E. Lee's decision to support the cause of the South in the Civil War.

25 The Fitzgerald Report, *supra* note 2, at 202-03.

26 But it should be noted that Fitzgerald, in the passage just quoted, suggests that skilled and experienced officers, likely to have reached a senior level, are the ones exposed to maximum temptation. In another passage, Fitzgerald suggests that senior officers do a lot to enforce the code:

Police observance of the code is substantially increased by the extent of the power which is held over ordinary police by the elite and the ruthlessness with which it has been exercised on those occasions when it has been considered necessary to do so (p. 205),

which suggests that they should not be trusted in the necessary way, or, at least, that they should not be trusted in circumstances such as prevailed in Queensland. In one of the sillier passages of the report, Fitzgerald also says:

Since a police force is drawn from the community (and from some sections of the community more than others), it is likely to reflect the general social culture, including its weaknesses (for example, materialism), and also to include a roughly representative proportion of individuals who break the law (p. 200).

If that reasoning had any soundness, it would, presumably, apply to senior officers too.

27 *Id.* at 202.

28 *Cf.* Wren, *supra* note 1, at 27-28.

29 See the quotation from Fitzgerald, *supra* note 13.

30 For an account of what constitutes a virtue and why the virtues are not simply a mixed bag of qualities of character, *see* R.E. Ewin, Co-operation and Human Values (1981).

31 There is an interesting and useful discussion of the nature of judgment in chapter one of Charles Larmore, Patterns of Moral Complexity (1987).

32 Even the most loyal of people, no doubt, might leave eventually, but loyalty displays itself in a willingness to give precedence to some extent to the interests of the object of loyalty over one's own and over those of others; somebody who left at the first sign of trouble would have no loyalty at all.

33 On first being offered a hamburger, such an officer might reason that there could be no harm given his or her upright nature: there is *really* no corruption, he or she might say, whatever might appear to be the case. But appearance is part of the relevant reality in such a case, as in many others: how one is perceived affects how others treat one, and that affects how a police officer can do his or her job.

34 See the suggestion by Wren, *supra* note 1, at 40.

[15]

The Problematic Virtue of Loyalty

John Kleinig

Professor Kleinig returns to the enduring theme of loyalty in the context of policing. He argues that loyalty is an associational virtue, which is necessary in terms of police bonding but must be reconciled with other necessities. A police service whose officers practise absolute loyalty to each other can neither uphold nor sustain a safe, just and tolerant society, since it will put its own interests above those of all others. The collective value of loyalty must be tempered by the individual virtue of integrity.

INTRODUCTION

Formal ethical constraints on police conduct—often characterised as codes of conduct or statements of values—are sometimes distinguished as 'rule-driven' or 'value-driven.' The 'or' is not exclusive: a well-formed formal document will include reference to both rules and values. Broadly speaking, a code will be rule-driven to the extent that it focuses on prescribed or (more commonly) proscribed behaviour. It will, for example, prohibit the taking of gratuities or smoking in public while on duty. A code will be value-driven to the extent that it focuses on the need for certain dispositions of character that might be expected to figure prominently in occupational decision-making. It will, for example, advocate team work, integrity, or, more generally, professionalism. Such values are often characterisable as virtues—excellencies of character that it is good for a person to have. In the case of professional virtues, they will be excellencies that help to constitute a person a good member of an occupational grouping.

Here we will prescind from questions about whether, for dispositions to be virtues, they have to be morally charged. Even if the so-called intellectual virtues (such as open-mindedness, thoroughness and imaginativeness) are not exclusively moral, the classic moral virtues (such as compassion, justice, and courage) are likely to be impoverished in the absence of the intellectual virtues. We shall also prescind from ongoing debates about the relation of rules to virtues and their relative priority. Again, it is generally accepted that any adequate ethic must give consideration to both: rules without appropriate dispositions will be eviscerated and dispositions without rules will be rudderless.

In the case of police ethics, development of the virtues is of particular importance. Police work involves a great deal of interpersonal interaction, often in ways that bear on sensitive areas of life. Moreover, such work involves discretionary judgment in which complex sets of facts must be accommodated in the process of decision-making. In addition, decisions will often have to be made under conditions that do not allow the luxury of casuistic deliberation, but instead demand that 'rightly trained instincts'—well-modulated virtues—are brought to bear on a complicated situation requiring a rapid response. Even if a course of action is, in some sense, rule-bound, determination that the rule is applicable and how it is to be implemented will require judgment informed by appropriate virtues. There are issues of spirit as well as letter.

Formal statements of virtues that are important to good police work are diverse and to some extent conditioned by local experience and needs. Codes of ethics are covenants between police and the communities they serve and are designed to assure those communities that the powers vested in police will be used in a manner that accords with communally recognised values. If the formal statement pledges compassion, courtesy, integrity, fairness, and respect, it is because these are considered significant as well as sensitive factors in good police–community relations. Good police work will manifest such virtues and is jeopardised if they are absent.

Although loyalty figures prominently in police culture, it is a virtue that has a much more ambiguous place than those already mentioned. Students of police culture will not usually characterise the 'working personality' of police officers in terms of their compassion, courtesy, and so on. They are, however, very likely to draw attention to their loyalty (or, more generally, solidarity). Formal statements of police values tend to be reticent about including loyalty—and the relatively few exceptions often underplay the importance that loyalty actually has in the dispositional life of police officers. One reason for this may be the fact that these formal statements tend to focus on 'sticking-points' in police conduct—dimensions of police behaviour that cause difficulties in police–community relations. If there is no lacking in loyalty as there may be in integrity or courtesy, there is little reason to emphasise it in a code or statement of values.

But the issue is almost certainly more complicated than this. Loyalty as a virtue, and particularly loyalty as a virtue in policing, has proven deeply problematic. In police culture loyalty has often functioned more actively as an underground virtue than as a public one, as a corruption of integrity rather than an expression of it. The community served by police most readily associates police loyalty with the blue wall of silence, a conspiracy to shield officers from public scrutiny and judgment. As one officer—no friend of the blue wall—put it to me: 'If an organization wants you to do right, it asks for your integrity; if it wants you to do wrong, it demands your loyalty.'

But even as a general virtue, loyalty has had its detractors as well as supporters. It is often considered a 'sham virtue', a form of commitment that is invoked to lend a patina of virtue to immoral behaviour—'the last refuge of rogues and scoundrels,' as Dr Johnson said of its political manifestation, patriotism. And even if not viewed as a cloak for immorality, it is interpreted as a flight from responsibility, the surrender of one's own judgment and freedom to that of another.

What, therefore, I propose, is first to focus on the problematic virtue of loyalty, exploring its nature and foundations. I then review its appropriateness to policing contexts, looking particularly at excesses and deficiencies. I conclude with a consideration of ways in which loyalty may be appropriately constrained.

LOYALTY AS A VIRTUE

As noted, not everyone considers loyalty to be a virtue. The cynical quotation above, in which loyalty is contrasted with integrity, captures one strand of the critique to which it has been subjected. Loyalty is construed as an amoral tribal bond that trumps the demands of moral conduct—a commitment to the 'us' that rides roughshod over 'them.' Such tribalism also lies at the heart of Dr Johnson's invective. An alternative critique sees loyalty as blind adherence—a sacrifice of one's independent judgment to the will of another, whether individual or collective. These claims reflect important concerns, and I will return to them later. For the present, though, it is more helpful if we become clearer about the kind of disposition that loyalty is, why it is a virtue, and how it may function as part of an ethical life.

At its most fundamental level, loyalty is an associational virtue. It is a virtue of interpersonal relations. What I mean by that is not simply that it is social in nature—as justice, kindness, or courtesy might be—but that it is a virtue of bonded groupings or associations, and particularly of groupings that have come to be considered intrinsically valuable by those who are members of them. Loyalty cannot exist apart from a sense of identification with those to whom one is loyal. I can be loyal only to my friends, my group, my community, and my country. I cannot be loyal to yours, unless they are also mine. It is in this sense that loyalty can be said to be a tribal virtue, though without the derogatory overtones. More neutrally, it is a particularistic virtue in the same way that gratitude is: one may owe it only to some other with whom one has a special relation.

Within such relations, loyalty is constituted by a disposition to secure the valued association against the ravages of self-interest that might otherwise tempt one to opt out. Those to whom I am loyal can count on my support in hard times, hard times for me as well as for them. Loyalty is no fair weather virtue: my loyalty is called for when someone to whom I regard myself as associationally bound needs my assistance in circumstances that may burden me also. Loyalty is shown when I render such assistance as I am able, despite the burdensomeness of doing so. Disloyalty occurs when I allow the blandishments of self-interest to override the claims of my bond to the other.

Loyalty is essential to some associations. Friendship, or, more narrowly, what is sometimes spoken of as end-friendship[1], is a relation in which the parties to it have each other's interests at heart. A so-called disloyal friend is often said to be no friend at all: disloyalty undermines the friendship. Certain other associations also tend to presume loyalty, though they have an ambiguous character that complicates the connection. Familial relations are frequently suffused with expectations of loyalty, but are more complex because they tend to be constituted by biological as well as social relations. To the extent that one focuses on the nurturing and supportive aspect of family relations one will expect loyalty to develop among family members. If that social dimension has been badly corrupted, and not much more exists than the biological connection, then loyalty will not seem so important.

---

[1] To be distinguished from means-friendship, an association forged only with the purpose of securing certain ends.

There are other associations, however, for which, even if loyalty is nonessential, it is often considered desirable. Teams, occupational societies, and employing organizations are primarily instrumental associations, but frequently operate more effectively if their members possess some loyalty to them. Indeed, if we assume that they have an endemic tendency to decline, then loyalty may be important for their long-term health. When members of such associations are committed to them to the extent that they are willing to make sacrifices to further the interests of such associations, the association will be more resistant to competition and more likely to achieve its goals.

It can be seen, then, that the virtue of loyalty possesses the important moral and social function of countering the corrosive effects of self-interest. The underlying presumption, of course, is that the associations to which loyalty is given are not merely *valued* by those who are party to them but also *valuable* in some more general sense. But that presumption cannot always be sustained. Even if friendship is a good to be realised, a valuable natural association, it is not the case that every friendship is a worthy one and that the loyalty of those who are participants is therefore justified. In the case of friendship, the point is not sometimes that the friends should be disloyal but that the friendship should not, or no longer, exist. In the case of other associations to which loyalty is not integral, it might be said that, when corrupted, the associational other cannot legitimately demand loyalty or has forfeited any claim to it.

This capacity for the objects of associational loyalties to fall short of or lose claim to the allegiance of others has led to the dissociation of loyalty from personal objects and its consignment to impersonal objects or the abstractions that might otherwise have been presumed to be exemplified in the primary associations. When mediaeval writers began to make a distinction between loyalty to the king and loyalty to kingship, their distinction reflected the painful reality that those vested with regal powers did not always possess the personal qualities that one might assume to be integral to the particular association. The distinction in such cases was intended to show that acts of disobedience—no doubt seen as acts of disloyalty—meant no disrespect for the office. They were therefore not to be seen as anarchistic or revolutionary, but were simply expressions of the fact that a particular officeholder had failed to live up to the demands of the office. If anything, they represented an effort to recall the officeholder to the high terms of his office. This dissociation has led to ideals and principles becoming secondary objects of loyalty.[2] It is reflected in Donald Schultz's dedication of his book on law enforcement 'to those police officers whose first loyalties are to principles, not men,' an interesting inversion of the original object.[3]

The vulnerability of loyalty to unworthy associations—and therefore the need to form associations worthy of loyalty—points to a further distinction between it and a number of other virtues, such as kindness and courage, in which there exists a greater presumption of appropriateness. Like sincerity, conscientiousness, and industriousness, loyalty is an executive virtue. It does not constitute a virtue of

---

[2] Sometimes this is taken even further. A person is said to be loyal to his or her own principles. But being true to oneself in this way is probably better characterised as a form of integrity.

[3] Schultz, D O (ed.) (1975), *Critical Issues in Criminal Justice*, Springfield, IL: Charles C Thomas, epigraph. A similar reversal is argued for in Souryal S S and McKay B W (1996), 'Personal Loyalty to Superiors', *Criminal Justice Ethics*, 15(2), Summer/Fall, pp. 44-62.

82 *John Kleinig*

relations in general, but only of particular relations, and then only if those relations possess other features that constitute them as worthwhile. This is why the classic contexts for loyalty encompass relations such as friendship, family, tribe, or nation—generally considered to be valuable in structuring and supporting human experience. But they can go wrong, as we well know, and so too can other associations that we enter into—teams and organizations that we join.

LOYALTY AS A POLICE VIRTUE

As noted earlier, police generally view loyalty as an important virtue within their own organizational culture. Indeed, I am tempted to say that it is informally viewed as the most important virtue. A considerable portion of police socialisation is devoted to the forging of loyal bonds among officers. At a certain level, that is both understandable and desirable. By its very nature, police work is hazardous. As a society we ask of police that they secure us against the encroachments of disorder and threat. As police often put it of themselves, they represent the thin blue line between civilisation and the jungle. To a degree, they occupy a social space in which they have only their fellow officers to rely on, and so, to cope with the emotional and physical demands individually placed on them they develop deep associational bonds through which they are assured that, should their well-being be jeopardised, they can rely implicitly on their fellows. Policing is an associational enterprise that unlikely to succeed in the absence of loyal bonding among its members.

Loyalty and fidelity
Police officers are called to be loyal to their communities, local or national, their departments and occasionally to their families. More often—no doubt in recognition of the ways in which personalised objects can fall short of the values that are supposedly implicit in them—they are called to be loyal to the Constitution, the law, their oath of office, their profession, their goals or mission, and sometimes to their own beliefs and ideals.[4]

---

[4] For statements in which loyalty is advanced as a professional value, see Singapore Police Force, Core Values (http://www.spinet.gov.sg/aboutus/mis/01mission.htm) (4/29/03); Pennsylvania State University Police Department, Organizational Values (http://www.psu.edu/dept/police/values.htm), (5/25/03); Garland (TX) Police Department, Conduct and Performance Values (http://www.ci.garland.tx.us/police/gpd1000.htm); Norton Police Department, Our Values (http://www.cityofnorton.org.Police/Values.htm) (5/25/03); Monroe (NY) Police Department, Our Mission (http://www.monroepd.org/ourmission.htm) (5/22/03); Punta Gorda (L) Police Department, Values (http://www.ci.punta-gorda.fl.us/police/police_about.htm) (3/14/03); Lake Havasu City (AZ) Police Department, Values (http://www.ci.lake-havasu-city.az.us/PD/Police.htm) (3/14/03); Pocatello (ID) Police Department, Department Values (http://www.ci.pocatelloid.us/departments/policedept/) (3/14/03); Ewing Township (NJ) Police Department, Organizational Values Statement (http://www.taylorapp.com/ewingpolice/mission.html) (3/14/03); Santa Monica (CA) Police Department, Values (http://santamonicapd.org/information/mission.htm) (3/14/03); Mountain Brook (AL) Police Department, Values (http://www.mtbrook.org/Pd/mission.htm) (3/14/03); Fremont (CA) Police Department, Our Values (http://www.fremontpolice.org/M_V_V/M_V_V.htm) (5/1/03); Calexico (CA) Police Department (http://www.calexicopd.org/mission/mission.htm) (5/1/03); and Fairfield (ME) Police Department, Values (http://www.fairfieldme.com/users/pd) (4/8/03) (almost identical to the Santa Monica PD statement).

These are all eminently understandable objects. We can easily accept that officers ought to be loyal to their communities, departments and families. Their role is to serve their communities, and to risk themselves in securing the members of those communities against the forces of disorder. Their departments will flourish only if their members can work together as a supportive team, subordinating personal ambitions to the larger structure. Their families promise an important source of personal stability, an intimate social centre that helps to steady them for the daily demands that are placed on them.

For the most part, our loyalties cohere with each other and also with other virtues and values that we possess. That is to be expected and desired: the choices we make—of friends, of occupation, of the community in which we reside—will be made against the background of values that we hold, leading to a relatively cohesive set of relations. And in the broader sphere, it is likely that the values that inform these choices will themselves reflect the associations that have nurtured us. Were this not the case, our lives would be characterised by anguished choices as one part of our identity was played off against another. Even so, there will almost certainly be occasions on which our loyalties will come into conflict with each other and also, perhaps, with other values that we hold, and we will confront a hard decision about the kind of person we will be.

Leaving aside for the moment how such decisions should be made, are there any generalities to which we might appeal—any ordering of loyalties that might assist in our decision making? Formal codes of ethics are often poorly crafted for such eventualities. They enunciate values to be observed without indicating how conflicts among them should be resolved. That is almost always true of conflicts between the general values they espouse, but it is also true of conflicts of loyalty that might arise.

However, not every code is deficient in this regard. In the *Conduct and Performance Values* promulgated by the Garland, Texas, Police Department, it is stated:

> Loyalty. Members shall recognise that their allegiance is first to the community, then to the department's mission and the government agency that employs them. Commitment to the department must be over and above that of any individual member of the department.

This is a worthy attempt to accommodate the potential for conflicting loyalties. In giving first place to the community, the statement acknowledges the source and purpose of police authority. Policing does not exist as a natural association, as friendship or even familial relations might be construed. It is a purpose-oriented institution, formed to serve specific even if broadly defined communal needs. Without that justification, policing lacks a *raison d'être*, and should it lose sight of its *raison d'être*, it loses its legitimacy. Wisely, it does not identify the department's mission with service to the community or the organization with the mission. Community needs may change; the mission may need to be rethought; and the agency may lose sight of its mission. What then follows addresses the most likely conflict of loyalties: that between the department as it seeks to fulfil its mission and the individual loyalty that members will come to have to each other. That loyalty is taken for granted: what cannot be taken for granted is the priority of other loyalties.

We might of course take issue with the statement if interpreted strictly. Communities may lose their legitimate claim on the loyalty of those who serve them. Thankfully, this will be rare, though statements that focus on loyalty to the Constitution or law might be said to grasp such possibilities. As is almost always the case with codifications of values and their prioritisation, any rankings will be presumptive or defeasible. Although we may generally wish to give departmental loyalty priority over loyalty to a fellow officer, it is surely possible to envisage cases in which corrupt departmental politics or the vindictiveness of superiors makes it reasonable to back up a fellow officer. For all its perversity, the blue wall of silence is often reinforced by the sense that departments operate in unfair and self-serving ways.

Nevertheless, by addressing the issue of loyalty and seeking to offer some prioritisation of the multiple loyalties that officers might be presumed to have, the Garland statement confronts what many other codes avoid, and does so about as well as one might expect from a formal statement. Codes of ethics are never complete manuals of decision making. They set parameters, at best, and if they try to do too much they may come to be treated as substitutes for judgment. Ethics will collapse into law.

EXCESSES AND DEFICIENCIES OF LOYALTY

Critics of loyalty tend to view it as blind adherence. Not only blind, but also absolute. There is some social basis for this criticism, particularly if one's focus is the blue wall of silence. Although the blue wall is buttressed by a variety of considerations, among them is the loyalist notion that one ought *never* to hurt another officer. Loyalty to fellow officers is deemed to override all other claims. It is the seeming detachment of such loyalty from moral boundaries that contributes significantly to the ambivalence, if not disdain, that loyalty attracts. It is not helped by the fact that loyalty has often been associated with what are seen as intrinsically distasteful objects—the loyalty of the Nazi, Mafioso or gang member is likely to exacerbate the evil they do. Loyalty appears to be particularly susceptible to excess.

Understandable though such reactions may be, they fail to show that there is something inherently problematic with loyalty. The fact that one may be sincere in one's devotion to Nazism or industrious as a gang member is not sufficient to exclude sincerity and industriousness from the pantheon of virtues. Sincerity may not be enough. That is true of the executive virtues in general: their limited or focused role cannot be used to criticise them for failing to be what they do not profess to be. Moreover, blind loyalty is just that: blind. But loyalty need not be blind, and a person in whom other virtues are strong will have reason to ensure that loyalties are well placed. There is nothing to prevent us from subjecting the objects of our loyalty to the kind of scrutiny that will determine whether they are worthy of it, or of our loyally seeking to make such objects more worthy in the event of their falling short.

For the most part, the process of developing a particular association will provide ample opportunities for assessing the worthiness of the object of our association. Friendships, though they may develop slowly and almost imperceptibly are not entered into in an ethical vacuum. To the extent that we become aware of deficiencies in the person with whom the association is developing we have opportunities to pause and reconsider or withdraw. Even if we have formed an association with others that has given rise to a loyal commitment, there is no reason to disengage our moral antennae. Although the loyalist will be inclined to support the object of loyalty, and might therefore not ask some of the questions that could be expected of a stranger, becoming aware of some problematic features in the situation might reasonably prompt questions that affect the response. In some cases, the loyal response might be to question what is being asked for; in other cases, continued loyalty may be inappropriate—what has been done or what is asked for may undermine the loyalty.

It is true that certain associational bonds—those to family and community—tend to be fostered before our abilities to assess them are fully mature. This can cause difficulties down the line. And some associational bonds may be demanded as a condition of membership. One suspects that those who enter police work will not always be aware of the associational demands that are going to be placed on them. Still these are practical challenges rather than deficiencies in loyalty as such. In his memoir, Bill McCarthy indicates how he avoided the awkward kinds of situations in which officers sometimes find themselves, such as when unexpectedly faced with the burden of protecting an errant officer:

> *Loyalty* in the police department means you're willing to lie for someone else. Loyalty to me meant that I would always be the way I promised to be for another person. I would never be an ambush. Any person I worked with, I had to tell them right away that I wasn't on any pad. They had to know from me that if I caught them stealing, *I* would be the one to lock up their ass.[5]

Although the executive virtues are particularly vulnerable to excess or misplacement, even the substantive virtues are not immune to subversion. One may be generous to a fault, or exact justice untempered by mercy. Any virtue, if not moderated by others, will result in excess. The implicit lesson of police codes, to the extent that they are value driven, is that the values they uphold are not to be viewed in isolation but as practical dispositions to be kept in some kind of balance. When the Garland Police Department advertises its commitment to: 'integrity, professionalism, loyalty, courage, compassion, fairness/equality, leadership, and teamwork,' it does not treat these as unbounded obligations, but as integrated pledges, in which loyalty will not undermine integrity, compassion will not subvert professionalism, courage will not undermine teamwork, and so on. The problem of course is to determine what that appropriate balance is, a determination that will depend on the particulars of situations and require judgment rather than the mechanical application of some formula.

If virtuous excess is a permanent danger, so too is virtuous deficiency. In some respects they are two sides of the same coin. Excessive loyalty is likely to involve a deficiency in integrity. But an excessive concern for integrity may also be associated with a deficiency in loyalty. Early in life we are taught the distastefulness of tattle telling. Although the tattle tale may be morally deficient in a number of respects, a key deficiency is his or her failure to stand on their own moral feet—a failure to

---

[5] McCarthy B and Mallowe M (1991), *Vice Cop: My Twenty-year Battle with New York's Dark Side*. New York: William Morrow, p. 42.

confront violations as breach of relationships calling for restoration rather than as infractions requiring outside intervention.

If the blue wall of silence represents an excess of loyalty, the reporting of every infraction—as departmental regulations often demand—can express a deficiency. Where loyal bonds exist, there is at least a *prima facie* reason to address infractions in a way that is compatible with a continuation or rejuvenation of the association. If I catch my daughter shoplifting, it is unlikely that I will respond by delivering her to the store security for arrest and charging. It is more likely that I will deal with the situation privately—no less seriously perhaps, but in a way that reflects and does not jeopardise the associational bond of father and daughter. So, too, one might expect police who become aware of relatively minor fraternal failures to deal with them 'horizontally' rather than 'vertically.' Obviously, as will be the case even between parent and child, there will be limits to the private handling of breaches.

The problem of course is that police culture is frequently hostile to any kind of vertical or even horizontal criticism, let alone criticism of a public nature. There is no room for a loyal opposition or 'second guessing.' As is it is understood in certain organizational contexts, loyalty is taken to demand unquestioning support, a 'yes-man' response to those to whom one is expected to be loyal. But this involves a corruption of loyalty.

CONSTRAINING LOYALTY

Even though loyalty is the source of many ethical problems in policing, it is not a dispensable virtue. The work to which police are called is often onerous and sometimes dangerous. We expect of them devotion to the community somewhat analogous to the devotion to country we expect of the military. But it is not only the community that lays claims on police loyalty; it is also expected by their departments and their fellow officers.

How are we to resolve such conflicts, and others that might arise between loyalty and other virtues? One partial solution is provided by the kind of prioritisation we observed in the Garland Police Department's statement of values. We can look at an occupation, determine its fundamental purposes, and then see how those purposes are best served by various personal characteristics possessed by those who enter it. If we see police fundamentally as social peacekeepers, we will give priority to certain communal commitments, recognising that they might be most effectively advanced by certain other commitments, but acknowledge the subordination of the latter to the former. That is the Garland strategy and it goes someway to providing a check on the development of loyalties.

Another way is to recognise that loyalty as a virtue does not exist in isolation from other virtues but must be expressed in ways that take account of those other virtues. And so, should loyalty and integrity conflict, the moral costs of compromising integrity should be given serious consideration. Even though loyalty to others may be a constituent of a person's integrity, it is unlikely that unfettered loyalty will be.[6] Or, to take a more generalised virtue, that of professionalism, we

---

[6] For an interesting discussion of this, with which I am in only partial agreement, see Thomas Wren, 'Whistleblowing and Loyalty to One's Friends,' in William C. Heffernan and Timothy Stroup (eds.), *Police Ethics: Hard Choices in Law Enforcement*, New York: John Jay Press, 1985.

will see that the public service ends of professionalism, the evolving commitment to providing the best service one can, will be compromised if certain loyalties are permitted too much influence. The blue wall of silence generally has a corrosive effect on police professionalism.

Whatever strategy we adopt, judgment will be involved. Officers will have to judge how their loyalties relate to each other and how those loyalties are to be balanced with other virtues they might, as officers, be expected to have. Occasionally those decisions will be very difficult. The case of an officer who sought release during a flash flood so that he could attend to the needs of his family—residing in the flood area—provides a poignant example. After having permission to leave his post twice denied, the officer decided that his family took priority and went to provide assistance to them. He was suspended and charged with insubordination, an offence justifying dismissal. Did he act improperly? One might argue that his professional responsibility (especially in an emergency situation) was to follow orders. On the other hand, had he been a member of the Queensland Police Service, he would have been able to take account of a provision allowing that 'while an officer will put his family responsibilities first, duty to the community of Queensland will always be given priority over the other private interests of officers.'[7] Judgment is required: not every family responsibility will take precedence over professional responsibilities any more than every professional responsibility will take precedence over family responsibilities.

Cultivation of the virtues does not relieve police officers of the need to make ethical judgments. What it does is to identify those virtues of which police ought to be particularly mindful, demanding that they be exercised in ways that give due weight to the purposes of policing and the particulars of a presenting situation.

---

[7] Queensland Police Service, *Code of Conduct*, issued by the Commissioner of Police, 1990, Sect. 1.

[16]

Three Types of Leadership

William C Heffernan

William C Heffernan is professor of Law, John Jay College of Criminal Justice and the
Graduate Center, City University of New York.[1] He sets out to examine the
contribution that policing can make in furthering the aims of a free and generally just
social order. In doing so, he considers three styles of leadership—exemplary,
reformist and counter-majoritarian, and concludes that police leadership needs on
occasion to be capable of all three. He believes that even in a generally just society
police leaders will be required to enforce specific laws that they consider morally
unacceptable—an issue which John Alderson also debates in *Chapter 3* and Roger
Scruton in *Chapter 6*, and of prime doctrinal significance he emphasises the
importance of the proper application of discretion.

INTRODUCTION

'I would absolutely not take a job as a police chief,' John Diaz, an assistant police
chief in Seattle, recently remarked during the course of an interview with a
reporter for *The New York Times*. 'The politics of being a police chief have become
so insane no one wants the job,' Diaz continued. 'I work an eleven-hour day, but
our chief is here before me every day and doesn't leave until I'm gone, and all he
gets is attacked in the media.'[2]

Diaz's claim that no one wants the job is clearly an exaggeration. Although
neither he nor any other assistant chief in the Seattle Police Department applied
for the top position after the city's chief resigned in the wake of rioting during
the World Trade Organization meeting held in the city in fall 2000, others did.
Unfortunately, the person selected, Gil Kerlikowske, formerly the police chief of
Buffalo, New York, discovered quickly just how thankless the position can be.
During the course of a Sunday afternoon jog not far from his downtown office,
Chief Kerlikowske happened upon a woman lying on the street who, it was
eventually established, had passed out as a result of a heroin overdose. While
still in his jogging gear, the chief stopped to give her mouth-to-mouth
resuscitation. When the woman began to breathe, he took her to the hospital. A
short time later, once the nature of the woman's condition became clear, the chief
had to return to the hospital, this time to get a hepatitis B shot for himself.

There is no reason to believe that Kerlikowske intervened to publicise
himself or his department, but his good Samaritanism was nonetheless
significant, if only as a reminder of the aid police officers frequently provide the
vulnerable and destitute. Seattle's TV stations did indeed mention the rescue.
However, they devoted only a few seconds to it. Their lead story was about a
police chase of a stolen car that struck a pedestrian—and for this, they provided
extensive footage, criticism of the police by eyewitnesses to the accident, and an

interview with the accident victim. The lesson for Chief Kerlikowske was clear. It's nice to help someone in distress. But what really matters is avoiding bad publicity. Doing the right thing by people is at most a sideline in police work.

This is the dreary lesson many police leaders insist upon when talking to their subordinates. I shall not expand on it here, however. Rather, what is needed is an essay on what police leadership might be, an essay that combines structural analysis with the good heart that impelled Chief Kerlikowske to aid the woman who had passed out on the Seattle streets.

I begin by surveying the conceptual terrain. In these opening sections, I consider some definitional points about police leadership and also the distinction between leadership of police organizations in democratic and authoritarian societies. The remainder of the essay is devoted to an analysis of three types of leadership: exemplary, reform, and counter-majoritarian in democratic polities. My inventory of categories is not meant to be exhaustive. Other types of police leadership—crime fighting and crisis management for example—can readily be imagined. I have confined myself to the three just mentioned in part because, given my professional training, I am not confident I could make a meaningful contribution to discussion of other types of leadership, in part because the three I do consider are critical to an account of policing democratic societies. My concern, in other words, is with the contribution policing can make in furthering the aims of a free, generally just social order.

THE POSSIBILITY OF POLICE LEADERSHIP

At first sight, the term 'police leadership' may seem to be an oxymoron. Police officers, whatever their rank, are members of a bureaucracy, and bureaucracies, it could be argued, are defined by their members' adherence to rules imposed from the outside. On this account, police leadership is impossible. In conforming to their rules of office, this argument maintains, the police are not led; rather, they simply adhere to the law.

Appealing as it is because of its simplicity, there are a number of fundamental problems with this thesis. One has to do with the nature of leadership. Even if it were conceded that all police behaviour is rule-governed, an important role could be found for leadership with respect to the way in which the police behave. Officers can honour their rules of office in a surly, rude manner, but they can also be courteous and considerate.

Given the bias of academics in favour of analytically difficult questions, it is easy to dismiss this factor as unimportant. I don't. Just as the president of a college sets a standard for the proper treatment of its students, a police leader sets a standard for the way in which his or her subordinates should treat civilians.

But there are further difficulties with the oxymoron thesis, all related to the issue of police fidelity to the law. One difficulty has to do with the fact that police often violate—indeed, *knowingly and egregiously* violate—the law. Leadership is critical to ensure that they do not. I shall have a good deal more to say in a later section about the nature of this leadership. It is sufficient now, as we define the intellectual terrain, simply to note that police leaders are constantly confronted with the challenge of making sure that their officers adhere to the law.

And what about leadership in settings where the law *is* honoured? Here, too, the oxymoron thesis is unsatisfactory, for police officers aren't simply rule-followers. They also have discretion as to the meaning of rules and the way in which they should be enforced and because discretion is an inevitable feature of the police role, leadership is not only possible, but necessary, for the police. The term 'discretion' is sometimes used in a broad sense to refer to unpunished violations of authoritative legal rules. I shall avoid this usage here. My concern instead is with those instances in which the police can reasonably infer, in light of the rule of recognition within their legal system, that they are entitled to interpret the meaning of a term contained in a rule or that they may determine whether and how extensively to enforce a rule.

The opportunities for these different kinds of discretion are endless. Numerous rules contain ambiguous terms that have not been interpreted by courts. Think, for example, about an officer's decision as to how to classify a child riding a tricycle when a city ordinance prohibits vehicles in public parks. Moreover, there are many instances in which courts have signalled that they are willing to let the police determine whether to enforce non-criminal statutes (motor vehicle codes, for instance), and there are other instances in which the police can decide how much enforcement is appropriate for a given type of action (consider questions related to the protection of demonstrators outside buildings). Some of these examples raise discretionary issues appropriately resolved in on-the-spot decisions. All, however, are potentially open to resolution by police leaders. Indeed, in his influential *Discretionary Justice,*[3] Kenneth Culp Davis advances a strong argument for the value of publicly announced decisions by police commanders as to the way in which their officers will exercise discretion. This is not the place to evaluate the merits of Davis's position. It is enough to note that his entire line of reasoning underscores the possibility of police leadership arising out of the opportunities for discretion provided by a legal system.

LEADERS OF POLICE ORGANIZATIONS VERSUS POLICE LEADERS

One more point must be considered in defining the conceptual terrain. There are numerous leaders of police whom I (at least) would say exhibit no qualities of police leadership. The fictional Baron Scarpia of *Tosca* was the chief of Rome's police, but he was not a police leader in the sense I am using the term. The all-too-real Heinrich Himmler and Lavrenti Beria were leaders of national police forces (Himmler of the Nazi SS and Beria of the Soviet Union's NKVD, subsequently known as the KGB), but they too do not qualify as police leaders on my analysis.

What is the identifying criterion of police leadership, then? As I use the term, a police leader is someone who (1) holds a high-ranking position in a police organization that operates in a generally just society and (2) seeks to use his or her discretionary powers to further the just aims of that society. Needless to say, there will be disagreement about when a society is generally just. The examples just provided demonstrate, however, that the concept is not infinitely contestable. Nazi Germany was committed to monstrous social injustice; the Stalinist Soviet Union comes off slightly better on this score. Any official who abetted the aims of these regimes that rounded up Jews on behalf of the SS, or prevented starving peasants from leaving their collective farms in the USSR, cannot possibly be considered a police leader in the normative sense that I am using the term. Leadership, as I understand it, promotes human welfare. It may result in a setback to the welfare of some (a setback that can include death), but this setback is justified only when it occurs in the context of a political regime that, on balance, promotes justice.

What, then, can be said about police organizations that operate in generally just societies where the police are legally required to carry out monstrously unjust acts? In my opinion, genuinely difficult cases are possible in such a setting. Because I shall *not* assume in the remainder of this essay that the police leaders I am discussing are legally required to carry out specific unjust acts, let me pause for a moment to consider the dilemmas that arise when the law does impose such obligations on them. Think, for example, about the difficulties that confronted police officers in northern cities of the United States when they were called upon to locate and render up, as per the terms of the Fugitive Slave Act of 1850, African-Americans who had fled from their southern slave masters. It is reasonable to assume that, apart from slavery and its treatment of native Americans, the United States of the mid-nineteenth century was a generally just society *for the majority of its residents*. It clearly was not, however, for African-Americans. Even those who were not slaves were ineligible for American citizenship; or so the Supreme Court held in *Dred Scott v. Sandford.*[4] And slaves lived under legal rules wholly inconsistent with the statements about human equality contained in the Declaration of Independence.

What options were open to a northern police chief of the 1850s when confronted with an order requiring the return of a fugitive slave? Three responses to this dilemma are worth considering. One possibility was to adhere to the law. Believing American society to be generally just, the chief might have concluded that the order should be executed. To fail to follow the legal obligations *he* views as unjust, the police chief might have said to himself, would encourage others (southerners, for example) to refuse to follow the obligations *they* view as unjust, thus jeopardising the security of a generally just society. Indeed, in adopting this line of reasoning, the chief might conclude that adhering to the obligation could have the effect of spurring northern public opinion into an even greater frenzy about slavery and so hasten its end. Second, a chief could have resigned and in doing so he could have stated publicly that his motive was to avoid enforcing the law. Resignation would not prevent the law's ultimate enforcement. Someone else would surely be found to do the job. But it would have found ways to ensure that the African-American in question was able to escape, thus frustrating the law while pretending to honour it.

I have no problem with either of the first two options. The second seems particularly attractive to me; it is the bureaucrat's equivalent of civil disobedience. However, the first option may actually do more to shape opinion, for enforcement of a patently unjust law in a generally just society can spur the public to consider change. In this instance, there is no doubt that questions about enforcement of the law not only influenced public opinion about the Fugitive

Slave Act but also about slavery itself. As the Boston textile magnet Amos Lawrence remarked after witnessing the scene in his city while federal marshals led a fugitive slave back to bondage, 'We went to bed one night old fashioned, conservative, compromise Union Whigs and waked up stark mad Abolitionists.'[5]

The third option is more problematic. It bears some resemblance to jury nullification in that a government official sworn to uphold the law frustrates a specific law while continuing publicly to champion the rule of law. But it is likely to be even less effective than jury nullification, which itself is usually haphazard in its effect, for the simple reason that stronger forces can be ordered by higher authorities on subsequent occasions to make sure that an odious law actually is enforced. Moreover, the third option blurs the central issue of injustice. It is certainly tempting, however, and this third option is likely to be particularly attractive in instances where the police are called upon *to* enforce laws that do not involve outrageous injustice. What this discussion makes clear, then, is that even in a generally just society, there will be occasions when leaders will be required to enforce specific laws they consider morally unacceptable.

EXEMPLARY LEADERSHIP

Let us now banish the moral cloud of unjust laws in generally just societies. This cloud can appear at any time and must be taken seriously indeed, but there are other issues of leadership that merit attention, and these are best addressed without having to consider the complications just mentioned. In thinking about what police leaders who accept the aims of a generally just society can do to further those aims, it is best to begin with leadership by example with the way in which a police executive demonstrates by means of his or her own conduct to those in the department how they should comport themselves.

Leadership by example matters in any organization. An executive who places personal interests ahead of the organization's takes a substantial step toward demoralising subordinates. But while this much is true across the board, there are three reasons why exemplary leadership is particularly important in a police bureaucracy. One has to do with the rule of law. Much as discretion matters in policing, there are many areas in which the law is sufficiently clear that the police must adhere to it. A leader who violates clear mandates of law or who even tests discretionary ones by interpreting ambiguous rules in his or her own self-interest helps to undermine subordinates' commitment to the rule of law.

Second, exemplary leadership matters because some police officers are routinely called upon to engage in acts of courage while all officers must live with the knowledge that they may, at some point in their careers, be called on to act courageously. In the former category, one would have to place members of a bomb squad or a hostage negotiation team. Elite units such as these tend to develop an *esprit de corps* of their own. But the strength of this spirit in turn often depends on the way in which department leaders comport themselves. These leaders must of course show respect for acts of courage. But they must also display courage within the bureaucracy that complements that of their squad members. As for the latter category, of which patrol officers are the best example, it must never be forgotten that routine police work can suddenly, and unexpectedly, require acts of great courage. On being summoned to a family quarrel, a patrol officer may witness an explosion of rage that places the officer in danger as well as others in the room. On stopping a car missing a headlight, an officer may find, on walking up to the driver's window, that someone has a gun pointed right at his or her head. Exemplary leadership establishes the context in which street officers accept the risks associated with encounters that can lead into the unknown.

Third, exemplary leadership can set the stage for courteous relationships between the police and the public. In a generally just society, the key to social order must lie in most citizens' willingness to refrain from self-interested violations of the law. The majority of citizens in a generally just society thus do not require repressive police measures. Rather, their encounters with the police will involve problems of co-ordination (making sure that traffic lanes are maintained, for example) and service (providing information to pedestrians and drivers, locating stray pets, and so on). A central, though often overlooked, question about policing in a free society is this: do the police perform these functions in a courteous manner in a manner that emphasises their role as public servants? Confining my observations to the police force I know best, the New York City Police, my answer to this is 'Sometimes'. I hope my answer errs on the side of pessimism; I hope that observers in other cities can deliver more positive reports about their police officers. To the extent I am right, though, there is surely a good deal of work to be done by exemplary police leaders. Good leaders will show by their example that the police need not be insular and suspicious, that they can instead be open and friendly. New York City Police Commissioners have been almost uniformly dour and unforthcoming in their remarks to the public; it is small wonder, then, that patrol officers are officious and often downright rude in their dealings with everyday New Yorkers.

How is exemplary leadership possible? What kind of bearing should a police executive have if he or she is to inspire subordinates to be law-abiding, courageous, and courteous? There are as many possibilities here as there are different types of human personality. One example, drawn from military rather than police history, will perhaps help to illustrate how someone can lead by example. Although plagued, at least to a degree, by alcoholism throughout his tenure in the Union army, Ulysses Grant was not only a formidable strategist but also an inspiring leader of troops.

According to Charles Dana, an observer sent by Secretary of War Edwin Stanton to report on Grant's unexpected victories in the Mississippi Valley at a time Union armies were being defeated in Virginia, the soldiers appreciated Grant's lack of 'superfluous flummery', his tendency to wear a plain uniform 'without scarf, sword, or trappings of any sort save the double-starred shoulder straps.' Grant, Dana asserted, was not a 'great man except morally, not an original or brilliant man, but sincere, thoughtful, deep and gifted with a courage that never faltered.'[6]

Grant, it should be noted, displayed these traits in a way that his subordinates found attractive and accessible. A private in Grant's army stated that the men 'seem to look upon him as a friendly partner of theirs, not as an arbitrary commander.'[7] Rather than cheer as Grant rode by, his soldiers would usually 'greet him as they would address one of their neighbours at home.'

140   *William C. Heffernan*

"Good morning, General", "Pleasant day, General," and like expressions are the greetings he meets everywhere ... There was no nonsense, no sentiment; only a plain businessman of the republic, there for the one single purpose of getting that command over the river in the shortest possible time.'[8]

There is no formula for producing 'thoughtful, deep and gifted' leadership that simultaneously inspires subordinates to act while remaining accessible to them. It is not even clear that people possessing such traits are randomly distributed among eras and countries; it may be that certain cultural factors—a particular concern for the cultivation of virtue, for example—must be present for such traits to emerge in young men and women. I can thus suggest only that those charged with selecting leaders should try to identify these traits. What can be expressed in more formulaic terms are the rules organizations should impose on their leaders. The first rule is that police organizations should (and, as far as I can tell, largely do) operate on the basis of a strong presumption of promotion from below. By recruiting through the ranks, police organizations provide incentives to younger officers, solidify morale and ensure that executives have experiences in common with line staff.

Standing alone, though, this rule is hardly sufficient to ensure strong leadership, for police executives promoted from below can all too easily forget their early days. There are many factors that can induce this type of moral amnesia: frequent contact with elite members of the community, a desk-bound work schedule, the development of a technocratic world-view, and, in particular, the sweet perquisites of office. Taken together, these can cause *nomenklatura syndrome*, a disorder that has the potential to afflict leaders of all organizations, in particular those who have risen from below. In the Soviet Union (where the term *nomenklatura* was first used), it was a mark in someone's favour that he hailed from the working classes. But working class origins often blended poorly with the special privileges available to the party elite. The result was a *nomenklatura* that was resented not simply for its unequal access to primary goods but also for the hypocrisy with which it defended its special position. A similar threat of hypocrisy is possible among police executives.

Our second rule for police organizations is designed to counter this syndrome: in selecting people for promotion, organizations must consider carefully whether someone's prior career indicates that the person will inspire subordinates to act as police officers should. Some cautionary words are needed about this rule. I am not suggesting that the value on which it is based is the only one that should be taken into account when promotion is at stake; analytic intelligence is certainly important as well. Nor am I suggesting, even when intellectual issues are set to one side, that leadership potential can be gleaned simply from an officer's performance in a subordinate position. Rather, I am arguing the rather obvious point that past performance is the best indication available of the likelihood of future achievement. I am also maintaining that high quality past performance can serve as an example to officers as to how they should conduct themselves while still in subordinate roles. And finally, I am maintaining that the logocentric civil service perspective should be revised to ensure that exemplary conduct is considered as well as intellectual ability. In particular, leadership positions should be limited to those who have served in line positions, faced the hardships typical of those positions, and performed well when confronted with those hardships.

This approach can be made concrete only by focusing far more carefully than most police departments now do on the quality of service an officer has rendered while serving in line positions. During their first two to three years of service, officers should be rotated out of different line positions on an annual basis, thus providing them with opportunities to serve in various capacities for their departments. Their superiors should carefully evaluate officers' performance in these positions, and these evaluations should receive substantial weight in promotion decisions. Frequent rotation of officers will reduce the likelihood that friendship and favouritism between subordinates and superiors will influence evaluations undertaken by the latter.

And how is *nomenklatura* syndrome to be prevented among those who have already been promoted? A third rule is needed here: police executives, we may hold, should have access to special perquisites only to the extent these are necessary to further the public interests their agencies are charged with pursuing. This rule does not prohibit limousines, secretaries, carpeted office floors, special cell phones, and so on. Rather, it enjoins the use of these and other special advantages of office in settings where they don't further the organization's legitimate aims. It thus prohibits *expensive* limousines and prohibits completely the use of a limousine for personal business. It prohibits luxurious carpeting and office furniture—and so gives no heed to the argument that a fancy office is necessary if a police executive is to mingle on equal terms with other members of the community's elite. Given the ubiquity of personal computers and laptops, the rule also alerts to the problem of redundancy associated multiple secretaries: one is usually enough to keep track of appointments and print the documents the boss has generated by typing on his or her own computer. It may sound as if the 'no unnecessary perquisites' rule is one that Cincinnatus would devise for modern police forces. I would accept that characterisation were someone to offer it. Cincinnatus embodies the simplicity, self-discipline, and exemplary leadership that propelled the Roman Republic to greatness. Police leaders who adopt this manner will earn the respect of the public at large and also their own subordinates.

But how is this rule of Cincinnatus to be administered? I see no way in which it can be imposed from above; after all, police leaders are the 'above' in a law enforcement organization. I of course hope that the politically accountable officials who appoint police chiefs will take it seriously. But although mayors and governors will almost surely derive political benefit from police chiefs known for their republican simplicity, it seems unlikely that politicians will make this a high priority in the selection process. The rule of Cincinnatus thus must be *self*-imposed. Moreover, only if police leaders *do* adopt it for themselves is it also likely that the leaders will adopt an approach that emphasises character among line officers.

Is everything I've advocated with respect to exemplary leadership unlikely to be achieved, then? I think not. The story about Chief Kerlikowske's rescue effort for a woman who had fainted on a Seattle sidewalk reminds us that many chiefs already practise what I am advocating. If I am right about this and right as well in assuming that exemplary leadership is likely to increase public

142 *William C. Heffernan*

satisfaction with the police, then it seems reasonable to assume that more and more police chiefs will adopt this strategy on their own as a sound way to do business. In this case, the right thing to do is also the one that is politically wise.

REFORM LEADERSHIP

Exemplary leadership is needed at all times. I turn now to leadership styles suited to particular problems—first to the leadership appropriate for a department demoralised by allegations of corruption and brutality, then to the style appropriate for police violations of civil rights. The former style I call 'reform leadership', the latter 'counter-majoritarian leadership'.

It is not entirely clear why reform leadership is of perennial importance in policing. Other government agencies are routinely beset by charges of corruption—think, for example, about the frequency with which building inspectors are alleged to take bribes. Charges of brutality are also lodged against officials other than the police—against prison officers, for example. In trying to identify why reform leadership has mattered so much in policing, we must consider the confluence of many different factors. Many agencies have to take one or two of these factors into account. Only the police have to consider all of them.

One factor has to do with the freelance nature of police work. Like building inspectors, police officers operate on their own, acting beyond the gaze of their superiors. The opportunities for self-dealing increase under such circumstances. Another factor is that police work is not accorded high status. There are, of course, elite units within police organizations, but police work is best classified as 'dignified blue collar' rather than 'white collar' labour. Because few police officers think of themselves as members of an elite occupation, they also lack the sense of themselves as being under a special obligation to refrain from self-dealing. Related to this is the grim nature of police work. Like those who work in hospital emergency rooms, police officers spend a vastly disproportionate amount of their time on the job with the most troubled members of society. Unlike hospital emergency workers, however, the police are charged with using force. These last two factors are particularly combustible. The officers who are worn down by the grimness of the encounters they have to endure on a daily basis are more likely than their peers to use excessive force in heated street encounters. In discussing the factors that contribute to corruption and brutality among the police, I am not of course advancing an excuse for officers. Most officers resist the temptations associated with money and with the vengeful use of force. I am simply noting why corruption and brutality are problems particularly associated with the police.

What can a police leader do about these problems, given the impossibility of modifying the factors just mentioned? The answer is that steps can be taken to prevent them in most instances and that other steps are possible in the few instances when they do. A necessary condition is exemplary leadership. If officers don't believe that their own leaders refrained from such wrongdoing while in line positions and don't see their leaders as now committed to the public interest, they are unlikely to act properly themselves. But this is hardly sufficient for reform leadership. What is needed, both for purposes of prevention and redemption, is a system of carefully measured accountability that constrains mid-range executives while still allowing them the flexibility to act creatively.

The key to this system of accountability is a principle of reasonable foreseeability. A mid-level executive should not be able to avoid censure simply by arguing that he or shedid not know about wrongdoing on their shift. On the other hand, such an executive should not be censured for every act of wrongdoing within their command. The principle of reasonable foreseeability holds that an executive is accountable for those acts of subordinates that a person well acquainted with police organizational behaviour can anticipate under circumstances that assume the executive is using proper standards of performance. The 'proper standards of performance' criterion holds mid-level executives to the review standards set by the leader of a police organization; given this criterion, a mid-level executive cannot deviate from the review standards established by a police leader and then avoid responsibility for the wrongdoing of subordinates. The criterion of acquaintance with a police organization limits blame to those acts that insiders are likely to anticipate given proper standards of performance review. It thus rejects blame for freak occurrences.

There will always be debate about when misconduct is freakish. Even here, though, a 'going rate' can be established. As time passes and decisions accumulate under the reasonable foreseeability standard, executives will understand fairly well the degree of supervision they are expected to undertake. Systematic corruption and brutality should always be detected; the executive who fails to detect practices by subordinates that have been underway for a substantial period of time—say, six months or more—will invariably by sanctioned under this standard. Random, unpredictable misconduct by a subordinate will not lead to an executive sanction. The hard cases will be those that fall between these extremes. Modest over-deterrence is, in any case, desirable in this context. That is, whenever an executive is uncertain about whether his or her failure to exercise oversight will lead to a sanction, it is surely desirable that the executive engages in such oversight.

COUNTER-MAJORITARIAN LEADERSHIP

Police leadership is counter-majoritarian when a chief takes politically unpopular steps to further the legitimate aims of policing in a generally just society. Although the distinction is not hard and fast, most reform leadership does not involve politically difficult measures. The public usually welcomes the steps leaders take to reduce corruption and brutality. An exception to this is found in cases where brutality is directed at unpopular minorities. If, for example, officers routinely engage in physical abuse of members of an unpopular ethnic group, a leader may antagonise the public by taking steps to eliminate this abuse. But while this problem is certainly real (consider, for example, the torture southern police officers routinely applied to African-Americans during the first half of the twentieth century), it seems fair to say that brutality and corruption are *generally* disfavoured by voters in modern democratic societies and that these central problems for reform leadership are therefore not central problems for counter-majoritarian leadership.

144   *William C. Heffernan*

What, then, is the central problem? Not brutality (or at least not brutality in today's political climate, though this statement is subject to revision) but rather the petty indignities associated with stops and frisks. There is practically no randomisation associated with stop and frisk in modern democracies. If someone is white, middle-aged, and moderately well dressed, that person has virtually no chance of being subjected to a stop and frisk. By contrast, if someone is identifiable by sight as a member of an ethnic minority and is also young and shabbily dressed, the chances of an intervention are substantial. These chances are not always the result of arbitrary public policy. For law-abiding members of ethnic minorities, however, they are the result of an arbitrary fate. It is not arbitrary public policy for the police to concentrate their attention on young members of ethnic minority groups; sadly, this is just the part of population the police must consider given the crime trends. But it is nonetheless a mark of cruel, arbitrary fate for law-abiding, young members of ethnic minority groups to have to be subjected to stops and frisks. No one chooses their race or age; to be subjected to routine police intervention —to intervention that has a degrading effect even when carried out politely—is to be reminded of the cruelty underlying the birth lottery.

Unfortunately, illegal stops and frisks provoke little outcry from the electorate in democratic societies. They thus pose a classic counter-majoritarian problem for proponents of human rights. The practice serves a useful social function and so is tolerated, if not applauded, because it places a burden on an ethnic minority segment of the population and provides a benefit for the majority segment. Courts perform an important role in trying to limit the practice. The legal systems of all western democracies offer monetary damages to victims of illegal stops and frisks. Some go further. Frustrated by the inefficacy of tort sanctions to deter police illegality in this context, some high courts (America's is the prime example) have also required suppression of the fruits of illegal interventions. But even this is far from foolproof. The suppression threat doesn't require return of illegally seized contraband, so officers often engage in what they know to be illegal stops and frisks in the hope of securing illegally possessed guns or drugs. And, in any event, suppression is required only in settings where trial courts find that officers acted illegally. If officers perjure themselves about an intervention—sometimes only modest shading is needed—then courts can uphold the officers' conduct and admit evidence.

If we step back from this, we can readily see that courts have adopted measures such as the exclusionary rule precisely because the police have been so reluctant to discipline themselves. And police reluctance in turn is understandable in light of the incentives democracies offer them. Politically elected officials appoint police leaders; the appointments are usually provisional; moreover, even when the appointments are for formally stated terms of office, they can often be terminated at the pleasure of elected officials. It is no wonder, then, that police illegality against ethnic minorities is a persistent problem in western democracies. The wonder is that police leaders are ever willing to take counter-majoritarian stands against such illegality.

How is it that counter-majoritarian leadership can be effective? In particular, how can police chiefs continue to survive in their positions when they are answerable to elected officials? The answer is to be found in the connection chiefs can forge with the courts. By reminding both their subordinates and the public at large that the police derive their authority from the law, chiefs can make it clear that adherence to judicially imposed limitations on stop and frisk is the price that must be paid in supporting the rule of law. 'The courts made me do it' is a refrain that may have limited resonance among the general citizenry. It has stronger resonance, however, among both the police and citizens-as-consumers-of-police-services once a chief makes clear that police illegality undermines the source of police authority. Needless to say, exemplary leadership is critical here as elsewhere. A chief who has risen to prominence by taking legal shortcuts will be in no position to guide his or her own officers in a different direction. But exemplary leadership is insufficient by itself in this context. A chief also must constantly reiterate that because officers are creatures of the law, they cannot use their authority to subvert it.

CONCLUSION

The typology of police leadership provided here is not proposed as an exhaustive one. As noted earlier, the list might be expanded to include crisis management and crime-fighting leadership. But important as these types of leadership may be, they do not, in my opinion, capture the moral seriousness associated with the three categories discussed in this essay. A Utopia can dispense with the police. I have reasoned in terms of the non-Utopian category of a generally just society. Police are essential to such a society. It is because policing is not a mechanical job that leadership of the kind I have discussed must be provided to further the aims of such a society.

REFERENCES

[1]   Acknowledgements are also due to John Laffey, a doctoral student at City University of New York and also a police leader, who provided helpful comments on an earlier draft of this chapter.
[2]   Butterfield, F (2001), 'City Police Work Losing its Appeal and its Veterans', *New York Times*, 30 July 2001.
[3]   Davis, K C (1969), *Discretionary Justice*, Baton Rouge: Louisiana State University.
[4]   *Dred Scott v. Sandford* (1857), 60 US 393.
[5]   McPherson, J (1989), *Battle Cry of Freedom: The Civil War Era*, New York: Ballantine Books.
[6]   Dana, C K (1902), *Recollections of the Civil War*, New York: Shamrock Hill Price.
[7]   Catton, B (1960), *Grant Moves South*, Boston: Little, Brown.
[8]   Foot, S (1963), *The Civil War: A Narrative*, Vol. 2., New York: Random House.

Part IV
Police Corruption

[17]

BECOMING BENT: MORAL CAREERS OF CORRUPT POLICEMEN[1]
Lawrence W. Sherman

> *I came finally to understand what*
> *corruption is and how it gets a man . . .*
> *rogues outside, but inside, honest men.*
>
> LINCOLN STEFFENS
>
> *Even a bent policeman has a conscience.*
>
> FRANK WILLIAMSON, Q.P.M.
> *H.M. Inspector of*
> *Constabulary (retired)*

My task here is to describe the process by which policemen become corrupt in two specific ways: how they come to accept bribes, and how they come to commit burglary. The central argument of this paper is that police grafters and burglars only "get that way" through a painful process of choices, and not because they are pathological "rotten apples." Though *which* choices will be taken cannot be predicted, the process should become clearer through a picture of how the choices are presented to policemen. As we rely totally on the available literature, we are unfortunately long on concepts and short on data.

[1] Paper presented to the National Deviancy Conference, University of York, England, April 15, 1973.

192   *AN INTERACTIONIST VIEW*

Data on the general moral careers of policemen is provided by Westley (1970), Wambaugh (1970), and Niederhoffer (1969), but they make little specific mention of corruption. Maas (1973) describes the moral career of an honest policeman, Frank Serpico. But with one exception, the life histories of *corrupt* policemen have been compiled exclusively by journalists. Steffens (1931) describes the moral career of a nineteenth-century New York policeman, Max Schmittberger, an extraordinary grafter who turned straight and became chief of police. Wittels (1949) describes a grafter's career in an eastern U.S. police department from 1930 to 1948. Stern (1962) and Smith (1965) interviewed policemen involved in the 1961 burglary scandal in Denver. Stoddard (1968), the lone social scientist, interviewed a convicted police burglar from another midwestern city.

The concepts used to explain police corruption in the past have relied upon *affinity* and *affiliation,* in Matza's (1969) terms. Vollmer (1936), Tappan (1960), and Sutherland and Cressey (1960) all stress that police recruitment attracts men who are predisposed to corruption, since they already have an *affinity* for deviance. Attacking that view, Stoddard (1968) (and Wilson, 1963) stresses the *affiliation* of the honest police recruit with a dishonest police subculture. Nowhere has the *signification,* or labeling, processes in police corruption been explicitly discussed.

This paper will ignore the affinity argument, since much data and experience suggest police recruits have a conception of police work as honest at the time they apply (see also McNamara, 1966). The focus will be on the process of affiliation with other policemen, and with other corrupt policemen, and with the way a corrupt policeman signifies, or defines, his behavior in relation to himself and others. For that, we shall look to those Matza (1969) calls the neo-Chicagoans.

THE CONCEPTS OF A MORAL CAREER

Howard Becker, Erving Goffman, and William Westley were all graduate students together at the University of Chicago's Department of Sociology, thirty years after the heyday of

Becoming Bent   193

the Chicago School. Thus, it is not surprising that they have all reformulated the early Chicago work on deviant careers in a similar fashion. The crucial difference between their work and such studies as Shaw's (1930) *Jack Roller*, is that Shaw et al. looked for careers *of deviants* from a correctional viewpoint, whereas the neo-Chicagoans look for careers *in deviance* from an appreciative standpoint. They have disentangled, though not very carefully, the *moral* career from the *occupational* career.[2]

Goffman (1961) defines career in a broad sense of "any social strand of any person's course through life" and a *moral* career as the "regular sequence of changes . . . in the person's self and in his framework of imagery for judging himself and others." Thus, the moral career is influenced by the occupational career, but does not *depend* on it; a businessman may begin to smoke pot and stop after intense usage while his business career progresses without interruption. Or a businessman may gradually compromise his ethics and enter into restraint of trade, then find his occupational career ended in prison. Moral careers and occupational careers *may* converge, but they do not *have* to.

The fundamental notion in a moral career is that of social process. Compare Becker's discussion of Mead's concepts with Steffens' similar discussion of Captain Schmittberger's life:

> George Herbert Mead . . . tells us that the reality of social life is a conversation of significant symbols, in the course of which people make tentative moves and then adjust and reorient their activity in the light of responses (real and imagined) others make to those moves. The formation of the individual act is a *process* in which conduct is continually reshaped to take account of the expectations of others, as these are expressed in the immediate situation and as the actor supposes they may come to be expressed. [Becker, 1966, italics added.]

> The *process* of corruption had begun so quietly with that first tip and proceeded so gradually in an environ-

[2] I am indebted to John Gagnon for this point.

194   *AN INTERACTIONIST VIEW*

ment where it was all a matter of course that [Schmitt-
berger] never realized what he was doing till the Lexow
Committee's exposure . . . exposed him to himself. "I
didn't know how it looked . . . till I saw the other
Lexow witnesses telling things." [Steffens, 1931, italics
added.]

And as both Becker and Steffens suggest, the process of a
moral career involves different *stages* of becoming bent. Goffman (1961) builds on that framework with the notions of
moral career *contingencies, moral experiences,* and an
equilibrium career stage of *apologia. Contingencies* are circumstances or problems which a person must face, often for
purely accidental reasons. The *moral experience* is a reaction
to contingencies, often involving an ethical decision of action,
that alters the "framework of imagery" in which a person
evaluates himself and others. The moral experience is a
benchmark between the *stages* in a moral career, which usually culminate (for the deviant) in an *apologia:* a distorted
image of one's life course that brings it into alignment with
the basic values of his society (Goffman, 1961, pp. 139–40).
    Thus, the moral career is a process of self-labeling that
takes place, for the policeman, within a context of affiliation.
As Matza (1969) notes, affiliation with a deviant group does
not preordain deviance, it only invites it: but the invitation
may be quite strong. Westley (1970) describes four strong
mechanisms of group social control which affect a man who
becomes affiliated as a policeman: expediency, categorical reactions, sanctions, and personal integrity.
    Expediency is simply the path of least resistance to find-
ing definitions of complex situations: following the prescriptions of older policemen and adopting the rules of the group.
Categorical reaction is the policeman's discovery that he has
been socially stereotyped: society has labeled him with the
reputation engendered by the actions of all other policemen.
(As a "cop" he is just as categorically defined as a "con" or a
"nigger.") The sanctions most often used against policemen
violating group norms are the refusal to share information
and the refusal to work with the wayward officer. The main-

Becoming Bent 195

tenance of personal integrity (self-esteem) in the face of a conflict between police group values and those of the larger society creates a pressure to break with one or the other value-sets; for the man who accepts the invitation to police affiliation, he must largely break with, or redefine, societal values. Goffman's apologia is a means of excusing that break, but Westley (1970) notes that a policeman's value conflict is never wholly resolved (see also Chwast, 1965).

Both Goffman's subjective view of the moral career and Westley's objective view of the forces that shape it may easily be misread as determinism, but they did not mean that. As Cohen (1955) notes, behavior is determined both by the facts of the situation (Goffman's contingencies) *and* by the individual's frame of reference for interpreting those facts: "the interests, preconceptions, stereotypes and values [he brings] to the situation" (p. 53). Cohen also notes that in order to deal effectively with many situations, the frame of reference, or values, of the individual must change. But that does not explain why one solution to a situation (one outcome of Goffman's moral experience) is chosen rather than another: "Different individuals *do* deal differently with the same or similar problems and these differences must likewise be accounted for" (Cohen, 1955, p. 55).

We cannot account for those individual differences with the available data. All we can do here is follow the careers of a few policemen to extreme forms of corruption while stressing that many other policemen drop out along the way. The interrelatedness of moral decisions about corruption to home life, sexual relationships, and other nonoccupational factors may be glimpsed in Chinua Achebe's novel, *No Longer at Ease* (1960).[3] But with the available data we can only focus on the situational contingencies and the changes in frame of reference which result from dealing with such decisions, without fully understanding the frame of reference the individuals *initially* brought to the situation.

[3] See also Colin McInnes, *Mr. Love and Justice* (London: MacGibbon and Kee, 1960) for the moral careers of both a policeman and a pimp, in novel form.

AN INTERACTIONIST VIEW

A final note on the situations of these moral careers is that there are wide differences in the values of police subcultures and opportunities for police corruption. Thus, each moral career described and analyzed below will be prefaced by a description of its organizational context (see p. 11 above).

BECOMING A POLICEMAN

The most important context for police moral careers, both in terms of situation and frame of reference, is of course the fact that the individual has become a policeman. Perhaps a key contingency in a policeman's moral careers is the system of appointment he must deal with. Wittels (1949) describes the great disillusionment of a young police applicant when he was visited by the ward (political) boss and told his application stood no chance without a six-hundred-dollar "contribution" to the party and the reregistration of his entire family to the "right" party. Few cities maintain such a system today, but Royko (1971) suggests it may persist in Chicago.

Recruit school, when there is one—and in half of our cases there was not—is usually an experience of great idealism and anticipation of an exciting career. Westley (1970) describes the recruit school as a *rite de passage* which detaches a man from his old experience and prepares him for the new by teaching the rough outlines of the job as it appears on the books (p. 156). But Niederhoffer (1969) describes the New York recruit school's "unrealistic" stress on ethics and professionalism as the first source of cynicism about the job.

Both Westley and Niederhoffer agree that contact with older police officers in the first day on duty teaches the recruit that the formal rules are largely a sham—a situation which is true for virtually all police departments and many bureaucracies (see Gouldner, 1954). From the older officers, the recruit learns what the *real* rules of the police subculture are, often in apocryphal form. While these rules vary widely, one universal rule of police departments is secrecy and not reporting the misdeeds of brother officers (Westley, 1970; Vollmer, 1930).

Though taking on this new peer definition of police work is something of a reality shock, more traumatic is the first contact with hostility from the public. As he begins to take responsibility for his actions, the rookie becomes emotionally involved in maintaining respect for his authority. From bitter experience, he sees that his lot is with other policemen, and that nonpolicemen are enemies. As Westley notes, "The rookie has then become a cop, and the group has gained a new member."

Thus, *allowing for individual differences*, the process of becoming a policeman is one of facing a set of contingencies that produce moral experiences which change a man's frame of reference. With his new uniform and group membership, he feels society has labeled him an "outsider"—and he in turn labels nonpolicemen as outsiders (Becker, 1963). As Becker's dance musicians hate "squares," so policemen hate "civilians." Since not very long ago the police recruit was a civilian himself, he has undergone a radical redefinition of self in a very short time. That change is even reflected in his life outside the job, which often relies exclusively on other police families for social contact.

BECOMING A GRAFTER

While the process of becoming a policeman is fairly universal to police work, the process of becoming a grafter is not. The key contingency for entering a moral career of grafting—i.e., accepting bribes—is the extent to which grafting already occurs in the work group the rookie is assigned to. This is not the place to explain why grafting subcultures arise in some police departments and not others (see p. 11 above), but we should again note that there are wide differences in the phenomena. Our two case studies of grafters both took place within a context of well-organized police graft, run by a corrupt political machine. The first is Max Schmittberger of the nineteenth century New York police, as told by Steffens (1931). The second is "Gus Blawker," a composite character of policemen known by Wittels (1949) between 1930 and 1949. Summaries of their cases follow:

198   *AN INTERACTIONIST VIEW*

CASE NO. 1.   Max Schmittberger was a tall, handsome, but naïve baker's apprentice in the 1880s when some Tammany (political) leaders offered to get this fine specimen on the police force—free! Without understanding, Max joined up and was soon directing traffic on Broadway. Since he pleased his superiors, he was transferred to the "fat" Tenderloin precinct, the major vice market of New York.

One night a brothel owner pressed ten dollars in his hand. Confused, he presented it to his captain. Angered by Max's honesty, the captain explained graft to him and began to assign him to posts more and more crucial to the graft system. He moved from liaison with the hack thieves to regulation of the brothels, finally to be promoted to the job of "bagman"—collecting twenty thousand dollars a month for the captain.

When the Lexow investigation began (1894), he was jarred back to honesty. As the star witness, he told the commission all of the details of the graft system. Though punished by his peers for years after, the forces of reform eventually had him appointed chief of police.

CASE NO. 2.   Gus Blawker had an idealistic conception of police work in 1930 when the ward boss told him the conditions of appointment to the force. Disillusioned, but desperately needing a job, he borrowed the necessary money.

In the first days on the beat, he witnessed the vice squad shake down a speakeasy that had skipped a payment. His attempts to arrest politically influential men for traffic violations were severely reprimanded, and he was assigned to a boring suburban beat.

Through luck he made a much publicized arrest of a famous robber, for which he was promoted to detective. But his zeal in raiding a protected gambling house was rewarded with demotion to his old beat.

When his son needed an expensive operation, he appealed to the ward leader for a promotion with a promise to "play the game." As head of a detective squad, he took no graft until the machine required him to fix an important case. When his payoff arrived, he stared at the envelope for an hour before taking out the money. When his son needed another operation, he shook down a gambling joint.

From that point on he collected regularly from gamblers. The next step was to shake down brothels and then drug pushers. When he was arrested ten years later, he was rich enough to fix the case against him and retire in luxury.

Though Blawker's experience is probably more representative than Schmittberger's, we may derive similar conclusions from both. Most important is the process of increased involvement by which they became grafters. That is, they became more accustomed to taking graft as the graft organization tested them with first petty graft, then graft for allowing more serious offenses. Most people would agree that drug pushing is a more serious crime than gambling; we may assume that neither Gus Blawker's morality (self-definition) nor the policies of the graft organization would let him begin his grafting career with drug pushers. Rather, he worked up a ladder of increasing self-perceived social harm of offenses, neutralizing any moral objection to the (crime-specific) graft at each rung of the ladder—each stage of his moral career. The same seemed to happen with Schmittberger.

If we generalize these cases to all possible sources of graft, we may hypothesize a continuum of graft stages which follows a policeman's initial frame of reference about the social harm of each source of graft. The first stage is police "perks" —free coffee and meals from restaurants on his beat. The moral experience about accepting these perks usually occurs in the recruit's first days on duty, and the peer pressure to accept them is great. If he does accept the minor perks, he then has a different image of self to contend with when a bar owner operating after closing hours offers him a drink. Again a moral experience; a decision to accept the drink and let the place stay open redefines the policeman's self, if only slightly.

The third step in the grafting career may be another regulative bribe—a motorist handing him a driver's license with a

200 AN INTERACTIONIST VIEW

five-dollar bill in it or a construction foreman giving him ten dollars to overlook materials left illegally on the sidewalk. He may either accept or reject the bribe, but acceptance is made easier if he is used to taking gifts from restaurants and bars.

If there are regular payoffs made by a local gambling operation, and if the rookie has passed the tests of accepting minor graft, the other policemen receiving the gambling payoffs may offer to cut him in. This moral experience is particularly difficult, because it is an invitation to solidarity with his, by now, *only* "significant others," an invitation he is loath to reject. Indeed, policemen I knew in New York who rejected the offer soon transferred out of the work unit to graft-free "inside" jobs. But most New York policemen seem to accept the offer (Knapp, 1972).

The fifth step in a grafting career may be prostitutes' bribes, either from pimps, lone streetwalkers, or more regularly, brothel operators. The relationships established in prostitution graft can lead easily into narcotics graft, since drug traffic is often closely linked with prostitution (Knapp, 1972). Accepting narcotics graft, however, is the most difficult moral experience of all, since the initial frame of reference of most policemen would abhor the thought of helping drug pushers. If that graft is accepted, though, it is not unknown for policemen to go on to selling drugs themselves.

To summarize the hypothetical stages of the moral career of a grafter:

1. Minor "perks"
2. Bar closing hours
3. Regulative crimes (traffic, construction)
4. Gambling
5. Prostitution
6. Narcotics

Again, the hypothesis is only that this career will be followed when situational contingencies make it available and then *only if the policeman accepts the invitation to bribery.* Even when all of the graft sources are available, a policeman may stop at a middle rung of his self-perceived ladder of

Becoming Bent 201

social harm. The stage at which he stops can become a key element in his apologia: "I might take money from gamblers, and whores, 'cause they don't hurt anybody—but I won't mess around with pushers!" Put another way: "I might be bad, but I'm not *that* bad."

Stoddard (1968) suggests that most policemen stop at a certain stage of deviance on the basis of group definition of "limits." An English police official told me that Manchester constables in the 1930s might brag about bribes from pub owners and gamblers, but they would never mention bribes from prostitutes. Cook (1971) notes the 1950s distinction between clean graft (gamblers, prostitutes) and dirty graft (drugs) in the New York police (that gradually disappeared during the 1960s).

Assuming there are group limits to bribery, some policemen go beyond them. A characteristic of deviance from group bribery norms is the switch from pure bribery to extortion, or from "reactive" to "proactive" graft (Reiss, 1971). The Knapp Commission has labeled the two kinds of grafters as "grass-eaters" (reactive) and "meat-eaters" (proactive). One possible explanation of the shift from grass to meat is that of secondary deviance (Lemert, 1967). In this case, the agent defining the individual as deviant is the individual himself, without the intervention of (another) agent of social control. Assuming the initial frame of reference of the grafter was morally opposed to graft, one of the moral experiences may be so severe that, if resulting in a decision for more graft, it may produce a "What the hell, I'm a crook, so I'll make the most of it" reaction. Subsequent career stages will then become proactive. Blawker, on the day that he received "the envelope," sought out a friend in tears and got very drunk. From then on he was a proactive grafter.

Individual differences in the initial frame of reference are important, since the switch from reactive to proactive graft does not occur at any particular stage of the grafting career. Policemen in vice-ridden Harlem have progressed to the extreme stages of grafting on an entirely reactive basis (virtually just standing on the corners and holding out their hands). Those more given to personality explanations of crime would

202   *AN INTERACTIONIST VIEW*

of course suggest that individual differences are paramount: some policemen join the force with an entrepreneurial affinity for proactive graft. But the data available so far suggest that secondary deviation is a more likely explanation.

One final contingency in the moral career of a grafter should be checked in future case study research. Both Schmittberger and Blawker (as well as the burglars described below) experienced a negative social reaction in their work group to acts of honesty or honest enforcement. This moral experience tends to occur early in the police career, and it clearly redefines the self in terms of perceived definitions of being a policeman. Future research should examine the extent to which such an experience is a necessary element in a grafting career.

BECOMING A BURGLAR

If individual differences and choice was important to stress in the moral careers of the grafter, it is an even more important caveat in the moral career of the police burglar. And as important as different individual frames of reference are the differences in situational contingencies.

Police burglary is not nearly as persistent a phenomenon as police graft. This is not the place to explain differences in the extent of burglary (see Wilson, 1963), but we should note that there was (1) a series of police burglary scandals all over the United States in the early 1960s, with few reports of it since, and (2) a police burglary group discovered in London in the mid-1960s, with no reports of it since.

Cook (1966), reviewing the 1961 Denver scandal, suggests a pattern that fits Cohen's (1955) description of the evolution of deviant subcultures. To restate Cook's analysis in Cohen's terms, policemen collectively face a status problem that can best be solved by acquiring more money. Many alternative means of supplementing a salary are available, but an easy route is to pick up "lying around" loot at the scene of a burglary. "Exploratory gestures" among the policemen are made at the scene of a burglary, and some goods or money is also

Becoming Bent 203

pocketed. Further gestures (suggestions) are made, and if well received, a burglary is planned. A successful burglary makes the idea more attractive to other policemen who are invited to join in. In Denver, when a transfer program inadvertently broke up the initial burglary subculture, its members spread the innovation to other patrol districts—making the exploratory gestures that established new subcultures.

Seen in this context, we may summarize the moral careers of two police burglars: the first from Denver, interviewed by Smith (1965), the second from another midwestern city, interviewed by Stoddard (1968).

CASE NO. 3.　Patrolman Hastings joined the Denver police to be an "eager beaver" cop, but discovered two policemen committing a burglary while he was still a probationary patrolman. Keeping his mouth shut, he stayed with honest, good police work.

His slated promotion to detective fell through when he arrested a politically influential man, who was immediately let off by the court.

Disillusioned, he agreed to his partner's suggestion one night to pick up "lying around" loot at the scene of a burglary, and his sergeant later took a cut of the loot.

A few nights later, they were called to a fur warehouse burglary, which turned out to be an insurance fraud done by the owner. The lieutenant's presence and the owner's offer of a free mink stole induced Hastings to "go along."

From then on he committed burglary on a regular basis, often at the request of insurance swindling businessmen.

CASE NO. 4.　Patrolman Smith began his police career with free meals at Sam Paisano's restaurant and immediately learned that Paisano was virtually immune from any kind of protection.

While still a rookie, he observed his partner steal candy bars from a supermarket. Refusing to share the loot, he was advised he should "go along" or face the consequence —social isolation.

204   *AN INTERACTIONIST VIEW*

When he did pass his "test," he joined in on picking up "lying around" loot. Eventually, his group began planning burglaries. When he was finally caught, he was surprised how alone he was, and he realized that "lying around" loot was the limit of theft by police standards; planned burglary was deviant.

A key contingency in Hastings' moral career was that he entered a police subculture of planned burglary and was invited to join it. In Smith's case, he was invited to join a subculture of "shopping" (picking up lying-around loot) and participated in the evolution of a subculture that exceeded the general group limits of theft. In both cases, they learned, while still rookies, that certain people had immunity from arrest and that other policemen committed criminal acts.

Whether a policeman joins an external burglary subculture or helps to form one, the case studies suggest the following stages in the moral career of the police burglar:

1. Learning the fallacy of impartial enforcement of the law
2. Learning that other policemen are dishonest
3. Picking up lying-around loot at the scene of a burglary ("shopping")
4. Joining in a planned burglary
5. Committing planned burglary on a regular basis

Evidence from the original case studies suggest that, just as in graft, the progression to each new stage in a burglary career depends upon a change in the frame of reference that allows a consistency with basic societal values. After the Denver scandal, several police burglars stressed in public interviews that "only the big chains and insurance companies, institutions that could afford it, had been hurt." And in Smith's case, where the peer influence had been stronger than rationalizations about insurance companies, his apologia was a perception of more policemen involved in planned burglary than was in fact the case. The societal value he used for justification of burglary was solidarity with his brother officers.

Becoming Bent 205

Again, individual differences are important. Some policemen may refuse even to "shop"; others may shop without ever planning a burglary; still others might pull off one planned burglary and then turn honest. As in the switch from reactive to proactive grafting, the switch from occasional to regular planned burglary may possibly be explained as *secondary* deviation. Whatever the individual moral experiences are, however, any progression is along the sequence of stages outlined here.

SOCIAL POLICY IMPLICATIONS

The central argument of this paper is, again, that police burglars and grafters become deviant only through a gradual process of confronting contingencies and making moral decisions. The social policy implications of that argument are clear for police graft, and not so clear for police burglary.

All of the contingencies of a grafter's moral career involve nonenforcement of what Schur (1965) calls "victimless crimes." Thus, police graft could be ended tomorrow if legislatures enacted Norval Morris's dictum (1970) that "everyone has a right to go to hell any way they please." But since modern Western society is ambiguous about that dictum, and clearly opposed to it in the area of opiate selling, this paper implies a less radical solution as well.

If a moral career must be a *gradual* process of redefining one's self to accept ever more serious deviance (as defined by the initial frame of reference), then grafting might be inhibited by making the process less gradual. If the graft steps from perks, to gambling, to prostitution, then to drugs, are small, a single step from perks to drugs is quite large. If gambling and prostitution were legalized, the narcotics pusher would not face policemen accustomed to taking large bribes; the moral experience of a policeman offered a large narcotics bribe would tend to decide against acceptance, since it would require too great a redefinition of self all at once. Thus, a society concerned with police *narcotics* graft is well advised to legalize gambling and prostitution.

206   *AN INTERACTIONIST VIEW*

Police burglary, a phenomenon we know much less about, seems to be an extension of the basic business ethics of American society: theft from large institutions doesn't hurt anybody in particular, so it's all right. Smigel (1956) found this attitude to exist generally in one American town, and Steffens (1931) suggests it permeates American business. Even though the police and the wider society seem to come to this value judgment gradually, the key question is what contingencies shape the formation of such attitudes. The "neo-Chicagoan" approach would seem to lose its explanatory power here, for what is at stake is no less than a critique of Western society. For that, one should turn to the macro-level concerns of a critical sociology, perhaps analyzing theft in terms of such basic institutions as private property itself (Birnbaum, 1972).

References

Becker, Howard L. (1963). *Outsiders*. Glencoe, Ill.: Free Press.

—— (1966). Introduction to Shaw, Clifford, *The Jack Roller*. Chicago: University of Chicago Press.

Birnbaum, Norman (1972). *Toward a Critical Sociology*. New York: Oxford University Press.

Chwast, Jacob (1965). "Value Conflicts in Law Enforcement." *Crime and Delinquency*, 11.

Cohen, Albert K. (1955). *Delinquent Boys: The Culture of the Gang*. New York: Free Press.

Cook, Fred J. (1966). *The Corrupted Land*. London: Jonathan Cape, 1967.

—— (1971). "The Pusher Cop: The Institutionalization of Police Corruption." *New York*, August 16, 1971.

Goffman, Erving (1961). *Asylums*. Garden City, N.Y.: Anchor Books.

Gouldner, Alvin (1954). *Patterns of Industrial Bureaucracy*. New York: Free Press.

Knapp, Whitman, et al. (1972). *Report of the Commission to Investigate Alleged Police Corruption* (City of New York). New York: George Braziller.

Lemert, Edwin (1967). *Human Deviance, Social Problems, and Social Control.* Englewood Cliffs, N.J.: Prentice-Hall, Inc.

Maas, Peter (1973). *Serpico.* New York: The Viking Press, Inc.

McNamara, John H. (1966). "Uncertainties in Police Work: The Relevance of Police Recruits' Background and Training." In *The Police*, edited by David J. Bordua. New York: John Wiley & Sons, Inc.

Matza, David (1969). *Becoming Deviant.* Englewood Cliffs, N.J.: Prentice-Hall, Inc.

Morris, Norval, and Hawkins, Gordon (1970). *The Honest Politicians Guide to Crime Control.* Chicago: University of Chicago Press.

Niederhoffer, Arthur (1969). *Behind the Shield: The Police in Urban Society.* Garden City, N.Y.: Anchor Books.

Reiss, Albert J., Jr. (1971). *The Police and the Public.* New Haven, Conn.: Yale University Press.

Royko, Mike (1971). *Boss.* London: Paladin, 1972.

Schur, Edwin (1965). *Crimes Without Victims.* Englewood Cliffs, N.J.: Prentice-Hall, Inc.

Shaw, Clifford (1930). *The Jack Roller.* Chicago: University of Chicago Press.

Smigel, Erwin (1956). "Public Attitudes Towards Stealing as Related to the Size of the Victim Organization." *American Sociological Review*, 21.

Smith, Ralph L. (1965). *The Tarnished Badge.* New York: T. Y. Crowell.

Steffens, Lincoln (1931). *The Autobiography of Lincoln Steffens.* New York: Harcourt, Brace.

Stern, Mort (1962). "What Makes a Policeman Go Wrong?" *Journal of Criminal Law, Criminology and Police Science* 53.

Stoddard, Ellwyn R. (1968). " 'The Informal Code' of Police Deviancy: A Group Approach to 'Blue-coat Crime.' " *Journal of Criminal Law, Criminology and Police Science* 59, no. 2.

208   *AN INTERACTIONIST VIEW*

Sutherland, Edwin H., and Cressey, Donald R. (1960). *Principles of Criminology*. Philadelphia: J. B. Lippincott Company.

Tappan, Paul (1960). *Crime, Justice and Correction*. New York: McGraw-Hill, Inc.

Vollmer, August (1936). *The Police and Modern Society*. Berkeley, Calif.: University of California Press.

—— (1930). To the U. S. National Committee of Law Observance and Enforcement. *Report on the Police*. Washington, D.C.: U. S. Government Printing Office.

Wambaugh, Joseph (1970). *The New Centurions*. New York: Dell Books.

Westley, William (1970). *Violence and the Police*. Cambridge, Mass.: Massachusetts Institute of Technology Press.

Wilson, James Q. (1963). "The Police and Their Problems: A Theory." *Public Policy*.

Wittels, David J. (1949). "Why Cops Turn Crooked." *Saturday Evening Post*, April 23, 1949.

[18]

Exploiting Police Authority

HOWARD COHEN

Precisely because police have wide-ranging authority and the latitude to exercise it in relatively unsurpervised ways, they also have ample opportunity to exploit their authority. The opportunities themselves are ubiquitous; police may respond to them by steadfastly ignoring them, resisting the temptation of them, taking what comes their way, or pursuing them rigorously. Most officers have no problem rejecting the opportunities to participate in serious crime for personal gain, but there is scarcely an officer in uniform who has not taken a free cup of coffee or a discounted meal. Are all forms of taking equally serious? The value of what is taken can range from thousands of dollars to the price of a cup of coffee. Is taking free coffee an exploitive act? A considered answer must begin from an understanding of what exploitation is. I would characterize exploitation in this context as follows: Acting on opportunities, created by virtue of one's authority, for personal gain at the expense of the public one is authorized to serve. The elements of exploitation, then, are (1) a position of authority, (2) an opportunity for personal gain created by that position, (3) a cost to those under one's authority, and (4) a causal relationship between the gain and the cost. On the face of it, all of these elements are plausibly present in the act of accepting free coffee.

Official police policy virtually always condemns all forms of taking, from theft and extortion to accepting petty gratuities. Departments standardly prohibit taking gratuities, as do police codes of ethics. Some police chiefs have gone so far as to claim to see no relevant difference between taking a cup of coffee and taking a television set from an appliance store. Pat Murphy once said, "Apart from your paycheck there is no honest buck." Police officers themselves tend to reject the claim that there is no difference between theft and accepting a gratuity. Even those officers who do not accept gratuities themselves generally do not condemn those who do and generally do not see the practice in moral terms. From their point of view, if taking free coffee is a sin at all, it is an extremely minor one. The question I am raising here is not whether all forms of "taking" are equally serious, but whether they deserve to be equally categorized as *exploitation* of police authority. The issue is important not as a way to encourage us to condemn the free cup of coffee but to understand what it is about the exploitation of authority that makes it a violation of our moral sensibilities. This is not an easy question to answer, and we will need to keep a range of cases in mind in order to sort it out.

Six Cases

CASE 1: THEFT An officer responding to a call to investigate a burglary alarm sounding at an appliance

Howard Cohen is Professor of Philosophy and Associate Dean of the College of Arts and Science at the University of Massachusetts–Boston.

store at 2:00 a.m. arrives to discover that the rear door is open and the alarm is ringing. The store is not in a residential neighborhood, and nobody is at the scene. The officer enters the store, sees that it has been ransacked, and determines that the thief is no longer on the premises. On the way back to his car, the officer takes a portable television set that is sitting on a shelf and puts it in his trunk. He then calls in to report the burglary and waits for the store owner to come down to secure the building and assess the losses.

CASE 2: EXTORTION An officer who regularly patrols a "skid row" neighborhood on the night shift is frequently called upon to break up fights in bar rooms. He has come to charge money for this service. Bar owners who call upon him for help are expected to offer him ten dollars for his efforts. Those who will not pay receive a very slow response. The officer might let the fight progress to the point where additional property is damaged or where other patrons are endangered by those fighting. Those who do pay receive quick, efficient responses. This is no unconscious pattern on the officer's part; he explicitly informs the uncooperative bar owners that they will get what they pay for.[1]

CASE 3: ACCEPTING A BRIBE An officer stops a motorist for speeding, approaches the car, and asks the driver to produce a license and registration. The driver hands over the required documents along with a $20 bill. The officer takes what is offered without saying anything and goes back to his cruiser to run a warrant check. Finding no outstanding warrants and determining that the license and registration are in order, the officer returns to the motorist and gives back the license and registration along with a warning. The officer keeps the $20.

CASE 4: GRATUITIES (AGGRESSIVE SHOPPING) An officer has organized his shift around the active pursuit of free goods. His first stop out of the station is a coffee shop that provides him with coffee and doughnuts. He then goes to one of four convenience stores (in rotation) that give him free cigarettes. He eats lunch for half price in the same place each day.

Once a week he stops at a liquor store for a free bottle. He does as much of his personal shopping as possible from merchants on his beat. His familiarity with them from his patrol duties yields discounts on cleaning, auto parts, food, equipment rental, and so on. This officer has worked very hard to keep his shift assignment and, indeed, has made his career decisions so as not to disrupt his work routine.

CASE 5: GRATUITIES (PASSIVE) An officer who is scrupulously honest about not taking money, goods, or favors nevertheless will not turn down a free cup of coffee when it is offered at a lunch counter or restaurant. This officer draws a sharp line between free coffee and all other forms of gratuity. He would never take anything other than coffee, and he takes that only when it is offered. He does not seek out places known to offer free coffee to police. Whenever he orders coffee, it is with the intent to pay. However, if the waitress or the proprietor says that police do not pay, this officer does not argue. He says thank you and leaves his change in his pocket.

CASE 6: GRATUITIES (COERCED) A new recruit on his first tour of duty is assigned to a Field Training Officer who regularly seeks out gratuities. The FTO takes free coffee, candy and cigarettes at virtually every opportunity. The recruit does not want to take any gratuities whatsoever. He knows that it is against departmental policy and that he is on probationary status. At first he pays for whatever he gets—coffee, cigarettes, and so on. He senses, however, that his FTO is becoming increasingly disgusted with him for maintaining his "academy" attitude and refusing to accept the realities of departmental customs concerning gratuities. In order to get along with his FTO, not to be labeled a "fink" throughout the patrol officers' grapevine, and receive a good evaluation, the new recruit begins to take coffee also.[2]

Key Differences

Are these six cases all examples of exploitation of their authority by police? Even without a very careful analysis of the elements of exploitation, the first four cases seem to be prime candidates for that category. The last two cases—involving gratuities—are less clear. They share some of the features of the first four cases, but they also differ from them in morally relevant ways. Some of these differences are relevant to the question of exploitation, but others may be set aside

> *If value alone determined the seriousness of taking gratuities, we might end up with an equation of four hundred cups of coffee to the television set.*

for our purposes. For example, in all six cases police officers have accepted or taken something of value, but that value differs significantly from case to case. The value in the theft case might be a few hundred dollars, and if the theft is not an isolated episode, the value of what is taken could be very great. The same might be said for the cases of extortion and accepting a bribe. The value of what is taken in the gratuities cases can mount up as well. If value alone determined the seriousness of taking gratuities, we might end up with an equation of four hundred cups of coffee to the television set. That would put a daily coffee drinker into the category of appliance thief in a little over a year. This suggests that it is not primarily the value of what is taken that will differentiate these cases as exploitive or not.

Another way in which these cases differ from one another is according to the intent of the officer. The officers in the first four cases make a conscious and intentional decision to take. The extortion and the aggressive pursuit of gratuities seem particularly avaricious. The theft and the acceptance of the bribe might be attributed to weakness of will, but in both of those cases the officer had time for second thoughts. In the case of the passive acceptance of gratuities, the officer does not seem to be intent on taking anything, and in the last case the officer himself feels coerced into taking the coffee. The differences in intent among these six cases do lead to differences in the severity of the judgment we might make of the officer in each of them. Although we do not generally approve of acts simply because they are done without evil or malicious intent, the absence of such intent does tend to mitigate our judgments. But even if we are inclined to judge officers who do not intend to do harm less harshly than we judge those who do, we must not forget that

exploitation does not depend upon intent. The elements of exploitation are the officer's authority, the officer's gain, and the public's expense. All of these elements can occur in circumstances quite independent of the officer's intent. The officer who uses his authority to gain at the public's expense may not see it that way, but we cannot let his blindness change the facts.

These six cases differ markedly as to whether what is taken is offered voluntarily. In the theft case it is not offered at all, and in the extortion case it is pretty clearly offered under threat. The "offerings" in the case of aggressive gratuities may or may not be voluntary, but it is hard to believe that they are offered joyfully. The bribe is no doubt offered voluntarily in case 3, as is the coffee in case 5. Whether or not the coffee is so offered in case 6 is an open question. The voluntariness of the offer is relevant here because one of the elements of exploitation is that the officer's gain occur at the public's expense. The fact that the offers are voluntary is sometimes used to show that the portion of the public that foots the bill in these cases

> *Police are in a position to take things because they have been put there in order to perform a particular function.*

treats them more like a contractual agreement than an exploitation. Whatever the moral defects of accepting a bribe might be, the cost to the motorist is hardly one of them. The cost in this instance is to the public, which does not receive the motorist's fine, or to the deterrent value of law enforcement, such as it is.

All six cases are cases of taking in which the officer's opportunities to take are based on his possession of police authority. This is not to suggest that others (nonpolice) do not have the opportunity to steal from appliance stores, get into the protection racket, accept bribes, and even have someone else pick up their tab at a lunch counter. Those opportunities can be made or found at the individual initiative of the taker, but they are not created by society *in the course of designating the authority of its own officials.* Police are in a position to take these things in these cases because they have been put there in order to perform a particular function. It is the authority to investigate crimes, keep public order, write traffic citations, and protect merchants that creates the opportunities for "taking." Thus, it is not merely the taking, but the taking *in an official capacity* that these cases share. This feature is an important element of exploitation.

"Exploitation" carries the connotation of a serious moral transgression, and it may seem inappropriate to apply the term to petty cases of taking. In some of the cases we are considering, the cost to society appears to be substantial; in other cases it seems quite minor. Those officers who defend accepting gratuities generally argue that the police do not behave any differently toward those who offer the gratuities than

they do toward other citizens. The fact that an officer has taken a cup of coffee from a merchant does not immunize the merchant from law enforcement, the argument goes. Many officers attest to having written tickets on such merchants (and to having received a shocked reaction). Given the officer's disposition to do his job as it should be done irrespective of prior favors, defenders of gratuities claim that there is a significant difference between accepting a gratuity and the morally indefensible forms of taking. In the cases of theft, extortion and accepting bribes, society more directly pays a price for the officer's personal gain, and that price, since it involves a failure to enforce the law, or violations of law by the officer himself, is higher.

The Social Costs

In some ways, then, the question of whether taking gratuities is exploitation of office turns on the seriousness of the impact of this practice on the public. There is no doubt that the police gain personally from the gratuities they receive, and no doubt that they receive them because they are police officers (with the authority that that implies). What is unclear is the cost of this practice to the community in which the police work. Since this is the pivotal issue, it will be worth our while to carefully examine the cost to society of all of the above-mentioned forms of taking by the police. We need to understand the cost of accepting gratuities *in relation to* the cost of theft, extortion, and accepting bribes if we are to determine whether or not there is a qualitative difference between cases 1–3 on the one hand, and cases 4–6 on the other.

The cost to society in the cases of theft and extortion by the police must be measured in terms of the betrayal of the public trust. These cases are nothing less than violations of the "Social Contract," and they strike at the very heart of the justification of social organization. The Social Contract is a conception of the basis of political authority that comes down to us from seventeenth-century English political philosophers Thomas Hobbes and John Locke. It is a conception that is still relevant to our contemporary understanding of governmental authority, and it is especially illuminating as a way of seeing what is so abhorrent about theft and extortion when they are practiced by the police.

The Social Contract seeks to justify the authority of the state in terms of a bargain struck by individuals in whom sovereignty originally resides. These individuals are imagined to live a life without political organization (life in the State of Nature) in which all are equal in authority. In Locke's scheme, each individual has rights to life, liberty, and property as well as the right to enforce those rights against the transgressions of others.[3] Locke calls the right to enforce one's rights the right of reparation and restitution. The State of Nature is a state of liberty, but it is not a state of security.

Hobbes imagined that life in the State of Nature would be "solitary, poor, nasty, brutish and short."[4] The strong would bully the weak, and the weak would seek their revenge as best they could. The State of

Police theft and extortion strike at the very core of our justification of authority.

Nature would be a state of war. Locke's State of Nature was, perhaps, a more peaceful world, but it was still a world of insecurity. People might accumulate property only to see it taken by those who would not respect their rights. Recovery of the property was the right, but also the responsibility, of the victim. If the victim were weaker or less resourceful than the thief, he had no higher recourse.

The difficulty of life in the State of Nature would drive rational people to renounce some of their liberty for security of life, liberty, and property. Rational people recognize that the creation of an authority over them all is a good bargain. They are willing, in Locke's terms, to assign the rights of reparation and restitution to a sovereign in exchange for security. They are thus willing to leave the State of Nature and enter a State of Civil Society. Thus, they contract to create a political authority that will enforce their rights and protect their lives and property.

If the Social Contract expresses the most cogent rationale for the creation and maintenance of political authority, then it is clear that police theft and extortion strike at the very core of our justification of authority. The police, as the enforcers of law, initiate the exercise of the rights of reparation and restitution that we have delegated to the sovereign. Their function in this regard is precisely the function we depend upon to secure life and property and, thus, make the Social Contract a good bargain. When police exploit this function by becoming thieves and extorters themselves, they directly assault the rationality of the bargain and, in theoretical terms, threaten to throw us back into the State of Nature. Or, more precisely, they create a situation in which the State of Nature is *more* secure than the State of Civil Society. At least in the State of Nature you do not have to worry about theft under cover of authority since nobody wears that cloak, and you retain your sense that protection is your own responsibility. In terms of political morality, few acts are more heinous than those in which persons in authority make us less secure than we would be without them.

Accepting Bribes vs. Accepting Gratuities

In terms of their cost to society, accepting bribes and accepting gratuities are not in the same league with theft and extortion by the police. Accepting bribes is not, on that account, a trivial matter. Rather, what makes accepting a bribe a serious moral transgression is not that the act threatens the life, liberty, or property of others but that it results in the injustice of preferential treatment based on the willingness to pay for it. The motorist who buys a warning ticket instead of a citation for his $20 bill has avoided the burden of conforming to the traffic laws, of paying what was likely to be a larger fine the proceeds of which can go to *public* purposes, and possibly of a surcharge on his insurance to cover the potential cost of accidents caused by scofflaw drivers. The officer who accepts the $20 has contributed to the unequal application of those laws and done an injustice to everyone who receives a citation for a similar offense. If the practice of accepting bribes were widespread and well understood by the public, it might easily have the effect of undermining conformity to the traffic laws. But even if the practice is relatively isolated and a relatively private matter between a small number of officers and citizens, the scale of the injustice does not diminish. The seriousness of the offense is measured in terms of all those who are not given preferential treatment when stopped by the police. While this level of injustice may not be of the magnitude of assaults on the Social Contract, it is no petty matter.

If we find that accepting gratuities is like accepting bribes, then they too must raise questions of justice. Most police officers argue that these are quite different kinds of taking, however. Some gratuities may, of course, be offered as bribes. A merchant may hope that by giving police officers a discount on merchandise, the officers will not write citations for violations of parking regulations in front of the merchant's place of business. The merchant may offer the gratuity in this hope, whether or not the officers are aware of his intent. And of course there may well be officers who would not write the citation because they had accepted a discount. In such cases, we would be dealing with accepting a bribe with all of the elements present in case 3. Accepting gratuities under those conditions would be an exploitation of authority. If we are willing to accept the possibility of the most innocent case of offering and accepting gratuities, however, the elements of bribery are absent. The merchant may offer the gratuity with no expectations of any benefit in return. More to the point, the officer may be resolved to give no special treatment to those who give gratuities.

Officers argue that the offer of free coffee or discounted meals is typically made with the expectation of any particular favor in return. In the clearest cases the free coffee is given by the establishment as a matter of policy to any uniformed officer. Some franchised food shops and restaurants have a policy of offering police gratuities which is set by high level executives rather than by shop managers. The gratuity is actually given by a waitress; the officer may not even know the merchant who is making the offer (much less the executive who set the policy). Even if the gratuity were intended as a bribe here, the officer might be excused for confusion about who is to receive the preferential treatment in exchange.

On the officer's side, most police agree that the acceptance of a cup of coffee will not alter the performance of their jobs. They argue that they would write a citation on a merchant or a waitress who gave them free coffee should they stop that person for a traffic violation. They further claim that they would enforce the laws in and around establishments which give gratuities no more selectively than they do in and around other establishments. In short, they do not

> *Police officers who do not disapprove of gratuities see the practice as a customary expression of appreciation for the work that police do.*

treat the gratuity as a payment for future service. This is not to say that officers do not admit to feeling badly about enforcing the law against the people who offer them gratuities. Many officers claim that after issuing a citation or ticketing cars in front of an establishment where they have taken gratuities, they would not go back to that place of business as a customer.

Police officers who do not disapprove of gratuities prefer to see the practice as a customary expression of appreciation for the work that police do. In their view, those who offer gratuities are, for the most part, genuinely friendly toward police. They appreciate a police presence in their neighborhoods, regard police work as somewhat underpaid and potentially dangerous, and wish to show support for an often

maligned group of public servants. The customary token by which merchants display this appreciation is

> *A less flattering model for the gratuity, but one which equally diminishes its moral seriousness, is the model of the "tip."*

food or beverage. Just as people might offer coffee to an officer in their own homes, so merchants offer it in their places of business.

A less flattering model for the gratuity, but one which equally diminishes its moral seriousness, is the model of the "tip." Just as the officer tips the waitress who serves him the coffee, the merchant tips the officer for the quality of the services rendered. The tip is not a bribe; it is offered for the past or present services performed well and makes no claim for future consideration. One does not tip in the hope of receiving better service in the future. To do so would be to undermine the disparity of status implied by the tip. Tips are for servants. They imply an evaluation of the quality of the service and an implication that the person giving the tip is in a position to make that evaluation. In other words, the tipper is the master in a master-servant relationship. To bribe a servant would be a show of weakness; to tip a servant is a show of superiority.

It is, perhaps, not surprising that merchants could treat police as servants by offering them free coffee or discounted meals. Tipping is a regular practice in their line of work and does not carry morally distasteful connotations. From the merchant's point of view, police *are* primarily servants (albeit public servants). They make the corner of the world in which the merchant works safe and orderly—the better to conduct business. They keep the traffic moving, prevent disputes from getting out of hand, and quell disturbances when necessary.

Although this conception of gratuities does diminish the cost of the practice to society, it surely does not present an appealing picture for the police. Its status and class connotation undermine the police sense of the proper authority relation between officer and citizen. How can someone who accepts a tip from another claim to have authority over that person? The question is rhetorical; it happens all the time. Police do claim to have authority over the merchants who offer them gratuities—and rightly so. But when they accept gratuities, they also engage in a practice which implies a contradictory authority relationship. It is probably this contradiction that makes many officers uncomfortable when they accept gratuities and unwilling to accept them again after they have exercised their authority on the merchant who offers them.

If we are willing to assume that in at least some cases accepting gratuities is nothing more than accepting a token of appreciation or a tip, we must still address the question of whether there is an element of exploitation of authority in the transaction. Although we have disassociated accepting gratuities from theft, extortion, and the corruption of taking bribes (in many cases), we have yet to consider whether by taking a free cup of coffee the officer is using his or her position of authority for pursuit of personal gain at the expense of the public.

Who is being exploited when the officer accepts a free cup of coffee, a discounted meal, or other goods or services? In the case of gratuities aggressively pursued, we might well argue that the merchants are being exploited. The officer's milking of the custom of giving token gifts or tips clearly strains the credibility of the claim that they are freely and happily given. Case 4 seems, on its face, to approach extortion, and it would take serious talking to convince all but the most naive to interpret it otherwise. In the other two cases of accepting gratuities, however, there is little reason

to believe that the merchants are being exploited. Indeed, there is some reason to believe that the transaction is to the merchant's benefit.

Some merchants feel that the reputation of being a regular stopping place for police officers will discourage thieves and robbers from making them targets.

Merchants may benefit from a police presence in their places of business in many ways. Some businesses attract an undesirable clientele (undesirable, that is, to the merchant). The regular presence of police may tend to discourage that group from patronizing such establishments. Some merchants feel that the reputation of being a regular stopping place for police officers will discourage thieves and robbers from making them targets. For others, having police on the premises sets a tone which discourages disturbances. For the price of a cup of coffee or a package of cigarettes, these merchants receive a service that they very much desire—police presence. But if the police are not exploiting the merchants who offer them gratuities, they may very well be exploiting others in the community who do not pay extra for their presence and their special attention.

The Police as a Social Resource

Because the police have the authority to enforce the laws and to keep peace, their presence is a social resource which may be to the benefit of virtually anyone in a time of need.[5] Because the police are a *social* resource, maintained through public funds as servants of the entire community, their presence should be allocated on the basis of need. That is, whoever needs police services should have an equal claim on them (subject, of course, to limitations on the availability of the service and to priorities of seriousness). When police accept gratuities, however, they allocate their presence on the basis of ability or willingness to pay for it. Merchants who do not offer

free coffee, cigarettes, half price meals, or discounted merchandise do not have the benefits of the regular, predictable police presence that is available to the merchants who do. Likewise, citizens who might benefit from police presence but who do not happen to live in the vicinity of the favored coffee shop receive less of a valuable social resource. This is not to say that the police will ignore calls for service, merely that the "freebies" may dictate how they allocate their presence between calls.

The cost to the public of any single instance of police allocating their presence on the basis of who is willing to pay for it is, in all honesty, not very great. As some officers like to point out, they have to eat their meals and drink their coffee somewhere. It is always possible that their presence would be more beneficial somewhere else. This may be regrettable, but it really cannot be helped. That argument has some plausibility when we focus on a single incident, but it is less convincing when we see accepting gratuities as a common and pervasive practice in a department. When the *pattern* of police deployment in a community is shaped by the location of establishments that offer gratuities, then the criterion for distribution of that resource is willingness to pay for it. The more pronounced the pattern, the more serious the inequity. If certain doughnut shops always have two or three police cars parked in front, then the community is paying a price. That price is the distribution of a valued resource through an inappropriate criterion.

When police accept gratuities, they exploit their authority in another way as well. The officer who always goes to the shop that offers free coffee makes a choice based on his personal interest. This is his own choice, made for his own reasons. The police, however, as public servants are a social resource. As such, the choice of where they are to be is not theirs to make. I do not mean that they must ask permission for every movement but rather that they must use public need (as opposed to personal interest) as a criterion for making those decisions. Officers should be where they judge that they can best serve the public, not where they can best be served themselves. To govern their movements by personal gain is to put an authority created for social ends to their own use. In this light, accepting gratuities undermines a public interest and becomes exploitive.

The aggressive pursuit of gratuities presents the clearest example of the substitution of "willingness to pay" for "need" as the criterion of distribution of police presence. The pattern of policing for personal profit is unambiguous. It is harder to find fault with the officer in case 5 who passively accepts gratuities, however. He makes a conscious effort to *not* use "willingness to pay" as the criterion for his presence. Since he is unlikely to return to a place where a gratuity was offered, he is undermining the point of the merchant's inducement and, to that extent, he is a counterforce to the merchant's effort to secure additional social benefits. The elements of exploitation are absent in this case because his gain is not at the expense of the public; his presence is not conditioned by the gratuity. He demonstrates this by his refusal to fall into the pattern of taking at selected establishments.

If certain doughnut shops always have two or three police cars parked in front, then the community is paying a price.

The last case, the recruit who feels coerced into taking coffee, presents an officer at the crossroads. Unlike his FTO, he does not take gratuities because he seeks personal gain. His inclination is to avoid gratuities, and he seems mildly coerced into accepting them. He rightly perceives that to make an issue out of this problem will earn him the scorn of his FTO—and any other officer who hears of it. Since he does not know how to resist his FTO, he falls into a pattern of accepting gratuities, which we have seen to be an exploitation of authority. The fact that he does not intend to exploit his authority should not obscure the fact that he is doing so. We may be less critical of the new recruit than of the officer who aggressively pursues his opportunities, but that is not the same as exonerating him. It is the practice, not the intent, that is the basis of the exploitation here. The recruit who is willing to fall into this practice in order to make a good impression is likely to maintain it in a department in which gratuities are customary.

Taking free coffee and accepting discount meals are not, as individual acts, grievous sins. This form of taking can, in the right circumstances, amount to extortion or accepting a bribe, but these are not the common cases. Taking free coffee and discount meals can also, in the right circumstances (case 5), be quite innocent. Yet the "right" circumstances are not the typical circumstances. The practice of accepting gratuities is typically a customary relationship between the police and some merchants. The effect of this custom is to substitute "willingness to pay" for "need" as the criterion for the distribution of one valuable social resource—police presence. The more widespread the practice, the more exploitive of police authority it becomes—measured from the point of view of the community rather than that of the individual officer. In comparison to theft and extortion, accepting gratuities is surely a petty sin. But, like theft and extortion, it tends to undermine the justification of police authority. By theft and extortion police take what they were authorized to protect. By accepting gratuities they accept a fee for services the community has a right to expect on the basis of need.

NOTES

I am indebted to my associate, Dr. Michael Feldberg, and to numerous police officers who attended our training sessions at the Law Enforcement Trainers Institute and the Institute for Humanities and Law Enforcement Training, for extended discussions of the issues that are raised in this paper.

1 This example is derived from a situation described by J. RUBINSTEIN in CITY POLICE 425 (1973).

2 This example is drawn from H. COHEN & M. FELDBERG, CURRICULUM GUIDE IN POLICE ETHICS, produced and distributed by the National Association of State Directors of Law Enforcement Training.

3 J. LOCKE, SECOND TREATISE OF GOVERNMENT (1952).

4 T. HOBBES, LEVIATHAN 107 (1958).

5 Rubinstein makes the point that one might object to police accepting gratuities on the grounds that they are a limited resource whose presence is widely desired, *supra* note 1, at 418.

[19]

The Dirty Harry Problem

By CARL B. KLOCKARS

ABSTRACT: Policing constantly places its practitioners in situations in which good ends can be achieved by dirty means. When the ends to be achieved are urgent and unquestionably good and only a dirty means will work to achieve them, the policeman faces a genuine moral dilemma. A genuine moral dilemma is a situation from which one cannot emerge innocent no matter what one does—employ a dirty means, employ an insufficiently dirty means, or walk away. In such situations in policing, Dirty Harry problems, the danger lies not in becoming guilty of wrong—that is inevitable—but in thinking that one has found a way to escape a dilemma which is inescapable. Dire consequences result from this misunderstanding. Policemen lose their sense of moral proportion, fail to care, turn cynical, or allow their passionate caring to lead them to employ dirty means too crudely or too readily. The only means of assuring that dirty means will not be used too readily or too crudely is to punish those who use them and the agency which endorses their use.

Carl B. Klockars is an associate professor of criminal justice at the University of Delaware. He holds a Ph.D. from the University of Pennsylvania. He is the author of numerous journal articles and The Professional Fence, a life history of a dealer in stolen property, and is coeditor of Deviance and Decency, a collection of essays on the ethics of research with deviant subjects.

34   THE ANNALS OF THE AMERICAN ACADEMY

WHEN and to what extent does the morally good end warrant or justify an ethically, politically, or legally dangerous means for its achievement? This is a very old question for philosophers. Although it has received extensive consideration in policelike occupations and is at the dramatic core of police fiction and detective novels, I know of not a single contribution to the criminological or sociogical literature on policing which raises it explicitly and examines its implications.[1] This is the case in spite of the fact that there is considerable evidence to suggest that it is not only an ineluctable part of police work, but a moral problem with which police themselves are quite familiar. There are, I believe, a number of good reasons why social scientists have avoided or neglected what I like to

call the Dirty Harry problem in policing, not the least of which is that it is insoluble. However, a great deal can be learned about police work by examining some failed solutions, three of which I consider in the following pages. First, though, it is necessary to explain what a Dirty Harry problem is and what it is about it that makes it so problematic.

THE DIRTY HARRY PROBLEM

The Dirty Harry problem draws its name from the 1971 Warner Brothers film *Dirty Harry* and its chief protagonist, antihero Inspector Harry "Dirty Harry" Callahan. The film features a number of events which dramatize the Dirty Harry problem in different ways, but the one which does so most explicitly and most completely places Harry in the following situation. A 14-year-old girl has been kidnapped and is being held captive by a psychopathic killer. The killer, "Scorpio," who has already struck twice, demands $200,000 ransom to release the girl, who is buried with just enough oxygen to keep her alive for a few hours. Harry gets the job of delivering the ransom and, after enormous exertion, finally meets Scorpio. At their meeting Scorpio decides to renege on his bargain, let the girl die, and kill Harry. Harry manages to stab Scorpio in the leg before he does so, but not before Scorpio seriously wounds Harry's partner, an inexperienced, idealistic, slightly ethnic, former sociology major.

Scorpio escapes, but Harry manages to track him down through the clinic where he was treated for his wounded leg. After learning that Scorpio lives on the grounds of a nearby football stadium, Harry breaks into his apartment; finds guns and other evidence of his guilt, and finally

1. In the contemporary philosophical literature, particularly when raised for the vocation of politics, the question is commonly referred to as the Dirty Hands problem after J. P. Sartre's treatment of it in *Dirty Hands*, (Les Maines Sales, 1948) and in *No Exit and Three Other Plays* (New York: Modern Library, 1950). Despite its modern name, the problem is very old and has been taken up by Machiavelli in *The Prince* (1513) and *The Discourses* (1519) (New York: Modern Library, 1950); by Max Weber, "Politics as a Vocation," (1919) in *Max Weber: Essays in Sociology*, eds. and trans. H. Gerth and C. W. Wills (New York: Oxford University Press, 1946); and by Albert Camus, "The Just Assassins,"'(1949) in *Caligula and Three Other Plays* (New York: Alfred A. Knopf, 1958). See Michael Walzer's brilliant critique of these contributions, "Political Action: The Problem of Dirty Hands" *Philosophy and Public Affairs*, 2(2) (winter 1972). Likewise the Dirty Hands/Dirty Harry problem is implicitly or explicitly raised in virtually every work of Raymond Chandler, Dashiel Hammett, James Cain, and other *Tough Guy Writers of The Thirties*, ed. David Madden (Carbondale, IL: Southern Illinois University Press, 1968), as they are in all of the recent work of Joseph Wambaugh, particularly *The Blue Knight*, *The New Centurions*, and *The Choirboys*.

confronts Scorpio on the 50-yard line, where Harry shoots him in the leg as he is trying to escape. Standing over Scorpio, Harry demands to know where the girl is buried. Scorpio refuses to disclose her location, demanding his rights to a lawyer. As the camera draws back from the scene Harry stands on Scorpio's bullet-mangled leg to torture a confession of the girl's location from him.

As it turns out, the girl is already dead and Scorpio must be set free. Neither the gun found in the illegal search, nor the confession Harry extorted, nor any of its fruits—including the girl's body—would be admissible in court.

The preceding scene, the heart of *Dirty Harry*, raises a number of issues of far-reaching significance for the sociology of the police, the first of which will now be discussed.

THE DIRTY HARRY PROBLEM I: THE END OF INNOCENCE

As we have phrased it previously, the Dirty Harry problem asks when and to what extent does the morally good end warrant or justify an ethically, politically, or legally dangerous means to its achievement? In itself, this question assumes the possibility of a genuine moral dilemma and posits its existence in a means–ends arrangement which may be expressed schematically as follows:

MEANS

		MORALLY GOOD (+)	MORALLY DIRTY (−)
E N D S	Morally good (+)	A + +	B − + The Dirty Harry Problem
	Morally dirty (−)	C + −	D − −

It is important to specify clearly the terms of the Dirty Harry problem not only to show that it must involve the juxtaposition of good ends and dirty means, but also to show what must be proven to demonstrate that a Dirty Harry problem exists. If one could show, for example, that box B is always empirically empty or that in any given case the terms of the situation are better read in some other means–ends arrangement, Dirty Harry problems vanish. At this first level, however, I suspect that no one could exclude the core scene of *Dirty Harry* from the class of Dirty Harry problems. There is no question that saving the life of an innocent victim of kidnapping is a "good" thing nor that grinding the bullet-mangled leg of Scorpio to extort a confession from him is "dirty."[2]

There is, in addition, a second level of criteria of an empirical and epistemological nature that must be met before a Dirty Harry problem actually comes into being. They involve the connection between the dirty act and the good end. Principally, what must be known and, importantly, known before the dirty act is committed, is that it will result in the achievement of the good end. In any absolute sense this is, of course, impossible to know, in that no acts are ever completely certain in their consequences. Thus the question is always a matter of probabilities. But it is helpful to break those probabilities into classes which attach to various subcategories of the overall question. In the given case, this level of problem would seem to require that three questions be satisfied, though not all with the same level of certainty.

In *Dirty Harry*, the first question is, Is Scorpio able to provide the information Dirty Harry seeks? It is an epistemological question about which, in *Dirty Harry*, we are absolutely certain. Harry met Scorpio at the time of the ransom exchange. Not only did he admit the kidnapping at that time, but when he made the ransom demand, Scorpio sent one of the girl's teeth and a description of her clothing and underwear to leave no doubt about the existence of his victim.

Second, we must know there are means, dirty means and nothing

2. "Dirty" here means both "repugnant" in that it offends widely shared standards of human decency and dignity and "dangerous" in that it breaks commonly shared and supported norms, rules, or laws for conduct. To "dirty" acts there must be both a deontologically based face validity of immorality and a consequentialist threat to the prevailing rules for social order.

other than dirty means, which are likely to achieve the good end. One can, of course, never be sure that one is aware of or has considered all possible alternatives, but in *Dirty Harry* there would appear to be no reason for Scorpio in his rational self-interest to confess to the girl's location without being coerced to do so.

The third question which must be satisfied at this empirical and epistemological level concedes that dirty means are the only method which will be effective, but asks whether or not, in the end, they will be in vain. We know in *Dirty Harry* that they were, and Harry himself, at the time of the ransom demand, admits he believes that the girl is already dead. Does not this possibility or likelihood that the girl is dead destroy the justification for Harry's dirty act? Although it surely would if Harry knew for certain that the girl was dead, I do not think it does insofar as even a small probability of her being saved exists. The reason is that the good to be achieved is so unquestionably good and so passionately felt that even a small possibility of its achievement demands that it be tried. For example, were we to ask, If it were your daughter would you want Harry to do what he did? it would be this passionate sense of unquestionable good that we are trying to dramatize. It is for this reason that in philosophical circles the Dirty Hands problem has been largely restricted to questions of national security, revolutionary terrorism, and international war. It is also why the Dirty Harry problem in detective fiction almost always involves murder.

Once we have satisfied ourselves that a Dirty Harry problem is conceptually possible and that, in fact, we can specify one set of concrete circumstances in which it exists, one might think that the most difficult question of all is, What ought to be done? I do not think it is. I suspect that there are very few people who would not want Harry to do something dirty in the situation specified. I know I would want him to do what he did, and what is more, I would want anyone who policed for me to be prepared to do so as well. Put differently, I want to have as police-officers men and women of moral courage and sensitivity.

But to those who would want exactly that, the Dirty Harry problem poses its most irksome conclusion. Namely, that one cannot, at least in the specific case at hand, have a policeman who is both just and innocent. The troublesome issue in the Dirty Harry problem is not whether under some utilitarian calculus a right choice can be made, but that the choice must always be between at least two wrongs. And in choosing to do either wrong, the policeman inevitably taints or tarnishes himself.

It was this conclusion on the part of Dashiell Hammett, Raymond Chandler, Raoul Whitfield, Horace McCoy, James M. Cain, Lester Dent, and dozens of other tough-guy writers of hard-boiled detective stories that distinguished these writers from what has come to be called the "classical school" of detective fiction. What these men could not stomach about Sherlock Holmes (Conan Doyle), Inspector French (Freeman Wills Crofts), and Father Brown (Chesterton), to name a few of the best, was not that they were virtuous, but that their virtue was unsullied. Their objection was that the classical detective's occupation, how he worked, and the jobs he was called upon to do left him morally immaculate. Even the most brilliant

defender of the classical detective story, W. H. Auden, was forced to confess that that conclusion gave the stories "magical function," but rendered them impossible as art.[3]

If popular conceptions of police work have relevance for its actual practice—as Egon Bittner and a host of others have argued that they do[4]—the Dirty Harry problem, found in one version or another in countless detective novels and reflected in paler imitations on countless television screens, for example, "Parental Discretion is Advised," is not an unimportant contributor to police work's "tainted" quality. But we must remember also that the revolution of the tough-guy writers, so these writers said, was not predicated on some mere artificial, aesthetic objection. With few exceptions, their claim was that their works were art. That is, at all meaningful levels, the stories were true. It is this claim I should next like to examine in the real-life context of the Dirty Harry problem.

THE DIRTY HARRY PROBLEM II: DIRTY MEN AND DIRTY WORK

Dirty Harry problems arise quite often. For policemen, real, everyday policemen, Dirty Harry problems are part of their job and thus considerably more than rare or artificial dramatic exceptions. To make this point, I will translate some rather familiar police practices, street stops and searches and victim and

3. W. H. Auden, "The Guilty Vicarage," in *The Dyer's Hand and Other Essays* (New York: Alfred A. Knopf, 1956) pp. 146–58.
4. Egon Bittner, *The Functions of Police in Modern Society* (New York: Jason Aronson, 1975) and "Florence Nightingale in Pursuit of Willie Sutton," in *The Potential For Reform Of the Criminal Justice System*, vol. 3, ed. H. Jacob (Beverly Hills, CA: Sage Publications, 1974) pp. 11–44.

318 *Police Ethics*

witness interrogation, into Dirty Harry problems.

Good ends and dirty means

The first question our analysis of street stops and searches and victim and witness interrogation must satisfy is, For policemen, do these activities present the cognitive opportunity for the juxtaposition of good ends and dirty means to their achievement? Although the "goodness" question will be considered in some detail later, suffice it to say here that police find the prevention of crime and the punishment of wrongful or criminal behavior a good thing to achieve. Likewise, they, perhaps more than any other group in society, are intimately aware of the varieties of dirty means available for the achievement of those good ends. In the case of street stops and searches, these dirty alternatives range from falsifying probable cause for a stop, to manufacturing a false arrest to legitimate an illegal search, to simply searching without the fraudulent covering devices of either. In the case of victim or witness interrogations, dirty means range all from dramaturgically "chilling" a *Miranda* warning by an edited or unemphatic reading to Harry's grinding a man's bullet-shattered leg to extort a confession from him.

While all these practices may be "dirty" enough to satisfy certain people of especially refined sensitivities, does not a special case have to be made, not for the public's perception of the "dirtiness" of certain illegal, deceptive, or subrosa acts, but for the police's perception of their dirtiness? Are not the police hard-boiled, less sensitive to such things than are most of us? I think there is no question

that they are, and our contention about the prevalence of Dirty Harry problems in policing suggests that they are likely to be. How does this "tough-minded" attitude toward dirty means affect our argument? At least at this stage it seems to strengthen it. That is, the failure of police to regard dirty means with the same hesitation that most citizens do seems to suggest that they juxtapose them to the achievement of good ends more quickly and more readily than most of us.

The dirty means must work

In phrasing the second standard for the Dirty Harry problem as "The dirty means must work," we gloss over a whole range of qualifying conditions, some of which we have already considered. The most critical, implied in *Dirty Harry*, is that the person on whom dirty means are to be used must be guilty. It should be pointed out, however, that this standard is far higher than any student of the Dirty Hands problem in politics has ever been willing to admit. In fact, the moral dilemma of Dirty Hands is often dramatized by the fact that dirty means must be visited on quite innocent victims. It is the blood of such innocents, for example, whom the Communist leader Hoerderer in Sartre's *Dirty Hands* refers to when he says, "I have dirty hands. Right up to the elbows. I've plunged them in filth and blood. But what do you hope? Do you think you can govern innocently?"[5]

But even if cases in which innocent victims suffer dirty means commonly qualify as Dirty Harry problems, and by extension innocent victims would be allowable in Dirty Harry problems, there are a num-

5. Sartre, *Dirty Hands*, p. 224.

ber of factors in the nature and context of policing which suggest that police themselves are inclined toward the higher "guilty victim" standard. Although there may be others, the following are probably the most salient.

1. The Operative Assumption of Guilt. In street stops and searches as well as interrogations, it is in the nature of the police task that guilt is assumed as a working premise. That is, in order for a policeman to do his job, he must, unless he clearly knows otherwise, assume that the person he sees is guilty and the behavior he is witnessing is evidence of some concealed or hidden offense. If a driver looks at him "too long" or not at all or if a witness or suspect talks too little or too much, it is only his operative assumption of guilt that makes those actions meaningful. Moreover, the policeman is often not in a position to suspend his working assumption until he has taken action, sometimes dirty action, to disconfirm it.

2. The Worst of all Possible Guilt. The matter of the operative assumption of guilt is complicated further because the policeman is obliged to make a still higher-order assumption of guilt, namely, that the person is not only guilty, but dangerously so. In the case of street stops and searches, for instance, although the probability of coming upon a dangerous felon is extremely low, policemen quite reasonably take the possibility of doing so as a working assumption on the understandable premise that once is enough. Likewise the premise that the one who has the most to hide will try hardest to hide it is a reasonable assumption for interrogation.

3. The Great Guilty Place Assumption. The frequency with which policemen confront the worst of people, places, and occasions creates an epistemological problem of serious psychological proportions. As a consequence of his job, the policeman is constantly exposed to highly selective samples of his environment. That he comes to read a clump of bushes as a place to hide, a roadside rest as a homosexual "tearoom," a sweet old lady as a robbery looking for a place to happen, or a poor young black as someone willing to oblige her is not a question of a perverse, pessimistic, or racist personality, but of a person whose job requires that he strive to see race, age, sex, and even nature in an ecology of guilt, which can include him if he fails to see it so.[6]

4. The Not Guilty (This Time) Assumption. With considerable sociological research and conventional wisdom to support him, the policeman knows that most people in the great guilty place in which he works have committed numerous crimes for which they have never been caught. Thus when a stop proves unwarranted, a search comes up "dry," or an interrogation fails, despite the dirty means, the policeman is not at all obliged to conclude that the person victimized by them is innocent, only that, and even this need not always be conceded, he is innocent this time.

Dirty means as ends in themselves

How do these features of police work, all of which seem to incline police to accept a standard of a

6. One of Wambaugh's characters in *The Choirboys* makes this final point most dramatically when he fails to notice that a young boy's buttocks are flatter than they should be and reads the child's large stomach as a sign of adequate nutrition. When the child dies through his mother's neglect and abuse, the officer rightly includes himself in his ecology of guilt.

guilty victim for their dirty means, bear upon the Dirty Harry problem from which they derive? The most dangerous reading suggests that if police are inclined, and often quite rightly inclined, to believe they are dealing with factually, if not legally, guilty subjects, they become likely to see their dirty acts, not as means to the achievement of good ends, but as ends in themselves—as punishment of guilty people whom the police believe deserve to be punished.

If this line of argument is true, it has the effect, in terms of police perceptions, of moving Dirty Harry problems completely outside of the fourfold table of means–ends combinations created in order to define it. Importantly as well, in terms of our perceptions, Dirty Harry problems of this type can no longer be read as cases of dirty means employed to the achievement of good ends. For unless we are willing to admit that in a democratic society a police arrogates to itself the task of punishing those who they think are guilty, we are forced to conclude that Dirty Harry problems represent cases of employing dirty means to dirty ends, in which case, nobody, not the police and certainly not us, is left with any kind of moral dilemma.

The possibility is quite real and quite fearsome, but it is mediated by certain features of police work, some of which inhere in the nature of the work itself and others, imposed from outside, which have a quite explicit impact on it. The most important of the "naturalistic" features of policing which belie the preceding argument is that the assumption of guilt and all the configurations in the policeman's world which serve to support it often turn out wrong. It is precisely because the operative assumption of guilt can

be forced on everything and everyone that the policeman who must use it constantly comes to find it leads him astray as often as it confirms his suspicions.

Similarly, a great many of the things policemen do, some of which we have already conceded appear to police as less dirty than they appear to us—faked probable cause for a street stop, manipulated *Miranda* warnings, and so forth—are simply impossible to read as punishments. This is so particularly if we grant a hard-boiled character to our cops.

Of course, neither of these naturalistic restrictions on the obliteration of the means–ends schema is or should be terribly comforting. To the extent that the first is helpful at all assumes a certain skill and capacity of mind that we may not wish to award to all policemen. The willingness to engage in the constant refutation of one's working worldview presumes a certain intellectual integrity which can certainly go awry. Likewise, the second merely admits that on occasion policemen do some things which reveal they appreciate that the state's capacity to punish is sometimes greater than theirs.

To both these "natural" restrictions on the obliteration of the means–ends character of Dirty Harry problems, we can add the exclusionary rule. Although the exclusionary rule is the manifest target of *Dirty Harry*, it, more than anything else, makes Dirty Harry problems a reality in everyday policing. It is the great virtue of exclusionary rules —applying in various forms to stops, searches, seizures, and interrogations—that they hit directly upon the intolerable, though often, I think, moral desire of police to punish. These rules make the very simple point to police that 'the more they wish to see a felon punished, the more they are advised to be scrupulous in their treatment of him. Put differently, the best thing Harry could have done for Scorpio was to step on his leg, extort his confession, and break into his apartment.

If certain natural features of policing and particularly exclusionary rules combine to maintain the possibility of Dirty Harry problems in a context in which a real danger appears to be their disappearance, it does not follow that police cannot or do not collapse the dirty means–good ends division on some occasions and become punishers. I only hold that on many other occasions, collapse does not occur and Dirty Harry problems, as defined, are still widely possible. What must be remembered next, on the way to making their possibility real, is that policemen know, or think they know, before they employ a dirty means that a dirty means and only a dirty means will work.

Only a dirty means will work

The moral standard that a policeman know in advance of resorting to a dirty means that a dirty means and only a dirty means will work, rests heavily on two technical dimensions: (1) the professional competence of the policeman and (2) the range of legitimate working options available to him. Both are intimately connected, though the distinction to be preserved between them is that the first is a matter of the policeman's individual competence and the second of the competence of the institutions for which (his department) and with which (the law) the policeman works.

In any concrete case, the relations between these moral and technical dimensions of the Dirty Harry problem are extremely complicated. But a priori it follows that the more competent a policeman is at the use of legal means, the less he will be obliged to resort to dirty alternatives. Likewise, the department that trains its policemen well and supplies them with the resources—knowledge and material—to do their work will find that the policemen who work for them will not resort to dirty means "unnecessarily," meaning only those occasions when an acceptable means will work as well as a dirty one.

While these two premises flow a priori from raising the Dirty Harry problem, questions involving the moral and technical roles of laws governing police means invite a very dangerous type of a priori reasoning:

Combating distrust [of the police] requires getting across the rather complicated message that granting the police specific forms of new authority may be the most effective means for reducing abuse of authority which is now theirs; that it is the absence of properly proscribed forms of authority that often impels the police to engage in questionable or outright illegal conduct. Before state legislatures enacted statutes giving limited authority to the police to stop and question persons suspected of criminal involvement, police nevertheless stopped and questioned people. It is inconceivable how any police agency could be expected to operate without doing so. But since the basis for their actions was unclear, the police—if they thought a challenge likely—would use the guise of arresting the individual on a minor charge (often without clear evidence) to provide a semblance of legality. Enactment of stopping and questioning statutes eliminated the need for this sham.[7]

Herman Goldstein's preceding argument and observations are undoubtedly true, but the danger in them is that they can be extended

7. Herman Goldstein, *Policing a Free Society* (Cambridge, MA: Ballinger Publishing, 1977), p. 72.

Police Ethics

to apply to any dirty means, not only illegal arrests to legitimate necessary street stops, but dirty means to accomplish subsequent searches and seizures all the way to beating confessions out of suspects when no other means will work. But, of course, Goldstein does not intend his argument to be extended in these ways.

Nevertheless, his a priori argument, dangerous though it may be, points to the fact that Dirty Harry problems can arise wherever restrictions are placed on police methods and are particularly likely to do so when police themselves perceive that those restrictions are undesirable, unreasonable, or unfair. His argument succeeds in doing what police who face Dirty Harry problems constantly do: rendering the law problematic. But while Goldstein, one of the most distinguished legal scholars in America, can follow his finding with books, articles, and lectures which urge change, it is left to the policeman to take upon himself the moral responsibility of subverting it with dirty and hidden means.

Compelling and unquestionable ends

If Dirty Harry problems can be shown to exist in their technical dimensions—as genuine means–ends problems where only dirty means will work—the question of the magnitude and urgency of the ends that the dirty means may be employed to achieve must still be confronted. Specifically, it must be shown that the ends of dirty means are so desirable that the failure to achieve them would cast the person who is in a position to do so in moral disrepute.

The two most widely acknowledged ends of policing are peace

keeping and law enforcement. It would follow, of course, that if both these ends were held to be unworthy, Dirty Harry problems would disappear. There are arguments challenging both ends. For instance, certain radical critiques of policing attempt to reduce the peace-keeping and law-enforcing functions of the police in the United States to nothing more than acts of capitalist oppression. From such a position flows not only the denial of the legitimacy of any talk of Dirty Harry problems, but also the denial of the legitimacy of the entire police function.[8]

Regardless of the merits of such critiques, it will suffice for the purpose of this analysis to maintain that there is a large "clientele," to use Albert Reiss's term, for both types of police function.[9] And it should come as no surprise to anyone that the police themselves accept the legitimacy of their own peace-keeping and law-enforcing ends. Some comment is needed, though, on how large that clientele for those functions is and how compelling and unquestionable the ends of peace keeping and law enforcement are for them.

There is no more popular, compelling, urgent, nor more broadly appealing idea than peace. In international relations, it is potent enough to legitimate the stockpiling of enough nuclear weapons to exterminate every living thing on earth a dozen times over. In domestic affairs, it gives legitimacy to the idea

8. *See*, for example, John F. Galliher, "Explanations of Police Behavior: A Critical Review and Analysis," *The Sociological Quarterly*, 12:308–18 (summer 1971); Richard Quinney, *Class, State, and Crime* (New York: David McKay, 1977).

9. Albert J. Reiss, Jr., *The Police and the Public* (New Haven, CT: Yale University Press, 1971), p. 122.

of the state, and the aspirations to it have succeeded in granting to the state an absolute monopoly on the right to legitimate the use of force and a near monopoly on its actual, legitimate use: the police. That peace has managed to legitimate these highly dangerous means to its achievement in virtually every advanced nation in the world is adequate testimony to the fact that it qualifies, if any end does, as a good end so unquestionable and so compelling that it can legitimate risking the most dangerous and dirtiest of means.

The fact is, though, that most American policemen prefer to define their work as law enforcement rather than peace keeping, even though they may, in fact, do more of the latter. It is a distinction that should not be allowed to slip away in assuming, for instance, that the policeman's purpose in enforcing the law is to keep the peace. Likewise, though it is a possibility, it will not do to assume that police simply enforce the law as an end in itself, without meaning and without purpose or end. The widely discretionary behavior of working policemen and the enormous underenforcement of the law which characterizes most police agencies simply belie that possibility.

An interpretation of law enforcement which is compatible with empirical studies of police behavior —as peace keeping is—and police talk in America—which peace keeping generally is not—is an understanding of the ends of law enforcement as punishment. There are, of course, many theories of punishment, but the police seem inclined toward the simplest: the belief that certain people who have committed certain acts deserve to be punished for them. What can one say of the compelling and unquestionable char-

acter of this retributive ambition as an end of policing and policemen?

Both historically and sociologically there is ample evidence that punishment is almost as unquestionable and compelling an end as peace. Historically, we have a long and painful history of punishment, a history longer in fact than the history of the end of peace. Sociologically, the application of what may well be the only culturally universal norm, the norm of reciprocity, implies the direct and natural relations between wrongful acts and their punishments.[10] Possibly the best evidence for the strength and urgency of the desire to punish in modern society is the extraordinary complex of rules and procedures democratic states have assembled which prevents legitimate punishment from being administered wrongfully or frivolously.

If we can conclude that peace and punishment are ends unquestionable and compelling enough to satisfy the demands of Dirty Harry problems, we are led to one final question on which we may draw from some sociological theories of the police for assistance. If the Dirty Harry problem is at the core of the police role, or at least near to it, how is it that police can or do come to reconcile their use of—or their failure to use—dirty means to achieve unquestionably good and compelling ends?

Public Policy and Police Morality: Three Defective Resolutions of the Dirty Harry Problem

The contemporary literature on policing appears to contain three

10. These two assertions are drawn from Graeme Newman's *The Punishment Response* (Philadelphia: J. B. Lippincott Co., 1978).

quite different types of solution or resolution. But because the Dirty Harry problem is a genuine moral dilemma, that is, a situation which will admit no real solution or resolution, each is necessarily defective. Also, understandably, each solution or resolution presents itself as an answer to a somewhat different problem. In matters of public policy, such concealments are often necessary and probably wise, although they have a way of coming around to haunt their architects sooner or later. In discovering that each is flawed and in disclosing the concealments which allow the appearance of resolution, we do not urge that it be held against sociologists that they are not philosophers nor do we argue that they should succeed where philosophers before them have failed. Rather, we only wish to make clear what is risked by each concealment and to face candidly the inevitably unfortunate ramifications which must proceed from it.

Snappy bureaucrats

In the works of August Vollmer, Bruce Smith, O. W. Wilson, and those progressive police administrators who still follow their lead, a vision of the perfect police agency and the perfect policeman has gained considerable ground. Labeled "the professional model" in police circles —though entirely different from any classical sense of profession or professional—it envisions a highly trained, technologically sophisticated police department operating free from political interference with a corps of well-educated police responding obediently to the policies, orders, and directives of a central administrative command. It is a vision of police officers, to use

Bittner's phrasing, as "snappy bureaucrats,"[11] cogs in a quasi-military machine who do what they are told out of a mix of fear, loyalty, routine, and detailed specification of duties.

The professional model, unlike other solutions to be considered, is based on the assumption that the policeman's motives for working can be made to locate within his department. He will, if told, work vice or traffic, juvenile or homicide, patrol passively or aggressively, and produce one, two, four, or six arrests, pedestrian stops, or reports per hour, day, or week as his department sees fit. In this way the assumption and vision of the professional model in policing is little different from that of any bureaucracy which seeks by specifying tasks and setting expectations for levels of production—work quotas—to coordinate a regular, predictable, and efficient service for its clientele.

The problem with this vision of *sine ira et studio* service by obedient operatives is that when the product to be delivered is some form of human service—education, welfare, health, and police bureaucracies are similar in this way—the vision seems always to fall short of expectations. On the one hand the would-be bureaucratic operatives—teachers, social workers, nurses, and policemen—resent being treated as mere bureaucrats and resist the translation of their work into quotas, directives, rules, regulations, or other abstract specifications. On the other hand, to the extent that the vision of an efficient and obedient human service bureaucracy is realized, the clientele of such institutions typically come away with the impression that no one in the institution truly cares about their problems. And, of

11. Bittner, p. 53.

course, in that the aim of bureaucratization is to locate employees' motives for work within the bureaucracy, they are absolutely correct in their feelings.

To the extent that the professional model succeeds in making the ends of policing locate within the agency as opposed to moral demands of the tasks which policemen are asked by their clients to do, it appears to solve the Dirty Harry problem. When it succeeds, it does so by replacing the morally compelling ends of punishment and peace with the less human, though by no means uncompelling, ends of bureaucratic performance. However, this resolution certainly does not imply that dirty means will disappear, only that the motives for their use will be career advancement and promotion. Likewise, on those occasions when a morally sensitive policeman would be compelled by the demands of the situational exigencies before him to use a dirty means, the bureaucratic operative envisioned by the professional model will merely do his job. Ambitious bureaucrats and obedient timeservers fail at being the type of morally sensitive souls we want to be policemen. The professional model's bureaucratic resolution of the Dirty Harry problem fails in policing for the same reason it fails in every other human service agency: it is quite simply an impossibility to create a bureaucrat who cares for anything but his bureaucracy.

The idealized image of the professional model, which has been responded to with an ideal critique, is probably unrealizable. Reality intervenes as the ideal type is approached. The bureaucracy seems to take on weight as it approaches the pole, is slowed, and may even collapse in approaching.

Bittner's peace

A second effort in the literature of contemporary policing also attempts to address the Dirty Harry problem by substituting an alternative to the presently prevailing police ends of punishment. Where the professional model sought to substitute bureaucratic rewards and sanctions for the moral end of punishment, the elegant polemics by Egon Bittner in *The Functions of Police in Modern Society* and "Florence Nightingale in Pursuit of Willie Sutton: A Theory of the Police" seek to substitute the end of peace. In beautifully chosen words, examples, and phrasing, Bittner leads his readers to conclude that peace is historically, empirically, intellectually, and morally the most compelling, unquestionable, and humane end of policing. Bittner is, I fear, absolutely right.

It is the end of peace which legitimates the extension of police responsibilities into a wide variety of civil matters—neighborhood disputes, loud parties, corner lounging, lovers' quarrels, political rallys, disobedient children, bicycle registration, pet control, and a hundred other types of tasks which a modern "service" style police department regularly is called upon to perform. With these responsibilities, which most "good" police agencies now accept willingly and officially, also comes the need for an extension of police powers. Arrest is, after all, too crude a tool to be used in all the various situations in which our peace-keeping policemen are routinely asked to be of help. "Why should," asks Herman Goldstein, in a manner in which Bittner would approve, "a police officer arrest and charge a disorderly tavern patron if ordering him to leave the tavern

326   *Police Ethics*

will suffice? Must he arrest and charge one of the parties in a lovers' quarrel if assistance in forcing a separation is all that is desired?"[12] There is no question that both those situations could be handled more peacefully if police were granted new powers which would allow them to handle those situations in the way Goldstein rhetorically asks if they should. That such extensions of police powers will be asked for by our most enlightened police departments in the interests of keeping the peace is absolutely certain. If the success of the decriminalization of police arrests for public intoxication, vagrancy, mental illness, and the virtually unrestricted two-hour right of detention made possible by the Uniform Law of Arrest are any indication of the likelihood of extensions being received favorably, the end of peace and its superiority over punishment in legitimating the extension of police powers seem exceedingly likely to prevail further.

The problem with peace is that it is not the only end of policing so compelling, unquestionable, and in the end, humane. Amid the good work toward the end of peace that we increasingly want our police to do, it is certain that individuals or groups will arise who the police, in all their peace-keeping benevolence, will conclude, on moral if not political or institutional grounds, have "got it coming." And all the once dirty means which were bleached in the brilliant light of peace will return to their true colors.

Skolnick's craftsman

The third and final attempt to resolve the Dirty Harry problem is offered by Jerome Skolnick, who in *Justice Without Trial* comes ex-

tremely close to stating the Dirty Harry problem openly when he writes:

. . . He (the policeman) sees himself as a craftsman, at his best, a master of his trade . . . [he] draws a moral distinction between criminal law and criminal procedure. The distinction is drawn somewhat as follows: The substantive law of crimes is intended to control the behavior of people who wilfully injure persons or property, or who engage in behaviors having such a consequence, such as the use of narcotics. Criminal procedure, by contrast, is intended to control authorities, not criminals. As such, it does not fall into the same *moral* class of constraint as substantive criminal law. If a policeman were himself to use narcotics, or to steal, or to assault, *outside the line of duty*, much the same standards would be applied to him by other policemen as to the ordinary citizen. When, however, the issue concerns the policeman's freedom to carry out his *duties*, another moral realm is entered.[13]

What is more, Skolnick's craftsman finds support from his peers, department, his community, and the law for the moral rightness of his calling. He cares about his work and finds it just.

What troubles Skolnick about his craftsman is his craft. The craftsman refuses to see, as Skolnick thinks he ought to, that the dirty means he sometimes uses to achieve his good ends stand in the same moral class of wrongs as those he is employed to fight. Skolnick's craftsman reaches this conclusion by understanding that his unquestionably good and compelling ends, on certain occasions, justify his employment of dirty means to their achievement. Skolnick's craftsman, as Skolnick understands him, resolves the Dirty

---

12. Ibid., p. 72.

13. Jerome Skolnick, *Justice Without Trial*, 2nd ed. (New York: John Wiley & Sons, 1975), p. 182.

Harry problem by denying the dirtiness of his means.

Skolnick's craftsman's resolution is, speaking precisely, Machiavellian. It should come as no surprise to find the representative of one of the classic attempts to resolve the problem of Dirty Hands to be a front runner in response to Dirty Harry. What is worrisome about such a resolution? What does it conceal that makes our genuine dilemma disappear? The problem is not that the craftsman will sometimes choose to use dirty means. If he is morally sensitive to its demands, every policeman's work will sometimes require as much. What is worrisome about Skolnick's craftsman is that he does not regard his means as dirty and, as Skolnick tells us, does not suffer from their use. The craftsman, if Skolnick's portrait of him is correct, will resort to dirty means too readily and too easily. He lacks the restraint that can come only from struggling to justify them and from taking seriously the hazards involved.

In 1966, when *Justice Without Trial* first appeared, Skolnick regarded the prospects of creating a more morally sensitive craftsman exceedingly dim. He could not imagine that the craftsman's community, employer, peers, or the courts could come to reward him more for his legal compliance than for the achievement of the ends of his craft. However, in phrasing the prospects in terms of a Dirty Harry problem, one can not only agree with Skolnick that denying the goodness of unquestionably good ends is a practical and political impossibility, but can also uncover another alternative, one which Skolnick does not pursue.

The alternative the Dirty Harry problem leads us to is ensuring that the craftsman regards his dirty means as dirty by applying the same retributive principles of punishment to his wrongful acts that he is quite willing to apply to others! It is, in fact, only when his wrongful acts are punished that he will come to see them as wrongful and will appreciate the genuine moral—rather than technical or occupational—choice he makes in resorting to them. The prospects for punishment of such acts are by no means dim, and considerable strides in this area have been made. It requires far fewer resources to punish than to reward. Secondly, the likelihood that juries in civil suits will find dirty means dirtier than police do is confirmed by police claims that outsiders cannot appreciate the same moral and technical distinctions that they do. Finally, severe financial losses to police agencies as well as to their officers eventually communicate to both that vigorously policing themselves is cheaper and more pleasing than having to pay so heavily if they do not. If under such conditions our craftsman police officer is still willing to risk the employment of dirty means to achieve what he understands to be unquestionably good ends, he will not only know that he has behaved justly, but that in doing so he must run the risk of becoming genuinely guilty as well.

A FINAL NOTE

In urging the punishment of policemen who resort to dirty means to achieve some unquestionably good and morally compelling end, we recognize that we create a Dirty Harry problem for ourselves and for those we urge to effect such punishments. It is a fitting end, one which teaches once again that the danger in Dirty Harry problems is never in their resolution, but in thinking that one has found a resolution with which one can truly live in peace.

[20]

Tragedy and "Noble Cause" Corruption

Edwin J. Delattre

> *Every rational being exists as an end in himself and not merely as a means to be arbitrarily used. Act so that you treat humanity, whether in your own person or in that of another, always as an end and never as a means only.*

IMMANUEL KANT[1]

Education directed to excellence of character and judgment is incomplete without some treatment of tragedy. The treatment is likely to be brief in criminal justice programs, since not all the features of general theory need be covered.

Tragedy may, but does not always, arise from a character flaw, as when blind ambition destroys a person of promise, or pride or hubris brings King Oedipus to grief in Sophocles' drama. Tragedy can also arise from the nature of the human condition itself.

Suppose that a doctor has two patients before him, both dying, but has the time and resources to save only one. The issue is not how he is to decide, but that he is to decide. If he cannot possibly save both—no matter what he does—he must decide. His deciding is not a case of "playing God"; it is a case of fulfilling the duties of a doctor.

That one patient dies, say, for lack of available blood, is tragic but not something the doctor could have prevented. By saving one—as many as he could—the doctor has done the right thing. In such circumstances, a doctor of fine character may feel regret bordering on remorse that he could not do more, even though he acted rightly in doing all he could. He faced the ordeal of judgment without shirking. Because he has behaved rightly and because only wrongful acts can logically be forgiven, we cannot respond to his regret or remorse with forgiveness. Instead, his friends and colleagues should offer comfort to him—and the humane reminder that sometimes the human condition causes tragedy, no matter how hard we try to prevent it.

Tragedy can also arise from the conflict of one undeniable good with another undeniable good, when no amount of effort, intelligence, or goodwill can bring the two into harmony. Sometimes we cannot have

182   CHARACTER AND COPS

things both ways. To make the public safe we must arrest and confine the criminally dangerous, but to make the public safe we must also restrain government from presumption of guilt and disregard for due process. Law enforcement officers sometimes know that someone is guilty of a serious crime but either lack evidence or have tainted evidence. The individual remains free to commit crimes against new victims. We are obliged to do everything in our power to safeguard the public and to make government just, but our best efforts cannot always prevent failure.

Despite the heartache, those who have to make practical decisions must acquire the fortitude to go on. They are obliged to give their best despite the stress that will otherwise grind down their aspirations. That is an irreducible element of taking the human condition seriously.

For those reasons, the possession of authority, discretion, and power leads reflective people from morally important but unproblematic cases to questions about extreme cases where tragedy may lurk. Often such cases are hypothetical, sometimes unrealistic. They are invariably extraordinary and distinct from commonplace decency in daily life. The principal value of examining them is that careful analysis can advance subtlety, good reasoning, and a sense of the tragic.

Although law enforcement officials do not always agree which cases are difficult, examples usually resemble the "lifeboat" type of problem. One question goes something like this:

> If you have a perpetrator in custody, and he has information that could save the life of an innocent victim, is it right to use extreme methods to get the information?

Such occurrences are removed from the daily realities of law enforcement. When the question comes up for discussion, I ask for more detail. Even hypothetical cases must be specific. Here is one response:

> Suppose that you have a perpetrator in custody who is known to have kidnapped a victim. The victim is known to be buried alive, and the perpetrator is known to have the information sufficient to rescue the victim.
>
> Time is short. The perpetrator will not divulge the information under ordinary legal interrogation, even though it is conducted very shrewdly. Is it morally right to exceed your authority and use physical coercion to get the information? Is saving the life of the innocent victim a sufficient end to justify such illegality? Does this noble cause justify a means we would normally consider wrong and evil?

Those types of questions are usually accompanied by others: Do

TRAGEDY AND CORRUPTION   183

ends justify means? Is there ever a cause so important that it justifies everything? Do noble causes justify illegality and immorality?

Many command personnel deny that this case is problematic or difficult. Police are sworn to uphold the law, they point out, and they have no right to violate it, certainly not by inflicting pain on a prisoner. The situation poses no ordeal, they argue, because the rules on prisoners are clear and unmistakable.

A smaller number admit that the rules are clear but still see a problem: What about the rights of the victim? They feel torn between a clear duty to obey the law and respect the rights of the suspect-perpetrator on the one hand and a sense of duty to try to save the life of an innocent victim on the other.

Some philosophers would direct the inquiry to another question. They say that mistreatment of the prisoner is wrong, but in such an instance—not as a rule—is it an excusable wrong? Should this person, who commits this wrong, under these conditions, this time, for the sake of this victim, be forgiven?

The questions raised by police can illuminate ways of thinking through such conflicts. Although character education would be incomplete without such illumination, hard cases cannot be the initial focus, and should not be the central focus, of academy programs in ethics.

Ends and Means

The meaning of the question, Do ends justify means? is neither simple nor clear. It might mean any or all of the following: (1) Do good ends make actions right? Do they contribute in part to the rightness of actions? (2) Should we take ends and consequences into account in deciding what to do? (3) Are a person's ends relevant to the quality of the person's character and to the praise or blame the person deserves for specific actions?

Clearly, having a good end contributes to the rightness of an act, just as having an evil purpose counts against it. And we do have to take consequences into account. A person's ends are relevant to the esteem the person deserves: one whose purpose is to benefit others deserves greater admiration than one whose purpose is to cause harm or than one utterly indifferent to everyone else.

But these answers do not lead to the conclusion that having a good end is sufficient to make an action right, or that ends and consequences are all we should consider in deciding what to do, or that having good ends is all that matters in a person's character. Furthermore, even if having good ends were the sole determinant of right action, we might still

184   CHARACTER AND COPS

encounter conflicts about what we should do. Good ends can conflict with each other. They can pull us in contrary directions, just as worthwhile principles do.

Accordingly, the answer to the question is, Ends do justify means up to a point, and in certain ways, depending on what you mean, but not simply or unqualifiedly. Human life is just not so simple.

This is the lesson that French Algerian author Albert Camus tried, in July 1943, to teach to a former German friend who had become a Nazi. Camus wrote to him:

> You said to me: "The greatness of my country is beyond price. Anything is good that contributes to its greatness. And in a world where everything has lost its meaning, those who, like us young Germans, are lucky enough to find meaning in the destiny of our nation must sacrifice everything else."
>
> "No," I told you. "I cannot believe that everything must be subordinated to a single end. There are means that cannot be excused. And I should like to be able to love my country and still love justice.[2]

Camus' love of justice is akin to Kant's recognition that people deserve consideration, deserve not to be just used, simply because they are people. A person is a repository of worth, of significance, even if that person appears without merit. This is the reason we oppose inordinate coercion; once we descend from reasoned persuasion—and respect for each other's freedom—to force, we deny the right to self-determination. Justice constrains us from going any further in this direction than we believe necessary.

American traditions affirm that principle. The right of due process and the prohibition against cruel and unusual punishment in the Eighth Amendment are based on the principle that human beings deserve to be treated as ends and never as mere means, never as objects, no matter how heinous their crimes. This moral tradition of America and other civilized nations contrasts with the gulags of the Soviet Union, where guilt was presumed, trials were a mockery, and cruel punishment routine. Where moral traditions are absent, the consequences are predictable.

Even in war, where enemy troops are often treated as mere obstacles to a nation's will, the Geneva Convention reflects the idea that nations still have an obligation to treat prisoners as human beings. Those standards prohibit torture because it is inexcusable brutality against a defenseless person. They should apply even to prisoners who refuse to divulge highly valuable information, but they are often violated. The North Vietnamese,

TRAGEDY AND CORRUPTION 185

for example, tortured American POWs to make them assist in their propaganda efforts. The Americans were routinely treated as mere means to their purposes.

American traditions stand squarely opposed to use of the third degree in interrogating suspects. Such methods violate at least the Fifth and Eighth Amendments, as well as *Miranda* and other judicial interpretations of those guarantees. Those amendments are not pieces of advice to law enforcement—they are fundamental law, the foundation of our way of life.

Yet in law enforcement as well as other national affairs, we are driven to the question whether illegal actions that violate the rights of citizens are ever morally right or excusable. I call that the question of "noble cause" corruption. Are police ever justified, or do they ever deserve to be excused, in breaking fundamental laws, not for personal gain, but for a purpose that appeals to our basic moral sensibilities? That is a question about extraordinary situations, when we cannot stand for all the goods we judge to be of the highest order, fulfill our highest principles, and respond to our most strongly felt duties in the treatment of all persons involved. The conflict between the rights of the innocent victim and the rights of the suspect-perpetrator is such a case.

Our response to that difficult question has crucial consequences. Since the literature about it leaves much to be desired, I have discussed it with philosophers and other scholars, lawyers, public officials, police chiefs, military officers, religious leaders, and corporate executives, whose counsel is paraphrased or quoted below. Sensible persons faced with hard problems should turn to the wisest people they know—the wisest friends, the best authors, and the historic figures and contemporaries they most admire. Their example is as precious as any moral precept and their judgment a powerful supplement to our own.

Three points are basic. First, since ends do not necessarily justify means, a good end cannot justify a means in a context that makes it wrong and evil. In a primitive setting where the law is nonexistent or ineffectual and where conditions of due process are not yet established, we might argue that physical coercion of a prisoner is at times justifiable. A lone champion of justice who behaves with regard for morality could be the only criminal justice system in existence. Or if a public official has thoroughly corrupted the system and become impervious to its sanctions, our main question might be one about what justice requires, not one about ends and means. But where civilizing law does have a hold, as in America, violations of fundamental civil liberties and laws, violations of oaths of

186   CHARACTER AND COPS

office, abuses of authority and power—all betrayals of the public trust—
are wrong and cannot be justified by any end.

Knowing this, however, does not help much in deciding what to do
or tell us whether as decent people we should ever use evil means. It
leaves open the question whether we should ever excuse the use of evil
means because the end is undeniably good, lesser means are ineffective,
and the motives of the agent are unquestionably noble.

Second, revising regulations and rules cannot eliminate tragedy and
conflicts of ideals. Although revisions can alter the mechanics of accountability, they cannot change elements of the human condition. After the
United States restricted the use of weapons by its ships defending tankers
from attack by Iran, thirty-seven Americans died in an attack on the U.S.S.
Stark. After the restrictions were relaxed, the U.S.S. *Vincennes* mistakenly
shot down an Iranian civilian airliner and killed all aboard. Both events
were tragic, despite efforts to establish the best policies.

Third, inflicting pain sadistically, with pleasure and without regret,
can never be excused. Even in a conflict in which allegiances have been
staked out and the pursuit of information has become brutal, thrilling to
the torture of others, viewing them at most as containers of information,
is wrong. It is depraved and inexcusable—even if the victim is loathsome.

Interrogators may pretend to be sadistic, however, and use fear
rather than pain as their instrument. In Bertolt Brecht's play, the pope—
who wants Galileo to recant his scientific discoveries—addresses the car-
dinal inquisitor:

> POPE (exhausted): It is clearly understood: he is not to be tor-
> tured. (Pauses.) At the very most, he may be shown the instruments.
> INQUISITOR: That will be adequate, Your Holiness. Mr. Galilei
> understands machinery.[3]

Who Is to Say (What to Do)?

To begin reflecting about a hard case, we should ask who should actually
have to suffer the ordeal of making the decision. Asking whom we should
trust differs from asking, What is the answer? Because hard cases must be
approached with a knowledge both of particulars and of general principles, we must determine who in a police department should be faced with
a moral issue so hard and of such profound consequence.

Most adults should reflect on and talk about painfully hard problems, which can contribute to the moral and intellectual maturation of
younger people as well. Certainly, many police of all ranks can meet the

challenge of demanding thought, but the issue here is, Who should actually have to make such a decision, not in thought, but in practice?

Not every moral question should require a decision by every officer, for some are beginners who are not qualified to decide problems of great magnitude. Beginners should not be asked to risk a career—for that may be at stake—in making decisions that go beyond their experience.

While citizens generally should try to develop informed opinions on public issues of all kinds, we would neither entrust policymaking to amateurs nor ask them to live with the trials of setting policy. As Walter Lippmann said, such decisions call for

> a kind of knowledge—not to speak of an experience and a seasoned judgment—which cannot be had by glancing at newspapers, listening to snatches of radio comment, watching politicians perform on television, hearing occasional lectures, and reading a few books. It would not be enough to make a man competent to decide whether to amputate a leg, and it is not enough to qualify him to choose war or peace, to arm or not to arm, to intervene or to withdraw, to fight or to negotiate.[4]

Although we may disagree with them, we want officials with "experience and a seasoned judgment" to have the authority to make such decisions.

As history teaches, the ordeal of judgment may be dreadful. When France fell to Germany in World War II, for example, the French government advocated alliance with Germany, not merely submission, so the French Navy seemed likely to become part of Germany's arsenal. Winston Churchill, as Britain's prime minister, had to decide whether to attack those ships, manned by former allies, to deny them to the enemy. He did so, thereby preventing German naval dominance. Although the decision was not compounded by any question of illegality, he described it as the most painful one of his life. Such hard decisions are part of the ordeal of command, not of lesser rank.

Police are the constituted authority for the use of force within society. They are uniformed as a mark of their authority and competence. Police departments have a structure of command just so that problems beyond the scope of junior personnel will not fall to them. Only in this way can the police live up to the public trust and safeguard against erosion of morale, which results when daily responsibilities simply cannot be met.

In many departments, policies on weaponry, ammunition, and the use of weapons other than sidearms are made by command rather than patrol personnel. In well-run departments, supportive and trustworthy

188 CHARACTER AND COPS

authority flows from the top. The hardest issues should therefore be faced by officers with the most seniority and highest rank. Officers who have risen to command rank are probably better qualified than anyone else inside or outside law enforcement to identify the hardest moral questions. They know from experience the temptation to twist the law or manipulate the facts in routine matters in the streets. They know the common view that some excesses in the use of authority are necessary. They should therefore consider where such views lead when the stakes are life, death, and fundamental law, and they may then help the next generation of police grapple with such issues.

Every person I have consulted on this issue insists that only mature adults with considerable experience should ever contemplate actually practicing extreme and illegal conduct. The moral burden is simply too heavy for personnel inexperienced in policing, who are not competent or prepared to make such decisions. They lack experience and information, they are less able to identify and apply legal means, and they have not had the opportunity to reflect on hard cases. Those police would more likely guess than think their way to a decision.

My colleagues do not mean to suggest that patrol and midrank personnel are without deep moral insight and great personal maturity. The moral character of police forces often rests as much on the influence and training provided by sergeants as on higher officers, they say, and seasoned officers of all ranks can arrive at compelling conclusions about such issues. Considerations both of authority and of fairness, however, imply that the highest ranking personnel ought to make such decisions and live with the consequences.

The consequences of extreme illegality within law enforcement are so grave that only those in a position to appreciate their gravity should be involved. Police officers who step so far beyond their authority as to coerce a prisoner physically have ceased to function as legitimate enforcers of the laws under the Constitution. They must be prepared to lose their job, to see the courts dismiss all charges against the suspect, or to deny the admissibility of evidence and to stand trial themselves for assault and battery or more severe charges.

If the suspect-perpetrator goes free because the evidence becomes inadmissible, the police official who violated the rights of the prisoner in custody will have turned loose on society a murderous kidnapper, who can again prey on the innocent. If the victim dies despite the efforts of police, the crime for which the perpetrator can no longer be prosecuted is

TRAGEDY AND CORRUPTION   189

first-degree murder. Furthermore, no matter how brutal the official becomes, the prisoner may still lie. In that case, the police official has forsaken duty and all else for nothing.

No less important, command personnel are obliged never to permit officers under their command to employ third-degree interrogations. Even if they are willing to act *in extremis* as individuals and accept the consequences, they cannot as officers tolerate such conduct in the ranks. And if they are hypocrites, they cannot lead their subordinates effectively or deserve their confidence.

If senior personnel have a right to consider such action, how can they avoid hypocrisy and remain faithful to the central duties of command? Since any attempt to justify illegal behavior after the fact would come too late, the question is, How should they stand on the record in advance?

With respect to policymaking, command personnel should keep in mind that most of us tend to go a bit beyond the set limits. If the speed limit is fifty-five miles per hour, for example, ordinary traffic will go sixty or more. Since minor illegal infractions are likely to be commonplace, setting the limits a bit tighter than we intend to hold is prudent, so long as doing so does not make policing impossible or render the limits ridiculous or yield an appearance of indifference to infractions. Departmental limits should therefore be set slightly tighter than the legal treatment of suspects allows. Then, minor and predictable infractions will not violate the law.

If command personnel take a realistic view toward slight overstepping, they can specify some limits as absolute. They can make clear, for example, that prohibition of third-degree methods is absolute and that they delegate no authority whatsoever in that matter. They can say candidly that, should any discretion ever be exercised on that issue, it will be reserved to the highest authority only—with no exceptions. To follow this path, the command officers must be forthright and not hide from the decisions of high office. Although they would avoid hypocrisy, they would still have to answer why rank carries a right to consider lawbreaking.

The answer is that the hardest moral questions cannot be reduced to questions of legality. Reserving the right of decision to the highest authority exhibits respect for the law, and it discloses that no principle—including the law—is utterly inviolable by absolutely everyone under all possible circumstances.

Article I, section 9, of the Constitution says, "The Privilege of the Writ of Habeas Corpus shall not be suspended, unless when in Cases of Rebellion or Invasion the public Safety may require it." Yet, when Abraham

190   CHARACTER AND COPS

Lincoln became president and feared that the Maryland legislature would vote to secede, he arrested many of its members and suspended habeas corpus. By that means, he preempted Maryland's possible secession and fulfilled his duty to preserve the Union. A state of rebellion may not yet have existed, however, and the danger to the public safety may not have "required" the action. And, certainly, there was no "invasion."

In practice, our moral sensibilities sometimes seem to call for things to be done, even though they are illegal. To make them legal would require too many specific details; otherwise, the law would be systematically abused. When we consider the morality of some illegal acts that we do not believe should be made legal, therefore, we recognize that no principle can be inviolable. Churchill and Lincoln perceived that inviolable principles can kill people. A refusal to fire on innocent French sailors in World War II might have enabled Germany to kill greater numbers with the French fleet and perhaps to win the war.

This ground is so slippery, especially in a nation that treats certain rights as inalienable, that only command personnel of the highest rank should ever step onto it. The complexity of human life seems to me to warrant their stepping onto it, to face the ordeal of judgment with all its consequences, rather than never to consider extreme measures. Not only does such a position foreclose future decisions; it also threatens command personnel in some future case with hypocrisy.

I understand why some in law enforcement say that no one ever has a right to consider illegal measures. They insist that command personnel should be told *never* and should be made to comply. They know the danger of a command officer's going beyond the law, and so do I. But I also believe that the human condition compels us to see that an unconditional position here is too strong.

Trying to Have It Both Ways

Since no one who can avoid it should ever step onto such dangerous ground, command personnel and departmental legal counsel must know the laws that may provide relief from a conflict between undeniable goods. The *Crimes Code of Pennsylvania*, for example, like many others, contains a section called General Principles of Justification:

> In any prosecution based on conduct which is justifiable under this chapter, justification is a defense. . . .
>
> (a) General rule. Conduct which the actor believes to be necessary to avoid a harm or evil to himself or to another is justifiable if

(1) the harm or evil sought to be avoided by such conduct is greater than that sought to be prevented by the law defining the offense charged.[5]

Such provisions may apply to command decisions in hard cases. Because such provisions may be overridden by other laws and by the Constitution, however, command personnel must use their intelligence, imagination, and experience to reduce the area of conflict.

A specific hypothetical case about physical coercion for information may help us test our suppositions to be sure that they do not draw us too hastily onto dangerous ground. In this case, the police know that the person in custody is the perpetrator, and not just a suspect. They know that the victim is buried and alive, and they know that the perpetrator knows where. They know that the perpetrator will not divulge the information under legal interrogation.

Are the police likely to *know* this much in the situations they face? Colleagues in domestic law enforcement and in military intelligence and interrogation say no. They stress the difficulty of knowing how much information a suspect has. Inexperienced officers often treat detainees disgracefully—and even commit atrocities—because they overestimate a prisoner's knowledge. Experienced officers would urge that the hypothetical situation be made more realistic by supposing that the suspect may have information on which a victim's life may depend. The victim may be alive, and whatever information is drawn from the prisoner by any means may be true and therefore may be useful in the preservation of life.

Those useful points show how the case becomes harder under plausible assumptions that call for intellectual humility. In such circumstances, a police command officer who is unsure of the facts contemplates the additional moral burden of wrongdoing, even while uncertain that the desired end can be achieved by any means. By contrast, he can be sure that a no-holds-barred interrogation is wrong.

This uncertainty of facts is quite different from the legal presumption of innocence. Police officers frequently know who committed a crime—they may even have apprehended someone in the act. Legally, however, the person remains a suspect entitled to due process of law and therefore to the presumption of innocence. Factual guilt and legal innocence are entirely compatible; if they were not, we could not bring evidence to a trial that proved beyond a reasonable doubt a suspect's legal guilt.

In the hypothetical case, my colleagues are not suggesting that the perpetrator be treated merely as a suspect. They are not saying that the

192   CHARACTER AND COPS

conditions for admissible evidence at a trial must be satisfied here, although they want to preserve those conditions if possible. Rather, they are pointing to an uncertainty about what the perpetrator knows. Accomplices, for example, may have decided where to bury the victim. The officers are also uncertain whether the perpetrator under duress would be telling the truth and whether any information could save the life of the victim.

Several of those colleagues point to extreme measures within the law that can be tried to obtain the information the perpetrator has. And some observe that a perpetrator may lie, even in pain or under threat of death, especially a perpetrator who would bury a victim alive. One wrote:

> A number of reasons might account for not telling the truth: buying time for an accomplice, placing blame on another person, and—the most difficult to deal with—complete lack of conscience with regard to the crime. If the perpetrator lacks a conscience and the attendant guilt, he has no interest in saving the endangered life as an act of personal redemption. To that type of individual, whom we can refer to as sociopathic, outwitting the police officer is a far more appealing goal than a cleansing confession. This would be the type of personality that would thrive on burying a child alive in the first place.
>
> Sociopaths may understand that what they have done is perceived as wrong by society, but they have absolutely no sense that their behavior is wrong, and, as a result, they have no remorse. Misleading a bothersome police officer would be predictable behavior from a sociopath, and provoking the officer to act outside the law in order to extract information would give the sociopath the last laugh that he seeks. Fooling the stupid officer and being very likely beyond prosecution *and* committing the original crime makes for the perfect sociopathic success.

The expertness of interrogators in such a case becomes a central issue. As one colleague noted, police must be "well enough trained in interrogation that they are not likely to rush into extreme measures." A poorly trained interrogator is more likely to panic under the pressure of trying to save a victim's life and ignore rules and policies. "The more urgent the need, the less rational a person is likely to be," one of my colleagues wrote. Although that may make us more tolerant of police behavior under pressure, it does not help the victim or achieve purposes within the law. Legal measures might have succeeded; at least they had as much potential as illegal ones.

Legal methods of interrogation may be distasteful, but they are preferable to illegal ones. If male perpetrators have kidnapped female victims, the interrogation may be more effectively conducted by women, so a department should have expert male and female interrogators.

As one colleague wrote:

> Scrupulous attention to detail, intelligent and practiced interrogation techniques based on an understanding of human psychology, and decisiveness . . . stand at least as good a chance of yielding the desired result [as physical coercion]. [T]hey do so without the risk of losing the admissibility of evidence. There are ways to flatter a suspect, gain his trust, convince him of his "rightness," enlist his assistance or enrage him, that yield information that can be acted upon. The lay person might very well be shocked by some of these techniques, and many police officers are uncomfortable using them because it requires their serious and convincing acting of roles which they find personally repugnant (such as telling a child molester that you understand perfectly how those little girls lead men on, and how they truly want to be screwed, and that you wish you had been screwed by someone strong and good-looking like the suspect when you were six years old), but they are not illegal, and they are remarkably effective. The U.S. Supreme Court has consistently affirmed the legality of the police use of these techniques.

And another concluded:

> The word "necessary" is slippery. It is often used merely for what appears efficient or expedient. "We had no choice" can be a lame and dishonest substitute for "It was the quickest way." There are many techniques for interrogation that are not violent.

In any deliberation about interrogation of great urgency, command personnel should be in close consultation with their legal personnel. A police department does not have to act alone in such a matter. A colleague wrote:

> Historically, our courts have sought to resolve and adjust the conflict of legitimate rights and interests in our society. Were I representing law enforcement authorities in the case you pose, I would naturally consider an emergency application to a court of competent jurisdiction. A compelling factual presentation would have to be made as to the life-threatening consequences of a suspect's refusal to provide information. I would ask the court to consider ordering the supervised administration of sodium pentathol or the employment of some alternative practice which has gained a degree of acceptance in the medical community. For purposes of analogy, I would cite those

194   CHARACTER AND COPS

instances where courts have ordered emergency medical intervention for minor children, despite the constitutionally protected religious scruples of their parents.

We should conclude that command officers who fail to exercise all the legal means at their disposal have failed in their duty. Those who proceed into flagrant illegality without doing so are neither justified nor excusable, and they thrust their departments into hazards of civil and criminal liability that might have been avoided.

Obviously, some illegal actions are more serious than others. Several of my colleagues point out that if they were questioning a suspect in a case of that sort in his home, they would listen illegally to a phone call from an accomplice if they could. Such a judgment would have to be made by an officer at the scene, without benefit of consultation or supervision. In my judgment, such an action, though illegal, would be morally appropriate; it is not a flagrant violation of the suspect's rights, and it seems less than extreme, given the peril to a life. Releasing a suspect to gain information by surveillance might be plausible in some cases, and it would be legal. An officer would be remiss, however, to spurn opportunities to secure information by intrusive but nonviolent means.

Thinking It Through

Given all those considerations, what should a conscientious high-ranking police official do in the extreme situation? Suppose that he is certain neither that the victim is alive nor that the suspect-perpetrator can be made to divulge what he does know. Suppose that the legal methods of interrogation have been tried, expertly (albeit quickly), and failed. The life of the victim may depend on information the suspect-perpetrator may have that physical coercion may yield.

Most thoughtful people will come down on one side of the issue with some feeling of respect and sympathy for those on the other. Even mature and experienced adults who agree with everything that has been said to this point will be divided on the issue. Certainly, my colleagues are. Some envision circumstances that would excuse the use of third-degree methods or drugs, but others do not. One wrote:

> If any end can justify all means, it would be the protection of innocent life. I would use all the instruments at my disposal to get information from someone who clearly possessed it to secure the safety of the blameless. And do so with the intention of taking the responsibility

TRAGEDY AND CORRUPTION 195

personally for such action. I would not consider putting such policy in writing; neither would I consider denying my actions afterward.

Another wrote:

> I think that, for roughly utilitarian reasons, getting information from a suspect by hurting him could be justified . . . but I think that saying or writing to policemen that it could be justified is probably not itself justified. This is because policemen, being human, may fall short of their convictions about hurting suspects and hurt them more and more often than they really think they should.

Still another observed:

> I think it unwise to offer a solution to this problem based on general principles. The problem for a real policeman is not so much what principles to apply but how to apply them. Much depends on the policeman's estimate of the suspect's knowledge, the urgency of the case, and the failure of successful interrogation by means less than physical coercion. . . . But I would want to make it clear that, when it is urgent to save human life, *any* rule is breakable.

Some who oppose those positions, including police, share the views of one colleague:

> I see the violation of rights as an easy way out. . . . I want to be able to look at myself in the mirror every day and believe that I have done the best I could have under the circumstances. To do so, I proceed under the belief that there is no situation that I can predict in which I will meet the circumstances with a studied and purposeful decision to violate a suspect's constitutional rights as the best—or only—solution.

Another colleague was even more direct:

> The rule of law requires all of us to submit to it. A cop who breaks the law, in order to enforce it more effectively, is a criminal. No one is above the law. If you can't live with it, quit. Anything else is a slope toward totalitarianism, and it is naive to have faith that command personnel or anyone else can avoid sliding downward once they break the law, and it is hypocrisy to say that anyone in law enforcement has the right to do so. It is wrong to agree to the slightest compromise in these matters.

Another concluded with a reflection on the human condition itself:

> My position is a simple *and plain* acknowledgment of a conflict between official duty and an obligation of a person to do all he can to save the life of another. We must refuse to blur the distinctions

196   CHARACTER AND COPS

between our official positions and our individual felt obligations. Thus, we should acknowledge on the one hand that using extreme measures to gain information from a "suspect" is never justified. On the other hand, *as individuals* we should be willing to consider acting *in extremis* and accepting the consequences of our actions. . . . In a sense my view is that this is one of the conflicts in the human condition (it is *not* a dilemma) for which there is no solution, even though individual human beings must, finally, decide. It is because the human condition can call for so much from the best of us that we should feel compassion for those who must face such conflicts.

When reasonable people of goodwill disagree about how to handle a complex problem, we can only hope that those who actually decide will do so with profound regard both for the status of the human beings involved as ends and for their own professional duties, including their duty not to bring the department into bad repute. They must not choose their methods in anger and passion, or in a vengeful or self-righteous spirit in the name of a supposedly all-justifying principle. They should recognize the moral peril of excess and take every measure to avoid it. Then, if they do choose to break the law and commit a wrongful act, they will at least not do so routinely or feel justified in cloaking their behavior in secrecy or perjury.

Terrorists and other extremists—in the name of justice—consider their murderous actions entirely justified. They are devoid of the humility that makes people trustworthy to bear authority or exercise power. Because they believe that they are entirely devoted to justice, they always believe themselves innocent as well. Human life is neither so easy, however, nor so simple.

The same tendency can be seen in law enforcement. In 1986 officers of the 106th Precinct in Queens, New York City, were convicted of assault in the second degree and coercion in the first degree for using stun guns to get confessions from misdemeanor suspects in custody. Also in 1986, in San Antonio, Patrolman Stephen Smith was shot to death by another officer, his closest friend, who believed that Smith was about to kill him. Smith was at the time suspected of a plot to assassinate city officials and of involvement in six vigilante murders. In an investigation by a local newspaper of what happens in a police department "when it has dangerous officers but cannot fire them because of union protection," City Manager Lou Fox had earlier declared, "I've got a killer cop I can't get rid of. . . . To know that there are renegade cops, dangerous people, on your force and to be unable for so long to do anything about it, that can scare hell out of you." Ballistics tests revealed that "bullets used in two unsolved murders matched slugs fired from one of Smith's AR15 rifles."[6]

This mentality of self-righteousness, which is absolutely incompatible with the public trust, was also exhibited by a Miami police officer on trial in 1988 for the murder of nine alleged drug dealers. According to the local press, his only regret was that he had not killed ninety-nine dealers before being caught. "I enjoyed what I was doing," he said, denying that he was a murderer because his victims were "not human beings." He acknowledged that he worshiped Hitler and said, "This is called absolute justice. . . . I took nine people with me. . . . They'll never sell drugs to your children." Prosecutors contended, however, that not all of his victims were involved with drugs.[7] Columnist William Safire put such behavior in perspective: "Toleration of the cop who deliberately kills a suspect threatens our way of life."[8]

A further problem, even for well-intentioned and normally restrained public officials, is the corrosive effect of extreme, illegal measures on restraint in future instances. Those who employ extreme measures may find it easier to do so the next time a hard case arises and perhaps easier in a case not quite so hard after that. Extreme measures can then become routine merely because they are convenient.

A point made in *A Man for All Seasons* applies here, because we are creatures of habit. After bribing someone to betray a trust, an official says, "There, that wasn't too painful, was it? . . . That's all there is. And you'll find it easier next time."[9] Once we go beyond the law for a noble purpose rather than a selfish one, we may feel that we have committed ourselves to illegal means, as further extremes become natural. As one of my colleagues observed, "When we violate a suspect's Constitutional rights, we deviate from fundamental principles. That can be the beginning of a substantial erosion. There's a fine line in these things, but once you step over it, you tend to justify subsequent acts by the former one." An intellectual and moral humility and an appreciation of the gravity of what we have done are the only bulwarks I know against such deterioration of character.

Dirty Harry

In a well-known article, Carl B. Klockars, professor of criminal justice at the University of Delaware, wrote, "The Dirty Harry problem asks when and to what extent the morally good end warrants or justifies an ethically, politically, or legally dangerous means to its achievement."[10] In the film *Dirty Harry,* a psychopathic killer, Scorpio, kidnaps a fourteen-year-old

198   CHARACTER AND COPS

girl, buries her alive, demands a ransom, and reneges on the promise to provide information when the ransom is delivered. The main character, Inspector Harry Callahan, illegally searches the suspect's room, confirms that he is Scorpio, tracks him down, shoots him in the leg, and then "stands on Scorpio's bullet-mangled leg to torture the information out of him." Scorpio divulges the location of the girl, who is, as Callahan suspected, already dead. Since the physical evidence and the confession are inadmissible in court, Scorpio walks away a free man.

Klockars denied that the most difficult problem is what Dirty Harry ought to do:

> On the contrary, I suspect that most people would want Harry to do something dirty in the situation. I know I would want him to do what he did, and what is more, I would want anyone who policed for me to be prepared to do so. I want to have men and women of moral courage and sensitivity as police officers.

All of us want morally courageous and sensitive police officers, and many audiences seemed thoroughly satisfied with Callahan's behavior. In fact, many would no doubt approve of inflicting pain as punishment on Scorpio even if Harry knew that the victim was dead.

Yet we must not allow moral outrage to blind us to facts. The inspector's behavior is justified, Klockars said, by the goodness of the purpose, by his knowledge that Scorpio has the information, and by the "small possibility" that the victim is still alive. "There appears to be no reason for Scorpio to confess to the girl's location without being coerced to do so," he added. Although Scorpio would not divulge the information from any goodness in his heart, a shrewd interrogator might enrage or trick him or use deceptively sympathetic tactics to draw out the information. Harry Callahan does not try any such means, nor does he try to comfort Scorpio as a way of gaining his confidence, however offensive such false compassion might feel. Neither does he seek assistance from a court of competent jurisdiction. He goes from asking a direct question at gunpoint to torture.

Callahan's excesses are no more a mark of courage or sensitivity than calling on interrogation experts and deferring to higher authority are marks of cowardice or insensitivity. Trying to fulfill the purposes of law enforcement within the limits of the law takes as much courage as any other course. Command personnel can help by being forthright and resolute about departmental policy in training. Klockars acknowledged that "the department that trains its personnel well and supplies them with the resources—knowledge and material—to do their work will find that its policemen will not resort to dirty means unnecessarily." He should add that a multitude of inexcusable moral wrongs has sought, and found, refuge under the slippery argument that it was "necessary." As Shakespeare wrote, necessity is the plea of tyrants. "The troublesome issue in the Dirty Harry problem," Klockars wrote, "is not whether a right choice can be made, but that the choice must always be between two wrongs. And in choosing to do either wrong, the police officer inevitably taints or tarnishes himself."

In conversation with me, Professor Klockars has explained his position: the fundamental tenets of one moral theory may be irreducibly at odds with those of another moral theory; since an individual cannot satisfy both, he is bound to be tainted by one or the other. Thus, if one moral theory holds that you must always try to achieve the best immediate consequences (such as saving the life of the victim) and another holds that you must honor fully the status of a person as an end and not as a means to some goal (such as torturing a suspect for information), then a dilemma results.

The conclusion does not follow, however, because a person who subscribes only to one theory or the other has no moral problem at all, let alone a dilemma. The person simply acts in accordance with the theory. The real conflict arises for a person who sees a measure of rightness in each tenet, when circumstances force a decision between them. The incompatibility of some moral theories with others, by itself, taints no one. If it did, a vicious moral theory holding that might makes right or that white males are superior to everyone else and have a right to all positions of power and authority would taint everyone who rejected it. Theories have no such power, because they are sometimes wrong, simplistic, or overstated, and sometimes foolishly applied.

Furthermore, when we use coercion to prevent a person from self-determination, we do so either with or without restraint. The two differ profoundly.

Still, is it in some sense inevitable that police will be tainted by tensions between the limits of the law and moral constraint on the one hand and noble purposes on the other? Is this what we expect courageous and sensitive police to accept as their fate? Shall we tell students at police academies that they must "inevitably" become "dirty"?

The answer is no. Although the world has in it the makings of tragedy, not everyone who faces its most grueling demands need become dirty. Is it not still true, however, as suggested by the Klockars argument,

200   CHARACTER AND COPS

that police officers who fail to use every means to achieve a high purpose are morally tainted? And are not officers who fail to abide by the law legally tainted or morally tainted by infidelity to their oath of office, to the Constitution, and to the public? I do not see why command officials would be morally tainted if they used all legal means at their disposal but declined to use illegal means that might be viewed by patrol personnel as a license for excess.

A more powerful consideration is that the suspect-perpetrator may go free if his rights are violated. The command officer may know that the prisoner is not suspected of other crimes that might lead to another arrest, that police surveillance of him will be prevented by charges of harassment, that no officers are available for surveillance, and that civic-minded private wealth cannot be enlisted to hire private surveillance. Moreover, the liberty of the suspect-perpetrator may be a murderous threat to other possible victims. The officer may imagine the eyes of the family of the next victim and hear their question, How could you have allowed the killer to walk away from his last murder?

That is, the command officer may see that using every conceivable means to save today's victim risks creating new victims tomorrow. What, then, is to be done? The slippery slope of physical coercion leads to the question whether false reports should be prepared to keep the perpetrator in custody and perjury should be committed to get a conviction. If the officer will do anything to save the victim and keep the suspect-perpetrator off the street, but he will not lie or commit perjury, then he cannot avoid the question whether he should murder the suspect-perpetrator.

I do not see how a person can be tainted by refusing to step onto this slope, toward which we are dragged by extreme illegal measures in law enforcement. Ignoring the slope, Klockars argued that the story of Dirty Harry is art, in the sense that at "all meaningful levels" it is "true." He meant that the Dirty Harry problem demands attention and analysis, not that all the particulars of the story are realistic.

After Scorpio goes free, Harry uses off-duty time to watch him until he is charged with harassment and ordered to stop. Scorpio then takes a bus full of elementary school children hostage. After Harry manages to force him away from the bus and they engage in a running gunfight, Scorpio takes yet another child hostage before Harry wounds him. When the child flees, the two at last confront each other. Now in a position to arrest Scorpio, Harry instead taunts him and dares him to try for the gun he has dropped. When Scorpio rises to the bait, Harry Callahan kills him. The shooting is calculated murder.

I do not know any police who would describe that denouement as realistic or "true" at "all meaningful levels" or describe Harry as a police officer of "courage and sensitivity." Klockars and others have said that Harry Callahan should be fired. After all, if arrested in those circumstances, Scorpio would almost certainly be prosecuted and convicted. For purposes of law enforcement or the safety of the public, murdering Scorpio is pointless. The murder does offer delicious gratification to the appetite for revenge, and it satisfies moral outrage and hatred of the perpetrator. Such gratification has no place, however, in real law enforcement. It is not extreme action for the sake of high purpose, but raw self-indulgence.

If police officials are not tainted by refusing to step onto the slope of illegal action, neither are officials of demonstrated probity necessarily tainted by a last-ditch illegal step. Such an act may be unjustifiable by any unconditional principle, but it also may be excusable. Even if committed without regard to self-interest and at great personal sacrifice, inflicting pain is an undeniably evil act when committed by one who has no right to punish. Although it would constitute a betrayal of the duties of office, it would not necessarily be condemned in any subsequent legal proceeding. An enlightened governor could justifiably pardon the act. Still less does it follow that those who commit such acts are bad, that their character is besmirched, or that their honor is tainted.

I doubt that we would describe officials who act either way as "dirty." Some would say that they should have done more, and some less. We may condemn their judgment, but we would not therefore think them worthy of disrespect. Our respect for proven decency in service to the public is deeper, and more subtle, than that.

Persons cannot be held morally responsible because the human condition has cast them into situations where highly desirable ends are at least temporarily at odds with each other. Neither can they be held blameworthy when they have undeniably done their best. We can scarcely say that those who have done their best are tainted for failing to do better. To say otherwise is to be fundamentally wrong about the nature of moral life.

"Noble Cause" Corruption

What does taint us as moral agents is an arrogant appraisal of ourselves that concludes, "I am entirely justified in my means because my end was noble," or a cowardly response to demands, such as, "I'm damned if I do and damned if I don't, so it makes no difference." Giving everything we

202   CHARACTER AND COPS

have when the issue is hardest does not taint us, but giving less suggests avoidable ignorance, weakness, or incompetence.

Such flattering self-appraisals and failures of nerve are the two forms of noble cause corruption. Arrogance and cowardice imperil the ideals of a constitutional republic, because they are marks of individuals who despair of rising to the ordeal of command. In my experience, the republic has little to fear from officials who face up to ordeals and do not try to get off the hook by complacently justifying themselves or by whining that "the world isn't fair." What is fearful are the officials who believe that their ends always justify or excuse their means or who give up in despair but remain in office nonetheless. The greater the responsibilities and authority of those officials, the less the country can afford such flight from tension and conflict. They are the marks of a human spirit that has admitted defeat. In practice, they undermine the judgment required to bear the public trust faithfully. Arrogance corrupts by obscuring the need for thought, and cowardice corrupts by denying the point of thought, thus forsaking judgment to the whims of impulse.

Excusable Wrongdoing

At this point, we may wonder whether we should consider well-intentioned and remorseful wrongdoing in terribly hard cases to be excusable. That is a tempting way to handle the problem of tragedy because it invites us to make a rule for excusing (or not excusing) high-minded wrongdoing. Then, when faced with a tragically difficult case, we can appeal to the rule and spare ourselves the ordeal of judgment.

That way of proceeding is dangerous. If certain considerations excuse illegal conduct in one case, they do so in sufficiently similar cases too, but each case must be treated in all of its particularity. The specifics force us to be morally humble and intellectually thorough. We sacrifice doing our best if we lapse into the self-assurance that what we are about to do is wrong, but we deserve to be excused. That form of complacency can be as remorseless as any other.

Temptations of this kind are another reason to avoid making beginners in ethics courses focus on hard cases, which are not the mainstream of moral life. Beginners are likely to look for simple rules when they are taught, to paraphrase Edmund Burke, "to make the extreme medicine of human life its daily bread." When that happens, Burke observed, people tend to become weak, because they develop the bad habit of speaking and thinking lightly about profoundly demanding matters, both before and after the fact.[11] That is as true in law enforcement as elsewhere.

The conclusion to be drawn is that illegal conduct in a specific case may or may not be excusable—and I believe that it could be, depending on the particulars and even the minute details of the case.

Deciding

On more than one occasion, I have been asked whether I—as a command officer who believed that all legal means had been exhausted and that physical coercion was the only means of saving an innocent victim—would consider using the third degree.

My response is yes, in that I would not absolutely foreclose consideration. I would consider it in light of all the relevant facts available at the time: the condition and reputation of my department; the levels of respect for law among my subordinates and peers; recent episodes of brutality and corruption for profit within; the prospect of loss of departmental autonomy in any resultant political firestorm; the legal means available for subsequently keeping the suspect-perpetrator off the streets; and other matters considered relevant by any competent command officer.

Would I actually use the third degree? I would be unlikely to, but I might. I would certainly seek the advice of counsel about the outer limits of the permissible throughout the ordeal. I would use every form of psychological pressure on the suspect, while making sure that he would have a difficult burden of proof if he sought to suppress evidence on grounds that his rights had been violated.

If I actually crossed the line to physical coercion, I would then request or commence a departmental inquiry, along the lines recommended by counsel, to minimize the hazards to the department and to try to keep the suspect in custody. I would not participate in a cover-up because such conduct betrays the law itself, inspires conspiracies against the rule of law, and undermines by deceit the public trust. But I would avail myself of all my rights under the Constitution, on the grounds that I had never casually or routinely disregarded anyone else's rights. At the same time, I would resign from my position—not necessarily from the department—to make clear that no one who has violated the standards of a position of authority should continue in it.

I hope that I would be decisive but aware of the shiver that ought to be felt by anyone facing the moral demands of the grimmest realities. I would have at hand words of theologian Reinhold Niebuhr:

> The tragic element in a human situation is constituted of conscious choices of evil for the sake of good. . . . Tragedy elicits admiration as well as pity because it combines nobility with guilt. . . . Our idealists are divided between those who would renounce the responsibilities of power for the sake of preserving the purity of our soul and those who are ready to cover every ambiguity of good and evil in our actions by the frantic insistence that any measure taken in a good cause must be unequivocally virtuous: We take, and must continue to take, morally hazardous actions to preserve our civilization.[12]

I hope that I would remember that some actions are not just morally hazardous, but morally suicidal. And I would have in mind the deepest reservation: that some of those I respect most in the world have said to me that they could never physically abuse any person in custody.

Notes 204a

Tragedy and Corruption

1. Immanuel Kant, *Foundations of the Metaphysics of Morals* (New York: Bobbs Merrill, (1959), pp. 46, 47.
2. Albert Camus, *Resistance, Rebellion, and Death*, trans. Justin O'Brien (New York: Vintage Books, 1974), p. 5.
3. Bertolt Brecht, *Galileo*, tr. Charles Laughton (New York: Grove Press, 1966), p. 110.
4. Walter Lippmann, *The Public Philosophy* (New York: Mentor Books, 1955), p. 27.
5. *Crimes Code of Pennsylvania*, secs. 502, 503 (Longwood, Fla.: Gould Publications, 1985), pp. 19, 20.
6. David Maraniss, *"Death of a Reputed Vigilante,"* Washington Post, September 21, 1986.
7. Joan Fleischman, *"Ex-Cop: 'I enjoyed shooting dealers"*, – Miami Herald, April 14, 1988.
8. William Safire, *"Stalker's Last Case,"* New York Times, June 30, 1986. Safire was writing in the context of his analysis of the "Stalker Affair," so named by Deputy Chief Constable of the Greater Manchester Police John Stalker in describing his investigation of alleged abuses of authority and power by the Royal Ulster Constabulary. The case was much more complex and murky than popular published accounts made it out to be, but Safire's statement of principle was nonetheless correct.
9. Robert Bolt, *A Man for All Seasons* (New York: Vintage Books, 1962), p. 43.
10. Carl B. Klockars, "The Dirty Harry Problem," in *Moral Issues in Police Work*, ed. Frederick A. Elliston and Michael Feldberg (Totowa, NJ.: Rowman and Allenheld, 1985), pp. 55-62.
11. See Edmund Burke, *Reflections on the French Revolution* and Other Essays (New York: E. P. Dutton, 1951), p. 60.
12. Reinhold Niebuhr, *The Irony of American History* (New York: Charles Scribner's Sons, 1952), pp. vii, viii, 5.

Part V
Deadly Force

[21]

[471 US 1]
TENNESSEE, Appellant

v

CLEAMTEE GARNER, etc., et al.

MEMPHIS POLICE DEPARTMENT, et al., Petitioners

v

CLEAMTEE GARNER, etc., et al.

471 US 1, 85 L Ed 2d 1, 105 S Ct 1694

[Nos. 83–1035 and 83–1070]

Argued October 30, 1984. Decided March 27, 1985.

Decision: Police use of deadly force to prevent the escape of an apparently unarmed suspected felon held to violate the Fourth Amendment.

SUMMARY

A citizen brought suit against the city of Memphis, its police department, and various individuals, alleging that the constitutional rights of his deceased son had been violated when a police officer shot the youth in order to prevent his escape from the scene of a burglary, even though he did not appear to be armed. The United States District Court for the Western District of Tennessee dismissed the complaint, ruling that the officer's actions were authorized by a Tennessee statute which allowed the police to use all necessary means to effect an arrest where a suspect fled or forcibly resisted after being notified of the intent to arrest, and that this statute was constitutional. The United States Court of Appeals for the Sixth Circuit reversed and remanded, holding that the statute violated the Fourth Amendment (710 F2d 240).

On certiorari, the United States Supreme Court affirmed. In an opinion by WHITE, J., joined by BRENNAN, MARSHALL, BLACKMUN, POWELL, and STEVENS, JJ., the court held that the Fourth Amendment prohibits the use of deadly force to prevent the escape of a suspected felon unless it is necessary to prevent the escape and the officer has probable cause to believe that the suspect poses a significant threat of death or serious physical injury to the

Briefs of Counsel, p 871, infra.

U.S. SUPREME COURT REPORTS   85 L Ed 2d

officer or others, and thus, the Tennessee statute was unconstitutional insofar as it authorized the use of deadly force to prevent the escape of an apparently unarmed suspected felon.

O'CONNOR, J., joined by BURGER, Ch. J., and REHNQUIST, J., dissented, expressing the view that the use of deadly force as a last resort to prevent the escape of a suspect from the scene of a nighttime burglary does not violate the Fourth Amendment.

HEADNOTES

Classified to U.S. Supreme Court Digest, Lawyers' Edition

Search and Seizure § 11 — seizure of person — deadly force — limits on use

1a–1c. The Fourth Amendment prohibits the use of deadly force to prevent the escape of a suspected felon unless it is necessary to prevent the escape and the officer has probable cause to believe that the suspect poses a significant threat of

---

TOTAL CLIENT-SERVICE LIBRARY® REFERENCES

3 Am Jur 2d, Arrest §§ 80, 81; 68 Am Jur 2d, Searches and Seizures §§ 2, 8, 22, 89

9 Am Jur Proof of Facts 2d 363, Police Officer's Use of Excessive Force in Making Arrest

15 Am Jur Trials 555, Police Misconduct Litigation—Plaintiff's Remedies

USCS, Constitution, 4th Amendment

US L Ed Digest, Search and Seizure § 11

L Ed Index to Annos, Arrest; Police; Search and Seizure

ALR Quick Index, Arrest; Deadly Force; Police; Search and Seizure

Federal Quick Index, Arrest; Force or Violence; Police; Search And Seizure

Auto-Cite®: Any case citation herein can be checked for form, parallel references, later history, and annotation references through the Auto-Cite computer research system.

ANNOTATION REFERENCES

When does police officer's use of force during arrest become so excessive as to constitute violation of constitutional rights, imposing liability under Federal Civil Rights Act of 1871 (42 USCS § 1983). 60 ALR Fed 204.

Modern status: Right of peace officer to use deadly force in attempting to arrest fleeing felon. 83 ALR3d 174.

TENNESSEE v GARNER
471 US 1, 85 L Ed 2d 1, 105 S Ct 1694

death or serious physical injury to the officer or others; thus, a state statute which authorizes officers to use all necessary means to effect the arrest of a suspect who flees or forcibly resists after being notified of the intent to arrest is unconstitutional insofar as it authorizes the use of deadly force to prevent the escape of an apparently unarmed suspected felon. (O'Connor, J., Burger, Ch. J., and Rehnquist, J., dissented from this holding.)

Search and Seizure § 11 — seizure of person — generally

2. Whenever an officer restrains the freedom of a person to walk away, he has seized that person within the meaning of the Fourth Amendment.

Search and Seizure § 11 — seizure of person — deadly force as seizure

3. The apprehension of a person by the use of deadly force is a seizure subject to the reasonableness requirement of the Fourth Amendment.

Search and Seizure § 11 — seizure of person — reasonableness

4. In order to determine the constitutionality of the seizure of a person by police, a court must balance the nature and quality of the intrusion on the individual's Fourth Amendment interests against the importance of the governmental interests alleged to justify the intrusion; because one of the factors is the extent of the intrusion, the reasonableness of the seizure depends on not only when it is made, but also how it is carried out.

SYLLABUS BY REPORTER OF DECISIONS

A Tennessee statute provides that if, after a police officer has given notice of an intent to arrest a criminal suspect, the suspect flees or forcibly resists, "the officer may use all the necessary means to effect the arrest." Acting under the authority of this statute, a Memphis police officer shot and killed appellee-respondent Garner's son as, after being told to halt, the son fled over a fence at night in the backyard of a house he was suspected of burglarizing. The officer used deadly force despite being "reasonably sure" the suspect was unarmed and thinking that he was 17 or 18 years old and of slight build. The father subsequently brought an action in Federal District Court, seeking damages under 42 USC § 1983 [42 USCS § 1983] for asserted violations of his son's constitutional rights. The District Court held that the statute and the

officer's actions were constitutional. The Court of Appeals reversed.

Held: The Tennessee statute is unconstitutional insofar as it authorizes the use of deadly force against, as in this case, an apparently unarmed, nondangerous fleeing suspect; such force may not be used unless necessary to prevent the escape and the officer has probable cause to believe that the suspect poses a significant threat of death or serious physical injury to the officer or others.

(a) Apprehension by the use of deadly force is a seizure subject to the Fourth Amendment's reasonableness requirement. To determine whether such a seizure is reasonable, the extent of the intrusion on the suspect's rights under that Amendment must be balanced against the governmental interests

3

in effective law enforcement. This balancing process demonstrates that, notwithstanding probable cause to seize a suspect, an officer may not always do so by killing him. The use of deadly force to prevent the escape of all felony suspects, whatever the circumstances, is constitutionally unreasonable.

(b) The Fourth Amendment, for purposes of this case, should not be construed in light of the common-law rule allowing the use of whatever force is necessary to effect the arrest of a fleeing felon. Changes in the legal and technological context mean that that rule is distorted almost beyond recognition when literally applied. Whereas felonies were formerly capital crimes, few are now, or can be, and many crimes classified as misdemeanors, or non-existent, at common law are now felonies. Also, the common-law rule developed at a time when weapons were rudimentary. And, in light of the varied rules adopted in the

States indicating a long-term movement away from the common-law rule, particularly in the police departments themselves, that rule is a dubious indicium of the constitutionality of the Tennessee statute. There is no indication that holding a police practice such as that authorized by the statute unreasonable will severely hamper effective law enforcement.

(c) While burglary is a serious crime, the officer in this case could not reasonably have believed that the suspect—young, slight, and unarmed—posed any threat. Nor does the fact that an unarmed suspect has broken into a dwelling at night automatically mean he is dangerous.

710 F2d 240, affirmed and remanded.

White, J., delivered the opinion of the Court, in which Brennan, Marshall, Blackmun, Powell, and Stevens, JJ., joined. O'Connor, J., filed a dissenting opinion, in which Burger, C. J., and Rehnquist, J., joined.

APPEARANCES OF COUNSEL

Henry L. Klein argued the cause for petitioners in No. 83–1070.
W. J. Michael Cody argued the cause for appellant in No. 83–1035.
Steven L. Winter argued the cause for Cleamtee Garner, et al.
Briefs of Counsel, p 871, infra.

OPINION OF THE COURT

[471 US 3]
Justice **White** delivered the opinion of the Court.

[1a] This case requires us to determine the constitutionality of the use of deadly force to prevent the escape of an apparently unarmed suspected felon. We conclude that such force may not be used unless it is necessary to prevent the escape and the officer has probable cause to believe that the suspect poses a significant

threat of death or serious physical injury to the officer or others.

I

At about 10:45 p. m. on October 3, 1974, Memphis Police Officers Elton Hymon and Leslie Wright were dispatched to answer a "prowler inside call." Upon arriving at the scene they saw a woman standing on her porch and gesturing toward the adja-

TENNESSEE v GARNER
471 US 1, 85 L Ed 2d 1, 105 S Ct 1694

cent house.' She told them she had heard · glass breaking and that "they" or "someone" was breaking in next door. While Wright radioed the dispatcher to say that they were on the scene, Hyman went behind the house. He heard a door slam and saw someone run across the backyard. The fleeing suspect, who was appellee-respondent's decedent, Edward Garner, stopped at a 6-feet-high chain link fence at the edge of the yard. With the aid of a flashlight, Hyman was able to see Garner's face and hands. He saw no sign of a weapon, and, though not certain, was "reasonably sure" and "figured" that Garner was unarmed. App 41, 56; Record 219. He thought Garner was 17 or 18 years old and

[471 US 4]

about 5' 5" or 5' 7" tall.[2] While Garner was crouched at the base of the fence, Hymon called out "police, halt" and took a few steps toward him. Garner then began to climb over the fence. Convinced that if Garner made it over the fence he

would elude capture,[3] Hymon shot him. The bullet hit Garner in the back of the head. Garner was taken by ambulance to a hospital, where he died on the operating table. Ten dollars and a purse taken from the house were found on his body.[4]

In using deadly force to prevent the escape, Hymon was acting under the authority of a Tennessee statute and pursuant to Police Department policy. The statute provides that "[i]f, after notice of the intention to arrest the defendant, he either flee or forcibly resist, the officer may use all the necessary means to effect the arrest." Tenn Code Ann

[471 US 5]

§ 40-7-108 (1982).[5] The Department policy was slightly more restrictive than the statute, but still allowed the use of deadly force in cases of burglary. App 140–144. The incident was reviewed by the Memphis Police Firearm's Review Board and presented to a grand jury. Neither took any action. Id., at 57.

---

1. The owner of the house testified that no lights were on in the house, but that a back door light was on. Record 160. Officer Hymon, though uncertain, stated in his deposition that there were lights on in the house. Id., at 209.

2. In fact, Garner, an eighth-grader, was 15. He was 5' 4" tall and weighed somewhere around 100 or 110 pounds. App to Pet for Cert A5.

3. When asked at trial why he fired, Hymon stated:
"Well, first of all it was apparent to me from the little bit that I knew about the area at the time that he was going to get away because, number 1, I couldn't get to him. My partner then couldn't find where he was because, you know, he was late coming around. He didn't know where I was talking about. I couldn't get to him because of the fence here, I couldn't have jumped this fence and come up, consequently jumped this fence and caught him before he got away because he was already up on the fence, just one leap

and he was already over the fence, and so there is no way that I could have caught him." App 52.
He also stated that the area beyond the fence was dark, that he could not have gotten over the fence easily because he was carrying a lot of equipment and wearing heavy boots, and that Garner, being younger and more energetic, could have outrun him. Id., at 53–54.

4. Garner had rummaged through one room in the house, in which, in the words of the owner, "[a]ll the stuff was out on the floors, all the drawers was pulled out, and stuff was scattered all over." Id., at 34. The owner testified that his valuables were untouched but that, in addition to the purse and the 10 dollars, one of his wife's rings was missing. The ring was not recovered. Id., at 34–35.

5. Although the statute does not say so explicitly, Tennessee law forbids the use of deadly force in the arrest of a misdemeanant. See Johnson v State, 173 Tenn 134, 114 SW2d 819 (1938).

5

Garner's father then brought this action in the Federal District Court for the Western District of Tennessee, seeking damages under 42 USC § 1983 [42 USCS § 1983] for asserted violations of Garner's constitutional rights. The complaint alleged that the shooting violated the Fourth, Fifth, Sixth, Eighth, and Fourteenth Amendments of the United States Constitution. It named as defendants Officer Hymon, the Police Department, its Director, and the Mayor and city of Memphis. After a 3-day bench trial, the District Court entered judgment for all defendants. It dismissed the claims against the Mayor and the Director for lack of evidence. It then concluded that Hymon's actions were authorized by the Tennessee statute, which in turn was constitutional. Hymon had employed the only reasonable and practicable means of preventing Garner's escape. Garner had "recklessly and heedlessly attempted to vault over the fence to escape, thereby assuming the risk of being fired upon." App to Pet for Cert A10.

The Court of Appeals for the Sixth Circuit affirmed with regard to Hymon, finding that he had acted in good-faith reliance on the Tennessee statute and was therefore within the scope of his qualified immunity. 600 F2d 52 (1979). It remanded for reconsideration of the possible liability of the city, however, in light of Monell v New York City Dept. of Social Services, 436 US 658, 56 L Ed 2d 611, 98 S Ct 2018 (1978), which had come down after the District Court's decision. The District Court was

[471 US 6]

directed to consider whether a city enjoyed a qualified immunity, whether the use of deadly force and hollow point bullets in these circumstances was constitutional, and whether any unconstitutional municipal conduct flowed from a "policy or custom" as required for liability under Monell. 600 F2d, at 54–55.

The District Court concluded that Monell did not affect its decision. While acknowledging some doubt as to the possible immunity of the city, it found that the statute, and Hymon's actions, were constitutional. Given this conclusion, it declined to consider the "policy or custom" question. App to Pet for Cert A37–A39.

The Court of Appeals reversed and remanded. 710 F2d 240 (1983). It reasoned that the killing of a fleeing suspect is a "seizure" under the Fourth Amendment,[6] and is therefore constitutional only if "reasonable." The Tennessee statute failed as applied to this case because it did not adequately limit the use of deadly force by distinguishing between felonies of different magnitudes—"the facts, as found, did not justify the use of deadly force under the Fourth Amendment." Id., at 246. Officers cannot resort to deadly force unless they "have probable cause . . . to believe that the suspect [has committed a felony and] poses a threat to the safety of the officers or a danger to the community if left at large." Ibid.[7]

---

6. The right of the people to be secure in their persons . . . against unreasonable searches and seizures, shall not be violated . . . ." US Const, Amdt 4.

7. The Court of Appeals concluded that the rule set out in the Model Penal Code "accurately states Fourth Amendment limitations

on the use of deadly force against fleeing felons." 710 F2d, at 247. The relevant portion of the Model Penal Code provides:

"The use of deadly force is not justifiable . . . unless (i) the arrest is for a felony; and (ii) the person effecting the arrest is authorized to act as a peace officer or is assisting a person whom he believes to be authorized to

TENNESSEE v GARNER
471 US 1, 85 L Ed 2d 1, 105 S Ct 1694

[471 US 7]

The State of Tennessee, which had intervened to defend the statute, see 28 USC § 2403(b) [28 USCS § 2403(b)], appealed to this Court. The city filed a petition for certiorari. We noted probable jurisdiction in the appeal and granted the petition. 465 US 1098, 80 L Ed 2d 122, 104 S Ct 1589 (1984).

II

[2, 3] Whenever an officer restrains the freedom of a person to walk away, he has seized that person. United States v Brignoni-Ponce, 422 US 873, 878, 45 L Ed 2d 607, 95 S Ct 2574 (1975). While it is not always clear just when minimal police interference becomes a seizure, see United States v Mendenhall, 446 US 544, 64 L Ed 2d 497, 100 S Ct 1870 (1980), there can be no question that apprehension by the use of deadly force is a seizure subject to the reasonableness requirement of the Fourth Amendment.

A

[4] A police officer may arrest a person if he has probable cause to believe that person committed a crime. E.g., United States v Watson, 423 US 411, 46 L Ed 2d 598, 96 S Ct 820 (1976). Petitioners and appellant argue that if this requirement is

satisfied the Fourth Amendment has nothing to say about *how* that seizure is made. This submission ignores the many cases in which this Court, by balancing the extent of the intrusion against the need for it, has examined the reasonableness of

[471 US 8]

the manner in which a search or seizure is conducted. To determine the constitutionality of a seizure "[w]e must balance the nature and quality of the intrusion on the individual's Fourth Amendment interests against the importance of the governmental interests alleged to justify the intrusion." United States v Place, 462 US 696, 703, 77 L Ed 2d 110, 103 S Ct 2637 (1983); see Delaware v Prouse, 440 US 648, 654, 59 L Ed 2d 660, 99 S Ct 1391 (1979); United States v Martinez-Fuerte, 428 US 543, 555, 49 L Ed 2d 1116, 96 S Ct 3074 (1976). We have described "the balancing of competing interests" as "the key principle of the Fourth Amendment." Michigan v Summers, 452 US 692, 700, n 12, 69 L Ed 2d 340, 101 S Ct 2587 (1981). See also Camara v Municipal Court, 387 US 523, 536–537, 18 L Ed 2d 930, 87 S Ct 1727 (1967). Because one of the factors is the extent of the intrusion, it is plain that reasonableness depends on not only when a seizure is made, but also how it is

---

act as a peace officer; and (iii) the actor believes that the force employed creates no substantial risk of injury to innocent persons; and (iv) the actor believes that (1) the crime for which the arrest is made involved conduct including the use or threatened use of deadly force; or (2) there is a substantial risk that the person to be arrested will cause death or serious bodily harm if his apprehension is delayed." American Law Institute, Model Penal Code § 3.07(2)(b) (Proposed Official Draft 1962).

The court also found that "[a]n analysis of the facts of this case under the Due Process Clause" required the same result, because the statute was not narrowly drawn to further a compelling state interest. 710 F2d, at 246–247. The court considered the generalized interest in effective law enforcement sufficiently compelling only when the the suspect is dangerous. Finally, the court held, relying on Owen v City of Independence, 445 US 622, 63 L Ed 2d 673, 100 S Ct 1398 (1980), that the city was not immune.

carried out. United States v Ortiz, 422 US 891, 895, 45 L Ed 2d 623, 95 S Ct 2585 (1975); Terry v Ohio, 392 US 1, 28–29, 20 L Ed 2d 889, 88 S Ct 1868, 44 Ohio Ops 2d 383 (1968).

Applying these principles to particular facts, the Court has held that governmental interests did not support a lengthy detention of luggage, United States v Place, supra, an airport seizure not "carefully tailored to its underlying justification," Florida v Royer, 460 US 491, 500, 75 L Ed 2d 229, 103 S Ct 1319 (1983) (plurality opinion), surgery under general anesthesia to obtain evidence, Winston v Lee, 470 US 753, 84 L Ed 2d 662, 105 S Ct 1611 (1985), or detention for fingerprinting without probable cause, Davis v Mississippi, 394 US 721, 22 L Ed 2d 676, 89 S Ct 1394 (1969); Hayes v Florida, 470 US 811, 84 L Ed 2d 705, 105 S Ct 1643 (1985). On the other hand, under the same approach it has upheld the taking of fingernail scrapings from a suspect, Cupp v Murphy, 412 US 291, 36 L Ed 2d 900, 93 S Ct 2000 (1973), an unannounced entry into a home to prevent the destruction of evidence, Ker v California, 374 US 23, 10 L Ed 2d 726, 83 S Ct 1623, 24 Ohio Ops 2d 201 (1963), administrative housing inspections without probable cause to believe that a code violation will be found, Camara v Municipal Court, supra, and a blood test of a drunken-driving suspect, Schmerber v California, 384 US 757, 16 L Ed 2d 908, 86 S Ct 1826 (1966). In each of these cases, the question was whether

[471 US 9]

the totality of the circumstances justified a particular sort of search or seizure.

B

The same balancing process applied in the cases cited above demonstrates that, notwithstanding probable cause to seize a suspect, an officer may not always do so by killing him. The intrusiveness of a seizure by means of deadly force is unmatched. The suspect's fundamental interest in his own life need not be elaborated upon. The use of deadly force also frustrates the interest of the individual, and of society, in judicial determination of guilt and punishment. Against these interests are ranged governmental interests in effective law enforcement.[8] It is argued that overall violence will be reduced by encouraging the peaceful submission of suspects

---

8. The dissent emphasizes that subsequent investigation cannot replace immediate apprehension. We recognize that this is so, see n 13, infra; indeed, that is the reason why there is any dispute. If subsequent arrest were assured, no one would argue that use of deadly force was justified. Thus, we proceed on the assumption that subsequent arrest is not likely. Nonetheless, it should be remembered that failure to apprehend at the scene does not necessarily mean that the suspect will never be caught.

In lamenting the inadequacy of later investigation, the dissent relies on the report of the President's Commission on Law Enforcement and Administration of Justice. It is worth noting that, notwithstanding its awareness of this problem, the Commission itself proposed a policy for use of deadly force arguably even more stringent than the formulation we adopt today. See President's Commission on Law Enforcement and Administration of Justice, Task Force Report: The Police 189 (1967). The Commission proposed that deadly force be used only to apprehend "perpetrators who, in the course of their crime threatened the use of deadly force, or if the officer believes there is a substantial risk that the person whose arrest is sought will cause death or serious bodily harm if his apprehension is delayed." In addition, the officer would have "to know, as a virtual certainty, that the suspect committed an offense for which the use of deadly force is permissible." Ibid.

TENNESSEE v GARNER
471 US 1, 85 L Ed 2d 1, 105 S Ct 1694

who know that they may be shot if they flee. Effectiveness in making arrests requires the resort to deadly [471 US 10] force, or at least the meaningful threat thereof. "Being able to arrest such individuals is a condition precedent to the state's entire system of law enforcement." Brief for Petitioners 14.

Without in any way disparaging the importance of these goals, we are not convinced that the use of deadly force is a sufficiently productive means of accomplishing them to justify the killing of nonviolent suspects. Cf. Delaware v Prouse, supra, at 659, 59 L Ed 2d 660, 99 S Ct 1391. The use of deadly force is a self-defeating way of apprehending a suspect and so setting the criminal justice mechanism in motion. If successful, it guarantees that that mechanism will not be set in motion. And while the meaningful threat of deadly force might be thought to lead to the arrest of more live suspects by discouraging escape attempts,[9] the presently available evidence does not support this thesis.[10]

The fact is that a majority of police departments [471 US 11] in this country have forbidden the use of deadly force against nonviolent suspects. See infra, at 18-19, 85 L Ed 2d, at 14. If those charged with the enforcement of the criminal law have abjured the use of deadly force in arresting nondangerous felons, there is a substantial basis for doubting that the use of such force is an essential attribute of the arrest power in all felony cases. See Schumann v McGinn, 307 Minn 446, 472, 240 NW2d 525, 540 (1976) (Rogosheske, J., dissenting in part). Petitioners and appellant have not persuaded us that shooting nondangerous fleeing suspects is so vital as to outweigh the suspect's interest in his own life.

[1b] The use of deadly force to prevent the escape of all felony suspects, whatever the circumstances, is constitutionally unreasonable. It is not better that all felony suspects die than that they escape. Where the suspect poses no immediate threat to the officer and no threat to

---

9. We note that the usual manner of deterring illegal conduct—through punishment—has been largely ignored in connection with flight from arrest. Arkansas, for example, specifically excepts flight from arrest from the offense of "obstruction of governmental operations." The commentary notes that this "reflects the basic policy judgment that, absent the use of force or violence, a mere attempt to avoid apprehension by a law enforcement officer does not give rise to an independent offense." Ark Stat Ann § 41-2802(3)(a) (1977) and commentary. In the few States that do outlaw flight from an arresting officer, the crime is only a misdemeanor. See, e.g., Ind Code § 35-44-3-3 (1982). Even forceful resistance, though generally a separate offense, is classified as a misdemeanor. E.g., Ill Rev Stat, ch 38, ¶ 31-1 (1984); Mont Code Ann § 45-7-301 (1984); NH Rev Stat Ann § 642:2 (Supp 1983); Ore Rev Stat § 162.315 (1983).

This lenient approach does avoid the anomaly of automatically transforming every

fleeing misdemeanant into a fleeing felon—subject, under the common-law rule, to apprehension by deadly force—solely by virtue of his flight. However, it is in real tension with the harsh consequences of flight in cases where deadly force is employed. For example, Tennessee does not outlaw fleeing from arrest. The Memphis City Code does, § 22-34.1 (Supp 17, 1971), subjecting the offender to a maximum fine of $50, § 1-8 (1967). Thus, Garner's attempted escape subjected him to (a) a $50 fine, and (b) being shot.

10. See Sherman, Reducing Police Gun Use, in Control in the Police Organization 98, 120–123 (M. Punch, ed 1983); Fyfe, Observations on Police Deadly Force, 27 Crime & Delinquency 376, 378–381 (1981); W. Geller & K. Karales, Split-Second Decisions 67 (1981); App 84 (affidavit of William Bracey, Chief of Patrol, New York City Police Department). See generally Brief for Police Foundation et al. as Amici Curiae.

9

others, the harm resulting from failing to apprehend him does not justify the use of deadly force to do so. It is no doubt unfortunate when a suspect who is in sight escapes, but the fact that the police arrive a little late or are a little slower afoot does not always justify killing the suspect. A police officer may not seize an unarmed, nondangerous suspect by shooting him dead. The Tennessee statute is unconstitutional insofar as it authorizes the use of deadly force against such fleeing suspects.

It is not, however, unconstitutional on its face. Where the officer has probable cause to believe that the suspect poses a threat of serious physical harm, either to the officer or to others, it is not constitutionally unreasonable to prevent escape by using deadly force. Thus, if the suspect threatens the officer with a weapon or there is probable cause to believe that he has committed a crime involving the infliction or threatened infliction of serious physical harm, deadly force may be used if necessary to prevent escape, and if, where

[471 US 12]

feasible, some warning has been given. As applied in such circumstances, the Tennessee statute would pass constitutional muster.

III

A

It is insisted that the Fourth Amendment must be construed in light of the common-law rule, which allowed the use of whatever force was necessary to effect the arrest of a fleeing felon, though not a misdemeanant. As stated in Hale's posthumously published Pleas of the Crown:

"[I]f persons that are pursued by

10

these officers for felony or the just suspicion thereof . . . shall not yield themselves to these officers, but shall either resist or fly before they are apprehended or being apprehended shall rescue themselves and resist or fly, so that they cannot be otherwise apprehended, and are upon necessity slain therein, because they cannot be otherwise taken, it is no felony." 2 M. Hale, Historia Placitorum Coronae 85 (1736).

See also 4 W. Blackstone, Commentaries *289. Most American jurisdictions also imposed a flat prohibition against the use of deadly force to stop a fleeing misdemeanant, coupled with a general privilege to use such force to stop a fleeing felon. E.g., Holloway v Moser, 193 NC 185, 136 SE 375 (1927); State v Smith, 127 Iowa 534, 535, 103 NW 944, 945 (1905); Reneau v State, 70 Tenn 720 (1879); Brooks v Commonwealth, 61 Pa 352 (1869); Roberts v State, 14 Mo 138 (1851); see generally R. Perkins & R. Boyce, Criminal Law 1098–1102 (3d ed 1982); Day, Shooting the Fleeing Felon: State of the Law, 14 Crim L Bull 285, 286–287 (1978); Wilgus, Arrest Without a Warrant, 22 Mich L Rev 798, 807–816 (1924). But see Storey v State, 71 Ala 329 (1882); State v Bryant, 65 NC 327, 328 (1871); Caldwell v State, 41 Tex 86 (1874).

[471 US 13]

The State and city argue that because this was the prevailing rule at the time of the adoption of the Fourth Amendment and for some time thereafter, and is still in force in some States, use of deadly force against a fleeing felon must be "reasonable." It is true that this Court has often looked to the common law in evaluating the reasonableness, for

TENNESSEE v GARNER
471 US 1, 85 L Ed 2d 1, 105 S Ct 1694

Fourth Amendment purposes, of police activity. See, e.g., United States v Watson, 423 US 411, 418–419, 46 L Ed 2d 598, 96 S Ct 820 (1976); Gerstein v Pugh, 420 US 103, 111, 114, 43 L Ed 2d 54, 95 S Ct 854 (1975); Carroll v United States, 267 US 132, 149–153, 69 L Ed 543, 45 S Ct 280, 39 ALR 790 (1925). On the other hand, it "has not simply frozen into constitutional law those law enforcement practices that existed at the time of the Fourth Amendment's passage." Payton v New York, 445 US 573, 591, n 33, 63 L Ed 2d 639, 100 S Ct 1371 (1980). Because of sweeping change in the legal and technological context, reliance on the common-law rule in this case would be a mistaken literalism that ignores the purposes of a historical inquiry.

B

It has been pointed out many times that the common-law rule is best understood in light of the fact that it arose at a time when virtually all felonies were punishable by death.[11] "Though effected without the protections and formalities of an orderly trial and conviction, the killing of a resisting or

[471 US 14]

fleeing felon resulted in no greater consequences than those authorized for punishment of the felony of which the individual was charged or sus-

pected." American Law Institute, Model Penal Code § 3.07, Comment 3, p. 56 (Tentative Draft No. 8, 1958) (hereinafter Model Penal Code Comment). Courts have also justified the common-law rule by emphasizing the relative dangerousness of felons. See, e.g., Schumann v McGinn, 307 Minn, at 458, 240 NW2d, at 533; Holloway v Moser, supra, at 187, 136 SE, at 376 (1927).

Neither of these justifications makes sense today. Almost all crimes formerly punishable by death no longer are or can be. See, e.g., Enmund v Florida, 458 US 782, 73 L Ed 2d 1140, 102 S Ct 3368 (1982); Coker v Georgia, 433 US 584, 53 L Ed 2d 982, 97 S Ct 2861 (1977). And while in earlier times "the gulf between the felonies and the minor offences was broad and deep," 2 Pollock & Maitland 467, n 3; Carroll v United States, supra, at 158, 69 L Ed 543, 45 S Ct 280, 39 ALR 790, today the distinction is minor and often arbitrary. Many crimes classified as misdemeanors, or nonexistent, at common law are now felonies. Wilgus, 22 Mich L Rev, at 572–573. These changes have undermined the concept, which was questionable to begin with, that use of deadly force against a fleeing felon is merely a speedier execution of someone who has already forfeited his life. They have also made the assumption that a "felon" is more dangerous than a misdemeanant untenable. Indeed,

---

11. The roots of the concept of a "felony" lie not in capital punishment but in forfeiture. 2 F. Pollock & F. Maitland, The History of English Law 465 (2d ed 1909) (hereinafter Pollock & Maitland). Not all felonies were always punishable by death. See id., at 466–467, n 3. Nonetheless, the link was profound. Blackstone was able to write: "The idea of felony is indeed so generally connected with that of capital punishment, that we find it

hard to separate them; and to this usage the interpretations of the law do not conform. And therefore if a statute makes any new offence felony, the law implies that is shall be punished with death, viz. by hanging, as well as with forfeiture . . . ." 4 W. Blackstone, Commentaries *98. See also R. Perkins & R. Boyce, Criminal Law 14–15 (3d ed 1982); 2 Pollock & Maitland 511.

11

numerous misdemeanors involve conduct more dangerous than many felonies.[12]

There is an additional reason why the common-law rule cannot be directly translated to the present day. The common-law rule developed at a time when weapons were rudimentary. Deadly force could be inflicted almost solely in a hand-to-hand struggle during which, necessarily, the safety

[471 US 15]

of the arresting officer was at risk. Handguns were not carried by police officers until the latter half of the last century. L. Kennett & J. Anderson, The Gun in America 150–151 (1975). Only then did it become possible to use deadly force from a distance as a means of apprehension. As a practical matter, the use of deadly force under the standard articulation of the common-law rule has an altogether different meaning—and harsher consequences —now than in past centuries. See Wechsler & Michael, A Rationale for the Law of Homicide: I, 37 Colum L Rev 701, 741 (1937).[13]

One other aspect of the common-

law rule bears emphasis. It forbids the use of deadly force to apprehend a misdemeanant, condemning such action as disproportionately severe. See Holloway v Moser, 193 NC, at 187, 136 SE, at 376; State v Smith, 127 Iowa, at 535, 103 NW, at 945. See generally Annot, 83 ALR3d 238 (1978).

In short, though the common-law pedigree of Tennessee's rule is pure on its face, changes in the legal and technological context mean the rule is distorted almost beyond recognition when literally applied.

C

In evaluating the reasonableness of police procedures under the Fourth Amendment, we have also looked to prevailing

[471 US 16]

rules in individual jurisdictions. See, e.g., United States v Watson, 423 US, at 421–422, 46 L Ed 2d 598, 96 S Ct 820. The rules in the States are varied. See generally Comment, 18 Ga L Rev 137, 140–144 (1983). Some 19 States have codified the common-law rule,[14]

---

12. White-collar crime, for example, poses a less significant physical threat than, say, drunken driving. See Welsh v Wisconsin, 466 US 740, 80 L Ed 2d 732, 104 S Ct 2091 (1984); id., at 755, 80 L Ed 2d 732, 104 S Ct 2091 (Blackmun, J., concurring). See Model Penal Code Comment, at 57.

13. It has been argued that sophisticated techniques of apprehension and increased communication between the police in different jurisdictions have made it more likely that an escapee will be caught than was once the case, and that this change has also reduced the "reasonableness" of the use of deadly force to prevent escape. E.g., Sherman, Execution Without Trial: Police Homicide and the Constitution, 33 Vand L Rev 71, 76 (1980). We are unaware of any data that would permit sensible evaluation of this claim. Current arrest rates are sufficiently low, however, that we have some doubt whether in past centuries the failure to arrest at the scene meant

that the police had missed their only chance in a way that is not presently the case. In 1983, 21% of the offenses in the Federal Bureau of Investigation crime index were cleared by arrest. Federal Bureau of Investigation, Uniform Crime Reports, Crime in the United States 159 (1984). The clearance rate for burglary was 15%. Ibid.

14. Ala Code § 13A-3-27 (1982); Ark Stat Ann § 41-510 (1977); Cal Penal Code Ann § 196 (West 1970); Conn Gen Stat § 53a-22 (1972); Fla Stat § 776.05 (1983); Idaho Code § 19-610 (1979); Ind Code § 35-41-3-3 (1982); Kan Stat Ann § 21-3215 (1981); Miss Code Ann § 97-3-15(d) (Supp 1984); Mo Rev Stat § 563.046 (1979); Nev Rev Stat § 200.140 (1983); NM Stat Ann § 30-2-6 (1984); Okla Stat, Tit 21, § 732 (1981); RI Gen Laws § 12-7-9 (1981); SD Codified Laws §§ 22-16-32, 22-16-33 (1979); Tenn Code Ann § 40-7-108 (1982); Wash Rev Code § 9A.16.040(3) (1977). Oregon limits use of deadly force to violent felons, but

TENNESSEE v GARNER
471 US 1, 85 L Ed 2d 1, 105 S Ct 1694

though in two of these the courts have significantly limited the statute.[15] Four States, though without a relevant statute, apparently retain the common-law rule.[16] Two States have adopted the Model Penal Code's

[471 US 17]

provision verbatim.[17] Eighteen others allow, in slightly varying language, the use of deadly force only if the suspect has committed a felony involving the use or threat of physical or deadly force, or is escaping with a deadly weapon, or is likely to endanger life or inflict serious physical injury if not arrested.[18] Louisiana and Vermont, though without statutes or case law on point, do forbid the use of deadly force to prevent any but violent felonies.[19] The remaining States either have no relevant statute or case-law, or have positions that are unclear.[20]

---

also allows its use against any felon if "necessary." Ore Rev Stat § 161.239 (1983). Wisconsin's statute is ambiguous, but should probably be added to this list. Wis Stat § 939.45(4) (1981–1982) (officer may use force necessary for "a reasonable accomplishment of a lawful arrest"). But see Clark v Ziedonis, 368 F Supp 544 (ED Wis 1973), aff'd on other grounds, 513 F2d 79 (CA7 1975).

15. In California, the police may use deadly force to arrest only if the crime for which the arrest is sought was "a forcible and atrocious one which threatens death or serious bodily harm," or there is a substantial risk that the person whose arrest is sought will cause death or serious bodily harm if apprehension is delayed. Kortum v Alkire, 69 Cal App 3d 325, 333, 138 Cal Rptr 26, 30–31 (1977). See also People v Ceballos, 12 Cal 3d 470, 476–484, 526 P2d 241, 245–250 (1974); Long Beach Police Officers Assn v Long Beach, 61 Cal App 3d 364, 373–374, 132 Cal Rptr 348, 353–354 (1976). In Indiana, deadly force may be used only to prevent injury, the imminent danger of injury or force, or the threat of force. It is not permitted simply to prevent escape. Rose v State, 431 NE2d 521 (Ind App 1982).

16. These are Michigan, Ohio, Virginia, and West Virginia. Werner v Hartfelder, 113 Mich App 747, 318 NW2d 825 (1982); State v Foster, 60 Ohio Misc 46, 59–66, 396 NE2d 246, 255–258 (Com Pl 1979) (citing cases); Berry v Hamman, 203 Va 596, 125 SE2d 851 (1962); Thompson v Norfolk & W. R. Co. 116 W Va 705, 711–712, 182 SE 880, 883–884 (1935).

17. Haw Rev Stat § 703-307 (1976); Neb Rev Stat § 28-1412 (1979). Massachusetts probably belongs in this category. Though it once rejected distinctions between felonies, Uraneck v Lima, 359 Mass 749, 750, 269 NE2d 670, 671 (1971), it has since adopted the Model Penal Code limitations with regard to private citizens, Commonwealth v Klein, 372 Mass 823, 363 NE2d 1313 (1977), and seems to have extended that decision to police officers, Ju-

lian v Randazzo, 380 Mass 391, 403 NE2d 931 (1980).

18. Alaska Stat Ann § 11.81.370(a) (1983); Ariz Rev Stat Ann § 13-410 (1978); Colo Rev Stat § 18-1-707 (1978); Del Code Ann, Tit 11, § 467 (1979) (felony involving physical force *and* a substantial risk that the suspect will cause death or serious bodily injury *or* will never be recaptured); Ga Code § 16-3-21(a) (1984); Ill Rev Stat, ch 38, ¶ 7-5 (1984); Iowa Code § 804.8 (1983) (suspect has used or threatened deadly force in commission of a felony, or would use deadly force if not caught; Ky Rev Stat § 503.090 (1984) (suspect committed felony involving use *or* threat of physical force likely to cause death or serious injury, *and* is likely to endanger life unless apprehended without delay); Me Rev Stat Ann, Tit 17-A, § 107 (1983) (commentary notes that deadly force may be used only "where the person to be arrested poses a threat to human life"); Minn Stat § 609.066 (1984); NH Rev Stat Ann § 627:5(II) (Supp 1983); NJ Stat Ann § 2C-3-7 (West 1982); NY Penal Law § 35.30 (McKinney Supp 1984–1985); NC Gen Stat § 15A-401 (1983); ND Cent Code § 12.1-05-07.2.d (1976); 18 Pa Cons Stat § 508 (1982); Tex Penal Code Ann § 9.51(c) (1974); Utah Code Ann § 76-2-404 (1978).

19. See La Rev Stat Ann § 14:20(2) (West 1974); Vt Stat Ann, Tit 13, § 2305 (1974 and Supp 1984). A Federal District Court has interpreted the Louisiana statute to limit the use of deadly force against fleeing suspects to situations where "life itself is endangered or great bodily harm is threatened." Sauls v Hutto, 304 F Supp 124, 132 (ED La 1969).

20. These are Maryland, Montana, South Carolina, and Wyoming. A Maryland appellate court has indicated, however, that deadly force may not be used against a felon who "was in the process of fleeing and, at the time, presented no immediate danger to . . . anyone . . . ." Giant Food, Inc. v Scherry, 51 Md App 586, 589, 596, 444 A2d 483, 486, 489 (1982).

13

[471 US 18]

It cannot be said that there is a constant or overwhelming trend away from the common-law rule. In recent years, some States have reviewed their laws and expressly rejected abandonment of the common-law rule.[21] Nonetheless, the long-term movement has been away from the rule that deadly force may be used against any fleeing felon, and that remains the rule in less than half the States.

This trend is more evident and impressive when viewed in light of the policies adopted by the police departments themselves. Overwhelmingly, these are more restrictive than the common-law rule. C. Milton, J. Halleck, J. Lardner, & G. Abrecht, Police Use of Deadly Force 45–46 (1977). The Federal Bureau of Investigation and the New York City Police Department, for example, both forbid the use of firearms except when necessary to prevent death or grievous bodily harm. Id., at 40–41; App 83. For accreditation by the Commission on Accreditation for Law Enforcement Agencies, a department must restrict the use of deadly force to situations where "the officer reasonably believes that the action is in defense of human life . . . or in defense of any person in immediate danger of serious physical injury." Commission on Accreditation for Law Enforcement Agencies, Inc., Standards for Law Enforcement Agencies 1–2 (1983) (italics deleted). A 1974 study reported that the police department regula-

tions in a majority of the large cities of the United States allowed the firing of a weapon only when a

[471 US 19]

felon presented a threat of death or serious bodily harm. Boston Police Department, Planning & Research Division, The Use of Deadly Force by Boston Police Personnel (1974), cited in Mattis v Schnarr, 547 F2d 1007, 1016, n 19 (CA8 1976), vacated as moot sub nom. Ashcroft v Mattis, 431 US 171, 52 L Ed 2d 219, 97 S Ct 1739 (1977). Overall, only 7.5% of departmental and municipal policies explicitly permit the use of deadly force against any felon; 86.8% explicitly do not. K. Matulia, A Balance of Forces: A Report of the International Association of Chiefs of Police 161 (1982) (table). See also Record 1108–1368 (written policies of 44 departments). See generally W. Geller & K. Karales, Split-Second Decisions 33–42 (1981); Brief for Police Foundation et al. as Amici Curiae. In light of the rules adopted by those who must actually administer them, the older and fading common-law view is a dubious indicium of the constitutionality of the Tennessee statute now before us.

D

Actual departmental policies are important for an additional reason. We would hesitate to declare a police practice of long standing "unreasonable" if doing so would severely hamper effective law enforcement.

---

21. In adopting its current statute in 1979, for example, Alabama expressly chose the common-law rule over more restrictive provisions. Ala Code § 13A-3-27, Commentary, pp 67–68 (1982). Missouri likewise considered but rejected a proposal akin to the Model Penal Code rule. See Mattis v Schnarr, 547 F2d

1007, 1022 (CA8 1976) (Gibson, C. J., dissenting), vacated as moot sub nom Ashcroft v Mattis, 431 US 171, 52 L Ed 2d 219, 97 S Ct 1739 (1977). Idaho, whose current statute codifies the common-law rule, adopted the Model Penal Code in 1971, but abandoned it in 1972.

TENNESSEE v GARNER
471 US 1, 85 L Ed 2d 1, 105 S Ct 1694

But the indications are to the contrary. There has been no suggestion that crime has worsened in any way in jurisdictions that have adopted, by legislation or departmental policy, rules similar to that announced today. Amici note that "[a]fter extensive research and consideration, [they] have concluded that laws permitting police officers to use deadly force to apprehend unarmed, non-violent fleeing felony suspects actually do not protect citizens or law enforcement officers, do not deter crime or alleviate problems caused by crime, and do not improve the crime-fighting ability of law enforcement agencies." Id., at 11. The submission is that the obvious state interests in apprehension are not sufficiently served to warrant the use of lethal weapons against all fleeing felons. See supra, at 10-11, 85 L Ed 2d, at 9, and n 10.

[471 US 20]

Nor do we agree with petitioners and appellant that the rule we have adopted requires the police to make impossible, split-second evaluations of unknowable facts. See Brief for Petitioners 25; Brief for Appellant 11. We do not deny the practical difficulties of attempting to assess the suspect's dangerousness. However, similarly difficult judgments must be made by the police in equally uncertain circumstances. See, e.g., Terry v Ohio, 392 US, at 20, 27, 20 L Ed 2d 889, 88 S Ct 1868, 44 Ohio Ops 2d 383. Nor is there any indication that in States that allow the use of deadly force only against dangerous suspects, see nn 15, 17–19, supra, the standard has been difficult to apply or has led to a rash of litigation involving inappropriate second-guessing of police officers' split-second decisions. Moreover, the highly technical felony/

misdemeanor distinction is equally, if not more, difficult to apply in the field. An officer is in no position to know, for example, the precise value of property stolen, or whether the crime was a first or second offense. Finally, as noted above, this claim must be viewed with suspicion in light of the similar self-imposed limitations of so many police departments.

IV

The District Court concluded that Hymon was justified in shooting Garner because state law allows, and the Federal Constitution does not forbid, the use of deadly force to prevent the escape of a fleeing felony suspect if no alternative means of apprehension is available. See App to Pet for Cert A9–A11, A38. This conclusion made a determination of Garner's apparent dangerousness unnecessary. The court did find, however, that Garner appeared to be unarmed, though Hymon could not be certain that was the case. Id., at A4, A23. See also App 41, 56; Record 219. Restated in Fourth Amendment terms, this means Hymon had no articulable basis to think Garner was armed.

In reversing, the Court of Appeals accepted the District Court's factual conclusions and held that "the facts, as found, did not justify the use of deadly force." 710 F2d, at 246.

[471 US 21]

We agree. Officer Hymon could not reasonably have believed that Garner—young, slight, and unarmed—posed any threat. Indeed, Hymon never attempted to justify his actions on any basis other than the need to prevent an escape. The District Court stated in passing that "[t]he

15

facts of this case did not indicate to Officer Hymon that Garner was 'non-dangerous.' " App to Pet for Cert A34. This conclusion is not explained, and seems to be based solely on the fact that Garner had broken into a house at night. However, the fact that Garner was a suspected burglar could not, without regard to the other circumstances, automatically justify the use of deadly force. Hymon did not have probable cause to believe that Garner, whom he correctedly believed to be unarmed, posed any physical danger to himself or others.

The dissent argues that the shooting was justified by the fact that Officer Hymon had probable cause to believe that Garner had committed a nighttime burglary. Post, at 29, 32, 85 L Ed 2d, at 21, 23. While we agree that burglary is a serious crime, we cannot agree that it is so dangerous as automatically to justify the use of deadly force. The FBI classifies burglary as a "property" rather than a "violent" crime. See Federal Bureau of Investigation, Uniform Crime Reports, Crime in the United States 1 (1984).[22] Although the armed burglar would present a different situation, the fact that an unarmed suspect has broken into a dwelling at night does not automatically mean he is physically

dangerous. This case demonstrates as much. See also Solem v Helm, 463 US 277, 296–297, and nn 22–23, 77 L Ed 2d 637, 103 S Ct 3001 (1983). In fact, the available statistics demonstrate that burglaries only rarely involve physical violence. During the 10-year period from 1973–1982, only 3.8% of all burglaries involved violent crime. Bureau of Justice Statistics, Household

[471 US 22]

Burglary 4 (1985).[23] See also T. Reppetto, Residential Crime 17, 105 (1974); Conklin & Bittner, Burglary in a Suburb, 11 Criminology 208, 214 (1973).

V

[1c] We wish to make clear what our holding means in the context of this case. The complaint has been dismissed as to all the individual defendants. The State is a party only by virtue of 28 USC § 2403(b) [28 USCS § 2403(b)] and is not subject to liability. The possible liability of the remaining defendants—the Police Department and the city of Memphis —hinges on Monell v New York City Dept. of Social Services, 436 US 658, 56 L Ed 2d 611, 98 S Ct 2018 (1978), and is left for remand. We hold that the statute is invalid insofar as it purported to give Hymon the authority to act as he did. As for the

---

22. In a recent report, the Department of Corrections of the District of Columbia also noted that "there is nothing inherently dangerous or violent about the offense," which is a crime against property. D. C. Department of Corrections, Prisoner Screening Project 2 (1985).

23. The dissent points out that three-fifths of all rapes in the home, three-fifths of all home robberies, and about a third of home assaults are committed by burglars. Post, at 26-27, 85 L Ed 2d, at 19. These figures mean only that if one knows that a suspect committed a rape in the home, there is a good chance

that the suspect is also a burglar. That has nothing to do with the question here, which is whether the fact that someone has committed a burglary indicates that he has committed, or might commit, a violent crime.

The dissent also points out that this 3.8% adds up to 2.8 million violent crimes over a 10-year period, as if to imply that today's holding will let loose 2.8 million violent burglars. The relevant universe is, of course, far smaller. At issue is only that tiny fraction of cases where violence has taken place and an officer who has no other means of apprehending the suspect is unaware of its occurrence.

TENNESSEE v GARNER
471 US 1, 85 L Ed 2d 1, 105 S Ct 1694

policy of the Police Department, the absence of any discussion of this issue by the courts below, and the uncertain state of the record, preclude any, consideration of its validity.

The judgment of the Court of Appeals is affirmed, and the case is remanded for further proceedings consistent with this opinion.

So ordered.

SEPARATE OPINION

Justice **O'Connor,** with whom The **Chief Justice** and Justice **Rehnquist** join, dissenting.

The Court today holds that the Fourth Amendment prohibits a police officer from using deadly force as a last resort to
[471 US 23]
apprehend a criminal suspect who refuses to halt when fleeing the scene of a nighttime burglary. This conclusion rests on the majority's balancing of the interests of the suspect and the public interest in effective law enforcement. Ante, at 8, 85 L Ed 2d, at 7. Notwithstanding the venerable common-law rule authorizing the use of deadly force if necessary to apprehend a fleeing felon, and continued acceptance of this rule by nearly half the States, ante, at 14, 16-17, 85 L Ed 2d, at 11, 12-13, the majority concludes that Tennessee's statute is unconstitutional inasmuch as it allows the use of such force to apprehend a burglary suspect who is not obviously armed or otherwise dangerous. Although the circumstances of this case are unquestionably tragic and unfortunate, our constitutional holdings must be sensitive both to the history of the Fourth Amendment and to the general implications of the Court's reasoning. By disregarding the serious and dangerous nature of residential burglaries and the longstanding practice of many States, the Court effectively creates a Fourth Amendment right allowing a burglary suspect to flee unimpeded from a police officer who

has probable cause to arrest, who has ordered the suspect to halt, and who has no means short of firing his weapon to prevent escape. I do not believe that the Fourth Amendment supports such a right, and I accordingly dissent.

I

The facts below warrant brief review because they highlight the difficult, split-second decisions police officers must make in these circumstances. Memphis Police Officers Elton Hymon and Leslie Wright responded to a late-night call that a burglary was in progress at a private residence. When the officers arrived at the scene, the caller said that "they" were breaking into the house next door. App in No. 81-5605 (CA6), p 207. The officers found the residence had been forcibly entered through a window and saw lights
[471 US 24]
on inside the house. Officer Hymon testified that when he saw the broken window he realized "that something was wrong inside," id., at 656, but that he could not determine whether anyone-either a burglar or a member of the household—was within the residence. Id., at 209. As Officer Hymon walked behind the house, he heard a door slam. He saw Edward Eugene Garner run away from the house through the dark and cluttered backyard. Garner crouched next to a 6-foot-high fence. Officer Hymon thought Garner was an adult and was unsure whether Gar-

17

ner was armed because Hymon "had no idea what was in the hand [that he could not see] or what he might have had on his person." Id., at 658–659. In fact, Garner was 15 years old and unarmed. Hymon also did not know whether accomplices remained inside the house. Id., at 657. The officer identified himself as a police officer and ordered Garner to halt. Garner paused briefly and then sprang to the top of the fence. Believing that Garner would escape if he climbed over the fence, Hymon fired his revolver and mortally wounded the suspected burglar.

Appellee-respondent, the deceased's father, filed a 42 USC § 1983 [42 USCS § 1983] action in federal court against Hymon, the city of Memphis, and other defendants, for asserted violations of Garner's constitutional rights. The District Court for the Western District of Tennessee held that Officer Hymon's actions were justified by a Tennessee statute that authorizes a police officer to "use all the necessary means to effect the arrest," if "after notice of the intention to arrest the defendant, he either flee or forcibly resist." Tenn Code Ann § 40-7-108 (1982). As construed by the Tennessee courts, this statute allows the use of deadly force only if a police officer has probable cause to believe that a person has committed a felony, the officer warns the person that he intends to arrest him, and the officer reasonably believes that no means less than such force will prevent the escape. See, e.g., Johnson v State, 173 Tenn 134, 114 SW2d 819

[471 US 25]

(1938). The District Court held that the Tennessee statute is constitutional and that Hymon's actions as authorized by that statute did not

18

violate Garner's constitutional rights. The Court of Appeals for the Sixth Circuit reversed on the grounds that the Tennessee statute "authorizing the killing of an unarmed, nonviolent fleeing felon by police in order to prevent escape" violates the Fourth Amendment and the Due Process Clause of the Fourteenth Amendment. 710 F2d 240, 244 (1983).

The Court affirms on the ground that application of the Tennessee statute to authorize Officer Hymon's use of deadly force constituted an unreasonable seizure in violation of the Fourth Amendment. The precise issue before the Court deserves emphasis, because both the decision below and the majority obscure what must be decided in this case. The issue is not the constitutional validity of the Tennessee statute on its face or as applied to some hypothetical set of facts. Instead, the issue is whether the use of deadly force by Officer Hymon under the circumstances of this case violated Garner's constitutional rights. Thus, the majority's assertion that a police officer who has probable cause to seize a suspect "may not always do so by killing him," ante, at 9, 85 L Ed 2d, at 8, is unexceptionable but also of little relevance to the question presented here. The same is true of the rhetorically stirring statement that "[t]he use of deadly force to prevent the escape of all felony suspects, whatever the circumstances, is constitutionally unreasonable." Ante, at 11, 85 L Ed 2d, at 9. The question we must address is whether the Constitution allows the use of such force to apprehend a suspect who resists arrest by attempting to flee the scene of a nighttime burglary of a residence.

TENNESSEE v GARNER
471 US 1, 85 L Ed 2d 1, 105 S Ct 1694

II

For purposes of Fourth Amendment analysis, I agree with the Court that Officer Hymon "seized" Garner by shooting him. Whether that seizure was reasonable and therefore permitted by the Fourth Amendment requires a careful balancing

[471 US 26]

of the important public interest in crime prevention and detection and the nature and quality of the intrusion upon legitimate interests of the individual. United States v Place, 462 US 696, 703, 77 L Ed 2d 110, 103 S Ct 2637 (1983). In striking this balance here, it is crucial to acknowledge that police use of deadly force to apprehend a fleeing criminal suspect falls within the "rubric of police conduct . . . necessarily [involving] swift action predicated upon the on-the-spot observations of the officer on the beat." Terry v Ohio, 392 US 1, 20, 20 L Ed 2d 889, 88 S Ct 1868, 44 Ohio Ops 2d 383 (1968). The clarity of hindsight cannot provide the standard for judging the reasonableness of police decisions made in uncertain and often dangerous circumstances. Moreover, I am far more reluctant than is the Court to conclude that the Fourth Amendment proscribes a police practice that was accepted at the time of the adoption of the Bill of Rights and has continued to receive the support of many state legislatures. Although the Court has recognized that the requirements of the Fourth Amendment must respond to the reality of social and technological change, fidelity to the notion of *constitutional*—as opposed to purely judicial—limits on governmental action requires us to impose a heavy burden on those who claim that practices accepted when the Fourth Amendment was adopted are now

constitutionally impermissible. See, e.g., United States v Watson, 423 US 411, 416–421, 46 L Ed 2d 598, 96 S Ct 820 (1976); Carroll v United States, 267 US 132, 149–153, 69 L Ed 543, 45 S Ct 280, 39 ALR 790 (1925). Cf. United States v Villamonte-Marquez, 462 US 579, 585, 77 L Ed 2d 22, 103 S Ct 2573 (1983) (noting "impressive historical pedigree" of statute challenged under Fourth Amendment).

The public interest involved in the use of deadly force as a last resort to apprehend a fleeing burglary suspect relates primarily to the serious nature of the crime. Household burglaries represent not only the illegal entry into a person's home, but also "pos[e] real risk of serious harm to others." Solem v Helm, 463 US 277, 315–316, 77 L Ed 2d 637, 103 S Ct 3001 (1983) (Burger, C.J., dissenting). According to recent Department of Justice statistics, "[t]hree-fifths of all rapes in the home,

[471 US 27]

three-fifths of all home robberies, and about a third of home aggravated and simple assaults are committed by burglars." Bureau of Justice Statistics Bulletin, Household Burglary 1 (January 1985). During the period 1973–1982, 2.8 million such violent crimes were committed in the course of burglaries. Ibid. Victims of a forcible intrusion into their home by a nighttime prowler will find little consolation in the majority's confident assertion that "burglaries only rarely involve physical violence." Ante, at 21, 85 L Ed 2d, at 16. Moreover, even if a particular burglary, when viewed in retrospect, does not involve physical harm to others, the "harsh potentialities for violence" inherent in the forced entry into a home preclude characterization of the crime as "in-

19

nocuous, inconsequential, minor, or 'nonviolent.' " Solem v Helm, supra, at 316, 77 L Ed 2d 637, 103 S Ct 3001 (Burger, C. J., dissenting). See also Restatement of Torts § 131, Comment g (1934) (burglary is among felonies that normally cause or threaten death or serious bodily harm); R. Perkins & R. Boyce, Criminal Law 1110 (3d ed 1982) (burglary is dangerous felony that creates unreasonable risk of great personal harm).

Because burglary is a serious and dangerous felony, the public interest in the prevention and detection of the crime is of compelling importance. Where a police officer has probable cause to arrest a suspected burglar, the use of deadly force as a last resort might well be the only means of apprehending the suspect. With respect to a particular burglary, subsequent investigation simply cannot represent a substitute for immediate apprehension of the criminal suspect at the scene. See President's Commission on Law Enforcement and Administration of Justice, Task Force Report: The Challenge of Crime in a Free Society 97 (1967). Indeed, the Captain of the Memphis Police Department testified that in his city, if apprehension is not immediate, it is likely that the suspect will not be caught. App in No. 81-5605 (CA6), p 334. Although some law enforcement agencies may choose to assume the risk that a criminal will remain at large, the

[471 US 28]

Tennessee statute reflects a legislative determination that the use of deadly force in prescribed circumstances will serve generally to protect the public. Such statutes assist the police in apprehending suspected perpetrators of serious crimes and provide notice that

a lawful police order to stop and submit to arrest may not be ignored with impunity. See, e.g., Wiley v Memphis Police Department, 548 F2d 1247, 1252-1253 (CA6), cert denied, 434 US 822, 54 L Ed 2d 78, 98 S Ct 65 (1977); Jones v Marshall, 528 F2d 132, 142 (CA2 1975).

The Court unconvincingly dismisses the general deterrence effects by stating that "the presently available evidence does not support [the] thesis" that the threat of force discourages escape and that "there is a substantial basis for doubting that the use of such force is an essential attribute to the arrest power in all felony cases." Ante, at 10, 11, 85 L Ed 2d, at 9. There is no question that the effectiveness of police use of deadly force is arguable and that many States or individual police departments have decided not to authorize it in circumstances similar to those presented here. But it should go without saying that the effectiveness or popularity of a particular police practice does not determine its constitutionality. Cf. Spaziano v Florida, 468 US 447, 464, 82 L Ed 2d 340, 104 S Ct 3154 (1984) ("The Eighth Amendment is not violated every time a State reaches a conclusion different from a majority of its sisters over how best to administer its criminal laws"). Moreover, the fact that police conduct pursuant to a state statute is challenged on constitutional grounds does not impose a burden on the State to produce social science statistics or to dispel any possible doubts about the necessity of the conduct. This observation, I believe, has particular force where the challenged practice both predates enactment of the Bill of Rights and continues to be accepted by a substantial number of the States.

TENNESSEE v GARNER
471 US 1, 85 L Ed 2d 1, 105 S Ct 1694

Against the strong public interests justifying the conduct at issue here must be weighed the individual interests implicated in the use of deadly force by police officers. The [471 US 29] majority declares that "[t]he suspect's fundamental interest in his own life need not be elaborated upon." Ante, at 9, 85 L Ed 2d, at 8. This blithe assertion hardly provides an adequate substitute for the majority's failure to acknowledge the distinctive manner in which the suspect's interest in his life is even exposed to risk. For purposes of this case, we must recall that the police officer, in the course of investigating a nighttime burglary, had reasonable cause to arrest the suspect and ordered him to halt. The officer's use of force resulted because the suspected burglar refused to heed this command and the officer reasonably believed that there was no means short of firing his weapon to apprehend the suspect. Without questioning the importance of a person's interest in his life, I do not think this interest encompasses a right to flee unimpeded from the scene of a burglary. Cf. Payton v New York, 445 US 573, 617, n 14, 63 L Ed 2d 639, 100 S Ct 1371 (1980) (White, J., dissenting) ("[T]he policeman's hands should not be tied merely because of the possibility that the suspect will fail to cooperate with legitimate actions by law enforcement personnel"). The legitimate interests of the suspect in these circumstances are adequately accommodated by the Tennessee statute: to avoid the use of deadly force and the consequent risk to his life, the suspect need merely obey the valid order to halt.

A proper balancing of the interests involved suggests that use of deadly force as a last resort to apprehend a criminal suspect fleeing from the scene of a nighttime burglary is not unreasonable within the meaning of the Fourth Amendment. Admittedly, the events giving rise to this case are in retrospect deeply regrettable. No one can view the death of an unarmed and apparently nonviolent 15-year-old without sorrow, much less disapproval. Nonetheless, the reasonableness of Officer Hymon's conduct for purposes of the Fourth Amendment cannot be evaluated by what later appears to have been a preferable course of police action. The officer pursued a suspect in the darkened backyard of a house that from all indications had just been burglarized. The [471 US 30] police officer was not certain whether the suspect was alone or unarmed; nor did he know what had transpired inside the house. He ordered the suspect to halt, and when the suspect refused to obey and attempted to flee into the night, the officer fired his weapon to prevent escape. The reasonableness of this action for purposes of the Fourth Amendment is not determined by the unfortunate nature of this particular case; instead, the question is whether it is constitutionally impermissible for police officers, as a last resort, to shoot a burglary suspect fleeing the scene of the crime.

Because I reject the Fourth Amendment reasoning of the majority and the Court of Appeals, I briefly note that no other constitutional provision supports the decision below. In addition to his Fourth Amendment claim, appellee-respondent also alleged violations of due process, the Sixth Amendment right to trial by jury, and the Eighth Amendment proscription of cruel

21

and unusual punishment. These arguments were rejected by the District Court and, except for the due process claim, not addressed by the Court of Appeals. With respect to due process, the Court of Appeals reasoned that statutes affecting the fundamental interest in life must be "narrowly drawn to express only the legitimate state interests at stake." 710 F2d, at 245. The Court of Appeals concluded that a statute allowing police use of deadly force is narrowly drawn and therefore constitutional only if the use of such force is limited to situations in which the suspect poses an immediate threat to others. Id., at 246–247. Whatever the validity of Tennessee's statute in other contexts, I cannot agree that its application in this case resulted in a deprivation "without due process of law." Cf. Baker v McCollan, 443 US 137, 144–145, 61 L Ed 2d 433, 99 S Ct 2689 (1979). Nor do I believe that a criminal suspect who is shot while trying to avoid apprehension has a cognizable claim of a deprivation of his Sixth Amendment right to trial by jury. See Cunningham v Ellington, 323 F Supp 1072, 1075–1076 (WD Tenn 1971) (three-judge court). Finally, because there is no indication that the use

[471 US 31]

of deadly force was intended to punish rather than to capture the suspect, there is no valid claim under the Eighth Amendment. See Bell v Wolfish, 441 US 520, 538–539, 60 L Ed 2d 447, 99 S Ct 1861 (1979). Accordingly, I conclude that the District Court properly entered judgment against appellee-respondent, and I would reverse the decision of the Court of Appeals.

III

Even if I agreed that the Fourth

Amendment was violated under the circumstances of this case, I would be unable to join the Court's opinion. The Court holds that deadly force may be used only if the suspect "threatens the officer with a weapon or there is probable cause to believe that he has committed a crime involving the infliction or threatened infliction of serious physical harm." Ante, at 11, 85 L Ed 2d, at 10. The Court ignores the more general implications of its reasoning. Relying on the Fourth Amendment, the majority asserts that it is constitutionally unreasonable to *use* deadly force against fleeing criminal suspects who do not appear to pose a threat of serious physical harm to others. Ibid. By declining to limit its holding to the use of firearms, the Court unnecessarily implies that the Fourth Amendment constrains the use of any police practice that is potentially lethal, no matter how remote the risk. Cf. Los Angeles v Lyons, 461 US 95, 75 L Ed 2d 675, 103 S Ct 1660 (1983).

Although it is unclear from the language of the opinion, I assume that the majority intends the word "use" to include only those circumstances in which the suspect is actually apprehended. Absent apprehension of the suspect, there is no "seizure" for Fourth Amendment purposes. I doubt that the Court intends to allow criminal suspects who successfully escape to return later with § 1983 claims against officers who used, albeit unsuccessfully, deadly force in their futile attempt to capture the fleeing suspect. The Court's opinion, despite its broad language, actually decides only that the

[471 US 32]

shooting of a fleeing burglary suspect who

TENNESSEE v GARNER
471 US 1, 85 L Ed 2d 1, 105 S Ct 1694

was in fact neither armed nor dangerous can support a § 1983 action.

The Court's silence on critical factors in the decision to use deadly force simply invites second-guessing of difficult police decisions that must be made quickly in the most trying of circumstances. Cf. Payton v New York, supra, at 619, 63 L Ed 2d 639, 100 S Ct 1371 (White, J., dissenting). Police are given no guidance for determining which objects, among an array of potentially lethal weapons ranging from guns to knives to baseball bats to rope, will justify the use of deadly force. The Court also declines to outline the additional factors necessary to provide "probable cause" for believing that a suspect "poses a significant threat of death or serious physical injury," ante, at 3, 85 L Ed 2d, at 4, when the officer has probable cause to arrest and the suspect refuses to obey an order to halt. But even if it were appropriate in this case to limit the use of deadly force to that ambiguous class of suspects, I believe the class should include nighttime residential burglars who resist arrest by attempting to flee the scene of the crime. We can expect an escalating volume of litigation as the lower courts struggle to determine if a police officer's split-second decision to shoot was justified by the danger posed by a particular object and other facts related to the crime. Thus, the majority opinion portends a burgeoning area of Fourth Amendment doctrine concerning the circumstances in which police officers can reasonably employ deadly force.

IV

The Court's opinion sweeps broadly to adopt an entirely new standard for the constitutionality of the use of deadly force to apprehend fleeing felons. Thus, the Court "lightly brushe[s] aside," Payton v New York, 445 US, at 600, 63 L Ed 2d 639, 100 S Ct 1371, a longstanding police practice that predates the Fourth Amendment and continues to receive the approval of nearly half of the state legislatures. I cannot accept the majority's creation of a constitutional right to flight for burglary suspects

[471 US 33]

seeking to avoid capture at the scene of the crime. Whatever the constitutional limits on police use of deadly force in order to apprehend a fleeing felon, I do not believe they are exceeded in a case in which a police officer has probable cause to arrest a suspect at the scene of a residential burglary, orders the suspect to halt, and then fires his weapon as a last resort to prevent the suspect's escape into the night. I respectfully dissent.

[22]

'Deadly Force'

P.A.J. Waddington

Introduction

Although the police have always used firearms they have been reluctant to acknowledge it too openly. Their fear, that to do so would promote public concern, has proven well-founded. Controversial incidents, especially tragic mistaken and accidental shootings, have raised not only issues of selection, training, and supervision, but also anxieties about an aggressive style of policing. It was seen in Chapter 2 that condemnation of 'trigger-happy' police has followed even the most apparently justified shootings of armed robbers by police. It was also noted how public anxieties were aroused by the sight of officers openly carrying what appear to be sub-machine-guns at Heathrow airport.

What seems to be at risk, so far as many onlookers are concerned, is whether the traditional commitment to the principle of 'minimum force' is in jeopardy. Therefore this chapter will consider whether tactics are unwarrantably aggressive and whether the weapons used are more lethal than they need be.

'Shoot to Kill'?

Perhaps one of the most serious worries is that armed officers are taught to 'shoot to kill'. This concern seems to underlie such casual remarks as that made by Tony Banks MP, following the Sir John Soane's Museum shooting: 'Too often police are shooting first and questioning later' (*People*, 8 February 1987). These anxieties have been most fully and forcefully articulated by Sarah Manwaring-White (1983) who, after an apparently thorough review of police weaponry and tactics, concludes:

it is obvious that an increasing number of officers are being trained to shoot to kill and more are trained every year. They are told to aim at the chest area and to do whatever is necessary to protect their colleagues and the public. . . . Training has become a matter of course and 'shoot to kill' has replaced the old instruction of using a gun as the last resort in self defence. (pp. 130–2)

This allegation is given apparent credence by her quoting the injudicious remarks of two Chief Constables: John Alderson, then Chief Constable of Devon and Cornwall, who is reported as saying, 'We are prepared to shoot to kill in the interests of society if necessary', and John Duke, the late Chief Constable of Hampshire, who is quoted as saying, 'The gun is not made for protection, nor made to injure or to frighten. It is made to kill, and police officers being trained to use it when necessary in Hampshire are being trained with this in mind' (Manwaring–White, 1983: 117). More recently, the then parliamentary adviser to the Police Federation, Sir Eldon Griffiths, MP, was quoted as saying that the police 'always shoot to kill' and do so as a matter of duty (*Sun*, 10 July 1987). Of course, the term 'shoot to kill' has acquired added significance in the context of allegations that security forces in Northern Ireland adopted a 'shoot to kill' policy, by which is meant 'summary execution'.

   In fact, Manwaring–White's case is flimsy and ill-informed. Let us consider the points made in reverse order. Perhaps the statements made by the two Chief Constables were ill-advised and made without consideration of how they might later be used by critics such as Manwaring-White. Yet, even as they stand, they do not offer support for Manwaring-White's extravagant conclusions. Alderson is saying no more than is and always has been the truth, for as 'monopolists of force in civil society' (Bittner, 1975) the police must be prepared ultimately to use lethal force to fulfil their mandate to protect the public. Thus, if it is necessary to shoot and kill a terrorist machine-gunning passengers in an airport lounge, this will be the duty of the police. This is not a revolutionary change: the police used firearms to engage anarchistic terrorists at the 'Siege of Sidney Street' (Gould and Waldren, 1986: ch. 7). What has changed is the scale of preparedness made necessary by the growth in armed crime and terrorism.

'Deadly Force'   77

Mr Duke, too, is uttering no more than a truism. A gun is not designed to fend off bullets: it is only effective when fired, and when it is fired at someone it is likely to prove fatal. When he says that Hampshire police officers are trained with this in mind, he is doing no more than repeating the generally accepted guidance on police use of firearms. Metropolitan Police policy, as taught to all AFOs, is quite explicit on this:

An authorized firearms officer is trained to shoot at a given area — usually the torso. Any shot aimed at that target area is likely to result in grievous bodily harm being caused. Therefore, if an officer shoots with the intention not to kill the suspect, but to stop him, he must realize that a possible consequence is the death of the suspect. He must therefore believe before he shoots that causing grievous bodily harm or possibly killing the suspect is reasonable under those particular circumstances and that the conditions of Section 3 Criminal Law Act 1967 apply.

It follows that, if the circumstances would not justify the killing, there must be no attempt to stop a suspect by shooting merely to wound him.

There are, then, two related but separable points to be considered. The first is that the purpose of shooting someone is not to kill them, but to stop them committing some extreme act. The goal is not death, but total and immediate incapacitation. The second point is that the consequence of shooting someone is probably, although not inevitably, that they will be killed. The policy is cautious, rather than cavalier in the manner suggested by Manwaring-White, because it insists that police can open fire only when they would be justified in killing the person, even if death does not result. In contrast to the impression conveyed by Manwaring-White, the policy is conservative, for it insists that firearms be used only as a last resort in the most extreme circumstances.

The reference made by Duke to using guns to 'frighten' people also leads, in fact, to the opposite conclusion to that arrived at by Manwaring-White. Two of the six safety rules which AFOs must learn by rote and be prepared to recite whenever challenged, state, 'Never draw your weapon from the holster unless you have occasion to use it' and 'Never point a firearm at anyone unless you are prepared to shoot'. In other words, officers are specifically warned *not* to draw their weapons and point them simply in order to intimidate someone. Drawing a gun from the holster is a serious matter, which must be reported to senior officers, and is not to be undertaken lightly.

If the purpose of shooting at suspects is to stop rather than kill them, why is it necessary to fire twice in 'sense of direction' shooting (see p. 293)? Police are trained to fire two shots in rapid succession when firing 'sense of direction' because these shots are fired at close range when immediate incapacitation is absolutely essential given the imminence of the threat. In view of the urgency of the situation and the lack of time in which to take aim, one shot might miss the armed person; and in the time it would take to appreciate this the suspect could have fired and killed the officer or some other innocent person. Moreover, if only one bullet struck the person there is no guarantee that it would totally incapacitate and prevent the suspect returning fire. The shooting at the Sir John Soane's Museum provides a good illustration of the difficulties that can arise in such circumstances. One of the bullets fired at Denis Bergin actually struck the butt of the shotgun he was carrying. Only one bullet struck his body. The other man who was shot was hit by a single bullet in the arm. In the confined space of the hallway of the museum, a failure totally to incapacitate an armed person could easily prove fatal to the police or other innocent people.

Returning fire?

If the police must only open fire when justified in using lethal force, should they not wait until their adversaries open fire upon them? In other words, are the police 'shooting first and questioning later', as Tony Banks, MP, suggested? This question has arisen, of course, most acutely in those cases where unarmed people have been mistakenly shot, but also when individuals carrying *unloaded* weapons or replicas have also been shot by police.

If officers were to be constrained only to draw their own weapon when confronted by a person who also had a weapon

'Deadly Force'

drawn, or only to point it when another was intending to shoot, or to fire only when fired upon, then this would be tantamount to inviting them to commit suicide. To draw a weapon from the holster, especially when that weapon is concealed under a tunic or jacket, would take much too long. A person armed with, say, a shotgun, would have ample time to aim and fire before the police officer's weapon had cleared the holster. Only to point a gun when an officer intends to fire it would, again, expose that officer to undue risk from a sudden attack. To fire only when fired upon is a prescription for serious injury or death. Thus, officers must be allowed to draw their gun from the holster when they reasonably apprehend that there is an armed threat. Similarly, it is essential that officers should fire their weapon when they reasonably anticipate that an armed person is *about* to open fire.

Warnings

The extent of the danger to which armed officers are exposed when confronting armed suspects is illustrated by the fate of three policemen engaged upon armed operations. The first, PC Peter Slimon, was shot as he shouted a warning to bank robbers in 1972. The second was Inspector Dwight Atkinson, who was shot in the leg as he called out a warning to armed bank robbers in Woolwich in 1987. The third, and most tragic, was PC Brian Bishop of the Essex Police, who was shot and killed by an armed robber whom he and his colleagues intercepted at Frimley in 1984. Bishop died as he challenged the robber to surrender with his gun drawn and pointing at the robber. Nevertheless, the latter was able to fire both barrels of his sawn-off shotgun from within a bag that he was carrying. The shots killed Bishop and seriously wounded his colleague standing near to him. A shot fired by a third officer armed with a shotgun gravely wounded the gunman, but was not quick enough to save Bishop and his colleague. Although having his gun drawn did not save Bishop, to require officers in similar circumstances to keep their weapon holstered would significantly increase the risk to them.

80   *'Armed Police'*

The fate of these officers puts other, more controversial, incidents into proper perspective. For example, the killing of Michael Calvey in 1978 has been criticized because he was hit in the back during a raid on a supermarket in Eltham by a shot fired by officers lying in wait. The pathologist explained at the inquest that the wound indicated that Calvey had been in the act of turning towards the officer when hit. A fully loaded double-barrelled shotgun was in his possession at the time, and was recovered from the scene. Had the officer not fired when he did, allowing Calvey to aim the shotgun towards him, he might well have suffered the same fate as Bishop. An even more striking parallel with the murder of Bishop was the shooting by police of two robbers at a North London sub-post office in 1984. When challenged, one of the robbers reached into a holdall he was carrying. Fearing that it concealed a shotgun, the officers opened fire, wounding the man and his accomplice. Upon inspection the bag was found not to contain a weapon (*The Times*, 15 June 1984). Of course, the officers could not have known that at the time, and had the bag indeed contained a gun they too might have been killed as Bishop was later to be killed. Inevitably, armed officers may be called upon to make a split-second decision which might, with hindsight, prove to have been made in error. An erroneous decision to open fire might lead to the injury or death of an innocent person; the opposite error may result in the death or injury of the officer himself.

Of course, the police cannot be licensed to fire upon suspects no matter what the circumstances, nor does the law allow them to do so. They can only use such force as is 'reasonable in the circumstances'. However, when it comes to judging what is 'reasonable in the circumstances', the actual hazards of armed operations must be kept in mind. The possession of a gun does not make a police officer invulnerable, and he must make split-second decisions upon which his life and the lives of others might depend. This undoubtedly creates a recurring dilemma, not least for the officer holding the gun, but it is not a dilemma that can be eliminated by imposing such restrictions on police officers as would repeatedly place their lives in jeopardy.

'Deadly Force'   81

'Shooting to wound'

A third point raised by the quote from John Duke regards so-called 'shooting to kill' as opposed to 'shooting to wound'. As Duke remarks, guns are designed to kill, not merely to injure, and the official guidelines explicitly forbid officers to attempt to stop a suspect by shooting to wound him or firing a warning shot. Why not shoot simply to wound or to knock a weapon from a person's hand? It would seem a humanitarian alternative to shooting with the knowledge that one is likely to kill. It would also seems to accord faithfully with the doctrine of 'minimum force'. Having passed the threshold at which recourse to firearms becomes necessary, this surely avoids inflicting more injury than is required to subdue an adversary. A person shot in the lower limb might well drop any weapon he was carrying and thus be rendered harmless. It seems difficult to disagree with Blom–Cooper (1988):

Even if prevention [of a crime] dictates some incapacitation of the terrorist before effecting his capture, it may be unnecessary or unreasonable to use deadly force. Warning shots overhead, or in an emergency to avoid an escape, a shooting to injure or maim but not to kill may suffice.

If such a policy were to be implemented, however, far from reducing death and serious injury, it would be likely to increase them.

There are four reasons why this is so: first, shots intended to wound are likely to miss. Limbs are very much more difficult to hit than the torso, especially in the highly charged conditions of an armed confrontation. It is, therefore, more likely that shots aimed at the limbs will miss their target completely (this, of course, being the intention of shots fired as warnings). In this event two dangers arise: the first is that, having missed its intended target the bullet will hit someone else and cause injury or death; the second is that, having missed the person at whom the shot was aimed, the intended target will carry out his threat.

Second, a wounded person is unlikely to be incapacitated either totally or immediately. Even if shots fired at the limbs strike their intended target, it is far from certain that they would have the intended effect. Compared to the trauma that normally follows being shot in the torso, gunshot wounds in the limbs inflict only relatively slight injury. Even if a person fell to the floor having been shot in the leg, he might still retain hold of a weapon and be capable of using it. There is a further danger: shots fired at the limbs are highly likely to pass through their target, retaining enough velocity to inflict serious injury or death upon anyone unfortunate enough to get in the way.

The third objection follows from the first two, for if shots aimed at the limbs failed to incapacitate totally and immediately, either because they missed or did insufficient injury, police officers would become inclined to open fire at a lower level of threat. To do otherwise would be to gamble with the life that was being threatened: a shot which failed to incapacitate, might allow the adversary to kill innocent people. There would need to be sufficient time to allow some assessment to be made of the effects of each shot. If the shot had missed or failed to incapacitate, a further shot may be necessary. Delaying to the last possible moment before opening fire would not leave enough time to make such an assessment and take *any* corrective action before the threat was executed.

This leads to the fourth objection; if police were to open fire at a lower level of threat, albeit with the intention of wounding, the result is likely to be an increase in serious injury and death. Mention has already been made of the danger posed to innocent bystanders by shots that miss or pass through a limb. There is also the likelihood that shots fired with the intention of wounding will actually kill. Errors of aim are likely to result in shots intended to hit the limb actually hitting a vital organ. Even when the bullet strikes its desired target, there is no guarantee that it will not ricochet off bone or a hard object carried by the person and cause unintended serious injury or death. For example, Errol Walker, shot as he stabbed his hostage at Northolt in 1985, was shot in the shoulder, but the bullet ricocheted, striking him in the side of the head, causing him serious injury although it did not kill him. If police officers were to follow the guidance offered by Blom–Cooper and fire at the lower torso, this likelihood becomes much greater, since, if the bullet misses the abdominal arteries, there is a strong probability that it will hit the pelvis and ricochet with unknowable consequences. These are more than hypothetical possibilities: evidence from Australia (Harding, 1970) and Canada (Chappell and Graham, 1985) suggests that a significant proportion of dubious killings by police arose from shots fired with the intention of warning or wounding.

It might be objected that even if *some* adversaries were inadvertently killed by shots intended to wound, this is preferable to *all* of them being shot with the intention of killing. This would be so if those shot at a lower level of threat would, in any case, have been shot at a later stage of the incident at an extreme level of threat. It is probable that at least some incidents would never reach the most extreme threat level, and so people would be shot with the intention of being wounded who would not be shot at all if the expectation was that they would be killed. Therefore, the likelihood is that a 'shoot to wound' policy would result in more people being shot, a proportion of whom would be killed.

The balance of advantage seems to lie — where policy currently places it — in favour of having recourse to firearms only *in extremis* and doing so with the intention of inflicting grievous, if not fatal, injury. To do otherwise would be to invite a lowering of the threshold at which recourse to firearms was made and thereby possibly to cause the unintended greater loss of life. The cost of this approach is that when shots *are* fired they must inflict sufficient injury to incapacitate immediately and utterly.

Man-Stopping Bullets

This brings us to the question of the weaponry issued to police, particularly the type of ammunition used and whether it is gratuitously injurious. Benn and Worpole (1986: 64) make the extraordinarily ridiculous claim that the .38-in

84 *'Armed Police'*

Smith and Wesson is 'a large calibre revolver originally developed for hunting in the US and known there as the "grizzly-bear killer". No other European countries issue their police with such large hand guns, guns which it seems lack the double-safety devices of other pistols.' In fact, the Model 10 Smith and Wesson was originally designated as the 'military and police' revolver, for this was always its intended market. The use of hand-guns for hunting is a relatively recent development, arising from the production of particularly powerful weapons, all of which chamber ammunition of much heavier calibre than the .38-in cartridge. Yet even these particularly powerful weapons would not be used against an animal as large as a grizzly bear.

Apart from these errors of fact, this and other similar comments reveal two areas of confusion: that between the revolver and the propellant power of the ammunition fired, and between revolvers and self-loading pistols. This section will examine the first source of confusion and the following section will consider the second.

There is no simple correspondence between the calibre of a gun and the power of the ammunition it can fire. A .38-in revolver may be capable of firing any one of several types of ammunition which vary in their power and, hence, muzzle velocity. The .380-in, or '.38-in short' as it is sometimes known, is the least powerful; the .38-in standard is next most powerful; that is followed by the .38-in special and the .38-in special + P; and finally the .357-in Magnum is the most powerful.

Contrary to the impression conveyed by television and cinema portrayals of armed police, there is no such weapon as the 'Magnum'. Thus, when Clint Eastwood says, in the 'soliloquy' from *Dirty Harry*, 'This is a Magnum .44-in, the most powerful hand-gun in the world . . . so all you've got to ask yourself is "Do I feel lucky today?"' he is talking nonsense: it is a Smith and Wesson Model 29 that he is pointing at the 'bad guy'. The term 'Magnum' refers, not to the gun, but to the propellant power of the round fired by the gun. In fact, just to confuse matters, the .357-in Magnum round is the same diameter as the .38-in round (the difference in nomenclature arising from where on the cartridge the measurement is taken). The difference between these rounds is the power of the propellant and the length of the cartridge case which accommodates it.

Confusion arises because not all .38-in rounds can be fired from the same gun. As the power of the round increases, so too does the length of the cartridge case. This is partly due to the need to accommodate the propellant itself, but also ensures that weapons which are not designed to withstand greater pressures cannot fire the more powerful cartridges. Thus, a .357-in Magnum round would fit into the chamber of a Smith and Wesson Model 10, but it would protrude beyond the length of the chamber, thus preventing the cylinder from being closed and the bullet fired. However, any of the various .38-in rounds could be fired from a revolver capable of firing Magnum ammunition, because the length of the cartridge would be less than that of the chamber. The round that is currently approved by the Home Office for issue to the police is the .38-in special + P 125 grain bullet, about which more will be written later.

Confusion is, perhaps, compounded by the fact that some police officers are issued with weapons which *are* capable of firing Magnum ammunition, even if they do not do so. For example, until recently Model 19s and 28s were issued to members of Level I teams, who also act as instructors. Why issue revolvers capable of firing the Magnum round, if this round is not actually used? Any gun designed to fire a Magnum round tends to be more robust than its counterparts designed to fire less powerful ammunition, because this round when fired imposes greater stress upon the weapon. Thus, an additional advantage of supplying Model 19s and 28s to instructors, who use them quite frequently in training and instruction, is that they are more durable. Moreover, heavier weapons tend to be more accurate. In short, the fact that some officers may be equipped with revolvers capable of firing more powerful ammunition does not mean that they will actually fire the most powerful ammunition the gun is capable of chambering. In sum, to say that the Smith and Wesson is a 'large-calibre revolver' (Benn and Worpole, 1986: 64) is simply to confuse the weapon and the power of the ammunition.

86   *'Armed Police'*

It is equally misleading to compare the Smith and Wesson
.38-in revolver with the 9-mm self-loading pistols traditionally used by Continental, and increasingly carried by
American, police forces. In fact, the 9-mm parabellum round
is almost exactly the same diameter as the .38-in round.
Moreover, just as .38-in ammunition has its more or less
powerful variants, so too does 9-mm ammunition. However, it should be added that, because of the enclosed
construction of self-loading weapons, as compared to the
open construction of the revolver cylinder from which gases
can escape other than through the barrel, 9-mm ammunition
actually has a *higher* muzzle velocity than comparable
revolver ammunition. This invalidates the second element of
Benn and Worpole's assertion.

Nevertheless, it must be acknowledged that there *has* been
a drift towards the use of more powerful ammunition by
police during the recent past. The 158-grain .38-in Special
replaced the .380-in, and more recently it in turn has been
replaced by the 125-grain .38-in special + P round. The
decision to change from the .380-in to the .38-in special was
dictated by problems in the supply of ammunition, which is
governed to a significant extent by the large American
market. The switch from the 158-grain .38-in special to the
125-grain .38-in special + P was made in order to provide the
police with ammunition which had greater stopping power.
However, it is a type of round which in 1973 was refused to
the Metropolitan Police (Gould and Waldren, 1986: 202) and
was described by the *Daily Telegraph* as being 'softer and flat-
nosed so as to spread on impact' (quoted in Gould and
Waldren, 1986: 201).

There may appear to be some substance, therefore, to
claims that the police are using more powerful ammunition
than they need and which, from the *Daily Telegraph's*
description, appears to be a form of 'dum-dum' bullet
apparently outlawed by international treaty. Indeed, the
decision to adopt semi-jacketed, semi-wadcutter ammunition (see p. 278) was taken in the knowledge that it departed
from the strict letter of the Hague Conventions of 1889,
1899, and 1907, the provisions of which British and
European governments have extended unilaterally to the

'Deadly Force'   87

police. These conventions stipulate that *military ammunition* must be fully jacketed round-nosed, and not designed to disintegrate or explode upon impact. It explicitly forbids 'hollow-point' bullets, commonly referred to as 'dum-dum' bullets. However, these conventions have never applied to policing; they have simply been extended by analogy.

The choice of a semi-wadcutter, semi-jacketed round departs from the Hague Convention in so far as the bullet is not fully jacketed and might, therefore, be seen as gratuit-ously lethal. In fact, the 125-grain revolver bullet and its 95-grain parabellum equivalent were chosen because, in practice, their fully jacketed predecessors were found to be *more* likely to disintegrate upon hitting a person. Specifically, it was discovered that the metal jacket became detached from the lead bullet after striking bone. Thus, it is contended that the semi-jacketed bullet, whilst departing from the strict letter of the Hague Conventions, complies with its spirit and is not *designed* to expand or fragment. At the same time, a lighter, faster bullet was thought to offer greater 'stopping power'.

Stopping power

This calls for some clarification of the notion of 'stopping power' — a discussion which for the moment will be re-stricted to low-velocity bullets like those fired from re-volvers. Bullets do not simply puncture the flesh, causing loss of blood, nor does the impact energy of the bullet knock a person off his feet. Low-velocity bullets fired from pistols, sub-machine-guns, and shotguns (and typically used by police) inflict catastrophic injury in the course of rapidly decelerating as they pass through bodily tissue. According to the size, shape, weight, and velocity of the bullet, the transfer of kinetic energy from it to the tissue creates a cavity of varying size and shape. The larger the cavity the more massive is the loss of blood and other bodily fluids, the greater the shock, and the more likely is damage to vital organs, causing rapid incapacitation and possibly proving lethal (Dawkins, 1989).

A bullet should be designed so that it is likely to come to

rest *within* the body of the person shot (in other words, it should not over-penetrate). This is for two reasons: first, it ensures that no other person is hit by a bullet that has passed through the 'primary target', unlike the holiday-maker hit by a bullet fired by the SAS soldiers in Gibraltar (*Independent*, 21 September 1988). Second, but more important, it results in *all* the kinetic energy of the bullet being deposited within the person shot, thus maximizing the amount of injury inflicted.

A failure to inflict maximum injury, and thereby fully to incapacitate, exposes innocent people to danger because the threat can be executed. There is always the real risk that, even as the adversary dies, he may fire a shot or detonate explosives that will injure or kill innocent people. Therefore, once the point is reached when opening fire is justified, the overriding consideration must be to incapacitate the opponent totally and immediately. Using ammunition which inflicts only limited injury, even though it too is often fatal, is to compromise the achievement of incapacitation. Since killing the adversary is justified in these conditions, and death is the likely consequence of being shot, compromising on the amount of injury inflicted is not only potentially dangerous to others but also an exercise in futility.

Is British police ammunition powerful enough?

Conformity with the stipulations of the Hague Conventions hitherto, and the continued reluctance to depart from them, testify to the conservative minimalist approach of the British authorities over the years. But the question must be asked: is policy on ammunition too conservative and minimalist? As noted above, police officers are instructed to fire two shots in rapid succession when firing by 'sense of direction' in order totally to incapacitate an armed antagonist. Experience gained at the Plumstead abattoir shooting in July 1987 indicated that when paired shots strike a person they may indeed incapacitate effectively. That same incident also demonstrated that where only a single shot hits a person, he is not necessarily incapacitated and might continue to pose a threat. At Plumstead the robber who survived, though knocked to the ground by the shot, still retained hold of his weapon and might have returned fire had he not been overwhelmed by other armed officers. This replicated the experience of the shooting at Sir John Soane's Museum, where one of the raiders was shot in the arm but was able to escape from the scene before being arrested by pursuing officers. Even more alarming was the fact that one armed robber was shot five times in an exchange of fire with detectives who intercepted a post office robbery in East Acton in 1988 whilst he, in turn, shot and wounded two of the detectives (*Independent*, 16 December 1988). Therefore, there is no guarantee that an armed person struck by a single shot will not be able to return fire, shoot innocent third parties, or detonate explosives. This raises the issue of whether there are good grounds for *increasing* the power of the ammunition supplied to armed officers.

If the police were to adopt more powerful ammunition, the most likely choice would be to use either .38-in special + P or .357-in Magnum hollow-point bullets. The .357-in Magnum hollow-point is virtually universal amongst American police forces, including the FBI, who set the standard of 'best practice' in these matters. The hollow-point configuration causes the bullet to expand rapidly upon hitting flesh and thereby to decelerate, creating a large cavity in the torso. The grounds for using the Magnum cartridge is that its enhanced velocity is needed to produce the expansion of the bullet upon impact. Indeed, there seems to be a trend amongst American police forces to use still heavier calibre ammunition such as .41-in, .44-in, and .45-in, because of the additional stopping power afforded.

Obviously, bullets of a hollow-point configuration, fired at greater velocity and possibly of heavier calibre, are likely to prove more lethal, but lethality should not be confused with stopping power. It is possible that ammunition that lacks stopping power can still prove lethal. The robber shot by PC Slimon in 1972 subsequently died, but did so some time later from loss of blood and was *not* immediately incapacitated by the .380-in bullet that struck him. Some people shot by police using the semi-jacketed, semi-wadcutter bullets have died, but others have survived. Nor does it seem that the use of hollow-point bullets will inevitably kill those who are shot by the police, since American experience indicates that only a third of police shootings prove fatal (Milton *et al.*, 1977).

Use of hollow-point ammunition is a clear breach of the Hague Conventions, but are the standards imposed by those conventions appropriate or prudent when applied to police work? The fully jacketed ammunition stipulated by the conventions tends to over-penetrate, thus proving less effective and more dangerous to innocent bystanders than alternative rounds which the conventions forbid. These are important considerations relating to any police ammunition, but are of particular significance in regard to close-protection officers, who are armed with .38-in Special + P ammunition, and riflemen, who are currently issued with .308-in or .223-in fully jacketed ball ammunition of military design.

Protection officers, for whom the most serious threat is an assassination attempt made at close quarters by someone in a crowd, need ammunition which is most likely to incapacitate a possibly drugged or crazed assassin with minimal risk of over-penetration. Greenwood argues that for this role it is 'irresponsible' to use anything other than hollow-point ammunition (1979: 296), whilst Yardley and Eliot (1986c) prefer the recently developed 'Glaser safety slug', a fully jacketed round containing a number of small pellets which are released within the body of a person shot once the outer casing strikes him, causing enormous injuries, and rejected by the Home Office for this reason. Either of these rounds is more likely to incapacitate even a determined attacker with little risk of over-penetration or ricochets than is currently issued ammunition. However, despite these purely technical advantages, the Home Office has rejected the use of this kind of ammunition because it would inflict injuries which are considered to be ethically unjustifiable and inconsistent with the Hague Conventions.

Achieving a balance between technical suitability and ethical acceptability is even more difficult in the case of high-velocity rifle ammunition. The police are currently permitted to use only ball ammunition of military design which strictly complies with the provisions of the Hague Conventions. However, high-velocity ammunition of this kind is almost

4. 'Deadly Force' 91

invariably lethal, because once the muzzle velocity of a bullet exceeds 2,000 feet per second (and the .308-in Steyr bullet has a muzzle velocity of 3,000 feet per second) it causes a particular kind of injury to the person. As it passes through the body the bullet creates a tremendous shock wave ahead of, and all around, its path. This causes the large exit wounds and enormous injuries for which these weapons have become notorious. Not only is the injury from such a weapon likely to prove fatal, but the bullet is almost certain to over-penetrate and, moving with such velocity, could hit others with devastating consequences.

The danger of over-penetration is illustrated by the injuries suffered by Governor Connally of Texas who was wounded during the assassination of President Kennedy in Dallas in 1963. One of the bullets, which is thought to have struck the president in the back of the neck, is then believed to have exited through the front of the throat and hit Connally, who was seated in front of Kennedy in the same car. The bullet hit Connally in the back and then exited from his chest and struck him in the wrist, eventually coming to rest in his thigh upon which his hand was resting. Fortunately, Connally survived; others might not be so lucky.

If the danger from ricochets is added to that of over-penetration, the unsuitability of this kind of ammunition becomes even more evident. A bullet that missed its target might have a range of up to two miles, and if it struck a substantial object and ricocheted its subsequent path could not be predicted. This could pose a considerable hazard to innocent people quite remote from the scene of the confrontation.

High-velocity weapons are necessary for riflemen because, used at long distance, they must retain their accuracy. The problems of over-penetration and ricochets could be mitigated, however, if not solved, by the adoption of some kind of soft-nosed bullet, such as the ROTA ammunition manufactured by Royal Ordnance which disintegrates upon impact and will not, therefore, ricochet. These rounds would cause horrendous injuries to anyone they struck, and would almost certainly prove fatal. However, the high-velocity ball ammunition now issued to riflemen is hardly less lethal. It seems that the desire not to be seen to adopt a type of ammunition most injurious to the suspect has overruled concern for the safety of innocent people who might suffer the fate of Governor Connally, or worse.

Treating the Hague Conventions as an analogy for the doctrine of 'minimum force' leads to the police being equipped with ammunition which is unsuitable to their role. The principle of 'minimum force' does not apply to military engagements in time of war, and the conventions do not apply to police confronting terrorists and armed criminals who, themselves, are not signatories to the conventions and cannot be expected to be bound by them. If the conventions are not treated as an analogy, and the doctrine of 'minimum force' is approached directly, then the ethical justification for more powerful, and thereby injurious, ammunition becomes evident. Yet such a conclusion invariably provokes a howl of outrage and the accusation that the doctrine of minimum force is being abandoned.

Minimum Force and Lethality

The objection that using more injurious ammunition would violate the principle of 'minimum force' is to appeal to an unduly simplistic conception of that principle. Put simply, the doctrine of minimum force means that no more force should be used than is *necessary* for the accomplishment of a lawful purpose. What goes unrecognized is that *necessity* has two quite distinct aspects which are of crucial operational importance to the use of firearms by police. The first is that force should not be employed until it becomes essential. Thus, although there may be occasions where a pre-emptive use of force may be expedient in order to extinguish any likelihood of threat, it is normally expected that force will only be used *in response* to some threatening action of the adversary. Force, in other words, should not be used 'just in case' the adversary poses a threat, but only after that threat has materialized.

The second aspect is that the force used should only be sufficient to overcome resistance. No matter how much

4. 'Deadly Force' 93

harm is threatened by an adversary, the amount of force used should be limited to that which is necessary to subdue him, otherwise the use of more force would be gratuitously punitive.

When police use non-lethal force, both corollaries of the doctrine are readily applicable. For example, a police officer should only strike someone with his truncheon if that person poses a threat sufficiently serious and imminent to make hitting him a necessity. Having struck him with sufficient force to disable, the police officer would be unjustified in administering any further blows. By contrast, the use of firearms entails crossing a threshold which precludes the application of this second restriction.

Because firearms are inherently lethal weapons, they can only be justifiably used in the most extreme conditions of an immediate threat to life. Primacy is thus accorded to the first element of the minimum-force doctrine — that firearms should only be used as a last resort. Paradoxically, this effectively renders other considerations redundant, for in life-threatening circumstances it is imperative that incapacitation be both total and immediate. To do otherwise might allow the adversary to carry out his threat after he has been hit. Instant and complete incapacitation entails inflicting nothing less than devastating injury, since the circumstances are so extreme that there is no room for error. This can *only* be achieved with any reliability by bullets that inflict the kind of injury that has hitherto been regarded as ethically unaccept-able. Inflicting such injury *is* to use no more force than is necessary, for to inflict lesser injury in such extreme circumstance might prove ineffective. If, instead, an effort is made to minimize the injury inflicted on an armed adversary, this merely transfers the risk of death and injury from him to the innocent. Using insufficiently injurious ammunition does precisely this — place innocent lives at risk.

Eliminating the threat and 'shooting to kill'

A similar problem arises in regard to the number of shots fired at an armed adversary. For although this issue has arisen with shootings in connection with terrorism in Northern

Ireland, it has implications for police on the mainland of Britain.

When terrorists and armed criminals mistaken for terrorists have been shot by the security forces, the great number of shots fired has been equated with a breach of the doctrine of minimum force. The pathologist at the Gibraltar inquest into the shooting of three Provisional IRA terrorists thought to be in possession of remote detonating devices capable of exploding a nearby bomb described the SAS soldiers' action as a 'frenzied attack' on precisely the grounds that each had suffered multiple gunshot wounds (*Independent*, 9 September 1988). It is taken to be axiomatic that shooting someone repeatedly, even after they have collapsed, cannot be consistent with using minimum force, simply because so much force is actually used. On the basis of the previous argument in relation to ammunition, there would seem to be every reason to use such devastating force when circumstances have reached such a perilous extremity. If they have not reached such an extremity there is no justification for shooting at all.

It might appear that to shoot someone twice in rapid succession is sufficient to achieve the purpose of total and immediate incapacitation, and so it might be in many instances. The trouble with relying on this measure of force alone is that it cannot reasonably assure total and immediate incapacitation in all circumstances, for some people show a tremendous capacity for sustaining injuries of this magnitude and still continuing to fight. This is illustrated by the armed confrontations between FBI agents and two armed bank robbers in the Miami suburb of Suniland in 1986, and between police and Palestinian terrorists at a Rome airport in 1985 (Edwards and Menzies, 1986). In both cases, adversaries continued to inflict death and injury upon others despite having sustained multiple and ultimately fatal gunshot wounds.

How can a person fail to be incapacitated after suffering such wounds? First, differences in physique affect the likelihood of incapacitation: more muscular, heavier, and larger people are able to sustain more injury than their smaller, lighter counterparts. Second, scientists have been aware for over a decade that people secrete 'natural opiates' when in a state of physical arousal which act as an analgesic and thereby immunize them against the pain and trauma of gunshot wounds (Snyder, 1986). Third, some criminals and terrorists may take synthetic drugs, such as heroin and its derivatives, which also have an analgesic effect. Fourth, and finally, there is the increasing likelihood that terrorists, in particular, will wear body armour, thus reducing their vulnerability to low-velocity bullets fired at the torso.

In these circumstances, to rely on firing (at most) paired shots only at the torso is to risk ineffective incapacitation of armed opponents and the consequent danger of injury and death being inflicted upon innocent people. The alternative is to use a significantly greater measure of force to ensure, so far as is possible, total and immediate incapacitation. It is reported that the FBI has changed its tactical procedures. The emphasis is now upon 'threat elimination', that is, agents are instructed to keep firing their weapon at their opponents until the threat posed by the suspect is eliminated (*Handgunner*, November 1988). Using the increasingly common 9-mm self-loading pistols, this could mean firing up to eighteen shots, and double this number with a change of magazines. This, of course, was the tactic employed by the SAS soldiers during their 'frenzied attack' on the terrorists in Gibraltar. Similar concerns were expressed after soldiers shot three betting-shop robbers on the Falls Road, Belfast, some thirty times (*The Times*, 15 January 1990).

In both incidents attention was also drawn to evidence that the deceased had been shot whilst lying on the ground, which led to the accusation that the soldiers had administered a gratuitous *coup de grâce* (Kitchin, 1988). As Blom–Cooper (1988) has noted: 'It is one thing to fire a fatal shot at an escaping prisoner, himself armed and intent upon shooting to kill. It is altogether different to use overkill—to do something more than is strictly appropriate.' Is firing a fusillade of shots at a person, even after he has collapsed, 'more than is strictly appropriate'? If a person poses an immediate armed threat such action is appropriate, for such a person will only be incapacitated if he is physically prevented from aiming the weapon and pulling the trigger. Firing repeated shots is most likely to achieve this purpose, for the impact of each bullet will cause at least momentary trauma until the person releases his grip on the weapon.

Not even the firing of repeated shots to the torso will necessarily prevent a terrorist from triggering an explosion even though he is lying gravely, even fatally, wounded. Such a threat would be eliminated only when *all* movement is arrested by shooting the person in the head, with the intention of severing the brain stem and thus preventing all motor functioning. Similarly, a gunman threatening a hostage could be prevented from reacting to having been shot himself only if shot in the head.

In short, in some circumstances it may be wholly justifiable under the doctrine of minimum force to inflict the most devastating injury upon an adversary by firing a fusillade of shots possibly at the head and even after the person had collapsed.[1]

Self-Loading Pistols: Firepower and Safety

It is the capacity to fire multiple shots in rapid succession that is the distinct advantage of the self-loading pistol when compared to the revolver. The Glock carries seventeen rounds in the magazine, and this fire–power is further enhanced by the speed with which magazines can be exchanged, so that in a sustained gun–fight an officer could have as many as thirty-four rounds readily available. It is this capability which has encouraged increasing numbers of American police forces to exchange revolvers for self–loading pistols. Its value was shown during an exchange of fire between police and armed robbers in Harrow, north London, when a PT17 officer expended fifteen rounds.

This kind of weapon also has attractions for critics of the police, for, unlike revolvers, the self-loading pistol is usually equipped with a safety catch. It is to this type of weapon that Benn and Worpole are invidiously comparing the .38-in revolver when they say that the latter 'seems to lack the double-safety devices of other pistols' (1986: 64). They are not alone in voicing such concern. The issue arose most

pointedly during the trials of PC Chester and Inspector
Lovelock. The defence in each of these trials was in essence
the same: that the gun was accidentally discharged by a
startled officer. This, not unnaturally, led to questions about
the safety of the revolvers issued to these officers and anxiety
that they seemed to lack 'safety catches'.

In fact, revolvers are not as a rule fitted with 'safety
catches': the safety of a revolver relies upon its firing
mechanism, for a revolver fired in 'double action' is an
inherently safe weapon. This calls for some explanation of
'double-action' versus 'single-action' shooting. Double action means that, when the revolver's hammer is in the closed
position and then the trigger is depressed, the cylinder rotates
and the hammer is forced back until it drops forward under
the pressure of a spring on to the firing pin, causing the round
in the chamber to be fired. This requires between 10 lb. and
13 lb. of pressure on the trigger of the Smith and Wesson
Model 10, and the trigger must travel some considerable
distance in order to operate the mechanism. This makes
double-action shooting an inherently safe procedure. Single
action, on the other hand, means that in the case of a revolver
the hammer is manually retracted until it locks (sometimes
called 'cocking' the hammer), which in consequence rotates
the cylinder, positioning the next round in line with the
barrel. Then the merest touch on the trigger (3 lb. in the case
of the Model 10) releases the hammer which fires the round.
The advantage of this mode of shooting is that the reduced
pressure upon, and shorter distance travelled by, the trigger
allows greater accuracy. For that reason, single action is
favoured by competition marksmen. However, it is obviously much less safe, since inadvertent pressure on the trigger
would be sufficient to fire a round accidentally.

Until the report of the Home Office Working Party
(1986a), Metropolitan Police officers were instructed in how
to fire the revolver in both single and double action. This was
justified as necessary because it was a feature of the weapon,
and it was important for officers to know how it operated. It
was also thought to have some operational value for carefully
aimed shooting at long distances; accuracy at 25 metres is
undoubtedly improved when firing single-action. However,
the evident dangers inherent in this procedure convinced the

Home Office Working Party that this mode of firing the weapon was too dangerous to be continued. There have been suggestions that under stress officers might place the gun in single action without realizing they have done so, and certainly news film of an armed incident in Oldham 1972 shows a supposedly trained AFO doing precisely this and then pushing the gun, still in single action, into his pocket!

The situation now is that AFOs are familiarized with single-action shooting, but are instructed never to use it operationally. What is not clear is why police revolvers continue to retain the facility for firing in single action. Some American police forces have adapted the internal mechanism of their revolvers to prevent this mode of firing, and the simple expedient of removing the hammer-spur would make it extremely difficult to cock the hammer. The fact that the Metropolitan Police have not taken such action, relying instead upon a simple proscription, seems to reveal a touching faith in the efficacy of rules and the influence they might have over officers in a tense and possibly frightening situation. Surely, if single-action shooting is inherently dangerous, then the means of doing it should be removed.

Critics seem not to be convinced of the inherent safety of revolvers, preferring instead the self-loading pistols that Continental police tend to use (Benn and Worpole, 1986). Indeed their preference is shared by many police officers in Britain and North America who find reassurance in the fire power of such weapons. Whether self-loading pistols are as suitable for police work as either side of the argument imagine is, at least, debatable.

Self-loading pistols: unsuitable complexity

It is important to recognize the important differences between the self-loading pistol and the revolver. In a revolver, each round is placed into its individual chamber and, as the gun is fired, the cylinder revolves, bringing each chamber in succession into line with the barrel and firing-pin. The round itself, once positioned in the chamber, does not move. By contrast, the rounds in a self-loading pistol are taken out of the magazine and pushed into the breech very rapidly. This is a complex and forceful mechanical process which is more likely to result in the weapon jamming because the round is not properly seated in the breech. Jamming may also occur if a bullet misfires and does not create sufficient pressure to operate the mechanism. When this occurs the slide has to be retracted manually, to eject the jammed round. Sometimes the round can be so badly jammed that the gun has to be disassembled to clear it. When a jam does occur, the weapon is incapable of firing any more shots until the jam is cleared. The Walther PP (a standard Continental police pistol) carried by Inspector Beaton when acting as Princess Anne's bodyguard was of this design, and jammed after he had fired one shot at the man attempting to abduct her. Once this occurred, and having been wounded, he was virtually powerless to protect the Princess (Rae, 1987). Revolvers, on the other hand, are mechanically much simpler, and therefore there is less likelihood that things can go wrong. If they do go wrong and the round does not fire for some reason, then all that is needed, save for the most improbable circumstances, is for the handler to squeeze the trigger once again, thus revolving the cylinder and bringing another round into position and firing it.

The sheer mechanical complexity of the self-loading pistol, which demands a very high standard of handling skill, makes this a weapon of limited use for police officers who may have to use the weapon in an emergency. Even in the safety of the practice range the complexities of handling the gun cause difficulties.

A further problem arises from the complexity of the firing mechanism: the need for the user to adopt a sound firing position. Unless the arms are locked so that the recoil from the gun can be fully absorbed by the user, the energy from the recoil can dissipate. This can result in the slide mechanism failing to work adequately and the gun jamming. Such a firing position is taught to users of both self-loading pistols and revolvers, but in an actual gun-fight an officer acting under stress or possibly injured might not be able to adopt an ideal firing position. For example, PC Slimon shot an armed robber after he himself had been shot and was lying on the pavement. It is highly improbable to suppose that he achieved this feat by adopting the prescribed firing position. Had he not been using a revolver, with its simple mechanism, it is less likely that he would have been able effectively to return fire.

Yet another problem arising from the complexity of the mechanism is the restrictions it places on the type of ammunition used. Because the round has to be transferred from the magazine to the breech before being fired, the gun is designed to fire fully jacketed, round-nosed bullets. A fully jacketed bullet has the lead bullet encased in a steel, copper, nickel, or brass sleeve or coat. This enables it to resist any distortion as it is wrenched from the magazine and slammed into the breech. Travel from magazine to breech is aided by a round-nosed bullet shape, which most readily slides up the ramp and into position. Unfortunately, as noted previously, fully jacketed round nosed bullets tend to over-penetrate. In 1986, therefore, it was decided to make available to officers authorized to carry the Browning or Glock an alternative semi-wadcutter, semi-jacketed round, that is, one with a flattened nose which is unsleeved and is therefore less likely to over-penetrate. Unfortunately, its shape means that it is rather less likely to travel easily up the ramp and into the breech. In particular, the condition of the magazine is critical, as any distortion of the lip might cause a jam to occur.

The complexity of this type of weapon demands not only the very highest handling skills, but also a degree of care and maintenance that could only reasonably be expected if it was the sole property of a particular individual, rather than being shared amongst a collection of AFOs.

Why, then, is this weapon so popular amongst firearms-trained police officers? What attracts users to such a weapon is its fire-power, rate of fire, speed of reloading (for all the user need do is remove the empty magazine, replace it with a full one, and release the catch), and its slim shape and lightness, which make it easier to carry and conceal. Perhaps another, but undeclared, reason for the popularity of self-loading pistols is that they are a 'prestige' weapon, restricted to the Force Firearms Unit and officers of the Heathrow airport Security Section.

The undoubted advantage of this type of pistol is its fire-power, and there are good grounds for issuing it to officers

4. 'Deadly Force' 101

who might become engaged in a sustained gun-fight with terrorists and determined criminals. Fortunately, very few armed officers can anticipate such confrontation, and for most police work the revolver seems adequate. The fire-power of revolvers can be enhanced by devices which speed reloading, and which are used by Level II teams. 'Jet loaders' carry six rounds in a cylinder which complements the revolver cylinder and a mechanism which allows all six rounds to be injected into their respective chambers simultaneously and rapidly. The only disadvantage with this is that it prevents topping up a revolver once a few shots have been fired; on the other hand, it offers a rapid and reliable method of reloading which enhances fire-power.

Whilst the self-loading pistol may be appropriate for officers who are highly skilled in their use, such as Level I teams, it would seem that the disadvantages of this kind of weapon outweigh the advantages for more general use. Only if the use of drugs by armed criminals becomes much more prevalent would the advantages of self-loading pistols outweigh their disadvantages. Even when this kind of weapon is issued to highly specialized officers, it would seem prudent (in view of the fact that armed police should always be deployed in pairs) for the partner to be equipped with the more reliable revolver. Alternatively, the British police may follow their American colleagues in allowing armed officers to carry an additional, back-up gun in case the primary weapon fails to operate or its ammunition becomes exhausted.

The catch in the safety argument

Another important difference between the two types of weapon is that, whereas revolvers can be fired in single or double action, a self-loading pistol is fired predominantly in the single-action mode. The mechanism of the self-loading pistol is operated by the recoil from the previously fired round, not by the depression of the trigger. Thus, each time a round is fired the mechanism pushes the hammer into the single-action position where the lightest touch on the trigger (5 lb. in the case of the Browning and 7 lb. for the Glock) causes the hammer to fall and the round in the breech to be fired, which in turn activates the mechanism and pushes the hammer into the single-action mode. Since a live round sits in the breech ready to fire and the hammer is cocked, there is always the danger that an inadvertent touch or even a jolt may cause a shot to be fired. It is because self-loading pistols are so delicately poised in single action that they are almost universally equipped with safety catches. Unlike the revolver, the self-loading pistol is not inherently safe and, therefore, safety has to be added by means of an external locking mechanism which prevents the trigger being depressed and a round being fired unintentionally. Once the safety catch is released in anticipation of opening fire, however, there is a greater risk of an accidental discharge than there would be with a revolver. Yet it seems strange that, when single-action shooting with revolvers has been discontinued on grounds of safety, there should be pressure from within the force and outside it to adopt a type of weapon that fires in single action.

Traditionally, self-loading pistols, like the Browning, operated *only* in single action and were carried 'locked and cocked'. When the gun is drawn from the holster, the safety catch is released by the thumb so that as soon as the gun is aimed it is ready to fire. Technical development has, paradoxically, both increased *and* decreased the safety of such weapons. On the one hand, many modern self-loading pistols incorporate a double-action mechanism for the first round fired, thereby enhancing safety. When the weapon is loaded, like all self-loading pistols, the first round is placed into the breech by 'racking' the slide manually. A catch is then depressed which causes the hammer to fall, but the gun does not fire because the hammer is not allowed to make contact with the firing-pin. When the first round comes to be fired, the trigger is depressed and this causes the hammer to open and fall onto the firing-pin as in double action (although, of course, there is no cylinder to rotate). This gives an extra margin of safety with respect to the first shot fired and obviates the necessity of applying a safety catch, but thereafter the recoil slide mechanism ensures that all subsequent rounds are fired single-action. On the other hand, manufacturers have made safety catches easier to release, thus arguably reducing the safety of the gun. The Glock 17, for example, incorporates the safety catch into the trigger so that as the user squeezes the trigger the first few pounds of pressure release the safety catch and the next few pounds cause it to fire, all in one action. The Heckler and Koch P7 incorporates the safety catch into the butt of the gun which, when gripped, releases the catch.

Safe handling

The safety of weapons is not guaranteed by safety catches or other mechanical features which can be disengaged. The way in which a weapon is handled is much more important for ensuring that it is safe. As the trials of PC Chester and Inspector Lovelock illustrate, there is the danger that innocent people might be accidentally shot as a result of an armed officer being startled. For example, Inspector Lovelock explained how, as a shape loomed out of the darkness, he tensed, causing the gun to fire.

The likelihood that such an accident will occur is increased by the stance adopted by armed officers. The 'isosceles' stance involves holding the butt of the gun with both hands, arms pushed forward and locked at the elbow, with the knees flexed. The reason for locking the elbows is that under extreme stress muscular control can be diminished, especially in the limbs, causing the condition known colloquially by some American police as the 'liquorice arm'. Massad Ayoob, whose system of gun-fighting is founded on the need to overcome stress, insists that the isosceles position is the most robust stance yet devised (Ayoob, 1984). Unfortunately, since the upper body is locked when adopting this stance, the muscles of the trigger finger are amongst the few parts of anatomy that are left free to contract if the officer is startled.

This danger is reduced by the practice of never fingering the trigger until the last possible moment—even a drawn weapon is held with the finger resting outside the trigger guard. In the event of the officer being startled, the trigger could not be inadvertently squeezed. However, there are difficulties concerning this practice, for normally the finger rests along the frame of the gun in the outstretched position and, if it becomes necessary to finger the trigger, it is simultaneously repositioned and bent around the trigger. Unfortunately, the weakness in this practice is that under stress there is a tendency to exaggerate the contraction of the finger muscles as the finger wraps around the trigger, thus making an accidental discharge likely. Ayoob recommends that, even when resting outside the trigger guard, the finger should always be kept bent, so that no further muscular contraction is required when fingering the trigger; all that is necessary is that the finger is repositioned, and the likelihood of accidental discharge is minimized. This seems to be a sensible recommendation which should be incorporated into training.

Non-Lethal Weapons

The prospect of non-lethal weapons being developed to replace the disagreeable necessity to use lethal firearms has long held a fascination for lay commentators. The impetus for the development of non-lethal alternatives to firearms in the USA came from the 1985 decision of the US Supreme Court in the case of *Tennessee* v. *Garner*, which restricted the right of American law enforcement personnel to shoot at a 'fleeing felon'. This has prompted the development and use of electrified batons ('sting sticks'), barbs that fasten to the skin and carry an incapacitating electric current ('Tasar'), bags containing shotgun pellets which expand upon being fired from a shotgun so as to stun and disable those who are hit ('bean bags'), and tranquillizing darts.

Unfortunately, no complete replacement for lethal firearms has yet been found. The reasons for this go to the heart of the problem of using minimum but effective force. To use a non-lethal weapon as a direct substitute for lethal firearms would require that it should incapacitate the adversary as totally and immediately as a lethal firearm. However, this would involve inflicting such trauma that it is likely to prove as deadly as a firearm, at least to some people. That is, an electric shock, or stunning impact from a 'bean bag', or anaesthetic drug capable of reliably causing total and immediate incapacitation would inflict so much injury that it is likely to prove fatal itself. If less injury is inflicted, then total and immediate incapacitation cannot be reasonably guaranteed.

What these kinds of weapon *can* offer, and have been used for in America, is a means of dealing with situations before they reach the stage at which the use of potentially lethal force is justified and where total and immediate incapacitation is *not* essential. A man holding police at bay with a knife or a person holding a gun, but not threatening anyone directly, might be overpowered with such a weapon. For example, had the police at the Northolt siege been able to disable Errol Walker when he appeared alone on the balcony adjoining the flat, they might not have had to shoot him as he attempted to stab his hostage.

The problem is one of calibrating a measure of injury needed to disable a dangerous person without its becoming life-threatening. This is immensely difficult given the vagaries of physical differences amongst human beings: the force needed to disable a body-builder could easily kill a 'seven-stone weakling'. Thus, although referred to as 'non-lethal', these weapons have actually caused the deaths of some of those against whom they have been used, whilst others seem to be have been almost totally unaffected by these weapons. As has been noted earlier, not even bullets will have the same effect on all those shot.

The introduction of this kind of weapon, far from resolving the problems of police use of deadly force, actually compounds them. If weapons of this type were to be employed, then potentially lethal force would be employed *not* as a last resort, but at a lower level of threat. True, the likelihood that these weapons would prove fatal is much less than that of firearms, but there remains a likelihood, however small, that they will kill. Thus, the police would need to make an even finer calculation than they now are obliged to make, between the amount of force to be applied as opposed to the level of threat presented by their adversary.

One weapon that seems particularly promising is the 'low energy' version of the ARWEN baton round, which contains a sack of CS powder that ruptures on impact. This, however, like any comparable weapon, is likely to inflict serious injury on at least some people and may even prove fatal in particular circumstances. This weapon was developed by Royal Ordnance in the early 1980s as a replacement for the baton gun used for riot control, in which capacity it has been the victim of the wider campaign waged against the use of plastic baton rounds (see pp. 195–208) and of financial restrictions on procurement by the Ministry of Defence (Waddington, 1989).

Sub-machine-guns

Of all the weapons issued to the police, those which have attracted most criticism are the Heckler and Koch MP5 and MP5K. It is the MP5 that is carried by some officers at Heathrow airport.

The issue is not whether terrorists pose a serious threat to diplomats, politicians, and airports. The fact that they do is evidenced by attacks such as the attempted assassination of Sholom Argov, the Israeli ambassador, in 1983 and the grenade and machine-gun attack at Rome and Vienna airports in December 1985, which resulted in two passengers being killed and forty-seven injured at Vienna and thirteen killed and seventy-six injured at Rome. The fact that Heathrow is not immune to terrorist activity was vividly illustrated in 1986, when Hussein Hindawi attempted to plant a bomb on board an El Al airliner departing from Heathrow, and, in 1988 by the destruction of Pam Am Flight 103 which blew up over Lockerbie *en route* from Heathrow to New York. Unfortunately, these are only the most recent of a series of similar attacks staged in different parts of the world over the past twenty years. The issue *is* whether the overt deployment of officers carrying the Heckler and Koch MP5 is operationally effective.

The grounds upon which the deployment of the MP5 was justified were twofold: as mentioned in Appendix A, its magazine of thirty rounds affords sufficient fire-power to engage terrorists in a prolonged gun-fight. At Rome and Vienna, terrorists attacked the El Al check-in queues with Kalashnikov AK47 assault rifles which had two magazines of thirty rounds each taped together, so that once the first magazine was exhausted the second could be inserted by the simple expedient of inverting the magazine and pushing it home. This meant that, within the space of a few seconds, the three terrorists at Vienna and the four at Rome each had the opportunity to fire sixty rounds at a rate of 600 rounds per minute. The total attack at Vienna, including a car chase and second gun-fight with police, lasted just seven minutes and that at Rome lasted only fifty-five seconds (Edwards and Menzies, 1986). Given that the police may need to confront that kind of fire-power, it is argued that *they* need the fire-power of a weapon like the Heckler and Koch MP5.

The second reason for requiring a carbine is that police may need to engage terrorists at relatively long distances. Terminal buildings provide large open areas affording little cover, and the piers connecting the various gates for boarding aircraft are enormously long corridors, again offering restricted cover. In addition, airports include large open areas where terrorists might attack airliners waiting to take off. The maximum effective range of the hand-gun is optimistically estimated at 50 metres. Rifles can fire accurately over much greater distances, but suffer from problems of over-penetration. A carbine firing a normal 9-mm pistol round can provide the additional range without much risk of over-penetration should a gun-fight occur under these circumstances. Fired single-shot from the shoulder and having little recoil, the MP5 is justified as much more accurate than any hand-gun but no more injurious.

The deployment of the MP5 at Heathrow created a furore, principally on the grounds that it was a sub-machine-gun unsuitable for use in a crowded airport. Yardley (1986) explicitly doubts whether it was meant to be fired from the shoulder, or whether it was intended to fire only single shots, and added that in any case the ammunition used was unsuitable. Like others, he sees it as a symbolic victory for terrorists, not only unlikely to deter further attacks but likely actually to increase the danger to armed officers, who would become the first targets for any attacker. What validity is there in these criticisms?

As already explained, the gun can only fire single shots and officers are instructed only to fire aimed shots from the shoulder. Why not, then, use a dedicated carbine which would not be confused with a sub-machine-gun, and avoid all the negative connotations of the latter? Yardley argues that such a weapon could fire a round more suitable to police needs. He points out that the Heckler and Koch MP5 normally fires a 9-mm, round-nosed, fully jacketed round, which, as mentioned previously, tends to over-penetrate, lacks 'stopping power' thereby, and tends also to ricochet. However, dedicated carbines are magazine-fed weapons which also normally fire round-nosed, fully jacketed rounds. Moreover, in fact the Metropolitan Police now issue a semi-wadcutter, semi-jacketed round of less power than the military 2Z round to which Yardley seems to be referring. This bullet does not over-penetrate as easily as its military counterpart, nor is it so likely to ricochet, although it is more prone to jam the firing mechanism. Of course, these same rounds could be used in a dedicated carbine with the same advantages and disadvantages. An advantage in doing so might be that they could not be confused with sub-machine-guns, and thus not convey such an aggressive militaristic image. However, dedicated carbines such as the Martini have the appearance of a rifle and must, like the MP5, be carried openly. It is doubtful whether they would be any more acceptable to public opinion.

A second, and altogether more substantial, challenge is contained in a report on the Rome and Vienna terrorist attacks written by Chief Superintendent Edwards and Detective Sergeant Menzies of the Sussex Police, who were at the time responsible for security at Gatwick airport (Edwards and Menzies, 1986). After visiting Rome and Vienna airports in the wake of the terrorist attacks of 1985, they too dispute the operational effectiveness of carbines or sub-machine-guns for use *within* airport buildings. Their report points out that, despite the fact that at least some of the officers who engaged the terrorists at both Continental airports were armed with sub-machine-guns only one officer used this weapon, and he did so in single-shot mode. The authors of this report remark that at Vienna: 'It is significant that although armed with the Steyr sub-machine-gun the offiers chose the 9-mm pistols as the more appropriate weapon for use inside the terminal.' At Rome: 'The majority of the rounds were fired from Beretta pistols . . . The sniper overlooking the concourse could not fire because of the confusion below.' They conclude: 'The use of machine-guns by police in the terminal building is not recommended because of the numbers of passengers that could be reasonably expected', and 'Hand guns used by trained officers can compete effectively against sub-machine-guns in close combat.'

Advocates of the Heckler and Koch MP5 amongst Metropolitan Police firearms instructors reply to this argument by pointing out that it is often the practice on the Continent, where officers are permanently armed with handguns, to use the sub-machine-gun as the back-up weapon rather than the primary weapon. Officers at Heathrow armed with the Heckler and Koch MP5 are trained to regard this as their primary weapon and their hand-gun as their back-up. Hence the Heckler and Koch MP5 is carried in the 'high port' position which facilitates ease of use, being very rapidly aimed and fired from the shoulder.

If, for whatever reason, officers at Rome and Vienna airports used pistols successfully against terrorists armed with AK47s, what purpose is served by equipping officers with carbines? What remains unclear from the Edwards and Menzies report (1986) is how much success the Rome and Vienna officers actually enjoyed. It appears that the terrorists were shot repeatedly but were not incapacitated until all their ammunition had been expended. Had the police used the fire-power of a sub-machine-gun, it is, perhaps, possible that they could have fired a sustained hail of bullets at the terrorists (aiming preferably for the head) and caused sufficient injury to disable them before they completed their murderous attack.

Where the report does undermine the justification for deploying the Heckler and Koch MP5 at Heathrow is in its finding that the only officers able to engage the terrorists were those immediately on hand, who did so at close range. At Vienna, the report notes: 'Of the number of police officers inside the terminal building only 2 were in a position to respond to the attack by using firearms, the remainder were

110   *'Armed Police'*

thwarted by the number of passengers who were running away from the attack.' A similar situation occurred at Rome, where only three of the ten or more officers on duty in the terminal were able to engage the attackers. Thus, the report concludes: 'Because of the number of passengers likely to be in the check-in area it is probable that a small number of officers will be able to respond to a terrorist attack.' Apart from pointing to the need to place available officers at strategic locations, this also suggests that the extra range afforded by the Heckler and Koch MP5 will not be needed. On the other hand, an attack on a pier or gate area may require officers to engage terrorists at some distance. Nevertheless, Edwards and Menzies do recommend that automatic weapons be available for the area outside the terminal, where confrontations might occur at greater distances.

Whether or not it is operationally effective, is the deployment of the MP5 a symbolic victory for terrorism? Whilst the sight of a police officer carrying what appears to be a sub-machine-gun will be commonplace to the international traveller, it obviously damages the unarmed image of the police in the eyes of the domestic population. Certainly, photographs of officers carrying this weapon seem frequently to adorn newspaper and magazine articles on the police, especially anything remotely to do with firearms. This might be an acceptable price to pay if it deterred terrorist attacks. On the one hand, it might be argued that the possession of such weapons did not deter the attacks on Rome and Vienna, where police are routinely and much more heavily armed than in Britain. On the other hand, it could be contended that the heightened security at airports since 1985 has caused terrorists to avoid any repetition of this kind of direct assault, even if they have simply changed their tactics in favour of hiding bombs on board aircraft. What cannot be validly argued is that carrying such a weapon endangers the police. Yardley claims: 'The irony is that high profile security is ineffective. At the most obvious level because walking around in uniform and carrying a sub-machine-gun is akin to walking around with a target pinned to you.' (1986: 20). The terrorists at Rome and Vienna had ample opportunity to shoot the police before opening fire on

'Deadly Force' 111

the passengers, but chose not to do so. Indeed, at Rome they paid no attention at all to two officers standing either side of the stairs from which they launched their attack.

Sub-machine-guns and 'minimum force'

Important though Heathrow airport has become as the most visible example of armed policing, the use of sub-machine-guns is not limited to this location. It was noted above that some protection officers may carry a sub-machine-gun under particular and closely monitored circumstances. Officers of PT17 train in its use both as a single-shot and as an automatic weapon. The advantage of using the MP5 in automatic mode is *not* that it can spray whole areas indiscriminately; on the contrary, automatic fire would be used in *close-quarters* encounters. A single burst lasting less than a second would discharge a number of shots faster than they could be fired as single shots. In a confrontation with terrorists or desparate criminals threatening to kill hostages, automatic fire at close range would allow the almost instant delivery of severely incapacitating force. An adversary hit by a hail of automatic gunfire would have much less opportunity to open fire or detonate explosives than had he been shot once or twice with single shots.

Although this can, as argued above (pp. 93–6), be justified within the doctrine of minimum force by the need to eliminate a threat by total and immediate incapacitation, the devastating injuries that the use of automatic fire is intended to inflict has caused controversy. What is ironic is that the controversy concentrates so exclusively upon the use of sub-machine-guns. It is this weapon that has come to symbolize the supposed threat to the principle of minimum force, whereas the shotgun is relatively publicly acceptable. This is so despite the fact that shotguns loaded with 'SG' (see pp. 283–4) have the potential.to hit a person with the equivalent of nine .32-in unsleeved bullets — the equivalent of a firing squad. Fired at more than 15–20 metres, there is a strong probability that some of the pellets will miss their target entirely and pose a danger to innocent bystanders. If any weapon is designed to spray bullets it is the shotgun. Loaded with a single rifled slug, the shotgun can achieve accuracy, but at a cost of inflicting massive injuries.

The sub-machine-gun, for all its negative public image, is a weapon whose use is much more consistent with the doctrine of minimum force. A single 9-mm round can be fired from a sub-machine-gun, or a succession of shots can be fired *depending upon the circumstances*. Thus, the amount of force used can depend upon the level of threat presented, whereas a shotgun will deliver a devastating hail of fire whatever the level of threat.

In view of this, there are strong grounds for arguing that shotguns should be weapons of last resort, and that the sub-machine-gun should replace them as the standard intermediate-range long-arm.

Overt versus Covert Carrying of Guns

It is not only the *fact* that police carry what appears to be a sub-machine-gun that seems to arouse so much public anxiety, but that they are *seen* to do so. In Britain, not only do armed officers in plain clothes covertly carry firearms, so too do armed officers in uniform. This is quite unusual, if not unique, amongst police forces throughout the world. On the one hand, this prevents the public being alarmed by the sight of visibly armed police, and avoids a distinction being drawn between armed and unarmed officers. On the other hand, it significantly hampers an armed officer who might need to draw his gun from the holster hidden under his tunic, as it did when PC Trevor Lock was overpowered by terrorists attacking the Iranian embassy before he could draw his gun. Officers in shirt-sleeves have an even greater problem, for the only opportunity for carrying the gun covertly is in a holster inside the trouser pocket, which makes the gun extremely difficult to draw in an emergency. Officers in some forces are equipped with a special pouch covered by a flap secured by velcron, which can quickly be ripped open and the gun drawn. Even so, this is obviously a more difficult manœuvre than simply drawing the gun from a holster worn openly on the hip.

There are also anomalies, especially at Heathrow airport,

where members of the Security Section are permanently armed. Amongst the officers in this section, a distinction is drawn between those who overtly carry the Heckler and Koch MP5, and who are, therefore, allowed also to carry their hand-gun overtly, and those who are simply armed with hand-guns which they must carry covertly. It is argued by some officers, first, that since the Heckler and Koch MP5 is carried overtly any damage to the unarmed image of the British police has already been inflicted, and second, that the justification for carrying the Heckler and Koch MP5 is that a terrorist attack may occur suddenly, without warning and be of such brief duration that an officer may need immediately to return fire. The same surely applies to other officers of the Security Section, each of whom might be impeded in drawing his covertly carried hand-gun from the holster under the same circumstances. A second anomaly is that officers who carry guns covertly cannot be easily distinguished from unarmed officers engaged on 'general duties'. In the event of a terrorist attack, insofar as police might be the targets of the attackers, unarmed officers will be at as much risk as their armed colleagues. However, there is a compensating advantage that not knowing which police officers are or are not armed may cause terrorists to overestimate the odds they might face in mounting an attack.

There seems little reason to doubt that the effectiveness of armed officers in combating a terrorist attack would be enhanced if they wore their firearms overtly. The difficulty lies in weighing these quite tangible benefits against the damage that this would do to the image of the unarmed, non-aggressive British bobby. The response of the Home Office Working Party (1986a) to the suggestion that weapons should normally be carried overtly was hostile. They insisted that overtly carrying weapons, such as the Heckler and Koch MP5, is an exceptional measure in response to exceptional conditions.

Guns for concealment

An issue related to the overt versus covert carrying of weapons is the type of weapon that should be issued to officers in plain clothes who must, of necessity, carry a firearm covertly. It was for officers engaged on these duties that the Walther PP was originally provided, because it is a compact weapon. However, when that weapon was withdrawn in 1974 it was replaced by the short-barrelled, five-chamber version of the standard Model 10 Smith and Wesson, the Model 36 (Home Office, 1972). In 1983 the Model 36 was, in turn, replaced with the six-chamber version of the same weapon, the Model 64, which is of stainless-steel construction.

The justification for choosing the Models 36 and 64 is that their two-inch barrels make them easier to conceal and less cumbersome to carry routinely. However, the disadvantage of this weapon is that it is less accurate over long distances (Greenwood, 1979; Harold, 1974). This is now officially acknowledged, since officers authorized to use the Model 64 need only qualify in aimed shooting at a maximum of 15 metres, compared to the 25-metre range of the Model 10. The short distance between the foresight and backsight on the Model 64 means that it is difficult to achieve accurate alignment, and any small error at the point of aim is magnified with increased distance. Moreover, the stainless-steel construction reflects light and often obscures the sight-picture, making this weapon particularly difficult to aim. On the other hand, it is thought that this weapon is unlikely to be used at long distances, for it is mainly issued to officers engaged on close-protection duty where they may have to combat an attack at close quarters. However, the only occasion to date where a protection officer has been called upon to use a short-barrelled revolver — the attempted assassination of Ambassador Argov — involved him shooting a carefully aimed shot at the escaping would-be assassin who was 15 metres away (see p. 64).

A further disadvantage is that the short barrel reduces the muzzle velocity of any round fired from the 800 feet per second of the Model 10 to approximately 600 feet per second. It was probably for this reason that detectives armed with Model 64s found that five shots were needed to incapacitate one of a gang who opened fire on them during the East Acton post office robbery (*The Times*, 16 December 1988). The reduced stopping power of a much slower bullet is particularly serious in regard to armed bodyguards, and further strengthens their need for more potent ammunition if the short-barrelled revolver is to remain the weapon with which they are issued.

The advantage of concealment over accuracy and stopping power would be more convincing if the length of barrel were critical to concealing a revolver. Unfortunately, the most difficult features of any revolver to conceal are the cylinder and the butt, which, in the case of the Model 64, are virtually identical to the Model 10. It seems difficult to disagree with Greenwood (1979) or Harold (1974), who argue that the balance of advantage lies with the longer-barrelled revolver, particularly since the 'pancake holster' makes even this bulky weapon easy to conceal. However, if concealment is of such overriding importance, then it would seem that a self-loading pistol, similar to the Walther PP, is what is required.

Armed-Response Vehicles

Just as the police are concerned about damaging their unarmed image by overtly carrying firearms, so they have sought to avoid the charge of having armed police 'roaming the streets of London'. Thus, instead of having a small number of armed officers on stand-by, ready to respond to incidents, divisional AFOs have been obliged to retire to the nearest station and draw a weapon specially from the armoury. It now seems likely that this will change, and that there will be a small number of vehicles on patrol which permanently carry firearms and whose crews are quite highly trained in their use. It will be they that will provide the initial response to armed incidents in future.

Hitherto, the police and the Home Office have been reluctant to endorse the deployment of armed-response vehicles for reasons which appear less than convincing. The Home Office Working Party (1986a) saw no reason 'to commend the practice to chief officers', apparently on the grounds that such vehicles require that crews be trained both as drivers and as AFOs. However, this is hardly a compelling objection, since dog-handlers have long been trained to drive emergency vehicles as an additional skill, and there seems no reason why AFOs should not similarly be trained. More- over, there seems to be a correlation between driving skill and marksmanship. The principal concern amongst policy- makers seems to have been the controversy that such a move might occasion. However, in the wake of the Hungerford massacre and the McLaughlin (1988) report, official attitudes seem ready to change. Indeed, they have already changed in many forces nationwide who now deploy armed-response vehicles. The irony is that, as the McLaughlin report made plain, armed-response vehicles would probably have made no difference to the outcome of the Hungerford massacre, save possibly to have increased police casualties.

Far from being viewed with trepidation, such a develop- ment has a number of advantages. In the past, when an armed incident was reported, the first police officers likely to arrive at the scene would have been unarmed. They would have done whatever they could to protect members of the public and contain the gunman, but their effectiveness in doing so was likely to have been hindered by their being unarmed. Moreover, these unarmed officers were highly vulnerable and may have fallen victim to a gunman, as did PC Brereton during the Hungerford massacre in August 1987 and PC Carlton who attempted to intercept armed robbers in Coventry in December 1988. When armed officers eventually arrived, they might have done so singly and have had to form themselves into pairs at the scene. This might have involved being paired with another officer whom they did not know, or had not worked with closely, or with whom they had not trained — an obviously unsatisfactory situation given the seriousness of the circumstances. An armed-response vehicle, by contrast, is not only likely to arrive first, but would contain a pair of officers of Level II standard who work and train together regularly. The weapons carried in the vehicle would be the same as those with which the crew regularly train, and not some unfamiliar and possibly unsuitable gun drawn from an armoury. Thus, the crew would be in a position to establish an effective containment from the outset.

What is less clear is why these vehicles need to *patrol*.

Clearly, the purpose that they will serve is one of an emergency response to armed incidents. Surely, it is imperative that they should be able to reach any point within the area for which they are responsible in the minimum amount of time. Patrolling means that, when armed officers are needed, they may be far from the scene of the incident and possibly engaged in some other task. Armed response is genuinely 'fire brigade policing', and it seems appropriate to adopt the same strategy as the fire brigade. Thus, the armed-response vehicle should be based at a static strategic location from where it can reach all points in the area in the minimum time. Officers on stand-by could then have weapons and body armour readily to hand, instead of being expected to stop their vehicle and don equipment. There could be no accusation that police were patrolling the streets with firearms, and the weapons themselves would remain securely inside a building rather than in a relatively insecure car. The officers could be occupied on duties which could quickly be abandoned. The only loss would seem to be to that shibboleth 'preventative patrol', which seems to achieve little besides the wasteful consumption of fuel.

Drifting Towards an Armed Police?

The prospect of certain police vehicles routinely patrolling with firearms on board raises the genuine issue of whether, in responding to armed crime and terrorism, the British police are drifting gradually but inexorably towards becoming routinely armed, as are virtually all their counterparts throughout the world. The danger is not only that, as the growth in crime and terrorism pose an increased threat, the police will be drawn towards ever more frequent deployment of armed officers, but also that it is more difficult to reverse direction once an escalatory step has been taken.

An example of this kind of 'ratchet effect' can be seen at Heathrow airport, where the Heckler and Koch MP5 was deployed in response to the attack on Rome and Vienna airports. Whilst until recently authority for carrying these weapons was granted each month by the Home Office

and the firm wish amongst senior officers of the Metropolitan Police to remove these weapons once it is safe to do so, it
is unlikely that they will be withdrawn in the foreseeable
future. If these weapons were to be withdrawn, and this
decision were to be followed by a terrorist attack at the
airport, it seems reasonable to suppose that the public outcry
would be enormous. The police and the Home Office would
be condemned for failing adequately to protect the public, as
they were following the Hungerford massacre, when a
spurious connection was made between that incident and
reductions in the number of AFOs (Edwards, 1988).

Only the clearest indication that the risk to airports has
been significantly reduced, if not eliminated, will encourage
those in authority to take such a decision. However, it is in
the nature of terrorist activity that it does not easily permit
such a conclusion to be drawn. It is difficult to identify a
point at which tension has lessened sufficiently to warrant a
degree of disarmament. Whereas a particularly horrendous
incident can precipitate an escalation towards armed policing,
few comparable events can prompt a compensating de-
escalation.

A Task for the Police?

If it is necessary for armed protection to be routinely
provided at airports and elsewhere, is it appropriate that this
should be a responsibility of the civil police, given the
damage that it inflicts upon their unarmed reputation? There
seems to be a strong case for assigning *some* armed tasks to a
separate agency.

The police, particularly the Metropolitan Police, have
always performed various guarding duties: there have always
been police bodyguards, and they have usually been armed.
The growth of international terrorism has caused this
function to be extended massively. Airports throughout the
UK are protected by armed police; the Royalty and
Diplomatic Protection Department (RDPD) guard persons
and places at risk from terrorist attack; beyond the civil
police, the Atomic Energy Authority police (see *Time Out*,
22 October 1986) and Ministry of Defence police both

provide armed protection for sensitive installations. Whether performed by members of the civil police or not, the tasks they perform are essentially the same, and distinguish them from the remainder of the police service. This is partially recognized in the case of the RDPD, whose vehicles have a distinctive maroon livery. All these departments of the Metropolitan Police or separate police forces perform a quasi-military, rather than police, role of providing protection from external attack. As already mentioned, it makes little sense to imagine police 'containing' a terrorist attack upon an airport terminal: the task of armed officers must be to engage and defeat.

Perhaps it is time that serious consideration is given to establishing a national paramilitary security force to perform these guarding duties. If they wore a uniform which distinguished them from the police, they would be free to carry weapons overtly without undermining the traditional image of the unarmed British police. Directly responsible to government, the cost of such a corps would not be obscured by its inclusion with other police functions and inevitable competition for resources within the police budget. In areas like airport terminals, the separation of function would avoid anomalies and confusion, leaving the police to deal with routine policing tasks whilst the security force simply guarded against terrorist attack.

Even if this strategy were adopted, it would not eliminate the need for some police to use firearms some of the time in connection with 'normal' crime. This is likely to amount to two or three armed operations per day in the Metropolitan Police District, as now, or even more. So long as this is a regrettable necessity, the police must commit themselves to maintaining and enhancing the professional approach that has been increasingly evident since the mid–1960s. There is no likelihood that PT17 will disappear — nor should they.

Conclusions

'Minimum force' is not what it seems: using less 'aggressive' tactics, weaponry, and ammunition may simply shift the

danger of death and injury from armed aggressors to
innocent victims; guns with safety catches may be more
dangerous than those without; a sub–machine–gun/carbine is
less lethal than a shotgun; the use of armed–response vehicles
would not amount to an escalation, but would allow fewer
specialized officers to provide an effective response to armed
incidents. However rationally defensible these propositions
and proposals, they confront the reality of 'public acceptability', which is often uninformed and emotional. Thus,
practices continue which not only are less effective, but in
some cases are more likely to result in error and needless
injury.

NOTES 120a

Chapter 4

1   It is an irony that the application of the Hague Conventions on military ammunition might encourage soldiers to fire a fusillade of shots in almost any event. Because full-metal jacketed bullets create little cavitation and over-penetrate, the amount of injury inflicted upon the adversary cannot be guaranteed to incapacitate. To compensate for the inadequate stopping power of military ammunition, soldiers may feel obliged to fire a fusillade of shots.

BIBLIOGRAPHY

Ayoob. M. (1984). *Stressfire.* M. and D. Ayoob, available from Police Bookshelf, Concord, NH.

Benn. M. and Worpole, K. (1986). *Death in the City.* London: Canary Press.

Bittner. E. 1975). 'A Theory of the Police', in H. Jacob (ed.), *Potential for Reform of Criminal Justice.* Beverly Hills, Calif.: Sage.

Blom-Cooper. L. (1988). 'Justifications for Homicide', *Independent,* 1 Sept. Bowden, T. (1977). *Beyond the Limits of the Law.* Harmondsworth, Middx.: Penguin.

Chappell. D. and Graham, L. P. (1985). *Police Use of Deadly Force: Canadian Perspectives.* Centre of Criminology, Univ. of Toronto.

Dawkins. K. (1989). 'Police Weapons (I): Soft-Nose Bullets', *New Zealand Law Journal,* Feb.

Edwards. C. (1988). Was Hungerford "a basic failure of the police"?', *Listener* 14 Jan.

Edwards. G. S. and Menzies, K. (1986). 'Visits to Leonardo Da Vinci Airport, Rome, and Schwechat Airport, Vienna, following Terrorist Attacks on 27th Dec., 1985'. Unpublished report, Gatwick Airport: Sussex Police.

Gould. R. W. and Waldren, M. J. (1986). *London's Armed Police.* London Arms & Armour.

Greenwood. C. (1979). *Police Tactics in Armed Operations.* Paladin, Colo.: Paladin Press.

Harding. R. W. (1970). *Police Killings in Australia.* Sydney: Penguin.

Harold. M. C. D. (1974). 'Armaments for Police Officers on Protection', *Police Journal,* Oct.

Kitchin. H. (1988). *The Gibraltar Report: Inquest into the Deaths of Mairead Farrell, Daniel McCann and Sean Savage, Gibraltar, September 1988.* London: National Council for Civil Liberties.

McLaughlin. C. (1988). *The Hungerford Incident.* Unpublished report.

Manwaring-White. S. (1983). *The Policing Revolution.* Brighton, Sussex: Harvester.

Milton. C. H. Halleck, J. W. Lardner, J. and Abrecht, G. L. (1977). *Police Use of Deadly Force.* Washington, DC: Police Foundation.

Rae. A. (1987). 'The Medals of the Met. ', *Police Review,* 30 Jan.

Snyder. S. H. (1986). *Drugs and the Brain.* New York: Scientific American.

Waddington. P. A. J. (1989). 'Beware the Shot in the Dark', *Police,* 21/6.

Yardley, M. (1986). 'Wrong', *Police,* 18/6.

[23]

Shootings by Police in Victoria: The Ethical Issues

SEUMAS MILLER

Introduction

Since 1986 over thirty-four people have died from police shootings in the state of Victoria, compared with about twelve in NSW over that period.[1] These recent killings raise the important philosophical issue of the moral justification for police use of deadly force.

Human life is a fundamental moral value and killing another person can only be morally justified in extreme circumstances. The basic such circumstance is that of self-defence. I am morally entitled to kill another person if that person is trying to kill me and will succeed if I do not kill him or her first. Self-defence is not the only justification for taking the life of another person; it is widely accepted that each of us has the right to kill in defence of the lives of others. I am morally entitled to kill someone attempting to kill my wife or husband if this is the only means of prevention.

With the establishment of police services in modern societies, the responsibility for defending myself, and especially for protecting others, has to a large extent devolved to the police. Crudely, the idea is that if someone's life is threatened, whether my own or someone else's, my first step should be to call the police.

According to the Australian National Committee on Violence, 'Recommendation 85.1, Uniform laws throughout Australia

206   Violence and Police Culture

regarding the use of firearms and other lethal force by police', 'These laws should reflect the principle that lethal force should only be used as a last resort, involving self-defence or the defence of others'.[2] In short, it is widely assumed that the only two morally acceptable justifications for killing are self-defence and the defence of others. But the recent killings by police in Victoria draw attention to the possibility of other *moral* justifications for use of deadly force. Whether or not these further putative moral justifications for police use of deadly force are also *legal* justifications is not something I am competent to judge. Nor do I pretend to offer authoritative accounts of what *in fact* took place in the various incidents of use of deadly force that I discuss.

Killing in Defence of Rights

Killing in order to defend one's own life or the life of another is morally justified on the grounds that each of us has a right to life.[3] We are entitled to defend that right to life by killing an attacker under three conditions. Firstly, the attacker is intentionally trying to kill someone—either oneself or another person—and will succeed if we do not intervene. We are not entitled to shoot dead an attacker whom we know is threatening us with a replica of a gun. Secondly, we have no way of preserving our own or the other person's life other than by killing the attacker—for example, we are not able to flee to safety. Thirdly, and more problematically, our attacker does not have a morally justifiable reason for trying to kill. For example, it may be that a legally appointed executioner has a decisive morally justifiable reason for carrying out the death penalty in the case of a serial killer, but that the serial killer does not have a decisive morally justifiable reason for trying to kill the executioner in self-defence supposing the opportunity arose.[4]

The police killing of Mark Militano in 1986 is evidently a case of justified killing in self-defence, and/or of killing in defence of the lives of others. Police were following Militano and had evidence in the form of an overheard conversation which was probably sufficient to charge him with conspiracy to commit armed robbery. Police cars converged on Militano, and one car swerved in front of Militano's vehicle causing him to brake. Militano reached for his handgun and pointed it at one of the police. A number of police fired at Militano. Militano, apparently unharmed, ran from his car. A police officer fired a shot in the air, calling for him to stop. Militano turned, raised his pistol and aimed at the police. Sergeant Ray Watson, the man who had overheard the conversation concerning the planned bank robbery, fired one shot from his .38 revolver. The bullet hit Militano in the head and minutes later he died.[5] Clearly, at the point when Watson shot Militano the above mentioned three conditions for justifiable killing in self-defence—or defence of the lives of others—obtained. Firstly, Militano was intentionally trying to kill someone—either Watson or another officer—and would have probably succeeded if Watson did not intervene. Secondly, Watson had no way of preserving his own or the other police officers' lives other than by killing Militano. Thirdly, Militano did not have a morally justifiable reason for trying to kill Watson and/or the other police officers.

The case of Gary Abdallah was apparently another instance of *justified* killing in self-defence, or at least *excusable* killing in self-defence. Abdallah was suspected by police of involvement in the Walsh Street killings of two police officers. However there was insufficient evidence to prosecute him. There was however evidence of his attempted murder of a senior policeman's son. Detectives Clifton Lockwood and Dermot Avon were sent to arrest Abdallah. It was alleged that Abdallah produced a revolver, aimed it at Lockwood, was warned by Lockwood to put it down, and was shot dead by Lockwood when he failed to do so. The revolver turned out to be an imitation gun. Detectives Lockwood and Avon were charged with murder but both were found not guilty. While the gun was an imitation gun, it was *reasonably believed* to have been a real gun.[6] Accordingly, the first of the above-mentioned conditions for justifiable self-defence—that the attacker will in fact kill the defender unless the defender intervenes—can be weakened to generate a set of conditions for morally *excusable* self-defence. The relevant new condition is that the defender *reasonably believes* the attacker will kill him unless he intervenes.

Police are entitled to kill in self-defence and to defend the lives of others. But a further point that needs to be stressed is that police on occasion have a legal and moral *duty* to kill to protect innocent lives. Indeed they can be held legally liable if they fail to take the opportunity to shoot dead an armed and dangerous criminal who then goes on to, say, take the lives of innocent citizens. While ordinary citizens have a right to kill in cases where there is an immediate threat to their own or someone else's life, it is by no means clear that they have a *duty* to kill to protect others, even in cases where the threat is immediate and beyond question.

Having outlined the standard account of killing in self-defence or in defence of the life of others, and illustrated it by recourse to some recent police killings in Victoria, let me now consider a different, or at least, an expanded kind of moral justification for killing, namely, what I will call killing in defence of rights. Clearly the rights in question are rights other than the right to life. However in speaking of killing in defence of rights one would obviously not want to include *all* moral rights, or at least *all violations* of all moral rights. For example, property rights are arguably moral rights, but for a police officer to kill someone to prevent them stealing a handbag would be morally unacceptable. So the question becomes: Are there any moral rights, apart from the right to life, the protection of which would justify police use of deadly force? Candidates for such rights might include a right not to be severely physically or psychologically damaged. Perhaps rape, serious child molestation and grievous bodily harm are actions the prevention of which might justify use of deadly force. Maybe police are justified in shooting a fleeing serial rapist if that is the only way to ensure his arrest. If we go further afield, geographically and historically, we find other kinds of possible case. What do we want to say of the current policy in Zimbabwe of police shooting rhino poachers on sight—given that rhinos are facing extinction and other methods have failed? Or what of the shooting on sight of cattle rustlers in the American West, in circumstances under which cattle rustling threatened ranchers' livelihoods? Again, what are we to say about shooting looters? The shooting of looters in disaster zones or in conditions of civil unrest has been an accepted policy in many parts of the world over a long period of time. Finally, there are the shootings of armed robber-murderers in South Africa by police. There has been a frightening increase in the robbery of businesses in South Africa by heavily armed gunmen who sometimes shoot dead unarmed shopkeepers and others in the process of the robbery. Some of these gunmen will shoot to kill police officers seeking to apprehend them. Such situations can escalate into quasi-military wars, with offenders and police treating each other as combatants.

Police use of Deadly Force to Enforce the Law

The first point to be made here is that many of the above-mentioned moral rights are enshrined in the law. They are protected by the law. So violations of many of these rights are regarded as serious crimes. The second point is that police forces exist (at least in part) to uphold the law, and especially laws against serious crimes. Accordingly, our question becomes: Are police officers morally entitled to use deadly force to protect citizens' moral rights, where the rights in question are not simply the right to life?

Let us take an example of a right, which is protected by the law, namely the right to property. Are police morally entitled to use deadly force to defend citizens' property rights?

There are certainly some cases in which they are not. Consider an unarmed pickpocket who is fleeing a police officer. The officer is not morally entitled to shoot and kill for such a minor offence. Moreover, it may even be that the police officer is not morally entitled to shoot and kill an unarmed burglar, notwithstanding the fact that the burglar is making off with a million dollars' worth of someone else's goods, and that the only way to prevent his escape is by shooting him dead.

It appears that there are at least some cases in which the police are morally entitled to use deadly force in order to uphold the law, and specifically the laws protecting property rights. Consider the case of someone who has successfully robbed a bank and gotten away with millions of dollars of other people's savings. Let's say this person is hiding out, and is armed and prepared to shoot in order to avoid capture, though if left alone with the money, he will not shoot anyone. There are two moral questions

210   Violence and Police Culture

here. Firstly, if an arrest attempt is to be made, how should it be done, and secondly, whether an arrest attempt should be made at all.

If an attempt is to be made, it will be a matter of deciding on the most effective method, ideally one that will minimise the risk to life. Perhaps the authorities should opt for a policy of containment and negotiation. Alternatively, the best option might be a surprise attack using forced entry. It may well be that in reality in situations of this kind, the Victoria Police have pursued the wrong options, and the nature of their training may come into this. Certainly the large number of killings by members of the Victoria Police relative to police in other states suggests Victoria Police officers have at the very least an unacceptably low level of professional competence in this area. Moreover if the methods of the Victoria Police are not best practice and if they should have known this, then they may well have been professionally negligent. Obviously the negligence of a professional group in relation to situations where lives are at risk is completely morally unacceptable.

Further, professional negligence may be a byproduct of the ethos or culture of an organisation. Perhaps members of a particular police service have developed an ethos of individual physical courage at the expense of reflection, and of 'machismo' rather than concern for the consequences, and that this ethos has tended to promote a tendency for early recourse to force rather than more considered methods such as negotiation. If so, then there would be cause for concern, and reason to reconsider the organisational structure and the education and training of the police service in question, including in particular education in the ethical principles underlying the legitimate and illegitimate use of force by police officers.

The former Victorian coroner Hal Hallenstein has taken the view that in some of the police shootings and killings in Victoria the wrong options have been pursued. For example, Joshua Yap ended up in a wheelchair after being shot by a police officer, Constable Steven Tynan, when Yap—armed with a hunting knife —attempted to rob a TAB agency with an accomplice, Chee Ming Tsen, who was 'armed' with an imitation revolver. Tynan had fired only after he had called upon Yap and Tsen to surrender, and Yap

had lunged at Tynan with the knife. However Hallenstein concluded that Tynan and fellow officer Constable Bodsworth ought
not to have entered the TAB in the first place but waited for
assistance and opted for containment and negotiation. He said
of their actions: 'arguably unnecessary, tactically unsound and in
circumstances considered as acceptable breach of police force
policy. A more satisfactory basis of acknowledgment would have
been non-exposure by police members, an active seeking of non-
firearms resolution of the situation and taking into account the
foreseeable risks'.[7]

Another example where forced entry was used when containment and negotiation were arguably the best option was the
police killing of Gerhard Alfred Sader. Four police officers led by
Sergeant Watson raided Sader's Melbourne bungalow at dawn.
Sader was wrongly suspected of illegal possession of arms and
drugs. The police had been issued with search warrants on the
basis of false information from an informer known to be unreliable. As it turned out the police used a sledgehammer to break
open an external gate before even getting to the door of the
house. This would certainly have alerted Sader. When they finally
broke open Sader's door, shouting 'Police. Open up!', they stared
at a figure in the darkness who later turned out to be Sader.
Watson shot three times at the figure in the dark on the grounds
that he believed him to be armed and about to shoot him. Sader
was at most armed with a baseball bat.[8]

In the light of these kinds of case let us assume that the
method most likely to minimise the risk to life is containment
and negotiation. It remains true that the police are institution-
ally required—whether or not they morally ought to be—not to
simply let wrongdoers go, and even in a situation of containment
and negotiation, the use of deadly force may turn out to be
necessary, albeit as a last resort. Consider in this connection a
gunman who having killed his wife in their home, refuses to give
himself up to police negotiators, and is preparing to escape,
notwithstanding the presence of police snipers. Should he be
allowed to escape? Martin Bryant, the Tasmanian mass murderer,
should not be allowed to escape, but what of the armed professional burglar seeking only to escape? In short, what is the
moral justification for the use of deadly force in cases in which

212   Violence and Police Culture

police confront a choice of either letting an offender go free or shooting him/her?

In these sorts of case the police are not necessarily engaged in self-defence. In many of these cases the best thing for police officers—if they were interested in self-defence—would be for them to get back into their patrol cars and return to the police station. Nor are they necessarily cases of killing in defence of others. The lives of ordinary citizens might not be at risk. For example, an offender (for instance, a burglar) might simply want to be left alone to spend his ill-gotten gains, and the above-mentioned husband might cease to be a threat to anyone once he had killed his wife.

It might be argued against this that the police are engaged in self-defence since they are doing their moral duty in trying to apprehend the suspect, he ought not resist them, and if he does resist them then their action of killing him is self-defence. After all, it might be claimed, he would have killed them if they had not killed him.

This response is flawed. It is simply false that he would have killed them if they had not killed him. The police had the option of not killing the suspect, or of retreating after they had begun the pursuit. What is true is that they have a duty to apprehend the suspect, and they cannot avoid shooting him on pain of failing to discharge this duty. But while the existence of this duty may render their killing of the suspect morally legitimate, it does not transform the killing into a case of self-defence (or killing in defence of the lives of others). Indeed to claim that it does is to obscure the moral considerations in play here—to make it appear that the moral predicament of the police is simply one of choosing between their lives and the life of the suspect, as would be so in a genuine case of self-defence.

I have argued that in the kinds of case in question the police are not simply engaged in self-defence or in the defence of the lives of others. Rather there is some more complex set of moral considerations here, to be pursued further.

Let us do so by first examining the case of the police killing of Pavel Marinoff, the psychopathic Bulgarian army deserter who had shot and wounded a number of police officers before being confronted by Sergeant John Kapetanovski and Senior Constable

Rod Macdonald on the Hume Highway outside Melbourne.[9] They pulled a van over to the side of the road, rightly believing it to be driven by Marinoff. They ordered the driver to place his hands outside the car. The driver drew his pistol, fired several shots and drove off. He had wounded both officers; however, Macdonald fired two shots from his shotgun through the rear window of the escaping car, killing Marinoff. Perhaps this was a case of killing a fleeing offender, rather than of killing in self-defence or in defence of the lives of others. After all presumably Marinoff was at this stage simply seeking to make good his escape. If so, it is nevertheless a morally justifiable killing of a fleeing offender. Marinoff's offences included attempted murder and grievous bodily harm.

There are various other cases of shootings of dangerous fleeing felons that can be drawn from other police services and used for illustrative purposes. For example, there are the shootings of fleeing suspected terrorists in Northern Ireland. And police have been held liable for not shooting at fleeing gunmen known to be terrorists.

Another case is that of Hussein Said who attempted to assassinate the Israeli ambassador in England. He fired one shot, which missed, and then his gun jammed. He took flight. He was pursued by a bodyguard who fired a warning shot and called upon Said to give himself up. When he continued to flee he was shot and wounded. In the ensuing court case the bodyguard's action was held by the judge to have been illegal, since Said no longer constituted an immediate threat to the life of anyone. Evidently, bodyguards and police can find themselves between a rock and a hard place. They might be held liable for murder if they shoot, and failure to discharge their duty if they do not.

Let me now consider the killing of Ian Turner by Constable Wayne Sherwell.[10] Sherwell stopped a car driven by Turner for speeding near St Arnaud in country Victoria. Turner had no ID and in the course of conversation aroused Sherwell's suspicions. Turner said he would look for ID in his bag but instead pulled a sawn-off .22 rifle on Sherwell. He then took Sherwell's police revolver. Sherwell grabbed Turner's hand and a struggle ensued. During the struggle Turner called on Sherwell to give up and simply let him go free. Sherwell disarmed Turner and now in possession of both weapons, ordered Turner to lie on the ground and allow himself to be handcuffed. He refused to do so, calling on Sherwell to let him go. When Sherwell refused his request and tried to radio for assistance, Turner blocked his way calling on Sherwell to shoot him. Sherwell fired his gun in the air. Turner ran to his car while Sherwell called on his radio for assistance. Turner ran back to his car and produced a sawn-off shotgun which he pointed at Sherwell. Sherwell fired a couple of shots. Both men hid behind their respective cars. Further shots were fired by Sherwell. Turner did not fire any shots at any time. When other officers arrived at the scene they found one of Sherwell's shots had killed Turner. Turner, it later emerged, was an armed robber.

At the point when Sherwell shot Turner he was acting in self-defence, and his killing of Turner was justifiable on grounds of self-defence. There is a further issue that the case raises.

It seems that throughout the whole episode Turner had no desire to kill Sherwell, but rather acted in order to escape from Sherwell. Thus initially Turner used the threat of deadly force pre-emptively in order to escape arrest, and subsequently he grabbed his shotgun because Sherwell was holding him prisoner and using the threat of deadly force to do so. So Turner essentially threatened, but never in fact used, deadly force in order to avoid arrest.

For his part Sherwell, while prepared to *threaten* to use deadly force to prevent Turner's escape, only in fact seemed prepared to use deadly force in self-defence. In other words if Turner had simply got into his car and driven off Sherwell would quite possibly not have shot him. Moreover, if Turner had known that Sherwell would not have shot him other than in self-defence, Turner would not have pulled a gun on Sherwell in the first place, but would simply have driven off.

The case illustrates the distinction between killing in self-defence and killing in order to prevent an offender escaping. Moreover it illustrates this distinction notwithstanding the fact that the offender is armed and is prepared to use deadly force to escape arrest.

This distinction between killing in self-defence (or defence of others) and killing (or not killing) in order to prevent an offender escaping is further illustrated in the following case of passive non-compliance involving the dangerous criminal, David Martin, in an underground subway in England in 1982. Cornered in the underground subway by armed police, Martin was persistently ordered to give himself up, but refused to do so. However he made no hostile movements against the police. The police were concerned that he might have a gun and might use it against them. Certainly his history indicated that this might be so. Finally, the police decided not to shoot him, but to rush and disarm him. He was found to be unarmed.

Three points need to be noted here. First, the police risked their lives in rushing Martin. He might have been armed, and if so, he may well have shot dead one or more of the police. Second, if Martin had been shot dead by the police, then the police may well have been found guilty of murder. Third, if Martin had been allowed to escape, he might have harmed, even killed, innocent people, and if so, the police might have been charged with criminal dereliction of duty, and might also have been liable in a civil court for damages.

Let us now consider the police killing of Graeme Jensen. Victorian police sought to arrest Jensen for murder. In fact he did not commit the murder. Nor did they have sufficient evidence to convict him of conspiring to rob a bank, the other matter for which he was under investigation. At most he could have been convicted of illegal possession of a firearm. Moreover, Jensen probably believed the police were out to kill him. At any rate he tried to escape the police when they tried to arrest him. Jensen was armed and allegedly pointed his gun at officers who first warned him and then shot at him. It later turned out that Jensen's gun was not loaded. Jensen was escaping when the second shot went through the back window and killed him. By one account Jensen was killed in self-defence. By a second account it was not a case of self-defence but of shooting a fleeing offender, the offence being illegal possession of an (unloaded) weapon.[11] On a third account it was unlawful for police to even try to arrest him. If so, Jensen was murdered.[12]

At any rate the Jensen killing raises at least two issues. In the case of Jensen, unlike Turner, the police initiated the threat of deadly force and Jensen at most threatened deadly force for the purposes of making his escape. Moreover, the police used an extent of force that was disproportionate to the offence committed.

Let me now summarise the moral considerations that the above-described cases illustrate.[13]

Firstly, there is the seriousness of the offence committed by the person shot dead by the police. In the case of a burglar the crime is a violation of the right to property, and one of far greater magnitude than the petty theft involved in picking someone's pocket. In the case of Marinoff the offence is far more serious still. This raises the issue of the proportionality of police use of deadly force.

Secondly, there is the question as to whether the offender is armed and prepared to kill in order to avoid imprisonment. Here we must distinguish between being prepared to kill to avoid imprisonment, and being prepared to kill for other reasons such as self-defence, revenge or to become rich.

These two considerations—the offence is a serious one and the offender is prepared to use deadly force to avoid arrest—are evidently held in Australian society to be jointly sufficient to justify morally the police use of deadly force as a last resort.[14] Australian society appears to take this view while at the same time being opposed to capital punishment. There is no obvious inconsistency here. On the one hand Australian society takes the view that killing is not justified as a punishment for criminals who are imprisoned and therefore no longer able to break its laws. On the other, society holds that police use of deadly force is justified if this is the only way to ensure that its laws against serious crimes are upheld, and in particular, if the perpetrators of serious crimes are themselves prepared to kill in order to avoid imprisonment.

While police use of deadly force in these kinds of case may well be in principle morally justifiable, the justification is nevertheless problematic in a number of ways. It needs first to be determined which crimes by *armed* perpetrators are sufficiently serious to warrant police use of deadly force. Secondly, it places an enormous responsibility—and a corresponding opportunity for abuse —on individual members of the police force.[15] For, as we have seen, if police are entitled to kill in order to ensure that the law is upheld, then police may kill an bank robber even thought he will not fire his gun if left alone. Moreover, in doing so they will kill this (alleged) bank robber prior to any considered judgement by a court of law that he has in fact broken the law. In such cases it is the responsibility of the individual police officer, initially, to make the judgement that the person is an armed bank robber who will kill in order to avoid apprehension, and then to go on to shoot this person dead in order that he not escape.

This latter problem raises perplexing questions concerning the moral balance to be struck between the right to life of a suspect, and the rights of citizens to be protected by police from serious rights violations, which nevertheless stop short of threatening their lives. Here there are a number of considerations. How serious and extensive are these rights violations? What moral weight, if any, is to be attached to the threat (posed by those who use arms to prevent their legitimate arrest) to the state's possession of overriding coercive power to uphold its morally legitimate laws? The problem also raises questions concerning the moral balance to be struck between the rights to life of citizens and/or suspects, and the right to life of police officers—or at least it does so if a situation develops where that choice has to be made by a police officer.

Conclusion

I conclude this chapter by outlining three main general conditions under which police use of deadly force might be morally justified, or at least might be morally justified if adequate police accountability can be ensured so as to prevent abuse of police powers. The use of police deadly force under condition 3 below is especially problematic in this latter respect. Needless to say, the conditions specified under 3 below make a number of implicit assumptions. One assumption is that the police officer has the degree of reasonable suspicion that is sufficient to justify making an arrest. However, killing an alleged offender to prevent his/her escape can presumably only be justified in situations in which there is certainty, or near certainty, that the alleged offender has in fact committed the offence. A higher standard of evidence than reasonable suspicion is required.

218   Violence and Police Culture

Another assumption is that there really are no possible ways of preventing escape other than by using deadly force. So, for example, letting the suspected offender escape in the knowledge that there is a reasonable chance he or she can be arrested at a later date is not an option.

1 *Self-defence.* A police officer is morally entitled to kill another person if that person is trying to kill, maim, rape or otherwise seriously harm the police officer, and will succeed unless the officer kills the person first.

2 *Defence of Others.* A police officer is morally entitled—and might be morally obliged—to kill another person if that person is trying to kill, maim, rape or otherwise seriously harm some third person(s), and will succeed unless the officer kills the would-be offender first.

3 *Armed Suspects.* A police officer is morally entitled—and might be morally obliged—to kill another person if that person has committed crimes that are serious rights violations, is attempting to avoid arrest, is armed and using those arms to avoid arrest, and if the only way to prevent the suspected offender from escaping is to kill him/her.

Notes

Shootings by Police in Victoria: The Ethical Issues

1   John Silvester, Andrew Rule and Owen Davies, *The Silent War: Behind the Police Killings that Shook Australia.*
2   National Committee on Violence, *Violence: Directions for Australia.*
3   For recent discussions of the moral justification for killing in self-defence, see J. J. Thomson, 'Self-defence'; S. Uniacke, *Permissible Killing*: The Self-defence Justification of Homicide; and Seumas Miller, 'Killing in Self-defence'.
4   But see J. Teichman, 'Self-defence', in her *Pacifism and the Unjust War.*
5   Tom Noble, *Untold Violence: Crime in Melbourne Today*, pp. 142–3.
6   Victoria, State Coroner, *Investigation into the Death of Gary John Abdullah: Inquest Findings.*
7   Victoria, State Coroner, *Investigation into the Death of Hia Foong Yap: Inquest Findings*, p. 164.
8   Victoria, State Coroner, *Investigation into the Death of Gerhard Alfred Sader: Inquest Findings.*
9   See Silvester et al., *The Silent War*, p. 3.
10 Ibid, pp. 125–30.
11 Ibid, p. 37.
12 Police were in fact charged with his murder but were not convicted.
13 For further discussion see Seumas Miller, John Blackler and Andrew Alexandra, *Police Ethics*, Chapter 6.
14 However this view is evidently controversial. It appears to be inconsistent with that advanced, for example, by Jerome Skolnick and James Fyfe in *Above the Law: Police and the Excessive Use of Force.*
15 See Seumas Miller 'Authority, Accountability and Discretion in Policing', inC. Sampford, N. Preston and C. Bois (eds), *Public Sector Ethics.*

Part VI
Rights of Suspects

[24]

Deception by Police

JEROME H. SKOLNICK

The ideal of legality implies that those convicted of crimes will not only be factually but legally guilty. A political commitment to legality is, after all, what distinguishes democratic governments from totalitarian ones. Yet for every ideal, there seems to be a practical challenge. The ideal of right to bail is challenged by the reality of the criminal's dangerousness, the presumption of innocence by the reality of factual guilt, the right to counsel by the triviality of certain offenses or the difficulties of providing counsel to those who have just been informed of their privilege against self-incrimination. Hard and fast rules limiting police conduct may challenge common sense, while the absence

Jerome H. Skolnick, author of Justice without Trial: Law Enforcement in a Democratic Society, *is Professor of Law and Director of the Center for the Study of Law and Society at the University of California, Berkeley.*

of such rules may invite arbitrary and abusive conduct. This paper discusses one of the most troubling and difficult questions pertaining to the ideal of legality: To what extent, if at all, is it proper for law enforcement officials to employ trickery and deceit as part of their law enforcement practices?[1]

Whatever the answer to that question—if, indeed, an answer can be formulated—it has to be measured against a hard reality of the criminal justice system. That reality is: Deception is considered by police—and courts as well—to be as natural to detecting as pouncing is to a cat. As we shall see, that is why it is so difficult both to control deceptive practices of detectives and to prescribe long-term measures to guarantee control.

A seminal, thought-provoking attempt has been made in Sissela Bok's important book on lying.[2] Bok does not deal explicitly with deception by detectives, as she does with deception by social scientists. But she does refer to certain police practices in what must be regarded as the central chapter of her book—that on justification of deception, where she introduces standards for backing away from the Kantian categorical imperative.[3] Essentially, she argues for combining two standards for justifiable deception, insisting, first, on a *public* offering of justification for a lie and, second, on

having the justification offered to an audience of *reasonable persons*. The chapter goes on to develop these notions in creative and original ways, but does not fully develop the implications of her guidelines for the detecting process. I would like to offer some observations, which have been stimulated by her analysis, about the detecting process itself.

The Normative Context of Detecting

Detecting occurs in the context of fluid moral constraints that are circumscribed by a tradition of due process of law, by ever-changing and not altogether clear interpretations of individual rights offered by the courts, and by the social organization of policing that develops its own moral norms and constraints. Finally, this amalgam of normative prescription is set within the context of an adversary system of justice.

If all that sounds complicated and confusing, it is. It suggests that, because of the multiple contexts of police action, there are unstable, even contradictory, norms. Is detecting to be considered akin to a poker game, where the players understand that deception is part of the game? It surely is not like the doctor-client, or even the social scientist-subject relationship. The detective is not treating the subject, nor is the detective merely observing.

The detective deceives in order to establish grounds for convicting and punishing. The detecting process is informed and controlled by notions of fairness and

dignity, but these notions, as embodied by law, are often unclear both in outcome and justification. The law often, but not always, supports police deception. The law permits the detective to pose as a consumer or purveyor of vice,[4] but does not allow the policeman to employ certain ruses to gain entry without a search warrant,[5] or to obtain a search warrant with a false affidavit.[6] The police subculture—the workaday normative order of police—permits, and sometimes demands, deception of courts, prosecutors, defense attorneys, and defendants but rarely, if ever, allows for deception of fellow policmen.[7] Police thus work within a severe, but often agonizingly contradictory, moral order which demands certain kinds of fidelities and insists upon other kinds of betrayals. The police milieu is normatively contradictory, almost to the point of being schizophrenogenic. Norms regarding deception, written and implied, abound in this moral order.

The Stages of Detecting

Deception occurs at three stages of the detecting process: investigation, interrogation, and testimony. If we place these three stages within the framework of a broad portrait of the moral cognition of the policeman, we observe that the acceptability of deception varies inversely with the level of the criminal process. Thus, deception is most acceptable to police—as it is to the courts—at the investigation stage, less acceptable during interrogation, and least acceptable in the courtroom.

If we inquire as to why that should be, the answer seems fairly obvious. Each stage is related to a set of

increasingly stringent normative constraints. Courtroom testimony is given under oath, and is supposed to be the truth, the whole truth, and nothing but the truth. Nobody is supposed to lie in a courtroom. When a policeman lies in court, he may be able to justify his deception on the basis of an alternative set of normative judgments (assuming that he is acting as a prosecution witness and is not himself the defendant), but he is still aware that courtroom lying violates the basic norms of the system he is sworn to uphold. Nevertheless, police do lie in the courtroom, particularly when they believe that judicial interpretations of constitutional limits on police practices are ill conceived or overly constraining in that they interfere with the policeman's ability to do his or her job as the police subculture defines it.

I shall argue in this paper that courtroom lying is justified within the police culture by the same sort of necessity rationale that courts have permitted police to employ at the investigative stage: The end justifies the means. Within an adversary system of criminal justice, governed by due process rules for obtaining evidence, the policeman will thus lie to get at the truth. The contradiction may be surprising, but it may be inevitable in an adversary system of justice where police perceive procedural due process norms and legal requirements as inconsistent obstacles to truth and the meting out of just deserts for the commission of crime.

Testimonial Deception

As I have indicated, it is difficult to prove a causal relationship between permissible investigative and interrogatory deception and testimonial deception. Police freely admit to deceiving suspects and defendants.[8] They do not admit to perjury, much less to the rationalization of perjury. There is evidence, however, of the acceptability of perjury as a means to the end of conviction. The evidence is limited and fragmentary and is certainly not dispositive. However, the evidence does suggest not only that a policeman will perjure himself—no surprise that—but that perjury, like corruption, does not lend itself to "rotten apple" explana-

tions.[9] Perjury, I would suggest, like corruption, is systematic, and for much the same sort of reason—police know that other police are on the take, and police know that other police are perjuring themselves. The following two items of evidence suggest that perjury represents a subcultural norm rather than an individual aberration.

Scholarly evidence of testimonial lying was revealed in a study conducted by Columbia law students in which they analyzed the effect of *Mapp v. Ohio*[10] on police practices in New York City. In *Mapp*, the Supreme Court held that the federal exclusionary rule in search and seizure cases was binding on the states. New York was the only large state that had not previously adopted the exclusionary rule as a matter of state law. (The exclusionary rule, of course, suppresses at trial evidence that was illegally obtained—usually in violation of the Fourth Amendment.) The students analyzed the evidentiary grounds for arrest and subsequent disposition of misdemeanor narcotics cases before and after the *Mapp* decision. Based on officers' accounts of the evidence for the arrest (see table) the student authors concluded that

uniform police have been fabricating grounds of arrest in narcotics cases in order to circumvent the requirements of *Mapp*. Without knowledge of the results of this study, the two Criminal Courts judges and the two Assistant District Attorneys interviewed doubted that a substantial reform of police practices had occurred since *Mapp*. Rather, they believe that police officers are fabricating evidence to avoid *Mapp*.[11]

Such lies came to be known as "dropsy" testimony since the police testified that those charged with drug possession were now dropping illicit drugs on the ground rather than keeping them where they were. Prior to *Mapp*, evidence obtained from unlawful

New York City Police Officers' Allegations Regarding Discovery of Evidence in Misdemeanor Narcotics Offenses, 1960–62

Percent of Arrests

Six-month period

How Evidence Found	Before Mapp	After Mapp	Difference
I. Narcotics Bureau			
(a) Hidden on person	35	3	−32
(b) Dropped or thrown to ground	17	43	+26
II. Uniform			
(a) Hidden on person	31	9	−22
(b) Dropped or thrown to ground	14	21	+ 7
III. Plainclothes			
(a) Hidden on person	24	4	−20
(b) Dropped or thrown to ground	11	17	+ 6

(Original source: Comment, "Effect of *Mapp v. Ohio* on Police Search and Seizure Practices in Narcotics Cases;" *Col. J. Law & Social Problems* 4 (1968): 94.)

searches of the person was admissible, even when illegally obtained. New York State was governed by the
famous 1926 dictum of Judge Cardozo, who, while he
was on the bench of the New York Court of Appeals,
had dismissed the federal rule with the observation
that under it "the criminal is to go free because the
constable had blundered."[12] Obviously, the New York
police had not been blundering prior to *Mapp*. Instead,
they simply and routinely ignored the requirements of
the Fourth Amendment.

In a more popular account, Robert Daley's fascinating *Prince of the City*, the former New York Deputy
Police Commissioner writes of a surveillance showing
that, on the one hand, defendants were guilty of hi-
jacking television sets and, on the other, that cops
were stealing some of the hijacked sets. The evidence
was obtained through a legal wiretap. The detectives
erased that part of the tape proving that the precinct
cops had stolen some of the sets. Daley writes,
"Tomorrow they would deny the erasure under
oath. . . . It was the type of perjury that detectives
. . . committed all the time in the interest of putting
bad people in jail."[13]

The point here is not whether to deplore the police
violations of the Fourth Amendment or the lying of
police in the testimonial context; rather, it is to understand how police who engage in it themselves come to
justify it, so that moral prescriptions might be given a
better chance of being persuasive to police who do not
find them compelling in practice.

The policeman lies because lying becomes a routine
way of managing legal impediments—whether to
protect fellow officers or to compensate for what he
views as limitations the courts have placed on his
capacity to deal with criminals. He lies because he is
skeptical of a system that suppresses truth in the interest of the criminal. Moreover, the law permits the
policeman to lie at the investigative stage, when he is
not entirely convinced that the suspect is a criminal,
but forbids lying about *procedures* at the testimonial

stage, when the policeman is certain of the guilt of the
accused. Thus, the policeman characteristically measures the short-term disutility of the act of suppressing
evidence, not the long-term utility of due process of
law for protecting and enhancing the dignity of the
citizen who is being investigated by the state.

I quote at this point from a passage in *Justice without
Trial* which recent discussions with police persuade me
is still essentially valid:

> The policeman . . . operates as one whose aim is to
> legitimize the evidence pertaining to the case, rather
> than as a jurist whose goal is to analyze the sufficiency
> of the evidence based on case law. . . .
>
> The policeman respects the necessity for "complying"
> with the arrest laws. His "compliance," however, may
> take the form of *post hoc* manipulation of the facts rather
> than before-the-fact behavior. Again, this generalization
> does not apply in all cases. Where the policeman feels
> capable of literal compliance (as in the conditions provided
> by the "big case"), he does comply. But when he sees the
> case law as a hindrance to his primary task of apprehending
> criminals, he usually attempts to construct the apearance
> of compliance, rather than allow the offender to escape
> apprehension. [14]

As I stated earlier, I am not aware of an ethical
theory that would condone perjured testimony. Bok's
standards for justifying deception would provide a
useful guideline here, because the lying policeman
would be required to justify courtroom perjury before
a relevant public. This is precisely the sort of test I
think Bok had in mind. Although police might justify
perjury to each other over drinks after work, or in the
corridors of the locker room, I can scarcely imagine any
policeman willing to justify such conduct in a public
setting—unless he was perhaps on a television talk
show wearing a mask and wig. But any hesitation on
the part of an officer to testify could be caused by fear
of a perjury charge, not by moral scruples about lying
in courtroom situations where criminals might go free.

Investigative Deception

Let us examine more closely the rationale for lying at
the investigative stage. Here, police are permitted by
the courts to engage in trickery and deception and are
trained to do so by the police organization. One might
properly conclude, from examining police practices

that have been subjected to the highest appellate
review, that the police are authoritatively encouraged
to lie. [15]

Detectives, for example, are trained to use informers
or to act themselves as informers or agents provoca-

teurs when the criminal activity under investigation involves possession or sale of contraband. The contraband itself does not much matter. From an enforcement perspective, the problems involved in apprehending those who sell counterfeit money are almost identical to those involved in trapping dealers of illegal drugs. Years ago, when I studied a vice squad intensively, the squad was asked to help the United States Secret Service in apprehending a counterfeiting ring. They were asked because vice squads are especially experienced in law enforcement practices involving use of informants, deception, security of information, and, most generally, the apprehension of offenders whose criminality is proven by the possession for sale of illegal materials. A similar point can be made with respect to burglary enforcement. Victims (or police) rarely observe burglars in action. In fact, burglars are usually apprehended when detectives are able to employ a decoy or an informer who tells them that so-and-so is in possession of stolen goods.

The line between acceptable and unacceptable deception in such enforcement patterns is the line between so-called entrapment and acceptable police conduct. How does the law presently define entrapment? From my reading, the definition is hazy, murky, unclear. Two approaches are employed in legal writing about entrapment. One, the subjective approach, focuses upon the background, character, and intention of the defendant. Was he or she the sort of person who would have been predisposed to have committed the crime, even without the participation of the government official or agent? The objective test, by contrast, sets its sights on the nature of governmental participation. Justice Frankfurter, concurring in *Sherman* v. *United States*, presented the objective test as follows: "The crucial question, not easy to answer, to which the court must direct itself is whether the police conduct revealed in the particular case falls below standards, to which common feelings respond, for the proper use of governmental power."[16] More recently, in *United States* v. *Russell*, Justice Rehnquist wrote the majority opinion affirming the prevailing rule—the subjective test—in a case where an undercover agent for the Federal Bureau of Narcotics and Dangerous Drugs told the suspect that he represented an organization that was interested in controlling the manufacture and distribution of methamphetamine.[17] The narcotics agent offered to supply Russell with a chemical that was an essential, hard-to-find ingredient in the manufacture of methamphetamine in return for half the drug pro-

duced. The agent told Russell that he had to be shown a sample of the drug in the laboratory where it was being produced before he would go through with the deal.

Russell showed him the laboratory and told the agent he and others had been making the drug for quite some time. The agent left and returned to the laboratory with the necessary chemical and watched while the suspects produced the drug. The narcotics agent did not actively participate in the manufacturing of the drug, but he was courteous and helpful to those who did. When a suspect dropped some aluminum foil on the floor, it was testified, the narcotics agent picked it up and put it into the cooker.

The majority of the court held that Russell was not "entrapped" because he had been an active participant in an illegal drug manufacturing enterprise that began before the government agent appeared on the scene and continued after the government agent left the scene. Russell was not an "unwary innocent," but rather, an "unwary criminal." The subjective test, in short, permits police to engage in deceptive practices provided that the deception catches a wolf rather than a lamb.[18]

The objective test, focusing on the activities of the government, seems to suggest a more high-minded vision of the limits of police deception. By a high-minded vision, I mean to suggest one which conceives

---

I find myself genuinely puzzled as to why informants are usually thought to be morally acceptable, while bugs are not.

---

of significant limitations on police conduct in the interest of maintaining a civilized or moral constabulary. For example, a civilized police should not be permitted to torture a suspect in order to obtain a confession, even if it should turn out that the tortured party was an unwary criminal, that is, even if torture should produce the truth.[19] Nor, to cite a real case, would a civilized police be permitted to pump the stomach of a suspected narcotics dealer to show that pills that he had just swallowed contained morphine, even if that is exactly what the pills did contain.[20]

But the objective test may lose its objectivity when it

relies on such concepts as "common feelings" or the "conscience of the community."[21] Although these concepts seem to imply enduring qualities or values, one could also argue that such concepts are variables. "Common feelings" might allow for far more latitude in police practices in a "high fear of crime" period than in a "low fear" period. Some might argue that values should be tested in the crucible of experience, and that flexibility is itself a virtue. The trouble is that one person's flexibility may be interpreted as another's lack of principle.

Moreover, "common feelings" may not be informative when we consider particular examples. I am reminded of a passage in Arthur Schlesinger's biography of Robert Kennedy, where Schlesinger tries to resolve the issue of whether Kennedy really knew about FBI wiretapping when he was Attorney General. Schlesinger relates a conversation between J. Edgar Hoover and Kennedy, where Hoover tells Kennedy that he had the situation "covered."[22] According to Schlesinger, Hoover felt that he had thus informed Kennedy of the wiretap, while Kennedy took the term "cover" to mean that a secret government informant had worked his way into the suspect's entourage.

Assuming for the purposes of argument that Kennedy did not know about the wiretapping, by what principle is a wiretap or bug to be considered less morally acceptable than a secret informant?[23] A wiretap or bug clearly invades expectations of privacy. But wiretaps and bugs enjoy two advantages over secret informants. First, the evidence they report as to what the defendant did or did not say is trustworthy. Second, and perhaps more important, a bug cannot encourage lawbreaking: It can neither advocate nor condone such conduct. It is not clear to me how an objective standard would distinguish between the two, and I find myself genuinely puzzled as to why informants are usually thought to be morally acceptable, while bugs are not. Indeed, an argument could be made that when the government attempts to modify dispositions (by employing secret informants who worm their way into the confidence of suspects, for example), that this is more violative of human dignity than the involuntary extraction of evidence from the body, even through stomach pumping. At least one whose stomach is being pumped can identify his adversary, while the secret informant "messes with the mind," as it were.

In any event, for the purpose of my more general argument, it is enough to acknowledge that both legal tests of entrapment—objective and subjective—permit police to employ an enormous amount of routine deception, although the prevailing subjective test permits even more. Even in the dissenting opinion in *Russell*, Justice Stewart, supporting the objective test, writes that "the government's use of undercover activity, strategy, or deception is [not] necessarily unlawful. Indeed, many crimes, especially so-called victimless crimes, could not otherwise be detected."[24] In short, police are routinely permitted and advised to employ deceptive techniques and strategies in the in-

The police may occasionally trap a lamb but the courts tacitly acknowledge that in the real world police deal mostly with wolves.

vestigative process. The police may occasionally trap a lamb but the courts tacitly acknowledge that in the real world police deal mostly with wolves—and in the eyes of the courts a wolf might be wearing the clothing of either a Congressman or a cocaine dealer.

Judicial permissiveness regarding investigative deception suggests how difficult it would be to defend a Kantian imperative against lying even in the abstract and how impossible it would be for any such defense to be accepted by courts, police, and the public. I shall conclude this discussion of investigative deception by suggesting a hypothesis: Judicial acceptance of deception in the investigation process enhances moral acceptance of deception by detectives in the interrogatory and testimonial stages of criminal investigation, and thus increases the probability of its occurrence.

This hypothesis does not suggest that every detective who deceives also perjures himself. It does suggest that deception in one context increases the probability of deception in the other. This hypothesis cannot be tested, and therefore may not hold. It cannot be tested because a true test would require an experimental design where we could manipulate the independent variable (authoritative permission to employ investigative trickery) and measure the dependent variable (courtroom perjury by police). Since we can neither manipulate the former nor measure the latter, the hypothesis, however plausible, must remain speculative.

Interrogatory Deception

In the remainder of this paper, I shall assume that the previously mentioned hypothesis is plausible and organize discussion around it. Thus, let us turn our attention to deception and interrogation—and here I shall confine my remarks to in-custody interrogation, although I recognize that the line between *custody* and *precustody* is unclear, and that the one between *conversation* and *interrogation* is also unclear. For the present, I simply want to make a historical reference to the in-custody interrogation problem which *Miranda* v. *Arizona*, decided in 1966, sought to resolve.[25] The holding of *Miranda* has now become so familiar as to be part of American folklore. The case held that the arrested person must be informed of his or her right to remain silent, must be warned that any statement he or she does make may be used as evidence, and must be told that he or she has the right to the presence of an attorney. The accused should also be informed that an attorney will be provided if he or she cannot afford one. The court also held that the government has a "heavy burden" to prove that a waiver of such rights was made voluntarily, knowingly, and intelligently.[26]

The *Miranda* decision was the evolutionary outcome of the Supreme Court's response to the admission, in state and federal courts, of confessions which, in the early part of the century, were based on overt torture, later, on covert torture (the third degree), and later still, on deception and psychological intimidation. Overt torture is exemplified by the facts in *Brown* v. *Mississippi*, where black defendants were beaten and whipped until they confessed. By 1936, the Supreme Court could no longer overlook the glaring fact that a confession so elicited was deemed admissible by the Supreme Court of the State of Mississippi.

But punitive in-custody interrogation was, of course, not confined to the South. The 1931 Wickersham Commission reported numerous instances of covert torture in many cities between 1920 and 1930.[27] The chief distinction between covert and overt torture is not in the severity of pain induced, but in its deniability. The Mississippi sheriffs did not deny whipping their black suspects. They were brutal, but truthful. By contrast, the third degree classically involved deniable coercion: starving suspects, keeping them awake day and night, confining them in pitch black airless rooms,

or administering beatings with instruments which left few, if any, marks. For example, a suspect might be hit over the head with a blackjack (though a telephone book would be placed between the blackjack and the head), or he might be hit with a rubber hose.[28]

Other types of in-custody interrogation might evoke forms of torture even more terrifying, but also more deniable. Detectives in one police department reportedly hanged suspects from their heels outside windows in tall buildings to induce confessions. Others simply required that defendants stand erect and be forbidden use of bathroom facilities. The dramatic impact of the sadism of the third degree[29] has tended to obscure the fact that, in using it, the police necessarily condoned systematic deception of the courts as well as torture of suspects. Thus, not only did the police subculture's norms of the period permit station house physical punishment of those whom the police might have felt deserved it, these norms also condoned wholesale perjury—disregard of the moral authority of the courts and of the oaths taken in them.[30]

Miranda overruled *Crooker* v. *California*,[31] and *Cicenia* v. *LaGay*,[32] both of which were cases where the accused asked to see a lawyer after he agreed to be interrogated. In Cicenia's case, not only did he ask to see a lawyer, but his lawyer, who had arrived at the police station, had asked to see his client. *Miranda* might well be interpreted as a case where the Supreme Court was concerned not only with whether a confession was coerced—that had long been a concern of the courts—but whether the right of the accused not to be coerced was being effectuated properly in the context of the adversary system. The dissenters in *Crooker*—Douglas, Warren, Black, and Brennan—took a strong position on the right to counsel at the pretrial stage, arguing:

The right to have counsel at the pre-trial stage is often necessary to give meaning and protection to the right to be heard at the trial itself. It may also be necessary as a restraint on the coercive power of the police[33]. . . . No matter how well educated, and how well trained in the law an accused may be, he is surely in need of legal advice once he is arrested for an offense that may exact his life[34]. . . . The demands of our civilization expressed in the due process clause require that the accused who wants a counsel should have one at any time after the moment of arrest.[35]

The dissent also wrote that "the third degree flourishes only in secrecy."[36] It is quite clear, I think, that Justices Warren, Douglas, Black, and Brennan (and later Fortas, with whom they were to form a majority in *Miranda*) simply did not trust police to behave noncoercively when they had a suspect in custody; only counsel, they believed, would constrain police.

Ironically, compelling evidence for the view that police custody is inherently coercive was elicited from a 1962 book by professional police interrogators Fred E. Inbau and John E. Reid, entitled *Criminal Interrogation and Confessions*.[37] This book was a revision and enlargement of the second half of Inbau and Reid's earlier book, *Lie Detection and Criminal Investigation*.[38] The book is replete with suggestions for coercive and deceptive methods of interrogation, which the authors clearly considered necessary and proper for police conducting an investigation. Inbau and Reid were not advocates of the third degree. On the contrary, their book, seen in historical context, was a reformist document, representing a kind of dialectical synthesis between the polarities of third degree violence and civil liberties for protection of human dignity: Such a synthesis would have been progressive in the 1930s.

The benchmark test employed by Inbau and Reid was: "Although both 'fair' and 'unfair' interrogation practices are permissible, nothing shall be done or said to the subject that will be apt to make an innocent person confess."[39] A more philosophically-based and sophisticated version of the Inbau and Reid position (and a more modern one) is Joseph Grano's "mental freedom" test of voluntariness. It is an objective test,

Deception and the inherent coercion of custody are inescapably related in modern interrogation.

asking "whether a person of ordinary firmness, innocent or guilty, having the defendant's age, physical condition, and relevant mental abnormalities (but not otherwise having the defendant's personality traits, temperament, intelligence, or social background), and strongly preferring not to confess, would find the interrogation pressures overbearing."[40] What might these pressures be?

It is worthwhile, I think, to quote substantially from

the *Miranda* decision itself, partly to understand the impact Inbau and Reid's books had on the courts, and partly to understand what sorts of police trickery might or might not be regarded as coercive. Justice Warren wrote:

> The officers are told by the manuals that the "principal psychological factor contributing to a successful interrogation is privacy—being alone with the person under interrogation." The efficacy of this tactic has been explained as follows:
>
> > If at all practible, the interrogation should take place in the investigator's office or at least in a room of his own choice. The subject should be deprived of every psychological advantage. In his own home he may be confident, indignant, or recalcitrant. He is more keenly aware of his rights and more reluctant to tell of his indiscretions or criminal behavior within the walls of his home. Moreover his family and other friends are nearby, their presence lending moral support. In his office, the investigator possesses all the advantages. The atmosphere suggests the invincibility of the forces of the law.
>
> To highlight the isolation and unfamiliar surroundings, the manuals instruct the police to display an air of confidence in the suspect's guilt and from outward appearance to maintain only an interest in confirming certain details. The guilt of the subject is to be posited as a fact. The interrogator should direct his comments toward the reasons why the subject committed the act, rather than court failure by asking the subject whether he did it. Like other men, perhaps the subject has had a bad family life, had an unhappy childhood, had too much to drink, had an unrequited desire for women. The officers are instructed to minimize the moral seriousness of the offense, to cast blame on the victim or on society. These tactics are designed to put the subject in a psychological state where his story is but an elaboration of what the police purport to know already—that he is guilty. Explanations to the contrary are dismissed and discouraged.
>
> The texts thus stress that the major qualities an interrogator should possess are patience and perseverance.[41]

The manuals also suggest that suspects be offered legal excuses for their actions, says the *Miranda* Court. The interrogator is instructed to tell the suspect something like:

> Joe, you probably didn't go out looking for this fellow with the purpose of shooting him. My guess is, however, that you expected something from him and that's why you carried a gun—for your own protection. You knew him for what he was, no good. Then when you met him he probably started using foul, abusive language and he gave some indication that he was about to pull a gun on you, and that's when you had to act to save your own life. That's about it, isn't it, Joe?[42]

If the suspect does not respond to the understanding interrogator, notes the Court, another investigator is brought in—Mutt, the tough guy who plays against Jeff's nice guy role.

In this technique, two agents are employed. Mutt, the relentless investigator, who knows the subject is guilty and is not going to waste any time. He's sent a dozen men away for this crime and he's going to send the subject away for the full term. Jeff, on the other hand, is obviously a kindhearted man. He has a family himself. He has a brother who was involved in a little scrape like this. He disapproves of Mutt and his tactics and will arrange to get him off the case if the subject will cooperate. He can't hold Mutt off for very long. The subject would be wise to make a quick decision. The technique is applied by having both investigators present while Mutt acts out his role. Jeff may stand by quietly and demur at some of Mutt's tactics. When Jeff makes his plea for cooperation, Mutt is not present. [43]

Although *Miranda* is generally interpreted as focusing on the inherently coercive aspects of custodial interrogation, it should be noted that interrogatory tactics employ both deception and coercion. It is questionable whether custodial interrogation would be effective without deception. Indeed, deception appears to serve as custodial interrogation's functional alternative to physical coercion. Hence, deception and the inherent coercion of custody are inescapably related in modern interrogation.

Miranda generated enormous controversy. Studies were conducted by scholars and law reviews to try to demonstrate the impact of *Miranda*. [44] (It would be interesting to conduct a new round of studies to see if the findings of the older ones still hold.) Basically, the studies came to much the same conclusion: The *Miranda* warning did not appreciably reduce the amount of talking that a suspect would do, nor did *Miranda* significantly help suspects in making free and informed choices about whether to talk. A nice statement of how *Miranda* warnings could be rendered ineffectual, written by an author of the *Yale Law Journal*'s study of *Miranda*'s impact, appeared in the *Yale Alumni Magazine* in 1968.

Even when detectives informed suspects of their rights without undercutting devices, the advice was often defused by implying that the suspect had better not exercise his rights, or by delivering the statement in a formalized, bureaucratic tone to indicate that the remarks were simply a routine, meaningless legalism. Instinctively, perhaps, detectives tended to create a sense of unreality

about the *Miranda* warnings by bringing the flow of conversation to a halt with the statement, ". . . and now I am going to inform you of your rights." Afterwards, they would solemnly intone: "Now you have been warned of your rights," then immediately shift into a conversational tone to ask, "Now would you like to tell me what happened?" By and large the detectives regarded advising the suspect of his rights as an artificial imposition on the natural flow of the interrogation. [45]

Miranda also generated a substantial law review literature—some might say an industry—because the United States Supreme Court has been unwilling to set the only standard that would eliminate practically all the *Miranda* problems. That standard would be: Once the *Miranda* warnings are given, the accused is *also* given a lawyer who explains the implications of the warning. [46]

The privilege against self-incrimination existed before *Miranda*. The *Miranda* ruling essentially argues that, as part of due process, the government should not be permitted to make its case on the basis of the defendant's ignorance. Defendants *must* be informed of their rights. If we accept *Miranda* and take it seriously, we also must acknowledge that suspects do not—across the board—possess the legal acumen to waive their *Miranda* rights. In the late 1960s, at least, persons of "ordinary firmness" interpreted—or misinterpreted—their *Miranda* rights in such a way so as not to exercise them. From the perspective of those who would like to see *Miranda* overturned, that might not be a problem. But it also suggests that the average suspect, however "ordinarily firm," is not legally competent.

Those who *are* legally competent (lawyers) will routinely advise suspects to maintain silence. The continuing debate over *Miranda* reflects an ambivalence over enforcing the rule that the values expressed by the *Miranda* majority seem to call for: There can be no confession without a genuinely *voluntary* and knowledgeable waiver, exercised after consultation with a lawyer. The *Crooker* minority was unquestionably correct in its assessment that people cannot fully understand the implications of legal warnings—offered, after all, in the rather coercive situation of arrest—without legal consultation. We apparently still prefer to offer the government an edge based on the defendant's ignorance. Knowledgeable defendants will remain silent. The ignorant will talk.

Grano's "ordinary firmness" test necessarily implies overruling *Miranda*. His test, which is oriented to crime control, would surely result in far more admissible evidence than a genuinely voluntary, lawyer-advised, waiver would. The present *Miranda* rule lies somewhere in between. Perhaps we tolerate *Miranda* because on the whole we have learned that it does not matter very much. Pressures of in-custody interrogation are such that, apparently, most suspects will talk despite the *Miranda* warning. In any event, most confessions are elicited in cases where there is a victim, where the confession is not the only evidence, and where the suspect is willing to plead guilty to a lesser offense.

Besides, once the suspect begins to talk, the very techniques the court sought to avoid are probably permissible. When a policeman says, in the kindliest of tones, "Look Joe, it will be better for you to confess," he is of course essentially deceiving the suspect into believing that he is the suspect's friend rather than his adversary.

In a recent article, Welsh S. White has argued that certain interrogation tactics are, nevertheless, likely to risk depriving the suspect of his constitutional rights.[47] Accordingly, White believes that the court should prohibit, via per se exclusions, "police conduct that is likely to render a resulting confession involuntary or to undermine the effect of required *Miranda* warnings or a suspect's independent right to an attorney."[48] What would some of these prohibitions be? One would be against deceiving a suspect about whether an interrogation was taking place, as in *Massiah* v. *United States*.[49] There, after indictment, one confederate, Colson, agreed to cooperate with the government, and deceptively interrogated his accomplice, Massiah. The resulting incriminatory statements were held inadmissible as a violation of the Sixth Amendment right to counsel. White argues that this right should be triggered at the point of arrest.

He also argues that statements elicited from "jail plants" should be prohibited, on grounds that someone who is experiencing the pressures of confinement is more likely to confide in a police agent.[50] Slightly different forms of trickery, which White also advocates prohibiting, are police misrepresentations of the seriousness of the offense or police use of threats or promises for confessing.

Finally, White argues for prohibition of "father figure" trickery, where a police officer falsely acts like a friend or counselor rather than an adversary. White offers as one example the famous Connecticut murder case, *State* v. *Reilly*, where the principal interrogating officer manipulated an eighteen-year-old into falsely confessing that he murdered his mother.[51] White treats the case primarily as an example of the officer pretending to be a father figure. White's discussion, however, omits entirely what two books about the case point to as the real culprit—the use of the polygraph during the interrogation of Reilly, who confessed after being told by the "father figure" that a machine, which could read his mind, had indicated that he actually was the murderer.[52]

The Polygraph as a Deceptive Device

Recall that Inbau and Reid were not only advocates of deceptive interrogation. They were also proponents and developers of polygraph examination techniques. The polygraph is an instrument which measures changes in blood pressure, pulse, respiration, and perspiration. Detection of lies via the examination of physical change is actually a throwback to early forms of trial by ordeal. There are reports of a deception test used by Hindus based on the observation that fear may inhibit the secretion of saliva.[53] To test credibility, an accused was given rice to chew. If he could spit it out, he was considered innocent; but if it stuck to his gums, he was judged guilty. Until 1895, however, nobody had ever used a measuring device to detect deception. In that year, the Italian criminologist Cesare Lombroso used a combination of blood pressure and pulse readings to investigate crime. Before the First World War, others experimented with blood pressure and respiratory recordings. John A. Larson, perhaps the most scholarly of the Chicago-Berkeley group which sought to advance the "science" of lie detection, built an instrument in 1921 which he called a "polygraph"; it combined all three measures—blood pressure, pulse, and respiration. His junior collaborator, Leonard Keeler, added galvanic skin response to the list. Contemporary lie detector machines basically employ all these measures, although there are some other technical improvements as well. For example, integrated circuits and other components reduce the margin of error in measurement.

According to a survey conducted by the *New York Times* in 1980, the lie detector is widely used by law enforcement groups:

The Federal Bureau of Investigation conducted 1900 polygraph examinations in 1979, an increase of about 800 from 1978. The number of polygraph examinations administered by the Army, Navy, Marines and Air Force increased by 18 percent in two years, from 5710 to 6751. Polygraphs are finding a steadily growing market among state and local law enforcement agencies, litigants in civil cases and private retailers, who use the device to screen job applicants and combat pilferage. [54]

It is understandable, but distressing, that the use of the polygraph should be increasing. It is distressing because the validity of polygraph results is flawed by fundamental theoretical problems, not by technical ones. The increase in use is understandable because even though the polygraph is not a dispositive truth-finding device, it is nevertheless an effective instrument of social control.

In the past, one problem of polygraph examination was imprecision of measurement. Thus, the machine recorded blood pressure, but there was a question as to whether it recorded blood pressure accurately. There is no doubt that imprecision of measurement was a problem in the past, but the problems with the lie detection process itself were far more fundamental and serious. These problems stem from the inadequacy of the theory behind lie detection. That theory involves the following premises: The act of lying leads to conscious conflict; conflict induces *fear* or *anxiety*; and these emotions are accompanied by measurable and interpretable physiological changes. [55]

But the assumptions of the theory are questionable. The act of lying does not always lead to conscious conflict. Some witnesses believe their own stories, even when they are false. Even when witnesses know they are lying, they may not experience much fear. Or, innocent witnesses may experience fear and anxiety just by being asked threatening questions. All this depends on witnesses' individual personalities, social backgrounds, what they are testifying to, and to whom they are testifying. Polygraph examiners acknowledge that subjects must "believe in" the lie detector.

Even if witnesses do experience fear and anxiety, these emotions may not consistently be expressed as changes in bodily response. If all bodily responses rose

and fell exactly with emotional states, the responses would have a precise relationship to each other. But that is not the case. Bodily responses do not vary regularly, either with each other or with emotional states. If they did, only a unigraph, not a polygraph, would be required. Four imprecise measures are not more accurate than one precise measure.

Since the relations among lying, conflict, emotion, and bodily responses are so fuzzy, the accuracy of the lie detector is not comparable to that of, say, blood tests or X rays. It is unlikely that a dozen lie detector examiners would consistently reach the same conclusions regarding truth or falsity if they depended only on the squiggles produced by a polygraph.

So why is the use of lie detectors sharply increasing? The fact that the polygraph is not reliable does not mean it is ineffective as a social control instrument. Crime suspects may confess when questioned by a skilled interrogator. When a suspect is strapped into what he or she would view as a technologically foolproof "lie detector," the coercive power of the interrogator is heightened. The interrogator is not an adversary, but an objective scientific observer. Even those suspicious of father figures may embrace the trappings of science.

Job applicants, in particular, are effectively "screened" with a lie detector. Consider the following lines of questioning. First, softballs: Is your name John Jones? Are you thirty-six years old? Were you born in New York City? Then, hardballs: Have you ever done anything you are ashamed of? Have you ever stolen anything? Have you ever known anyone who has stolen anything? Who? Have you ever engaged in

It is unlikely that a dozen lie detector examiners would consistently reach the same conclusions.

homosexual acts? And so forth. This sort of questioning may well produce results.

There are thus two quite different empirical issues regarding the polygraph. Is it highly accurate, like X rays and blood tests? The answer is no. Is it effective in eliciting information from subjects who believe in it? The answer is yes. Whether the lie detector ought to be used by police—or by employers—is ultimately an ethical question. Should we allow deceptive, intrusive, yet nonviolent methods of interrogation in various institutions of a free society? Different people will have different answers to that question. But at least we should ask the right questions when considering the role of the so-called lie detector in American society.

The ethical problem is even more complicated because some who employ the lie detector actually believe that it detects lies, while others use it primarily as a technique of psychological intimidation. The police sergeant who told Peter Reilly that "this machine will read your mind" and then falsely persuaded Reilly that he had killed his own mother, thus eliciting from Reilly a critical but untrue confession, may himself have believed that the polygraph detects lies. Did the sergeant also believe that the lie detector reads the mind?

The lie detector is symbolically scientific, and its technologically sophisticated trappings commend it to the most thoughtful and professional segments of the policing community. Thus, police use the polygraph because they believe in it. Yet the technique's results can convict innocent people, where old-fashioned techniques of deception would not. An instance of this, the case of F. B. Fay, is reported by psychophysiologist David T. Lykken.[56] Fay was asked by a police polygraphist in Toledo in 1978, "Did you kill Fred?" and "Before age twenty-four did you ever think about doing anyone bodily harm to get revenge?" It was

assumed that, if Fay were innocent of Fred's murder, the second or "control" question would frighten Fay more, and that this would, in turn, "dampen" his autonomic reaction to the first or "relevant" question. Unfortunately for Fay, he responded more strongly to the "relevant" questions. The examiner, therefore, testified that Fay's denials were deceptive, and he was found guilty of murder and sentenced to prison for life. In October 1980, the actual killers were identified, and Fay was released after serving two and a half years.

In sum, then, we have to educate the law enforcement community as to the realistic limits of the polygraph. This will be difficult, partly because there is, as I have noted here, considerable controversy over use of the polygraph, and partly because, for the reasons I have already suggested, it is a uniquely valuable tool of interrogation. I myself have no hesitancy in stating where I stand on use of the instrument. I would argue against its use—first, because the false claims for its accuracy permit the highest degree of nonviolent coercion, and second, because cool nonreactors (sociopaths, skilled con men, the mildly self-drugged) can beat the test. Finally, if one of the important reasons for the *Miranda* rule is the inherent coerciveness of police interrogation, then how much more coercive is an interrogation by a questioner who is armed with a deceptively scientific instrument that can "read the mind"?

Conclusion

I have tried in this article to offer several observations about deception in the detecting process. First, I have suggested that detecting is a process moving from investigation, often through interrogation, to testimony. Police are offered considerable latitude by the courts during the investigation stage. This latitude to deceive, I have argued, carries over into the interrogation and testimonial stages as a subculturally supported norm. I have suggested that there is an underlying reason for this. When detectives deceive suspects in the course of criminal investigations or interrogations, they typically are not seeking to promote their own self-interest (as a detective would if he had lied about accepting bribes). On the contrary, the sort of deception employed to trap a narcotics dealer or dealer in stolen goods, or to elicit a confession from a murderer or rapist, is used for

the public interest. The detective—and here I am speaking of the professional detective who explicitly condemns the use of physical violence but accepts employing psychological intimidation during interrogation—is also interested in eliciting truth. This results, I have suggested, in a paradox. The end of *truth* justifies for the modern detective the means of *lying*. Deception usualy occurs in the interest of obtaining truth.

Both the detective and the civil libertarian, I have suggested, employ a utilitarian calculus. In so doing, each reveals the obvious limitations of such a calculus for resolving major issues of public policy. The detective measures the costs of the act of lying against the benefits to the crime victim and the general public. The civil libertarian is also concerned with the public interest but measures it in terms of rules protecting the long--range interests of all citizens in a system of governance, as opposed to the shorter range interests of punishing perpetrators.

The law reflects the tension between due process and crime control imperatives by establishing different—and inconsistent—standards for investigation and interrogation. At the investigative stage, the law's subjective test of entrapment comes perilously close to tests like Inbau and Reid's "innocent person" or

Apparent inconsistency makes law look more like a game than a rational system for enforcing justice.

Grano's more sophisticated "mental freedom" test: Both permit deceptive and coercive interrogation against wolves but not lambs.

Is there a moral justification for distinguishing between governmental deception at the investigative stage and at the interrogation stage? One could approach this issue by asking: What would be the rule of law regarding police deception in a moral society? It seems clear that in a moral society, authorities such as police would not be permitted to employ tactics that are generally regarded as immoral against those suspected, or accused, of a crime.

Indeed, we already have such rules: Police are not permitted to coerce a suspect physically. The police may, however, subject suspects to psychological coercion provided they consent to be interrogated. Unreliability is one reason we prohibit the admission of evidence obtained from physically coerced confessions. But we could have a rule distinguishing between a pure mea culpa confession and one which produces material evidence, such as a gun or a body. We do not have such rules partly because we deplore physically coercive tactics even when used against the guilty; we also do not have them because we fear that physical coercion would become a routine aspect of police interrogation. Physical coercion is clearly indistinguishable from deceit and trickery, and few of us would, really, I suspect, choose to be smashed in the face with a rifle butt, or hung from a high window, rather than be betrayed by a friend who is actually and

secretly a police informant gathering incriminating evidence.

The more difficult question is whether deception—which we accept at the investigative stage—is as morally offensive as psychological coercion. Recall that earlier I discussed the distinction between gathering information by a secret informant and gathering it by electronic eavesdropping. I suggested there that I could not see any principle by which one was, on balance, worse than the other, even though we can perceive different sorts of objections to each. The wiretap or bug clearly invades privacy, while the secret informant invades both privacy—in some ways more, in some ways less, than electronic eavesdropping—and personality. Not only is the secret informant privy to actions and conversations one would never consent to have had overheard; the secret informant also modifies personality by deliberately attempting to impair judgment. The wiretap is, in social science jargon, an "unobtrusive measurer." By contrast, the informant necessarily produces a reaction—speech, behavior—on the part of the observed, and may prove influential in determining that reaction.

If there is a distinction between investigative and interrogatory trickery and deceit, it has to be based on situational ethics, the morality of practical necessity. Practically speaking, it is impossible to enforce consensual crime statutes—bribery, drug dealing, prostitution—without employing deception. This need for deception may not be as clear at the interrogation stage. Often, evidence can be produced independently of confessions, and occasionally, false confessions are elicited.

But confessions may also be a practical necessity in many cases, particularly when dealing with the most serious sorts of criminals, such as murderers, rapists, and kidnappers. Miranda himself, it may be recalled, had confessed to the forcible kidnapping and rape of a nineteen-year-old woman. Why should situational ethics permit lying to a drug dealer, but forbid in-custody conversational questioning of a forcible rapist? That question can be answered on historical and constitutional grounds, but it is hard to see how to make consistent common sense out of it.

I cannot here reconcile such inconsistencies, nor am I writing to lobby the Supreme Court. But I would like to conclude by suggesting that apparent inconsistency makes law look more like a game than a rational system for enforcing justice. Because of this appear-

Deception by Police / 53

ance of inconsistency, police are not likely to take the stated rules of the game seriously and are encouraged to operate by their own codes, including those which

affirm the necessity for lying wherever it seems justified by the ends.

NOTES

1 See generally, Welsh S. White, "Police Trickery in Inducing Confessions," *U. Pa. L. Rev.* 127 (1979): 581–629; Welsh S. White, "Interrogation without Questions: Rhode Island v. Innis and United States v. Henry," *Mich. L. Rev.* 78 (1980): 1209–51.

2 Sissela Bok, *Lying: Moral Choice in Public and Private Life* (New York: Pantheon, 1978).

3 See, for example, the discussion in Chapter VII, "Justification," of the group decision to deceive the public. Bok says it is based on the shared belief that the group's norms are good, and that any means used to achieve group ends would therefore also be good (Bok, *Lying*, p. 97). See also the discussion of unmarked police cars as justifiable deception because the practice is publicized, while entrapment is not deemed justifiable unless the public agrees this is proper police behavior (Bok, *Lying*, pp. 98–99).

4 See, generally, Gary Marx, "Undercover Cops: Creative Policing or Constitutional Threat?" *Civ. Libs. Rev.* 4 (July/August 1977): 34–44.

5 United States v. Ressler, 536 F. 2d 208 (1976), and list of cases cited in the body of that opinion.

6 Franks v. Delaware, 98 S.Ct. 2674 (1979).

7 As to "code of honor" regarding deception, see Lawrence W. Sherman, *Scandal and Reform: Controlling Police Corruption* (Berkeley and Los Angeles: University of California, 1978), pp. 46–67. As to existence of police subculture, see Ellwyn R. Stoddard, "A Group Approach to Blue-Coat Crime," in *Police Corruption: A Sociological Perspective*, ed. Lawrence W. Sherman (Garden City, N.J.: Doubleday, Anchor Books, 1974), pp. 277–304.

8 Jerome Skolnick, *Justice without Trial*, 2nd ed. (New York: Wiley & Sons, 1975), p. 177.

9 *The Knapp Commission Report*, City of New York Commission to Investigate Allegations of Police Corruption and the City's Anti-Corruption Procedures (New York, 1972), discussed in Sherman, *Scandal and Reform*, p. 160.

10 Mapp v. Ohio, 367 U.S. 643 (1961).

11 Quoted and discussed in Dallin Oaks, "Studying the Exclusionary Rule in Search and Seizure," *U. Chi. L. Rev.* 37 (1970): 665–757.

12 People v. Defore, 242 N.Y. 13 (1926).

13 Robert Daley, *Prince of the City: The True Story of a Cop Who Knew Too Much* (Boston: Houghton Mifflin Co., 1978), p. 73.

14 Skolnick, *Justice*, pp. 214–15.

15 For a discussion of institutional support for trying to cover up misuse of force charges, see Paul Chevigny, *Police Power* (New York: Pantheon, 1969), p. 139. For case law and discus-

sion of trickery and deception at the investigative stage, see Yale Karnisar, *Police Interrogation and Confessions* (Ann Arbor: University of Michigan Press, 1980).

16 Sherman v. United States, 356 U.S. 369 (1958).

17 United States v. Russell, 411 U.S. 423 (1973).

18 Welsh S. White, "Policy Trickery."

19 Brown v. Mississippi, 297 U.S. 278 (1936).

20 Rochin v. California, 342 U.S. 165 (1952).

21 Ralph A. Rossum, "Entrapment Defense and the Teaching of Political Responsibility: The Supreme Court as Republican Schoolmaster," *Amer. J. Crim. L.* 6 (1978): 287–306.

22 Arthur M. Schlesinger, Jr., *Robert Kennedy and His Times* (Boston: Houghton Mifflin, 1978), p. 285.

23 Provisions for issuing a warrant to wiretap are stringent. The rule is that wiretaps may be conducted only after a warrant has been issued. Title III of 18 U.S.C. §§2510–20 prescribes a careful procedure for obtaining a warrant to use electronic surveillance, and the federal law preempts state law on this subject. By contrast, an informant paid by the D.E.A., for example, may freely roam about southwestern Florida, working his way into any corner of the drug subculture, without specific judicial authorization. See Stuart Penn, "The Informer," *Wall Street Journal*, 10 May 1982.

24 United States v. Russell, 411 U.S. 423 (1973).

25 Miranda v. Arizona, 384 U.S. 486 (1966).

26 Lego v. Twomey, 404 U.S. 477 (1972) (Voluntariness must be proven by a preponderance of evidence).

27 *Report on Lawlessness in Law Enforcement*, National Commission on Law Observance and Enforcement (Washington, D.C.: United States Government Printing Office, 1931).

28 Ernest J. Hopkins, *Our Lawless Police: A Study of the Unlawful Enforcement of the Law* (1931; reprint ed., New York: Da Capo Press, 1972), pp. 236–63.

29 A list of such tactics is found in the Wickersham Report; see note 27.

30 Modern commentators claim that the most outrageous examples of the third degree tactics are no longer employed in American police departments. See Robert M. Fogelson, *Big City Police* (Cambridge, Mass.: Harvard University Press, 1977), p. 302.

31 Crooker v. California, 357 U.S. 433 (1958).

32 Cicenia v. LaGay, 357 U.S. 504 (1958).

33 Crooker v. California, 357 U.S. 433, 443 (1958).

34 Ibid., p. 446.

35 Ibid., p. 448.

36 Ibid., p. 443.

37 Fred E. Inbau and John E. Reid, *Criminal Interrogation and Confessions* (Baltimore: Williams and Wilkins Co., 1962).

38 Fred E. Inbau and John E. Reid, *Lie Detection and Criminal Interrogation*, 3rd ed. (Baltimore: Williams and Wilkins Co., 1953).

39 Inbau and Reid, *Criminal Interrogations and Confessions*, p. 208.

40 Joseph Grano, "Voluntariness, Free Will, and the Law of Confessions," *Va. L. Rev.* 65 (1979): 906.

41 Miranda v. Arizona, 384 U.S. 436, 449–50 (1966), citing Charles O'Hara, *Fundamentals of Criminal Investigation* (Springfield, Ill.: Charles Thomas Publishing Co., 1956), p. 99.

42 Ibid., pp. 451–52, citing Inbau and Reid, *Criminal Interrogation and Confessions*, p. 40.

43 Ibid., p. 452, citing O'Hara, *Fundamentals*, p. 104, and Inbau and Reid, *Criminal Interrogation*, pp. 58–59.

44 Project, "Interrogations in New Haven: The Impact of Miranda," *Yale L.J.* 76 (1967): 1519–1648; Richard H. Seeburger and R. Stanton Wettick, Jr., "Miranda in Pittsburgh—A Statistical Study," *U. Pitt. L. Rev.* 29 (1967): 1–26; Cyril D. Robinson, "Police and Prosecutor Practices and Attitudes Relating to Interrogation," *Duke L.J.* 1968: 425–524.

45 Richard E. Ayers, "Confessions and the Court," *Yale Alumni Magazine* (December, 1968): 18, 20. Cited in Yale

Kamisar, Wayne R. LaFave, and Jerold H. Israel, *Modern Criminal Procedure: Cases, Comments, Questions*, 5th ed. (St. Paul, Minn.: West Publishing Co., 1980), p. 632.

46 John Baldwin and Michael McConville, "Police Interrogation and the Right to See a Solicitor," *Crim. L. Rev.* 1979: 145–52; Welsh S. White, "Police Trickery."

47 Welsh S. White, "Police Trickery," p. 586.

48 Welsh S. White, "Police Trickery," pp. 599–600.

49 Massiah v. United States, 377 U.S. 201 (1964).

50 United States v. Henry, 100 S.Ct. 2183 (1980).

51 State v. Reilly, No. 5285 (Conn. Super. Ct. Apr. 12, 1974), vacated 32 Conn. Supp. 349, 355 A.2d 324 (Super. Ct. 1976).

52 Donald S. Connery, *Guilty Until Proven Innocent* (New York: G. P. Putnam's Sons, 1977); Joan Barthel, *A Death in Canaan* (New York: E. P. Dutton, 1976).

53 David T. Lykken, *A Tremor in the Blood: Uses and Abuses of the Lie Detector* (New York: McGraw-Hill Book Co., 1981), p. 26.

54 Robert Pear, "As Use of the Polygraph Grows, Suspects and Lawyers Sweat," *New York Times*, 13 July 1980.

55 Jerome Skolnick, "Scientific Theory and Scientific Evidence: An Analysis of Lie Detection," *Yale L. J.* 70 (1961): 699.

56 David T. Lykken, "Review: The Art and Science of the Polygraph Technique," *Contemporary Psychology* 26 (1981): 480.

[25]

Who Really Gets Stung?
Some Issues Raised by
the New Police Undercover Work

Gary T. Marx

In the last decade covert law enforcement has expanded in scale and changed in form. Factors responsible for this are briefly considered. The advantages and successes of recent undercover work have been well publicized. Yet the mere fact that a practice is legal should not be sufficient grounds for its use. Its ethical, practical, economic, and social implications must also be taken into account. Without denying the positive aspects of undercover work, the paper discusses some disadvantages, costs, and risks which have received inadequate public attention. These are discussed with respect to (1) targets of the investigation who may be subjected to trickery, coercion, excessive temptation, and political targeting, (2) undercover police work, which may cause police severe stress, entail lack of supervision, and present police with unique opportunities for corruption, (3) informers, the weakest link in the system, who may exploit their undercover role in a variety of ways, (4) third parties victimized as a result of undercover operations, and (5) the potential of undercover work to contribute unintentionally to crime, through such factors as generation of a market or the provision of ideas, motives, or scarce resources.

Recent undercover practices such as ABSCAM and police-run fencing fronts may be portents of a subtle and perhaps irreversible change in how social control is carried out. It is important to reflect on whether this is the direction in which we wish to see our society move.

THE CHANGING NATURE
OF UNDERCOVER WORK

Recent federal investigations, such as ABSCAM, MILAB, and BRILAB, and the many local variations, such as police-run fencing fronts and anticrime decoy squads, call attention to changes in an old police tactic: undercover work. In the last decade, covert law enforcement activity has expanded in scale and changed in form. At the local level, for example, the

GARY T. MARX: Professor of Sociology, Departments of Urban Studies and Humanities, Massachusetts Institute of Technology, Cambridge. This paper is drawn from testimony delivered to the House Subcommittee on Civil and Constitutional Rights during its hearings on proposed guidelines for FBI undercover work (Feb. 25, 1981). The author is grateful to Sissella Bok, Jay Wachtel, and Chuck Wexler for their comments.

proportion of all police arrests involving undercover work has roughly doubled in the last fifteen years. This represents in part an increase in work countering drug offenses. But new federal aid for strike forces, the Witness Protection Program, fencing stings, and anticrime decoys has been a major stimulus. With increased attention given to organized and white collar crime, the Federal Bureau of Investigation has dropped J. Edgar Hoover's policy of prohibiting sworn agents from playing undercover roles. Funding for FBI undercover operations increased from $1 to $4.8 million from 1978 to 1981. Recent FBI investigations into political corruption, insurance fraud, and labor racketeering have received extensive media attention. Moreover, other government agencies in addition to law enforcement appear to be making increased use of undercover tactics as part of their audit and general inspection procedures.

Undercover tactics have, of course, been used for vice and political crimes since the turn of the century; yet, within professional police circles, these tended to be seen as insignificant and marginal activities. These traditional undercover practices have been supplemented by new and more complex forms and changing emphasis and attitudes.

Undercover work is increasingly viewed as an important and innovative police tactic carried out by carefully chosen, elite units. In many big city police departments, competition for assignment to such units, such as anticrime decoy squads, is intense: Assignment to tactical or special squads which use undercover tactics in new ways brings increased prestige and professional recognition. Their use has been extended to white collar corruption and street offenses, and to consumers of activities constituting vice crimes (reaching beyond the customary targets, the providers of those activities). Examples of the latter can be seen in decoy police women posing as prostitutes and arresting men who proposition them, and undercover officers offering to sell (rather than buy) drugs. The lone undercover worker making isolated arrests has been supplemented or replaced by highly coordinated and staged team activities, involving technological aids and many agents and arrests. Informers have always been central to undercover work for information, introduction, and often participation. Recent complex undercover operations have relied heavily upon unwitting informers, persons unaware that they were part of a police operation, and who therefore were not bound by the legal and administrative restrictions under which police operate.

With such consensual crimes as prostitution or gambling, the undercover transaction has been restricted to the consenting adults involved. But recent undercover work in other types of consensual crimes (such as the buying and selling of stolen property, with police posing as fences) may entail victimization of third parties. Goals and targeting have also changed. Traditionally, undercover work has been used in a targeted fashion as part of a criminal investigation after a crime has occurred, where there is a suspect and his apprehension is the goal. Today, its range is broader, as undercover work has become part of efforts to anticipate crimes not yet committed, where there is as yet no suspect, and where deterrence is an important goal.

There is neither a single nor a simple reason for changes in the nature and scale of undercover work. Multiple factors are involved, and they interact in complex ways. At a very general level, there appears to be a decline in the acceptance of coercive means to control people, with a concomitant rise in deceptive means. Values of rational organization, planning, and prevention are increasingly important in varied institutions, whether medical, educational, or criminal justice.

For those concerned with criminal justice reform, one of the most interesting issues involves the possible link between the success of demands to change police priorities and limit past abuses by police and increases in undercover work. In the case of the former, the FBI's new white collar and organized crime priorities led easily to increased undercover work as an effective tactic for dealing with consensual or skilled offenders.

While rightfully focusing on continuing abuses and some retreat from earlier gains, civil libertarians can note considerable progress with respect to some aspects of police reform. The legal environment in which police work has changed markedly in recent decades. While the new limitations they face can easily be exaggerated, it is clear that the conditions of police work have altered. The rights guaranteed citizens under the Constitution are better honored than in the past. Supreme Court decisions, legislation, and departmental policies have restricted the conditions under which police can gather information, whether through search and seizure, electronic surveillance, or stressful and coercive interrogation after arrest. Police must build stronger cases in order to arrest and convict, and there is less tolerance in the courts of extralegal techniques for effecting an apprehension.

One response to the exclusionary rule, *Miranda*, *Escobido*, and the like, is for police simply to do less for fear of running afoul of departmental and court rulings. But another is to seek imaginative ways around the rulings, as in the increased use of informants and undercover work involving anticrime decoys, false fencing fronts, and infiltration. There need be little problem with rules of evidence, interrogations, the search for a suspect, testimony, and guilt if the undercover officer is a direct party to the offense, and the crime has even been videotaped in living color. Better still if (as was the case with ABSCAM) an assistant attorney general or prosecutor can monitor the videotape as the action unfolds and even place a call to undercover agents warning them if their behavior verges on entrapment.

As the police use of coercion has been restricted, their use of deception has increased. Restricting police investigation after a crime occurs has increased the attention paid to anticipating crimes. Restricting the conditions under which the police can carry out searches and seizures, participate in violence or felonies, or engage in coercive persuasion as part of undercover investigations has meant increased use of civilians (knowing and unwitting informants, private detectives), who are less accountable than the police. Thus, increased police respect for individual liberties and rights may come partly at a cost of widening manipulation of citizens by informants and other civilians used by law enforcement. What police want to have done but cannot themselves do legally may be delegated to others.

This ironic link between reform and the spread of undercover practices is an intriguing example of the unintended consequences of reform, a topic that is finally beginning to receive the serious academic attention it deserves.[1]

As police departments have become more bureaucratic, modern management techniques have been adopted. For example, one can see a greater emphasis on measuring output as a means of accountability and an attempt to anticipate and sometimes even create demand. Increased conflict with minorities and the politically and culturally disenchanted may also have made it more difficult for the police to gain crime information or to obtain complaints or testimony from alienated or intimidated citizens. This also means greater reliance on informers and undercover work to gain information and witnesses.

New crime problems are also important. The increase in street crime over the last decade has led to the search for better methods of crime control. The spread of organized crime's activities has stimulated expanded and more sophisticated undercover work, as have the proliferation of heroin and other serious drugs and establishment of sophisticated international distribution networks.

Beyond the provision of new federal financial resources and guidance for undercover work, technical innovations appear to be relevant. The development of highly intrusive and easily hidden surveillance technology has encouraged undercover work. But whatever is responsible for the changes in undercover investigation, it is clear that important policy questions are at stake. Executive and legislative bodies responsible for general police policy and accountability, courts, police managers, and policy analysts have not adequately confronted these questions.

The advantages and successes of recent undercover work have been well publicized. For example, for certain offenses, such as bribery and drug sales, the tactic can permit arrests rarely possible using overt methods. This is also the case for crimes in which a well-organized, skilled, or particularly intimidating group is involved. Knowledge that anyone on the street could be a police officer may deter some offenders and increase feelings of safety among citizens. Conviction rates are high when an undercover officer has been party to a crime, and even higher when

---

1. See, e.g., Sam Sieber, *Fatal Remedies* (New York: Plenum, 1981).

videotaped evidence is presented. And the courts' willingness to accept complex undercover activities such as ABSCAM as legal has diverted attention from problematic questions.

Given the favorable press that recent undercover work has generally received and the secrecy that surrounds such operations (the relative ease with which agents may overlook or disguise mistakes, abuses, and costs), the public perceptions probably reflect an overestimation of the advantages and underestimation of the disadvantages of the tactic. The mere fact that a practice is legal should not be sufficient grounds for its use. Its ethical, practical, economic, and social implications must also be considered. Without denying the positive aspects of undercover work or arguing that it should be categorically prohibited, I will discuss some disadvantages, costs, and risks which have received inadequate public attention. I also wish to offer reasons why undercover tactics can be more troubling than overt police methods, and, as a result, require greater restrictions and closer supervision. Determining the frequency of unintended consequences of undercover work and weighing the competing values and trade-offs are important tasks for research and policy analysis, and much work remains to be done. Identifying the issues at stake is a crucial first step. I will consider these as they bear upon targets of the investigation, informers, police, third parties, and society in general.[2]

TARGETS: TRICKERY, COERCION, TEMPTATION

In considering the targets of undercover investigations, European observers are often surprised at how far American police are permitted to go in generating conditions for crime. The law and courts are very tolerant here. Recent decisions, such as those in the Hoffa, Lewis, Osborne, Russell, Hampton, and Twigg cases,[3] continue this support. The predisposi-

---

2. The discussion here continues my interest in covert forms of interdependence between rule breakers and enforcers. See also the following: "Thoughts on a Neglected Category of Social Movement Participant: Agents Provocateurs and Informants," *American Journal of Sociology*, September 1974, pp. 402–42; "Double Agents," *New Republic*, Oct. 18, 1975, pp. 8–13; "External Efforts to Damage or Facilitate Social Movements," in *The Dynamics of Social Movements*, Mayer Zald and John McCarthy, eds. (Cambridge, Mass.: Winthrop, 1979), pp. 94–125; "The New Police Undercover Work," *Urban Life and Culture*, January 1980, pp. 400–46; "Ironies of Social Control: Authorities as Contributors to Deviance through Escalation, Non-Enforcement, and Covert Facilitation," *Social Problems*, February 1981, pp. 221–46; "Types of Undercover Operation and Activities" (Paper delivered at Hastings Center Conference on Undercover Activities, Hastings-on-Hudson, N.Y., 1981); "Undercover Police Tactics," *Encyclopedia of Crime and Justice*, forthcoming.

3. Hoffa v. U.S., 385 U.S. 293 (1963); Lewis v. U.S., 385 U.S. 323 (1966); Osborn v. U.S., 385 U.S. 323 (1966); U.S. v. Russell, 411 U.S. 423 (1973); Hampton v. U.S., 425 U.S. 484 (1976); U.S. v. Twigg, 588 F.2d 373 (3rd Cir. 1978).

tion of the offender, rather than the objective methods of police, tends to be seen as the key factor in determining entrapment at the federal level. The fact that the crime could not or would not have occurred had the government not been involved is usually not considered legally relevant if the person is thought to have been predisposed to engage in the prohibited activity. Yet, for understanding causes of behavior, and developing guidelines for the use of scarce law enforcement resources, issues related to the behavior of government agents is crucial. The fact that a tactic is legal does not necessarily imply that its use is ethical. In addition, because of the secrecy surrounding undercover work, it can easily be used in ways that are illegal. This section considers issues bearing on the targets of undercover operations.

Three types of agent behavior are of particular interest: the use of excessive trickery, the use of coercion, and the offer of extraordinarily seductive temptations. Where the behavior of the undercover agent exhibits any of these characteristics, it may be questionable whether the suspect acted with autonomy and full knowledge of the illegal nature of his behavior. Let us consider each of the above.

Trickery

Three common forms of trickery are (1) offering the illegal action as a minor part of a very attractive socially legitimate goal, (2) hiding or disguising the illegal nature of the action, and (3) weakening the capacity of the target to distinguish right and wrong (or choosing a suspect who is already so weakened). In the first case, targets are lured into the activity on a pretext. The goal put forth is legal and desirable, and the illegality is secondary. Thus, in the most questionable ABSCAM case, that in Philadelphia, the defendants were told that their involvement could bring a convention center and possibly other means of financial gain to the city. They were led to believe that the project would not come to Philadelphia if they did not accept the money. Judge Fullam, in his ruling on the Philadelphia case of Schwartz and Jannotte, indicates that neither of the defendants asked for money and both indicated that no payment was necessary.[4]

In another example, Rommie Loudd, the first black executive with a professional sports team, organized the Orlando, Florida, franchise in the World Football League. With the failure of the league, Loudd went broke. A man whom he did not know called and offered him $1 million to reorganize his team. The caller promised to bring wealthy colleagues into the deal, but Loudd was told he first had to loosen up the financiers with

---

4. John Fullam, "Memorandum and Order," U.S. District Court for the Eastern District of Pennsylvania, U.S. v. Harry P. Jannotte, George Schwartz, no. 80-166, November 1980.

cocaine. He resisted the offer, but eventually introduced the caller (an undercover agent) to two people who sold him cocaine. Loudd, with no previous criminal record, was sentenced to a long prison term. On tape, the agent involved said to his partner, "I've tricked him worse than I've tricked anybody ever."[5]

Ignorance of the law is, of course, not an excuse for its violation. However, the situation seems different (at least, ethically) when one is led into illegal activities by a government agent who claims that no wrongdoing is occurring. Here the agent creates a subterfuge in order to make it appear to the suspect that nothing illegal is happening.

In several ABSCAM cases, defendants were led to believe that they could make money without having to deliver any promises. The videotape from the case of New Jersey Senator Harrison Williams reveals the main informant coaching the senator in what to say, almost putting words in his mouth: "You gotta tell him how important you are, and you gotta tell him in no uncertain terms—'without me, there is no deal. I'm the man who's gonna open the doors. I'm the man who's gonna do this and use my influence and I guarantee this.' " The senator is then assured that nothing wrong is happening: "It goes no further. It's all talk, all bullshit. It's a walk-through. You gotta just play and blow your horn."[6]

Some ABSCAM defendants were told that, in accordance with the "Arab mind" and "Arab way of doing business," they must convince the investors that they had friends in high places. In order to do this, money had to be accepted from the apparent investors, although the defendants were not required by the undercover agents to offer any commitments contingent on accepting the payment. The key element was appearances. In Philadelphia, the situation was structured so that the acceptance of money would be seen as payment for private consulting services and not as the acceptance of a bribe.[7] The defendants were not asked to behave improperly.

Another problematic situation involves the use of trickery against people with diminished capacity, such as the mentally limited or ill, juveniles, and persons under extreme pressure or in a needy or weakened state (e.g., addicts in withdrawal). Such persons may be more susceptible to persuasion and less able than most citizens to distinguish right from wrong. As part of the investigation, the undercover agent may attempt to create or may aggravate such conditions in the target. Senator Williams refused the first offer of cash. However, he eventually took money after resourceful government agents (who had concluded that he was an alcoholic) gave him liquor.

5. *Newsweek*, Nov. 15, 1976.
6. Nat Hentoff, *Village Voice*, Dec. 31, 1980. In a useful series of articles from November to January, Hentoff gives forceful consideration to the civil liberties issues raised by ABSCAM. In general, these issues have received only cursory attention in the media.
7. Fullam, "Memorandum and Order."

172   **Gary T. Marx**

Coercion

Participation may stem from a fear of the failure to cooperate rather than from free choice. An element of this seems inherent in certain sham criminal situations, or in employing as informants those accustomed to using threats of violence to get their way.

For example, two federal agents and a convicted armed robber became involved in a gambling and prostitution front in Alaska. This was part of an anticipatory plan to deal with organized crime, believed to be coming into the area because of opportunities offered by the pipeline project. The agents helped finance a bar which was to be the center of the operation and actively sought participants for the scheme. One of the agents posed as the organization's "heavy muscle"—and appears to have played a heavy-handed role in intimidating and prodding some participants.[8]

In a case growing out of a Washington, D.C., fencing sting, former Assistant United States Attorney Donald Robinson was accused of taking money for information from persons he thought were organized crime figures, but who were actually police. He eventually won his case on the grounds of entrapment. Robinson had at first ignored their approaches, but became involved after persistent telephone calls, a threatening call to his wife, and a warning that he might end up missing.[9] When coercion is mixed with temptation, the incentive to participate can be very strong.

Temptation

Recent undercover actions have transformed the Biblical injunction to something like, "lead us into temptation and deliver us from evil." Temptation raises different issues than coercion or trickery. An act is no less criminal because it is engaged in as a response to a very attractive temptation than if it is committed without the presentation of temptation. The concerns raised are instead the assumptions on which the tactic is based, the questionable fairness of such a technique, and whether scarce resources ought to be used to pose temptation.

Defenders of these tactics usually make the assumption that the world is divided clearly between criminal and noncriminal citizens. It is assumed that presenting a temptation will not endanger the uprightness of the latter, while the former will commit the offense if given any opportunity to do so. Numerous critics have questioned this, noting the importance in criminality of situational factors. A well-known story captures something of this disagreement regarding the nature of motivation to engage in deviant behavior. A man encounters a woman in a fancy bar and asks her, "Would you accompany me to my hotel room for $10,000?" She says yes.

8. *Los Angeles Times*, Nov. 17, 1977.

9. *Newsweek*, Nov. 15, 1976; John Lardner, "How Prosecutors Are Nabbed," *New Republic*, Jan. 29, 1977, pp. 22–25.

Whereupon he asks her whether she would come to his room for $10. She indignantly says, "No, what kind of a girl do you think I am?" He responds, "Madam, we have already established that, what we are haggling about is the price." Depending on the side taken in this story, deviance is seen as either an inherent or a conditional attribute.

Of course, much depends on the type of offense. For some, the line between the criminal and noncriminal can be easily blurred through the offer of secret temptations. Al Capone captured this insight (if going too far) when, in response to a reporter's question, he said something like, "Lady, when you get down to cases, nobody's on the legit." Or, put differently, in the immortal words of Mel Weinberg, the key figure in the ABSCAM case, "You put the big honeypot out there, all the flies come to it."

It is certainly not true that everyone has his price or can be tempted. The imagery of turning on a faucet or providing sticky flypaper is overdrawn. However, there are certain types of behavior in which undercover tactics can turn up offenses a goodly proportion of the time among persons not thought of as criminals. This is the case for sexual encounters, underage drinking, marijuana use, minor traffic violations, and certain forms of illegality related to routine job performance. For example, a building inspector or purchasing agent may take a bribe or accept a gift for issuing a permit or purchasing goods that would have been issued or bought anyway; merchants and manufacturers will buy needed goods very cheaply without asking questions; and it is usually little problem to sell consumers goods such as televisions and stereos when offered at big discounts. The number of arrests possible from certain undercover actions is astounding. In situations were illegality is so easy to generate, the secret provision of state opportunities should be handled in accordance with a clear set of priorities with respect to both types of offense and offender. The necessity to make the best use of scarce resources, as well as fairness, requires that seriousness rather than the technical ease of making a case be a major criterion governing law enforcement's uses of culpability.

When there is a well-documented pattern of prior serious infractions or reasons for suspicion, secret testing may be appropriate. It may also be appropriate for persons in positions of special trust or temptation, if they are warned beforehand that the tactic may be used. But there is a danger that, once resources are provided and skills developed, the tactic will be abused. It may have been appropriate for God to test Job. The conditions under which it is appropriate for humans to test one another need careful specification. Some of the new police undercover work has lost sight of the profound difference between carrying out an investigation to determine whether a suspect is, in fact, breaking the law, and carrying it out to determine whether an individual *can be induced* to break the law. As with God's testing of Job, the question "Is he corrupt?" may be replaced with the question "Is he corruptible?" Questions of police discretion are

involved here. With limited resources, how much attention should authorities devote to crimes that appear in response to the opportunity they
themselves generate or that can be subtly ferreted out through secret tactics, rather than focusing on offenses that appear without their inducement? As Judge Frankfurter wrote in *Sherman* v. *U.S.*, "Human nature is
weak enough and sufficiently beset by temptations without the government adding to them and generating crime."[10]

Even if temptations are not offered, most complex activities, whether of
businessmen, legislators, or academics, have legally gray areas wherein
secret investigations could turn up violations. In many bureaucratic settings, "creative bookkeeping" may be illegal or at least violate internal
policy, but organizational functioning would be much inhibited without
it. Those who get ahead in organizations are often the persons who make
things happen by breaking, bending, and twisting rules and by cutting
through red tape. Rules are often general, contradictory, and open to varied interpretations. As those in law enforcement bureaucracies know too
well, organizations have a vast number of rules that are overlooked until
a supervisor wants to find fault with someone. In such cases, morality and
conformity are often not the simple phenomena that the record of rule
violation may make them out to be. The use of secret forms of information gathering, without there even being temptations, can thus be problematic.

POLITICAL TARGETING AND
MISUSE OF RESULTS

The vagaries and complexities of motivation aside, questions can also be
raised about how targets are chosen and how the results of an investigation are used. Undercover operations can be contrasted with conventional
investigations which appear in response to the complaint of a victim. The
latter offer some controls not present in secret investigations undertaken
at police initiative. Openness in an investigation (with respect to the fact
that it is being carried out and the means used to do so) and the presence
of a complainant as a concerned outside party reduce discretionary power.
Secret investigations carried out at police initiative that involve testing of
integrity are a powerful means for the discovery or creation of discrediting
information. They can offer a powerful way to control a person through
arrest, the threat of exposure, or damage to a reputation through leaks of
information. The potential for political and personal misuse of undercover work appears to be greater than that with overt police methods.

The last decade offers many examples of undercover targeting of radical activists, who could not be arrested for their political beliefs, for drug
and other arrests. In Los Angeles, a top mayoral aid, unpopular with

10. *Sherman* v. *U.S.*, 356 U.S. 369, 372 (1974).

Issues in New Police Undercover Work

police because of his role in police department changes, was arrested on a morals charge under questionable circumstances. He lost his job.

Even persons who reject an undercover temptation may still be harmed. Involvement as a suspect in the apparatus of a covert government investigation cannot help but cast a shadow on a person's reputation. To be secretly videotaped or tape recorded and then to have this made public will convey a presumption of guilt to the uncritical. For the unprincipled, undercover tactics may offer a tool for character assassination.

Investigations may be carried out with no intention of formal prosecution. In cases where there is no prosecution because of insufficient evidence, rejection of the offer, or improper official behavior, the subject may still be damaged through leaks to the media. The government's unregulated power to carry out integrity tests at will offers a means of slander, regardless of the outcome of the test. In the case of politicians, for whom matters of public reputation are central, the issue is particularly salient. The breadth of some criminal laws (e.g., conspiracy) in the absence of internal guidelines gives police wide discretion in deciding whom to investigate. This routine discretion can mask the political motivation that may be behind an investigation.

As with other privacy-invading tactics, such as electronic surveillance or access to confidential records, there is the potential in undercover work for blackmail and coercion. Information gained may never be used in court, but may be filed away as long as those implicated continue to cooperate with the controlling agent—in legal ways, such as by offering information or setting up others, or in illegal ways, such as through pay-offs.[11] Getting information on the extent of this type of coercion is very difficult,

---

11. J. Edgar Hoover, with his files on important people, was a master at the use of this technique. Watergate has been interpreted as an effort to gather data for blackmail and political leverage rather than for publication. In a shocking example, Southern Bell Company executives used wiretap material in an effort to coerce local officials into agreeing to rate increases (George O'Toole, *The Private Sector: Rent-a-Cops, Private Spies and the Police-Industrial Complex* [New York: W. W. Norton, 1978], p. 70). As the main "headhunter" of the Internal Affairs Unit, and later as Chief of Police, William Parker is said to have used such tactics to control the Los Angeles Police Department and its broader political environment. The myth of secret knowledge can be a powerful control factor spreading fear among those who have things to hide. Rumors of the secret information Parker supposedly had worked to his advantage. Joseph Woods ("The Progressives and the Police: Urban Reform and the Professionalization of the Los Angeles Police" [Ph.D. diss., University of California at Los Angeles, 1973], p. 420) observes, "Newspaper reports implied that Parker knew dreadful things about one or another public figure, and that his secret files made him and the Department invulnerable to political interference." Within bureaucracies such as the police, holding in abeyance negative information that can always be used against a person is a major (and unstudied) form of internal control. One policeman notes, "It was like being in a game where the umpires had two rule books and wouldn't tell you which one you were playing under" (Sonny Grosso and Philip Rosenberg, *Point Blank* [New York: Avon, 1979], p. 189).

since undercover police and those blackmailed have a shared conspirational interest in keeping silent.

In some jurisdictions where employees are required to report illegal activities, they may face double testing. Thus, an employee of New York City's Buildings Department was approached by an undercover investigator who offered him a bribe if he would submit falsified architectural plans. The bribe was rejected. However, the inspector was suspended from his job for failing to report the bribe attempt.[12] Although legal, this action takes the traditional integrity test to a new extreme. A person may become the target of an undercover opportunity scheme, not because of suspected corruption, but merely to see whether requirements that bribes be reported are followed. The potential for misuse is clear. This technique can be a tool for getting rid of employees seen as troublesome for other reasons.

EFFECTS ON POLICE

Undercover work offers great risks and temptations to the police involved. As is the case with informants, the secrecy of the situation, the protected access to illegality, and the usual absence of a complainant can be conducive to corruption and abuse. As noted, undercover operations can offer a way for agents to make easy cases or to retaliate, damage, or gain leverage against suspects not otherwise liable to prosecution. Issues of entrapment, blackmail, and leaks were considered in the section on targets. Here the focus is on direct implications for police.

The character of police work, with its isolation, secrecy, discretion, uncertainty, temptations, and need for suspicion, is frequently drawn upon to explain (1) poor relations between police and the community, (2) the presence of a police subculture in conflict with formal departmental policy, and (3) police stress symptoms. These characteristics are even more pronounced in the case of undercover work, which also involves other factors that may be conducive to a variety of problems. Beyond the threat of physical danger from discovery, there may be severe social and psychological consequences for police who play undercover roles for an extended period of time.

Undercover situations tend to be more fluid and unpredictable than is the case with routine patrol or investigative work. There is greater autonomy for agents, and rules and procedures are less clear. The expenses in setting up an undercover operation are often significant; thus, the financial costs of mistakes or failure are much higher than in conventional investigations. The need for secrecy accentuates problems of coordination and concern over the great potential for error. Undercover police may

12. *New York Times*, May 17, 1979.

unknowingly enforce the law against one another or have it enforced against themselves, sometimes with tragic consequences.

Undercover agents are removed from the usual controls of a uniform, a badge, a visible supervisor, a fixed place of work, radio or beeper calls, and a delineated assignment. These have both a literal and a symbolic significance in reminding the officer who he or she is.

Unlike conventional police work, activities by the undercover agent tend to involve only criminals, and the agent is always carrying out deception; thus, a criminal environment and role models assume predominance in the officer's working life. The agent is encouraged to pose as a criminal. His ability to blend in, to resemble criminals, and to be accepted is central to effectiveness. It also serves as an indication to the agent that he or she is doing a good job. As positive personal relationships develop, the agent may experience guilt, and ambivalence may develop over the betrayal inherent in the deceptive role being played. The work is very intense; the agent is always "on." For some agents, the work becomes almost addicting, as they come to enjoy the sense of power the role offers and its protected contact with illegal activity.

Isolation from other contacts and the need to be liked and accepted by members of a criminal subculture can have unintended consequences. "Playing the crook" may increase cynicism and ambivalence about the police role and make it easier to rationalize the use of illegal and immoral means, whether for agency or for corrupt goals. In his novel *Mother-Night*, Vonnegut tells us that "we are what we pretend to be, so we must be careful about what we pretend to be."[13] Police may become consumers or purveyors of the very vice they set out to control.

A good example of this can be seen in the case of a northern California police officer who participated in a "deep cover" operation for a year and a half, riding with the Hell's Angels. He was responsible for a very large number of arrests, including heretofore almost untouchable high-level drug dealers, and was praised for doing a "magnificent job." But this came at a cost of heavy drug use, alcoholism, brawling, the break-up of his family, an inability to fit back into routine police work after the investigation was over, resignation from the force, several bank robberies, and a prison term.[14]

Other examples include a Chicago policeman whose undercover work involved posing as a pimp and infiltrating a prostitution ring. He continued in the pimp role after the investigation ended and was suspended.[15] A

13. Kurt Vonnegut, *Mother-Night* (New York: Dell, 1975).
14. Lawrence Linderman, "Underground Angel," *Playboy*, July 1981, pp. 134–36, 142, 220–235, 244.
15. *Chicago Daily News*, Sept. 24, 1975.

member of an elite drug enforcement unit in the Boston area became an addict and retired on a disability pension.[16]

The financial rewards from police corruption, particularly in gambling and narcotics, can be great and the chances of avoiding detection rather good. Ironically, effectiveness and opportunities for corruption may often go hand in hand.[17] Police supervisors and lawbreakers may face equal difficulties in knowing what undercover police officers are really up to. Awareness of the problematic aspects of undercover activity helps explain J. Edgar Hoover's opposition to having sworn agents in such roles. The stellar reputation of the FBI for integrity is attributable, in part, to Hoover's refusal to allow the agents to face the temptations confronting police in agencies routinely involved in undercover activities.

Other costs to police, while not raising ethical or legal issues, can be wasted resources and even tragic consequences. The secrecy, presence of multiple enforcement agencies, and nature of many undercover activities can mean that police end up enforcing the law against one another. Sometimes the instances are merely comical, as in the case described by Whited.[18] Here, an effeminate man wearing mascara went for a walk with another man he met at a gay bar. After a series of suggestive comments, the former, an undercover officer, sought to arrest his companion. He discovered that the companion, also an undercover officer, was hoping to arrest him. Other times, however, the results are far more serious, as undercover police are shot or killed by other police. In recent years in the New York area alone, eight black police officers in undercover roles or working as plainclothesmen have been shot (five fatally) by other policemen who mistook them for lawbreakers.[19]

INFORMERS

Exploitation of the system by informers can be a major problem. The frequency and seriousness of the problems informers can cause make them the weakest link in undercover systems. But most undercover operations must rely to some degree on such persons in the criminal milieu for information, technical advice, "clients," contacts, and introductions involving legitimation of the agents' own disreputability. A heavy price may be paid for this. Although informers face exceptional risks, they also face exceptional opportunities.

16. *Boston Globe*, Oct. 26, 1979.
17. See, e.g., Peter K. Manning and Laurence Redlinger, "Invitational Edges of Corruption: Some Consequences of Narcotics Law Enforcement," in *Politics and Drugs*, Paul Rock, ed. (New York: E. P. Dutton/Society Books, 1977), pp. 279–310; Robert Daley, *Prince of the City* (Boston: Little, Brown, 1978).
18. Whited, *Chiodo* (Chicago: Playboy Press, 1974).
19. *New York Times*, July 30, 1978.

Issues in New Police Undercover Work   **179**

Some recent cases appear to represent a significant delegation of law enforcement investigative authority. Informers can be offered a license to pursue whatever target they choose, as long as they assert that the person selected is predisposed to commit illegal actions. Verification of such assertions is often difficult. Control agents are dependent on persons whose professional lives routinely involve deceit and concealment. When the informer has a motive to lie, as is often the case, matters are even worse. Because of charges they are seeking to avoid, the promise of drugs or money, or a desire to punish competitors or enemies, informers may have strong incentives to see that others break the law. This can mean false claims about past misbehavior of targets and ignoring legal and departmental restrictions. Whether out of self-interest or deeper psychological motives, some informers undergo a transformation and become zealous super-cops, creating criminals or sniffing them out using prohibited methods.

The convicted swindler in ABSCAM (described by Judge Fullam as an "archetypical, amoral, fast-buck artist") had a three-year prison sentence waived and received $133,150 for his cooperation in the two-year investigation. Accounts in an internal Justice Department memorandum indicate that he "would be paid a lump sum at the end of ABSCAM, contingent upon the success of the prosecution." In testimony at Representative John Jenrette's trial, the informer acknowledged that he expects to make more than $200,000 from his undercover activities. He also received a $15,000 advance for a book on his exploits.[20] In an age where "books by crooks" (not to mention movies and the lecture circuit) can mean big money, informers have a further incentive for dramatic discoveries.

The bridge to the truth and respect for law may be further weakened when brokers or middlemen are drawn into the operation. The latter do not even know they are part of a police operation. For example, a device used by some fencing stings is to employ street persons to spread the word that a new fence is paying good prices. A commission is paid the unwitting informer for each transaction he is responsible for. The informer may also collect a fee from the person selling the property. One of the most

20. Fullam, "Memorandum and Order"; Irving Nathan, "ABSCAM—Production of Supplemental Information to Defense Counsel" (memorandum: Washington, D.C.: Justice Department, Jan. 6, 1981); Stephen Kaufman and Daniel Rezneck, "Post-Hearing Memorandum in Support of Defendant Frank Thompson, Jr.'s Motion to Dismiss the Indictment on Due Process Grounds," March 1980, U.S. v. Frank Thompson, Jr., et al., no. CR-80-00291 (Pratt, J.); *Boston Globe*, July 18, 1980. In the classic fashion of the double agent, some of Weinberg's compensation appears to have come from his deceiving the government, beyond the intended targets of the deception. He was paid a $15,000 reward for helping to recover $2 billion worth of supposedly stolen certificates of deposit. However, there is evidence to suggest that the certificates were counterfeit and were never actually stolen, but rather were created under Weinberg's tutelage. He then "recovered" them for the reward money (Jack Anderson, United Features Syndicate, May 28, 1981).

troubling aspects of many of the ABSCAM cases is the role played by middlemen. For example, Joseph Silvestri, one such middleman, was apparently led to believe that he could earn a $6 million broker's fee for helping an Arab sheik invest $60 million in real estate. A condition for his earning the fee was gaining the cooperation of political figures, to be sure that all would work smoothly. It is not surprising that he apparently cast a wide net in seeking to gain "cooperation" from public officials.[21] Claims about past misbehavior or the predisposition of potential targets become even more suspect when this circuitous path is followed. This may help account for why, under the very tempting conditions of ABSCAM, it appears that only half of those approached took the bait.

Informers and, to an even greater extent, middlemen are formally much less accountable than are sworn law officers and are not as constrained by legal or departmental restrictions. As an experienced undercover agent candidly put it, "Unwitting informers are desirable precisely because they can do what we can't—legally entrap." This need not involve police telling informers to act illegally. But the structure of the situation, with its insulation from observability, skills at deception, and strong incentives on the part of the informer, makes supervision very difficult. Videotapes and recordings are a means of monitoring informer behavior. But the crucial and generally unknowable issue is what takes place off the tape recording. To what extent are events on the tape contrived? Informers and middlemen are well situated to engage in entrapment and the fabrication of evidence. Furthermore, the structure of the situation may enable informers to commit crimes of their own, apart from their role as law enforcement agents.

The informer-controller relationship is usually seen to involve the latter exercising coercion over the former. Through a kind of institutionalized blackmail—the threat of jail or public denouncement as an informer—prosecution is held in abeyance as long as cooperation is forthcoming. What is less frequently realized is that the situation can be reversed. When not able to hide criminal behavior, the skilled or fortunately situated informer may be able to manipulate or coerce the controller as well, with neither able to react.

The relationship can be exploited in other ways. Informers may secretly and selectively "give up" sworn undercover agents. The informer's knowledge of police can be a resource traded within criminal milieus. Or informers may sell the same information to several law enforcement agencies, in each case concealing the similar transactions with the other agencies. This leads to the possibility of confrontations between undercover agents from different agencies who are unaware of each other's identity.

---

21. Nick Kotz, "ABSCAM's Loose Cannons," *New Republic*, Mar. 29, 1980, pp. 21–25, citing the account of *Newsday* correspondent Anthony Marro.

Issues in New Police Undercover Work

The price of gaining the cooperation of informers may be the necessity to ignore their rule breaking. But beyond this "principled nonenforcement," these situations lend themselves well to exploitation by informers for their own criminal ends. Major cases may require the government to deal with master con artists operating in their natural habitat. They are likely to have a competitive edge over police.

An insurance expert playing an undercover role in "operation frontload," investigating organized crime in the construction industry, was apparently able to obtain $300,000 in fees and issued worthless insurance "performance bonds." As part of his cover, he was certified as an agent of the New Hampshire Insurance Group with the power to issue bonds. The problems in this expensive case, which resulted in no indictments, became known through a suit against the government.[22] How many other such cases are there that we do not hear about because no one brings suit?

An informer in the ABSCAM case was apparently able to exploit his role and the false front that had been set up (Abdul Enterprises, Ltd.) to swindle West Coast businessmen. Realizing they had been taken, the businessmen complained to the FBI. However, the informer was able to carry on for a year and a half. The FBI took no action, essentially covering up his crime until after ABSCAM became public.[23]

Here we see a type of immunity that undercover work may offer. In this case, it was only temporary, serving to protect the secrecy of an ongoing investigation. Once the investigation was over, the informer was indicted, although one can speculate on the harm done (and lack of compensation) to the victims. Their victimization was indirectly aided by the government, first through its helping to provide the opportunity and then in its failing to intervene to warn others. Even more troubling are cases in which informers can essentially blackmail police into granting them permanent immunity. This happens when a trial and related publicity would reveal dirty tricks and illegality on the part of government agents,

---

22. *New York Times*, May 18, 1979. Another potential hidden cost in undercover operations involves the goods or money that is exchanged. In a Seattle case a judge ruled that patrons of a bar who purchased color televisions and stereos from undercover agents did not have to return them. The goods were not actually stolen, but purchased by police through an LEAA grant. The status of the nearly $500,000 which the government paid out in nine ABSCAM cases is less clear; only $50,000 had been recovered by the end of 1981 (*New York Times*, Sept. 18, 1981). In a related vein is the dispute over what should happen to a $5,000 bribe paid by an FBI operative as part of a "staged crime" to the police superintendent of Bridgeport, Connecticut. The superintendent arrested the former convict bearing the bribe and took possession of the FBI's bugging equipment. Moments later FBI agents appeared and unsuccessfully sought the release of the operative and return of the equipment and money. The mayor of Bridgeport ordered that the $5,000 be spent to buy Christmas toys for poor children, while the FBI continued to demand that the money be returned (*New York Times*, Aug. 21, 1981).

23. *New York Times*, June 4, 1980.

secret sources, techniques of operation, projects, or classified information.

A related phenomenon is crimes committed by persons who have been given new identities and relocated as a result of the Federal Witness Protection Program. The fact that such persons may eventually be prosecuted does not detract from the damage caused to third parties through the government's indirect complicity. Furthermore, prosecution for later crimes is not assured, either because of the witnesses' continuing usefulness, because of what they know, or because of the nature of the offense. For example, no matter what kind of bad debts (including unpaid child support) protected witnesses incur using their phony credentials, the Justice Department apparently will not reveal their identity. A relocated witness may even be moved again and again. Graham cites the example of a witness provided with a new identity who was relocated from Oklahoma to Minnesota to North Carolina, to protect him from the bad debts he continually ran up.[24] The ethical and practical consequences of helping career criminals relocate with a false identity in the midst of an unsuspecting community have received little attention.

THIRD PARTIES

The possible damage to third parties is one of the least explored aspects of undercover work. Because of the secrecy and second-order ripple effects, much of the damage never comes to public attention. Those who are hurt may not even be aware of it to complain or seek damages. Its invisibility makes the harm even more problematic.

One type of damage to third parties has already been considered, crimes committed by informers under the protection of their role, but unrelated to an investigation. A second type more directly involves the intended law enforcement role. The most obvious cases involve the victims of government-inspired or facilitated crimes. These may be of a collateral nature, as in a Lakewood, Colorado, case, where two young men learned that a local "fence"—in reality a police sting—was buying stolen cars. They stole several cars and sold them to the sting. They showed the undercover officers a .45 caliber automatic taken in a burglary, stole another car, killed its owner in the process with this gun, and then sold the car to the "fence." They repeated this again and were then arrested.[25]

24. Fred Graham, *The Alias Program* (Boston: Little, Brown, 1977). See also the poignant case of Tom Leonhardt. His former wife, their two children, and her new husband, a criminal witness, were relocated by the Witness Protection Program. Leonhardt spent eight difficult years trying to find his children. The story is told in Leslin Waller's *Hide in Plain Sight* (New York: Dell, 1980) and in a film of the same title.

25. *National Law Journal*, Oct. 20, 1980. Of course, it is also possible to argue that third parties may be saved from victimization because such undercover work prevents crime that would have occurred in its absence. This may be through deterrence or incapacitation (e.g., some unknown proportion of persons may be saved from victimization while those arrested through a sting are in jail). But cases such as the one in Colorado have a reality and poignancy that make it hard to give equivalent attention to this argument.

Issues in New Police Undercover Work 183

According to one estimate, only about half the property stolen for the purpose of sale to a police-run fencing operation is actually returned to its owners.[26] People may not report their loss, or the property may lack distinctive identification. Even when people do get their property back, it can be argued that the trauma of their victimization should entitle them to some special compensation because of the government's role.

For security reasons or to gain compliance, citizens or businesses approached about cooperating with an undercover operation may not be given the full and candid account necessary for truly informed consent. Such was apparently the case with the informer in "operation front-load." In seeking his certification as an insurance agent with the power to issue bonds, FBI agents described him to the insurance company in question as a former police officer and "a straight arrow," and used a false name. The insurance company was not told of his criminal record, nor of the fact that he had agreed to be an informer to avoid a nine-year prison sentence and a fine. Because of the misbehavior of this informer, as of May 1979 damage suits had been filed in five states against the New Hampshire Insurance Group, the certifying insurance company. Company officials claim that his actions in issuing fake performance bonds to construction companies cost them and insurance brokers more than $60 million in business losses. The head of a Chicago insurance firm states, "What the FBI did was a disgrace. . . . They've ruined us." He is suing for $40 million dollars.[27]

26. Department of Justice, *What Happened* (Washington, D.C.: Govt. Printing Office, 1979), p. 4. Even were documentation presented, a high rate of return might simply be an artifact of the method. For example, undercover agents may be encouraged to purchase only easily identifiable stolen goods that can be returned to their owner. Adequate understanding of the effect of government fences on victimized persons requires knowing (1) what percentage of property brought to a government fence by a thief is stolen in the expectation that it will be purchased by the fence, (2) what percentage of this property is actually purchased by the fence, and (3) what percentage of the goods that are purchased is returned? The first question presents the most difficult measurement issues. Yet in many cases it seems clear that the theft is undertaken with a government fence in mind. For example, an El Paso, Texas, fencing sting conducted by local police and the United States Customs Agency set up in a storefront called JRE Apartment Complex Maintenance and Repair Shop. In the year the sting was in operation almost $2 million in stolen property was purchased. A major contributor to this was a man and his girl friend who, over a five-month period, sold the project seventeen stolen automobiles, four trucking rigs with five semi-trailers, and two trailer loads of merchandise. The total recovery value of the items purchased from this couple was put at $575,909 (Catherine Cotter and James Burrows, *Property Crime Program: A Special Report: Overview of the Sting Program and Project Summaries* [Washington, D.C.: Justice Department, January 1981]). Making such a large number of purchases from the same persons over a period of time certainly seems questionable policy. Issues related to how long an operation should go on, how many buys should be made from a person after sufficient evidence for prosecution has been obtained, and how many times a target should be approached after initially refusing an illegal offer have received little policy attention, particularly at the local level. Most departments have no guidelines for the conduct of undercover activities.

27. *New York Times*, May 18, 1979.

The web of human interdependence is dense, and by trifling with one part of it for deceptive purposes one may send out reverberations that are no less damaging for being unseen. Have any small businesses been hurt by the competition from proprietary fronts run by police? To appear legitimate, such fronts may actually become competitors during the investigation. Government agents with their skills and no need to make a profit would seem to have an obvious competitive edge over many small businessmen.

The damage to third parties need not be only economic. The most private and delicate of human emotions and relationships may be violated under the mantle of government deceit. As part of an attempt to infiltrate the Weather Underground, a federal agent developed a relationship with a woman. She became pregnant. After considerable indecision and at the urging of the agent, she decided to have an abortion. The agent's work then took him elsewhere and he ended the relationship, with the woman apparently never knowing his secret identity and true motives.[28] One can imagine the publicity and law suits if she had kept the child and the circumstances of the paternity had become known, or if she had died in childbirth, or become mentally unstable.

Another form of damage to innocent third parties may lie in the harmful publicity resulting from having their names mentioned on tapes which become public. This was the case for at least three senators mentioned as possible targets for ABSCAM. The frequent reliance of such investigations on con artists with a proclivity to lie, boast, and exaggerate is conducive to colorful and damaging exchanges or mistaken investigation. The fact that a person wrongly named by an informer may later receive a letter from the Justice Department indicating that an intensive investigation "disclosed no evidence of illegality that warranted our further investigation" seems small compensation once he has been implicitly tried by the newspapers.

While likely infrequent, another problem involves "good samaritans" who happen upon undercover operations and take action through benign motives which police may misinterpret. In a Boston case, for example, two college students heard a woman scream and intervened in what they thought was a crime in progress. They were then arrested and charged with assault and battery and helping a prisoner escape. The "crime" involved a decoy squad trying to arrest the woman's male companion.[29] In

---

28. Cyril Payne, *Deep Cover* (New York: Newsweek, 1979).

29. Four Philadelphia policemen from a decoy squad were recently indicted by a federal grand jury on the grounds that they had framed eight suspects on robbery charges. In one of these cases two suspects claimed they were arrested as they bent over to help the decoy pick up a roll of bills he had dropped. The police were members of an aggressive squad whose arrest totals easily exceeded those of other decoy squads working in the central business district (*New York Times*, Sept. 13, 1981).

Issues in New Police Undercover Work

New York, a minister and a former medical student were arrested as a result of what they claimed was an effort to help a "drunk" decoy with an exposed wallet. Charges were dropped. The minister reported feeling shaken and humiliated. He spent thirteen hours in custody after trying to aid the apparently unconscious decoy.[30]

Such occurrences are probably rare, but given the lack of systematic research, one cannot maintain this with certainty. The need to meet arrest quotas and desire to protect the decoy from assault may mean immediate police action once a person bends over or touches a sprawled decoy. This means that arrest of persons without criminal intent will occur.

Indirect damage to third parties may be seen in a possible increase in police impersonators as undercover work becomes more prevalent. Impersonators are offered role models and their initial tales made more credible by the public's knowledge that undercover work is common. Classic con games, such as the game in which the "mark" is persuaded to draw money from his bank in order to test secretly the honesty of bank employees, may be made more believable by public knowledge that various kinds of secret government integrity tests are carried out. Official statistics probably greatly underestimate the extent of police impersonation, since the persons preyed upon are often prostitutes, homosexuals, and persons seeking to buy or sell narcotics, who are relatively unlikely to report their victimization.

CONVENTIONAL MEASURES OF EFFECTIVENESS

In assessing the consequences of undercover work with respect to crime, a distinction should be made between operations directed against subjects whose identity is known in advance, as with the infiltration of particular organizations, the disguise of police as hit men, or the offer of an opportunity for corruption to a person under suspicion, and operations directed against a more general "market" of suspects, as with decoys and fencing stings. The former type of undercover work is judged by its success in the case in question. Was a serious crime prevented? Were convictions obtained that would not have been possible otherwise or that were achieved at less expense than would be possible with conventional methods? The goal in such cases is not general deterrence, but apprehension. Such offenses tend to involve victims or witnesses who can report an incident, rather than being so defined only as a result of arrest actions, as is the case with consensual crimes. Analyzing the consequences of undercover work is easier with the former type of operation than with work directed against a more general suspect group, in which deterrence is also a goal.

30. *New York Post,* Mar. 29, 1978.

The case for the newer forms of undercover work, such as stings and decoys, rests on a number of inadequately tested assumptions, a fact that is ignored in the public relations efforts of advocates of these tactics, as well as by the media, which appear infatuated with the new investigative techniques. They are heralded as tactics that finally work in the war against crime, and as the only way to deal with conspirators. The dramatic effect of suddenly making a large number of arrests and recovering substantial amounts of property is stressed. But far less attention is given to other questions. What happens to crime rates during and after the operation? Who is being arrested? How does the number of arrests made or amount of property recovered compare with the accomplishments that would be expected over the same period using conventional methods? What is the cost per arrest or value of property recovered as compared with the gains under conventional methods? Any assessment of costs must include the sometimes long waiting periods aimed at establishing credibility and undercover efforts that had to be closed down because of leaks. An operation shut down because its cover is blown is far less likely to receive media attention than is one stopped after a large number of arrests. High vulnerability to discovery is an additional cost.

The research evidence on anticrime decoys and fencing stings is limited and not very reassuring. An analysis of New York City's much heralded Street Crime Unit (which specializes in decoy operations), while laudatory of the group's arrest and conviction record, did not find that the unit was ". . . decreasing either robberies or grand larcenies from a person."[31] Nor did a careful analysis of Birmingham's experiment with an antirobbery unit, which relied heavily on decoys, find it to have any effect on rates of larceny or robbery.[32]

A 1979 Justice Department study, entitled *What Happened*, makes rather grandiose claims for the success of sixty-two antifencing sting operations carried out since 1974.[33] But in a reanalysis, Klockars casts serious doubt on the quality of these data and their interpretation. Klockars concludes that there is no sound statistical evidence to suggest that the sting operations produced a decline in the rate of property crime.[34] An analysis of the use of federal funds for antifencing projects in San Diego over a five-year period concluded that neither the market for stolen prop-

---

31. Abt Associates, *New York City Anti-Crime Patrol—Exemplary Project Validation Report* (Washington, D.C.: National Institute of Law Enforcement and Criminal Justice, 1974).

32. Mary Ann Wycoff, Charles Brown, and Robert Petersen, *Birmingham Anti-Robbery Unit Evaluation Report* (Washington, D.C.: Police Foundation, 1980).

33. Dept. of Justice, *What Happened*.

34. Carl Klockars, "Jonathan Wilde and the Modern Sting," in *History and Crime: Implications for Criminal Justice Policy*, James A. Inciardi and Charles E. Taupel (Beverly Hills, Calif.: Sage, 1980).

erty nor the incidence of property crimes had been reduced.[35] Walsh notes that police engaged in antifencing operations were positive in their reactions to the experience, but had ". . . serious questions as to what had really been accomplished."[36]

In general, the stings do not result in the arrest of minors because of concern over civil liability and fear of a bad press (i.e., agents are contributing to the delinquency of minors, or are leading unwary innocents into crime). Yet this age group is disproportionately responsible for property crime. Nationally, slightly over half those arrested for burglary are seventeen and under,[37] yet, in the stings studied, only 3 percent of those arrested were seventeen or under.

If we view the relation between police and criminals (especially those who are highly skilled) not as a war that is ultimately to be won, but as a continuing struggle with each side reciprocally responding to the other's temporary tactical advantage, then a diminishing returns effect is likely to be present. While the costs and risks of the illegality may be increased, committed criminals may simply become more clever. They are likely to make increased use of antibugging devices and engage in more sophisticated investigations and testing of potential co-conspirators.

Although the arrest of street criminals is an appropriate goal, it is important to determine what proportion of such persons are arrested. Seasoned observers note that some street criminals are adept at identifying decoys. Some of those arrested are derelicts or poverty-stricken persons in great need, or children, who cannot resist the temptation of what seems to be easy money, rather than regular street criminals. In a New York City study one in four, and in Birmingham four in ten, of those arrested through decoy operations had no previous arrest record.[38] Of course nonarrest may attest to a person's cleverness rather than purity of character. But given the transparent quality of, and publicity around, exposed wallet decoy operations, what is most striking about those who are arrested is their lack of competence. It thus seems unlikely that a large proportion of such first-time arrestees are criminals skilled in avoiding arrest. What ratio of criminals to noncriminals, or derelicts, arrested in such operations justifies a conclusion that the tactic is appropriate?

Awareness of the above can lead to a revised set of questions about the

35. Susan Pennell, "Fencing Activity and Police Strategy," *Police Chief*, September 1979, pp. 71–75.

36. Mary Walsh, *Strategies for Combatting the Criminal Receiver of Stolen Goods* (Washington, D.C.: Law Enforcement Assistance Administration, 1975), p. 114.

37. Federal Bureau of Investigation, *Uniform Crime Reports* (Washington, D.C.: Govt. Printing Office, 1977), p. 174.

38. New York City Police Department, "Survey of Criminal Records of Perpetrators Arrested by Members of the Street Crime Unit" (memorandum; Apr. 5, 1974); Wycoff, Brown, and Petersen, *Birmingham Anti-Robbery Unit Evaluation*.

effects of undercover work. That is, are there conditions under which undercover work may cause crimes that would not have otherwise occurred? There are many individual examples of this, although evidence in the aggregate is lacking. Among the ways in which undercover work may cause or contribute to crime (at least for the particular offense in question and in the short run) are the following:

It may generate a market for the purchase or sale of illegal goods and services and the indirect generation of capital for other illegality.

It may generate the idea for the crime, for example, vice and bribery operations that involve unwary innocents.

It may generate a motive. In political cases, for example, agents provocateurs may question the commitment or courage of those they seek to goad into illegal actions or may greatly encourage hostile actions which increase intramovement conflict.

It may provide a missing resource, such as chemicals for drug manufacturing or plates for counterfeiting, a resource essential for the commission of the crime. Or it may offer a seductive temptation to a person who would be unlikely to encounter such temptations were it not for police actions.

It may entail coercion or intimidation of a person otherwise not predisposed to commit the offense.

It may generate a covert opportunity structure for illegal actions on the part of the undercover agent or informant.

It may lead to retaliatory violence against informers.

It may stimulate a variety of crimes on the part of those who are not targets of the undercover operation (e.g., impersonation of a police officer, crimes committed against undercover officers).

Highly complex questions with difficult measurement problems are involved here, and they pose a severe task for research. However, there is a need to ask hard questions about these operations. If claims about the effectiveness and benefits of the operations are to be accepted, the Justice Department must go much farther in permitting research by disinterested outside evaluators. Such research should be concurrent with the investigation, and not restricted to evaluations done six months after its close.

Of course, undercover operations and the behavior within them are not all of one kind. Efforts to prevent versus efforts to facilitate a crime raise different sets of issues. Having an undercover agent attempt to purchase illegal goods and services involves questions different from those related to agents' attempts at the sale of such goods and services. In general, problems appear more likely as we move from operations undertaken in response to crimes that have already occurred, or are occurring, to those

Issues in New Police Undercover Work

that anticipate crimes that might occur. Among the latter, providing a target for victimization, as with the decoy squads, tends to raise fewer problems than do co-conspiratorial operations where the undercover agent is a willing participant in the offense. Undercover investigations which increase the opportunity for self-selection and are organized on the basis of prior intelligence or complaints, and stay close to real-world criminal conditions, seem superior to random integrity testing, or the creation of a highly artificial criminal environment with unrealistically attractive temptations.

BROAD CHANGES IN SOCIAL CONTROL

Whatever the variations among undercover operations with respect to their legal and ethical implications, or short-term effects, actions such as ABSCAM and police-run fencing operations may be portents of a subtle and perhaps irreversible change in how social control in our society is carried out. It is well to reflect on whether this is the direction in which we wish to see our society move. It was roughly half a century ago that Secretary of War Henry Stimpson indignantly observed, in response to proposed changes in national security practices, "Gentlemen do not read each other's mail." His observation seems touchingly quaint in light of the invasions of privacy and the institution of routine surveillance that subsequent decades have witnessed. How far we have come in such a short time.

Fifty years from now will observers find our wondering about the propriety of attempts by police agents to bribe congressmen, distribute pornographic film, and run fencing operations equally quaint?

Broad changes in the nature of American social control appear to be taking place. We are experiencing a general shift away from some of the ideas central to the Anglo-American police tradition. The modern English police system, which Robert Peel established in 1829, worked to prevent crime by a uniformed, visible, twenty-four-hour presence. As societal conditions have changed and as the deterrent effect of this visible and predictable police presence has been questioned, an alternative conception has gradually emerged.

Rather than only trying to decrease the opportunity for crime through a uniformed police presence, or through more recent "target hardening" approaches that increase physical security and educate citizens in crime prevention, authorities now seek to *increase* selectively the opportunity structures for crime ("target weakening"), operating under controlled conditions with nonuniformed police. Anticipatory police strategies have become more prominent.

In this respect, police strategies may be paralleling those of the modern corporation, which seeks not only to anticipate demand through market research, but also to develop and manage that demand through advertising, solicitation, and more covert types of intervention. By secretly gathering information and facilitating crime under controlled conditions, the police obtain a degree of control over the "demand" for police services hardly possible with traditional reactive practices.

Whenever a market is created rather than being a response to citizen demand, there are particular dangers of exploitation and misuse. This is as true for consumer goods as it is for criminal justice processing. Some of the "demand" for undercover police practices may be spurious. In legal systems in which authorities respond to citizen complaints rather than independently generating cases, liberty is likely more secure. There is a danger that once undercover resources are provided and skills are developed, the tactics will be used indiscriminately.

Where there is a well-documented pattern of prior infraction, the use of undercover tactics may be appropriate. Yet, given pressures on police to produce, and the power of such tactics, it is an easy move from targeted to indiscriminate use of integrity tests, and from investigation to instigation.

The bureaucratic imperative for intelligence can easily lead to the seductions of counterintelligence. On this relationship, former FBI executive William Sullivan observed, "As far as I'm concerned, we might as well not engage in intelligence activities without counterintelligence. One is the right arm, the other the left. They work together."[39]

The allure and the power of undercover tactics may make them irresistible. Just as most societies that have discovered alcohol have seen its use spread, once undercover tactics become legitimate and resources are available for them, they are likely to spread to new areas and be put to questionable use. To some observers the use of questionable or bad undercover means is nevertheless justified because it serves good ends. Who, after all, cannot be indignant over violations of the public trust on the part of those sworn to uphold it, or the hidden taxes we all pay because of organized crime? One of the problems with such arguments is, of course, that there is no guarantee that bad means will be restricted to good ends.

An important party to the elaboration and diffusion of undercover tactics is likely to be police trained in government programs, who may face mandatory retirement at age fifty-five if they are not attracted to the more lucrative private sector long before that. The police lieutenant who was the central figure in the widely publicized stings in Washington, D.C., retired and opened his own securities investigation firm—"Sting Security, Inc."—and Mel Weinberg has started his own private investigation agency, called "Abscam Incorporated."[40] Perhaps we will reach the point

39. William Sullivan, *The Bureau: My Thirty Years in Hoover's FBI* (New York: W. W. Norton, 1979), p. 128.

40. Charles Conconi and Toni House, *The Washington Sting* (New York: Coward, McCann & Geoghegan, 1979); *Newsweek*, Oct. 26, 1981. Of course, undercover tactics are certainly not new to the private sector. Indeed, such tactics were largely brought to federal police agencies from the private sector through persons such as Alan Pinkerton and William J. Burns.

where some type of registration will be needed for former government agents trained and experienced in highly "sensitive" operations who continue such work in private enterprise. The case of the former CIA agents working for Libya could easily have its domestic counterparts.

From current practices, we may not be far from activities such as the following. Rather than infiltrating criminal enterprises or starting up their own sham enterprises, police agents (such as accounting specialists) might infiltrate legitimate businesses to be sure they are obeying the law, or to ensure that they would obey it if given a government-engendered chance not to. The IRS might secretly sponsor a promotion sweepstakes and then prosecute those who fail to report their winnings accurately. Following a wonderful Don Quixote tale, husbands or wives, or those considering marriage, might hire attractive members of the opposite sex to test their partner's fidelity. Businesses might create false fronts using undercover agents to involve their competitors in illegal actions for which they would then be arrested. A business could be sabotaged through infiltration by disruptive workers, or its public image could be damaged by a rival's taking false front actions in its name.

In the case of ABSCAM, we have the irony of Congress giving the FBI funds for undercover activities that were then used to finance actions against Congress. With Watergate not yet a decade past, one can imagine a more sinister reciprocal pattern. This would involve using some of the money and undercover dirty tricks to help elect friendly congressmen, who would then increase the appropriation, generating an endless cycle.

The deterrence sought through the use of undercover tactics comes, in the words of an experienced undercover agent, through "[creating] in the minds of potential offenders an apprehension that any 'civilian' could, in fact, be a police officer." Whether this tactic deters or merely makes sophisticated criminals more clever, while also encouraging new crimes on the part of the weak and the gullible, is a question for research. One can also ask what is the effect of ever more sophisticated ruses and elaborate surveillance on trust among law-abiding citizens? To many observers, American society is fragmented enough without the government's adding a new layer of suspiciousness and distrust. It is possible that, the greater the public's knowledge of such tactics, the greater the mutual distrust among American citizens.

In recent decades, undercover police activities such as COINTEL and the many local varieties damaged the protected freedoms of political dissenters. But now, through a spill-over effect, they may be inhibiting the speech of a much broader segment of society. The free and open speech protected by the Bill of Rights may be chilled for everyone. After ABSCAM, for example, people in government cannot help but wonder who it is they are dealing with. Communication may become more guarded and the free and open dialogue traditionally seen as necessary in high levels of government inhibited. Similar effects may occur in business and private life.

A major demand in totalitarian countries that undergo liberalization is for the abolition of the secret police and secret police tactics. Fake documents, lies, subterfuge, infiltration, secret and intrusive surveillance, and the creation of apparent reality are not generally associated with United States law enforcement. However, we may be taking small but steady steps toward the paranoia and suspicion that characterize many totalitarian countries. Even if unfounded, once such feelings are aroused and become part of the culture, they are not easily dissipated.

Soothsayers of doom are likely to become increasingly apparent as we approach 1984. The cry of "wolf" is easy to utter and hence easy to dismiss. Liberty is a complex condition, and under democratic government there are forces and counterforces serving both to jeopardize and protect that condition. That is, tactics that threaten liberties can also be used to protect them. However, neither complexity, sophistry, nor the need for prudence in sounding alarms should blind us from seeing the implications of recent undercover work for the redefinition and extension of government control. Lewis, in *It Can't Happen Here*, argues that if totalitarianism comes to America, it will be in traditional American form.[41] It will be by accretion and the gradual erosion of traditional liberties, rather than by cataclysmic changes. The issues raised by recent police undercover actions go far beyond whether a given congressman was predisposed to take a bribe or the development of effective guidelines.

Such police actions are part of a process of the rationalization of crime control that began in the nineteenth century. Social control has gradually become more specialized and technical, and, in some ways, more penetrating and intrusive. The state's power to punish and to gather information has been extended deeper into the social fabric, although not necessarily in a violent way. We are seeing a shift in social control from direct coercion used after the fact to anticipatory actions entailing deception, manipulation, and planning. New technocratic agents of social control are replacing the rough-and-ready cowboys of an earlier era. They are a part of what Foucault refers to as the modern state's "subtle calculated technology of subjection."[42]

Here, undercover practices must take their place beside varied technological advances:

> New or improved data-gathering techniques, such as lasers, parabolic mikes and other bugs, wiretaps, videotaping and still photography, remote camera systems, periscopic prisms, one-way mirrors, various infrared, sensor, and tracking devices, truth serum, polygraphs, voice print and stress analysis, pen registers, ultraviolet radiation, and helicopter and satellite surveillance.

41. Sinclair Lewis, *It Can't Happen Here* (New York: New American Library, 1973).
42. Michel Foucault, *Discipline and Punish: The Birth of the Prison* (New York: Pantheon, 1977).

New data-processing techniques based on silicone computer chips, which enable inexpensive storing, retrieval, and analysis of personal information that previously was not collected—or, if collected, not kept; or, if kept, not capable of being brought together inexpensively in seconds. To this must be added the increased prominence of computers (with their attendant records) in everyday affairs, whether involving commerce, banking, telephones, medicine, education, employment, criminal justice, pay television, or even library transactions.

An increase in the amount and variety of data available as a result of new reporting requirements (e.g., at one extreme, the pressure for some form of a national identification system), and an increase in private entrepreneurs who collect and disseminate personal data.

The vast and continuing expansion of the private security industry (which is, according to some estimates, now three times the size of the public police force). This is staffed by thousands of former military, national security, and domestic police agents schooled and experienced in the latest control techniques while working for the government, but now much less subject to its control.

Increasing centralization, standardization, and integration of law enforcement agencies (e.g., regionalization and merger plans at the local level; the absorption of the Alcohol, Firearms and Tobacco Agency into the Secret Service and suggestions to add the Drug Enforcement Agency to the FBI at the federal level; joint local-state-federal enforcement efforts; a new domestic role for the CIA; and standardized operating procedures inspired by new Justice Department funding efforts).

Evolving techniques of behavior modification, manipulation, and control, including operant conditioning, pharmacology, genetic engineering, psychosurgery, and subliminal communication.

Taken in isolation and with appropriate safeguards, each of these technological advances may have appropriate uses and justifications. However, the techniques become more problematic when seen in consort and as part of an emerging trend. Observers will differ as to whether they see in this an emerging totalitarian fortress, or benign tools for a society ravaged by crime and disorder. But regardless of how the trend is seen, it is clear that some of our traditional notions of social control are undergoing profound change. There is a need for careful analysis and public discussion of the complex issues involved.

[26]

THE SERPENT BEGUILED ME AND I DID EAT: ENTRAPMENT AND THE CREATION OF CRIME

GERALD DWORKIN

ABSTRACT. This paper examines the legitimacy of pro-active law enforcement techniques, i.e. the use of deception to produce the performance of a criminal act in circumstances where it can be observed by law enforcement officials. It argues that law enforcement officials should only be allowed to create the intent to commit a crime in individuals who they have probable cause to suppose are already engaged or intending to engage in criminal activity of a similar nature.

In the past few years a number of criminal prosecutions have brought to public attention the issue of entrapment: Abscam, the DeLorean cocaine trial, Operation Greylord, various sting fencing operations. The investigative techniques used in, say, Abscam while highly elaborate, expensive and ingenious are only one example of the range of investigative techniques with which I shall be concerned in this essay. What these techniques have in common is the use of deception to produce the performance of a criminal act under circumstances in which it can be observed by law enforcement officials. I shall use the term "pro-active enforcement" to cover such techniques and the question I shall be discussing is under what circumstances, if any, is the use of such measures legitimate.

1.

Let me begin by saying something more about the nature of pro-active law enforcement and also by giving a fairly extensive sample of the use of such techniques. The sample will not only make clearer the nature of such operations but also provide a range of cases for testing judgments about the acceptability of such techniques.

Traditionally, law enforcement in our society has left most of the burden of reporting criminal offenses to private citizens. It is left to individuals, usually victims, to come forward with a complaint of criminal action and to provide much of the evidence in identifying and prosecuting the criminal. Government's role has been limited to various patrol activities and to reaction to complaint. Hence, the traditional notion of reactive law enforcement.

Recently the existence of "invisible offenses" has posed challenges to reactive law enforcement. Invisible offenses include not only the so-called victimless crimes, i.e. those crimes in which there are no complaints because all parties to the transaction are willing (drugs, vice, gambling) but also a variety of cases in which the victims are not aware of any criminal act. The patrons of a hotel are not aware of code violations whose existence is protected by the bribery of a building inspector. The purchasers of General Electric products were not aware of the fact that the price of the products they bought was affected by a price-fixing agreement. The customers of a bank are not aware of the loss of funds due to the embezzlement of a teller. There is another class of offenses which produces knowing victims but where, for a variety of reasons, the victims are not prepared to complain — blackmail, extortion, sexual harassment. We know from crime surveys that many victims of robbery and theft do not report these crimes either because of fear of harassment or because they believe it to be a waste of time.

Faced with the failure of the traditional modes of notification and investigative aid, law enforcement officials have turned to modes of investigation in which the reporting, observation and testimony can be done by the officials themselves. Detection of crime and investigation of crime procede simultaneously. This is the arena of pro-active law enforcement. Originally used mainly in drug and vice investigations such techniques are now being used increasingly for many other kinds of crime. I shall enumerate a list of such techniques.

Entrapment   **19**

Decoy Operations

The New York City Street Crime Unit is a unit of the New York City Police Department which specializes in the techniques of "decoying and blending". The decoy is a police officer who assumes the role of a potential victim. He (or she) may play the role of derelict, shopper, grandmother, drunk, "john", cab driver, potential rape victim. The decoy is placed in an area where experience indicates it is likely the decoy will become a victim. The back-up blends into the street area near the decoy. When the decoy indicates that a crime has been committed the back-up team moves in for the arrest. A similar idea using inanimate objects occurs when decoy letters are sent to trap postal thieves.

In most decoy cases the potential offender is not targeted. But the same techniques can be used against specific suspects. In one case a Manhattan dentist was targeted after three patients had complained that they had been molested while under anaesthesia. An undercover policewoman posed as a patient, accepted anaesthesia, and was kept under surveillance by a hidden camera. The dentist was arrested and the video evidence led to a conviction.

Sting Operations

Undercover agents take over a warehouse and announce that they are in the market to purchase stolen goods. They purchase goods brought to them and, after some period of time, arrest the sellers of the stolen property. Similar operations have involved running a pornographic bookstore in order to arrest film wholesalers.

Manna from Heaven Operations

Police leave a piece of luggage unattended at the Port Authority bus terminal and arrest those who attempt to walk off with it. As an integrity test for policemen money is left in an apartment, the door is left open, and an "open-door" call is put through to the police.

Honey-pot Operations

Undercover agents provide opportunities for various criminal acts without actively soliciting them. They may, for example, open a garbage business in the hopes of becoming targets for extortion, or operate a bar in the hopes of being solicited for bribes by city inspectors.

Solicitation Operations

The most common mode of drug enforcement involves government agents offering to buy drugs from dealers. Similar methods are used to enforce laws against counterfeit currency and illegal firearms. In one of the more creative uses of such techniques the police fencing detail in Portland, Oregon purchased color television sets at wholesale prices (under an LEAA grant) and then made the rounds of bars offering to sell the sets very cheaply, claiming they were stolen. As part of the same operation randomly chosen appliance stores were approached with the same offer.

In the recent Operation Greylord in Cook County, Illinois, undercover agents staged a crime and arrest so that they could solicit offers to drop the charges for a payment.

In the course of soliciting a crime the government may play an active role in a criminal operation. In one extreme case involving liquor regulations an agent contacted two defendants with whom he had been previously involved in the production of bootleg alcohol and pressured them to re-establish operations. He offered to provide a still, a still-site, equipment and an operator. He then provided two thousand pounds of sugar at wholesale. The operation lasted for three years during which the government agent was the only customer.

Although the Ninth Circuit reversed this conviction it did not do so on grounds of entrapment. It did argue, however, that "the same underlying objections which render entrapment objectionable to American criminal justice are operative."[1] To see both

---

[1] Greene v. United States, 454 F. 2nd 783 (9th Cir. 1971).

why the court did not find entrapment, and what the underlying objectives referred to consist in, we must now examine the nature of the entrapment defense. Although my concern is with the normative issues raised by pro-active law enforcement, the legal doctrine of entrapment has been the focus of much of the discussion of such issues, and many of the conceptual and normative distinctions are present in the legal discussion.

2.

Entrapment is a defense to a criminal charge. The defendant asserts a claim that he ought not to be held legally liable for some criminal act. It is a defense which originally was a judicial creation although it has since been codified in a number of states including Illinois, New York and Alaska. It is also interesting to note that as a bar to criminal liability it is virtually exclusive to the criminal jurisprudence of the United States.

It is a very narrow defense in that it only applies when the entrapment is performed by a government agent. It is not available to those who are enticed into criminal acts by private citizens. The term government agents, however, includes all employees of government, and in certain circumstances private citizens working for a government agent will count as government agents.

Entrapment occurs when government agents procure the commission of a criminal act by someone who, except for the solicitation, persuasion, or enticement, would not have committed the crime. Both the conditions under which entrapment will be found and the theoretical foundations of the defense are matters of legal dispute. Originally, state and federal courts based the defense on estoppel and public policy. But in 1932 the Supreme Court replaced these with the legal fiction that Congress implicitly excludes entrapment whenever it enacts a criminal statute. The court held that if the police implant in the mind of an innocent person the disposition to commit an offense it is unfair to find such a person guilty. We see here the two elements which recur through the future development of the doctrine — the innocence or predisposition of the offender and the inducement to commit the offense.

Sorrells contains the two main views about the justification of the entrapment defense.[2] The majority focuses on entrapment as a defense in the standard sense of the term, i.e. as a factor affecting the culpability or innocence of the offender. If somebody is found innocent by virtue of entrapment then, on this view, it is similar to being found innocent by virtue of mistake of fact. The offender is not, or not as, culpable. As an excuse, entrapment is focused on the conduct of the defendant and his relative blameworthiness.

The concurring view, on the other hand, focuses not on the culpability of the offender but on the integrity of the judicial process and the legitimacy of the methods used by the police. The defendant is excused, not because he is less culpable, but because the government has acted in an illegitimate fashion. The point of the defense is not to exculpate offenders but to monitor police behavior.

Parallel to these different views of the nature and function of the defence has been the development of two different standards for the applicability of the defense. What has come to be called the "subjective" test concentrates on the offender's state of mind. With whom did the intent to commit the crime originate? Was the defendant pre-disposed to commit the crime? Would this particular defendant have committed this particular crime in the absence of the government's conduct? On the view that the defense affects culpability, only those not predisposed to commit the offense will be excused. That is why the defendant in Greene, who had a prior history of violation of liquor regulations, could not invoke entrapment.

The "objective" test, sometimes called the "hypothetical person" test focuses on the conduct of the police, not the defendant. It asks whether the methods used would have led a hypothetical law-abiding citizen to commit the crime in question. As

---

[2] Sorrells v. United States, 287 U.S. 435 (1932).

the California Supreme Court put it:

[We] are not concerned with who first conceived or who willingly, reluctant-ly, acquiesced in a criminal project. What we do care about is how much and what manner of persuasion, pressure and cajoling are brought to bear by law enforcement officials to induce persons to commit crime. ... The proper test of entrapment in California is the following: was the conduct of the law-enforcement agent likely to induce a normally law-abiding person to commit the offense.[3]

Note that on this view it does not matter whether or not this defendant was predisposed. If a hypothetical nonpredisposed person would have been likely to commit the crime because of the actions of the police this defendant is let off, not because he is innocent, but because the government conduct cannot be con-doned.

The two views cannot be integrated into a single theory. For on the view which emphasizes the innocence of those induced to per-form criminal acts it should be irrelevant whether or not the entrapping parties are government agents or private citizens. And on the view which emphasizes the conduct of government agents, it should be irrelevant whether or not the suspect was predisposed to commit the crime.

Because the dominant opinion in the Supreme Court has favored the subjective test of entrapment, and most defendants have a criminal record which makes it difficult to demonstrate lack of predisposition, the entrapment defense remains limited in scope, rarely used, and even less rarely successful.

The legal literature on entrapment consists almost exclusively in expositions of the Supreme Court's various views about the doc-trine, and normative questions are usually confined to arguing the

---

[3] People v. Barraza, 23 Cal. 3rd 675 (1979).
[4] Some exceptions include Park, *The Entrapment Controversy*, 60 Minn. L. Rev. 163 (1976). Goldstein, *For Harold Laswell: Some Reflections on Human Dignity, Entrapment, Informed Consent and the Plea Bargain*, 84 Yale L.J. 683 (1975). *Causation and Intention in the Entrapment Defense*, 28 UCLA Law J. 859 (1981).

24 *Gerald Dworkin*

relative merits of subjective vs. objective tests.[4] The much larger and important issue of the legitimacy of government created crime is ignored. What values are threatened by the use of pro-active methods of law enforcement? Ought we to distinguish between public officials and private citizens as targets of such techniques? Ought criminals have a right to complain about efficient methods of investigating and detecting their crimes? If certain crimes, e.g. bribery, can only (or most efficiently) be detected by these methods then does a norm of equal enforcement of the law favor such techniques?

3.

The central moral concern with pro-active law enforcement techniques is that they manufacture or create crime in order that offenders be prosecuted and punished. They do not discover criminal activity; they create it. I take it that there is some common understanding of these terms such that if this were an accurate and apt description of certain law enforcement methods there would be a decisive objection to their use.

Consider, for example, the scenario of *U.S. v. Ordner.*[5] Ordner, a commercial blaster and firearms manufacturer, with no previous history of lawbreaking, was approached by a government informer at a gun show. The informer, working with the government in the hope of reducing his sentence in a pending case, offered to introduce Ordner to a contractor who might have some blasting work for him. When Ordner went to meet the contractor, he was instead confronted with an elaborate scheme concocted by agents of the Bureau of Alcohol, Tax and Firearms to resemble a meeting of an underworld gang. Ordner eventually provided the blueprint and directed the assembly of five hundred "penguns". This is clearly an instance of the creation of criminal activity by law enforcement agents. What are the elements that distinguish the creation or manufacture of crime from its investigation and detection?

---

[5]   554 F. 2d 24 (2d Circ.), 434 U.S. 824 (1977).

If one looks back at the range of operations listed earlier one sees that there are various means by which agents contrive to have criminal acts performed in their presence (other than maintaining surveillance of the suspect or a potential crime scene). They can suggest the crime be committed, offer various incentives, use coercion, provide some of the means needed to commit the crime, participate in the commission of the crime, arrange the presence of a potential victim, arrange the presence of a valuable object in an unsecure context, offer to buy or sell contraband, appeal to sentiments of friendship.

On at least one view all of these might count as the creation of criminal activity. Suppose we defined the creation of criminal activity as occurring whenever the police acted in such a way that they caused criminal activity to occur. According to one idea of cause which has played an important role in tort law, one event is said to cause another if it is a necessary condition for its occurrence. This is referred to as "but for" causation. But for the presence of the event in question the other event would not have occurred. Now it is a feature of all pro-active techniques that but for the actions of law enforcement officials the crime for which the defendants are charged would, almost certainly, not have been committed.

Thus, if a policeman rides on a bus with a wallet in his back pocket, and his pocket is picked, but for the actions of the policeman his wallet would not have been stolen. If an officer, suspecting short weighting, makes a purchase of meat at a supermarket, weighs it and finds it short weighted, then this particular fraudulent sale would not have been committed if the government had not acted. Yet, in these cases, it does not seem that the culpability of defendants is reduced, or that the methods go beyond some idea of what is fair.

One way to see this is to note that in an ordinary mugging the presence of the victim is a but for cause of the crime. If this little old lady had not been walking her dog in the park, her mugging would not have occurred. But, surely, she did not create or manufacture crime. The contribution of the state has to go beyond simply providing a potential victim, as in decoy operations.

If, however, the decoy is made to look particularly vulnerable and the "reward" particularly attractive, then questions of temptation and the overcoming of the will raise issues of causation and responsibility. If the crime is made sufficiently "easier" or sufficiently attractive then, as social scientists who leave wallets lying about in phone booths find out, almost any of us is likely to commit a crime.

It is relevant here to note that the increased probability does not occur simply as a forseen consequence of governmental action. A case of this would be the decision to shift patrols to a high-crime area foreseeing that there would be an increase in crime in the section of town with reduced patrols. But in the cases we are considering the point of the action is to increase the likelihood that a crime will be committed in the presence of the police.

If somebody commits a crime, and would not have done so absent the efforts of the state to make the crime easier, has the state created crime? To help in thinking about this let us look at other parts of the law which have developed theory on similar matters. In tort law it is common to invoke the idea that if one neglects to take precautions against harm one is liable for the harm that comes about, even if the harm is brought about by others. Thus a house painter was held liable for the loss of goods stolen by a thief who entered when the painter failed to lock the front door. But the language of the courts in such cases is not that the negligent party causes the wrongdoer to do what he does, or that he causes the harm that results. Rather it is that one has a duty to guard against such harm. Providing others with the opportunity to do harm may ground liability but not because it causes the harm.

In the criminal law there is also a distinction drawn between providing an opportunity to commit a crime and inducing others to commit crime. With respect to criminal responsibility a person is only held to have caused another to act if he makes use of threats, lies or the exercise of authority to induce another to act. With respect to civil liability for the acts of others the accepted view is that one individual must do something which is directly addressed to the other person such as uttering a threat, or making a false statement, or exploiting personal influence. It is only when the agent led to act is less than fully competent, as in the case of young children, that the mere providing of a temptation counts as causing another to act — as in the doctrine of "attractive nuisance."

Both on grounds of conformity with other legal doctrine and harmony with commonsense notions of causation it is reasonable not to count the mere provision of opportunity to commit a crime as the manufacture or creation of crime. It is only if the opportunity is made sufficiently attractive that creation of opportunities can be regarded as temptation. The danger of such techniques is that they may lead persons to commit crimes who have not engaged in similar activities before. The person who walks away with the "abandoned" suitcase in the Port Authority building may not have been disposed to steal anything at all. In such cases there is the danger that one may not merely shift the scene of criminal activity but create crime that otherwise would not have occurred.

The offer to buy drugs, sex or stolen goods from those already engaged in their sale, or letting it be known that one is available for a bribe, does more than merely make it easier to commit a crime. It invites the criminal to act. Again, this does not seem sufficient to categorize the activity as the creation of crime since although the particular sale might not have taken place had it not been for the offer to engage in the transaction, by hypothesis one is dealing with those already engaged in criminal activity. Leaving aside complications, such as the fact that sting fencing operations may encourage individuals to commit burglaries by providing a ready outlet at above-market prices, such offers are on the portion of the spectrum closer to shifting the scene of criminal activity.

An interesting comparison is between the offer to sell as opposed to buy contraband. This seems a more questionable practice but it is not apparent where the difference lies. It is a crime to buy as well as sell contraband. Both transactions rely on the willingness of an offender to engage in the transaction. While it is true that the danger to society is usually greater from the seller than the buyer this seems to be relevant to what crimes to aim at, not at which techniques are permissible. Moreover, it does not seem particularly outrageous to let it be known that one is willing to sell one's services as a contract murderer (for the purpose of apprehending a buyer of such services).

I believe this is explained by the contingent fact that the offer to sell is more likely to be made without knowledge that a particular individual is already embarked on a course of criminal conduct. This is why the Orgeon case of going into bars and offering to sell supposedly stolen televisions seems to be the creation of crime, while the offer to sell one's services as a contract murderer does not. In the former the state is, in effect, making a random test of the corruptability of the general public.

The next step up from merely providing an opportunity, or merely offering to engage in a criminal transaction, is to provide the necessary means for the commission of a crime. Consider for example the facts in the Twigg case.[6] Robert Kubica after being arrested on charges of illegally manufacturing speed, pled guilty and agreed to assist the Drug Enforcement Administration in prosecuting other offenders. At the request of DEA officials he contacted an acquaintance, Henry Neville, and proposed they set up a laboratory for manufacturing speed. Kubica assumed responsibility for acquiring the necessary equipment, raw materials and a production site. The DEA supplied all of these plus an ingredient essential to the manufacture which, while legal, was difficult to obtain. Twigg joined the operation at the invitation of Neville. Kubica alone had the technical knowledge and skills necessary to manufacture the drug and had complete charge of the laboratory. The Court reversed on the grounds that when Kubica contacted him, Neville

was not engaged in any illicit drug activity. Using Kubica, and actively participating with him, the DEA agents deceptively implanted the criminal design in Neville's mind.... This egregious conduct on the part of government agents

---

[6] U.S. v. Twigg, 558 F. 2d 373 (3d Cir. 1978).

generated new crimes by the defendant merely for the sake of pressing criminal charges against him when, as far as the record reveals, he was lawfully and peacefully minding his own affairs. Fundamental fairness does not permit us to countenance such actions by law enforcement officials and prosecution for a crime so fomented will be barred.[7]

I should suppose fundamental fairness would raise some problems about this case even if the intent to commit the crime arose in Neville. Imagine that he approached Kubica saying he would like to manufacture some speed but, unfortunately, lacked the raw materials, the technical skills, the capital, and the equipment. Kubica then supplies them all and Neville is then arrested. What is the harm that the state seeks to avoid by such prosecutions?

Nevertheless the court is focusing on the right factor in the creation of crime — the origin of criminal intent. The essential question for determining when crime has been created is what the role of government is in causing the offender to form the specific intent to commit the crime in question. The issue of pre-disposition, which runs through the entrapment commentary, is a red herring. We are not interested in the general willingness of an offender to commit crime but in whether he has formed the intent to engage in a specific crime if the opportunity presents itself. In so far as only an opportunity is offered, then if the offender is using it to realize a pre-existing purpose the origin of intent is in him. If the government, in Learned Hand's phrase, "solicits, proposes, initiates, broaches or suggests" the offense then the origin of the intent lodges with the state.

Real situations are, of course, complicated by overdetermination. Suppose, for example, I form the intent to commit a crime if and only if I am solicited to do so by someone else. Or suppose I form the intent to steal something, but cannot overcome a residual fear of being apprehended, and it is only your encouragement that enables me to carry out the original intent.

The fact that there are difficult questions about determining

---

[7] Id. at 381.

the origin of intent only shows that the question of whether crime has been manufactured is often hard to settle. And that is something we already knew. If the ambiguities and difficulties in determining the origin of intent match those in deciding whether crime has been created that is all one can demand in terms of a satisfactory analysis.

Given our understanding of the idea of the creation of crime in terms of origin of intent we can now pass to the normative issues. Is it legitimate, and if so under what conditions, for the government to create criminal activity?

4.

To answer this question one must have some general view about the underlying purpose and rules of fairness which are embedded in the particular system of criminal law-enforcement we have adopted. The legitimacy of particular law-enforcement techniques is necessarily relative to a particular conception or model of criminal justice. At most an argument for condemning particular modes of enforcement will be of the form "If you accept a particular ideal of the purposes and fairness of attaching criminal sanctions to rules of conduct, then these methods will be inconsistent or not cohere with such an ideal."

I shall sketch the outlines of what I believe to be an ideal of the principles of distribution applied to criminal sanctions embedded in our current practice and jurisprudence.

1. Criminal sanctions constitute an interference with the liberty of the members of a society.

2. They are justified, at least in part, by their contribution to the adherence of citizens to justifiable standards of conduct.

3. Individuals ought to have a broad area of autonomy, i.e. self-determination, in the choice of behavior and the formation of goals and purposes.

4. There is a conflict between maximizing autonomy and promoting fundamental human goods such as security of possessions, personal integrity and opportunity. One way of mitigating

this conflict is to allow individuals to choose whether or not to become subject to criminal sanctions by presenting them with reasons against certain conduct (sanctions) and letting them make the decision to comply or not. Individuals who are legitimately punished have self-selected themselves for such treatment.

5. The criminal law is not to be thought of as a price system, i.e. as it being indifferent whether a citizen obeys the law or violates it but pays the price of the sanction. The criminal law is meant to be obeyed. Certain behaviors are forbidden and others are required, and while the citizen is given a choice (in the sense that the behaviors are not made impossible) his will is constrained to make the correct choice.

These propositions have implications for very different aspects of the criminal justice system. They affect the substantive content of legal standards, e.g. standards which are very difficult or impossible to obey would be ruled out. They affect procedural issues, e.g. laws should be prospective in application. They affect the excusing conditions we ought to allow. And they affect the types of law-enforcement techniques we should regard as legitimate.

In light of the above propositions the normative issue may be phrased in the following manner: what methods of apprehending and detecting offenders are consistent with the view of a system of criminal sanctions as a choosing system and as the enforcement of law, i.e. authoritative rules backed by sanctions. I am claiming that it is not consistent with such a system that law enforcement officials attempt to see if they can cause a person to commit a crime by suggesting or encouraging in any way that a crime be committed.

It is not that such suggestions are improper only if they are such as to overwhelm the will. The use of coercion, excessive temptation, and fraud are obviously inconsistent with the view that we are only entitled to punish those offenders who willingly choose to commit crimes. I am arguing for the much stronger view that it is not proper to solicit, encourage, or suggest crime even if this is done by no stronger means than verbal suggestion. It is not that the offender can complain after the fact that his will was overborne. It is that we, any of us, can complain before the fact that it is not the purpose of officers of the law to encourage crime for the purpose of punishing it.

For the law is set up to forbid people to engage in certain kinds of behavior. In effect it is commanding "Do not do this." And it shows that it is commanding, as opposed to requesting or advising by saying that it will impose sanctions on those who refuse to conform. It will "humble the will" to use Fingarette's language.[8]

But for a law enforcement official to encourage, suggest, or invite crime is to, in effect, be saying "Do this." It is certainly unfair to the citizen to be invited to do that which the law forbids him to do. But it is more than unfair; it is conceptually incoherent. Of course this incoherence does not appear to the person being entrapped since he is not aware of the official capacity of his entrapper. And the incapacity is concealed from the official since he thinks of himself as trying to detect a criminal — the thought being that an honest citizen will simply refuse the invitation. From the standpoint of one trying to understand and evaluate the system, however, the conflict is clear.

It is important to note that we are not literally involved in a contradiction as we would be, for example, if the Statutes both commanded and forbade that a certain action be done. Nor is it a pragmatic contradiction, in the sense of being self-defeating. The person who says "P but I do not believe P" takes back with the latter part of his assertion what he implies with the former part. Nor is it self-defeating in the sense that it cannot be useful to engage in such behavior in order to increase overall compliance with the legal system. It is not as if one part of the criminal justice system (the police) are trying to undo what another part (the legislature) is trying to accomplish.

It is not always incoherent to invite someone to do the very act which one is trying to get them to avoid doing. Consider a parent trying to teach a child not to touch the stove. In the case of a

---

[8] H. Fingarette, *Punishment and Suffering*, Proceedings and Addresses of the American Philosophical Society, v. 50, 1977 p. 510.

particularly recalcitrant child the most effective technique might be to encourage the child to touch the stove in one's presence. The slight pain now will teach the child to avoid a greater pain later. But this is surely not the model being used by the police. They are interested either in deterring others or in punishing guilty people. The end being served is not that of the person being invited to commit the crime.

I suppose we can (barely) make sense of a system of rules forbidding certain behavior which is enforced by inviting people to commit the forbidden acts and then punishing them for doing so. But such a system violates elementary standards of coherence and fairness.

To encourage the commission of a crime in the absence of any reason to believe the individual is already engaged in a course of criminal conduct is to be a tester of virtue, not a detector of crime.

As a way of insuring against such testing of virtue I suggest that whenever the action of creating an intent to commit a criminal act would render a private citizen liable to criminal charges as accessory or co-conspirator, public officials should be allowed to perform such acts as would create such an intent only if they have probable cause to suppose that the individuals approached are already engaged or are intending to engage in activity of a similar nature. If they offer to buy contraband from specific individuals they should have probable cause to believe those individuals are already engaged in such transactions. If they offer to sell stolen goods to individuals, they ought to have probable cause to believe such individuals are already buying stolen goods. If they offer bribes to public officials, then they should have probable cause to suppose that the officials are already corrupt; not just corruptible.

To use an analogy we do not think it proper for police to engage in random searches of homes in order to detect possible criminal activity. Why then should we allow random solicitation or encouragement of criminal activity? I have heard it argued that on grounds of equitable law enforcement it is wrong to allow those who may have corrupt dispositions, but have been fortunate enough not to have been given the opportunity to exercise them, to escape punishment when their less fortunate counterparts are caught. After all if we had offered them a bribe they would have taken it. This counter-factual seems to me an interesting piece of data for God, but not for the FBI. Suggesting the commission of a crime, even to wicked people, is not a legitimate function of a system of law enforcement.[9,10]

APPENDIX

Although my discussion has been much broader than the topic of Abscam I would like to apply the discussion to Abscam, partly because it has caused so much controversy and partly because it is a difficult case to form a judgment about. Abscam is not one case but many since there were a number of different public officials involved. But basically the actual solicitation of crime involved

---

[9] I have ignored in my argument any discussion of the practical consequences of law enforcement officials engaging in the creation of crime. My argument has been addressed to matters of principle rather than practice. I believe, however, that considerations of likely consequences strengthens the argument. The work of Gary Marx, a sociologist from MIT, is the best source for the dangers of undercover police work in general. Here are some of the problems that he worries about.
(a) the lack of effective supervision of informers and police.
(b) The possibility of damage to unwitting victims and third parties.
(c) The possibility of police participating in real crimes to gain the confidence of the targeted suspects.
(d) The use of selective targeting against political opponents.
(e) The corrupting effect on police of pretending to be corrupt.
(f) Excessive invasion of privacy.
(g) Stimulation of criminal activity, e.g. through offering to purchase stolen goods.
[10] A version of this paper was read at the Eastern Division Meetings of the American Philosophical Association. My commentators at the meeting were Gerald Postema and Patricia White. I am indebted to them, and in particular to Postema, for helpful suggestions and criticisms.

either offering money to secure residency for the "shiek" or the offer to finance a titanium mine in return for using political office to secure government contracts: It is the latter case (Senator Williams) that I wish to focus upon.

The charges against Williams and his attorney related .to a titanium mine and processing plant. Williams' investment group consisting of himself, his attorney Feinberg, Katz, Errichetti (the mayor of Camden) and Sandy Williams sought financing to acquire the titanium enterprise. Through Errichetti the group contacted Melvin Weinberg a convicted swindler who was working for the government, and an undercover agent, Anthony Amoroso. The latter pair posed as members of Abdul Enterprises, an investment firm pretending to represent wealthy Arabs. Criminal charges arose out of the promise requested by the undercover agent as a condition for the financing, that Williams would use his power and influence to obtain government contracts for purchasing the titanium to be produced.

My own reading of the trial transcripts and the due process hearings that followed the conviction of Williams convinces me that Senator Williams acted in a corrupt and morally indefensible manner. Quite independently of the outcome of the criminal charges the Senate Ethics Committee acted entirely correctly in recommending that Williams be expelled from the Senate — an outcome he avoided by resigning.

On the legal issue of entrapment the trial judge denied Williams' motions to dismiss the indictment on grounds of entrapment and the Supreme Court concurred. What this shows, in my view, is that the current legal doctrine of entrapment is too narrowly construed because I believe the best reading of the evidence shows that Williams' crime was created and manufactured by the state, that there was no probable cause for targeting Williams, and that, in accordance with my earlier argument, it was improper to procede with prosecution. I can, in this appendix, only briefly highlight what I believe to be the grounds supporting my reading of the evidence. I shall be ignoring various aspects of the investigation which raise due process questions of their own, such as the reliability of Weinberg, the chief government informant, the absence of control over Weinberg by government agents, the absence of written reports summarizing conversations that were not recorded. I will focus only on the entrapment issues.

Was there probable cause for targeting Williams? The U.S. Attorney who supervised the investigation stated that he "had no reason to question the integrity of Senator Harrison Williams." The Special Agent in Charge, John Good, testified the government was "starting with a clean slate." Nowhere is there evidence of a predicate to investigate. It is the absence of such a predicate, not the question of predisposition, which I regard as crucial to the legitimacy of soliciting or encouraging crime.

As to the question of where the suggestion for criminal activity arose one has to read the evidence and note when and how often the suggestion for illegal conduct arose with the informant or government agents. The titanium venture itself was a legitimate business venture. The criminal elements included using political influence to get government contracts, concealing one's interest in the mine, and so forth. Consider these conversations. MW is Melvin Weinberg, the government informant. SW is Sandy Williams friend and business associate of Senator Williams. TD is an FBI agent. AF is Williams attorney and business associate. GK is a business associate of Williams.

MW: Allright, now what about, uh, let me ask you a question. There's a lot of government contracts that, ya know, on the chemicals. .

SW : Right.

MW: Now, can Williams get us the bids on them.

SW : Well, I don't know about that. The main thing is with this Cyanamid thing ...

MW: Yeah.

SW : They've got customers they've had for twenty, thirty, forty years ... And if we wanna increase our business, we'll have to, we'll have to go into like Sherman-Williams and people like that and try to get their business away from somebody else.

TD : Is he going to be able to steer any kind of contracts from the Committees that he's going to get involved with? I mean ...

AF : Well, this I didn't know until now I have to ask him that.

GK : He's not a guy, he's not a doer, you know, quietly behind the scene, you know, he, uh, may move a little bit ... but let me tell you this here between you and me, he's in a very, very powerful position here, the committees that he heads, you understand?

MW: Yeah.

GK : But he doesn't use that power for any advantages.

MW: Oh, how can we make him use it?

. . .

In this exchange the associates of Williams did not raise the issue of government contracts, and in every case where the government did so, they acted in a neutral or discouraging fashion. With respect to concealing his interest in the mine notice how in this conversation between Feinberg, Weinberg and Da Vito, the suggestion of concealing the interest arises from the government.

MW: That's in the mine though. But on the other thing there he, in fact you may we may put the 20 percent in his name even. I don't think he can though.

TD : Well, if he puts ...

AF : I don't know, we haven't decided yet. We're gonna both examine the law involving his side investments which he ...

MW: I don't think he can.

AF : He can put it in his wife's name or someone else.

MW: They could chase that too fast.

TD : Yeah.

MW: Come on, you're an attorney, you know that.

AF : I know that.

TD : Any, anything that he puts ...

AF : I'm not sure that he's forbidden.

MW: Sure he is if he's going to get us open doors. Come on, you know that's a conflict of interest. He'll be sitting with Nixon out in Clemente there.

Perhaps the most controversial aspect of the investigation involves the coaching session between Weinberg and Williams just prior to Williams' meeting with the "shiek". This is the backstage maneuvers before the on-camera performance. Here is Weinberg telling Williams what to say.

MW: Forget the mine. Don't even mention the mine ... [Tell him] How high you are in the Senate ... He's interested in you ... Who you know in the Senate can do you favors ...
Without you there is no deal. You are the deal. You put this together. You worked on this and you got the government contracts. Without me there is no government contracts ...
Mention, you know, come on as strong as possible ... You gotta just play and blow your horn. The louder you blow and mention names, who you control.
And that's it, it goes no further. It's all talk, all bullshit.

But with all this effort the meeting with the shiek proves inconclusive. In November 1979, the prosecutors held a meeting to review the evidence against Williams and came to the conclusion that further investigative efforts were required.

Relative to the matter concerning US Senator Harrison Williams of New Jersey, the following was decided:
1. It will be necessary to recontact US Senator Williams to attempt to obtain an overt action on his part regarding the sponsorship of some type of legislation, i.e. tax cover for titanium mine and/or import quotas for titanium mine.
2. It was also suggested that attempts should be made to elicit from US Senator Williams whether or not he wanted his shares hidden, through discussions concerning reporting of personal taxes and official acts that he promised to provide.

The prosecutors subsequently decided to add the "asylum scenario" that had been used so successfully against other Congressmen. A meeting between Williams and the sheik was held in which the sheik offered Williams money to obtain permanent residency in the United States. Williams refused the money, although he did go on to link his assistance on the immigration matter to the financing of the titanium venture. Incidentally, this meeting which was video-taped and observed by the investigators was interrupted at one point by a phone call by an FBI agent who instructed the sheik as to what he should say to Williams. The agent later testified as to the purpose of the interruption: "It was clear from the way the conversation was going on that it wasn't quite as specific as we would have liked it to have been."

I suggest that what we had in this case was not an investigation of whether Senator Williams was breaking the law but an effort to see if he could be induced to do so. That he was apparently quite willing to be so induced is not at issue. The issue is whether it is legitimate to substitute for the question. "Is this individual, who we have reason to suspect of corrupt activity, acting in a corrupt manner?" the question "Can we corrupt this individual who we have no reason to believe is corrupt?"

I do not deny that political corruption is a very difficult crime to detect by normal investigative techniques. I also do not believe that it is impermissible to use deception and trickery in the attempt to uncover such corruption. But I do not believe that it is legitimate to solicit and encourage such corruption unless we have evidence that the targeted individuals are already engaged in such corruption.

Dept. of Philosophy
University of Illinois at Chicago
Chicago, IL 60607
U.S.A.

[27]

The Ethics of Deceptive Interrogation

JEROME H. SKOLNICK AND RICHARD A. LEO

I Introduction

As David Rothman and Aryeh Neier have recently reported, "third degree" police practices—torture and severe beatings—remain commonplace in India, the world's largest democracy.[1] Police brutality during interrogation flourishes because it is widely accepted by the middle classes.[2] Although this may seem uncivilized to most Americans, it was not so long ago that American police routinely used physical violence to extract admissions from criminal suspects.[3] Since the 1960s, and especially since *Miranda*, police brutality during interrogation has virtually disappeared in America. Although one occasionally reads about or hears reports of physical violence during custodial questioning,[4] police observers and critics agree that the use of physical coercion during interrogation is now exceptional.

This transformation occurred partly in response to the influential Wickersham report,[5] which disclosed widespread police brutality in the United States during the 1920s; partly in response to a thoughtful and well-intentioned police professionalism, as exemplified by Fred Inbau and his associates; and partly in response to changes in the law which forbade police to "coerce" confessions but allowed them to elicit admissions by deceiving suspects who have waived their right to remain silent. Thus, over the last fifty to sixty years, the methods, strategies, and consciousness of American

police interrogators have been transformed: psychological persuasion and manipulation have replaced physical coercion as the most salient and defining features of contemporary police interrogation. Contemporary police interrogation is routinely deceptive.[6] As it is taught and practiced today, interrogation is shot through with deception. Police are instructed to, are authorized to—and do—trick, lie, and cajole to elicit so-called "voluntary" confessions.

Police deception, however, is more subtle, complex, and morally puzzling than physical coercion. Although we share a common moral sense in the West that police torture of criminal suspects is so offensive as to be impermissible—a sentiment recently reaffirmed by the violent images of the Rodney King beating—the propriety of deception by police is not nearly so clear. The law reflects this ambiguity by being inconsistent, even confusing. Police are permitted to pose as drug dealers, but not to use deceptive tactics to gain entry without a search warrant; nor are they permitted to falsify an affidavit to obtain a search warrant.

The acceptability of deception seems to vary inversely with the level of the criminal process. Cops are permitted to, and do, lie routinely during investigation of crime, especially when, working as "undercovers," they pretend to have a different identity.[7] Sometimes they may, and sometimes may not, lie when conducting custodial interrogations. Investigative and interrogatory lying are each justified on utilitarian crime control grounds. But police are never supposed to lie as witnesses in the courtroom, although they may lie for utilitarian reasons similar to those permitting deception at earlier stages.[8] In this article, we focus on the interrogatory stage of police investigation, considering (1) how and why the rather muddled legal theory

---

Jerome H. Skolnick, author of Justice Without Trial: Law Enforcement in a Democratic Society, *is Claire Clements Dean's Professor of Law at the University of California at Berkeley; Richard A. Leo, a graduate and law student at the University of California at Berkeley, is currently researching police interrogation for his doctoral dissertation.*

authorizing deceptive interrogation developed; (2) what deceptive interrogation practices police, in fact, engage in; and —a far more difficult question— (3) whether

police should ever employ trickery and deception during interrogation in a democratic society valuing fairness in its judicial processes.

II   The Jurisprudence of Police Interrogation

The law of confessions is regulated by the Fifth, Sixth, and Fourteenth Amendments. Historically, the courts have been concerned almost exclusively with the use of *coercion* during interrogation. Although a coerced confession has been inadmissible in federal cases since the late nineteenth century, the Supreme Court did not proscribe physically coercive practices in state cases until 1936.[9] In *Brown v. Mississippi*, three black defendants were repeatedly whipped and pummelled until they confessed. This was the first in a series of state cases in which the Court held that confessions could not be "coerced," but had to be "voluntary" to be admitted into evidence.[10]

Whether a confession meets that elusive standard is to be judged by "the totality of the circumstances." Under that loose and subjective guideline, an admission is held up against "all the facts" to decide whether it was the product of a "free and rational will" or whether the suspect's will was "overborne" by police pressure. Over the years, however, certain police practices have been designated as presumptively coercive. These include physical force, threats of harm or punishment, lengthy or incommunicado interrogation, denial of food and/or sleep, and promises of leniency.[11]   In 1940, the Supreme Court ruled—in a case in which a suspect was first threatened with mob violence, then continuously questioned by at least four officers for five

> *An interrogation is presumed to be*
> *coercive unless a waiver is obtained.*

consecutive days—that psychological pressure could also be coercive.[12]

One reason for excluding admissions obtained through coercion is their possible falsity. But, beginning with *Lisenba v. California*[13] in 1941, and followed by *Ashcraft v. Tennessee*[14] three years later, the Supreme Court introduced the criterion of *fairness* into the law. Whether in the con-text of searches or interrogations,

evidence gathered by police methods that "shock the conscience" of the community or violate a fundamental standard of fairness are to be excluded, regardless of reliability.[15] This rationale is sometimes twinned with a third purpose: deterring offensive or unlawful police conduct.

In its watershed *Miranda* decision, the Supreme Court in 1966 prescribed specific limitations on custodial interrogation by police.[16]   The five-to-four majority deplored a catalog of manipulative and potentially coercive psychological tactics employed by police to elicit confessions from unrepresented defendants. In essence, the court could not reconcile ideas such as "fairness" and "voluntariness" with the increasingly sophisticated and psychologically overbearing methods of interrogation. In response, it fashioned the now familiar prophylactic rules to safeguard a criminal defendant's fifth amendment right against testimonial compulsion. As part of its holding, *Miranda* requires that (1) police advise a suspect of her right to remain silent and her right to an attorney, and (2) the suspect "voluntarily, knowingly and intelligently" have waived these rights before custodial interrogation can legally commence. An interrogation is presumed to be coercive unless a waiver is obtained. Once obtained, however, the "due process-voluntariness" standard governs the admissibility of any confession evidence. In practice, once a waiver is obtained, most of the deceptive tactics deplored by the majority become available to the police.

In retrospect, *Miranda* seems to be an awkward compromise between those who argue that a waiver cannot be made "intelligently" without the advice of an attorney, who would usually advise her client to remain silent, and those who would have preferred to retain an unmodified voluntariness standard because police questioning is "a particularly trustworthy instrument for screening out the innocent and fastening on the guilty," and because the government's obligation is "not to counsel the accused but to question him."[17]

In sum, then, three sometimes competing principles underlie the law of confessions: first, the truth-finding rationale, which serves the goal of *reliability* (convicting an innocent person is worse than letting a guilty one go free); second, the substantive due process or *fairness* rationale, which promotes the goal of the system's integrity; and third, the related *deterrence* principle, which proscribes offensive or lawless police conduct.

The case law of criminal procedure has rarely, however, and often only indirectly, addressed the troubling issue of trickery and deceit during interrogation. We believe this is the key issue in discussing interrogation since, we have found, interrogation usually implies deceiving and cajoling the suspect.

Police deception that intrudes upon substantive constitutional rights is disallowed. For example, the Supreme Court has ruled that an officer cannot trick a suspect into waiving his *Miranda* rights. But apart from

these constraints, the use of trickery and deception during interrogation is regulated solely by the due process clause of the Fourteenth Amendment, and is proscribed, on a case-by-case basis, only when it violates a fundamental conception of fairness or is the product of egregious police misconduct. The courts have offered police few substantive guidelines regarding the techniques of deception during interrogation. Nor have the courts successfully addressed the relation between fairness and the lying of police, or the impact of police lying on the broader purposes of the criminal justice system, such as convicting and punishing the guilty. As we shall see, the relations among lying, conceptions of fairness, and the goals of the criminal justice system raise intriguing problems.

III A Typology of Interrogatory Deception

Because police questioning remains shrouded in secrecy, we know little about what actually happens during interrogation. Police rarely record or transcribe interrogation sessions.[18] Moreover, only two observational studies of police interrogation have been reported, and both are more than two decades old.[19] Most articles infer from police training manuals what must transpire during custodial questioning. Our analysis is based on Richard Leo's dissertation research. It consists of a reading of the leading police training manuals from 1942 to the present; from attending local and national interrogation training seminars and courses; from listening to tape-recorded interrogations; from studying interrogation transcripts; and from ongoing interviews with police officials.

A *Interview" versus "Interrogate"*
The Court in *Miranda* ruled that warnings must be given to a suspect who is in custody, or whose freedom has otherwise been significantly deprived. However, police will question suspects in a "non-custodial" setting— which is defined more by the suspect's state of mind than by the location of the questioning—so as to circumvent the necessity of rendering warnings. This is the most fundamental, and perhaps the most overlooked, deceptive stratagem police employ. By telling the suspect that he is free to leave at any time, and by having him acknowledge that he is voluntarily answering their questions, police will transform what would otherwise be considered an interrogation into a non-

custodial interview. Thus, somewhat paradoxically, courts have ruled that police questioning outside of the station may be custodial,[20] just as police questioning inside the station may be non-custodial.[21] The line between the two is the "objective" restriction on the suspect's freedom. Recasting the interrogation as an interview is the cleanest deceptive police tactic since it virtually removes police questioning from the realm of judicial control.

B *Miranda Warnings*
When questioning qualifies as "custodial," however, police must recite the familiar warnings. The Court declared in *Miranda* that police cannot trick or deceive a suspect into waiving *Miranda* rights.[22] The California Supreme Court has additionally ruled that police cannot "soften up" a suspect prior to administering the warnings.[23] However, police routinely deliver the *Miranda* warnings in a flat, perfunctory tone of voice to communicate that the warnings are merely a bureaucratic ritual. Although it might be inevitable that police would deliver *Miranda* warnings unenthusiastically, investigators whom we have interviewed say that they *consciously* recite the warnings in a manner intended to heighten the likelihood of eliciting a waiver. It is thus not surprising that police are so generally successful in obtaining waivers.[24]

C *Misrepresenting the Nature or Seriousness of the Offense*
Once the suspect waives, police may misrepresent the nature or seriousness of the offense. They may, for

example, tell a suspect that the murder victim is still alive, hoping that this will compel the suspect to talk. Or police may exaggerate the seriousness of the offense—over-stating, for example, the amount of money embezzled—so that the suspect feels compelled to confess to a smaller role in the offense. Or the police may suggest that they are only interested in obtaining admissions to one crime, when in fact they are really investigating another crime. For example, in a recent case, *Colorado v. Spring*, federal agents interrogated a suspect on firearms charges and parlayed his confession into an additional, seemingly unrelated and unimportant, admission of first-degree murder.[25] Despite their pretense to the contrary, the federal agents were actually investigating the murder, not the firearms charge. This tactic was upheld by the Supreme Court.

D *Role Playing: Manipulative Appeals to Conscience*

Effective interrogation often requires that the questioner feign different personality traits or act out a variety of roles.[26] The interrogator routinely projects sympathy, understanding, and compassion in order to play the role of the suspect's friend. The interrogator may also try to play the role of a brother or father figure, or even to act as a therapeutic or religious counselor to encourage the con-fession. The best-known role interrogators may act out is, of course, the good cop/bad cop routine, often played out by a single officer. While acting out these roles, the investigator importunes—sometimes relentlessly—the suspect to confess for the good of her case, her family, society, or conscience. These tactics generate an illusion of intimacy between the suspect and the officer while downplaying the adversarial aspects of interrogation.

The courts have routinely upheld the legitimacy of such techniques—which are among the police's most effective in inducing admissions—except when such role-playing or manipulative appeals to conscience can be construed as "coercive," as when, for example, an officer implies that God will punish the suspect for not confessing.[27]

E *Misrepresenting the Moral Seriousness of the Offense*

Misrepresentation of the moral seriousness of an offense is at the heart of interrogation methods propounded by Inbau, Reid, and Buckley's influential police training manual.[28] Interrogating officials offer suspects excuses or moral justifications for their misconduct by providing the suspect with an external attribution of blame that will allow him to save face while confessing. Police may, for example, attempt to convince an alleged rapist that he was only trying to show the victim love or that she was really "asking for it"; or

they may persuade an alleged embezzler that blame for her actions is attributable to low pay or poor working conditions. In *People v. Adams*, for example, the officer elicited the initial admission by convincing the suspect that it was the gun, not the suspect, that had done the actual shooting.[29] Widely upheld by the courts, this tactic is advertised by police training manuals and firms as one of their most effective.

F *The Use of Promises*

The systematic persuasion—the wheedling, cajoling, coaxing, and importuning—employed to induce conversation and elicit admissions often involves, if only implicitly or indirectly, the use of promises. Although promises of leniency have been presumed to be coercive since 1897, courts continue to permit vague and indefinite promises.[30] The admissibility of a promise thus seems to turn on its specificity. For example, in *Miller v. Fenton*, the suspect was repeatedly told that he had mental problems and thus needed psychological treatment rather than punishment. Although this approach implicitly suggested a promise of leniency, the court upheld the validity of the resulting confession.[31]

Courts have also permitted officers to tell a suspect that his conscience will be relieved only if he confesses, or that they will inform the court of the suspect's cooperation, or that "a showing of remorse" will be a mitigating factor, or that they will help the suspect out in every way they can if he confesses.[32] Such promises are deceptive insofar as they create expectations that will not be met. Since interrogating officials are single-mindedly interested in obtaining admissions and confessions, they rarely feel obliged to uphold any of their promises.

G *Misrepresentations of Identity*

A police agent may try to conceal his identity, pretending to be someone else, while interrogating a suspect. In *Leyra v. Denno*, the suspect was provided with a physician for painful sinus attacks he begun to experience after several days of unsuccessful interrogation.[33] But the physician was really a police psychiatrist, who repeatedly assured the defendant that he had done no wrong and would be let off easily. The suspect subsequently confessed, but the Supreme Court ruled here that the confession was inadmissible. It would be equally impermissible for a police official or agent to pretend to be a suspect's lawyer or priest. However, in a very recent case, *Illinois v. Perkins*, a prison inmate, Perkins, admitted a murder to an undercover police officer who, posing as a returned escapee, had been placed in his cellblock.[34] The Rehnquist Court upheld the admissibility of the confession. Since Perkins was in

QM LIBRARY
(MILE END)

jail for an offense unrelated to the murder to which he confessed, the Rehnquist Court said, Perkins was not, for *Miranda* purposes, "in custody." Nor, for the same reason, were his Sixth Amendment *Massiah* rights violated.[35] Thus, the profession or social group with which an undercover officer or agent identifies during the actual questioning may—as a result of professional disclosure rules or cultural norms—be more significant to the resulting legal judgment than the deceptive act itself.[36]

H Fabricated Evidence

Police may confront the suspect with false evidence of his guilt. This may involve one or more of five gambits. One is to falsely inform the suspect that an accomplice has identified him. Another is to falsely state that existing physical evidence—such as fingerprints, bloodstains, or hair samples—confirm his guilt. Yet another is to assert that an eyewitness or the actual victim has identified and implicated him. Perhaps the most dramatic physical evidence ploy is to stage a line-up, in which a coached witness falsely identifies the suspect. Finally, one of the most common physical evidence ploys is to have the suspect take a lie-detector test and regardless of the results—which are scientifically unreliable and invalid in any event—inform the suspect that the polygraph confirms his guilt.[37] In the leading case on the use of police trickery, *Frazier v. Cupp*, the Supreme Court upheld the validity of falsely telling a suspect that his crime partner had confessed.[38]

IV The Consequences of Deception

Although lying is, as a general matter, considered immoral, virtually no one is prepared to forbid it categorically. The traditional case put to the absolutist is that of the murderer chasing a fleeing innocent victim, whose whereabouts are known by a third party. Should the third party sacrifice the innocent victim to the murderer for the cause of truth? Few of us would say that she should. We thus assume a utilitarian standard regarding deception. So, too, with respect to police interrogation.

Interrogatory deception is an exceedingly difficult issue, about which we share little collective feeling. How are we to balance our respect for truth and fairness with our powerful concern for public safety and the imposition of just deserts? We are always guided by underlying intuitions about the kind of community we want to foster and in which we want to live. Which is worse in the long run—the excesses of criminals or the excesses of authorities?

Few of us would countenance torture by police in the interests of those same values. One reason is that violence may produce false confessions. As Justice Jackson observed in his dissent in *Ashcraft*: "...[N]o officer of the law will resort to cruelty if truth is what he is seeking."[39] But that is only partly correct. Cruelty can also yield incontrovertible physical evidence. We reject torture for another reason—we find it uncivilized, conscience-shocking, unfair, so most of us are repelled by it. That leads to a third reason for opposing torture. If effective law enforcement requires public trust and cooperation, as the recent movement toward community-oriented policing suggests, police who torture can scarcely be expected to engender such confidence.

What about police deception? Does it lead to false confessions? Is it unfair? Does it undermine public confidence in the police? A recent and fascinating capital case in the Florida Court of Appeal, *Florida v. Cayward*, the facts of which are undisputed, is relevant to the above questions.[40] The defendant, a nineteen-year-old male, was suspected of sexually assaulting and smothering his five-year-old niece. Although he was suspected of the crime, the police felt they had too little evidence to charge him. So they interviewed him, eventually advised him of his rights, and obtained a written waiver.

Cayward maintained his innocence for about two hours. Then the police showed him two false reports, which they had fabricated with the knowledge of the state's attorney. Purportedly scientific, one report used Florida Department of Criminal Law Enforcement stationery; another used the stationery of Life Codes, Inc., a testing organization. The false reports established that his semen was found on the victim's underwear. Soon after, Cayward confessed.

Should this deception be considered as akin to lying to a murderer about the whereabouts of the victim? Or should police trickery, and especially the falsification of documents, be considered differently? We unsystematically put this hypothetical question to friends in Berkeley and asked about it in a discussion with schol-ars-in-residence at the Rockefeller Study Center in Bellagio, Italy. The answers, we discovered, revealed *no* common moral intuition. For some, the answer was clear—in either direction. "Of course the police should lie to catch the murdering rapist of a child," said one. "I don't want to live in a society where police are allowed to lie and to falsify evidence," said another. Most were ambivalent, and all were eager to know how the Florida court resolved the dilemma.

Citing *Frazier v. Cupp* and other cases, the court recognized "that police deception does not render a confession involuntary *per se*." Yet the court, deeply troubled by the police deception, distinguished between "verbal assertions and manufactured evidence." A "bright line" was drawn between the two on the following assumption: "It may well be that a suspect is more impressed and thereby more easily induced to confess when presented with tangible, official-looking reports as opposed to merely being told that some tests have implicated him."[41]

Although we do not know the accuracy of the conjecture, it assumes that false police assertions such as "Your fingerprints were found on the cash register" are rarely believed by suspects unless backed up by a false fingerprint report. But in these deception cases, we do not usually encounter prudent suspects who are skeptical of the police. Such suspects rarely, if ever, waive their constitutional rights to silence or to an attorney. As in *Cayward*, and many deception cases, the

The decision in Cayward *is bedeviled by the classic problem of determining whether* Cayward's *confession was "voluntary."*

suspect, young or old, white or black, has naively waived his right to remain silent and to an attorney.

Would such a suspect disbelieve, for example, the following scenario? After two hours of questioning, the telephone rings. The detective answers, nods, looks serious, turns to the suspect and says: "We have just been informed by an independent laboratory that traces of your semen were found, by DNA tests, on the panties of the victim. What do you say to that?"

A verbal lie can be more or less convincing, depending upon the authority of the speaker, the manner of

speaking, its contextual verisimilitude, and the gullibility of the listener. False documentation adds to verisimilitude, but a well-staged, carefully presented verbal lie can also convince. The decision in *Cayward*, however well-written and considered, is nevertheless bedeviled by the classic problem of determining whether Cayward's confession was "voluntary."

No *contested* confession, however, is ever voluntary in the sense of purging one's soul of guilt, as one would to a religious figure. "The principal value of confession may lie elsewhere, in its implicit reaffirmation of the moral order," writes Gerald M. Caplan. "The offender by his confession acknowledges that he is to blame, not the community."[42] That observation focuses on the offender. Sometimes that is true, oftentimes it is not. Those who contest their confessions claim that they were unfairly pressured, and point to the tactics of the police. The claim is that the police violated the moral order by the use of unfair, shady, and thus wrongful tactics to elicit the confession. Had the police, for example, beaten a true confession out of Cayward, it would indeed seem perverse to regard his confession as a reaffirmation of the moral order.

If Cayward had been beaten, and had confessed, we would also be concerned that his confession was false. Assuming that all we know are the facts stated in the opinion, which say nothing of corroborating evidence or why Cayward was suspected, should we assume that his confession was necessarily true? However infrequent they may be, false confessions do occur. Moreover, they do not result *only* from physical abuse, threats of harm, or promises of leniency, as Fred Inbau and his associates have long maintained;[43] nor are they simply the result of police pressures that a fictionalized reasonable person would find "overbearing," as Joseph Grano's "mental freedom" test implies.[44] They may arise out of the manipulative tactics of influence and persuasion commonly taught in police seminars and practiced by police and used on Cayward.

Psychologists and others have recently begun to classify and analyze the logic and process of these false confessions,[45] which are among the leading causes of wrongful conviction.[46] Perhaps most interesting is the "coerced-internalized" false confession, which is elicited when the psychological pressures of interrogation cause an innocent person to temporarily internalize the message(s) of his or her interrogators and falsely believe himself to be guilty.[47] Although Cayward was probably factually guilty, he might have been innocent. Someone who is not altogether mature and mentally stable, as would almost certainly be true of a nineteen-year-old accused of smothering and raping his five-year-old niece, might also have a precarious and vague memory. When faced with fabricated, but supposedly incontrovertible, physical evidence of his guilt, he might falsely confess to a crime of which he has no recollection, as happened in the famous case of Peter Reilly,[48] and, more recently, in the Florida case of Tom Sawyer,[49] both of which were "coerced-internalized" false confessions.[50]

If Cayward was, in fact, guilty, as his confession

> *Rarely do advocates of greater latitude for police to interrogate consider the effects of systematic lying on law enforcement's reputation for veracity.*

suggests, the court was nevertheless willing to exclude it. Presumably, he will remain unpunished unless additional evidence can be produced. Characterizing the falsified evidence as an offense to "our traditional notions of due process of law," the Florida court was evidently alarmed by the *unfairness* of a system which allows police to "knowingly fabricate tangible documentation or physical evidence against an individual."[51] In addition to its "spontaneous distaste" for the conduct of the police, the court added a longer-range utilitarian consideration. Documents manufactured for such purposes, the court fears, may, because of their "potential of indefinite life and the facial appearance of authenticity,"[52] contaminate the entire criminal justice system. "A report falsified for interrogation purposes might well be retained and filed in police paperwork. Such reports have the potential of finding their way into the courtroom."[53] The court also worried that if false reports were allowed in evidence, police might be tempted to falsify all sorts of official documents "including warrants, orders and judgements," thereby undermining public respect for the authority and integrity of the judicial system.

Yet the slippery slope argument applies to lying as well as to falsification of documents. When police are permitted to lie in the interrogation context, why should they refrain from lying to judges when applying for warrants, from violating internal police organization rules against lying, or from lying in the courtroom? For example, an Oakland Tribune columnist, Alix Christie, recently received a letter from a science professor at the University of California at Berkeley who had served on

an Alameda County (Oakland) murder jury. He was dismayed that a defendant, whom he believed to be guilty, had been acquitted because most of the jurors did not believe the police, even about how long it takes to drive from west to east Oakland. "The problem," writes Christie, "predates Rodney King. It's one familiar to prosecutors fishing for jurors who don't fit the profile of people who distrust cops." She locates the problem in "the ugly fact that there are two Americas." In the first America, the one she was raised in, the police are the "good guys." In the other, police are viewed skeptically.

Police misconduct—and lying is ordinarily considered a form of misconduct—undermines public confidence and social cooperation, especially in the second America. People living in these areas often have had negative experiences with police, ranging from an aloof and legalistic policing "style" to corruption, and even to the sort of overt brutality that was captured on the videotape of the Rodney King beating in Los Angeles. Community-oriented policing is being implemented in a number of American police departments to improve trust and citizen cooperation by changing the attitudes of both police and public.

Police deception may thus engender a paradoxical outcome. Although affirmed in the interest of crime control values by its advocates like Fred Inbau—who, along with his co-author John Reid, has exerted a major influence on generations of police interrogators—it may generate quite unanticipated consequences. Rarely do advocates of greater latitude for police to interrogate consider the effects of systematic lying on law enforcement's reputation for veracity. Police lying might not have mattered so much to police work in other times and places in American history. But today, when urban juries are increasingly composed of jurors disposed to be distrustful of police, deception by police during interrogation offers yet another reason for disbelieving law enforcement witnesses when they take the stand, thus reducing police effectiveness as controllers of crime.

Conservatives who lean toward crime control values do not countenance lying as a general matter. They approve of police deception as a necessity, measuring the cost of police deceit against the benefits of trickery for victims of crime and the safety of the general public. Police and prosecutors affirm deceitful interrogative practices not because they think these are admirable, but because they believe such tactics are necessary.[54]

The Florida police officers who fabricated evidence did so for the best of reasons. The victim was a five-year-old girl, and the crime was abhorrent and hard to prove. Nevertheless, the Florida court excluded the confession on due process grounds, arguing that police must be discouraged from fabricating false official documents. Many persons, but especially those who, like Fred Inbau, affirm the propriety of lying in the interrogatory context, tend to undervalue the significance of the long-term harms caused by such authorized deception: namely, that it tends to encourage further deceit, undermining the general norm against lying. And if it is true that the fabrication of documents "greatly lessens," as the Florida court says, "the respect the public has for the criminal justice system and for those sworn to uphold and enforce the law,"[55] doesn't that concern also apply to interrogatory lying?

There is an additional reason for opposing deceitful interrogation practices. It does happen that innocent people are convicted of crimes. Not as often, probably, as guilty people are set free, but it does happen. Should false evidence be presented, a suspect may confess in the belief that he will receive a lesser sentence. In a study in 1986 of wrongful conviction in felony cases, Ronald Huff and his colleagues conservatively esti-

> *Those who affirm the propriety of lying in the interrogatory context, tend to undervalue the significance of the long-term harms caused by such authorized deception.*

mated that nearly 6,000 false convictions occur every year in the United States.[56] Hugo Bedau and Michael Radelet, who subsequently studied 350 known miscarriages of justice in recent American history, identified false confessions as one of the leading sources of erroneous conviction of innocent individuals.[57]

There are no easy answers to these dilemmas, no easy lines to suggest when the need to keep police moral and honest brushes up against the imperatives of controlling crime. Phillip E. Johnson, who has proposed a thoughtful statutory replacement for the Miranda doctrine,[58] would not allow police to "intentionally misrepresent the amount of evidence against the suspect, or the nature and seriousness of the charges,"[59] as well as other, clearly more coercive tactics. But he would allow feigned sympathy or compassion, an appeal to conscience or values, and a statement to the suspect such as "A voluntary admission of guilt and sincere repentance

may be given favorable consideration at the time of sentence."[60] Johnson states no formal *principle* for these distinctions, but does draw an intuitively sensible contrast between, on the one hand, outright *misrepresentations*, which might generalize to other venues and situations; and, on the other, *appeals* to self-interest or conscience, which seem to draw upon commonly held and morally acceptable values. If, however, as we have argued, rules for police conduct, and the values imparted through these rules, produce indirect, as well as direct, consequences for police practices and the culture of policing, Johnson's distinctions are persuasive. This resolution, we suggest, is quite different from the direction recently taken by the Rehnquist Court.

We have earlier argued that when courts allow police to deceive suspects for the good end of capturing criminals—even as, for example, in "sting" operations—they may be tempted to be untruthful when offering testimony. However we think we ought to resolve the problem of the ethics of deceptive interrogation, we need always to consider the unanticipated consequences of permitting police to engage in what would commonly be considered immoral conduct—such as falsifying evidence. The Supreme Court has moved in recent years to soften the control of police conduct in interrogation. In *Moran v. Burbine*, for example, the Court let stand a murder conviction even though the police had denied a lawyer—who had been requested by a third party, but without the suspect's knowledge, prior to his questioning—to the suspect during interrogation. The dissenters decried the "incommunicado questioning" and denounced the majority for having embraced "deception of the shabbiest kind."[61]

More recently, the notoriety of the Rodney King beating overshadowed the significance of the Rehnquist Court's most significant self-incrimination decision, *Arizona v. Fulminante*.[62] Here, a confession was obtained when a prison inmate, an ex-cop who was also an FBI informer, offered to protect Fulminante from prison violence, but only if he confessed to the murder of his daughter. In a sharply contested five-to-four opinion, the Court reversed the well-established doctrine that a coerced confession could never constitute "harmless error." Whether the ruling will be as important in *encouraging* police coercion of confessions as the King videotape will be in discouraging future street brutality remains to be seen. But in concert with other recent U.S. Supreme Court decisions that have cut back on the rights of defendants, the *Fulminante* decision may also send a message that police coercion is sometimes acceptable, and that a confession elicited by police deception will almost always be considered "voluntary."

NOTES

For helpful advice, criticism, and counsel, we would like to thank the following individuals: Albert Altschuler, Jack Greenberg, James Hahn, Sanford Kadish, Norman LaPera, Paul Mishkin, Robert Post, Peter Sarna, Jonathan Sither, Amy Toro, Jeremy Waldron, and, especially, Phillip Johnson.

1 Rothman & Neier, *India's Awful Prisons*, N.Y. REV. BOOKS, May 16, 1991, at 53-56.

2 *Id*. at 54.

3 *See* E. HOPKINS, OUR LAWLESS POLICE: A STUDY OF UNLAWFUL ENFORCEMENT (1931), and E. LAVINE, THE THIRD DEGREE: A DETAILED AND APPALLING EXPOSE OF POLICE BRUTALITY (1930).

4 "Confession at Gunpoint?" 20/20, ABC NEWS, March 29, 1991.

5 NATIONAL COMMISSION ON LAW OBSERVANCE AND ENFORCEMENT, LAWLESSNESS IN LAW ENFORCEMENT (1931).

6 Richard Leo, From Coercion to Deception: An Empirical Analysis of the Changing Nature of Modern Police Interrogation in America (paper presented at the Annual Meeting of the American Society of Criminology, Nov. 19-23, 1991).

7 *See* G. MARX, UNDERCOVER: POLICE SURVEILLANCE IN AMERICA (1988).

8 *See* Skolnick, *Deception by Police*, CRIMINAL JUSTICE ETHICS, Summer/Fall 1982, at 40-54.

9 Brown v. Mississippi, 297 U.S. 278 (1936).

10 Caplan, *Questioning Miranda*, 38 VANDERBILT LAW REVIEW 1417 (1985).

11 The Supreme Court's very recent ruling that coerced confessions may be "harmless error" will undermine this general rule. Arizona v. Fulminante, U.S. LEXIS 1854 (1991).

12 Chambers v. Florida, 309 U.S. 227 (1940).

13 314 U.S. 219 (1941).

14 322 U.S. 143 (1944).

15 *See* Rochin v. California, 342 U.S. 165 (1952), Spano v. New York, 360 U.S. 315 (1959), and Rogers v. Richmond, 365 U.S. 534 (1961).

16 Miranda v. Arizona, 384 U.S. 436 (1961).

17 Caplan, *supra* note 10, at 1422-23.

18 The state of Alaska requires, as a matter of state constitutional due process, that all custodial interrogations be electronically recorded. *See* Stephan v. State, 711 P.2d 1156 (1985).

19 Wald, et al., *Interrogations in New Haven: The Impact of Miranda*, 76 YALE L. J. 1519-1648 (1967), and N. MILNER , COURT AND LOCAL LAW ENFORCEMENT: THE IMPACT OF MIRANDA (1971).

20 Orozco v. Texas, 394 U.S. 324 (1969).

21 *See* Beckwith v. United States, 425 U.S. 341 (1976), Oregon v. Mathiason, 429 U.S. 492 (1977), and California v. Beheler, 463 U.S. 1121 (1983).

22 However, police may deceive an attorney who attempts to invoke a suspect's constitutional rights, as to whether the suspect will be interrogated, and the police do not have to inform the suspect that a third party has hired an attorney on his behalf. People v. Moran, 475 U.S. 412 (1986).

23 People v. Honeycutt, 570 P.2d 1050 (1977).

24 See O. STEPHENS, JR., THE SUPREME COURT AND CONFESSIONS OF GUILT 165-200 (1973) for a useful summary of studies assessing the impact of Miranda in New Haven, Los Angeles, Washington, D.C., Pittsburgh, Denver, and rural Wisconsin. These studies indicate that police obtain waivers from criminal suspects in most cases. Additionally, the Captain of the Criminal Investigation Division of the Oakland Police Department told one of the authors that detectives obtain waivers from criminal suspects in 85-90% of all cases involving interrogations.

25 Colorado v. Spring, 107 S.Ct. 851 (1987).

26 Consider the following passage from R. Royal and S. Schutt, THE GENTLE ART OF INTERVIEWING AND INTER-

Jerome Skolnick and Richard Leo / 12

ROGATION (1976): "To be truly proficient at interviewing or interrogation, one must possess the ability to portray a great variety of personality traits. The need to adjust character to harmonize with, or dominate, the many moods and traits of the subject is necessary. The interviewer/interrogator requires greater histrionic skill than the average actor. . . .The interviewer must be able to pretend anger, fear, joy, and numerous other emotions without affecting his judgment or revealing any personal emotion about the subject" (p. 65).

27 People v. Adams 143 Cal.App.3d 970 (1983).

28 F. INBAU, J. REID, & J. BUCKLEY, CRIMINAL INTERROGATION AND CONFESSIONS (1986).

29 People v. Adams, *supra* note 27.

30 Bram v. United States, 168 U.S. 532 (1897).

31 Miller v. Fenton, 796 F.2d 598 (1986).

32 Kaci &Rush, *At What Price Will We Obtain Confessions?* 71 JUDICATURE, 256-57 (1988).

33 Leyra v. Denno, 347 U.S. 556 (1954).

34 Illinois v. Perkins, 110 S.CT. 2394 (1990).

35 In Massiah v. United States, 377 U.S. 201 (1964), the U.S. Supreme Court held that post-indictment questioning of a defendant outside the presence of his lawyer violates the Sixth Amendment.

36 *See* Cohen, *Miranda and Police Deception in Interrogation: A Comment on Illinois v. Perkins,* CRIMINAL LAW BULLETIN 534-46.(1990).

37 *See* Skolnick, *Scientific Theory and Scientific Evidence: Analysis of Lie Detection,* 70 YALE LAW JOURNAL 694-728 (1961); and D. LYKKEN, A TREMOR IN THE BLOOD: USES AND ABUSES OF THE LIE-DETECTOR (1981).

38 Frazier v. Cupp, 394 U.S. 731 (1969).

39 Ashcraft v. Tennessee, *supra* note 14, at 160.

40 Florida v. Cayward, 552 So. 2d 971 (1989).

41 *Id*. at 977.

42 Caplan, *Miranda Revisited,* 93 YALE L. J. 1375 (1984).

43 F. INBAU, LIE-DETECTION AND CRIMINAL INTERROGATION (1942).

44 Grano,*Voluntariness, Free Will, and the Law of Confessions,*

65 VA. L. REV. 859-945 (1979).

45 *See* Kassin & Wrightsman, *Confession Evidence,* in THE PSYCHOLOGY OF EVIDENCE AND TRIAL PROCEDURE (S. Kassin & L.Wrightsman eds. 1985). G. GUDJONSSON & N. CLARK, SUGGESTIBILITY IN POLICE INTERROGATION: A SOCIAL PSYCHOLOGICAL MODEL (1985); Ofshe, *Coerced Confessions: The Logic of Seemingly Irrational Action,* 6 CULTIC STUD. J. 6-15 (1989); Gudjonsson, *The Psychology of False Confessions,* 57 MEDICO-LEGAL J. 93-110 (1989); R.Ofshe & R. Leo, The Social Psychology of Coerced-Internalized False Confessions (paper presented at the Annual Meetings of the American Sociological Association, August 23-27, 1991).

46 Bedau & Radelet, *Miscarriages of Justice in Potentially Capital Cases,* 40 STAN. L. REV. 21-179 (1987).

47 Kassin & Wrightsman, *supra* note 45.

48 *See* J. BARTEL, A DEATH IN CANAAN, (1976); AND D. CONNERY, GUILTY UNTIL PROVEN INNOCENT (1977).

49 State of Florida v. Tom Franklin Sawyer, 561 So. 2d 278 (1990). *See also* Weiss, *Untrue Confessions,* MOTHER JONES, Sept.. 1989, at 22-24 and 55-57.

50 Ofshe & Leo, *supra* note 45.

51 Florida v. Cayward, *supra* note 40, at 978.

52 *Id.*

53 *Id.*

54 Inbau,*Police Interrogation—A Practical Necessity,* 52 J.CRIM. L,. CRIMINOLOGY, & POL. SCI. 412 (1961).

55 Florida v. Cayward, *supra* note 40, at 983.

56 Huff, Rattner & Sagarin, *Guilty Until Proven Innocent: Wrongful Conviction and Public Policy ,* 32 CRIME & DELINQ. 518-44 (1986). *See also* Rattner, *Convicted But Innocent:: Wrongful Conviction and the Criminal Justice System,* 12 L.& HUM. BEHAV. 283-93 (1988).

57 Bedau & Radelet, *supra* note 46.

58 P. JOHNSON, CRIMINAL PROCEDURE 540-50 (1988).

59 *Id.*. at 542.

60 *Id..*

61 Moran v. Burbine, 475 U.S. 412 (1986).

62 Arizona v. Fulminante, *supra* note 11.

Name Index

Douglas, Justice 453, 454
Doyle, Arthur Conan 317
Doyle, James F. 149–70
Duke, John 382, 383, 387
Dworkin, Gerald 493–515
Dworkin, Ronald 154, 155, 161

Eastwood, Clint 390
Edwards, C. 424
Edwards, Chief Superindendent G.S. 400, 413,
    414, 415, 416
Eliot 396
Ericson, R. 241, 242
Errichetti, Mayor 511
Ewin, R.E. 247–59

Fay, F.B. 458
Feinberg, Attorney 511, 513
Feldberg, Michael xiv, 15–30
Filmer, Robert 18
Fingarette, H. 508
Fitzgerald, Lord 238, 241, 247, 249, 250, 251,
    254, 257, 258
Fortas, Justice 454
Foucault, Michel 490
Fox, Lou 344
Frankfurter, Justice 451, 472
Fullam, Judge 468, 477
Fuller, Lon 156, 157, 162
Fyffe, James 237

Galileo 334
Garner, Edward Eugene 361, 362, 371, 372, 373,
    374
Geller, W. 370
George III 20
Goffman, Erving 286, 287, 288, 289
Goldstein, Herman 166, 234, 321, 322, 325, 326
Goldstein, Joseph 105
Goldwater, Barry 222
Good, Special Agent John 512
Gould, R.W. 382, 392
Gouldner, Alvin 290
Graham, Fred 480
Graham, L.P. 389
Grano, Joseph 454, 456, 522
Grant, Ulysses 276
Greenwood, C. 420, 421
Griffin, James 60, 61
Griffiths, Eldon 382

Halleck, J. 370
Hallenstein, Hal 240, 434, 435
Hamilton, Alexander 20
Hammett, Dashiell 317
Hanewicz, Wayne 48
Harding, R.W. 389
Harold, M.C.D. 420, 421
Hart, H.L.A. 156, 157, 162
Hastings, Patrolman 297, 298
Hawkins, Chief Inspector 107
Heffernan, William C. xiii, 83–104, 197, 271–82
Hill, Richard 59
Himmler, Heinrich 273
Hindawi, Hussein 412
Hitler, Adolf 345
Hobbes, Thomas 16, 17, 18, 175
Hoover, J. Edgar 452, 476
Huff, Ronald 524
Hymon, Elton 360, 361, 362, 371, 372, 373, 374, 377

Inbau, Fred E. 454, 456, 520, 524

Jackson, Justice 521
James II 18
James, Steve 233–45
Janowitz, Morris 204, 215
Jay, John 20
Jefferson, Thomas 16, 19
Jenrette, John 477
Jensen, Graeme 439
Johnson, Dr 262
Johnson, Phillip E. 524
Joy, Constable 107

Kadish, Mortimer 159
Kadish, Sanford 159
Kant, Immanuel 329, 332
Kapetanovski, Sergeant John 436
Karales, K. 370
Kasachkoff, Tziporah 197
Katz, Attorney 511
Keeler, Leonard 456
Kennedy, President John F. 397
Kennedy, Robert 452
Kennett, L. 368
Kerlikowske, Gil 271, 272, 278
King, Rodney 517, 523, 524
Kitchen, H. 401
Klein, Henry L. 360
Kleinig, John xiv, 31–53, 185–99, 261–70

WITHDRAWN
FROM STOCK
QMUL LIBRARY